Direct Practice in Social Work

Scott W. Boyle   **Grafton H. Hull, Jr.**
Jannah Hurn Mather   **Larry Lorenzo Smith**   **O. William Farley**
University of Utah

PEARSON
and

Boston   New York   San Francisco
Mexico City   Montreal   Toronto   London   Madrid   Munich   Paris
Hong Kong   Singapore   Tokyo   Cape Town   Sydney

Series Editor: Patricia Quinlin
Development Editor: Shannon Steed
Editorial Assistant: Sara Holliday
Marketing Manager: Kris Ellis-Levy
Editorial-Production Administrator:
   Annette Joseph
Editorial-Production Service:
   Omegatype Typography, Inc.

Text Designer: Joyce C. Weston
Electronic Composition:
   Omegatype Typography, Inc.
Composition Buyer: Linda Cox
Manufacturing Buyer: JoAnne Sweeney
Cover Administrator: Linda Knowles
Cover Designer: Studio Nine

For related titles and support materials, visit our online catalog at www.ablongman.com.

Between the time website information is gathered and then published, it is not unusual for some sites to have closed. Also, the transcription of URLs can result in typographical errors. The publisher would appreciate notification where these errors occur so that they may be corrected in subsequent editions.

Cataloging-in-Publication Data

Direct practice in social work / Scott W. Boyle . . . [et al.].
       p.   cm.
   Includes bibliographical references and index.
   ISBN 0-205-40162-7
       1. Social service. 2. Social service—United States. I. Boyle, Scott W.

HV40.D587 2006
361.3'2—dc22

                                              2004063376

Printed in the United States of America

10 9 8 7 6 5 4 3 2   RRD-VA   10   09   08   07   06   05

Brief Contents

Contents

Chapter 3   Values, Ethics, and Ethical Dilemmas   67

PART II THE HELPING PROCESS 103

Chapter 4 Basic Skills for Engagement 105

Chapter 5   Knowledge and Skills for Assessment   143

Chapter 6   Knowledge and Skills for Planning   177

Chapter 7   Knowledge and Skills for Intervention   215

Chapter 8 Developing Clients' Coping Skills 249

Chapter 9 Empowerment and Strengths-Based Practice 281

Chapter 10 Strengthening Family Functioning 311

Chapter 11 Improving Group Functioning 347

Chapter 14   Knowledge and Skills of Termination   445

This text is a guide to direct practice in social work. It is intended to help students understand the multiple areas of knowledge, skills, and values that underpin this important social work practice arena. The text is divided into two sections. The first focuses on basic information required in all areas of social work practice. Thus, Chapters 1–3 are devoted to understanding the definition of and roles involved in direct practice as well as the major theories that support direct practice interventions. The first section also describes the social work values and ethical principles that govern the profession's work with client systems.

The second section, Chapters 4–14, covers the steps in the helping process, including engagement, assessment, planning, intervention, evaluation, and termination. The intervention chapters provide detailed information on working with individuals, families, groups, and larger systems within the direct practice paradigm. Consistent with the thrust of direct practice, we have emphasized the knowledge and skills necessary for helping at the micro and mezzo levels with the understanding that many of these will be useful in working with systems of other sizes. For example, the chapter on helping clients improve their coping skills can be used as readily with families as with groups. Likewise, group work skills can be employed when necessary for addressing problems in organizations or larger systems.

Ultimately, this book underscores the importance of the generalist perspective of social work practice that is required by the Council on Social Work Education for first-year MSW programs. It also builds on and is distinguished from the generalist practice model used throughout BSW programs in the United States. It is our hope that students and faculty will find the text an important addition to the resources currently available in social work education.

A Note from the Publisher: Instructor's Supplements

Instructor's Manual

For each chapter in the text, the Instructor's Manual includes learning objectives, chapter summaries, key terms with definitions, classroom discussion questions, and related web links. The Instructor's Manual is available in print and electronically.

Test Bank

The Test Bank contains a multitude of questions in multiple choice, true/false, and essay formats. The Test Bank is free on request to adopters and is available in print and electronically.

Computerized Test Bank

The printed Test Bank is also available through Allyn and Bacon's computerized testing system, TestGen EQ. This fully networkable test generating software is available on a multiplatform CD-ROM for Windows and Macintosh. The user-friendly interface allows you to view, edit, and add questions, transfer questions to tests, and print tests in a variety of fonts. Search and sort features allow you to locate questions quickly and to arrange them in whatever order you prefer. TestGen EQ is free on request to adopters.

PowerPoint Presentation

A PowerPoint presentation created for this text provides dozens of ready-to-use lecture outlines with graphics. The presentation is available electronically for Mac or Windows.

A Note from the Publisher: Student Supplements

Companion Website with Online Study Guide

This website includes case studies with application questions, flash cards of key terms, practice tests, professional series of web links, as well as a Navigating Direct Practice section dedicated to Research Navigator™.

Research Navigator™ for the Helping Profession: Resources for College Research Assignments

Pearson's new Research Navigator™ for the Helping Professions is the easiest way for students to start a research assignment or research paper. Complete with extensive help on the research process and three exclusive databases of credible and reliable source material, including EBSCO's Content Select Academic Journal Database, *New York Times* Search by Subject Archive, and "Best of the Web" Link Library, Research Navigator™ helps students quickly and efficiently make the most of their research time. Research Navigator™ requires a Pearson Access Code, which is included in our Allyn & Bacon Research Navigator™ Guide for the Helping Professions. These guides facilitate appropriate academic use of the Internet by helping students to strengthen their research skills and to quickly and easily find and cite reliable sources. Available FREE when packaged with a new Allyn and Bacon text. See your publisher's representative for bookstore order codes. Access Research Navigator™ at **www.ablongman.com/researchnavigator**.

The Career Center

Allyn and Bacon realizes that making the jump from student to professional is challenging. We're dedicated to making this transition as smooth as possible with our new career assistance service, offered FREE to any student using a new Allyn and Bacon textbook. Employing qualified career specialists, the Career Center addresses the wide range of preparation and life stages of individuals attempting to develop their career through education. Students who register for our service are entitled to eight 30-minute sessions, a total of four hours of career consultant time. Services offered include career advice, resume review and critiquing, networking and relationship building, interviewing skills, portfolio review in education, and more. Contact your publisher's representative for more details and order codes.

(Special package ISBN is required.) Access the Career Center at **www.ablongman.com/careercenter**.

Social Work Career Packs

Allyn and Bacon combines our two most popular career preparation resources into one unique package to make the leap from student to professional that much easier. Both the Career Center and *Thinking about a Social Work Career? 2/e* by Leon Ginsberg provide students with up-to-date information on social work education, finding employment, salaries and benefits, and licensing and legal regulation. Students who register for the Career Center are entitled to eight 30-minute sessions, a total of four hours of career consultant time. Contact your publisher's representative for more details and order codes.

Acknowledgments

Writing a text can be a time-consuming and frustrating endeavor punctuated by deadlines, reviewer suggestions, and editor feedback. It is a pleasure to note that while the time-consuming characteristic could not be avoided, the rest of the process of preparing this manuscript proceeded without many of the usual vexations. Much of the credit for this degree of smoothness goes to Patricia Quinlin, acquisitions editor for Allyn and Bacon, and to Shannon Steed, development editor. Their continued creativity, thoughtfulness, and commitment to this book are greatly appreciated.

Reviewers

It is also important to mention the many colleagues who agreed to review all or parts of the book and to provide enormously useful comments that contributed to the overall quality of the manuscript. Their support and encouragement are also appreciated. These individuals include: Chrystal Barranti, California State University, Sacramento; Nancy Brown, University of South Carolina; Terry Carilio, San Diego State University; Miriam Clubok, Ohio University; Jacqueline Cocoran, Virginia Commonwealth University; Dan Coleman, Portland State University; Helen Crohn, Columbia University; David Droppa, Seton Hall University; James Hanson, University of Northern Iowa; Robert Jackson, University of Washington, Tacoma; Larry Livingston, University of Illinois, Springfield; Tony Maltese, Southern Connecticut State University; Diana Mirabito, New York University; Susan Mittendorf, Louisiana State University; Mary Montminy-Danna, Salve Regina University; Robert Ortega, University of Michigan; George Patterson, New York University; Ellen Ryan, Florida Atlantic University; Sally Speer, University of South Florida; Mimi Tracey, University of Georgia; Nancy Udolph, Ashland University; Ruth Anna Van Loon, University of Cincinnati; Dexter Voisin, University of Chicago; Tanya Voss, University of Texas; Ellen Whipple, Michigan State University; and Stephen Wong, Florida International University.

Voices from the Field Contributors

In addition to the reviewers, we are grateful to the contributors who have shared their stories in our Voices from the Field feature. We would like to thank the following students of social work and social work professionals: Paula

Allen-Meares, Dorothy S. Becvar, Edward R. Canda, Barry Cournoyer, Leon Ginsberg, Kim Jeanson, Della Marshall, Kenneth McCoy, Zoe Minor, John Nickisson, Maria Puig, Frederic G. Reamer, María Janet Rodriguez, Dennis Saleebey, and Jessica Whitney.

Others who contributed to preparation of the manuscript include Cheryl Gibson, Jeana Lee, and Becky Lübbers, of the University of Utah College of Social Work. Jane Boyle (Scott's better half) and Mary Farley (Bill's better half) also assisted. We would also like to extend a special thank you to Bonnie Lantz, our colleague at the University of Utah, for her help in creating the Applications to Practice features and also the Writing Skills for Social Workers appendix. We would be greatly remiss if we did not thank the legions of students who have passed through our classrooms over a cumulative 135 years of teaching. Many have challenged our thinking and led us to revise our pedagogy while simultaneously inspiring us with their curiosity and enthusiasm. It is for their benefit that we undertook this project.

Finally, we would like to acknowledge the many author colleagues whose contributions to the literature of social work have encouraged us to continue a Utah tradition. Those with the Utah connection include Amanda Barusch, Barry Cournoyer, Dean H. Hepworth, Jo Ann Larsen, Rex O. Skidmore, and Milton Thackeray, to name just a few. We are pleased to add our contribution to theirs.

Scott W. Boyle is Associate Professor in the B.S.W. program at the University of Utah College of Social Work. His academic experience includes teaching at both the M.S.W. and B.S.W. levels for the past sixteen years. His focus has centered on micro and mezzo practice as well as on human behavior in the social environment. He holds an M.S.W. from the University of Southern Mississippi and a Ph.D. from Brigham Young University. He began his teaching career at Grambling State University, where he served as chair of the Mental Health Concentration Committee for eight years. He has coauthored two social work texts as well as a number of articles related to the profession. Boyle's practice experience has centered on the field of mental health and rehabilitation. He has been employed by numerous psychiatric, rehabilitation, and general medical hospitals providing both inpatient and outpatient clinical services. He has also maintained a private practice for the past twenty years. His hobbies include fly-fishing, golf, and traveling.

Grafton H. Hull, Jr., is Director of the B.S.W. program at the University of Utah College of Social Work and has taught at the B.S.W., M.S.W., and Ph.D. levels over the past thirty years. His academic appointments include Director of the School of Social Work at Southwest Missouri State University and of the Division of Social Work at Indiana University Northwest. Hull holds Ed.D., M.S.W., and B.S. degrees, and his practice experience is in mental health, child welfare, delinquency services, and family services. Hull is licensed as an independent social worker in Wisconsin. He is coauthor of seven social work texts and has contributed many articles to social work journals. In addition, Hull is a consulting editor for three social work journals and has held leadership positions in state and national social work organizations, including NASW, BPD, the Institute for the Advancement of Social Work Research, and CSWE. He serves as a frequent consultant to graduate and undergraduate social work programs in the United States and Canada. His hobbies include coin collecting and golf.

Jannah Hurn Mather is Dean of the College of Social Work at the University of Utah. She is coauthor of three social work texts and many articles in peer-reviewed journals. Mather has twenty-four years of experience as a social work educator and has taught at all levels of social work education. Her practice experience includes mental health, family services, and therapy with children. All three of Mather's degrees are in social work. She has served on the CSWE Commission on Accreditation and is a site visitor for the organization. She also serves as a consultant for social work education programs. Prior roles included private practitioner in Florida, dean of the Faculty of Social Work at Wilfrid Laurier University in Waterloo, Ontario, and associate dean of the Florida State University School of Social Work. Her hobbies include pottery and collecting antique furniture and quilts.

Larry Lorenzo Smith received his B.S., M.S.W., and D.S.W. degrees from the University of Utah. He has been a full-time faculty member at the College of Social Work since 1974, the Director of Admissions at the

College of Social Work for the past eleven years, and M.S.W. director for the past five years. Smith is a licensed clinical social worker and a marriage and family therapist and supervisor. He has published articles on crisis intervention, health, mental health, and corrections along with an earlier book on crisis intervention, and is also the coauthor of two social work textbooks.

O. William Farley received his B.S., M.S.W., and Ph.D. degrees from the University of Utah. Following his graduation from the M.S.W. program, Farley served for three years in the U.S. Air Force as a captain in the Medical Services. At his last assignment, he was the chief psychiatric social worker at the USAF Hospital at Travis Air Force Base in California. In 1962, Farley became a full-time faculty member at the University of Utah Graduate School of Social Work. He has held many different positions within the College of Social Work, including director of the master's program, director of the doctoral program, associate dean for research, and director of the Social Research Institute. Farley is also a licensed clinical social worker and marriage and family therapist. He has published extensively in the fields of health, mental health, and clinical practice and coauthored a number of textbooks related to the social work profession. He has been the principal investigator on many research grants, including an NIMH grant on case management strategies.

Part One

Introduction

THIS SECTION OF THE TEXT provides the foundation that underlies the knowledge and skills of direct practice in social work. To establish this foundation, we recognize three important areas of the profession that need to be addressed: (1) a brief history of social work practice, (2) an orientation to the theories that support direct practice, and (3) the values and ethics of the profession that play such a critical role in practice.

To understand the present status of practice within the profession, students need to understand the past and how social work has evolved over the last century and more. We have learned much, yet the process is ongoing and will continue as we mature as a profession and learn from our successes as well as our mistakes.

One of the primary features that separates the trained practitioner from the well-intentioned individual is those skills applied in practice that are grounded in sound theory and research. Without this foundation, the helper is no different from the neighbor, family member, or barber. Although the person may be sincere in their advice, it may lead to more harm than good or potentially interfere with the progress or remediation of the problem. Further, we live in a litigious society. If direct practice is grounded in recognized theory and techniques and practitioners are able to defend their plan, they will be seen as providing an acceptable standard of care. Our understanding of theory also provides us with a fund of knowledge that allows us to communicate, at a professional level, with other helpers and to be recognized as credible providers of services.

Another distinguishing feature of trained professionals is that their work is guided by values and ethical principles and standards for practice. The values adhered to by social workers make their profession unique. The standards set forth lay the foundation for entering into a professional relationship with a client as well as aiding in the selection and implementation of intervention models and techniques.

Chapter 1

Direct Practice in Social Work

■ Chip Vu read his agency's intake form on the Sawyer family as he prepared to meet with them. This was Chip's first case since graduating with his MSW degree, and he wanted to do a good job. However, the more he read, the more he began to worry. The Sawyer family was not your typical family and their needs were incredibly complex. This case looked like it was going to require all of his knowledge and skill if he was to be successful in helping the family. As he read the intake worker's notes, Chip made a list of the challenges facing the Sawyers:

- David Sawyer, the father, unemployed following the closure of his plant, was experiencing high levels of stress, saying cryptically that he felt like he wanted to jump out of his skin.
- Helen Sawyer, the mother, was showing signs of postpartum depression.
- The family was in danger of being evicted from their apartment for failure to pay the rent due to Mr. Sawyer's unemployment.
- Six-year-old Matt Sawyer had been diagnosed with attention deficit hyperactivity disorder.
- Baby Samantha, now four months old, was born with a cleft palate and would need surgery in the future.
- Finally, there were suspicions that Matt was reacting strongly to the new baby; he had talked about hurting her.

As he finished reading the intake report, Chip took a deep breath and headed for the agency's waiting room to meet the Sawyers and begin his first case.

Social work has a long history of providing a wide variety of services to clients, ranging from counseling and therapy for individuals, families, and groups to community organization and social action designed to change some aspect of the larger environment. The practice of social work has thus encompassed an enormous area and brought social workers into arenas as diverse as schools, mental health agencies, housing authorities, prisons and correctional facilities, domestic violence shelters, group homes, and child welfare agencies, to name only a few. To understand this diversity, we need to look at several topics. These include the definition of social work practice and its history, mission, and purposes. It also requires distinguishing between direct practice and generalist practice and identifying the knowledge, values, and skills that are required for success in this profession.

This chapter begins by addressing these issues and concludes with a review of the remaining chapters. Our purpose is to clearly communicate the richness of the social work profession and to help prepare direct practitioners for the roles they will play as social workers.

Purpose and Function of Social Work

Barker (1999) describes social work as "the applied science of helping people achieve an effective level of psychosocial functioning and effecting societal changes to enhance the well-being of all people" (p. 455). This definition reflects the twin concerns of the social work profession, namely helping individuals function better and working for societal conditions that benefit everyone. The National Association of Social Workers (NASW) expands slightly on Barker's definition in describing social work as "the professional activity of helping individuals, groups, or communities enhance or restore their capacity for social functioning and creating societal conditions favorable to this goal" (NASW, 1973, p. 4). Here is a recognition that social workers also assist systems besides the individual. There is also a clear understanding that social workers deal with at least two types of people: those who need assistance to get back to a healthier stage in their lives (restoration) and those who have the capacity to develop increased competence in their lives (enhancement). The Sawyer family, for instance, illustrates the first situation, in that they were once better able to manage their lives. Clients of the second type are not necessarily considered deficient in some aspect, but it is assumed they can get better at what they do.

The preamble to the NASW Code of Ethics provides a different but related view of the mission of social work. This document notes that *"the primary mission of the social work profession is to enhance human well-being and help meet the basic human needs of all people, with particular attention to the needs and empowerment of people who are vulnerable, oppressed, and living in poverty"*

(NASW, 1999, p. 1). This statement reflects the traditional role of the profession that traces its roots back to the settlement house movement and early efforts to help those without adequate resources.

Defining Social Work Practice

NASW further defines social work practice as

> the professional application of social work values, principles, and techniques to one or more of the following ends: helping people obtain tangible services; providing counseling and psychotherapy with individuals, families, and groups; helping communities or groups provide or improve social and health services; and participating in relevant legislative processes. The practice of social work requires knowledge of human development and behavior; of social, economic, and cultural institutions; and of the interaction of all these factors. (1999, p. 5)

This is certainly the case with the Sawyer family, which needs tangible services such as financial assistance and medical care as well as counseling.

One important characteristic of social work that helps set it apart from most other groups is "the profession's focus on individual well-being in a social context and the well-being of society" (NASW, 1999, p. 1). This focus results from a basic conviction that there is a mutual interaction between the individual and the larger society that affects both systems. Gordon Hamilton, an early social work functional theorist and practitioner, talked about this concept as the "person-situation" perspective (Shoshani, 1984). Today, social work refers to this focus as *person-in-environment*, a framework that helps set the profession apart from many others in the human services field.

The person-in-environment concern of social work means that as change agents we give "attention to the environmental forces that create, contribute to, and address problems in living" (NASW, 1999, p. 1). This perspective grew in favor with the development of the ecological model of social work practice, which saw the individual within the larger environment as an ecosystem. Within this ecosystem, social workers could work with the individual, the family, or the larger environment. In addition, social workers could focus on the intersection or interface of the person with the environment, looking at whether transactions between the two benefited both (Johnson & Yanca, 2004). The influence of the environment on the individual can be seen in the case of Mr. Sawyer, whose loss of employment has contributed to his high levels of stress and reduced his ability to adequately support his family.

Another key characteristic of the profession is its historic concern about *social justice* and a commitment to social change. Barker (1999) defines social justice as "an ideal condition in which all members of a society have the same basic rights, protections, opportunities, obligations, and social benefits" (p. 451). The concern about social justice arises from an awareness that resources, opportunities, and benefits are not distributed equitably within society. This inequality is fostered by a variety of factors ranging from discrimination and oppression to bad luck and poor life choices. As a profession, social work is committed to bringing about social justice and eliminating the barriers that prevent people from meeting their needs.

At the same time, social workers are expected to "enhance the capacity of people to address their own needs" while seeking to promote social institutions that are responsive to "individuals' needs and social problems"

(NASW, 1999, p. 1). This responsibility can involve helping clients develop their own problem-solving skills, teaching them how to navigate resource systems, and building their capacity for dealing with future challenges. The Code of Ethics states that social work activities may be carried out "in the form of direct practice, community organizing, supervision, consultation, administration, advocacy, social and political action, policy development and implementation, education, and research and evaluation" (NASW, 1999, p. 1).

The preamble to the code makes it clear that direct practice is considered a primary practice activity for social workers that can be employed alone or in conjunction with other activities. Some social workers' entire careers are devoted to providing direct practice, whereas other social workers are engaged in efforts to change organizations and communities to make them more responsive to the needs of individuals and families. Some social workers have supervisory or administrative roles in agencies or engage in policy development at levels ranging from the individual agency to legislative arenas. Still others teach and some engage in research and evaluation activities designed to build the knowledge base of the profession and identify ways to improve the well-being of all members of society. All of these activities are considered appropriate for and consistent with common definitions or understandings of social work practice.

Historical Perspectives on Social Work Practice

As noted earlier, social work has had a long tradition of concern for social justice and social change on behalf of vulnerable and at-risk populations. The early Charity Organization Society and the settlement house movement demonstrated this commitment as social workers acted to improve living and working conditions for people, taught immigrants how to read and speak English, and pushed for laws to protect children from abuse and neglect. The profession was clearly committed to a goal of improving society and bringing about change whenever and wherever possible. This two-pronged focus on helping the individual directly and bringing about changes in society captured what social work was all about in the early part of the twentieth century. Interestingly, these goals and related activities were closely connected as demonstrated by one social work pioneer, Edith Abbott, who observed that good social workers both help people out of the ditch and simultaneously try to eliminate the ditch (Abbott, 1919, p. 313).

At the same time, much of what social workers actually did involved simply doing things for the client (Shulman, 1999). To a large extent, social workers were trying to socialize immigrants, the poor, and other downtrodden segments of society to the values and beliefs of the middle class. In general, those being helped were viewed as not yet possessing the characteristics needed to successfully navigate within the norms of society.

Social Work as a Profession

During the early part of the twentieth century, social work was less an identified profession and more a collection of threads, each one sufficiently different to challenge the idea that a single profession was possible. One thread was composed of those who saw in social action the raison d'être of the profession, mainly settlement house workers and others who believed that society must change in order for individuals to achieve their goals. However, their focus remained largely on helping the individual, a process described as social casework.

A second thread was made up of group workers who shared some characteristics with the settlement house practitioners but who saw groups as a potential means of helping individuals cope with the hazards of life. The third strand was composed of social workers dedicated to fund-raising and coordination of services, an early emphasis on community organization. By the 1930s, these three threads—casework, group work, and community organization—were all associated with social work in spite of their different theoretical perspectives.

The three threads were officially recognized as a single profession in 1955 with the founding of the National Association of Social Workers, an organization made up of seven existing social work bodies. At the same time, each specialization was recognized as separate and distinct despite sharing an ethical code, similar values, a common knowledge base, and a basic skill set.

Although this evolution might seem smooth and effortless, it was in fact characterized by multiple fissures, disagreements, and disputes. For example, social workers were challenged early on by Abraham Flexner (Austin, 1983), who argued in 1915 that social work was not a profession because it did not meet several conditions necessary for such a designation. Over the next twenty-five or more years, social workers undertook several steps that they believed would lead to increased status for social work. Perhaps one of the most controversial steps was the gradual adoption of a diagnostic school of thought that used medicine as its model. The work of Freud and others seemed to offer social work a body of theory that could be used to better understand clients. The diagnostic school emphasized identifying specific causes for the difficulties clients faced, just as a physician does in diagnosing a physical illness. Although the theories used to understand human behavior in the social environment changed over time, the predominant focus remained on diagnosing the individual's problem.

As other theorists developed different approaches to understanding the human being, an additional school of thought developed, that of functionalism. Based on the works of Otto Rank and others, the functionalist school was most closely associated with Jessie Taft, dean of the Pennsylvania School of Social Work. Other theorists such as Carl Rogers aligned with this alternative school of thought (Gilbert, Miller, & Specht, 1980). The functional school challenged the diagnostic or medical school at a time when social work was enthralled with Freud's theory of human development. Functionalism rejected the idea that the individual's personality was formed almost entirely by early childhood experiences. This new school did not consider the client as either "sick or deviant but rather as a person requesting a specific service" (Johnson & Yanca, 2004, p. 23). The functional school was concerned with time-limited interventions that were directly related to the function of the social worker's agency. The focus of the social worker–client interaction was to work together to achieve the client's identified goals. The functional school has been labeled a "growth model" in which "the worker's major responsibility is to use his or her self in providing a relationship in which consumers can discover, reaffirm, and tap the growth impulses of their true selves, or at least the sense of true self sufficient to mobilize their own resources to deal with their specific problems in social living" (Anderson, 1981, p. 166). Clients are viewed as having the capacity to change and grow, a perspective that is consistent with the strengths-based approaches used in social work today (Furman, 2002).

The threat to the diagnostic school posed by the functionalist school was particularly unwelcome. The result was that the functionalists "found themselves excluded from the mainstream of the field. They were not invited to present at conferences, and the peer review process worked to exclude their publications from journals" (Shulman, 1991, p. 17).

The Freudian emphasis on the individual and the diagnostic/medical model left little room for consideration of other factors that might be responsible for the client's situation. As a consequence, some have argued that this model took social work far away from its roots in the community and its focus on social action and social justice (Specht & Courtney, 1994). Today, aspects of both diagnostic and functional schools can be seen in social work practice. However, the profession recognizes that factors in the environment can and do influence the client's ability to meet needs and realize aspirations. It also values the strengths that clients bring to their work with social workers and is aware of the deleterious effects of deficit models that focus on shortcomings and problems.

Current Challenges

At the same time, changes in the practice arena have produced multiple challenges for social workers. Managed care, once relegated to the realm of physical illness, is now a part of the practice of a large proportion of social workers. Short-term treatment models are heavily used and supported by both efficacy research and managed care companies. Social workers, even those who believe strongly in recognizing a client's strengths, face the prospect of having to use a diagnostic label in order to ensure that the client receives services that will be paid for by insurance.

Another challenge that social workers face today is the devolution of social policies and the programs they provide. Many of the social programs that were routinely available and to which clients had some measure of entitlement have been replaced with new ones that no longer recognize that the client has any rights. Programs that were originally federally structured and funded are now often passed down to the states or municipalities with less funding than was originally the case. Changes in philosophy about the poor and other commonly encountered groups now mean that these groups must earn the services they receive. The combination of reduced funding, the movement of programs from federal to state auspices, and the resultant challenges make the task of social workers that much more complicated. On the other hand, the devolution of programs to the state also means that decision makers are closer at hand, and the opportunity for influencing social policy development is perhaps greater than in the past. As the saying goes, one door closes and another door opens.

An additional challenge facing social workers is the continued emphasis on professionalism that has resulted in all states licensing social workers at the MSW level and in over thirty states licensing BSW social workers. Often these licensing laws provide for multiple levels within the same state, such as certified social worker (CSW), certified independent social worker (CISW), and licensed clinical social worker (LCSW). No longer is it sufficient to graduate with a social work degree and go to work. Practitioners now are required to pass state-mandated examinations and meet other criteria in order to practice their craft. In the case that began this chapter, Chip Vu had already passed the examination required to be an LCSW but would have to spend two more years under supervision in order to achieve this certification.

At the same time, social work professional organizations such as the National Association of Social Workers have created a series of credentials to recognize increased competence on the part of practitioners. These include the Academy of Certified Social Workers and the Diplomate in Clinical Social Work. The social worker can also achieve additional certifications, including such things as certified substance abuse counselor or certified social work manager.

Social work educational programs offered at colleges and universities are also subject to a certification process. Accreditation of college and university social work programs began in 1932 and is continued today by the Council on Social Work Education (CSWE), which accredits both BSW and MSW programs throughout the United States (Berengarten, 1986). These programs now number about 600, with about 450 accredited undergraduate programs and around 150 graduate programs. Often, licensing by the state requires a student to graduate from a school accredited by CSWE. Chip Vu, for example, had earned his MSW from a school of social work that was accredited by CSWE. As the president of the student organization, Chip had met with the CSWE site team that visited the school, an experience of which he was quite proud.

The social work field has developed different terms to refer to what members of the profession do. These include concepts such as generalist practice, generalist perspective, direct practice, and micro, mezzo, and macro practice. We discuss each of these in the following pages.

Generalist Practice and the Generalist Perspective

The *generalist perspective,* a term used by the Council on Social Work Education, captures the unique way that social workers practice their profession. The **generalist perspective** is an approach to helping that reflects social work's commitment to comprehensive assessments and planning. The approach recognizes the social environment's influence on the client's quality of life, and the worker takes this into consideration when assessing client problems, strengths, and capacities. Planning and interventions must be equally comprehensive to address the factors that prevent people from achieving their goals.

The use of the term *generalist perspective* is one way that CSWE distinguishes between social workers prepared at the graduate (MSW) level and those at the undergraduate (BSW) level. The mission of undergraduate social work programs is to prepare students to "apply the knowledge and skills of generalist social work practice with systems of all sizes" (CSWE, 2003, p. 33). Generalist practice has been defined somewhat differently by various authors but tends to be characterized by a common set of elements. For our purposes, we define generalist practice as the use of the problem-solving process to intervene with systems of various sizes, including individuals, families, groups, organizations, and communities. By problem-solving process, we are referring to a step-by-step model that includes engaging with the client, assessing problem areas and identifying strengths, creating and carrying out an intervention plan, evaluating the success of that intervention, and terminating the client–practitioner relationship. The generalist operates within a systems and person-in-environment framework and recognizes that many problems require intervention with more than one system. By the very nature and definition of undergraduate social work education, graduates are generalists who possess a knowledge base and skills required for entry-level positions in the social welfare enterprise.

The broad mandate associated with generalist practice at the BSW level does not mean that these graduates will be prepared to handle all of the problematic situations they will encounter in their practice. They do, however, have the ability to practice with multiple system sizes while recognizing the limits of their educational preparation. Clients who need extensive direct practice assistance are likely to be referred to graduate-level practitioners who possess the higher level of knowledge and skill required to deal with more complex situations.

In contrast to BSW programs, graduate education prepares students with "the knowledge and skills of a generalist social work perspective to practice with systems of all sizes" (CSWE, 2003, p. 33). However, in addition, graduates are prepared for advanced professional practice in an area of concentration or speciality. Although neither CSWE nor NASW define the term **generalist social work perspective,** it is clear that those completing a graduate program will possess the ability to use a problem-solving process with systems of various sizes while also operating within a person-in-environment framework that is endemic to the profession of social work. Graduate practitioners will have the capability, in concert with the client, to engage, assess, plan, intervene, evaluate, and terminate with clients but with the added ability that arises from the concentration or specialization completed in the second year of the MSW program. They will be able to engage clients who are experiencing more serious problems, develop plans that reflect greater levels of depth, and undertake more complex interventions. They will be able to do this, however, within the same generalist perspective that most in the field associate with the profession of social work.

Both generalist social workers and specialists with a generalist perspective are needed in the field and both contribute to the purpose and mission of the social work profession. Careful consideration of the levels of practice for which each is competent is an ongoing task for social work agencies, organizations, state licensing bodies, and the profession itself. BSW- and MSW-prepared social workers complement one another in addressing the enormous variety of human and social problems encountered today.

Defining Direct Practice

The decision by NASW to identify direct practice as one method of delivering social work services was a recognition that practitioners play a wide variety of roles. The direct practice role has usually been associated, or used interchangeably, with clinical practice (Shulman, 1999; Pinderhughes, 1995). Barker (1999) defines *direct practice* as "the term used by social workers to indicate their range of professional activities on behalf of clients in which goals are reached through personal contact and immediate influence with those seeking social services. It is to be distinguished from *indirect practice*" (p. 130). His definition highlights the importance of personal contact between the practitioner and the *client,* a term that encompasses at least individuals, families, groups, and, in some instances, larger systems. For our purposes, **direct practice** is the provision of services to individuals, groups, and families that includes therapy, counseling, education, and other roles designed to enhance the problem-solving capacities of clients, improve their well-being, and assist them in meeting basic human needs.

The focus in direct practice is on face-to-face interactions with clients, which is sometimes called *micro practice.* It differs from other social work activities that do not necessarily involve direct contact with clients. Supervisors and agency administrators, for example, certainly play an important role in serving the needs of agency clients, but they are not responsible for providing services directly to those clients. Likewise, social workers engaged in community organizing, program development, and legislative advocacy are much less likely to have face-to-face contact with those who will ultimately benefit from their efforts. Historically, the work of supervisors, administrators, and community/organizational change agents has been called *indirect practice.* This term reflects the fact that although clients or groups of clients will certainly benefit from the social worker's activities, these activities are one step removed from direct contact with the client. Although some social workers in direct practice will provide consultation to other practitioners, this is not their primary function in their agency or organization. Likewise, the experience of serving multiple clients with similar needs may result in the direct practitioner becoming involved in efforts to develop new programs serving these needs. Albeit important, these are considered ancillary activities for direct practitioners. The concept of multiple client needs is evident in the Sawyer case. Chip Vu's agency considers him a direct practitioner.

Micro, Mezzo, and Macro Practice

Whereas social workers once described their activities as either casework, group work, or community organization, new terminology has been used more recently. The terms *micro, mezzo,* and *macro* have been used to distinguish between social workers helping an individual (micro level), a family or group (mezzo level), or an organization or community (macro level). Unfortunately, there has been confusion over the meanings of the individual terms. Some describe work with families as micro practice, whereas others believe it is mezzo-level practice. The term *clinical practice* is sometimes used interchangeably with *micro practice,* especially if families are included in the mezzo level. The level of intimacy is generally higher in micro practice.

Mezzo-level practice is considered less intensive than micro level because the client may be a member of a self-help group or therapy group, and the relationship between worker and client is thought to be less intimate. The focus of mezzo practice is on modifying the various systems with which the client interacts, including the family or peers.

Social workers operating at the macro level are engaged in activities such as community organization, social action, administration of services, program evaluation, and other activities generally not involving face-to-face interactions with clients. Social policy issues affecting clients are also a concern of macro-level social workers who might focus their efforts on legislative advocacy or planning. Sometimes macro-level work is considered indirect practice because the social worker is not working directly with clients. This is one way of differentiating this level of activity from direct practice. However, overlap between direct and indirect practice often exists.

Direct Practice Roles

Direct practice may involve any number of roles that assist the client in meeting identified needs. These roles include that of therapist/counselor, educator, broker, case manager, case advocate, group leader, and mediator (Shulman, 1999; Hepworth, Rooney, & Larsen, 2002; Knox & Roberts, 2002).

Therapist/Counselor

The role of therapist/counselor is typically one of the most attractive to social workers. It is the one students most often gravitate to during their graduate work, and it tends to be the most highly rewarded role in social work. At the same time, it is only one of several important social work roles or activities. Activities associated with the role of therapist/counselor include:

- Building relationships with clients
- Assessing client strengths and needs
- Developing an intervention plan in concert with the client
- Implementing an intervention plan
- Monitoring and evaluating client progress and intervention plan activities
- Terminating the client–professional relationship

Therapists attempt to understand client behavior and situations using a variety of theories and models and employing techniques and approaches that seek to enhance the client's quality of life. Maguire (2002) identifies some of the characteristics of the clinical therapist's role, noting that these interventions require an advanced level of "knowledge, skills, and expertise" and a "repertoire of the appropriate behavioral, cognitive, psychodynamic, problem-solving and other developing methods required to resolve complex psychosocial problems" (p. 36). Clinical work is also characterized as "systems based in that it recognizes the effects of the interacting social environment and particularly the need to increase social supports and decrease sources of stress and negative forces in the client's system" (p. 36). The social work focus on the "biopsychosocial" factors that influence human behavior requires this type of systemic approach because single explanations of cause and effect fail to capture the enormous interplay among systems and their environments. Moreover, the techniques used by direct practitioners are often drawn from the specific theory or theories on which we base our assessments. Again, this requires a broad base of knowledge and skills to choose and apply the appropriate technique(s).

Maguire (2002) also comments that the methods therapists use must be "integrative," involving both a wide knowledge base and a careful focus on the appropriate strategies to be used. Clinical work must also be "empirical," in the sense that it uses the results of research to inform practice, and "eclectic," by virtue of its use of different theories and methods to achieve the goals of intervention (pp. 36–37).

The therapist/counselor role may be employed one-on-one with a single client, or with multiple individuals, as might occur in a family therapy setting. Likewise, it may be carried out in groups serving clients with similar issues such as depression, anger management, or self-destructive behavior. Therapists/counselors, in many of their activities, combine this role with others such as that of educator. Chip will certainly be engaging in this role with the Sawyer family.

Educator

A significant component of the work done by direct practitioners is educational in nature. In the role of educator, the direct practice social worker might be helping clients to develop new skills, teaching more effective ways of parenting, or orienting clients to new experiences they will face. They may be providing information on services with which the client is unfamiliar or helping group members deal with a family member suffering from a psychiatric disorder. As educators, social workers must be aware of what clients already know, judge their capacity for additional learning, adapt teaching activities to the individual's learning

style, and support and recognize client learning as it occurs (Lloyd, 1980; Hoffman & Sallee, 1994).

Of course, education does not need to be focused on an individual client system. One can, for example, provide education on preventing suicide aimed at the "general public, mental health professionals, and agency personnel regarding the characteristic thinking and behavior of suicidal persons" (Gilliland & James, 1993, p. 155). In a sense, this is an indirect practice role because there is no face-to-face interaction with a client system.

In addition, clients can be provided reading material to help them better understand certain issues in their lives. The adult children of alcoholics, for example, might be given readings that help provide different perspectives on their past experiences and potential risks. Educational activities might be directed at women who have survived battering, those dealing with multiple life stressors, or others facing serious medical problems such as surgery. Like therapy/counseling, the educational role can be carried out with an individual client, families, or groups. It can also be used to work for change in larger systems such as helping police officers develop appropriate responses in cases involving sexual assault or domestic violence. The Sawyer family may need information on what is involved in helping their son who has been diagnosed with attention deficit hyperactivity disorder.

Broker

Referring clients to available community services is a primary role for direct practitioners. This role is essential because clients often have multiple needs and the direct practitioner cannot hope to meet all of them. Knox and Roberts (2002), for example, identify brokering as a key activity of social workers in the field of forensic social work. Brokering is also one component in the work of case managers, a role described in the next section.

Brokering requires a solid knowledge of community services so that referrals can be made appropriately. Clients may need any number of resources, and the social worker must be familiar with everything from sources for concrete services such as financial help, to support and treatment services. Figure 1.1 gives an example of the types of needs one client might have. As you can see from the list, social workers must be able to offer some services themselves and to help clients and their

---

Figure 1.1

Identifying Multiple Client Needs

Lorenzo, age nineteen, was referred to the Mountain Mental Health Center with a long history of schizophrenia. Although he often would go several months without an episode, he usually relapsed, refused to take his medication, and became difficult for his sister to handle. Over the years, he had been hospitalized several times, stabilized, and released back to the community.

When Owen received the referral, he reviewed the initial information and prepared for his interview with Lorenzo and members of Lorenzo's family. During the interview, it became clear that both Lorenzo and the family had several needs. After his last stay in the hospital, Lorenzo had lost his job working in a car wash. Employment was important for him because it both gave him something to do during the day and produced an income. He would need to locate suitable employment soon.

Lorenzo also needed assistance staying on his medication and avoiding the tendency to quit whenever he began to feel better. His sister Annie, who cared for him, was experiencing doubts about whether she could continue to help Lorenzo and was feeling the exhaustion and anger that is common in these situations. Other family members, though they cared about him, seemed to have little understanding of Lorenzo's disorder and played a very small role in his life.

Owen assessed the needs of Lorenzo and his family as including the following:

- Employment that matched Lorenzo's abilities.

- A vocational rehabilitation program designed to increase Lorenzo's level of job skills.

- A support group for Annie designed for family members providing care for other members experiencing chronic mental illness. The group would provide emotional support, motivational techniques, and management skills to assist Annie in her efforts to care for Lorenzo.

- A psychoeducational group focused on informing family members about the nature of schizophrenia, common treatments, and appropriate community resources while also helping to reduce the family's anxiety about Lorenzo.

- Regular meetings with Owen designed to encourage continued use of medication and provide ongoing assessment of Lorenzo's needs.

- A community program offering respite care to allow Annie to take some time off from her caregiving responsibilities.

families locate other needed resources. In the case of the Sawyer family, the father may need help locating employment or acquiring job training, services about which Chip must be knowledgeable.

Case Manager

Rubin (1992) has defined case management as

> an approach to service delivery that attempts to ensure that clients with complex, multiple problems and disabilities receive all the services they need in a timely and appropriate fashion. It is a boundary-spanning approach in that, instead of providing a specific direct service, it utilizes case managers who link the client to the maze of direct service providers. (p. 5)

Case management is an important role for direct practitioners in many fields. Mather and Hull (2002) identify the role that case managers play in the child welfare field and describe three specialized models: community-based, strengths-based, and integrated case management. Walsh (2002) notes that case management is used frequently with "clients having serious mental illnesses such as schizophrenia, major depression, bipolar disorder, personality disorders, and substance abuse disorders" (p. 472). Typically, clients experiencing these disorders will have multiple needs that include financial help, counseling, medical care and medication, job training, housing, social support, and daily living skills.

Rothman (2002) identifies a series of functions that a direct practitioner carries out while doing case management. These include helping clients access the agency, conducting intake, providing assessment, setting goals, planning interventions, identifying resources, linking clients to agencies and programs, linking clients to families and social networks, moni-

toring progress, reassessing, and evaluating outcomes (pp. 467–469).

Of course, it should be emphasized that the case management role is often played simultaneously with other roles. For example, Hall, Carswell, Walsh, Huber, and Jampoler (2002) report the combined use of case management activities and brief, solution-focused therapy for rural clients receiving treatment for substance abuse. Similarly, Moxley (2002) has focused on the intersection of therapy and case management with clients experiencing serious mental illness. Harris and Bergman (1988) describe the inherent connection between therapy and case management in the therapeutic activities of the case manager. Figure 1.2 highlights their assessment of these activities.

Figure 1.2

Therapeutic Activities of Case Managers

- Forging a relationship or making a positive connection with a client. This may unfold in a variety of ways depending on a particular client's characteristics, and may range from high levels of interaction to the maintenance of interpersonal formality and distance.

- Modeling healthy behaviors to facilitate a client's movement from a position of dependency through one of imitation to an internalization of the case manager's qualities. When this is successful, the client internalizes assumptions such as that separate events can be organized into a coherent whole; that action can influence the course of events; that events unfold in a predictable, understandable way; and that he or she has unique needs, goals, and skills.

- Altering the client's physical environment through processes of creation, facilitation, and adjustment.

Source: Harris & Bergman, 1988 (pp. 5–13).

There is increasing evidence that case management services using a strengths-based approach are more effective for a variety of clients, including those receiving public assistance, dealing with substance abuse, or experiencing severe mental disabilities (Coffey, 1999; East, 1999; Sullivan, 2002; and Rapp, 2002).

It is important to differentiate the role of case manager from that of broker. Whereas the broker role is usually limited to locating and referring clients to appropriate resources, the case manager has the major responsibility for actually overseeing the case from start to finish. Not only do they make appropriate referrals, but they also work to ensure that services are coordinated for the client. They will likely work with other professionals and agencies to facilitate the delivery of services based on a specified service plan created in concert with the client. The level of their involvement with the client can vary depending on the individual's needs. In some situations, the case manager manages only the service plan while others provide the specific services required by the client. In other scenarios, the case manager may also be providing other services and playing other roles such as counselor or case advocate.

Case Advocate

Brill (1998) has described the advocate as "one who pleads the cause of another" and "one who argues for, defends, maintains, or recommends a cause or proposal" (p. 212). Advocacy in direct practice is often focused on activities that assist specific clients. Typically, this is referred to as case advocacy, in contrast to cause advocacy. *Case advocacy* is concerned with helping a client, whether that be an individual, family, or group. *Cause advocacy,* on the other hand, is concerned with achieving or enforcing rights for classes or groups of people such as all those with physical disabilities or all

those in a given neighborhood. It may grow out of a social worker's awareness that multiple families or clients encounter the same problem. Direct practice workers are not precluded from engaging in cause advocacy, but in most cases, employers do not sanction their direct practice social workers to carry out cause advocacy during working hours. Although cause advocacy is an appropriate activity for all social workers according to the NASW Code of Ethics, it is often done outside of their employment hours.

Typically, case advocacy is employed when the client is having difficulty obtaining benefits, services, or resources from an appropriate organization or agency. The difficulty may be the result of a misunderstanding, communication barriers, or discrimination based on gender, race, sexual orientation, or some other client characteristic.

The case advocate role can be carried out in a multiplicity of situations. For example, some schools have adopted "zero tolerance" policies against drugs, policies so stringent that an asthmatic student can be expelled from school for bringing an inhaler, a device that may be needed to save his life. In such situations, a school social worker or other direct practice social worker could advocate with the school to apply a more reasoned standard to the child's case. Case advocacy could be needed when a client is turned away from a medical facility because she lacks the financial resources to pay for a procedure that is critical to her health. In this case, the medical facility would be the target of the advocacy effort. In the Sawyer family's situation, Chip may need to play the role of an advocate with the family's landlord.

Group Leader

Social workers lead a variety of groups in direct practice. These can include both treatment groups, as mentioned earlier, and task groups, depending on the particular situation and needs of the client. Walsh (2000), for example, identifies the importance of establishing and leading support groups for families whose members are receiving case management services for such things as chronic mental disorders and substance abuse. Often these groups will have a psychoeducational focus combining both therapeutic interventions and education. Walsh also discusses the direct practitioner's role in leading treatment groups and facilitating self-help groups.

Mediator

The role of mediator is aimed at intervening "in disputes between parties to help them reconcile differences, find compromises, or reach mutually satisfactory agreements" (Barker, 1999, p. 294). Direct practitioners provide mediation in divorce or custody situations to help couples resolve disagreements and reach amicable resolution of contested issues. Much of what occurs in work with families involves mediation as the social worker helps family members communicate with one another (Barker, 1999). Mediation is also a common element in case management as the direct practice worker intervenes in disputes "between clients, between clients and community services, or between personnel in agencies who are involved with your clients" (Frankel & Gelman, 2004, p. 40–41). Mediators attempt to be neutral in their approach and try to help both sides find a way to resolve their differences. This is in striking contrast to advocates, who are clearly serving as partisans on the client's side.

Other Roles

Direct practice social workers may be called on to play other roles in their careers. For example, a therapist may find herself working with others to provide mental health services to homeless individuals currently being unserved or underserved. This is clearly an indirect practice role, again because of the lack of direct contact with client systems. Likewise, a case manager role may evolve into a community planner role as the manager becomes part of a task group wishing to expand the number of clubhouse programs offered to assist in rehabilitation of people with serious mental illnesses. In the process, the case manager becomes concerned with building a sense of community for these clients as a way of preventing relapse and ensuring continued functioning (Jackson, 2001).

Another potential role is that of outreach worker tasked with helping underserved clients receive services. This may involve providing educational programs about available services, developing advertisements and other methods for attracting the attention of the target population, or delivering services outside of the usual agency setting.

It should be clear by now that these many roles can be carried out sequentially or simultaneously, depending on such factors as client need, practitioner expertise, and agency policies. In some situations, the direct practice social worker may also need to refer a client to other services or practitioners better able to meet the client's needs.

Knowledge, Skills, and Values for Direct Practice

This text is designed to help students acquire the knowledge, skills, and values essential for direct practice in social work. Each of these components is critical to the tasks that direct practitioners face. Without knowledge, there is little that social workers can do except listen to what clients tell us. Knowledge without skill is useful for understanding people and situations but too often leads nowhere. The phrase "it's academic" conveys the message that knowledge by itself is of limited use for dealing with real problems. By themselves, skills are useful, but without corresponding knowledge about which skill should be employed in what situations, they are more characteristic of the technician than the professional. Finally, both knowledge and skill must be applied within a value context appropriate to the social work profession. Without values guiding the application of knowledge and skill, even well-meaning individuals can end up harming others. Knowledge helps us understand client situations better and suggests possible alternative courses of action, whereas skills provide a means of demonstrating this understanding and assisting clients in weighing their options. Values, on the other hand, guide us in deciding what to do or not do in the process of helping others. They also give rise to a set of ethical principles, a characteristic common to all professions. These principles allow our work to be judged by others, adding an important benchmark for direct practitioners. In the following sections, we identify the knowledge, skills, and values essential for direct practice in social work that are described throughout this text.

Knowledge

The knowledge needed for direct practice in social work cannot be acquired through a single course or even a series of courses. Learning what we need to know to help clients is a never-ending process. It is our intent in this text to provide a solid beginning for the practice theory and knowledge used in direct practice. The Council on Social Work Education, the accrediting body for bachelor and master of social work programs in the United States, has established a more detailed description of the minimum content needed for practicing social work. This information is contained in the Educational Policy and Accreditation Standards (EPAS) currently used to evaluate the quality of social work education programs (CSWE, 2001). The EPAS require that both BSW and MSW students be provided foundation content in the areas of values and ethics, diversity, populations-at-risk and social and economic justice, human behavior and the social environment, social welfare policy and services, social work practice, and research. They also require that students have a field education component that "occurs in settings that reinforce students' identification with the purposes, values, and ethics of the profession; fosters the integration of empirical and practice-based knowledge; and promotes the development of professional competence" (CSWE, 2003, p. 36). In addition, the EPAS require graduate programs to provide advanced curriculum content that builds on the foundation content previously described. Advanced curriculum content is designed to address each of the foundation areas "in greater depth, breadth, and specificity."

In this text, we focus on knowledge that includes the following areas:

- The planned change or problem-solving process
- Theories and models useful for understanding human behavior in the social environment
- Use of an integrated model of helping
- Strengths versus a focus on problems
- Knowledge for engagement
- Knowledge for assessment
- Cultural diversity factors in direct practice
- Goals, contract development, and planning
- Models of intervention
- Evaluation approaches for direct practice
- Tasks and planning of termination

Voices from the Field

What are the likely possibilities for social work careers for those who read this book in its early years of publication? One of the beauties of a professional career in twenty-first-century America is that the possibilities are not fully known and may change dramatically between the time one studies and the time one is in midcareer.

Leon Ginsberg

In social work, when I began in the profession some forty-six years ago, social workers were involved in public assistance programs, child welfare, and leisure time and recreational programs such as those of the YM and YWCAs, the Jewish Community Centers, and the Catholic Youth Organizations.

In the late 1950s, social work was just entering the mental health field with support from the federal government's National Institute of Mental Health, which eventually provided financial assistance to virtually every social work education program in the United States. Social work also became heavily involved in rehabilitation services and continued in the hospital and health care fields, in which it had been engaged for years. But many fields that are now commonplace continued to unfold. For example, during my career, I worked with the first social worker who served older adults and was involved in aging. Some of my friends were astonished when they met their first social work PhD. Now, of

course, aging programs are a strong source of jobs for social workers. There are over sixty doctoral programs educating social workers, and professional social workers are not as heavily involved as they once were in public assistance, child welfare, and leisure time and recreational organizations.

What about the future? It is likely that social workers will continue to be heavily involved in managing human service programs, training for human service programs, and helping make policy for human service programs. More than a few social workers are members of state legislatures and the U.S. Congress. Many more are staff members to committees that deal with social services, budgets, and other high government priorities. And there are also many jobs in aging, children's services, family counseling, and community mental health. Whatever the case, the abundance of social problems that Americans want to solve provides great opportunities for social workers.

How did I get into this business? I've observed over the years that social workers enter the field somewhat differently than people enter many other professions. People either have a job they like that requires social work education or an advanced degree such as the MSW, or they see jobs they like for

Of course, social workers must have knowledge of themselves and an awareness of their own strengths and limitations. This extends to our value system and what we believe about human nature. Those whose values clash with the values required of social work-

which they would want to prepare. They choose social work because they realize that it involves a job they would like to do and they recognize, as I did, that most people spend most of their lives on their jobs. So I thought—and most prospective social workers think—that I wanted to spend that time doing something I cared about.

I was heavily involved in a Jewish youth organization that became my primary reference group and almost my life as a teenager. My youth organization offered me a staff position and a scholarship to study for the MSW at Tulane in New Orleans where the regional headquarters were located. So after a stint as an Army artillery officer and turning down an invitation to apply for the Central Intelligence Agency, I went to school to become an MSW. That initially seemed to be the biggest mistake of my life. Coming out of an executive army position to a female-dominated settlement house field placement with colleagues who were almost all women from places like the Tennessee Department of Public Welfare caused a shock that was almost more than I could take. However, with the guidance of a very able field instructor, I adjusted, or perhaps more than adjusted, to a social work career.

By that time, I decided that the chosen agency that had brought me to social work in the first place wasn't for me at all. So I left as soon as my commitment was over and went to the Tulsa, Oklahoma, Jewish Community Council, where I was able to organize youth and senior citizen programs, parent education workshops, a summer day camp, and many other activities that were new to the Tulsa Jewish community. I also worked in a children's mental hospital, did training for a state mental hospital, and just did some of many things, based on what I had learned in school and done in field instruction.

Then I offered my services to the University of Oklahoma School of Social Work and was hired. And that led to hundreds of experiences—working with American Indian communities, getting involved in training Peace Corps volunteers and War on Poverty workers, writing and publishing, and getting a doctorate in political science. Then I became dean of the School of Social Work at West Virginia University, took a sabbatical in Latin America where I perfected my Spanish, and taught students social work management. I was then invited to be the commissioner of human services for West Virginia, and served as chancellor of higher education there. Later I came to South Carolina as a distinguished professor and became dean of the College of Social Work.

So social work for me has been many different careers and I suppose the best thing about it is its possibility for variation. It should be difficult to become bored in social work, and the possibilities are usually wide open for those who like our kind of work.

ers usually find themselves moving into different career paths. Social workers must also know the limits of their education and professional preparation so that they do not attempt to offer services that are beyond their level of knowledge and skill. They must know what kinds of situations are likely to raise issues that will make working with a specific client especially difficult. Finally, they must also know the laws, regulations, and policies that govern their work with clients. These may be based on state licensing requirements or the rules of a specific agency. It should be clear by now that social workers need a great deal of knowledge to be effective. In addition, because knowledge grows rapidly, social workers must keep abreast of new research, practice approaches, and services in order to continue to maintain a high quality of service to their clients. Consider for a minute what kinds of knowledge would be important for Chip as he begins working with the Sawyers.

Skills

Skills are essential to the effective practice of social work. They are employed in every step of the problem-solving process and, appropriately applied, can have a major impact on whether our work with clients succeeds. Barker (1999) identifies direct practice skills as "the ability to put social work knowledge into effective intervention activities" with systems of various sizes (p. 130). He describes the skills as "inner (perception and cognition), interactional (setting the stage, dealing with feelings and information), and strategic (dealing with behavior and coping with conflict)" (p. 130). Additional skills include those needed for working with groups, such as group building and facilitation skills. These skills and others are addressed in this text. Specifically, the text includes discussions of the following:

- Skills needed for engagement, including empathy, listening, and paraphrasing, among others
- Professional use of self
- Skills for assessment, including leading and following and observation, among others

- Skills for planning, including contracting and identifying tasks and priorities
- Selecting appropriate interventions, partializing, and focusing skills
- Practice skills for evaluation and termination
- Techniques for developing clients' coping skills
- Empowerment strategies
- Skills for strengthening family functioning
- Skills for improving group functioning and leading groups
- Skills for modifying environmental barriers

No single course or text can cover all of the skills required of social workers. Each of the broad categories listed includes multiple subskills that must be mastered before a direct practitioner can be effective. Likewise, any skills the student learns in school must be maintained and strengthened over time. Social workers must take advantage of opportunities to learn new skills through continuing education and other methods. Relying solely on the skill set one learned in school is a recipe for disappointment for both the social worker and the client. Which of the skills listed here are most likely to be needed with the Sawyer family?

Values

The NASW Code of Ethics notes that the profession is rooted in core values that affect every aspect of our work. Those values are service, social justice, dignity and worth of the person, the importance of human relationships, integrity, and competence. In turn, these values provide the underpinning for ethical principles and standards that govern the activities of all social workers. These values, principles, and standards are discussed in detail in Chapter 3. Among the ethical principles discussed are:

- Social workers' ethical responsibilities to clients
- Social workers' ethical responsibilities to colleagues
- Social workers' ethical responsibilities in practice settings
- Social workers' ethical responsibilities as professionals
- Social workers' ethical responsibilities to the social work profession
- Social workers' ethical responsibilities to the broader society

Each of these ethical principles means that the social worker has many specific responsibilities toward and with clients. For example, an ethical responsibility to clients also requires the social worker to hold client information in confidence, disclose it only under certain restrictions, and safeguard client records, to name just a few.

Moreover, social workers must deal with three value areas in their role as professionals. First, social workers need to be aware of their own values. Knowing your own values requires thinking about them and examining them periodically. Social work education provides an excellent opportunity to facilitate this process. Often one's personal values are consistent with those of the profession, but this is not always the case. When there is a divergence, the social worker must be prepared to manage such situations in a manner that is responsive to client needs.

A second value area involves learning the values of the profession of social work and being able to apply these in a wide variety of situations. For example, it is important to know what the profession expects of you if you want to be a social worker. What behaviors are expected of you when you demonstrate a commitment to clients—or to your colleagues? What do the values of the profession say should be done when you think a colleague is impaired or incompetent? These and a host of other questions are raised and answered in the NASW Code of Ethics. Social workers must have a working knowledge of these ethical principles and the requirements of the code.

A third value area concerns situations in which two or more ethical principles are in conflict. This might occur, for example, when the duty to maintain client information in confidence clashes with the duty to report suspected child abuse. Sometimes the decision about which duty has higher value is clear. In other situations, it is not. Thus, the social worker must learn how to resolve ethical dilemmas in a manner that respects the intent of the Code of Ethics and upholds the practitioner's obligations to the profession or to broader society. This text addresses these issues in some depth. Can you think of any particular value issues the Sawyer case might engender?

Design of the Text

This text is conceptualized and divided into two sections. Part I, which encompasses Chapters 1 through 3, provides an introduction to and background for direct practice in social work. The first chapter places direct practice in its historical context and describes the generalist perspective used in most advanced social work programs. It also defines direct practice as well as identifying the knowledge, skills, and values that are essential for this level of practice.

Chapter 2 provides a detailed orientation to direct practice, focusing on the knowledge base and theories used when working with individuals, families, and groups. The chapter defines the terms *theory* and *model* and

Case Example

Mrs. Smith, the sixth-grade teacher at Underlake Elementary School, has asked Olivia, a social work intern, to talk to Loretta. In the past two weeks, Loretta has been coming to school late, falling asleep in class, and sitting alone on the lawn during recess and lunch hour. Mrs. Smith has tried several times to call Loretta's mother but has been unable to reach her by telephone. Olivia sets a time to stop by the class, pick up Loretta, and take her to the counseling office. Loretta sits with her head down and says she doesn't feel well and doesn't want to talk. Olivia sits in the chair next to Loretta and takes out paper and crayons and asks Loretta if she would like to sit and draw with Loretta. During the time they are together, Loretta says her mother had to get a second job because Johnny, her mother's boyfriend, has moved out. Loretta reports that she must go straight home from school and do chores every night to help out her mother. She makes her own dinner, watches television, and gets ready for bed. She reports that she is afraid to go to sleep until her mother gets home at 11:00 p.m. Loretta starts to cry and says, "I don't want my mother to get into trouble."

Key words: School social work; latchkey.

The local Aging Office, where you are a student intern, has just received a call from Lonnie Smart about his mother, Orla, who has just been released from a rehabilitation center following hip replacement surgery and physical therapy. Orla has always been very independent and lives alone in a settled middle-income neighborhood where the family has lived for fifty years. Lonnie is concerned that his mother may not be able to take care of herself, but she has said she doesn't need any help. The social worker from the rehabilitation center, Cinda Jones, said his mother needs some regular daily activities so she wouldn't be so isolated and will be up walking around. Lonnie lives out of state and took two weeks of vacation to be with his mother during her surgery and subsequent rehabilitation. He needs to return home and get back to work next week. He has asked the agency to send someone out to visit with his mother and discuss ways to get her involved in the community.

Key words: rehabilitation; home health care.

Critical Thinking Questions

The following questions relate to the two preceding cases and to Figure 1.1 (p. 13).

1. How do you decide who is the client?
2. What obligations do you have to the caretaker, the parent, or the son?
3. What should you tell the client (Loretta, Lonnie, or Orla) about collateral contacts in the two previous case examples?

Research Activity

Go to the library's electronic catalog and put in a key word from one of the cases (use one of the key words listed or one of your own). Get a call number for a relevant book and locate the book. Read a chapter and prepare a one-page report of what you learned. The report should include the bibliographic citation for the book, including which pages you read, followed by one to three paragraphs about what you learned.

Using the Research Navigator™ website www.

researchnavigator.com, find an article or website and read information that might be salient to your work with one of these clients. Create a one-page report about what you learned and use the American Psychological Association style manual to cite your electronic source.

Practice Activity

Role playing is an activity in which participants assume "roles" (much like in a movie or TV show) and act out an event. Ask a friend, relative, or classmate to be the client and have him or her read the scenario. Then practice introducing yourself and asking how you can help. Follow the opening statements with listening to the client and asking open- and close-ended questions to continue gathering information and building a connection (a goal-oriented relationship of helping) with the client.

Social work intern: Hi, I'm _____, a social work intern at _____. _____ asked if I'd talk to you about _____.

e.g., Hi, I'm Owen Farmer, a social work intern at Mountain Mental Health Center. Your sister Annie asked me to talk to you about how things are going and how you are feeling. So, how have things been the last couple of months? (open-ended question)

Lorenzo: Not so good. I'm hearing voices again and I lost my job.

Social work intern: I'm sorry to hear you're having problems (empathic response). I'm glad you came into the agency. That shows such good judgment on your part to get help when you are having difficulties. (compliment and encouragement) Let's look at "hearing voices again" first, and then we'll look at the job loss second. Would that be all right with you? (showing respect and including the client in the process)

Lorenzo: Yes, my last therapist explained that if I was taking my medicine as I've been told and I start to hear voices, I should come and talk to someone here because it meant that my medicine may need to be increased or changed.

Social work intern: So, it looks like you are currently taking 20 mg of Stelazine every day. Is that what you've been doing?

Lorenzo: Yes, Annie gives me my medication every day when I get up.

Social work intern: Well, then, maybe we had better have you make an appointment to see Dr. Coleman, the psychiatrist, to have your medications reviewed. We'll make that appointment before you leave today.

Lorenzo: Oh, good, because I really like working, but it's impossible to concentrate when I have these voices in my head telling me stuff.

Social work intern: So, are there things you can do to get some relief when the voices come into your head?

Lorenzo: Sometimes I say, "Hey, get out of my head, I know you're not real." Or sometimes I can say, "I don't have time to listen to you right now so go away." If I sing or play a video game, sometime I can make them go away for a while. But now they are there most of the time and these things don't work to make them go away.

(continued)

APPLICATIONS TO PRACTICE, cont.

Social work intern: Lorenzo, I'd like to check with my supervisor to make sure I do what will be the best for you right now. Would it be okay if you just sit in my office here while I go and talk to Mrs. Heart?

Lorenzo: Oh, yah, sure. She used to be my caseworker.

In this example, the social work intern could see that Lorenzo seemed to be coping pretty well, but because Lorenzo reported the voices were happening all the time and he couldn't stop them, and because his sister Annie, his caretaker, reported feeling overwhelmed, Owen wanted to check with his supervisor to see if Lorenzo needed to be seen by a psychiatrist right away or hospitalized immediately rather than waiting to see the psychiatrist in a few days.

Practice Activity

Reread the two cases and write down what the client might say and what you might say in both situations. Think about and write down questions you might want to ask in class.

Critical Thinking Questions

1. What do you believe are the reasons that people are mentally ill?
2. How might your beliefs about the reasons for depression influence how you treat a depressed person?

---

identifies five domains for understanding human behavior: biological/physiological, psychological, emotional, behavioral, and environmental domains. The chapter discusses an integrative model the authors consider useful for direct practice. The model is eclectic in orientation and identifies the importance of selective borrowing of models and techniques rather than wholesale adoption of any particular approach.

The strengths perspective is also introduced in this chapter as an approach that is consistent with the goals of social work practice. The last section of the chapter reviews a variety of theories important for direct practice, including biological/genetic, ego psychology, cognitive, classical, operant, social learning, person-centered, general systems, and multicultural theories.

Chapter 3 describes in detail the role of values and ethics in social work practice. It discusses the differences between personal and professional values as well as identifying the critical social work values of service, social justice, dignity and worth of the person, the importance of human relationships, integrity, and competence.

Following this introduction to values, the chapter identifies the ethical standards of the social work profession, particularly those incorporated in the NASW Code of Ethics. These include the social worker's ethical obligation to clients, to colleagues, in practice settings, as professionals, to the social work profession, and to the broader society. Finally, the chapter presents the Loewenberg and Dolgoff Ethical Principles Screen, which is extremely useful for dealing with ethical dilemmas that social workers are likely to encounter in practice.

The second part of the book focuses on the helping process. Chapter 4 looks at the knowledge and skills needed for engaging clients in direct practice. These include the skills of listening and facilitative conditions for helping such as empathy, positive regard (respect), congruence (genuineness, authenticity), paraphrasing, summarizing, clarifying, and questioning. Although especially important during the engagement phase, these skills are also useful throughout the direct practice helping process.

Chapter 5 considers the knowledge and skills needed for assessment. It discusses assessment as both a process and a product and looks at theoretical aspects of assessment. Three major tasks of assessment are introduced, and the inner and outer forces model is described in detail. The chapter also looks at assessment from various theoretical perspectives including ego and cognitive psychology, person-centered, behavioral (classical and operant), social learning, systems, and strengths-based. It also considers assessment as used by task-centered practitioners, the use of the *Diagnostic and Statistical Manual* of the American Psychiatric Association, and specialized assessments with cases involving substance abuse, suicide, and the elderly.

Chapter 6 covers the planning process beginning with developing a contract, identifying and selecting goals, considering tasks and priorities, and planning for the evaluation and measurement of goals. The chapter highlights the importance of client input in the planning process.

Chapter 7 addresses the knowledge and skills needed for intervention, including integrating assessment and planning. In particular, the chapter identifies the specific techniques used within different theories to achieve change. For example, techniques and approaches drawn from ego and cognitive psychology theory, person-centered theory, behavioral theory, systems theory, and strengths-based models are described, as well as those that are effective in multicultural situations.

Chapters 8 through 12 identify and discuss specific intervention approaches that a direct practitioner will be expected to carry out. For example, Chapter 8 looks at ways of developing and enhancing clients' coping skills. In particular, it discusses how the social worker can teach clients how and when to use these skills. Specific approaches are described based on cognitive theory. Among the coping skills discussed in depth are assertiveness training, anger management, stress management, and crisis management strategies. Spiritual and humanistic strategies are also covered along with a variety of other life management approaches. Finally, the chapter identifies cultural and diversity issues that influence coping skills.

Chapter 9 presents empowerment and strengths-based strategies that can be employed with different client systems. Guidelines for empowerment are discussed, along with a strengths-based practice model that social workers will find useful. The chapter also looks at an array of intervention techniques that are consistent with a strengths-based approach. These include using confrontation, emphasizing motivation and commitment, maintaining focus, checking for ambivalence, rehearsing, story and narrative building, using natural helping networks, and complimenting success. The chapter ends with discussions about empowerment of women, older individuals, gays and lesbians, and people of color.

Chapter 10 is devoted to the topic of strengthening family functioning. It discusses family therapy and considers the application of general systems concepts to families. Various unique family therapy models are reviewed, including structural family, experiential, strategic, cognitive–behavioral, psychoanalytic/ ego psychology, feminist, and narrative therapy.

The chapter also takes the practitioner through the stages of initial contact with the family, assessment, and intervention techniques and processes. Family assessment looks at topics such as identifying family problems, understanding family life cycles, and exploring family functioning and environmental factors that affect the family, including issues of cultural and other diversity. Ecomaps and genograms are also described as useful tools for assessing families. Processes and techniques discussed include family sculpture, homework assignments, questioning, multiple family therapy, and approaches to changing family communication.

Chapter 11 is dedicated to working with groups, particularly to ways of improving group functioning. The chapter explores task groups and identifies such issues as leadership, composition, and procedures and exercises appropriate to this type of group. Similar attention is paid to treatment groups. Group development is discussed, with each stage of the group identified and described.

Group assessment is also considered, with a specific focus on assessing group members, the group as a whole, and the group's environment. Applications to Practice features are provided to suggest how a social worker might handle situations occurring in the group.

Chapter 12 considers the role that environmental barriers play in preventing clients from meeting their needs. The chapter begins by discussing several barriers such as physical, policy and procedural, emotional/social, cultural, and informational. The goal of the chapter is to identify and describe ways in which environmental barriers can be modified or overcome using approaches that include advocacy, case management, and coordination. It also briefly describes some other environmental change strategies used in social work, including social action, social planning, and organizational change. Ethical, cultural, and diversity issues are also incorporated in the chapter.

Chapter 13 is devoted to the process of evaluation of direct practice. It looks at the rationale for evaluating our work, describes multiple evaluation approaches, and explores the advantages and disadvantages of each. Reviewed are single-subject designs, goal-attainment scaling, target-problem scaling, task-achievement scaling, satisfaction studies, and quality assurance methods of evaluation. Also discussed are group designs including experimental and quasi-experimental methods. Threats to the internal and external validity of evaluation designs are identified, and both cultural and diversity issues in evaluation are described.

The last chapter looks at the termination process in direct practice with individuals, families, and groups. It reviews how termination is approached in various theories and models while identifying some general termination guidelines. The chapter also covers the types and tasks of termination. The chapter describes planning for ending and how to incorporate termination approaches that will maintain change and prevent relapse. Cultural and diversity issues in termination round out the discussion.

SUMMARY

This chapter provides an introduction to direct practice in social work. It begins by discussing the purpose and function of social work and looks at some definitions of the social work profession. A brief historical overview of social work practice includes a discussion of efforts made to professionalize social work.

Current challenges facing the field are also identified.

In addition, the chapter distinguishes between generalist practice and the generalist perspective required for direct practice. Direct practice is defined and several direct practice roles are described. These include therapist/counselor, educator, broker, case manager, case advocate, group leader, mediator, and other roles.

The chapter provides a basic explanation of the categories of knowledge, skills, and values required for direct practice. Finally, the last section identifies the design of the text as a way of orienting the reader.

The purpose of this text is to help prepare students for direct practice in social work. It is based on the premise that learning is a lifelong undertaking and that students will continually need to upgrade their knowledge and skills to accommodate new challenges and to cope with a changing social environment. It is our hope that students enjoy the process of learning as much as we have enjoyed writing this text.

Navigating Direct Practice

An access code for Research Navigator™ is packaged within your text. Use this code to register at www.researchnavigator.com and then use the key words listed below to research articles related to the chapter's content. Research Navigator™ helps you quickly and efficiently make the most of your research time.

❏ Generalist perspective
❏ Direct practice
❏ Indirect practice
❏ Case manager

Chapter 2

Theoretical Perspectives on Direct Practice: An Overview

■ Sarah Savant is a twelve-year-old who has been referred to juvenile court for missing school and smoking behind the school building. Sarah recently moved in with her grandmother, who lives alone in a small apartment about three miles from school and works twelve hours a day at the local tractor factory. Bessie Cummins has taken the day off work to bring her grandchild to the appointment and states that she would like to get back to work today so she doesn't have to use up all the time she has been saving for a vacation. Sarah is about 4 feet 6 inches tall and weighs about ninety pounds. She has an olive complexion and long straight brown hair. She sits with her knees drawn up to her chest and her hair hangs in front of her face. Bessie reports the following information without prompting. Bessie's daughter, Liz, has just remarried, and her new husband, George Seward, and Sarah don't get along. George issued an ultimatum a week after the marriage: "It's either her or me," so Liz arranged with Bessie to take Sarah. Sarah's father, Mark Savant, went off to work one night when Sarah was two years old and was never heard from again. Two years ago Mark was declared legally dead. Sarah has never had any contact with Mark's parents or family. Liz felt so lost when Mark disappeared that she kept Sarah with her all the time and didn't send Sarah to school until she was seven. Evidently, a neighbor reported Liz and Sarah to child services, and the protective service investigator said Sarah needed to be in school or they would both be breaking the law. Sarah has always been a quiet child and was often sent home from school because she said she was sick. Although she was regularly examined by a pediatrician, no medical problems were found. The school says she won't do her work, doesn't talk in class, doesn't play with the other kids, and pretty much stays by herself. Bessie is not sure how long Sarah has been smoking. "All the women in my family have always smoked, and I guess I started smoking when I was eight and Liz started when she was ten." Bessie also reports that Sarah isn't any trouble at home. "She heats something in the microwave for dinner, cleans up after herself, and is in bed by the time I get home at 9:00 p.m. I thought she was getting herself up in the morning, eating breakfast, and going to school until you called."

Two major goals of this text are to reflect current trends in the profession and identify models of best practice. A third goal is to help both instructors and students understand theories, models, and techniques that can be used with clients at multiple levels within a direct practice framework.

A vast array of theories and models is presently available to professionals. As far back as 1981, Corsini identified some 250 counseling models. Obviously, it is unrealistic for professors to teach and students to learn them all. Therefore, this text incorporates largely mainstream theories and models that have adequate research support. We believe that once they have learned the skills and theoretical underpinnings from the selected models, direct practitioners will be able to adapt to other methods or models. As they mature through professional growth and experiences and incorporate their ongoing discovery of disseminated knowledge and ideas regarding direct practice and human behavior, their capacity to help will improve accordingly.

Another goal of this text is consistency with current curriculum policy as identified in the Council on Social Work Education's (CSWE) *Educational Policy and Accreditation Standards* (EPAS) (2001). The text has a comprehensive focus and uses a deductive model, starting from a broad perspective or paradigm and then working toward specific theories, models, and ultimately techniques.

Because we recognize that no single theory or model can explain the complex nature of human beings and the environment in which we exist, this text uses an integrative model to direct practice. This model allows readers to see that the components of the biopsychosocial, cultural, and spiritual perspectives are important cornerstones to practice. In addition, the text addresses the fundamental contrast between a strengths perspective favored in social work with a problem-oriented perspective frequently encountered in direct practice.

Direct Practice Skills

The 2001 CSWE curriculum policy identifies broadly what practice content must be incorporated in the foundation level curriculum as students begin their progress toward self-directed practice. Practice content is to include the skills of "engaging clients in an appropriate working relationship, identifying issues, problems, needs, resources, and assets; collecting and assessing information; and planning for service delivery . . . ; practice content also includes identifying, analyzing, and implementing empirically based interventions designed to achieve client

goals" (p. 10). This is to be accomplished by focusing on clients' capacities and strengths as they interact with their environment. All of this is to be incorporated within the values and ethics of the profession.

To summarize, direct practice skills include:

- Knowing how to develop and maintain a professional/helping relationship
- The collection and assessment of information about a problem/situation
- Recognizing the client's strengths and abilities
- The development of a plan to improve the problem/situation
- The use of legitimately recognized and researched interventions
- Working within the values and ethics of the profession

Based on the concepts of the problem-solving model, these recommendations provide a general structure for the development of direct practice skills yet at the same time allow enough latitude for the injection of a variety of ideas, concepts, and preferences that are part of our current and past history as a profession. A clear understanding of the basic concepts of a theoretical approach to direct practice becomes vital to the practitioner. Specifically, the theory or model a practitioner aligns with will influence many aspects of the practitioner–client relationship. It will direct the social worker to establish a particular kind of relationship, determine which problems and needs are focused on, determine the types of questions asked and information sought when the social worker collects and analyzes assessment information, and influence the selection and implementation of goals as well as the interventions used to remedy the problem.

The Effectiveness of Direct Practice

As previously noted, Corsini (1981) identified 250 different forms or systems of counseling and psychotherapy, and as of 1994, he believed the number had risen to more than 400 (Corsini & Wedding, 1995). Garfield and Bergin (1994) also reported that techniques associated with the 200-plus therapy models exceed 400. Based on these estimates, what course of action ought colleges and universities take when deciding which model(s) to teach to students in the helping professions? The obvious answer should simply be: those that provide the best results. But how can practitioners be sure which are best when professionals in various camps believe the ones they ascribe to are superior while assuming other theories and models to be weak, incomplete, missing the mark, or completely wrong (Corsini & Wedding, 1995)? What if no one model is far superior to the others? Each may have aspects or components that are helpful in alleviating certain disorders. How do direct practitioners work out of this conundrum to provide the best practice for clients? One solution is to turn to the current state of research to answer some of these questions.

The first question to ask is whether therapy (counseling) works. The straightforward answer is yes. "More than 40 years of outcome research make clear that therapists are not witch doctors, snake oil peddlers, or over-achieving do-gooders" (Hubble, Duncan, & Miller, 1999, p. 1). Literature reviews and meta-analyses have supported counseling and psychotherapy as a viable and legitimate method of helping people. According to Smith, Glass, and Miller (1980), the average person, at the end of treatment, is better off than 80 percent of those not treated. With these positive results and increased legitimacy, the profession has grown, with a 275 percent increase in the number of therapists from the mid-1980s to the late 1990s (Hubble, Duncan, & Miller, 1999).

Further positive support for counseling is that treatment for the majority of persons need not be long and drawn out. In session-by-session studies and meta-analysis of client progress, 50 percent of clients were found to have made positive changes in eight to ten sessions, and 75 percent showed improvement after six months of weekly psychotherapy (Howard, Kopta, Krause, & Orlinsky, 1986; Kadera, Lambert, & Andrews, 1996).

With the increase in the number of therapeutic models and techniques, the growing number of therapists providing services, and the push from insurance companies and governments to contain costs, many are looking for standardized treatment for specific disorders, a movement that promotes a more traditional medical model. Furthermore, from years of teaching practice methods to undergraduate and graduate students, we have often witnessed the panic in their eyes and trembling in their voices as they realize they are about to role-play working with a client while believing they do not know what to do. Students often seek a how-to guide, hoping for the "perfect" method of treatment for the client.

The medical model is the predominant model that has been used among helping professionals since at least Freud's introduction of his theory of psychodynamics. The medical model essentially seeks to identify and isolate the cause or root of the problem and then prescribe treatment to eradicate or rehabilitate it. Treatment following this model often follows a protocol or a process based on a theoretical model and successful outcome studies for a particular disorder or diagnostic group. Based on these positive outcome studies over a period of the past forty years, this model has served the helping professions well. Occasionally, a particular model has been found to be more effective in achieving a desired outcome for a specific disorder, such as cognitive or behavioral interventions for anxiety-related disorders (Barlow, Craske, Cerny, & Klosko, 1989), but research does not suggest the overall superiority of one model over another (Norcross & Newman, 1992).

Common Elements in Effective Practice

The positive effects from various counseling models are now considered to be the result of commonalities rather than differences across different therapeutic models. The common factors believed to be associated with the different models of psychotherapeutic intervention that result in positive change or improvement in clients have been reported by Asay and Lambert (1999). These include four general areas: (a) extra therapeutic change; (b) therapeutic relationship; (c) techniques; and (d) expectancy–placebo effects. *Extra-therapeutic factors* were found to account for 40 percent of the improvement. These factors include a client's level of motivation, strength of ego, ability to identify a problem, and ability to relate interpersonally, along with "psychological mindedness" and social support (Lambert & Andersen, 1996). These factors are believed to aid in the client's recovery, whether or not the client has been in counseling.

The second most significant factor, *therapeutic relationship*, accounts for 30 percent of client improvements. The components of this factor have been identified as the "facilitative conditions": empathy, genuineness, positive re-gard, and warmth (Rogers, Gendlin, Kiesler, & Truax, 1967), skills that are compatible with the curriculum policy's statement on the establishment and maintenance of a working relationship. The importance of this factor cannot be overestimated because it is the single most important element the helper is able to control.

The remaining two factors, *techniques* and *expectancy–placebo effect,* each account for 15 percent of the change. Most research examines interventions based on a particular theory. This is often done by comparing a treatment group with a non-treatment control group. Although many studies have found that those who receive treatment have been better off than those in the non-treatment group, a different picture emerges when interventions from different theoretical models are compared against one another. "Overall, in many comparative studies completed to date, little evidence to suggest superiority of one school or technique over another has been obtained. While expectations occur in the research literature, . . . specific techniques are estimated to account for only 15% of the improvement in psychotherapy" (Asay & Lambert, 1999, p. 39).

As previously cited, some therapies have produced better results for specific disorders, such as therapy for simple phobias, agoraphobia, and compulsions, thus indicating the need for practitioners to stay current on research regarding specialized treatment. However, this approach currently appears to be limited in scope. Therefore, we consider it important for practitioners to acquire knowledge of a range of theories and models that will assist them in their present as well as future professional development. A solid foundation of the theoretical knowledge behind a particular model, combined with the development of skills of associated techniques and attention to the research supporting those models and techniques found to be more successful with specific groups of clients or disorders, also appears to influence positive practice outcomes.

The expectancy and the placebo effect, described by Asay and Lambert (1999), is considered to be a commonly held belief by clients no matter which theoretical model is applied by the practitioner. It is defined as having "hope" in the process of treatment. According to Garfield (1994), a significant correlation has been found between positive expectations held by the client and improvement, especially in the early stages of therapy. This client expectation is that the client will experience some form of relief from the presenting problem. Hope is believed to increase through the helper's ability to explain the rationale of the techniques being applied and the client's acceptance of the explanation. This finding supports the rationale for limiting the number of theories that students learn in order to increase their level of understanding and the skillful application of the techniques in the provision of therapeutic services. The practitioner's knowledge and mastery of skill tends to increase the practitioner's level of competence and self-confidence that has been found to correspond with increases in the client's sense of hope and trust in the helper.

In summary, Asay's and Lambert's (1999) findings suggest the following:

- Therapy is a viable treatment for psychological disorders. Clients in therapy do better than 80 percent of those persons who do not receive help.
- For the most part, the various theories, models, and accompanying techniques do not differ significantly in terms of the positive outcomes of psychotherapy.
- For some disorders, specific techniques have been found to produce better out-

comes. When appropriate, the literature on outcome studies regarding various disorders ought to guide practitioners in the choice of which techniques to use.

- Long-term therapy is not necessary. Fifty percent of clients were found to have positive changes after eight to ten sessions, with 75 percent showing positive changes after six months, or approximately twenty-five sessions of weekly psychotherapy.
- Four common factors have been identified as accounting for client improvement. They include extra-therapeutic change (40 percent), therapeutic relationship (30 percent), techniques (15 percent), and expectancy–placebo effects (15 percent).

Whether a practitioner is a novice or a master therapist, continual effort and importance ought to be placed on nurturing the therapeutic relationship and developing skill in the use of appropriate techniques. By relying on techniques alone, the helper may be knowledgeable and proficient in the delivery of services, but without demonstrating the human quality of caring and connecting through the development of a strong therapeutic relationship, the client will likely not benefit from the help provided. We see that the more knowledgeable and skilled practitioners are in the provision of services, the more likely it is they will be confident and proficient, generate hope in the client, and achieve their goals in a shorter period.

Theories and Models

Theories are developed in an attempt to explain why things happen. A **theory** is "a group of related hypotheses, concepts, and constructs, based on facts and observations, that attempts to explain a particular phenomenon" (Barker, 1999). Applied theory becomes a means of understanding and describing a person and his or her presenting problem. With regard to human behavior, theories attempt to answer "why" questions, such as why is a person hallucinating, or why does a client attempt to hurt himself. To answer these questions, current theories might examine the individual's biochemistry, past trauma that has not been addressed, development through childhood and adolescence, status as a member of a family or an ethnic group, relative sense of safety in a neighborhood, or status as a member of an organization.

Theories are then conceptualized in the form of a **model** or are mapped out as a representation of the relationships, concepts, or constructs described in the theory. The model often allows the reader the opportunity to "visualize" the theory.

When clients seek professional help, it is often because some aspect of their lives is not right, as defined either by the client or by society. The professional seeks to "join" with clients in understanding their personal condition as well as their environment. The trained professional will apply theoretical knowledge, along with its accompanying model, to the assessment of the biopsychosocial–cultural conditions surrounding the problem, as well as identify the client's strengths and available resources. How this actually plays out in direct practice is evidenced by the types of questions a professional asks. The direction taken by the helper will be directly influenced by the theory, model, and values believed to be important when solving or ameliorating the client's problem. Thus, the theoretical model applied by the practitioner will strongly influence how and what is assessed and the extent to which the client's weaknesses, deficits, strengths, and ca-

pabilities are incorporated into the intervention used. The specific techniques applied need to be congruent with the theory. This is best determined based on current research and professional training, along with professional experience and judgment.

Five Domains for Understanding Human Behavior

Though there are many ways of categorizing theories and models to explain the human condition and reasons for behavior, the following system is easy to use and helps in conceptualizing and organizing them in a general yet useful manner. On close examination of theories and models of human behavior, most people place a particular emphasis on one of the five domains, especially as it focuses on what is to change and is directly involved with the process of assessment and interventions in direct practice. The factors may generally be identified as either personal or environmental. More specifically, they are broken down into the following: biological/physiological, psychological, emotional, behavioral, and environmental.

Biological/Physiological Domain

The *biological/physiological domain* consists of all the systems and processes necessary for physical functioning. These include the following systems: physiological, organ, cell, and biochemical (Nurcombe & Gallagher, 1986). Each system will "develop and change as a consequence of genetically guided maturation, environmental resources such as nutrition and sunlight, exposure to environmental toxins, encounters with accidents and diseases, and life habits related to daily exercise, eating, sleeping, and use of drugs" (Newman & Newman, 1995, p. 5).

Psychological Domain

The *psychological domain* focuses on change that occurs in the mind. The change may be in mental structures (schema) as in cognitive therapy of the psyche (conscious or unconscious levels) from an ego psychology perspective. From cognitive psychology, a person's thoughts are believed to largely determine how one feels and behaves (Ellis, 1994). From an ego psychology perspective, the ego has two basic functions: (1) continually seeking to master reality and (2) acting as the negotiator between unconscious impulses or drives (id) and the constraints (rules and expectations) placed on us from the environment (superego). In the case of cognitive psychology, when problems arise the primary technique is first to identify then alter irrational or self-defeating thoughts. With ego psychology, the goal is to help clients learn how to better cope and adapt to the world by providing insight, explaining the motivation behind behavior and interpreting previous life experiences and dreams to help resolve conflict as it continues to influence clients in their present day life.

Emotional Domain

The *emotional domain* has as its focus the identification and accurate, uninhibited expression of feelings. As a foundation of humanistic theory and therapy, expression of feeling is considered to be the only way that people can genuinely learn about themselves. This can be achieved by turning one's attention to one's feelings and getting in touch with their meaning. Only by accurately symbolizing feelings are people able to come to know who they are (Rychlak, 1981).

Behavioral Domain

During the early years of behavioral psychology, Watson (1924) rejected the notion of mentalism because of its excessive subjectivity.

Feelings and thoughts were recognized as existing but incapable of being accurately measured and studied. Only overt, observable, and measurable human behaviors could be studied with any real accuracy. Thus, primary emphasis was placed on changing a person's behavior by externally controlling antecedents and consequences of a specific behavior.

Environmental Domain

The *environmental domain* identifies and attempts to alter those factors outside the person that influence behavior. One's environment consists of family, friends, employment, religion, culture, neighborhood, school, state and national factors, and quality of air, food, and shelter, to name but a few. Environmental factors believed to hinder or harm the client are seen as a threat to the growth and development of the individual, family, community, or group and therefore need altering or changing, most often by group action or through policy implementation.

Selection of a Domain

How does a practitioner select or become associated with one or more of the preceding domains? Three basic areas appear to influence how a practitioner self-identifies. The following areas are not written in any particular order or by strength of influence; they are all areas of significant influence. First is the discipline or academic field in which one receives training. For example, if training and education today are sought in the field of medicine and psychiatry, the biological/physiological model will be most significant, with peripheral learning acquired in psychological and environmental factors.

Another variable influencing academic fields is the period of time in which the practitioner received his or her education. Was it during the 1960s and 1970s, when behavioral psychology strongly competed with Freud's psychoanalytic theory and Rogers's humanistic theory, or was it during the 1980s and 1990s, which saw the addition of the cognitive component to treatment? Or was it during the beginning of the twenty-first century, when an increased emphasis was placed on the role of diversity and its importance in understanding human behavior?

Social work, in its attempt to be more comprehensive, has moved toward a broader perspective in explaining human behavior by examining the individual from the biological, psychological, and sociological perspectives, most often doing this by incorporating a systems theory approach to practice, along with integration of particular cultural and spiritual influences on the person(s). In more recent years, a significant effort has been made to emphasize environmental influences beyond the control of the individual as important factors in explaining behavior and as potential foci for intervention. For example, economic shifts at the local, state, national, and now international levels that are beyond the control of the individual may have a significant impact on quality of life and the potential for growth and psychological well-being of the individual, couple, family, group, or community. Thus, acquiring knowledge and skills needed to ameliorate environmental factors is deemed vitally important but not the sole method of intervention.

In the early 1900s, Freud's theory of psychoanalysis, based on his work with individuals, became one of the first theoretical approaches, beyond that of a moralistic perspective, in describing the source of personal problems. It strongly influenced our history and continues to be a recognized and viable method of practice, especially in the fields of clinical or direct practice, health, and mental health. However, direct practice at multiple levels (micro, mezzo, and macro) is the preferred model of practice being taught in social work education today.

Psychology studies the inner workings of the mind and the behavior of the individual. Much effort is placed on assessing and predicting human behavior based on psychological instruments of measurement that identify certain learning styles or deficits as well as adaptive and maladaptive behavioral and personality characteristics or traits. Interventions are primarily directed toward changing the individual's behavior or psyche.

Students of marriage and family therapy have been schooled on systems theory, examining individuals in relationship to the forces and influences of those significant persons within their immediate world (family). The individual is important as the identified client and as the person with the problem, but students are taught to look beyond the individual to the interactions between and among family members as the focal point for influencing change.

Another area of influence is the practitioner's own personality, values, and sense of which theory/model seems to match his or her personal style and belief system. It may be that the person's value system leans more to the belief that what is needed for people to grow or change is a supportive environment, one that is nondiscriminatory and allows equal access to resources. Others see the past as having a strong influence on present behavior. Therefore, the past must be examined and worked through before progress in the present will occur. Then there are those who believe that the expression of emotions in a safe and healthy way is necessary in order to obtain maximum health and well-being of the client. Yet others look for answers in the hard sci-

Voices from the Field

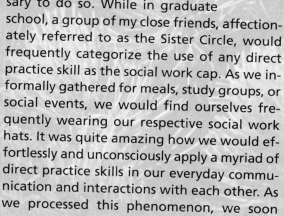

In life we all wear many hats. Mother, father, daughter, son, sister, brother, and friend are some of the many roles we all occupy. The unique thing about wearing different hats is that putting one on normally requires taking off the one before it. This makes sense because normally the roles are so distinctly different that it is necessary to do so. While in graduate school, a group of my close friends, affectionately referred to as the Sister Circle, would frequently categorize the use of any direct practice skill as the social work cap. As we informally gathered for meals, study groups, or social events, we would find ourselves frequently wearing our respective social work hats. It was quite amazing how we would effortlessly and unconsciously apply a myriad of direct practice skills in our everyday communication and interactions with each other. As we processed this phenomenon, we soon

Zoe Minor

found that wearing our social work caps had permeated our relations beyond the Sister Circle as well. It had touched virtually every aspect of our lives. It soon became clear to us that our social work caps were one hat we were always wearing. It became a constant. What we were unaccustomed to, however, was the fact that we didn't wear our social work caps to the exclusion of other hats. It simply became an addition that we could add others to and wear simultaneously. For me, that is the beauty of our profession. Our social work skills add to the richness that we already embody and enhance our ability to fulfill not only our roles as practitioners, but also the other roles we occupy in life. It becomes how we carry ourselves, how we interact with others, and how we see the world.

ences, which can improve biological functioning through the use of chemotherapy. More recently, models have veered away from viewing the client as having deficits; instead they look for strengths and resources on which to build change.

The last area comes from the influence of a mentor or significant person in the life of a developing practitioner. Some may have received assistance from a professional and as a result of the positive influence became "converted" to the model used by the helper. Oth-

ers were likely to have been influenced by a professor or supervisor in a particular college class or seminar or during internship or training. Because of the positive influence, it is likely that the mentor seemed to have many, if not all, of the answers to questions in a manner that "felt right," or that produced positive results with at least a significant number of clients.

Once the novice practitioner feels connected to a particular theory, learning begins to take on a sense of excitement and wonder.

There is often a search for the one true method, an attempt to find the key that unlocks the door to the questions about why individuals, couples, families, organizations, and communities with problems function as they do. What is it that leads to a breakdown in the individual or the system? Novices search for concrete answers about how to deal with a specific type of disorder or population. Novice practitioners often believe or assume that once the answers to these questions are found, all the helper needs to do is to share the knowledge with the client or client system in the form of giving advice, counsel, or insight. This sharing will in turn bring about change leading to an improvement in the conditions that led up to treatment or the delivery of services.

An Integrative Model

Academic fields of study find it inappropriate to limit teaching to one or two theories. This would not only hobble the learning and growth of students through limited exposure, but it would also make it difficult, if not impossible, to reach agreement among scholarly experts about which model(s) to teach. Over the years, one way out of this box has been through the use of the "eclectic" paradigm, teaching an array of models at a general level but often doing so without educating the student with any depth in the specific workings of a particular model. This is all done while pointing out the relative strengths and weaknesses of each model (Nichols & Schwartz, 2001). What often happens with this type of learning is that as students enter the field and engage a client in a therapeutic relationship, they feel intimidated or impotent. Even though hundreds of hours have been spent learning theories about the human condition and applicable interventions, students are not sure where to go with the client. Once they have moved beyond rapport building, they report lacking specificity in skill development when conducting an assessment and, more specifically, when implementing interventions. Some report feeling frustrated, others angry, whereas still others have a sense of incompetence or wonder why they were not better prepared before entering the field. Although some in education believe the real hands-on learning takes place during the practicum or internship, in reality this does not happen enough.

At the other end of the continuum are those who have often, on their own, gravitated to a particular model and received additional education and training that prepares them well for practice. However, as most have come to realize, rarely does one model seem to fit all clients and client conditions or problems. What works well for a depressed or anxious client, for example, does not necessarily work when intervening with someone who has a particular personality disorder, nor does it always work with multibarrier families. Thus, the practitioner may come to question the entire premise of the theory, along with its techniques. The response may be either to define the client as being "resistant" to therapy or to drop the current therapeutic approach only to go in search of another, more perfect one (Nichols & Schwartz, 2001).

An integrated model is a way of moving out of these dilemmas. It allows practitioners to learn a variety of theories and techniques in greater detail yet stay with the theories and models that are congruent with their personality, values, philosophy, and training. Further, practitioners have the leeway to implement techniques deemed appropriate or helpful depending on the client, the presenting problem, environmental circumstances, cultural and ethnic background, or current research in the field.

The concept of an integrative model in the helping professions is relatively new. Nichols and Schwartz (2001) have written about it in *Family Therapy: Concepts and Methods*. There are multiple ways of applying this concept, and various ways are addressed in this chapter. It allows for an inclusive, albeit limited, framework in the assessment and implementation of interventions. The integrative model is conceptualized as a blending of a limited number of theories, models, and techniques as they apply to direct practice. The techniques written about may or may not easily cross over from one model to another, but they should be used based on a solid understanding of the theoretical model from which they originate. Techniques should not be randomly applied to every client in one's practice, no matter what the problem or disorder, just because the practitioner has heard, seen, or read about them as some miracle cure.

In order to deliver services effectively, practitioners must be well versed with regard to particular theories and models, along with the techniques associated with these theories. These theories, models, and techniques need to be mastered in order for services to be delivered appropriately and effectively. Techniques used because they were modeled by another practitioner, but not understood and applied as they pertain to a specific theoretical perspective, may not be the best practice model or the best delivery of services.

Nichols and Schwartz (2001) identify three approaches to integration: eclectism, selective borrowing, and specifically designed integrative models. The *eclectic* perspective is one that gathers ideas and practices from various sources and systems (*Webster's New World Dictionary,* 1999). Although incorporating information from various sources may be an appropriate method in direct practice,

there is a risk that our understanding and attempts to help will become diluted or fragmented when working from this perspective. The merging of many sources may cloud rather than clarify the problem for the practitioner, and therefore may hinder the practitioner from arriving at a clear line of thinking or achieving consistency in the implementation of therapeutic strategies.

Selective borrowing is evident in clinicians who have deliberately aligned themselves with a particular theoretical model or camp and who choose to remain loyal to it. This is most likely to happen because of significant training and development with the model and because of the "goodness of fit" between the model and the helper's values, personality, and belief system. However, over time, these helpers may selectively integrate techniques and ideas from other modalities as a way of strengthening their skills and increasing the repertoire of available interventions without losing the heart and soul of that which has carried the practitioner through the years. Unfortunately, sampling techniques without a solid conceptual understanding will likely produce a muddled form of eclecticism in which the therapist shifts back and forth without consistency or conviction (Nichols & Schwartz, 2001). Selective borrowing is about the incorporation of knowledge and skills that can serve as an addendum to an existing model.

The third approach to integration is that of purposely trying "to create something new out of complementary aspects of existing models" (Nichols & Schwartz, 2001, p. 416). Within this approach, Nichols and Schwartz have identified various *specifically designed* models. One model is an attempt to bring together well-developed aspects of various models that focus on narrow areas of human behavior in order to create a more comprehensive model. Another way of conceptualizing this approach is through the integration of two models into one, such as strategic family therapy with behavioral psychology (Alexandar & Parsons, 1982), or psychodynamic psychotherapy with systems theory (Sander, 1979; Nichols, 1987; Scharff, 1989), or cognitive theory with behavioral theory (Bandura, 1986; Ellis, 1973). Further, some integrative models are designed specifically for a particular disorder or population such as substance abuse or abusers (Piercy & Frankel, 1989).

Strengths versus Problem Perspective

Throughout their history, the helping professions in general, and social work in particular, have relied heavily on the problem, disease, and deficit model. This remains an important perspective or paradigm for students to understand, if only as a way of interacting and relating with professionals from other fields (medicine, psychology, nursing, government leaders, and lawyers, to name a few) and with clients. Additionally, much has been learned from this paradigm and clients have been helped by it, as evidenced by the positive outcomes from counseling over the past forty years.

The problem-solving model is a model commonly applied to this paradigm, and it is often used in the generalist perspective of social work practice. Also common is the incorporation of the medical model, with its specific diagnostic categories found in the *Diagnostic and Statistical Manual of Mental Disorders* (DSM) (American Psychiatric Association, 2000). These two models, along with others (psychodynamic psychotherapy, behavioral theory, systems theory, the person-in-environment perspective, the use of genograms and

ecomaps, social histories, and psychological tests, to name a few), all examine the individual, the family, the group, the organization, or the community from the viewpoint of what is missing, out of balance, defective, abnormal, pathological, or deficient. The assessment burden falls primarily on the professionals and their knowledge of the particular disorder, assessment instrument, or theory/model that guides the professional's perspective in determining the source of a problem and what causes its continuance. The professional collaborates with the client inasmuch as the client offers information to aid the professional in the assessment and decision of which problem will be addressed. Once an assessment is completed, the professional then implements techniques aimed at remediating, curing, or rehabilitating that aspect of the client (biological, psychological, spiritual) or the environment (sociological, cultural) that is dysfunctional.

Because of the prevalence of the problem paradigm within the profession of social work and related helping professions, and the positive effects that have been achieved in the last forty-plus years (such as medication for the treatment of mental disorders, behavioral and cognitive behavioral therapies for specific disorders, family therapy from a systems perspective), discussions of those theories and models that reflect this line of thinking are included in this text. Our goal is to help students understand the theoretical base and underpinnings of these theories and models as well as develop skills in the techniques that stem from each perspective.

At the same time, the social work profession has moved more in the direction of a strengths-oriented focus on understanding and helping people. In recent years, people in the profession (Saleebey, 2002; Weick, Rapp, Sullivan, & Kisthardt, 1989) have called on professionals to depart from our history of relying on the problem–medical model when working with clients. They recommend shifting to a **strengths** perspective.

> The strengths perspective is a dramatic departure from conventional social work practice. Practicing from a strengths orientation means this—*everything* you do as a social worker will be predicated in some way on helping to discover and embellish, explore and exploit clients' strengths and resources in the service of assisting them to achieve their goals, realize their dreams and shed the irons of their own inhibition and misgiving, and society's domination. (Saleebey, 2002, p. 1)

Saleebey believes that little more than lip service has been paid to clients' strengths, and he calls on the profession to use this way of thinking in a direct fashion by incorporating the values associated with it in the direct practice of social work. The strengths approach does not ignore the problems that exist with individuals, families, groups, organizations, and communities, but "it emphasizes the client's assets that are used to achieve and maintain individual and social well being" (Barker, 1999, p. 468). Recently, Saleebey (2002) reported that strengths-based practice has been developed for use with a variety of clients, including the chronically mentally ill, people with addictions, the elderly, and troubled youth, as well as a variety of generalizable models and perspectives, including solution-focused therapy, resilience, wellness and healing, and assets-based community development.

Review of Theories

As previously suggested, theories bring together a group of concepts and related hy-

potheses in an attempt to explain a particular phenomenon. The intent of this text is not to provide an exhaustive, detailed review of theories, but to provide information to be used as a guide to assist practitioners in their awareness of theories. In addition, it is important to understand how these theories influence the practitioner throughout the processes of engaging clients, assessing clients' problems and resources, goal setting, and implementing therapeutic interventions and techniques in direct practice.

The following material identifies and briefly reviews theories and models of counseling psychotherapy and human behavior that are commonly used in direct practice and that reflect the five domains of human behavior (biological/physiological, psychological, emotional, behavioral, and environmental). Although any selection of representative theories is open to debate, this list provides an adequate foundation to guide the new practitioner toward an understanding of the common theoretical concepts and their application in the engagement, assessment, goal setting, treatment, and termination phases of direct practice.

The principal theories reviewed for the five domains of human behavior are genetic/neurological theory (biological/physiological domain); ego and cognitive psychology (psychological domain); person-centered psychology (emotional domain); classical, operant, and social theories (behavioral domain); and general systems theory (environmental domain). Based on these theories, specific models of practice attempt to explain or diagram human behavior and the nature or occurrence of problems within human existence. The integrative model does not prescribe a how-to method of integration and implementation of the various theories, models, and techniques. Instead, it provides an understanding of each so that the practitioner becomes knowledgeable and develops skills based on the different theoretical schools and applied techniques. It is at this point that clinical judgment, along with the art and skill of the professional and current research findings on best practice, can be applied to the integration of models and the provision of services.

Biological–Genetic/ Neurological Theory

Biologically based theories are generally oriented toward the study of two areas of human behavior: personality and psychological disorders. One avenue focuses on the study of **genetics** and those traits and diseases considered to be inherited. The second avenue seeks to understand the **neurochemical** and **neurophysiological** occurrences within the brain. This section briefly reviews theories associated with both areas of study.

"Behavioral genetics is the study of genetic influences on behavioral qualities" (Carver & Scheier, 1996, p. 134). People with a clear and specific genetic disease (e.g., Down syndrome, PKU) are affected by a single gene or chromosome. Depending on the disease, a part of a chromosome will be missing or added on to, a part will be in the wrong place, or an abnormality will be present on a particular gene. Included in this field of study are cognitive and emotional processes, psychological disorders, personality traits, and behaviors hypothesized to have been inherited. This section focuses on those traits and disorders believed to be genetically influenced.

For the last thirty or more years, the primary method of research in this field has been the study of twins, comparing identical with fraternal twins, as well as of adopted children. These foci help researchers to control environmental factors in an attempt to isolate and examine the influence of genetics on human behavior. One focal point of research has been the inheritability of psychological traits. However, in infancy and childhood, the term *temperament* has been used in lieu of *traits* because the latter has been less well defined and developed. Both refer to the "inherited personality traits present in childhood" (Buss & Plomin, 1984, p. 84). Temperaments are thought to be inherited and to affect what people do and how they do what they do (Carver & Scheier, 1996). Believed to be present in childhood, temperaments are also thought to continue on and be an influence in adulthood.

Three specific components of temperament often cited in the literature are activity level, sociability, and emotionality (Buss & Plomin, 1984). *Activity level* relates to a person's behavior and level of energy. *Sociability* refers to the tendency to be with others or to be alone, whereas *emotionality* is the level of arousal in upsetting situations and consists of the emotions of anger, fear, and distress. Twin studies have supported the inheritability of emotionality, activity level, and sociability. Intelligence, not considered a trait, has also been found to be genetically influenced (Bouchard, Lykken, McGue, Segal, & Tellegen, 1990).

More recent investigations have noted that heredity associated with traits appears to weaken over time. According to McCartney, Harris, and Bernieri (1990) in their meta-analysis of twin studies on this topic, as twins grow older, they have a tendency to become less alike, except for intelligence, in which the tendency toward alikeness actually increases. Although these researchers believe that genetics plays a part in influencing personality, the effects may not always be great.

As with the study of temperaments and intelligence, researchers have used twin and adopted children studies to investigate the influences of genetic inheritability for psychological disorders (cognitive, emotional, and behavioral). Specifically, many studies have focused on schizophrenia, bipolar disorders, and alcoholism. Concerning schizophrenia, Gottesman and Shields (1972) found a 50 percent concordance rate among identical twins compared to a 9 percent concordance rate for fraternal twins. It has also been determined that first-degree relatives of a person diagnosed with schizophrenia have a 10 percent chance of having the disorder, compared to a 1 percent chance among the general population (Kaplan & Sadock, 1998).

Bipolar disorder, evidenced by mood swings from severe depression on the one end to mania on the other, has also been identified in families. Twin studies have found a higher rate among identical twins (Tsuang & Faraone, 1990). According to Kaplan and Sadock (1998), concordance rates for monozygotic twins range from 33 to 90 percent. First-degree relatives were found to be eight to eighteen times more likely to have bipolar I disorder when compared with rates among the general population.

Although genetics has been found to influence alcoholism, according to Dodes (2002), "there is no such thing as a 'gene for alcoholism', nor can you directly inherit alcoholism" (p. 81). Current research suggests there are likely many genes that indirectly influence the susceptibility to the development of alcoholism, but a specific gene for alcoholism has not been found.

Dodes (2002) reviewed the literature on genetic factors for alcoholism that have been investigated through the study of families, twins, and adopted children. The following is a synopsis of his findings. There is a tendency for alcoholism to show up in families from one generation to the next. For people with alcoholism, about 25 percent of their fathers and 5 percent of their mothers tend to have also been diagnosed with alcoholism (Merikangas, 1990). If genetics were to be the primary factor, it would be hypothesized that the incidence of alcoholism would be greater for first-degree than for second-degree relatives. This, however, was not found to be the case in a number of studies. These data do not disprove a genetic influence, but instead suggest that a genetic factor is probably too small to be significant or found in such a small number of people that it is difficult to detect.

On average, among identical twins a 40 percent concordance rate was found for alcoholism. However, in these studies the influence of environmental factors was not eliminated. The twins were reared together, thus allowing other factors beyond genetics to be involved when determining the concordance rate. According to Pickens et al. (1991), heritability analyses based on twin studies "showed genetic factors to have only a modest influence on the overall risk of both sexes, . . . approximately 0.35 for male subjects and 0.24 for female subjects" (p. 19), which left approximately 70 percent of the remaining influence to nongenetic/environmental factors.

The findings from adoptive studies (children removed from their biological parents while in infancy) have been inconsistent. Some have found no significance, whereas others have found a correlation between adopted male children and their biological fathers. Apparently, the correlation was greater for those male children removed after they had reached an average age of eight months compared to children placed in adoptive homes at an even younger age. Again, adoption studies suggest "a minor to insignificant role for genetic factors in the majority of people with alcoholism, and a more significant role in susceptibility in a smaller group" (Dodes, 2002, p. 89).

Dodes (2002) summarized the data by reporting that a genetic factor appears to have a minimal influence on alcoholism for the majority of people. Rather than a single gene for alcoholism, it is more likely that multiple genes may be involved within a subgroup of people, making them more susceptible. However, the "increased incidence in this subgroup is unknown, but in any case it is an influence of susceptibility . . . , rather than there being a 'gene for alcoholism' " (p. 89).

Neurochemistry is the study of communication processes at the neuron level of the brain. In recent years, significant energy has gone into the study of neurotransmitters and neuron receptors and their influence on human behavior. Along with this research has been the introduction of psychoactive medications for the treatment of numerous psychological disorders. Currently, a predominant theory focuses on restoring "biochemical imbalances" at the neuronal level through the administration of drugs.

A neurotransmitter is a chemical that flows from the end of one neuron, called the **presynaptic nerve,** into and across the **synaptic cleft,** the gap between two neurons, to the end of another neuron, the **postsynaptic nerve.** Neurotransmitters signal the postsynaptic neurons to either increase or decrease the likelihood that an action potential—an electrical charge that transmits information along the neuron—will occur.

Postsynaptic cells are also regulated by hormones, referred to as neurohormones. Unlike neurotransmitters, which are released directly into the synaptic cleft, hormones are released into the bloodstream. Through the bloodstream, they are capable of arriving at the neuronal space and thus have an effect on neurons (Kaplan & Sadock, 1998).

There are three primary types of neurotransmitters in the brain: biogenic amines, amino acids, and peptides. Of the three, biogenic amines are the most understood and the first to have been discovered (Kaplan & Sadock, 1998). Following is a synopsis of Kaplan and Sadock's (1998) overview of neurochemistry. The neurotransmitters classified as biogenic amines are dopamine, norepinephrine, epinephrine, serotonin (also referred to as 5-hydroxytryptamine, or 5-HT), acetylcholine, and histamine. The **dopamine** hypothesis for schizophrenia suggests that too much dopamine is being made available at the neuronal site. This hypothesis appears to be substantiated by the induced psychotic symptoms that occur from the ingestion of drugs that stimulate the release of dopamine. For example, the amphetamine drugs have this stimulative effect. Further supporting this hypothesis are the positive effects from antipsychotic drugs (e.g., Haldol) that "block" the receptor neurons from accepting the neurotransmitter dopamine. Additionally, it is hypothesized that dopamine is associated with mood. When levels are too low, a person experiences depression, and when levels are too high a person may become manic. Evidence for this hypothesis is found through stimulant medications that improve a depressed person's mood and through the drug Levodopa (a drug used in the treatment of Parkinson's disease), which has been found to trigger manic and psychotic symptoms in some patients diagnosed with Parkinson's.

It is hypothesized that **serotonin** also affects mood. Too little serotonin is believed to cause depression and too much is associated with mania. Alternatively, the "permissive hypothesis" views low levels of serotonin as allowing abnormal levels of norepinephrine (too high or too low) to occur, which in turn causes manic or depressive moods. More recent research has also suggested that a link exists between serotonin and anxiety and schizophrenia. Studies have found positive benefits from medications (called SSRIs) that inhibit the reuptake of serotonin in neurons. Schizophrenia is hypothesized as occurring due to imbalances in both dopamine and serotonin. A more recent antipsychotic medication, Clozaril, has had remarkably positive results through its combined direct effects on dopamine and serotonin.

Norepinephrine is believed to be associated with depression, but the pathophysiology is not clear. The drugs with norepinephrine used for the treatment of depression are the tricyclic antidepressants and MAO inhibitors (MAOIs), along with the more recent antidepressants—Serzone, Effexor, and Remeron. The theory behind these drugs is the need to increase the levels of norepinephrine. This is achieved by blocking the reuptake of norepinephrine back into the neuron, thus increasing the levels of the neurotransmitter in the synaptic cleft. It also has the effect of increasing the levels of serotonin.

This review of genetic and chemical influences on human behavior is limited but is provided to help readers gain an appreciation for potential biological conditions that may need to be examined and possibly treated by medical professionals. An understanding of the current state of the science can assist both clients and health care providers in the provision of services.

Ego Psychology

A number of theorists have followed after Freud and maintained aspects of his theory yet differed in their view of the structure and the development of personality. They are often divided into various groups depending on their primary emphasis. One group, referred to as *neo-Freudians*, places more emphasis on "soci-

ocultural factors, interpersonal relationships, and psychosocial development into and through adulthood" (Barker, 1999, p. 324). This group includes Karen Horney, Harry Stack Sullivan, and Erich Fromm. The second group, *ego analysts*, emphasizes the influence of the ego on the development of an individual's personality and includes writers such as Anna Freud, Heinz Hartmann, and Ernst Kris. A third group, called *object relations theorists*, places an emphasis on the early relationships one has with significant caregivers and on the process of separating from them. This group is often associated with Margaret Mahler, Donald Winnicott, Melanie Klein, and Ronald Fairbairn. The last group, referred to as *self-psychologists*, focuses on how people view themselves and their parents and how this view influences other relationships in their lives. This approach is most closely associated with Heinz Kohut.

We selected the ego psychology theorists to review as part of this section because "ego psychology embodies a more optimistic and growth-oriented view of human functioning and potential than do earlier theoretical formulations" (Goldstein, 1995, p. xi). Ego psychology focuses on the adaptive functioning of the ego, and therefore it has "opened the way for psychoanalytic theory to become, not only a study of psychopathology, but of a normal developmental psychology as well" (Blanck & Blanck, 1994, p. 8). Further, ego psychology, primarily through the works of Erikson (1950), emphasizes the influence of environmental factors on the ego's development. Erikson believed that Freud neglected to adequately describe the influence of cultural, interpersonal, and environmental factors on the ego and personality, and that these factors continue to influence the individual's development throughout his or her life.

Some who followed Freud, including his daughter Anna, sought to strengthen the role of the ego on personality development. Heinz Hartmann and Anna Freud were among the first to introduce the expanded role of the ego, focusing on a person's "ability to solve problems and deal with social realities" (Barker, 1999, p. 149). Their writings began in the 1930s, with this branch of psychodynamic theory increasing in popularity following World War II. This newer generation of psychoanalysis "emphasized the ego's innate, conscious, rational, and adaptive capacities, the autonomous or conflict-free areas of ego functioning, the adaptive role of defense, the importance of interpersonal and environmental factors, and the capacity for growth and change all through the life cycle" (Goldstein, 1995, p. 34). Thus, the goal of human behavior according to the ego psychologists, is adapting to one's environment. This process of adaptation is both physical (learning how to use our body to get what we want) and psychological (learning to control our impulses in order to obtain what we want through appropriate behaviors) (Hartmann, 1958).

Freud's drive theory placed primary emphasis on the id as the origin of psychic energy. The ego, he believed, developed from the id and took on the role of mediator to manage conflict between the id and the superego as well as external reality. Ego psychology agrees with Freud on this role of the ego but extends the role by viewing it as possessing energy separate from the id. This gives it some innate or separate qualities beyond that of dealing with the id and superego. "Whereas id psychology assumes that the ego serves only a defensive function in trying to find a safe and satisfying balance in the ongoing conflicts between instincts and the rules of society, ego psychology assumes that there are conflict-free

spheres of the ego (Hartmann et al., 1947) that involve the individual's adaptation to reality and mastery of the environment (Hendricks, 1943)" (Prochaska & Norcross, 1999, p. 48). The ego's striving to master reality is its foremost motivation in the development of personality.

Ego theorists believe that the conflict-free sphere derives energy from its innate desire to adapt to objective, external reality. Ego psychology views this function of the ego as being equally important to that of mediating the unconscious structures of the mind. To achieve this development, the ego must be capable of investing energy in other areas. "Learning visual motor coordination, discrimination of color, and language skills, for example, are some of the tasks that individuals can be motivated to master, independent of longings for sexual or aggressive gratification" (Prochaska & Norcross, 1999, p. 48).

Based on this expanded concept of the role of the ego, Goldstein (1995) lists seven propositions on human functioning from an ego psychology perspective:

- People have the innate ability to function in their environment. The ego serves as a force in this lifelong process by learning how to cope with, adapt to, and shape the world around us.
- The ego has the function of leading people toward adaptation to their environment. This function is innate yet develops over time as a person interacts at the biopsychosocial level. Among the important biopsychosocial factors are heredity; the quality of one's relationships, especially during childhood; and the impact the environment has on a person, including the sociocultural values, economic circumstances, and social institutions.

- The development of the ego is sequential. Development takes place as one learns and reaches mastery of developmental tasks and develops coping and problem-solving skills for both internal and environmental conditions, meeting one's basic needs, and learning.
- Although the ego functions as an autonomous structure, it also works in relation to internal drives and needs as well as those cultural values, standards, and mores that are brought to bear from the environment.
- Besides mediating between the environment and the person, the ego also mediates internal conflicts that are part of the personality. For example, the ego can implement defense mechanisms to deal with anxiety and conflict. When defense mechanisms are called on, they may serve adaptive or maladaptive purposes.
- Personality is shaped by the social environment. Environmental conditions either promote or hinder the development of positive coping. When assessing the functioning of the ego, a person's cultural, racial, and ethnic background; age; gender; and sexual orientation must be accounted for and understood.
- As problems with social functioning occur, we must examine them in relation to the individual's environmental resources and conditions; that individual's needs; and the possible limits in the person's ability to cope (pp. xii–xiii).

Freud viewed development as a sequence of stages. To stay congruent with his structural theory, he placed primary emphasis on explaining where the instinctual or id drives were focused. Erik Erikson (1968), a student of Anna Freud, also observed stages of development, but he de-emphasized the role of sexual energy and instead focused on the normal aspects of development, as well as recognizing the influences of the social environment. Erikson also viewed development as a process that continued beyond adolescence and throughout the life span.

A primary concept in Erikson's theory is that of *ego identity*. "Ego identity is the consciously experienced sense of self, which derives from transactions with one's social reality. A person's ego identity changes constantly in response to changes in the social environment" (Garver & Scheier, 1996, p. 303). A person with a strong sense of identity will be able to adjust to different environmental conditions, but individuals struggling with their identities will likely experience difficulties.

Erikson also applied the *epigenetic* principle to psychosocial stages of development. This concept essentially means that development is an unfolding process. It occurs in an orderly sequential process and is influenced by both biologic makeup and the social environment.

At each stage, Erikson identified a crisis or demand that needs to be negotiated. By doing so successfully, individuals will be prepared for the next crisis. With successful negotiation of all the crises leading up to the establishment of identity, they will be able to integrate all of those aspects into their ego identities. If a crisis task is not adequately mastered, a person will experience difficulties when facing later crises (Sharf, 2000). Although perfect resolution of a crisis is the ideal, it is not necessary. However, resolution needs to be on the positive side of the continuum for the person to successfully transition through the stage. See Chapter 5 on assessment for a brief overview of the psychosocial stages, along with the approximate age for each stage and the crisis that needs to be resolved.

The ego is therefore theorized as having two basic or essential functions. The first consists of incorporating defense mechanisms in response to the unconscious conflicts (see Figure 2.1) that were described by Freud. However, when the ego relies on defense mechanisms for extended periods, it interferes with the ego's ability to resolve the conflict that initiated the anxiety. As a result, during times of extreme stress the anxiety may reemerge and produce more severe symptoms such as panic or phobias.

The second function of the ego is to learn, perceive, and have a memory of experiences that occur outside of or apart from the conflicts that arise in the unconscious region of the psyche, or in what is referred to as the "conflict-free sphere" of the psyche. As long as this conflict-free sphere of the ego can function separately from the id, it is under conscious control. When the ego is dominated by the id or is unable to stay in reality, psychological problems arise.

Cognitive Theory

During the 1970s, a major shift occurred in the field that resulted in an increased interest in the

---

Figure 2.1

Common Defense Mechanisms

Repression—Considered the most basic defense mechanism; all other defense mechanisms involve repression to some degree. Repression occurs when the id's impulses and drives are not allowed into consciousness but instead are kept in the unconscious.

Displacement—The transfer of instinctual drives from the original object to another, less threatening object.* This allows for a safer expression of the drive.

Fixation—As a result of unresolved conflict or trauma occurring at one of the stages of psychosexual development, the person remains fixed or stuck at that stage.

Projection—Involves attributing one's own unacceptable drives and instinctual needs to another person.

Rationalization—Elaborate, self-serving, yet incorrect explanations of one's unacceptable behaviors in an attempt to make them appear socially acceptable.

Reaction formation—One way of avoiding an anxiety-evoking instinctual drive is to substitute or express behaviors, thoughts, or feelings that are completely opposite or diametrically opposed to those unacceptable instincts.

Regression—Occurs when the individual reverts to an earlier and safer stage of development, one already transitioned through, as a way of coping with stress or trauma.

Sublimation—A form of displacement through which unacceptable impulses are diverted and channeled into prosocial activities (e.g., sports, academics, activism).

---

*Note: An "object" in psychodynamic theory may represent a person, oneself, an item, or a desired state of affairs. It may literally be anything that can lead to satisfaction of an instinct (Rychlak, 1981).

influence of cognitive factors in learning, such as the importance of "the individual's perception and interpretation of external events rather than the direct influence of the surroundings themselves" (Kazdin, 1978, p. 307). The shift was influenced most from the work of Albert Ellis and Aaron Beck. Practitioners became increasingly interested in the influence of cognitive factors on a person's mood and behavior. "The individual's perception and interpretation of external events rather than the direct influence of the surroundings themselves" (Kazdin, 1978, p. 307) became the point of focus.

"Probably the most general meaning of cognition is the act of knowing, which suggests that there is a process going on mentally that permits a person to gain insights and understanding of experience" (Rychlak, 1981, p. 522). According to Mancuso, "The development of comprehensive, cognitively based theories of behavior began in the latter part of the 1950's" (1970, p. 22). Since then, behaviorists have focused on integrating this variable into their theory in order to provide a more comprehensive understanding of human behavior. The critical factor associated with cognitive theories is the emphasis on a person's thought process.

Tolman and Honzik (1930) hypothesized the existence of what they referred to as "cognitive maps." This concept relates to one's ability to mentally organize or learn a structure. They believed they had observed this phenomenon in their study of rats in a maze. They found that even when the animals were not being rewarded for their efforts they still appeared to have learned the maze, suggesting that latent learning had occurred.

George Kelly's theory is often used as a comprehensive model of cognitive theory (Mancuso, 1970). According to Kelly, "human beings come at life with an active intellect, one that is not under control by events but that puts events under control by posing questions from experience and then seeking answers to them" (Rychlak, 1981, p. 712). For Kelly, learning is a process of our functioning as living organisms, and therefore we are constantly moving forward, asking and seeking answers to questions. As people pose questions, they find new answers, which in turn motivates people to change.

Cognitive theory is specifically applied to counseling through the models of cognitive therapy (Beck, Rush, Shaw, & Emery, 1979) and rational emotive therapy (Ellis & Harper, 1975). Beck's "cognitive therapy is based on a theory of personality which maintains that how one thinks largely determines how one feels and behaves" (Beck & Weishaer, 1995, p. 229). The basic concept of this theory is that humans take in information, process it, and then develop a plan based on what was processed. When information is processed in a faulty way, the person may begin to feel such emotions as depression, anxiety, or anger and behave in a manner congruent with those feelings and related thoughts.

Beck, Rush, Emery, and Shaw (1979) identified a number of ways in which people incorrectly process information. Among these are **arbitrary inference,** arriving at a conclusion without evidence to support it; **selective abstraction,** attending to a particular detail while ignoring the total situation; and **overgeneralization,** arriving at a general rule that is based on only one or a few incidents. Three other ways include **magnification and minimalization,** evaluating an event in such a way that it is blown up or minimized out of proportion to what actually occurred; **personalization,** connecting external events to oneself when there is no evidence to support the connection; and absolutistic, dichotomous thinking, seeing things from one extreme or another, such as all good or all bad, smart or stupid, handsome or ugly. A change in a person's cognitions results in a change in emotions and behavior.

Behavioral (Learning) Theories

For centuries, theorists have addressed the concepts and processes of how people learn. With specific reference to personality, these theories examine the learned tendencies a person obtains from experience. Three theories have made recent significant contributions to the field and are reviewed in this section: (a) classical conditioning, (b) operant conditioning, and (c) social learning.

At the foundation of psychodynamic theories is the view that current psychological disorders exist due to a root cause that can be traced back to past events that resulted in some form of conflict. Behavioral theorists, on the other hand, do not look for underlying psychopathology or past conflict. Instead, they focus on the exhibited maladaptive behaviors themselves. They pay little attention to uncovering how the behavior was acquired but instead focus on how it is currently maintained and how the environmental conditions associated with the maladaptive behaviors can be changed. Behaviorists rely strongly on the scientific approach.

Classical Conditioning

Classical conditioning, also referred to as *respondent conditioning,* is best recognized from the works of Ivan Pavlov, a Russian physiologist. While investigating the physiological response in dogs of salivation and digestion to meat powder, Pavlov discovered that some of the dogs in his study began salivating before the meat powder was introduced to them. Because of the dogs' reactions, he refocused his attention on this behavior. What was later referred to as classical conditioning became his primary focus of study.

For classical conditioning, or learning, to occur, two conditions must be met. First, the response emitted must occur naturally or automatically (reflex). Second, the stimulus causing the reflex reaction has to be associated with another stimulus that causes no specific response, yet it must be noticed (Carver & Scheier, 1996). In the experiment with the dogs, Pavlov did not need to teach the dogs how to salivate; it occurred automatically when they saw and/or smelled the meat powder. The meat powder elicited this response from the dogs and was identified as an unconditioned stimulus (US). The salivation, in response to the meat powder, was identified as an unconditioned response (UR) (a natural reflex). Pavlov began presenting the meat powder (US) at the same time or immediately after ringing a bell, referred to as "pairing." The ringing bell became the conditioned stimulus (CS), because on its own it elicited no response, but when paired with the meat powder, it began to influence the dogs' salivation response. Over time, the bell alone (now a conditioned stimulus) began to elicit salivation from the dogs. The salivation had become a conditioned response (CR) because it occurred in the presence of the ringing bell. Figure 2.2 illustrates this theory.

Once the relationship between the CS and the CR is established, the CS will continue to elicit the response, although it will need occasional pairing with the US in order for the association to be maintained. Without occasional pairing of the US with the CS, the CS will lose strength and the CR will stop occurring, resulting in extinction (Carver & Scheier, 1996). Pavlov did, however, find that even

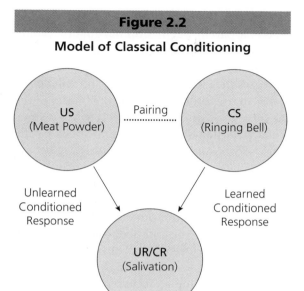

Figure 2.2

Model of Classical Conditioning

US
(Meat Powder)

Pairing

CS
(Ringing Bell)

Unlearned
Conditioned
Response

Learned
Conditioned
Response

UR/CR
(Salivation)

when extinction occurred, fewer trials were needed to reestablish the relationship between the CS and the CR when compared with the original learning trials. Further, Pavlov found that the CR rarely stops being emitted all at once. From this, he hypothesized that learning is not totally lost, but instead inhibited.

More recent research has revealed that cues or stimuli in the environment that are identifiable by the subject become significant as a signal that the unconditioned stimulus is about to be presented (Davey, 1987). Labeled anticipatory learning (Rescorla, 1972), this phenomenon suggests that the CS reflects the anticipation of the presentation of the US, one stimulus providing direct information about the occurrence of another stimulus. Such might be the case when a person with a drug disorder sees drug paraphernalia and immediately anticipates the use of a psychoactive chemical.

Two other findings are important when using this model. First, stimulus generalization occurs when a CR is elicited not only from the CS but also from a stimulus that is similar to the CS. For example, at the sight of a line of cocaine, the CS brings about the craving for the drug. But when an addict sees a spilled box of baking powder (US), he may also begin to experience similar cravings because the two powders resemble each other. The degree of generalization is dependent on the amount of similarity between the stimuli. The second finding is the potential for stimulus discrimination, which is the opposite of stimulus generalization. Stimulus discrimination allows a person to discriminate between two stimuli, whereas stimulus generalization does not. The sight of gin or vodka in a bottle elicits from an alcoholic the craving to drink, whereas a bottle of water has no significant effect on the same person (Carver & Scheier, 1996).

Classical conditioning also can be applied to the study of emotions. Negative emotional reactions that are believed to be conditioned are labeled conditioned responses (CR). This model has been used to understand and treat anxiety-related disorders as well as anger. For example, fear, a normal rational emotion when one is faced with a dangerous object or situation such as a snarling dog, can turn into anxiety, an irrational response, when one merely thinks about encountering a dog. What is hypothesized is that a naturally occurring stimulus that becomes associated with a pleasant event creates a positive preference, but linking a naturally occurring stimulus with an event that creates fear leads to an aversion.

Operant Conditioning

Thorndike (1898) studied cats' learning habits by placing cats in "puzzle boxes." The puzzle boxes required a specific response that allowed the cats to escape and obtain food. He observed a trial-and-error strategy the cats used to solve the problem, a strategy that did not suggest any form of insight. Thus, Thorndike theorized that learning comes about by the connections we make between responses that are voluntarily emitted and the stimuli that follow them. Thorndike called this the "law of effect." If the behavior is followed by a positive response, the person is more likely to engage in the same behavior again. If the response that follows is perceived as negative, the behavior is less likely to occur in the future (Carver & Scheier, 1996).

Aware of the work of both Thorndike and Pavlov, B. F. Skinner focused his work on the law of effect. Skinner, like Thorndike, focused on those behaviors that are voluntarily emitted. He considered that classical conditioning best describes those behaviors that are automatically (innate) emitted by certain stimuli. Skinner believed that the consequences, whether positive or negative, following the occurrence of voluntary behaviors cause the organism to continue the behavior, reduce its frequency, or stop emitting it.

Skinner's model of operant conditioning includes both reinforcers, defined as anything that increases the likelihood that a behavior will be produced, and punishers, anything that decreases the likelihood (Ewen, 2003). Confusing to many is Skinner's concept of reinforcers as being both positive and negative. Remember that reinforcers, whether positive or negative, both *increase* the likelihood that a behavior will continue to be produced. A **positive reinforcer** increases a behavior when it is "present" after the behavior occurs. Positive reinforcers might consist of rewards of food, a smile, a token or a coin, or a word of congratulation, to name but a few. A **negative reinforcer** also increases the likelihood that a behavior will continue to be emitted, but does so when it (the consequence) is "removed" or

"stopped" when the behavior occurs. For example, a parent might stop nagging or yelling when his or her son begins to do the dishes. Ending the nagging (negative reinforcement) increases the likelihood that the son will do the dishes in the future. Similarly, the buzzer in the car serves as a negative reinforcer when it stops when we fasten the seat belt to the buckle. The dishwashing and the seat belt fastening behaviors are likely to continue because doing so is a way of "avoiding" the nagging and yelling or the annoying buzzer noise.

Punishers, on the other hand, are used to *decrease* a behavior and, like reinforcers, may be "present" or "removed" at the time the behavior is produced (Newman & Newman, 1995). For example, if parents wish to decrease a child's behavior, such as running into the street, they might present a punisher in the form of a spanking each time the child runs out into the street. Alternatively, when parents wish to decrease a child's TV watching behavior, they may choose to take away, or remove, points their child has earned (response cost) toward a treat or activity. Another punishing approach is to restrict the child's involvement in pleasant activities by use of a timeout each time the behavior occurs. The way to judge whether something is a reinforcer or a punisher is by measuring the target behavior to see if it increases or decreases based on the consequences that occur following the emitted behavior.

Skinner used the term **shaping** to describe the process by which learning a task can be quickened. If the desired task is for a child to place a ball in a box, the child, never having done this before, does not know what to do. To achieve this goal, the experimenter would give instructions to the child and then positively reward successive approximations of the child doing this behavior. For example, the child would be positively rewarded as she picks up the ball, then again as she turns toward the box, again as she moves toward the box, and ultimately when she places the ball in the box. If a behavior moves away from the goal, positive reinforcement is withheld. The child is led in a step-by-step direction toward the desired outcome (Ewen, 2003).

The rate at which a behavior is reinforced has also been found to have an influence on the learning and maintenance of that behavior. The fastest way to increase the rate of learning of a new behavior is to reinforce it each time it occurs. However, the reinforcer will lose some of its strength at this rate of reinforcement because of "satiation"—that is, for example, if food is used as the reinforcer, at some point the subject will no longer be hungry or will tire of the particular type or taste of food used, and thus the reinforcer loses its strength. To overcome the obstacle of satiation, Skinner devised different schedules of reinforcement (Rychlak, 1981). Once the response is acquired from continuous reinforcement, an alternative schedule is implemented.

Four variables, when combined, make up the schedules of reinforcement. The first is based on the reinforcer being given following an interval of "time" or by a "number" of times the behavior is emitted. Time is referred to as an "interval," whereas the number is identified as a "ratio." The next two variables indicate whether the responses are fixed or variable. *Fixed* refers to a specific or fixed number of times a behavior needs to be emitted or an amount of time that needs to transpire before a reward is provided. *Variable* refers to a varying or random number of times a behavior needs to be emitted or a random amount of time that must pass before the subject is rewarded. Figure 2.3 illustrates the four possible combinations.

Figure 2.3

Schedules of Reinforcement

Fixed	Variable
Fixed Ratio	Variable Ratio
Fixed Interval	Variable Interval

Operant conditioning is used most in education, in which young people are provided feedback about their level of mastery in learning, and in therapy, to decrease maladaptive behaviors and increase adaptive behaviors. This is done through the use of reinforcers (representative or physical rewards) and punishers (timeout, token economy).

Social Learning

Bandura disagreed with Skinner's belief that all behavior is controlled by the environment (through rewards and punishments). Instead, Bandura believed that a combination of "behavior, environmental influences, and internal personal factors (including beliefs, thoughts, preferences, expectations, and self-perceptions) all cause and can be caused by each other (**reciprocal determinism**)" (Ewen, 2003, p. 367). "In the social learning view, people are neither driven [solely] by inner forces nor buffeted by environmental stimuli. Rather, psychological functioning is explained in terms of a continuous reciprocal interaction of personal and environmental determinants" (Bandura, 1977, pp. 11–12).

Social learning, also called observational learning, takes place in a social context. That is, people observe others performing a task and learn how to do it without being directly rewarded or punished. Best known for his study using Bobo dolls, Bandura (1965) identified how children learn aggressive behavior by observing adults. In this study, children watched an adult hitting and kicking a large plastic doll. The children were divided into three groups and observed the adult model receiving different consequences for his or her aggressive behavior. One group observed the model being punished for the behavior, while another group observed the model being rewarded for the behavior. A third group observed the model being ignored. When the groups of children were placed in a room with the Bobo dolls, it was found that the children who observed the adult model being punished for the aggressive behavior demonstrated less aggressive behavior toward the doll when compared with the other two groups.

Social, or observational, learning is influenced by a number of factors. First are the consequences (reinforcements) the model receives, as observed by the learner. Depending on whether the consequences are negative or positive, it is less or more likely that the observer will attempt the behavior. Another characteristic found to be helpful in observational learning is when the behavior to be learned is paired with *participant modeling*, or guided participation. Bandura, Blanchard, and Ritter (1969) determined that when a person observed a model doing a task and at the same time participated or interacted with the model, learning was more effective when compared with *symbolic modeling* (observing the model on film).

People are also more likely to follow a model when the model has certain characteristics, such as being perceived to have high status, or to have personal characteristics similar to those of the observer. Multiple models have also been found to be more effective than a single model (Bandura, 1969; Bandura, Adams, & Menlove, 1968).

Person-Centered Theory

Humanistic psychotherapies are also referred to as phenomenological. The humanistic approach was developed primarily in the United States, whereas the existential approach has its roots in Europe. Abraham Maslow began encouraging work toward a "third force" in the study of human behavior and psychology (Maslow, 1968). Maslow held that "the individual is basically sound, whole, healthy, and unique, with an innate drive for growth and self-actualization; that mankind is by nature active, resourceful, purposive, and good; and that human suffering comes from denial of this basic good" (Davison & Neale, 1990, p. 52).

Under the umbrella of these theories is Carl Rogers's humanistic or client/person-centered therapy; Eric Berne's transactional analysis; existential therapy based on the philosophies of Kierkegaard, Nietzsche, Jaspers, Heidegger, and Sartre; and Fritz Perls's gestalt therapy. Basic characteristics of these therapies include the following:

- Each person experiences life in a unique and subjective way.
- To understand a person, you must understand his or her subjective experience.
- Emphasis is placed on the relationship between client and therapist.
- Each person has an innate tendency toward self-actualization or self-fulfillment.
- An emphasis is placed on the wholeness (gestalt) of a person as well as his or her uniqueness.
- Treatment occurs when a client gains insight.

- Emphasis is placed on a person's free will and freedom of choice (Davison & Neale, 1990; Rychlak, 1981; Corsini & Wedding, 1995).

This section addresses Rogers's humanistic theory. A basic tenet of humanistic psychology is that each person has unique experiences that occur within what Rogers referred to as the "phenomenal field" (Rogers, 1951). The phenomenal field is that which is known by the individual and includes "all that is experienced by the organism, whether or not these experiences are consciously perceived; . . . only a portion of that experience and probably a very small portion, is consciously experienced" (Rogers, 1951, p. 483). One's experiences include "everything that is available to your awareness at any given moment: thought; emotions; perceptions, including those that are temporarily ignored (such as the pressure of the chair on which you are sitting); and needs, some of which may also be momentarily overlooked (as when you are engrossed in work or play)" (Ewen, 2003, p. 199). The majority of things, however, are experienced below the level of consciousness or subception.

Included in the phenomenal field are experiential processes that are both mental (thoughts, consciousness) and bodily (feelings, biology). Rogers did not consider the basic neurobiological processes within an organism to be a part of the phenomenal field, because a person cannot, through introspection, become aware of their occurrence. We are aware of their effects when they do not function properly, such as when one's stomach is upset from improper digestion of food (Rychlak, 1981). The phenomenal field becomes important to each person because it defines that person's subjective reality.

We may or may not be able to symbolize bodily sensations, whether sensory or visceral.

A symbol is an image or a word that comes to mind as representing something else. It is possible to experience a feeling in the body (physiology) yet not be able to define it in the mind. Learning to understand these feelings is vital to understanding what different situations mean to an individual or developing the ability to symbolize them. The more unafraid we are to experience all that we feel, the greater the opportunity to know oneself, or one's phenomenal field, and have a sense of freedom to communicate these experiences to others (Rogers, 1951, p. 496). The only way to truly understand ourselves is to attend to our feelings (bodily experience) and to attempt to understand the meaning behind them (mind experience). To do this, feelings need to be accurately symbolized because they define our subjective reality.

In order to come to know ourselves, we need to develop what Rogers termed *self* or *self-concept*. Self-concept is a "learned, conscious sense of being separate and distinct from other people and things" (Ewen, 2003, p. 201). It is a gestalt based on what we see as our basic characteristics (such as those based on professional identity or physical characteristics), the perceptions we have of our relationships with others (e.g., a father, employee, student), along with the values we attach to these perceptions.

A core assumption embedded in Rogers's theory is that of self-actualization, which is an innate tendency that motivates people, through growth, to maintain, enhance, and actualize their self and their experiences (Rogers, 1951). "Behavior is purposive and goal-directed; people do not respond passively to the influence of their environment or to their inner drives. They are self-directive" (Davison & Neal, 1990, p. 525). Rogers believed that when people are free from the negative influences of others (e.g., the conditional acceptance by others), self-actualization will occur and motivate a person toward positive qualities and characteristics.

As organisms we have needs defined as physiological tensions. As tension from needs increases, we behave in ways that reduce the tension. Our general feelings of needs have their roots in our physiology, but the specific needs of the individual are influenced by individual experiences. "Behavior is not 'caused' by something which occurred in the past. Present tensions and present needs are the only ones which the organism endeavors to reduce or satisfy" (Rogers, 1951, p. 492). Therefore, it becomes important to allow a person to come to know the meaning of his or her present behavior and not to focus on the past.

Needs directly felt by the body (organism) are not always congruent with the needs of the self. The self needs (the "I" or "me" portion of the phenomenal field) may not always take us in the direction of enhancing the organism needs by moving in the direction of spontaneous and naturally felt emotions (Rychlak, 1981). For example, a self need for wealth may take us in the direction of dishonest business dealings that are in conflict with organismic needs (those felt directly in the body) to be an honest person.

Many of the values we incorporate into our self-concept are taught to us by our culture, primarily by our parents. If a particular deep-felt need or value (our gut feeling) does not mesh with what we consciously tell ourselves, a conflict arises between the two. At this point, we confront what it is we really believe. Although both needs are seeking to be satisfied, this can occur only when both are consistent with the organized concept of self.

A person achieves psychological adjustment when she or he is free from inner tension. This state occurs only when the self is congru-ent with all of the experiences of the organism (Rogers, 1951). Congruence is a matching of our awareness with whatever attitude or feeling we are experiencing (Rogers, 1961). Incongruence can come about by various means. It may occur as a result of being insincere with oneself or others, of not committing to those values taught to us by our parents, of not being open to experience, or of mimicking others instead of being oneself (Rychlak, 1981). Rogers would recommend that people admit to their feelings (such as fear, anger, confusion, discouragement, sadness) and then seek to do those things that will bring about change or growth.

Before individuals are able to sense congruence, they must first feel a sense of worth or being without shame. People must feel positive about their complete organism and comfortable with what it is. The need for positive regard is basic to our relationships with other humans. It occurs when we have a perception that our experience with another makes a positive difference. It includes attitudes of acceptance, liking, warmth, and respect (Rogers, 1959, p. 203). In order to have positive regard, we must have a sense of personal acceptance. This in turn will allow us to feel a sense of congruence.

When a person perceives a difference between the concept of self and the organismic experience, he or she feels anxiety. During these times, Rogers identified defense mechanisms as methods of dealing with the differences. The defense mechanisms include introjection, repression, distorted symbolization, rationalizations, and locus of evaluation.

General Systems Theory

Systems theories make up a broad approach to understanding how the world works and can be applied to different settings. General systems theory is a subset of systems theories that focus primarily on living entities such as families and organizations. "General systems theory is a conceptual orientation that attempts to explain holistically the behavior of people and societies by identifying the interacting components of the system and the controls that keep these components (subsystems) stable and in a state of equilibrium" (Barker, 1999, p. 191). General systems theory was first written about by Ludwig von Bertalanffy (1968), a biologist. This theory examines entire systems along with the components and interactions among and between components. It also contends that the best way to understand any component of the system is by studying it in the context of the entire system.

General systems theory, like other systems theories, incorporates terms and concepts that describe the interactions and relationships between parts of the system and from one system to another. The following terms are used in relation to this theory. A **system** is a functioning whole composed of all the interrelated parts and processes. Systems may include an individual, a family, a community, an organization, or a nation. The human system is made up of one person, whereas social systems are made up of interacting people (Longres, 1995).

Boundaries are defined as the repeatedly occurring patterns of behavior that define who or what elements are included in a system. "The boundary defines the subject system. In so doing, it also defines the appropriate roles that will be enacted by those comprising the system, for example, student, professor, secretary, or department chair. Like our skin, one purpose of a boundary is to protect the system so that its function is not adversely affected by external influences" (Chess & Norlin, 1991, p. 18). Boundaries exist within families. They define who is a part of the family and who is

not, as well as the role of each person, such as parents being the providers of the physical needs of the children. Healthy boundaries are neither too closed nor too open. They are closed enough to protect the system yet open enough to receive the resources needed to sustain and allow growth.

Subsystems are subordinate or smaller systems within the entire system. They are also defined and regulated by boundaries. Just as with systems, subsystems need boundaries that are healthy. For example, a single adult parent in the role of provider functions as a subsystem in a family; she likely associates with other adult subsystems yet also makes time to associate with her children, another subsystem.

Systems that remain relatively stable or steady are said to be in a state of **homeostasis** (Nichols & Schwartz, 2001). If the system becomes unstable or out of balance, an effort will be made to return it to a constant state. However, what is stable does not always equate to healthy or effective. Therefore, a system that is homeostatic may be functioning well or it may not, yet it is maintaining the status quo. An example of a homeostatic organization is one in which the employees are following the policy and procedures while providing services as conceptualized in the mission statement and fulfilling assignments in a timely and consistent manner according to their job descriptions.

A **role** is "concerned with specifying the attitudes and behaviors expected of people in particular positions" (Longres, 1995, p. 58). A person's role is defined by three variables: the expectations of the person in the role, the expectations of others about the person in the specific role, and how the person in the role actually behaves (Deutsch & Krauss, 1965). Each person in a system or subsystem takes on a role and is expected to behave in a certain way. For example, students are expected to

APPLICATIONS TO PRACTICE

Practice Tip

When considering the following questions, please refer to the chapter opening case on page 29.

What should you do next? Your supervisor has told you that the purpose of completing the intake process with a juvenile and guardian is to gather information about the family history and individual growth, development, emotional, social, and environmental concerns. Mrs. Cummins has provided you with basic information about herself, Liz, and Sarah. At this point it is probably important to get more detail about the problem and circumstances. You may also want to ask Sarah some questions about how she sees what is happening. Depending on what you decide needs to be done next, your questions and response will reflect that action. Here are some ideas for next steps:

If you want to have information from Sarah, you might say, "Mrs. Cummins, I really appreciate your taking time off work to bring Sarah in for this meeting. Sarah, I wonder if you could tell me what you think about what's happening?"

If Sarah doesn't say anything to your question, you might then ask, "Sarah, would you rather talk to me with your grandmother in the room with us or would you rather talk to me alone?" (Notice this question limits the choices and assumes that Sarah will talk.)

Once a decision is made about whether Grandma is going to stay in the interviewing room, your next step might be to get Sarah to engage in talking about nonthreatening things such as what she likes to do, what she watches on television, what she likes to eat, and so on. During this conversation, it is helpful to find ways to agree with what Sarah is saying or to echo ("Me too") with the things that you also like. Remember, agreeing and echoing must be honest and genuine. You wouldn't agree or echo something that was part of the referral problem. If Sarah talks about a television show that you also watch, you might say, "Yeah, did you see last week how Jim and Joanie hid from Mary? Was that funny or what?" This part of the warming-up conversation shouldn't last more than fifteen minutes. As you are listening to Sarah, your next step will be to make a transition from what the two of you are talking about to an exploration of the issues that you need to address. "So, it sounds like one way you keep busy while Grandma is at work is watching *The Collisters* on TV. Did you watch that show at home with your mother?" And then, "What was it like for you at home with your mother?" Now you have a way to shift the conversation to Sarah's relationship with her mother, her step-father, and her grandmother and other issues of importance.

Some agencies have interview outlines that identify what needs to be covered in a first interview. You may want to inquire about a format. Also, some agencies have forms that clients can fill out that cover the basic information that you need to gather during the first interview. Check with your agency to see what materials might be available.

Before the Interview

Before you actually talk with the client, it can be helpful to read the file. After you have read the materials, ask yourself:

1. How do I want to introduce myself and what do I want to say is the purpose of the interview?
2. What questions do I want to ask when Sarah and Mrs. Cummins come into the office? Jot down some ideas of topics you want to ask about.

APPLICATIONS TO PRACTICE, cont.

3. Do I want to talk with them together or separately? If separately, who do I want to talk with first?
4. What should we have accomplished before we end the interview?

Critical Thinking Questions
1. How am I the same as others of my same age?
2. How am I different from others of my same age?

3. How might I be different from a client or group of people my same age?
4. How might people who are older or younger than me see me?

behave in a particular way in class as they interact with the professor, a way of behaving that is significantly different from the way they interact with their peers.

Input and **output** involves the flow of information or energy among different systems. Once input has been received, the system processes it and then decides how to respond. A community that receives information about an increase in drug-related crimes may decide to organize a community watch program that informs the sheriff's department when apparent drug deals are occurring. **Positive feedback** is input or information to the system that tells it that what it is doing is right or good and to continue in the same direction to maintain growth.

When a mutual exchange occurs between two or more systems or individuals with a connection at the affective, behavioral, and cognitive levels, a **relationship** is said to have occurred (Barker, 1999). Parents and teens who communicate with each other about their goals, responsibilities, and needs are involved in a relationship.

Interface is the point at which two systems come in contact with each other. It may be a client meeting with a mental health therapist, a teen being assisted by a police officer, or the parents from two different families discussing their children's behavior while the children play in the neighborhood.

Differentiation, entropy, and **negative entropy** are terms used to describe the positive or negative growth of a system. *Differentiation* is the tendency for a system to move from being simple to developing greater levels of complexity. As an agency adopts the new federal HIPAA guidelines, it becomes more complex because of the greater demands placed on it. *Negative entropy* is a term associated with growth. As an agency expands from three to thirty employees, it experiences negative entropy. *Entropy* is the opposite of negative entropy. It occurs when systems move toward disorganization and even death. An example would be a family service agency that loses key employees as it shrinks because of budget cuts and lower reimbursement rates from managed care organizations.

Equifinality is a term that suggests there is more than one way to achieve a result. It means that systems can be creative when confronting the need to change by considering all possible alternatives rather than examining only one perspective.

Multicultural Theory

When addressing the topic of theories, models, and techniques that embrace diversity and a multicultural perspective toward practice, the task becomes daunting, just as it did when we attempted to distinguish those theories and models that reflect the biopsychosocial emotional aspects from more traditional Euro-American theories of counseling and psychotherapy. One of the most representative theories comes from the work of Sue, Ivey, and Pedersen (1996) and their book, *A Theory of Multicultural Counseling and Therapy*. Multicultural counseling theory (MCT) appears to provide the most comprehensive, organized, and inclusive approach to this topic. Although this approach is labeled as a theory, the three authors actually describe it as a metatheory, or a theory about theories, because they subscribe to the belief that no single theory is adequate when we attempt to help people from diverse backgrounds (religious, cultural, political and economic, ethnic, sexual). Thus, MCT offers "an organizational framework for understanding the numerous helping approaches that humankind has developed. It recognizes that both theories of counseling and psychotherapy developed in the western world and those helping models indigenous to non-western cultures are neither inherently right or wrong, good or bad. Each theory represents a different worldview" (Sue, Ivey, & Pedersen, 1996, p. 13).

The term *worldview* has been used by a number of authors on the topic of multicultural counseling and psychotherapy as a way of explaining how each theory, model, or technique (e.g., psychoanalytic, humanistic, behavioral, structural) is based on a philosophy about human behavior and what is needed to help people change, cope, or improve their circumstances. "Worldviews are the reservoirs for our attitudes, values, opinions and concepts; they influence how we think, make decisions, behave, and define events" (Sue, Ivey, & Pedersen, 1996, p. 7).

Worldviews are believed to be influenced by a person's culture. The more traditional schools within the behavioral and physical sciences are seen by multicultural specialists as being strongly influenced by Euro-American perspectives and values (Sue, Ivey, & Pedersen, 1996). One such value is that of "individualism." Against this value, clients may be assessed as either healthy or unhealthy, functional or dysfunctional, self-actualized or inhibited based on the level of separateness or individuation they have achieved. Although this value is neither good nor bad, it may be very different from that learned by an Asian client whose culture places higher value on the success of the family, group, or community over that of the individual.

Because theories and models are grounded in certain worldviews, practitioners must realize that, no matter how well intentioned, the interventive approaches they use with clients from diverse backgrounds may be providing help that is in opposition to or at variance with the client's basic values or beliefs. For this reason, as well as other differences that may exist between people, MCT has been developed in an effort to provide a structure for the study of theories and techniques applied to people from varying cultures and backgrounds. The theory proposed by Sue, Ivey, and Pedersen (1996) consists of six propositions with multiple corollaries for each proposition. Following is a review of the propositions and corollaries that underlie MCT.

Proposition 1 identifies MCT as a metatheory that provides structure for the evolution of counseling and psychotherapy theories. MCT is an inclusive, rather than exclusive, theory. It suggests that individual theories be examined from a worldview perspective—placing each theory in the context of the culture and cultural values that influenced the theory—as an important method of understanding and appreciating the applicability of each theory to certain cultural groups. Further, MCT also allows for the integration of diverse theories and techniques and the modification of them as they appear to have a goodness-of-fit for clients.

The corollaries for Proposition 1 are as follows:

- It is assumed that all counseling theories and models of therapy are tied into a culture and its beliefs. Therefore, the philosophical base, the assumptions, and values on which theories are predicated need to be identified and fully examined.
- It is believed that any counseling theory developed in a particular culture will automatically favor that culture and be prejudiced toward others. Thus, the MCT approach attempts to employ theories or models that are consistent with the client's life and culture while being open to the use of ideas and perspectives from different cultures.
- Practitioners' worldviews will influence how and what they define to be the client's concern (unconscious, behavioral, spiritual problem) as well as the mode of treatment. MCT instead views the client in context, seeking to understand cultural background and using culturally appropriate methods.
- One benefit of MCT is the way it incorporates and combines elements of Western psychology while taking into account the client's cultural background. For example, a practitioner using behavioral theory would look within the client's culture for the factors that reinforce particular behavior patterns. At the same time, a social worker using cognitive theory would focus on those experiences that influence the client's view of self and the internal messages that reflect this view.
- The client is viewed as an equal in the helping relationship. Together, the client and social worker coconstruct solutions as well as define problems.
- MCT attempts to aid clients (individual, couple, family, organizations, etc.) in generating new ways of feeling, thinking, and acting within their own cultural beliefs as well as respecting other cultural viewpoints.
- MCT believes it qualifies as a "theory by predicting failure from overemphasis of either cultural differences or cultural similarities and success from a combined perspective" (Sue, Ivey, & Pedersen, p. 15). Overemphasizing cultural differences limits its understanding of clients and promotes stereotypes. This, in turn, encourages exploitation of groups or individuals who are vulnerable, less powerful, or marginalized.

Proposition 2 recognizes that people are influenced at multiple levels by the experiences they have. The totality of those experiences needs to be considered when the client is being assisted by a professional. We are all connected as human beings, yet we may differ based on our cultural or family ties.

The corollaries for Proposition 2 are as follows:

- All people have multiple levels of identity (individual, group, and universal). We all share one level of identity as human beings and a unique identity as part of a reference group (culture, race, religion, sexual orientation, etc.). These identities are in flux and their relative importance will change over time. Those in the helping professions have tended to view and interact with clients at the levels of the individual and universal while ignoring the importance of the client's group.
- MCT sees that a person's identity is influenced by his or her context. It is important

to recognize the person–environment interaction, specifically the client's place in a family and how the family is influenced by a multicultural society.

- While differences exist between the client and helper, because of the complexity of identity, clients will be able to recognize their similarities and commonalities, with the social worker helping to create a functional worker–client relationship.
- At the same time, because of the complexity of cultural identities, it is believed that client and helper will be able to identify things that are unique about each one of them, no matter how similar they may appear to be. These cultural differences also make it possible that misunderstandings will occur.
- The specific concerns expressed by clients are almost always underlaid by cultural influences. For example, a couple seeking marital counseling to resolve difficult interpersonal problems will also be dealing with cultural factors such as gender and language differences that influence the identified areas of discontent.
- Social workers and other helpers are likely to operate under the influence of their own worldviews informed by membership in their own social and cultural backgrounds. Such influences can interfere with accurate assessment and limit the full range of potentially effective interventions.
- A skilled and knowledgeable helper will know and be able to track clients when they change from one cultural referent to another (individual, group, universal).
- Both client and practitioner experience a cultural identity that is dynamic and continually evolving.

The third proposition focuses on the developmental process (stages) of one's cultural identity. One's cultural identity may influence one's self-identity as well as one's view of self in relation to others of one's own reference group, to members of the dominant group, and to those of other minority groups. One's identity will also likely influence the helper–helpee relationship based on the respective sense of power. The setting of goals is also likely to be influenced by one's stage of cultural identity. For a complete review of the stages of racial and cultural identity development, see Sue and Sue (1990), *Counseling the Culturally Different: Theory and Practice.*

The following are the corollaries to Proposition 3:

- The development of cultural identity occurs through a series of identifiable stages that encompasses cognitive, emotional, and behavioral aspects of an individual. The stages appear to follow a sequence from being naive or unaware of oneself as a cultural being, to confronting the reality of culture, to the reflection of oneself as a cultural being, to arrival at a multiperspective thought about oneself in a larger system that encompasses many cultures. Each stage brings a new and different awareness about oneself and others (both one's referent group and other groups).
- Although each client has multiple cultural identities (e.g., man, Catholic, Italian, democrat, heterosexual) at the same time, MCT may help the client to recognize the influence of cultural issues on his or her identity.
- Based on the previous corollary, MCT recommends changing "self-concept" to "conceptions of self-in-relation" (Sue, Ivey, & Pedersen, 1996, p. 17). Help is given

only in context with interconnections to others.

- At present, the helping profession has not adequately understood the power differential as it relates to the helper's role and theories for intervention. MCT recognizes the potential power imbalances and puts effort into mutually constructing goals and strategies between client and helper.
- MCT helpers continually strive to increase awareness of cultural identity concerns and problems for clients, as well as themselves.
- Theories of identity that disregard or do not acknowledge that one's identity is developed in context to one's culture are likely to misconstrue clients' basic learned assumptions that influence the formation of their identity.
- MCT recognizes the importance that power differences have on a group's or an individual's own identity and how they view others.
- If behavior is not interpreted or assessed based on its cultural context, it will likely be misunderstood.
- A person's identity is complex. It is learned from one's culture. Therefore, a client's perspective must be viewed as a gestalt, the parts in context with the whole.
- When people from different cultural backgrounds disagree, it does not necessarily mean that one is right and one is wrong. Their reasons, based on differing cultural values and beliefs, may lead them to separate conclusions.
- MCT uses flexibility in incorporating both linear and nonlinear thinking. The one that is applied depends on its appropriateness to the client's way of thinking.

- Cultural differences are not viewed as being equal to or the same as individual differences.
- Both intentional as well as unintentional forms of racism are considered to be dangerous.

The fourth proposition suggests that the therapeutic goals that are established and the techniques that are implemented must be congruent with the values and experiences of the client. Therefore, multicultural helpers need to enhance their knowledge of ways and methods of intervening with clients.

The corollaries to Proposition 4 are as follows:

- MCT recognizes that there are at least two culturally sensitive approaches, namely, the universal and the culture-specific. MCT adheres to the universal approach, yet recognizes that on an individual basis the culture-specific approach may be more helpful.
- By utilizing a cultural frame of reference, new theories can be developed. This will help to expand treatment alternatives stemming from the predominant Western European theories that currently influence the profession.
- MCT recognizes that counseling and psychotherapy are based on language and that worldviews also stem from language. As such, helpers must be attuned to the dominant culture's influence and power as they affect our understanding of the client and our choice of theories.
- Assuming that a client wants a helper with a similar cultural background is a form of stereotyping. The matching of a client with a helper ought to be according to the client's preference.

- Helpers need to have a variety of skills or types of interventions to draw on when helping clients and should not assume that one technique will work with all.
- Empathy, not sympathy, is viewed as the appropriate response for helpers to have for clients.

Proposition 5 recognizes the importance of being able to help people by employing numerous roles, in particular the roles commonly utilized by helpers from various cultures. The helper may not want to be restricted by traditional one-on-one counseling roles. This is in line with the generalist practice perspective that social work adheres to, that of being involved at multiple levels with clients (micro, mezzo, and macro) as well as serving in various roles (therapist, broker, mediator, case manager, and advocate). This proposition also suggests the inclusion of others (minister, community leader) as adjuncts toward the accomplishment of clients' goals.

The following are the corollaries for Proposition 5:

- Helpers applying MCT will network with others to develop alternative treatments and to better use community resources.
- MCT encourages helpers to be open and flexible toward the setting and methods of services that are delivered. Instead of scheduling the classic one-hour session once a week, an "as needed" appointment may be more appropriate.
- Counseling is viewed in broad terms. It occurs whenever one person is helping another with a personal problem.
- Depending on the culture, some may be offended if they are referred to as a *counselor*. This may be because of a past negative connotation held toward counselors and their profession.

- Multicultural helpers may find that the values and ethics of their profession may need to be reframed to provide ethically appropriate counseling. This may occur because the ethics of the profession are founded on narrowly based cultural perspectives about what constitutes counseling.
- MCT recognizes that each client's problem occurs within a cultural context and that one-on-one counseling to help solve the problem may be inadequate. The client's network of support systems also needs to be considered.
- Successful outcomes need to be considered based on the individual-in-context model (individual, family, and community).
- Assessment from a multicultural perspective increases accuracy beyond merely working with minority groups.

The sixth proposition subscribes to the need for a "liberation of consciousness." MCT places an emphasis on viewing the individual, family group, and organization in a context. The expansion encourages helpers to look beyond the person, family, or the group to see them in relation to their world. It also encourages the use of traditional methods or means of healing, from one's culture, as an additional aspect of the helping process.

The following corollaries stem from Proposition 6:

- Clients must always be viewed in relationship with their context.
- As part of the process, helpers educate clients about underlying cultural aspects of their present problems.
- Helpers applying MCT incorporate aspects from Western and non-European methods of helping. These methods are adapted to meet the needs of the client

based on the client's cultural background (Sue, Ivey, & Pederson, 1996).

SUMMARY

This chapter focused on the importance of using an integrative perspective in direct practice. This perspective builds on an awareness of particular theories and models stemming from five domains involved in the human experience (biological/genetic, psychological, behavioral, emotional, and environmental). Characteristics of an integrative model draw on theories relating to these domains. This chapter provided a detailed review of major theories: genetic/ neurological, ego and cognitive psychology, learning (behavioral, social learning), humanistic-phenomenological and existential (person-centered), general systems, and multicultural theory. Each provides a unique perspective on the human condition that can be employed in social work practice with clients. Practitioners need to be grounded in the rationale (theory) behind techniques and strategies utilized in the process of direct practice to maintain organiza-

tion and continuity of services, to be able to evaluate client progress along with the delivery of services, and to be flexible in the delivery of services to better meet the needs of the client.

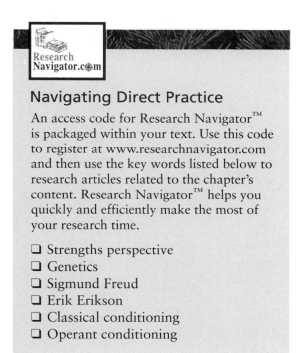

Navigating Direct Practice

An access code for Research Navigator™ is packaged within your text. Use this code to register at www.researchnavigator.com and then use the key words listed below to research articles related to the chapter's content. Research Navigator™ helps you quickly and efficiently make the most of your research time.

❑ Strengths perspective
❑ Genetics
❑ Sigmund Freud
❑ Erik Erikson
❑ Classical conditioning
❑ Operant conditioning

Chapter 3

Values, Ethics, and Ethical Dilemmas

■ "When I see Tone again, I'm going to pop a cap in his head." The words came out from his client's mouth with such vehemence that Masoud was shocked and more than a little perplexed. "I can see that you are very angry with Tone, but why do you want to buy him a cap?" he responded, trying to understand his client's anger. The client rolled his eyes and said, "He's the reason I spent two years in the slammer and I ain't forgiving or forgetting. Now he's sleeping with my ex-wife. I should do both of them."

This was Masoud's third week on the job providing direct services to clients transitioning from a halfway house to full integration into the community. His client, having served his entire sentence, would be free at the end of the week. Masoud recognized that the client was harboring strong feelings toward someone named Tone and perhaps his ex-wife as well. But he was not sure whether to try to talk to his client about the anger, remonstrate with him about the consequences of hurting someone, or just assume the client was blowing off steam. He wanted to be empathetic and not push his values on a client whose language use was a bit confusing. At the same time, he recognized that the client's anger had been partly responsible for his previous incarceration. Because the client's outburst came at the end of their session, Masoud decided to talk to his supervisor about the situation and perhaps get some guidance. Although he did not know what to do, he did recognize that he needed to do something.

This case involves some of the most challenging aspects of social work practice, namely the application of professional values and ethics. One mark of a profession is the fact that it is governed by an ethical code that affects every decision we make. This chapter addresses several topics including the roles of personal and professional values, critical social work values that underlie the NASW Code of Ethics, and strategies for dealing with ethical dilemmas.

The Role of Values in Social Work

Values are, by definition, things that we consider good, positive, or important in our lives. For most people, values dictate the decisions we make about our behavior and what we expect from other people. If individuals think that acquiring money and consumer goods is important, that value will drive the actions they take in their daily lives. If others value relationships, this too will color the decisions they make every day.

Everyone holds a set of values, yet there are enormous differences among people with respect to specific values. Value differences are evident in every area of our existence. They show up in the world in the form of hatred and harm directed at others whose values are not the same. They are reflected in decisions made about the activities or services on which governments spend taxpayer money. If people value acquiring wealth above helping those with less, they will be reluctant to share their resources. If we believe that social problems in the United States such as poverty and illiteracy should be given higher priority than spending on foreign aid, we are reflecting a set of values about the relative importance of these two competing issues. This leads us into a discussion of personal and professional values.

Personal versus Professional Values

Competing values underlie political parties, differentiating, for example, Democrats from Republicans and conservatives from liberals. It should come as no surprise that all of our clients will have values and that we ourselves possess values. Social work, like many professions, recognizes that social workers have a right to their own values. The profession also has a set of values, and ethical standards drawn from those values, that circumscribe how social workers are expected to act. These professional values sometimes set limits on the extent to which social workers are free to exercise their personal values. This is a challenge for many individuals who are considering social work as a career. If you believe, for example, that life begins at conception, you will probably have strong values about abortion. If you believe that life begins at birth, this likely gives you a different set of values about abortion. If you value a woman's right to control her own body, you will likely have a different take on attempts by others to restrict women's ability to exercise that right.

All of these differences in values can be interesting and help make us a diverse society and world. However, the decision to become a social worker places most of us in a position of deciding whether we can accept different values. We become acutely aware of this situation when clients have values that differ from ours. When a client seeks our help, we are expected to make every effort to ensure that the assistance we provide is appropriate and effective. A client seeking help for an unplanned pregnancy should be able to expect that her social worker will inform her about options, discuss honestly the advantages and disadvantages of each, and see that she gets the help she needs. Just as a client seeking help from a lawyer expects the attorney to defend him to the best of his ability, social work clients have a similar right to expect that we will do our very best to help them. If attorneys took the position that "I don't like to defend anyone who might be guilty," few of us would ever seek legal representation because we would distrust that person's ability and willingness to help us.

The pregnant client will not be served well by a social worker who decides that she will offer the client only one choice because she does not personally believe in the other alternatives. Again, it would be like an attorney who, after hearing your situation, says, "Well, why don't you consider pleading guilty?" Most of us would feel, correctly, that the lawyer has not behaved professionally, because she has a duty to inform us about the options from which we can choose. Likewise, if we seek medical help for a problem, we would like the physician to explain to us what our choices are. We would be put off by a doctor who has only one solution: "You will need surgery to cure that infection." In fact, we would likely accuse the person of malpractice because the doctor failed to explain alternatives and the risks for each option.

Social work clients have the same rights as others to get the best care and service we can provide. This means that we have a professional obligation to ensure that the services we provide are complete, appropriate to the client's needs, and reflect the best information currently available. The inability to meet this standard should be an indication that the social worker is unsuited for this profession. Although some prospective social workers respond to this challenge with statements like, "Well, I'd just refer the client to another social worker," this is not always an option. In some cases, you may be the only social worker serving an area. In other situations, clients would need to go through the entire process of explaining their situation to yet another social worker, a step that causes needless delay and inconvenience.

As you can see, it will be a challenge for some social workers to fulfill their ethical obligation to clients when their personal values are different from those of the profession. Having to wrestle with these challenges is a standard component of social work education and one that will confront the social worker at different stages of his or her career.

So far we have talked about social work values in the abstract without delineating what they are. In the following section, we look specifically at critical social work values that undergird practice within this profession.

Critical Social Work Values

The NASW Code of Ethics identifies six **core values** of the social work profession (NASW, 1999). They include service, social justice, dignity and worth of the person, importance of human relationships, integrity, and competence. These values are the basis for the ethical principles underlying the ethical standards incorporated in the code. We discuss each of the values and the ethical principle derived from the value. Later in this chapter, we

address each of the social worker's ethical responsibilities.

Service

Social workers believe that **service** to others is the core value that characterizes the work of the entire profession. Service to others trumps self-interest and is an obligation of all social workers. The ethical principle drawn from this value is that "social workers' primary goal is to help people in need and to address social problems." Volunteering one's time and energies without expectation of remuneration is also consistent with this value.

Social Justice

The existence of vulnerable groups and populations at risk in society requires that social workers pursue social change activities designed to enhance economic and **social justice.** The ethical principle growing from this value is that "social workers challenge social injustice" wherever it exists. Goals for social workers include recognition of the importance of cultural diversity, equitable distribution of resources, and elimination of poverty and discrimination, among other social ills.

Dignity and Worth of the Person

Social workers believe in the inherent **dignity and worth** of every person and demonstrate this in the ways we treat other people. We acknowledge differences and diversity among individuals and groups and seek to ensure that all people have the maximum opportunity to develop their capacities. Social work values self-determination, the right of individuals to make decisions about their lives, even when we disagree with that decision. At the same time, social workers are responsible to both the client and the larger society and are committed to resolution of conflicts between the two systems. The related ethical principle is that "social workers respect the inherent dignity and worth of the person."

Importance of Human Relationships

Relationships among people are important to social workers for several reasons. First, it is from these relationships that people acquire the supports and strengths they need to succeed in life. Second, social work practice is based on the premise of a helping relationship between the client and the social worker. One tenet of practice is that social workers work to enhance the well-being of people by supporting and strengthening human relationships. The ethical principle arising from this value is that "social workers recognize the central importance of human relationships."

Integrity

Integrity has to do with basic honesty. Social workers are expected to engage in ethical practice that honors their obligation to the client and to their employer. The ethical principle devolving from this value is that "social workers behave in a trustworthy manner." A social worker who fails to do so is violating a basic tenet of the profession.

Competence

It should come as no surprise that social work values **competence** in its practitioners. By this we mean that social workers have an obligation to acquire and maintain the highest level of knowledge, skills, and values. Whenever possible, social workers should contribute their wisdom in ways that further the knowledge base of the social work profession. This can include evaluating one's practice and sharing the results with colleagues through conference presentations, workshops, and publications. The related ethical principle is

that "social workers practice within their areas of competence and develop and enhance their professional expertise."

The Social Work Code of Ethics

For purposes of this chapter, we look specifically at the Code of Ethics of the National Association of Social Workers. In doing so, we freely acknowledge the existence of other codes of ethics, including the Canadian code and those promulgated by other social work organizations. It is not our intent to suggest that one ethical code is superior to another. Rather, we anticipate that the vast majority of students using this book will be expected to conduct their practice guided by the NASW Code of Ethics. In addition, it is entirely possible that individual agencies or social service organizations will have their own ethical codes and expectations of their employees. Having acknowledged the existence of other codes, however, we note that most such ethical standards have similar provisions and place like obligations on the practitioner.

Within the NASW Code of Ethics are six broad ethical standards, each placing a specific obligation on social work practitioners. These include:

- Social workers' ethical responsibilities to clients
- Social workers' ethical responsibilities to colleagues
- Social workers' ethical responsibilities in practice settings
- Social workers' ethical responsibilities as professionals
- Social workers' ethical responsibilities to the profession
- Social workers' ethical responsibilities to the broader society

Voices from the Field

Frederic G. Reamer

I first discovered the complex world of social work ethics in the mid-1970s. At the time, I was a doctoral student at the University of Chicago and was working in the criminal justice field. During those years, I began to understand how clinical and policy decisions that social workers make sometimes involve difficult ethical issues.

During the last quarter century, I have witnessed many dramatic changes in social work ethics, especially the remarkable evolution of the most prominent set of ethical standards in the field—the National Association of Social Workers' Code of Ethics—from a one-page document (the 1960 code) to the current twenty-nine page code. During my tenure as chair of the committee that wrote the current NASW code, I had the opportunity to wrestle with a wide range of ethical issues that were unimaginable to social work's earliest pioneers, for example, dilemmas involving social workers' use of the Internet to provide clinical services, clients who are HIV positive and pose a health threat to third parties, and providing mental health services within strict managed care guidelines.

Today's social workers have so much more to learn about ethics than did earlier generations of practitioners. My succinct advice is for you to learn as much as you can about (1) core social work values and their relevance to your professional goals (for example, values related to client confidentiality and privacy, self-determination, paternalism, informed consent, conflicts of interest, professional boundaries, social justice); (2) the ways in which social work values and ethical standards sometimes conflict (for example, when a client's right to confidentiality conflicts with your duty to protect third parties from harm, your client's right to self-determination conflicts with your client's wish to engage in self-harming behavior, or your personal values conflict with social work's values); (3) conceptual frameworks designed to help social workers make difficult ethical decisions; and (4) practical steps that you can take to prevent ethics complaints (filed with state licensing boards or NASW) and lawsuits that allege ethics-related negligence (for example, the violation of clients' rights).

Each of these ethical standards has many components, and we address these in the following pages. It should be noted, however, that the first and foremost responsibility is to clients, hence the placement of this item at the start of the list.

Social Workers' Ethical Responsibilities to Clients

This ethical principle is composed of sixteen separate but related areas. Each is discussed in detail, beginning with the social worker's commitment to clients.

Commitment to Clients

The Code of Ethics states clearly that **the social worker's primary obligation is to his or her clients** and their well-being. All things being equal, the worker's responsibility to the client supersedes other duties. At the same time, there may well be situations in which other obligations require that the social worker breach this commitment to the client. For example, it is common for states to have laws requiring that social workers and other professionals report suspected cases of child abuse to the proper authorities. In such instances, the legal requirements dictate the social worker's course of action, and clients are so informed. In the case that opened this chapter, we encountered such a situation. The client tells the social worker about his intent to hurt or kill another individual. In such cases, the social worker has a duty to warn the individual who is threatened and to inform the police of the intended harm. Social workers cannot allow a client to hurt another individual under the guise of obligation to the client.

Our responsibility to the client also means that we sometimes have to advocate for benefits or policies that help clients achieve their goals. For example, we have an ethical obligation to challenge managed care organizations that recommend specific treatments that we believe are either not appropriate or unhelpful to our clients. The first step in such situations is to talk with the managed care organization staff to determine if there is room for compromise. If efforts to get the organization to reconsider its decision are unsuccessful, it follows that social workers should "appeal denials of reimbursement for services they see as necessary" even under the threat of being removed from provider lists (Welfel, 2001b).

Self-Determination

Self-determination is the worker's obligation to ensure that clients have the right to set their own course in life even if we disagree with the direction. Clients should be assisted to identify their options and choose the one that makes the most sense to them. This does not mean that the client has complete latitude, however. Like all citizens, clients face limitations on their freedoms. Social workers can restrict a client's right to self-determination if the client's "actions or potential actions pose a serious, foreseeable, and imminent risk to themselves or others" (NASW, 1999, p. 7). Thus, it would be the worker's responsibility to try to prevent a client from killing herself or another person.

The importance of this exception was illustrated by the 1976 court case, *Tarasoff v. Regents of the University of California,* which established the therapist's duty to warn in situations in which danger to the public can be foreseen. In that case, a client had threatened a woman who had rejected his advances, and the therapist reported this fact to the campus police. However, the therapist did not share this information with the intended victim, who was subsequently murdered by the therapist's client. The court found that the therapist had not fulfilled his duty to warn. A social worker who fails to fulfill this now well-accepted duty is at risk of both civil charges of negligence and disciplinary action by licensing boards and NASW.

Informed Consent

Clients have to be fully informed about such things as their right to accept or decline services and the possible consequences of their decisions. This is called **informed consent.** Making an informed decision means knowing as much as possible about the risks and rewards of specific choices, including any related to things such as health insurance coverage and costs for services. When clients give their consent for treatment, it is always for a predetermined period of time with the understanding that consent can be withdrawn at any time.

One way in which social workers can violate this standard is when they fail "to disclose to clients the extent of disclosure of confidential client information to MCOs [managed care organizations] for fear of scaring them away" (NASW, 1999, p. 496). Clients must be informed about the amount of information the MCO will receive in order to comply with requests for reimbursement.

There may be times when the client's condition or characteristics may inhibit the ability to make an informed decision. This might occur when a client lacks fluency in the language used in treatment, has diminished capacity to make decisions, or is involuntarily required to participate in a program. Even in these cases, the social worker should do everything possible to ensure that the client is provided sufficient information and understands the risks of participating. In the case of a client mandated by the court to participate in an anger management group, a decision not to attend sessions may result in returning to the court to face further consequences.

If the social worker wishes to record practitioner–client sessions or allow others to view them, the client must give permission. Although the primary purpose may be to aid in helping the client, permission must still be sought.

Competence

Being **competent** at what you do is the mark of a professional. Social workers have an obligation to the client to have the knowledge and skill necessary to be of assistance. If the client's

problems appear outside of or beyond the social worker's ability, a referral to a more competent helper is required. At no point should a social worker profess to be competent in areas or with respect to specific approaches unless actually possessing this acumen. Careful use of consultation and supervision can assist the social worker in this area. We have a **duty to protect** clients from harm, including potential damage that we ourselves may cause.

An ethical problem can arise in situations in which managed care organizations approve only specific treatment approaches and the social worker lacks adequate training or supervision in the use of the approved methods. Providing services using treatment approaches in which one is not competent is unethical (Welfel, 2001b).

Cultural Competence and Social Diversity

One aspect of competence is known as **cultural competence,** or fluency with cultures different from one's own. This means that learning as much as possible about the cultures of our clients is critical, particularly in terms of theories, techniques, and skills that are culturally sensitive. It also means learning about all aspects of diversity, including gender, sexual orientation, race, ethnicity, and other characteristics that affect clients.

Conflicts of Interest

A **conflict of interest** exists when one's professional judgment is potentially impaired by factors other than concern for the client. For example, a social worker's need for income should never result in a client receiving services for longer than is required. In such cases, there is a conflict between the private interests of the social worker and those of the client. In the event of such potential conflicts, we should inform clients and, if needed, refer them to other practitioners.

Another potential area for conflict is dual relationships. Dual relationships exist whenever the social worker and client have relationships that extend beyond that of practitioner–client. An example is a social worker who agreed to serve as a field instructor for a student for whom she had previously provided therapy. The dual relationships of practitioner–client and field instructor–student were potentially at odds. In this particular situation, the conflict was compounded because the social worker, in an ethical lapse that is beyond understanding, hired the ex-client to clean her house. Thus, three separate relationships existed, necessitating elimination of the placement and reporting of the problem to the social worker's supervisor.

Dual relationships cannot always be avoided, and in some cases may be harmless. For example, social workers practicing in smaller communities may end up sitting next to their clients at the local baseball game or attending the same church. A client's cultural traditions might require the social worker to accept a small gift from the client or to share a meal. Certain theoretical orientations such as feminist theory tend to encourage a blurring of boundaries as the distance and power differentials between worker and client are reduced from those of traditional male-dominated approaches (Freud & Krug, 2002). Other situations pose questions about the right thing to do. For example, is it a boundary violation for the therapist to attend the graduation of a client whom he helped following the client's adolescence marked by drug use and self-destructive behavior? Is it wrong to inform a client about an employment opening in a friend's company when the job opportunity matches the client's qualifications and interests? Would it be improper to accept as a client an individual you met at a party thrown by a mutual friend? These and other situations arise frequently in the lives of social workers. The real challenge is to decide when an action might endanger the client and when it may be beneficial.

Conflicts of interest can also arise when we provide services to individuals who already have relationships with one another. This could happen in the course of working with a wife and husband separately or when social workers are required to testify in court proceedings affecting one or both parties. Whenever possible, clients should be informed about the potential conflict, and the worker should take steps to eliminate one of the situations.

Any situation in which there is risk of exploiting a client is ripe for a conflict of interest. Consider the social worker providing services to a college admissions counselor who makes decisions about which high school seniors get into her college. The social worker's own child is seeking admission and the social worker is tempted to mention this to the counselor. To do so creates a potential for exploiting the practitioner–client relationship for the social worker's benefit, an ethical violation.

Privacy and Confidentiality

Clients have a right to **privacy,** a right shared by most citizens according to the U.S. Supreme Court. In practice this means that social workers request only information they need in order to assist clients. It also means that whatever information is shared by the client is governed by **confidentiality.** Releasing confidential client information requires getting the client's permission and protecting this information whenever possible. Breaches of confidentiality are permissible in situations in which the social worker is responsible for preventing harm to the client or others or when required by law.

When information must be released, the minimum amount of data required should be used, and clients must be informed about this action.

Clients are to be told about the limits of confidentiality at the start of the professional relationship. When multiple clients are involved, as might occur with groups or families, the importance of maintaining confidentiality should be discussed. Clients should be warned, however, that the worker cannot guarantee that each member of the family or group will abide by this expectation.

Ultimately, clients have the right not to agree to release their information, and we should abide by this requirement whenever possible. We are obligated not to share this information with others nor to talk about a case in any setting where the conversation might be overheard. Failure to follow this admonition has resulted in punitive action against many social workers. Breaches of confidentiality "are the most frequently identified form of unethical behavior reported by practicing mental health professionals" (Welfel, 2001a, p. 448).

An important area of confidentiality involves situations in which the social worker is required to testify in court or similar proceedings. In such cases, we are obligated to request that the least amount of information be divulged and provide only such information as is legally required.

Another area in which confidentiality plays a large role is in record keeping. Information recorded in files should be restricted to only what is needed. Records should be protected from access by others who have no such right. This means keeping files locked away and ensuring that electronic files are available only to those with a need to know. The advent of technology has complicated this matter in several ways. First, computerized records can often be accessed by others not involved in a case. Second, messages transmitted by e-mail can be intercepted or read by others, although the risk may be relatively low. Third, answering machines and services can often be accessed by family members, roommates, and others. Leaving any message on these services that identifies the individual as a client or contains confidential information can breach our obligation of confidentiality. Figure 3.1 lists some of the risk factors in using common technology.

Figure 3.1

Risk Factors in Using Technology

The use of technology in social work practice is increasing, as it is in other areas of our lives. In many instances, technology has increased the efficiency and productivity of social work practitioners, possibly freeing more time for contact with clients. At the same time, the potential for harm from this technology increases apace. Welfel and Heinlen (2001) point out some of the pitfalls that await unsuspecting or novice users.

Fax Machines
1. Common errors include misdialing and sending the document to the wrong fax machine.
2. Unrestricted access to recipient's fax machine by others.

Computer Records
1. Potential vulnerability to "loss, theft, or unauthorized duplication" by hackers (p. 485).
2. Inadvertent access by coworkers and other staff.
3. Risk of deletion of critical information.

Voice Mail
1. Unauthorized access to voice mail and message machines by other family members, roommates, etc.

Using client information for teaching or other educational purposes is permitted if no identifying data about the client are revealed. If there is potential for revealing this type of information, the client's permission must be acquired. Likewise, it is common for the social worker's supervisor to have access to the client's file because is often necessary for supervisors to fulfill their educational and training role with the social worker.

The obligation to protect the client's records extends after that person's death. It also requires that social workers ensure that their own health or wellness does not place the client's records at risk. This suggests that client records not be routinely taken out of the office or otherwise exposed to potential loss. It is also important to avoid having the files of clients on your desk when others are in your office. Client records should not be left lying on the desk when the social worker is out of the office, whether for an evening or a longer period. See also Figure 3.2.

Access to Records

Reasonable **access to records** should be provided to clients whenever possible. In some cases, it may be necessary to explain records or notes so that clients do not misunderstand the meaning or nature of our assessment. Unless clients may be harmed in some identifiable way by releasing their records to them, we should grant their request. At the same time, we must ensure that no information is available to the client that would breach our duty of confidentiality to others. For example, if we have

---

Figure 3.2

Privilege and Privileged Communications

We should perhaps distinguish between the concepts of confidentiality and privilege. *Privilege* is a "legal right of clients to prevent mental health professionals from offering testimony or written documents in a legal proceeding involving the client" (Welfel, 2001a, p. 448). The right to privileged communication can be provided for in laws or granted as a result of court rulings. If a social worker is covered by privileged communication requirements, it is essential to inform the court and attorneys about the inability to discuss any aspect of the case without the client's specific permission. Normally, courts will recognize the existence of privilege, but this is not always the case. "If a judge ultimately orders that privilege does not hold in the current case, the clinician has three options: to submit the requested testimony or records as ordered, to appeal the order to a higher court, or to risk a contempt-of-court charge" (Welfel, 2001a, p. 448). The wisdom of consulting legal counsel in such cases should be obvious. Although state laws vary considerably in the extent to which they recognize privilege for social workers, the U.S. Supreme Court in *Jaffee v. Redmond* (1996) extended this protection to social workers and psychologists testifying in federal courts.

Claims to privilege are not absolute, and in certain situations information normally covered by privilege can be released. Examples include situations in which the client waives privilege, in which courts order the release of privileged information, in which clients sue the social worker, in which state or federal laws specifically limit privilege (for example, mandatory reporting of child or elder abuse cases), or in which clients are dangerous to others or to themselves (Welfel, 2001a; Danzinger, 2001). In such cases, the social worker is justified in abridging or obligated to abridge privilege to the degree necessary to comply with legal requirements and to meet the challenges they encounter.

recorded information in the client's file that was provided by others, this information may need to be removed. Requests by clients to see their files and any limitations inherent in that access should be recorded in the files.

Sexual Relationships

Although the **prohibition against sexual relationships** with clients should be easily understood by everyone, it remains one of the more problematic aspects of social work practice. The Code of Ethics is clear that "social workers should under no circumstances engage in sexual activities or sexual contact with current clients, whether such contact is consensual or forced" (NASW, 1999, p. 13). This prohibition extends to "clients' relatives or other individuals with whom clients maintain a close, personal relationship where there is a risk of exploitation or potential harm to the client" (p. 13). It also applies to "former clients" (p. 13).

Social workers are also forbidden to "provide clinical services to individuals with whom they have had a prior sexual relationship" (NASW, 1999, p. 13). This and the preceding prohibitions are based on the premise that any mixing of professional and sexual relationships violates boundaries, produces dual relationships, and has the potential to exploit the client. Many of these provisions of the Code of Ethics are also incorporated in licensing laws and other state regulations. Not only can violations of these prohibitions result in sanctions from NASW (including loss of membership), but they can also lead to termination of one's license to practice and possibly to criminal charges.

Social workers who do not maintain appropriate boundaries with clients are especially at risk when clients file complaints with state licensing boards or ethics committees. The presumption from the start is that the responsibility for maintaining boundaries rests squarely with the professional social worker. Boundary issues may arise with specific clients, such as those characterized by borderline personalities. They may also occur when the social worker's own needs become involved in work with a client. Another source of boundary problems is the use of nonsanctioned interventions that are not generally recognized as appropriate or effective. Examples might include holding therapies, use of repressed memory, or other alternative approaches (Welch, 1999).

The prohibition against sexual relationships with clients is part of an overall concern about maintaining appropriate boundaries with clients. It is based on a recognition that engaging in dual or multiple relationships with clients is problematic from several perspectives. First, there are clear power differentials between clients and social workers that place the former in a vulnerable position subject to exploitation. Second, dual relationships can carry mixed messages that confuse the client and create conflicting responsibilities for the social worker. This can lead to hurt feelings and a sense of betrayal (Herlihy, 2001).

Physical Contact

Physical contact between client and social worker should be avoided when there is any risk of psychological harm to the former. The obligation to maintain appropriate boundaries in this area also rests with the social worker. Physical contact can carry the risk "that a client might misinterpret or sexualize such a gesture," and social workers "should proceed only after first securing the client's permission" (Herlihy, 2001, p. 468).

Sexual Harassment

Sexual harassment "includes sexual advances, sexual solicitation, requests for sexual favors, and other verbal or physical conduct of a sexual nature" (NASW, 1999, p. 13). Social workers are prohibited from sexually harassing clients.

Derogatory Language

Social workers may not use **derogatory language** in either written or verbal communication regarding their clients. In all cases, we should use language that demonstrates respect and professional courtesy toward clients.

Payment for Services

As **fees for service** become a relatively common practice in many agencies, social workers must exercise care in their use. For example, fees should be "fair, reasonable, and commensurate with the service performed. Consideration should be given to the client's ability to pay" (NASW, 1999, p. 14). Clients should know the nature and amount of all fees, and under no circumstances should a social worker accept or solicit fees beyond those imposed by the agency. It is generally unethical to accept goods or services from clients as a means of payment. Such bartering can lead to conflicts of interest, exploitation, or other harm to the client. In rare instances in which bartering is a common practice in the client's community, special care must be exercised to avoid even the appearance of impropriety. Complete responsibility for obeying this provision rests with the social worker.

Clients Who Lack Decision-Making Capacity

In some areas of social work, we will encounter clients with diminished ability to make their own decisions. When clients **lack the decision-making ability,** it is the social worker's obligation to ensure that the client's rights are respected and that all actions taken are in the client's best interests.

Interruption of Services

There may be times when services to clients are in danger of disruption. **Interruption of services** may occur when the worker is ill or incapacitated or when the client moves to a new community. In such situations, the worker should attempt to ensure "continuity of service" (NASW, 1999, p. 14) to clients.

Termination of Services

We have identified termination as one step in the problem-solving process employed by social workers. **Termination** carries with it several admonitions. First, termination should occur when clients no longer require our services. Second, we should always try to get help for clients for whom services are terminated if a need still exists. Whenever possible, clients should be referred to other helpers, and any potential harm to clients should be minimized.

Third, although clients may be terminated for failure to pay for services, this must be explained to the client at the beginning of the relationship and discussed prior to removal of services. Services should not be terminated when the client poses an imminent threat to self or others.

Fourth, services may not be terminated if the goal is a "social, financial, or sexual relationship with a client" (NASW, 1999, p. 15). Withdrawing services under these circumstances is clearly unethical. Finally, when services must be terminated, it is the obligation of the social worker to notify clients beforehand, offer assistance in transferring the client, and discuss the benefits and risks of continuing services either in the present agency or in another setting.

Welfel (2001b) notes that it is considered unethical to terminate "treatment (without a specific referral to alternative care) when reimbursement ends if they believe clients may benefit from additional services but may be unable to pay for them" (p. 496). In such situations, social workers are obligated to provide service themselves or to provide an appropriate referral.

It should be clear by now that the social worker's obligations and responsibilities to clients are numerous and complex. They cover everything from professional relationships to record keeping to termination of services. They place a clear burden on the social worker to act in ways that are beneficial to the client, professionally sanctioned, and clinically appropriate. They do not allow the needs or wishes of the social worker to take precedence over those of the client, and they limit significantly situations in which client's rights can be abridged.

Social Workers' Ethical Responsibilities to Colleagues

As with clients, social workers have an ethical duty to colleagues in social work and other professions. These obligations cover eleven separate areas.

Respect

The social worker's first obligation to one's colleagues is to show them **respect.** The Code of Ethics states, "Social workers should treat colleagues with respect and should represent accurately and fairly the qualifications, views, and obligations of colleagues" (NASW, 1999, p. 15). It further requires that social workers "avoid unwarranted negative criticism of colleagues in communications with clients" and other professionals (p. 15). Negative criticism includes demeaning a colleague's competence or other characteristics such as race, ethnicity, disability, sexual orientation, or other factors. The social worker is obligated to cooperate

with colleagues from social work and other professions when this serves clients' well-being.

Confidentiality

Information provided to us by colleagues in the context of professional relationships should be maintained with the same degree of **confidentiality** as client data. At the same time, it may be necessary to warn colleagues about the limits of our ability to maintain confidential information in specific instances, such as arise when the social worker has a legal or ethical duty to warn or divulge certain information. If another professional informs us, for example, about a case of suspected child abuse, social workers may have no choice but to report this information based on their duty as mandated reporters under state child abuse law.

Interdisciplinary Collaboration

Interdisciplinary collaboration is common for social workers in certain fields. In school and hospital settings, for example, it is typical for social workers to collaborate with psychologists, physicians, nurses, psychiatrists, and many other professionals dealing with specific client situations. In such situations, social workers are obligated to contribute the knowledge, skills, and values of the profession to the deliberations.

Because individual professions have their own ethical standards, there may be times when these are in conflict with the social worker's ethical obligation. When ethical conflicts occur in interdisciplinary teams and similar settings, the social worker should address these issues within the group. If such disagreements cannot be resolved, and social workers believe the ethical issues are sufficiently serious, social workers "should pursue other avenues to address their concerns consistent with client well-being" (NASW, 1999, p. 16).

Disputes Involving Colleagues

Having a dispute with a colleague is neither unusual nor unexpected. Differences in perceptions, theories, approaches, and values often arise in the process of working with other professionals, including other social workers. Recognizing this, the NASW Code of Ethics provides some guidance about how best to handle **collegial disputes.** The social worker's first obligation is to not exploit or take advantage of disputes in order to further his or her own interests. This obligation also extends to clients and prohibits social workers from inappropriately involving them in disputes between or among practitioners. Such involvement can be detrimental to clients who may come to see the professionals they count on as siblings squabbling over issues that the clients neither understand nor appreciate. It also undermines the profession's image, a fragile thing in the best of situations.

Consultation

Although colleagues may sometimes be a source of conflict, more often they represent an opportunity for wisdom and sound advice. Seeking the advice and counsel of colleagues in order to benefit clients is a common practice among social workers and is supported by the Code of Ethics. At the same time, social workers should be aware of their colleagues' areas of expertise and seek **consultation** only from appropriate sources. If we seek consultation on a case involving child sexual abuse, for example, we would want to talk with those who are experts on this topic. Even then, the amount of information shared with the expert should be limited to only that which is absolutely necessary. Though we are seeking help on behalf of our client, we are not free to divulge unneces-

sary details of their lives without appropriate permission to do so.

Referral for Services

There may be times when clients can benefit greatly from **referral** to other professionals, in either social work or other disciplines. This might occur when the other professional has greater knowledge in the client's area of difficulty, or when the services needed cannot adequately be provided by the social worker's agency. In some instances, referral may be required when it is clear that the social worker is not helping the client to reach identified goals.

Handling referral situations requires care and involves ethical considerations. For example, the process of facilitating the transfer is the social worker's responsibility. We are obligated to get the client's permission to divulge information to the new professional and to carefully explain each step in the process. Ethically, the referring social worker may not accept payment from the client or anyone else for making a referral to another professional. A social worker who receives such a referral may not pay the referring social worker for making the referral. Such payment arrangements give at least the appearance of impropriety and undermine the social work profession's declared dedication to the client's best interests.

Sexual Relationships

Because **sexual relationships** between colleagues can have serious consequences for their well-being, the Code of Ethics contains specific language about such situations. For example, "Social workers who function as supervisors or educators should not engage in sexual activities or contact with supervisees, students, trainees, or other colleagues over whom they exercise professional authority" (NASW, 1999, p. 17). The need for this prohibition should be clear. The potential conflict of interest in the dual roles of sexual partner and supervisor/educator is obvious. Even if such conflicts could be eliminated, the power differential between social workers in these respective positions is substantial and places one person in a potentially risky situation.

Human nature being what it is, the code also makes provision for situations in which social workers have stepped over the line. In such an event, the social workers have a duty to transfer professional responsibilities to others to eliminate the conflict of interest that has arisen or may arise. Practically speaking, this means that the supervisor must inform his or her superior about the situation, transfer supervisory responsibility to another supervisor, and avoid any appearance of a conflict of interest.

The prohibition against sexual relationships does not apply to two colleagues at equal positions in an organization, nor is it intended to infringe on the freedom of individual social workers. However, the potential damage that can occur to the professional reputations of one or both parties when supervisors and supervisees or educator and student engage in sexual relationships is great. Moreover, the organization or agency environment can experience problems with morale, public respect, and confidence in its ethical standards when such situations are allowed to continue.

Sexual Harassment

The frequency with which **sexual harassment** is discussed in the media should be sufficient guarantee that social work practitioners would avoid this behavior. Organizational consequences such as termination, demotion, and suspension are often coupled with professional loss of license and sometimes financial costs associated with defending or losing court cases. Nevertheless, the Code of Ethics contains a clear statement about this topic: "Social workers should not sexually harass supervisees, students, trainees, or colleagues. Sexual harassment includes sexual advances, sexual solicitation, requests for sexual favors, and other verbal or physical conduct of a sexual nature" (NASW, 1999, p. 17).

Although the items included in the code regarding sexual harassment are limited for purposes of definition, it is common for a much broader definition to be applied within organizations. For example, sexual harassment legally includes creating a hostile or demeaning work environment through such activities as telling sexist jokes, posting pictures that others consider obscene, and/or making comments that demean women. In such situations, the absence of explicit sexual advances or solicitations will not protect the accused individual.

Impairment and Incompetence of Colleagues

Impairment of colleagues is one of three areas, along with incompetence and unethical conduct, that requires the social worker to take specific actions toward another professional. Impairment of a colleague may arise from "personal problems, psychosocial distress, substance abuse, or mental health difficulties" (NASW, 1999, p. 17). The ultimate concern regarding a colleague's impairment is the way it interferes with the ability to practice effectively.

When we believe a colleague is sufficiently impaired so as to prevent the individual from doing his or her best for clients, our first obligation is to try to talk to the person about taking appropriate steps to get help. In an ideal world, this step would be sufficient to prompt the colleague to seek remediation. However, this is not always possible, sometimes due to the nature of the impairment itself. For example, many substance abusers deny being addicted despite the obvious toll drug use is taking on their lives. In such situations, the social worker is obligated to "take action through appropriate channels established by employers, agencies, NASW, licensing and regulatory bodies, and other professional organizations" (NASW, 1999, p. 18). This may mean informing the individual's supervisor or agency director, filing a grievance through NASW, and/or notifying the state social work licensing bureau.

Incompetence of a colleague may occur when a social worker offers services to clients while lacking the proper training needed for the kind of problem being experienced by the client. Perhaps the colleague has a higher regard for his own skill than is justified by prior education or experience. Perhaps the social worker felt embarrassed to admit that a client's problems were beyond her competence. Either way, the problem remains the same—the client is at risk of not getting appropriate assistance.

Incompetence of a colleague can also happen when an agency places assignments on a social worker that are well above his or her level of competence. One would not assign a BSW graduate, for example, to provide psychotherapy to a depressed client. However, some agencies, in an effort to reduce costs, have placed BSW staff in positions for which their education has not prepared them. In such situations, it is the responsibility of both the BSW and MSW staff members to challenge this situation. As in the case with impairment, we begin by talking first to the colleague whose competence is in doubt and then, if needed, to other appropriate authorities.

Unethical Conduct of Colleagues

A colleague whose behavior we consider to be unethical presents another situation in which we are obligated to take specific action. The code specifies that "social workers should take adequate measures to discourage, prevent, expose, and correct the unethical conduct of colleagues" (NASW, 1999, p. 18). This poses a special challenge because sometimes a situation creates an ethical dilemma within which two or more ethical obligations collide. We address this issue later in the chapter and provide some recommendations for managing such scenarios. Keep in mind, however, that different people may have divergent views on what is ethical behavior in a given situation.

The first step in attempting to deal with what we believe to be **unethical conduct** is to become familiar with the policies and procedures that govern our professional behavior. For example, in many states this involves presenting information to the state licensing board for social work. NASW maintains state and national inquiry committees for investigating allegations of unethical conduct by social workers.

The second step is to talk directly with the colleague if such discussions are likely to be effective. In some situations, the colleague will not be open to such a direct intervention and in others may retaliate against the messenger. When talking directly about the matter is not feasible, it is appropriate to follow the steps identified earlier for dealing with the impairment or incompetence of a colleague.

On the other hand, colleagues may sometimes be accused of unethical behavior although they have done nothing improper. This can occur, for example, in situations involving child protective services when parents try to divert attention from their own shortcomings by accusing the social worker of ethical violations. In such situations, social workers should do all in their power to support, defend, and help their colleagues.

Social Workers' Ethical Responsibilities in Practice Settings

Practice settings are the locations in and auspices under which we conduct our social work activities. These can be a social service agency, educational setting, medical center or hospital, community organization, or private practice, among many others. The social worker's ethical responsibilities in these settings cover supervision and consultation, education and training, performance evaluation, client records, client billing, client transfer, administration, continuing education and staff development, commitment to employers, and labor–management disputes.

Supervision and Consultation

As you might expect given the importance consistently placed on competence, those who provide supervision and consultation are expected to have the requisite knowledge and skill to assume these responsibilities. It therefore follows that providing consultation or supervision outside of your area of competence is unethical. Not only does it hurt the colleagues you are assisting, but it also does equal disservice to the clients they serve.

When we do provide consultation and supervision, we are obligated to set "clear, appropriate, and culturally sensitive boundaries" (NASW, 1999, p. 19). This is especially important because the opportunity for dual or multiple relationships often exists in these situations. The supervisor is resonsible for avoiding these types of relationships that involve "risk of exploitation of or potential harm to the supervisee" (p. 19). It is also the supervisor's duty to evaluate the work of supervisees fairly and respectfully. Maintaining dual relationships of supervisor and personal friend with another social worker can impair the ability to do both.

Education and Training

The code places an equal burden on those who "function as educators, field instructors for students, or trainers" in that they must operate within the scope of their competence and "provide instruction based on the most current information and knowledge available in the profession" (NASW, 1999, p. 19). Like supervisors, educators and trainers must fairly evaluate the work of their students and avoid the dual or multiple relationships that can harm the student. Also like supervisors, it is the educator or field instructor who has the burden of setting appropriate boundaries.

One other obligation of field instructors and educators is to ensure that clients are aware that the services they receive are being provided by students. Neither agency personnel nor the student should give the impression that the social worker is other than a learner. Rather, they have an active obligation to inform clients of the student's status.

Performance Evaluation

We have established that fair and respectful evaluation of supervisees and students is an expectation for all social workers. One way of helping to ensure such an outcome is to insist that evaluation systems have "clearly stated criteria" that articulate the expected performance of those being evaluated (NASW, 1999, p. 19). Using vague, nonspecific evaluation methods is inherently unfair to those being evaluated, contributes to confusion and misunderstanding, and increases the likelihood of grievances and other personnel difficulties.

Client Records

Documenting social worker activities and client characteristics in the form of case records is a common expectation in almost all agencies. MacCluskie (2001) points out that

> there are numerous organizational entities that might require documentation to communicate about a client or service processes: insurance companies or other third-party payers (e.g., Medicaid); governing bodies (e.g., County Board of Mental Health); accrediting bodies (e.g., Joint Commission of Accreditation of Healthcare Organizations, JCAHO); and internal agency requirements (i.e., quality assurance) to ensure compliance with the first three groups. (p. 461)

In addition, we have previously addressed the social worker's responsibility with regard to allowing clients to access their own records. However, providing access to files is only one of several obligations covering the records we keep on our clients. Another requirement is that information contained in the client's file be "accurate and reflect the services provided" (NASW, 1999, p. 20). This is important because the record is the official repository of information gleaned by the social worker and may be the basis for all kinds of decisions affecting the client. Files that contain inaccurate information can result in a client being considered ineligible for services and cause insurance companies and other third-party payers to deny payment for services rendered. Because files can be subpoenaed into court, they are open to inspection by others who don't share the social worker's experience with the client.

In addition, files must be kept current so that another practitioner picking up a client's case will understand what was occurring and what progress was being made. A supervisor may need to become involved in the case in an emergency, or something could happen to the social worker, necessitating a change in practitioner. Current files help keep people informed in such situations.

Sometimes, failure to keep files accurate and up-to-date is reported in quality assessments completed as part of the agency's overall program evaluation. Failure to keep accurate and current records can have negative consequences. Wiger (1999) suggests that "without good documentation, there is no clear record of the course and progress of therapy. Sloppy clinical procedures are not only unfair to the client, but they may border on malpractice" (p. 1). Moreover, good record keeping can be of enormous benefit in the event that a client charges a social worker with malpractice. Careful documentation helps reduce a social worker's liability if a client or family member sues the practitioner or when a regulatory body pursues an investigation into the quality of care provided. MacCluskie (2001) recommends that when social workers must report suspected child abuse, they should enter into the record the actions they took and the individuals to whom they provided relevant information. Any written reports filed should also be included in the client's record.

Other information should be included in the client's record. For example, if a managed care company has denied the client treatment that has been recommended by the social worker, this information should be described in the record. Every contact with a client whether by phone or in person should be documented. Cancellations of appointments should also be noted. If at termination the social worker recommends additional treatment, it is essential to record this information along with any referral provided. This is especially important if the client is terminating prematurely.

At the same time, some items should probably not be recorded in the client's file. These might include personal revelations that would be unduly embarrassing to the client and are unnecessary to your work with the client. A client's fantasies, dreams, or private behaviors that are incidental to the situation should be excluded. Putting comments, observations, or other items in the file that are unnecessary can place the client at risk should the file be accessed by other individuals.

Recent changes mandated by the Health Insurance Portability and Accountability Act (HIPAA) place even greater obligations on the social worker to maintain adequate documentation (Welch, 2003a) (See Figure 3.3).

The recommendation to abide by the most stringent requirements also applies in cases in which the social worker has a duty to warn, as when a client threatens harm to self or others. Although state laws may differ on the legal requirement to warn an intended victim, the social worker should err on the side of caution and detail in the record the identified victim and actions taken to warn that person and notify authorities. Clients who are at risk for suicide also should have this information entered into the record, along with steps the social worker took to protect the client. Record keeping should note the "client symptoms, verbalizations, behaviors, and diagnostic impressions" (MacCluskie, 2001, p. 461).

Typical documentation will vary somewhat from agency to agency but will usually include the initial assessment and intervention plan along with periodic progress reports. Copies of correspondence, release-of-information forms, and other pertinent items should also be retained. At the point of termination, a summary of the client's situation and progress should be prepared for the record. Social workers should focus their comments on client behaviors to the extent possible and avoid broad generalizations or interpretations that go beyond what is evident.

An additional ethical requirement regarding client records involves storage of files. Once services are terminated, client files should be retained in case the client needs help in the future. The length of time records should be retained is often governed by state laws, agency policies, or other guidelines. Although

---

Figure 3.3

HIPAA

The Health Insurance Portability and Accountability Act of 1996 mandated multiple changes in the way information is handled in the health care field. Failure to meet the law's provisions can lead in extreme cases to fines and potentially imprisonment. In some cases, HIPAA privacy requirements are stricter than state rules with which the practicing social worker will already be familiar. This necessitates learning what the law means for you. If a state law has more stringent requirements than HIPAA, the social worker must adhere to the laws of the state. Some of the more salient requirements of HIPAA (Welch, 2003b) include the following:

- Social workers are required to have written privacy policies.

- Clients must be provided a consent form detailing how information will be used.

- Social workers must keep client process notes separate from the client's file.

- Social workers must maintain a log of all information released about a client.

using electronic record-keeping systems such as computers can greatly facilitate entering and retrieving information, just as with written records social workers must be alert to concerns about unauthorized access.

Client Billing

Billing clients for services is common in some areas of practice. In others, the worker may never be directly involved in this process. The important consideration here is that billing practices "accurately reflect the nature and extent of services provided" and "identify who provided the services in the practice setting" (NASW, 1999, p. 20). This allows others who do the billing to know precisely what should be charged and who should be paid. Keeping accurate billing information is another way of showing respect for one's employing organization.

Client Transfer

It is not uncommon to encounter clients who wish to transfer from other agencies or practitioners. Before automatically agreeing to accept a transferring client, carefully consider the client's needs and whether you or your agency can meet them. Transfers can occur for many reasons and involve both positive and negative elements. Is it in the client's best interests to transfer? What information, if any, should be sought from the previous service provider? These questions need to be discussed with the client prior to arranging transfer.

Administration

Along with social workers, agency administrators have ethical obligations associated with their responsibilities. For example, they are expected to "advocate within and outside their agencies for adequate resources to meet client's needs" (NASW, 1999, p. 20). Moreover, the al-locations of resources should be fair and known to other staff. Distribution of resources must be "nondiscriminatory and based on appropriate and consistently applied principles" (p. 21).

Of course, financial and similar resources are not the only ones important to social workers and clients. For example, administrators are expected to "provide appropriate staff supervision" (NASW, 1999, p. 21). This obligation is related to the administrator's duty to create working environments that are in compliance with the NASW Code of Ethics. Conditions, activities, or behaviors that interfere with code compliance should be eliminated. An example would be an agency in which the administrator is billing clients for the work of practicum students while not informing the clients about the students' learner status.

Continuing Education and Staff Development

A major ethical responsibility of both employers and supervisors is the provision of continuing education and staff development opportunities for their staff. This requirement is intended to ensure that social work staff remain current in their knowledge and skills and capable of providing the best service to clients.

Commitment to Employers

When we agree to accept a position, regardless of the type of agency, there is an implicit agreement with employers that we will meet our commitments to them. This includes fulfilling our job responsibilities, meeting our obligations to our clients, and adhering to organizational policy. At the same time, we are ethically bound to work to improve agency policies or procedures that impair our effectiveness in helping clients. To the extent that we can identify more effective or efficient means of delivering services, we should share this knowledge with the employer.

You may be thinking about situations in which an agency's policies need revision. It is well within our ethical obligation to work for changes in policies, procedures, regulations, or other aspects of the agency that interfere with our ethical responsibilities. This can involve advocating for changes in rules or other areas that prevent us from doing our ethical duty. If, for example, our agency has a procedure that discriminates against people with disabilities, we should seek to change these arrangements. Ethically, we cannot tolerate discriminatory practices that conflict with our values about the worth and dignity of human beings, deny social and economic justice to others, or place populations at risk.

Social workers should not accept employment or supervise social work practicum students in agencies that use unfair personnel policies. This not only places the employee at risk, but it also needlessly undermines the learner's opportunity to observe effective organizational practices.

As employees, we are also obligated to "be diligent stewards of the resources" of our employing agencies (NASW, 1999, p. 22). This means not wasting resources, making wise decisions about cost, and maintaining the fiscal health of the organization.

Labor–Management Disputes

Although it is permissible for social workers to "engage in organized action, including the formation of and participation in labor unions to improve services to clients and working condition," there are guidelines about what is appropriate (NASW, 1999, p. 22). Our actions, for example, while on strike or engaged in job actions must remain consistent with the values and ethical standards of the profession. Be-

cause involvement in some of these activities drastically affects services to clients, it is important to recognize that this is an area about which social workers disagree on the best way to resolve various issues. The possible effects on clients should be a consideration as we contemplate an appropriate decision.

Social Workers' Ethical Responsibilities as Professionals

In addition to our responsibilities to clients, to colleagues, and to practice settings, social workers have obligations as members of the social work profession. These obligations are designed to help ensure a positive image of social work professionals and to avoid situations that would cast aspersions on other social workers. These responsibilities cover the areas of competence, discrimination, private conduct, dishonesty, impairment, misrepresentation, solicitation, and acknowledging credit.

Competence

Competence, the possession of the knowledge and ability needed to meet the demands of a particular position, is a sine qua non for any social worker. Competence is indispensable, and social workers should accept "responsibility or employment only on the basis of the existing competence or the intention to acquire the necessary competence" (NASW, 1999, p. 22). Competence, however, is a condition that is never fully met in the sense that social workers must continually upgrade their knowledge and skill to deal with emerging issues. This entails keeping abreast of literature in the field, attending conferences and workshops, and participating in in-service training opportunities.

By extension, this requirement means that the activities we carry out in practice with client systems should be based on "recognized knowledge, including empirically based knowledge, relevant to social work and social work ethics" (NASW, 1999, p. 22). Consequently, we are not permitted to include in our practice untested theories or ideas, particularly those that have the potential to harm our clients. Doing so undermines our ethical obligation to our clients and endangers the reputation of the social work profession.

An emerging area of practice that has significant ethical implications involves what has been termed *e-therapy* or electronic counseling. Because this is a relatively untested practice venue and method, it bears special consideration. Figure 3.4 addresses this issue.

Discrimination

Discrimination involves treating people with partiality and making unjust distinctions between groups or individuals. Under no circumstances should a social worker engage in "any form of discrimination on the basis of race, ethnicity, national origin, color, sex, sexual orientation, age, marital status, political belief, religion, or mental or physical disability" (NASW, 1999, pp. 22–23). This obligation sometimes clashes with those of the practice setting, especially when the setting services certain groups to the exclusion of others. Social workers must be mindful of such situations and sensitive to the inherent ethical dilemmas.

Private Conduct

Private conduct includes all actions taken by the social worker as a citizen and not within the scope of his or her employment. Although social workers have the same rights as other citizens when it comes to their private conduct, they do have an obligation to "not permit their private conduct to interfere with their ability to fulfill their professional responsibilities" (NASW, 1999, p. 23). An example is a social worker who placed a bumper sticker on her car that stated her strong antiabortion position. Her job responsibilities included making home visits to clients, including some who were pregnant. A danger of her private expression of opinion is that some clients might feel sufficiently intimidated or unsure about whether she could be helpful should they wish to end their pregnancy. To the extent that this happened, her private expression of position interfered with her professional obligation to assist clients.

Dishonesty, Fraud, and Deception

Dishonesty, fraud, and deception include behaviors such as lying, deceitfulness, cheating, unscrupulousness, and deviousness. Social workers are not permitted to engage in dishonesty, fraud, or deception in any aspect of their professional work, nor to be associated with such behavior. To do otherwise is to place the entire profession in a bad light and undermine the public's faith in social workers. An example of how this might occur comes from Welfel (2001b), who cites social workers "giving inaccurate diagnoses to meet managed care requirements for reimbursement even when they believe alternative (unreimbursable) diagnoses better described the client's concerns" (p. 496). Although the social workers are interested in the well-being of their clients, this action is an example of fraud and deception.

Impairment

Impairment can include any behaviors that diminish the social worker's performance of duty. As professionals, "social workers should not allow their own personal problems, psychosocial distress, legal problems, substance abuse, or mental health difficulties to interfere with their professional judgment and performance or to jeopardize the best interests of

Figure 3.4

Ethical Issues in E-Therapy

Kanani and Regehr (2003) and Maheu and Gordon (2000) highlight some of the ethical issues that arise in the use of e-therapy. E-therapy includes such things as using e-mail, videoconferencing, web-based counseling, and real-time chat, among others. The ethical issues surrounding use of e-therapy can be both complex and serious. The following are a few of the potential problems that can occur when a social worker decides to offer services over the Internet.

- Lack of informed consent about the limitations and risks of web counseling

- Loss of confidentiality on either the worker or client ends of the communication

- Potential access by hackers during sessions

- Maintenance of e-mail records by third parties such as Internet service providers

- Inhibition of social worker's fulfillment of duties to warn and protect due to physical inaccessibility of, and distance between, client and social worker.

- Licensing complications arising from clients in one state and social workers in another

- Social worker unfamiliarity with state laws governing telecounseling

- Inhibition of worker's ability to recognize nonverbal clues such as body language, gestures, or facial expressions due to absence of face-to-face contact

- Requirement that social workers learn unique Internet communication skills including "emotional bracketing, descriptive immediacy, and the use of similes, metaphors, and stories" (Kanani & Regehr, 2003, p. 158)

- Necessity of adopting special computer security systems to reduce the risk of others accessing worker–client communications

- Transmission errors allowing others to see communication meant for the client

- Misapplication of e-therapy to clients whose problems are not susceptible to this methodology (such as clients who are suicidal or experiencing eating disorders)

- Potential boundary issues arising from enhanced intimacy associated with use of the Internet to build relationships

- Inadequate research showing the effectiveness of e-therapy

Concerns about the ethics of using the Internet for counseling extend to worries about clients. For example, it may be difficult for the client to verify the credentials of the person offering services. If there is a problem, the client may have limited access to out-of-state licensing boards that govern the social worker. Social workers who elect to use the Internet as a component of their practice must carefully consider licensing issues, develop competence in the use of communication based entirely on text, obtain appropriate consent from clients, and adopt security systems designed to maintain confidentiality. They must also be sensitive to the ways in which boundaries can be crossed on the Internet that would not likely occur in face-to-face interactions. Finally, social workers must develop plans about how they will fulfill their duty to protect and to warn third parties should this become an issue during electronic counseling (Kanani & Regehr, 2003).

people for whom they have a professional responsibility" (NASW, 1999, p. 23). When such situations arise, it is the social worker's duty to seek immediate help and take the actions needed to ameliorate conditions. These actions can include seeking "professional help, making adjustments in workload, terminating practice, or taking any other steps necessary to protect clients and others" (p. 23). In short, we cannot help clients and meet our obligations to colleagues, our agency, or our profession when we are overcome by our own impairments.

Misrepresentation

Misrepresentation involves holding oneself out as representing the views of others without sanction. At no point should social workers allow their private comments or behavior to be seen as representative of their agency or the profession at large. Although there may be times when we are authorized to speak on behalf of our organization, we should make it clear when we are doing so and when we are simply expressing our own opinion. When we do have authorization to speak on behalf of an organization, what we say must be in line with the "official and authorized positions of the organization" (NASW, 1999, p. 23).

At the same time,

> social workers should ensure that their representations to clients, agencies, and the public of professional qualifications, credentials, education, competence, affiliations, services provided, or results to be achieved are accurate. Social workers should claim only those relevant professional credentials they actually possess and take steps to correct any inaccuracies or misrepresentations of their credentials by others. (NASW, 1999, p. 23)

For example, if your agency inaccurately lists you as having a doctorate or a certification as a substance abuse counselor, you should make every effort to correct this information.

Solicitation

Solicitation is any attempt to attract clients already being served by other practitioners. It is considered unethical to attempt to solicit potential clients who are in vulnerable positions. In such situations, solicitation can be perceived as manipulation or coercion in order to benefit the social worker. An example is an adjunct (part-time) faculty member teaching a class on eating disorders. In the course of her teaching, she becomes aware of a student who has a serious eating disorder and is being seen at the campus counseling center. The social worker, a clinician in private practice, discusses the student's disorder after class and then drives the student to an inpatient treatment facility with which the clinician is affiliated. This is unethical from at least two perspectives. First, the social worker had a conflict of interest by removing the client from one treatment program and taking her to another facility in which she had a financial interest. Second, the social worker was effectively soliciting clients—in this case, a very vulnerable client—from other practitioners. Even if such actions are well-meaning, we have an obligation to avoid these kinds of situations.

Another prohibition is soliciting client testimonial endorsements as a means of increasing one's own business. Clients tend to be vulnerable to social worker's requests for validation and should not be placed in such a position.

Acknowledging Credit

Acknowledging credit means accurately identifying the author or producer of a given work product. The responsibility to acknowledge credit is a simple one. According to the Code of Ethics, "social workers should take responsibility and credit, including authorship credit, only for work they have actually performed and to which they have contributed" (NASW, 1999, p. 24). When social workers use the work or contributions of other people, they should give appropriate credit to the material's creator. Plagiarism—taking credit for the work of another—is thus considered unethical and a violation of the code.

Social Workers' Ethical Responsibilities to the Social Work Profession

The social work profession holds a unique place in society, reflecting public sanction to engage in specific types of helping behaviors. Social workers must behave in ways that maintain and enhance the profession's image and standing. The two areas to which this obligation is most applicable are the integrity of the profession and evaluation and research.

Integrity of the Profession

Maintaining the integrity of the social work profession involves several activities. First, we must work to ensure that the profession is characterized by "high standards of practice" (NASW, 1999, p. 24). This means that we must always strive to provide high-quality services consistent with client needs.

Social workers must also "uphold and advance the values, ethics, knowledge, and mission of the profession" through research, appropriate criticism, and enhancing our own practice skills. They must engage in activities that "promote respect for the value, integrity, and competence of the social work profession. These activities may include teaching, research, consultation, service, legislative testimony, presentations in the community, and participation in their professional organiza-

tions" (NASW, 1999, p. 24). Social workers can also contribute to the profession's knowledge base by presenting at professional conferences and submitting material for publication.

Finally, "social workers should act to prevent the unauthorized and unqualified practice of social work" (NASW, 1999, p. 25). This means working for licensing laws that ensure that only those with appropriate education and training may provide services to the public. The frequent news stories dealing with child welfare cases often make reference to failure on the part of "social workers" without any concern about whether those people are professionally prepared social workers. In many states, those providing basic services may lack any professional education yet be labeled as social workers. This practice casts an unfavorable and undeserved negative light on the profession, and social workers should work to prevent such misrepresentation.

Evaluation and Research

Evaluating the outcomes of our own work with clients and the programs with which we are associated is an ethical obligation of those in the social work profession. Because knowing whether what we are doing is working is critical to the welfare of both clients and the profession, we should do everything in our power to encourage outcome research. The profession itself benefits when we have evidence of the effectiveness of our interventions and programs.

A corresponding responsibility is to ensure that evaluation and research activities are conducted in ways that protect the rights of participants. This means adhering to informed consent obligations, making sure that participants understand any risks involved and are familiar with what will happen to them during their participation. We must also take special

Case Example

Susan Ellison is a student intern at a well-baby clinic. Susan is married with three children in grade school and is active in her religion. Her supervisor, Ellen Jones, has asked Susan to see Marsha Winters, who brought her baby into the clinic for a checkup. Mrs. Winters is crying and wiping her eyes in the waiting room as Susan calls her name. As Mrs. Winters picks up the diaper bag, Susan says, "It looks like you have your hands full. Would you like me to carry the baby?" Mrs. Winters nods yes. After they enter the office, close the door, and are seated, Mrs. Winters starts the interview before Susan can explain who she is.

Mrs. Winters: I'm sorry. I don't mean to cry and be a burden. . . .

Susan: We all are sad from time to time (connecting with Mrs. Winters by responding to what Mrs. Winters is doing and letting her know that it is okay to have and show feelings). I know I sometimes got the baby blues after I had my babies. I'm a social work intern here and my supervisor, Ellen Jones, asked me to see you.

Mrs. Winters: I don't think it's baby blues. . . . I've had those before. My husband is out of work and I'm pregnant again. My baby is only four months old and we've got three more children, under four years of age, at home. I don't know from day to day how we are going to feed them, let alone another one. I want to have an abortion, but George, that's my husband, says no. I'm almost three months along, so I've got to decide soon.

Susan: It sounds like you have your hands full and are overwhelmed by your current situation, with your husband out of work, three children under four, and being almost three months pregnant (paraphrasing and summarizing what the client has said). Have you tried to think through the pros and cons of your choices?

Mrs. Winters: No, I just know I cannot take care of another child no matter what George thinks.

Susan: Would it help if we tried to think this through together?

Mrs. Winters: Yes, I'd like that.

Critical Thinking Questions
1. What values do you have strong feelings about? (Values aren't just about religious beliefs but extend to beliefs about relationships, decision making, and so forth.)
2. How might these values conflict with a client's values?
3. What things will you need to do to maintain and separate who you are and who the client is in this human relationship?
4. Talk to other students and your supervisor about how they maintain boundaries between what they individually believe and what their clients believe.

Case Example

Charles Livingston is a social work student. He works part time at the prison and has been assigned an internship at the county drunk driving (DUI) treatment agency. While walking into the waiting room, Charles sees Mac Lawrence, who he knows has just gotten out of prison for drug trafficking. Charles has worked with several prisoners who have been released into the community and knows that while they are

APPLICATIONS TO PRACTICE, cont.

on parole, they are required to remain drug free. One of the other counselors comes into the waiting room and calls Mac's name. Mac gets up and follows the counselor into the hall where the offices are. Charles has taken an oath as an officer of the law to report any knowledge of a crime being committed

or planned. In this internship placement, Charles has signed a volunteer statement that says he will maintain confidentiality about who his clients are and what they say except in the cases of child abuse, domestic violence, and acknowledgment of plans to hurt self or another.

Critical Thinking Questions

1. How might the client's knowing you from one setting and seeing you in another setting affect the client and the service delivered?

2. How might your knowledge of the client from one setting affect your seeing him in another setting?

Practice Activity

Identify which social work ethical obligations are illustrated in the Charles Livingston case.

Research Activity

Using the Research Navigator™ website, www.researchnavigator.com, find two codes of ethics from other professions to compare with the NASW Code of

Ethics. Prepare a short paper in which you identify three to five similarities and three to five differences among these codes.

care when dealing with participants who have limited capacity to give informed consent. Further, participants must be informed that they can refuse to continue their participation in the research at any point without any negative consequences. In some cases, agencies may have internal review boards for the protection of human subjects that must approve research efforts affecting their clients. It may be necessary to provide clients with informed consent information in their own language if it differs from English and to make extra effort to ensure that they understand what is being asked of them.

In some cases, those who participate in research may need special assistance. For example, a survey of experiences related to sexual assault may trigger issues for which the partic-

ipant will need assistance. It is our obligation to protect clients from "unwarranted physical or mental distress, harm, danger, or deprivation" (NASW, 1999, p. 26). Protocols should ensure participants' privacy and anonymity and inform them of any risks to confidentiality that may occur through their involvement in the research.

Once data have been acquired, it is incumbent on the social worker to report findings accurately and fairly. Falsifying data is unethical. If errors later become known, the social worker should ensure that this information is provided to everyone involved.

At no point should social workers engage in research that involves a conflict of interest with their other obligations to participants. Dual relationships should be avoided, as well as any other situation that places participants at risk. One of the best ways of staying out of trouble when doing research and evaluation is to educate yourself about "responsible research practices" (p. 26).

Social Workers' Ethical Responsibilities to the Broader Society

Social workers also have an ethical obligation to the larger society in which we live and practice. This obligation involves four areas: social welfare, public participation, public emergencies, and social and political action.

Social Welfare

> Social workers should promote the general welfare of society, from local to global levels, and the development of people, their communities, and their environments. Social workers should advocate for living conditions conducive to the fulfillment of basic human needs and should promote social, economic, political, and cultural values and institutions that are compatible with the realization of social justice. (NASW, 1999, pp. 26–27)

As a result of this obligation, social workers must be concerned with what occurs elsewhere in the world and not get overly focused on their own little sphere of operations. The nature of a global economy means that things occurring in another country or on another continent can have profound impacts on our own world. Political refugees forced from their homelands in the Balkans, for example, may become clients and/or members of our community. Companies that outsource their operations by moving them to countries with lower wages impact the economic health of the communities and workers they leave behind in the United States.

Likewise, decisions of the U.S. government to engage in military activities elsewhere in the world can have profound implications for the rest of our society. These may include death and injury to military personnel, family breakups, and redistribution of resources from social programs designed to help vulnerable populations to foreign aid and military spending. In other words, the systemic nature of the world means that almost every decision or action taken somewhere has the potential to produce consequences elsewhere.

Public Participation

Social work believes that the public, to the extent possible, should participate in shaping social and economic policies and institutions. We should take steps to facilitate this process by encouraging other citizens to understand critical issues and share their perspectives with elected representatives.

Public Emergencies

Public emergencies provide opportunities for social workers to render services on behalf of those affected. This means volunteering to assist in whatever ways are appropriate and within the competence of the social worker.

Social and Political Action

The knowledge and experience that social workers acquire in the course of their professional activities places them in a unique position to help members of the public understand critical social issues. Social workers are much more likely to be familiar with problems of the poor, mental health issues, trends in family life, and other situations in society. We should pursue social and political action that advances the needs of vulnerable populations. Similarly, we should alert elected representatives to the potential consequences of proposed legislation and work for programs and policies that are responsive to human needs.

Social workers have an obligation to "act to expand choice and opportunity for all people, with special regard for vulnerable, disadvantaged, oppressed, and exploited people and groups" (NASW, 1999, p. 27). We should also work for services and conditions that reflect sensitivity to and respect for cultural differences and other forms of diversity. This also entails efforts to "prevent and eliminate domination of, exploitation of, or discrimination against any person, group, or class on the basis of race, ethnicity, national origin, color, sex, sexual orientation, age, marital status, political belief, religion, or mental or physical disability" (p. 27).

Although some social workers will encounter ethical obligations on a daily basis, some specific sections of the code may be of concern only rarely in a social worker's professional life. A major limitation of any set of ethical standards is the fact that no code can take into account all of the situations a practitioner might encounter in social work practice. For example, in many situations the obligations we have to one group conflict with those we owe to another, such as duty to an employer and to the client. Because the code does not establish priorities among the social worker's respective obligations, it does not provide guidance on what should be done. In yet other cases, ethical obligations may collide with one another, as when a social worker owes a client both confidentiality and safety. We deal with these clashes of ethical obligations in the following section.

Managing Ethical Dilemmas

Any time a social worker has two or more ethical duties in a given situation, the possibility for conflict exists. This is the crux of an ethi-cal dilemma—an obligation of a social worker to two conflicting duties. Consider the case cited at the beginning of this chapter in which a client announces, in the course of treatment, his intention to harm another individual. We know from our review of our ethical obligations to clients that confidentiality should be maintained whenever possible and that clients have the right to self-determination. At the same time, these obligations are contrary to our responsibility to intervene when "clients' actions or potential actions pose a serious, foreseeable, and imminent risk to themselves or others" (NASW, 1999, p. 7). From the information shared by the client at the start of this chapter, there clearly is a potential for risk to another person.

In cases like this, making an ethical decision is easier because of the relative risk and benefits inherent in each choice of action. In other cases, there may be conflicts between our personal values and those of the profession. Whenever possible we should look to the Code of Ethics for guidance regarding what action to take. The code, for example, takes precedence over our personal values. In other situations, the resolution of ethical dilemmas may not be so easy or obvious. In some situations, there may also be conflicts between one's ethical obligations and legal requirements. As Freud & Krug (2002) observe, "most dilemmas do not fall neatly into the ethical domain, but combine ethical, legal, and clinical issues with different emphases in different situations" (p. 478). To help us deal with these more difficult ethical dilemmas, several writers have come up with approaches that social workers can use. Although other authors have focused on different models when addressing the issue of managing ethical dilemmas, we focus our attention on the work of Loewenberg, Dolgoff, and Harrington (2000).

An Ethical Decision-Making Process

Loewenberg et al. (2000) note that before we can begin to resolve an ethical dilemma several factors must be considered. First, we must be aware of three sets of values that may be operating in a given situation. These include our own personal values, those values held by general society, and the values of the profession of social work.

Second, we must identify what ethical options we have that could be employed in this situation. In doing so, we consider what alternatives provide the greatest protection of the client's rights and those of others. We must also think about which alternatives will protect society.

Third, we must consider ways in which clashes among the three sets of values can be mitigated. We must do the same for the alternatives that protect the client, others, and society. By being creative, we may find a way to reduce conflict among these different value sets and alternatives and identify an appropriate course of action.

Fourth, we must carefully consider which alternative actions available to us do the "least harm" possible (NASW, 1999, p. 67). Because we do not wish to harm anyone by our actions, we must think about each alternative in view of what harm will come to the client, others, or general society if we take a specific action.

Fifth, we must rate each alternative in terms of its relative degree of efficiency, effectiveness, and ethicalness. For example, one alternative may be more efficient but may prove unsuccessful, thereby reducing its effectiveness.

Sixth, we must consider and rate the ethical consequences (both long and short term) of any action we are considering. Short-term negative consequences may be of less concern, for example, than long-term effects. To assist in sorting out the various alternatives and conse-quences, Loewenberg et al. (2000) have created what they call the Ethical Principles Screen, a tool we discuss in the next section.

The Ethical Principles Screen

Loewenberg et al. (2000) have considered a series of ethical principles that can be helpful to social workers as they grapple with ethical dilemmas that are not easily resolved. Their **Ethical Principles Screen** provides a rank ordering of ethical principles that can be used in these more difficult situations. By rank ordering we mean that some ethical principles have greater importance than others. Whenever possible, we make decisions that reflect the ethical principle with the highest priority. There are seven principles, including "protection of life, equality and inequality, autonomy and freedom, least harm, quality of life, privacy and confidentiality, and truthfulness and full disclosure" (NASW, 1999, p. 69). Figure 3.5 depicts the hierarchical nature of these principles as a ladder, with the highest rung indicating the most important principle.

Protection of Life

The highest priority among the seven principles is **protection of life,** including that of the client and of other people. The right to life supersedes all other rights because without it none of the other rights can be enjoyed. This is the concept behind most efforts to help people with serious physical or emotional problems, although it can have other consequences for the individual. For example, a person suffering from a terminal illness who is in great pain may not want to continue living because the quality of his life is so poor and he has no hope of recovery. These are issues that social workers sometimes must deal with as they try to balance values such as client self-determination, sanctity of life, and quality of life.

Figure 3.5

Ethical Principles Hierarchy

Protection of Life
Equality & Inequality
Autonomy & Freedom
Least Harm
Quality of Life
Privacy & Confidentiality
Truthfulness & Full Disclosure

Equality and Inequality

The second highest priority among the rights to which people are entitled is to be **treated equally**, all things being equal. Using this principle, the social worker would not discriminate against a client because of sexual orientation, age, ethnicity, or other factors. At the same time, it is often necessary to discriminate on other grounds. For example, some clients are at greater risk than others. The frail elderly may have higher priority for services than younger adults without physical limitations. A family with children living in their car may have higher priority than a couple living in the same circumstances. This is what we mean by the notation *all things being equal*. When the situation is not equal and one group has greater or more emergent needs than another, the one with fewer needs receives lower prior-ity. You may have experienced this principle in action if you have ever been treated in a hospital emergency room. It is not unusual for someone suffering from the flu who arrived first to be treated after someone else who arrived later. If the late arrival has an injury that could result in loss of limb or life, the medical personnel are going to treat this person first. Their reasoning has nothing to do with valuing one person more than another but rather with an awareness that the two situations are not equal.

Autonomy and Freedom

Social workers are committed to providing clients with the maximum degree of **autonomy** possible because this is the underlying factor in client self-determination. Likewise, they value the individual's **freedom** to make choices in life. This value is shared by most in the helping professions, including medicine. A patient is almost always accorded the right to refuse medical treatment even to the point of being allowed to sign out of a hospital against medical advice (sometimes referred to as AMA). However, autonomy and freedom can be limited by other factors that have higher priority. The patient who is bleeding profusely and may die from loss of blood is likely going to be prevented from leaving. The client who announces that she is going to go home and kill herself may find the social worker taking action to prevent this occurrence despite the profession's belief in individual freedom. Maintenance of life has higher priority than an individual's freedom to take her own life.

Similarly, a child may not be allowed to pursue a course of action that would be permitted an adult. This is because children are not equal in the eyes of the world, and we believe they must be protected, sometimes against their own wishes. The twelve-year-old girl who is talking about running away from home to join the Internet boyfriend she has been corresponding with will be prevented from doing this. The competence of a person of this age to make such a significant life decision is judged by most people as inadequate to the task. Thus, we are more likely to limit the degree of autonomy or freedom when we deem the person unable to make a competent choice.

Least Harm

Least harm means we have a duty to ensure that any harm an individual experiences is as slight as possible. Under most circumstances, we would not want any harm to befall another person. But there will be times when it is necessary to take an action that may cause harm to a client. When confronted with this challenge, we err on the side of the least harm possible. Consider, for example, an individual who is experiencing a major depressive episode and is considering suicide. The client's social worker has several choices to consider. First, the seriousness of the threat to kill oneself must be taken into account. If the threat is considered serious, the social worker must look at the remaining options. If the client is allowed to go ahead and kill himself, this is perhaps the greatest harm one can experience. If the client is restrained and admitted to an inpatient mental health facility, this is likely to cause him additional emotional anguish and bitter feelings toward his social worker. Of the two possibilities, death or emotional anguish, the latter causes the least harm for the shortest possible time.

Quality of Life

The concept of **quality of life** is somewhat elusive, but most people know when their life's quality is good or bad or somewhere in between. Quality of life is influenced by access to resources for meeting basic and other human needs and some degree of control over one's environment. The ability to make choices has a great deal to do with the individual's sense of quality of life. As social workers, we are interested in ensuring a decent quality of life for both our clients and others in society. Given options, social workers choose the one that enhances quality of life over one that reduces it.

Privacy and Confidentiality

As you can see, **privacy and confidentiality** are way down the list of priority rights that social workers must be aware of when working with clients. Although we believe in the importance of maintaining confidentiality in our communications with clients, we cannot allow this to have priority over other values with higher priority. This fact is recognized by state laws that make social workers mandatory reporters of child abuse. Despite the risk to our relationship with the client when we disclose our knowledge of such abuse, protecting the child from harm has to have greater priority. At the same time, we may rightly decide to refuse a lawyer's request for a client's files pursuant to a lawsuit because we believe that maintaining client confidentiality has greater priority.

Truthfulness and Full Disclosure

Truthfulness and full disclosure have the lowest priority in the Loewenberg et al. (2000) Ethical Principles Screen. Despite this, whenever possible social workers conduct their work with an emphasis on telling the truth and fully disclosing information needed by the client or other professionals (subject to the client's permission). We do not lie to clients or tell them only some of the limits to confidentiality or some of the risks inherent in a particular treatment. At the same time, truthfulness, like confidentiality, has its limitations. Consider a client who arrives for a meeting with the social worker, is armed, and threatens to hurt anyone who tries to take her child away. In such situations, the social worker would be expected to say whatever was needed to diffuse the situation and protect human life. No one would challenge the decision to lie or to stretch the truth under those circumstances.

On the other hand, consider a seriously depressed client who is getting ready to undergo electroconvulsive therapy. The social worker's failure to mention the risks associated with such procedures is unwarranted. Clients have a basic right to expect that the social worker will be truthful and honest in communications as well as in what is written into the client's records.

As we have seen, each of the ethical principles has a specific priority in relation to each of the others. Whenever possible, we ensure that the rights with the highest priority are observed before those with lowest priority. The principles provide a useful yardstick against which to measure choices we make as professionals. Although they will not solve all dilemmas, they provide an excellent starting point from which to consider our options.

Ethical Complaints

Ethical complaints can be brought against a social worker by a client, another professional, or a member of the public. Complaints that involve violations of state licensure laws, which may also involve ethical issues, can be brought to the attention of the state-level body responsible for overseeing licensing of social workers. In Utah, for example, this body is the Division of Professional Licensing, whereas in Wisconsin it is the Department of Regulation and Licensing. These bodies usually follow formal steps or procedures in investigating whether a violation occurred and in considering appro-

priate sanctions. The results of actions taken by these licensing bodies are often listed in quarterly newsletters sent to all licensed professionals.

Consequences of violating licensing laws can include loss of the license to practice, suspension of the license for a designated period of time, remedial education, or some other action. In some cases, such as engaging in a sexual relationship with a client, a social worker may be charged with a criminal violation.

Ethical violations can also be brought to the attention of the National Association of Social Workers at the state level. Each state NASW chapter has a Commission on Inquiry (COI) that hears accusations of unethical behavior by social workers and social work agencies. The COI is made up of three social workers from the state in which the violation is alleged to have occurred. The results of an NASW Commission on Inquiry indicating that a social worker has violated the Code of Ethics will be published in the *NASW News* and sometimes in state NASW newsletters. Common COI decisions might include corrective actions such as additional

> training, supervision, or consultation, as appropriate, notification of respondent's supervisor or employer when such notification is necessary in order to provide information needed for supervision recommendations contained in the Report, private censure by the NASW, restitution (including financial restitution) by the respondent to an individual, group, or organization harmed by the respondent's unethical behavior, [or] correction of a record. (NASW, 2004, p. 1)

If a respondent fails to fulfill the terms of an agreement reached with the COI (such as undertaking additional education), or if the ethical violation is particularly egregious, more

---

Figure 3.6

NASW Sanctions for Ethics Violations

- Publication in the *NASW News* and/or the chapter newsletter of adjudication findings, conclusions, and sanctions imposed

- Suspension of membership or expulsion from membership in NASW

- Suspension of ACSW standing or other NASW issued credentials (including forfeiture of dues or fees paid)

- Revocation of ACSW standing or other NASW issued credentials (including forfeiture of dues or fees paid)

- Notification to state regulatory boards of adjudication findings, conclusions, and sanctions imposed

- Removal from the Register of Clinical Social Workers (including forfeiture of dues or fees paid)

- Notification to credentialing bodies, societies, and specialized practice groups in which the individual may hold membership of adjudication findings, conclusions, and sanctions imposed

- Notification to employers of adjudication findings, conclusions, and sanctions imposed

- Letter of censure

- Notification to respondent's malpractice insurer of findings and conclusions

- Notification to the Disciplinary Action Reporting System (administered by the Association of Social Work Boards) of findings and conclusions

---

serious actions called sanctions can be imposed. These are listed in Figure 3.6 and taken from NASW's national guidelines for handling ethical violations. Because of the seriousness of sanctions, these must be approved by the national Executive Committee of NASW.

When considering what consequences to impose on a social worker who has violated the Code of Ethics, NASW considers a variety of factors. These mitigating items are listed in Figure 3.7.

Although the risk of any one social worker being charged with an ethical violation is small, it is wise to carry malpractice liability insurance to help protect against these and other complaints that a client might bring. Often this insurance is provided by one's agency or organization, but social workers in private practice will generally need to purchase their own coverage.

SUMMARY

It should be clear by now that social workers are governed by a Code of Ethics that is at once broad and specific. The code covers the profession's obligations to clients, to colleagues, in practice settings, as professionals, to the profession itself, and to the broader society. These ethical standards are based on values that are considered underpinnings of the profession. Ethical practice is an obligation for every social worker regardless of educational level, type of employment, or nature of services provided. On the one hand, adherence to the NASW Code of Ethics can help ensure that

---

Figure 3.7

Mitigating Circumstances in Ethics Violations

- Vulnerability of individuals affected by the misconduct

- Cooperation in professional review proceedings

- Understanding effects of behavior, attitude

- Infraction intentional/unintentional

- Resources available to implement recommendations

- Incidence/number of persons harmed

- Degree of danger to clients

- State regulatory laws (assess how potent notification is)

- Voluntary change of practice setting; transfer of cases with a specific (limited) clientele

- Available research or literature to inform recommendations

---

social workers meet their duty to clients, colleagues, practice settings, the profession, and the broader society. On the other hand, the code does not prioritize the social worker's responsibilities well. This can be problematic when situations arise that present the worker with an ethical dilemma, a clash between two or more ethical obligations. In order to respond to these situations, the chapter discusses the importance of using an ethical principles screen to assist in selecting the best option. Competent social work practice requires more than just a repertoire of skills and a sound knowledge base of theories. It also requires that social workers honor their ethical obligations as professionals serving the most vulnerable members of society.

Research Navigator.com

Navigating Direct Practice

An access code for Research Navigator™ is packaged within your text. Use this code to register at www.researchnavigator.com and then use the key words listed below to research articles related to the chapter's content. Research Navigator™ helps you quickly and efficiently make the most of your research time.

- ❏ Ethics
- ❏ Values
- ❏ Cultural competence
- ❏ Confidentiality
- ❏ Health Insurance Portability and Accountability Act

Part Two

The Helping Process

THIS SECTION OF THE TEXT is written in a format that illustrates the process of helping. The problem-solving model serves as the general guide for the provision of services. Essentially, it covers the tasks of developing rapport with the client and understanding the problem(s) the client confronts while assessing his or her circumstances from multiple perspectives. Through a collaborative effort, both client and helper establish goals and a plan of intervention. The plan is then implemented using whatever theories and techniques are most likely to lead to successful accomplishment of the client's goals. Evaluation is incorporated as part of an ongoing process in order to determine the effectiveness of the plan. On completion of the helping process, the relationship between client and social worker is terminated.

At each stage of the problem-solving model, we took care to examine how different theoretical models approach each task. For example, for social workers who select cognitive psychology as the preferred model, this model is discussed from the perspective of what cognitive psychology considers important to be assessed. Readers will be able to compare this model with others, such as traditional person-centered and behavioral perspectives. Readers will thus be able to recognize how models differ in their goal development and planning as well as the techniques that are applied. Finally, we examine the goals or process of termination from the perspectives of different models.

With an awareness of the varying theories and an increased skill level in the use of techniques, students will be better prepared to provide services to clients. They will be guided by principles instead of good intentions, thus leading them to greater professionalism. By being grounded in the basic knowledge and skills discussed in this section, novice practitioners will be better able to develop what is often referred to as the "art" of the profession. They will also be able to understand and adopt or adapt new techniques and models that arise in the future, as well as be able to test out various theories and techniques to determine those with which they are most comfortable.

This section also takes an in-depth look at the application of models and techniques of direct practice in specific areas. Of particular note are chapters on enhancing clients' coping skills and practicing with families and groups. Also included is an exploration of empowerment and strengths-based strategies that are of increasing importance to the delivery of social work services.

Chapter 4

Basic Skills for Engagement

■ Manola, a twenty-three-year-old single female, is struggling with low self-esteem and a lack of confidence, especially when it comes to employment, her social life, and academic ability. She has a high school education and a good history of employment working in restaurants, telephone marketing, and retail work before she sustained a head injury in an automobile accident. She has been in a rehabilitation setting, both inpatient and outpatient, for the past six months relearning words (reading and writing) and how to speak, along with regaining basic control of her body (walking, eating, personal care, and so forth). Currently, Manola walks with a limp and has arm and leg weakness on the left side of her body (the injury was to the right side of her head). At this time, she appears to speak normally, but she occasionally struggles to remember a person's name or certain nouns. She associates these problems with feelings of frustration and anxiety. She is worried about being on the job and not learning tasks fast enough, not understanding some aspect of a task, or being found incompetent and then feeling embarrassed. Manola's speech, physical, and occupational therapists seem to think she is ready to take the necessary steps toward employment but that she needs help managing anxiety and building up her self-confidence.

A s noted in Chapter 2, the development of a positive therapeutic relationship is essential to any model of direct practice. Whether a practitioner is a novice or a master therapist, continual effort and importance ought to be placed on nurturing the therapeutic relationship as well as skill development in the application of theories and specific therapeutic techniques. By relying solely on theory and techniques, the social worker may be knowledgeable and proficient in the delivery of services but still not demonstrate the human qualities of caring and the ability to engender trust in the client. These two last skills are essential for the creation of a strong therapeutic relationship, without which the client may not benefit from the help provided. This chapter focuses on the basic relational skills found to be useful when engaging and working with clients. Specifically, this includes the skills associated with effective listening, the facilitative conditions, and other basic helper skills considered necessary for building a strong helper–client relationship and assisting with engagement, problem identification, assessment, remediation, and ongoing evaluation.

Listening

Before social workers can be effective in making an assessment, developing a plan, or offering advice or recommendations, they must be willing to listen to and hear the client's story. Listening, something most everyone has done since childhood, is a skill that needs to be refined while the helping professional performs his or her responsibilities. In general, listening skills are often dulled, compromised, or reduced because we are not actively attending to the other person in a holistic way. If listeners are distracted, this may cause their energy to become divided between the client and something or someone else. Divided energy can occur when social workers are feeling pressure to complete the interview or when they are feeling put upon and don't really want to be involved. It may also occur when they give the appearance of listening to the other person but find their thoughts are focused more on what they are going to say or how to say it in response to the client's remarks. Divided energy can also occur when practitioners get caught up in their own reaction to the client's experience as it brings back memories, or when they try to focus on two things at the same time, such as watching television and reading the newspaper or using the computer.

In general conversations, people often listen to others while at the same time thinking about how they can be involved in the conversation by sharing a similar experience. Although this is not necessarily a negative quality in informal conversations, it is not recom-

mended in formal helping relationships. The social worker's energy needs to be directed to and focused on hearing and understanding what the client is saying. A good example is the case that begins this chapter. The breadth and depth of feelings and reactions expressed by the client require a social worker who can hear what the client is saying, focus on the most salient issues, and demonstrate sensitivity to what the client is experiencing.

Five Ways of Listening

Long (1996) identifies five basic ways that people listen. They include "nonlistening, pretend listening, selective listening, self-focused listening, and empathic (other-focused) listening" (pp. 156–157). The first two, **nonlistening** and **pretend listening,** are similar in that the listener is essentially not registering the delivered message. With the first type, the listener is simply not paying attention, as when you talk to someone who is changing the stations on the radio and responding with an "uh

---

APPLICATIONS TO PRACTICE

Research Activity

To complete these activities, refer to the chapter opening case study on page 105.

Now that you have basic information about Manola's case, you may want to look up some studies about treatment for clients who have neurological damage and are experiencing frustration and anxiety. Using the Research Navigator™ website www.

researchnavigator.com, identify at least two articles, and after you have reviewed them, write a brief summary of each that suggests what treatment techniques might be helpful.

Critical Thinking Questions
1. When listening to Manola, what kind of things will you want to say to show that you are listening?

2. Think about what you do when you are feeling anxious. What do you usually suggest to others around you who are feeling anxious?

3. What might you say to your client about feelings of anxiety and when such feelings might be normal?

huh." A moment or two later the person asks, "What were you talking about?" The second type is reflected in the person who is looking right at you but whose mind is a million miles away.

With **selective listening,** the listener hears at least a portion of what the other person is saying. Unfortunately, what was heard may lead to erroneous conclusions because of the lack of complete understanding. This can also happen when the listener focuses on only the content portion of the message or just the feeling portion. Social workers cannot afford to allow their lack of attentiveness or their own biases to interfere by filtering out pertinent information that does not fit their frame of reference.

The **self-focused** listener is hearing the client's message but becoming anxious to respond. This can occur when listeners hear something to which they want to respond. Because concentration is focused on responding, the rest of the message is missed.

The goal of social workers is to develop the skills of being an **empathic listener.** In this mode, the message receiver accurately understands what the sender is feeling and thinking,

as well as the details associated with the experience.

Nonverbal Behaviors in Listening

Effective listening behavior is an essential skill that contributes to the development of trust. It is an active behavior that involves more than hearing the client's verbal utterances; it involves the social worker's ongoing search to understand the meaning, feelings, and context accompanying the client's spoken words. In order to do this, the practitioner must attend to the whole message, nonverbal as well as verbal, all the while placing what has been said in context with previous messages. Parts of nonverbal messages include the client's tone of voice, facial expressions, and body language. Verbal messages include the specific words selected by the client. The active listener will attend to all of these forms of communication in an attempt to better understand clients' experiences (feelings and thoughts) and the messages they are trying to convey.

Egan (2002) has listed important nonverbal behaviors that are communicated by both

---

APPLICATIONS TO PRACTICE

Practice Activities

During the week, notice what type of listening behavior you exhibit in a variety of circumstances (such as on the phone, in person with a friend, when you are in a hurry, when you don't want to talk about the subject or to the person). This will help you notice the different ways you personally may need to change how you listen to clients.

Have a friend or relative tell you something that happened during the day. Listen to three or four sentences and then make an empathic response. Tape-record or write down your response and rate it according to the chapter information.

helpers and clients. It is imperative that practitioners first understand how they express themselves nonverbally and then acquire skills in observing these qualities in clients, as both a form of assessment and a way to understand the sender's complete message. The factors include:

- Bodily behavior, such as posture, body movements, and gestures
- Eye behavior, such as eye contact, staring, and eye movement
- Facial expressions, such as smiles, frowns, raised eyebrows, and twisted lips
- Voice-related behavior, such as tone of voice, pitch, volume, intensity, inflection, spacing of words, emphasis, pauses, silences, and fluency
- Observable automatic physiological responses, such as quickened breathing, blushing, paleness, and pupil dilation
- Space—that is, how close or far apart people sit from one another during a conversation
- General appearance such as grooming and dress (p. 67)

Positive Listening Skills

Ivey, Normington, Miller, Morrill, and Haase (1968) first identified four dimensions of attending as components of positive listening skills. Ivey and Ivey (2003) revisit the original work and describe the components as visual/eye contact, vocal qualities, verbal tracking, and attentive and authentic body language (p. 37). Among many peoples, eye contact is appropriate and demonstrates interest and attention to what a person is communicating. The social worker, as listener, more often makes the greater amount of eye contact, whereas the speaker tends to glance away. This is not a recommendation to stare at the client,

which can create uncomfortable feelings. The listener's eyes ought to glance away from the eyes of the speaker on occasion.

But eye contact is also culturally influenced. For example, among some Native American peoples, depending on the level of acculturation and specific tribal traditions, eye contact may or may not be appropriate. Ivey and Ivey (1999) suggest that eye contact may also be a problem for some Latinos and African Americans. Thus, special attention should be paid to the client's behavior. A good rule to follow when you are uncertain about a particular behavior or belief is to ask the person, or someone close to or familiar with the person's customs or family rules, what is appropriate or customary.

Vocal quality ought to be congruent with the words and expression used. "Your voice is an instrument that communicates much of the feeling you have toward another person or situation" (Ivey & Ivey, 2003, p. 43). Listen to the volume and emphasis people place on the words they use to describe their situation. These elements often lend insight into items of importance to clients.

Careful listening entails verbal tracking. By this we mean that the practitioner must follow the path the client sets based on the information previously communicated. At times, multiple paths or problem situations may be introduced. However, if the practitioner has attended to what was communicated, it should be possible to paraphrase or summarize this information. The goal is to help clients decide which direction or path is most important for them to take at the present time. As the social worker trying to stay on track with the client, it may be helpful to consider some questions. For example, you can ask yourself, "What seems to be important to the client? What theme or main point keeps coming to light? What does the client want me or others to understand? What would he like to see happen?" When you believe you understand the message, present this information to your client, but be willing to alter your point of view based on the feedback you receive.

Body language is a form of communication and is culturally influenced. Italian men who are good friends, for example, may be seen walking arm in arm while discussing an important topic. Teenagers in the United States can often be observed sitting in a relaxed, laid-back position when talking with their peers and often with adults. Although these behaviors might be considered disrespectful, unusual, or inappropriate in some cultures, in others they are not.

Paying attention to how clients express themselves through body language may help you understand the significance of their messages. Clients may look away and turn their head when feeling guilt or shame. When they are excited, they may rise up in the chair and lean forward. Drooping shoulders along with minimal body movement may signal a depressed or hopeless feeling. The practitioner also should be aware of how clients respond to the social worker's body language. Do they feel smothered by the social worker leaning too close, or feel that the practitioner is showing disinterest by adopting a laid-back posture? With all of the listening skills identified earlier, the goal is to gain a holistic understanding of what is being communicated.

Often a client's message or story will come in parts, like a puzzle. It is vital for the quality and potential success of the relationship for the practitioner to accurately hear and understand as many pieces of the client's story, experiences, and life as possible. Then the practitioner's task is to help the client piece this

Voices from the Field

Della T. Marshall

What is it like to sit across from a client for the first time? What do you say? How do you connect with the client? These questions and many more ran through my mind as a social work student getting ready to meet my first client. Theories, concepts, and techniques all came into the room with the client and me. But I will always remember the words my first supervisor spoke that were just as important as all of the ideas taught in the classroom. She said, "Never underestimate the power of being present with your clients, and genuinely listen to them." So when I sat in session with my first client, something magical happened. After completing the intake assessment, I turned off my self-monitoring instinct and really witnessed the client's experience. When the session ended, the young woman told me how good it felt to talk to someone who took the time to listen to her and not judge her or tell her what to do. It is a validating experience when someone listens carefully to you. For many people, it is a rare experience to be "really heard."

information together to provide a clear picture of what the client is communicating.

Distractions to Listening

Listening may be hindered by noise or distractions, which can be defined as anything that distorts or causes interference with the message that has been sent. Noise and distractions may include sounds occurring around or within the area of the interview, such as a client's child crying or attempting to gain parental attention, a ringing phone, a knock at the door, the routine noises of a not-so-private office, or a TV or radio that is turned on. Most of these distractions can be dealt with by planning ahead to meet in an environment and under conditions that are free from these interferences.

Other forms of distraction may occur within the receiver of the message, as when the social worker has preconceived, prejudicial, stereotypic, or biased thoughts about the client or the client's experience. This results in the receiver hearing only pieces of what is conveyed and then jumping to conclusions about the message or the sender of the message.

One common example of having a preconceived notion that may interfere with understanding occurs in people who cannot believe that a child, teenager, or adult survivor of domestic abuse or violence did not react "differently." Because of this preconceived notion, the practitioner may not listen but instead question the client's reactions to the event, thus ineffectively listening to what the client is saying. Self-awareness, continuing education, and supervision are ways in which social workers can help protect themselves, as well as their clients, from the negative effects of these types of interference.

Social workers must also be on guard against the negative influence that their own personal problems may have as they listen to clients. Examples might include personal struggles with relationships (marital/partner, parent/child, employee/boss); mood or affective disorder, alcohol or substance abuse problems, or other psychological disorders; or burnout and fatigue from work. Any of these problems can rise to a level that makes it difficult to listen to one more story of pain, suffering, or struggle. The practitioner may be influenced by his or her own past experiences to the point of jumping to conclusions about or hearing selectively the client's unique experience. At the very least, practitioners may be preoccupied with their current problems to such an extent that they become distracted and inattentive.

An example of the last situation is the social worker who has been assigned to difficult cases with clients who are dealing with gambling and substance abuse. While meeting with her client, the social worker finds it a struggle to attend to and hear what the client is saying because the practitioner is preoccupied with the care of her elderly mother just recently admitted to a nursing home. The social worker had promised her father that she would never place her mother in institutional care, but following her father's death and her mother's deteriorating health (both physical and mental), she finds herself no longer able to manage her own family, her career, and her ailing mother. Although finding support from her mother's physician and friends, not all of the social worker's family agrees with her decision to move mother to a nursing home, which adds to her sense of guilt. Thus, she finds her thoughts drifting in an effort to find an alternative plan for her mother while at the same time interviewing her client about recent problems.

Practitioners are not immune, by virtue of their training, from personal struggles, being hurt, or having to deal with life's problems. Setting aside one's personal problems while engaging in a professional relationship with clients is a learned behavior. However, the social worker may experience a problem at a crisis level and therefore may temporarily need to seek help or take a break from seeing clients. A colleague or supervisor may be a good support system while the social worker is engaged in the evaluation and decision-making processes. This should not be viewed as a weakness but rather as a strength, first recognizing and then putting into practice what one believes to be helpful.

Skill Development for Listening

After you have studied the do's and don'ts of active listening (see Figure 4.1), divide up members of your classroom into small groups of two or three. One person should role-play a client seeking help for the problem of stress. Specifically, the client is in school taking fifteen credits of course work, is working fifteen to twenty hours a week, and has recently married a spouse who is also trying to survive under the same conditions. The client feels exhausted, overwhelmed, confused, and discouraged because graduation is at least a year away for both of them and they never seem to have time for themselves.

As the social work intern at the university's student counseling center, it is your assignment to do the intake interview to learn about clients' presenting problems and to begin building a relationship with them so that they will feel encouraged to return. To do this, you will need to demonstrate your listening skills. To determine your level of competence, you may use the system provided in Figure 4.2.

The raters may include the client, the third person as an observer, and yourself. Practice your listening skills for five to ten minutes and then discuss those behaviors that were effective and those that need more work.

Figure 4.1

Do's and Don'ts of Active Listening

Some basic do's and don'ts of active listening are:

- Do focus on what is being communicated.

- Attend to both verbal and nonverbal expressions.

- Give encouragement to the client to continue talking by nodding your head or by uttering an occasional "uh huh" or "I see."

- Within reason, try to match the client's mood or level of expression. For example, if your client is sad, show an expression of concern; if your client relates something humorous, allow yourself the opportunity to laugh along with, but not at, your client.

- Do not try to second-guess what your client is trying to express by finishing his or her sentence or thought.

- Do not start solving clients' problems for them.

- Do not get too anxious about silence.

- Do not jump to conclusions.

- Avoid allowing an attitude of superiority to enter into the meeting.

Silence

One aspect of the practitioner–client relationship with which helpers need to be comfortable is silence. As novice social workers begin working with others, they often place unrealistic demands on themselves to have answers for all of their clients' concerns. Therefore, when there is a pause in the conversation, they begin to feel anxious. In response to the anxiety, and to avoid looking as though they are solutionless with respect to the client's problems, they rapidly interject some form of verbal communication.

Figure 4.2

Listening Behaviors and Attitudes Checksheet

Listening Behaviors & Attitudes	N/A	Improve	Adequate	Excellent
1. Undivided attention—not distracted				
2. Client's speech is uninterrupted				
3. Nonprejudicial, nonjudgmental listening				
4. Body behavior—posture, gestures, body movements				
5. Eye behavior—eye contact, staring, eye movement				

6. Facial expressions—congruent with client's affect
    overexpression
    underexpression				

7. Vocal behavior—volume, intensity, emphasis, pauses				

8. Observable physiological responses—
    breathing
    blushing
    tension
    comfortable				

9. Space—too close, too far, adequate				
10. Tracking—helper's responses follow client's statements, summarizes				

Silence may be occurring for many reasons, and as it is happening the helper commonly begins to infer what the meaning may be. "Consider these possible meanings of silence: 'I don't want to be here.' 'It's hopeless.' 'Leave me alone.' 'I don't trust you.' 'I don't trust your words.' 'You might think you are in control, but you can't make me talk.' 'I don't understand a thing you are saying'" (Miley, O'Melia, & DuBois, 2004, p. 180). In addition to these possibilities, silence may have a neutral or positive slant to it, such as, "That's a really good question and I'm not sure how to respond"; "No one has asked me that before; let me think about it for a minute"; "It feels good to finally be feeling better. I want to enjoy the moment"; "That's a lot to take in. I need a minute to process it."

It is best not to take the inference to an automatic conclusion. Realize that clients need time to sort through the questions being asked of them, determine how they are feeling, reexperience the images and thoughts associated with past events, and consider the impact the therapeutic relationship is having on them. Silence may also be connected to culture. It may be a demonstration of respect for the helper, as is common in the Japanese culture.

Getting comfortable requires realizing that silence is not necessarily negative nor a threat to the social worker's credibility as a help agent. As this occurs, helpers will be able to relax and then attempt to understand, from their clients' point of view, the meaning behind the silence. You can ask clients directly, "What was going through your mind?" or "What were you feeling just a moment ago?" If, on the other hand, you seem to understand the meaning behind the silence, you can verbalize this understanding in an empathic statement such as "It must be overwhelming for you as you confront all these problems at once."

Facilitative Conditions

The core qualities or relationship conditions found to be effective when demonstrated by social workers are referred to as the "facilitative conditions" (Rogers, Gendlin, Kiesler, & Truax, 1967). The roots of these conditions are found in the theory of humanistic psychology developed by Carl Rogers (1951). Originally referred to as client-centered therapy, it has evolved into what is currently recognized as person-centered therapy (Raskin & Rogers, 1995).

At the foundation of person-centered therapy is the belief that people have the ability to change their self-concept, their attitudes toward others, and their behaviors, along with having the resources to understand themselves. According to this theory, the social worker provides a climate that allows these qualities to emerge. This is achieved through the demonstration of three fundamental qualities. (Raskin & Rogers, 1995): empathy (accurate understanding), positive regard (respect), and congruence (genuineness, authenticity). These three characteristics are considered essential qualities for professionals that must be communicated to the client (Rogers, 1951). These three conditions have been reported by clients as being the most helpful during the process of the therapeutic relationship (Paulson, Truscott, & Stuart, 1999).

Empathy (Accurate Understanding)

The concept of **empathy** refers to the ability of the practitioner to understand, as accurately as possible, what it is that a client is experiencing from the client's frame of reference. Clients may express their experience by describing what they felt (emotions) or what they were thinking (cognition), by describing an experience from one of the forms of sensory perception (sight, smell, hearing, touch, taste), or by any combination of the above. Once the social worker understands the client's experience, this is communicated back to the client. According to Egan (1998), this process helps to build and strengthen the rapport between client and practitioner. Further, it will positively influence the client's disclosure of pertinent information, based on the ability of the social worker to show understanding.

The client also ought to sense that the listener is relating to him or her in a nonjudgmental or noncritical way for having had and expressed the experience, thus keeping the line of communication open. By being able to convey these qualities, the practitioner is better able to demonstrate that both parties are working on the same problem or concern. Clients therefore can feel and believe that they have been heard and understood while gaining the impression that someone else comprehends their experience.

A basic way to demonstrate empathic listening is by using the following formula (Egan, 2002). Begin communicating to the client by using the phrase "You feel . . . " followed by the insertion of the word for the feeling reported by the client, or by identifying a feeling that is assumed to be accurate based on what the helper reviewed. Once the feeling is stated, follow up with "because . . . " Then comes the insertion of the experience identified by the client that accompanied the feeling. The following are examples of this basic formula. "Jason, you <u>feel</u> betrayed <u>because</u> your best friend went behind your back and dated your girlfriend," or "Megan, you <u>feel</u> anxious <u>because</u> you have to stand up in front of your class and give a seven-minute speech on domestic violence."

There are different ways to communicate this understanding to the client. At a very basic level, one way is to nonverbally inform the client that he or she was heard. This can be expressed through listening behaviors that demonstrate interest and attention to what the client is saying. This behavior often consists of sitting so that you appear to be slightly leaning forward with eyes focused on the client (except with clients from cultures in which this might be inappropriate) and nodding occasionally in response to what is communicated.

The practitioner's facial expression is also important and should demonstrate concern and interest. An inappropriate look of shock, disgust, or anger will likely send the message that you are upset or disgusted with the client or their personal experience, thus discouraging or interfering with the helping process.

Carkuff (1969) sought to identify and teach skills that demonstrate increasing or decreasing levels of empathic or nonempathic responses by practitioners. In an effort to simplify this model, we follow Ivey and Ivey's (2003) recommendation and use three levels of responses. A level 1 response indicates that what the client expressed was not recognized, understood, or legitimized by the practitioner. It may be a response that ignores what the client said, or it may be a response that is in some way critical or expresses contempt for the client.

Level 2 responses accurately repeat back to the client what the listener heard. At this level, it is common to hear the practitioner parrot what the client previously stated. Such a response might also include matching the client's tone of voice and, nonverbally, a look of concern. Occasionally, practitioners may even decide (based on clinical judgment and skill) to accentuate their response in order to help the client perceive that the message was received with significant understanding.

Level 3 responses not only reflect that the practitioner's understanding of the message matches the client's intended message, but also include indications of an additional, greater appreciation and sensitivity to the client's thoughts, feelings, and experiences. Most often this additional understanding comes about because the practitioner has been listening intently to what the client has said and is able to accurately surmise additional feelings and thoughts based on practice experience, knowledge of human behavior, and a synthesizing of data previously presented by the client. With practice, clinicians are able to reach this higher level of empathic response.

The following are examples of client statements, followed by the three levels of empathic responses:

1. **Client:** I've been feeling really discouraged about my grade in biology. I need at least a B+ or better.

   Practitioner—Level 1: So, how are you and your roommate doing? You're in the dorms this semester, aren't you?

   Level 2: You're feeling discouraged because your biology grade is below a B+.

   Level 3: Because you have your goal set on going to graduate school, you feel pressure to maintain a B+ average in all of your classes, including biology. Currently, your grade in biology is below a B+ and now you're wondering if you will be accepted into graduate school. If you don't, you'll feel as if you've failed.

2. **Client:** I was injured on the job. My leg was crushed by a backhoe. That was a year ago and I'm still in so much pain I can't work, and my insurance benefits and worker's comp are running out.

   Level 1: I'm sure if you just talk with the caseworker at worker's comp everything will be just fine.

   Level 2: You're feeling discouraged because you are still unable to work since your accident.

   Level 3: You're still in significant pain from the injury and surgery. Because of it, you're unable to work, and now you see your insurance benefits running out. You're worried about how you'll be able to support your family, and it scares you.

The use of empathy, like any skill, needs to be applied appropriately. Novice helpers have a tendency to use it too often. Allow your clients the opportunity to express information about themselves, their experiences, what is important to them, and what problems they are struggling with. As you listen to their stories and observe their behaviors, you will be able to sense and hear what is important to them. At this point, you will be able to communicate that awareness.

Avoid using empathic statements for each client statement, because it will make you sound like a robot going through the motions of listening but not connecting with the client. Another common error of beginning practitioners is to respond to or follow a client's statement about a pertinent item of concern by asking a question about something that seems unrelated. This was illustrated in the first example when the practitioner asked about the roommate situation following the client's statement about a biology grade. This type of behavior suggests that the practitioner is not listening to the client or that what was communicated was not important. It can also happen when social workers do not know what to do about the client's concern and therefore ignore it. Sometimes it occurs when practitioners are worried about items on their own agendas that seem to be more important than what the client is experiencing and reporting. A good rule of thumb is to respond with an empathic statement when a client has communicated something you judge to be significant, especially with regard to feelings.

Skill Development

The following are possible statements made by clients. In a role-play setting, one person plays the part of a client and the other person the social worker. The client repeats the statement written below, which is followed by an empathic response by the person playing the social worker. The goal is to respond with at least a level 2 empathic response. When you are comfortable, attempt a level 3 response to increase the quality and depth of the helper's response.

1. **Client:** "I'm so angry with my brother. My mom never makes him own up to his actions."

2. **Client:** "For the past twenty-two years, we have had at least one child living at home. This is the first time it has just been the two of us. It feels strange."

3. **Client:** "Smoking some weed is no big deal. Everyone is doing it. My parents forget what it's like to be a teenager. We aren't hurting anyone; we're just having a little fun, that's all."

4. Helena Kosovic, a refugee from Bosnia, speaks very little English. She is trying to find work yet still feels unsure in her new surroundings.

   Client: "I don't know where find job. Need money, send money mama, papa. Very difficult here. Always feel tired, not sleep good."

5. A seventeen-year-old female diagnosed with an eating disorder is meeting with you for the first time.

   Client: "They expect me to be perfect. I have to get all A's or they won't let me use the phone. I have to practice the piano one hour a day, plus they expect me to take care of the twins because they need a break. Well, when do I get one?"

6. LaToya is a twenty-four-year-old single parent of two children, ages five and three. She is seeking assistance for housing. She only has $25 to her name. She also fears for her safety.

   Client: "I was told you could help me and my kids. We need a place to stay. We were kicked out of my boyfriend's apartment last night and we had to sleep in my car. It's too dangerous to go back to him. I don't trust him. He scares me when he starts drinking. He says it's my fault he lost his job and he can't pay for a woman with two kids."

7. Jimmy is an eighty-three-year-old retired steelworker residing in a nursing home. His Medicare and pension cover his nursing home expenses, and he receives a monthly allowance of $88.

   Client: Agitated, he states angrily, "Montell said he'd take me to the bank this morning. Where is he? It's my money and I want it and I'm not waiting any longer. I'm calling my daughter, and she'll get me out of this jailhouse today if I don't get my money."

8. A twelve-year-old girl who has been fondled by her brother while attempting to sleep.

   Client: "I woke up when he was touching me. I was scared and didn't know what to do. I pretended to be asleep and tried to roll over."

9. Manny is the stepfather of four children ages seventeen, fifteen, twelve, and seven. He married Lupita six months ago.

   Client: "I work very hard at my job. I take care of these kids when their father does nothing for them. All I get in return is disrespect. They do nothing around the house, and their mother lets them get away with it. If things don't change, I'm leaving."

10. **Client:** "Antoine is the guy I've been dating for a year now. He's the first guy who's

been really nice to me. He just told me he's been offered a job in Washington, D.C. He wants me to go with him, but I don't know. I'm so confused."

Positive Regard (Respect)

"When the social worker is experiencing a positive, nonjudgmental, accepting attitude toward whatever the client *is* at that moment, therapeutic movement or change is more likely. It involves the practitioner's willingness to let the client feel whatever immediate feelings are going on—confusion, resentment, fear, anger, courage, love, pride. When the social worker prizes the client in a total rather than a conditional way, forward movement is likely" (Rogers, 1986, p. 198). The social worker's "regard for the client" ought not to be affected by the client's "particular choices, characteristics, or outcomes" (Raskin & Rogers, 1995, p. 129.).

Positive regard is a condition in which the helper conveys a sense of acceptance, warmth, and nonpossessive caring for the client's self-concept and experienced feelings (Ewen, 2003). Positive regard, also referred to as respect, is the ability to value the client as a person of dignity and worth (Rogers, 1957). According to Ivey and Ivey (2003), positive regard can be defined as noting those positive parts of the client's statements and stories and attending to them.

Four Aspects of Respect

Egan (1998) identified four aspects of respect: commitment to the client, suspending critical judgment, working to understand the client, and showing care and competence. **Commitment** is exhibited by the attitude of being there for the client during the good as well as the difficult times. Further, it is showing interest in and attention to what the client is saying as well as what he or she reports experiencing.

Suspending critical judgment means withholding judgment about the client and the client's thoughts, feelings, and behavior. To be able to demonstrate this characteristic, social workers need to develop self-awareness of their own personal values, ongoing experiences, and facial, as well as verbal, expressions in response to what clients report.

To **understand the client,** practitioners must focus their full attention on what the client expresses both verbally and nonverbally. Practitioner questions ought to both seek to gain a better understanding of what the client is reporting and also demonstrate to the client that the social worker is attempting to accurately understand his or her feeling, perceptions, and experiences.

Being **competent** means working within the area of one's training, expertise, or competence. It means obtaining supervision, training, and education in those areas in which the social worker is less qualified. Further, it means staying current in the field on research and practice through continuing education. It also means ensuring that clients receive the highest quality of care no matter what their race, religion, culture, gender, or socioeconomic status.

One method of evaluating the quality of a social worker's positive regard is to rank the helper's response based on his or her ability to reflect back those positive aspects about a client—the client's experience, abilities, or strengths (Ivey & Ivey, 2003). The following are examples of using the three-point scale as a method of evaluating this skill:

1. **Client:** I've been so anxious lately. It has been hard to get up and go to work, but somehow I've been able to do it. I find it's worse when I stay home.

Level 1: Sometimes you just have to suck it up and do it.

Level 2: Even though you found it hard to get up and go to work, you did it anyway.

Level 3: You seem to be very aware of yourself and how the anxiety affects you. You realize that by going to work, you'll feel better in the long run, so you found the strength to get up and to go, even when you didn't want to.

2. **Client:** I screw up all the time. Everything I touch ends in disaster. My family has left me and I'm about to lose my job because my boss doesn't trust me. What else could go wrong?

   Level 1: You need to get into a support group.

   Level 2: Even though a number of very important things in your life are not going well for you, at least you had the courage to come here and seek help.

   Level 3: With all of these negative things happening in your life at this time, I could see how you might feel like giving up, but you haven't. Instead, you are willing to seek help and find ways to work through your problems. It takes a strong person to be willing to do this, and I respect you for it.

Work by yourself or with a partner to create level 2 and 3 responses to the following client statements:

1. Dave is a thirty-year-old male. He has been diagnosed with generalized anxiety, which he has experienced for the past fifteen years or more.

   Client: "I'm so tired of feeling anxious all of the time. I worry about everything, but I want you to know that I haven't quit. I'm willing to try whatever you suggest."

2. **Client:** "My husband is a workaholic. We have two children and I end up taking care of them and doing all the work. I had pictured the two of us raising the children together. Don't get me wrong, I love my children. I just need some help once in awhile."

3. A fifteen-year-old male is brought to therapy by his mom. He is struggling with school but excels in sports.

   Client: "I just don't like school; it's not helping me any toward a baseball contract. I'm better off going to the gym and working out. I'll be stronger and faster. School is for preppies and computer geeks. What do I need that stuff for?"

4. Your client went through a messy divorce eighteen months ago, and his wife is still angry with him.

   Client: I haven't been able to see my children on a regular basis for the past ten months. My ex won't work with me and my busy schedule. I really miss my kids and I want to see them."

5. You are employed as a school social worker. One of your assignments is to help those children whose parents have separated or divorced. Your client is a ten-year-old girl.

   Client: "I felt real sad when my dad moved out. I miss him a lot. I wait for him to call every night. I wish he would come home and live with us again. I think he's lonely."

6. Your client was date raped. She is in counseling for post-traumatic stress disorder.

   Client: "It was happening so fast and I didn't know what to do. It was surreal, nothing like that had ever happened to me before. I just froze, I was so scared. What should I have done?"

7. Your are a counselor at Workforce Services and a new client reports to you the following.

   Client: "I've been out of work for over a month now. No one wants to hire me. It's like there aren't any jobs out there. It's to the point where all I do is drive down a street and apply at every place."

8. You work for a teen services program, and a seventeen-year-old young woman tells you the following:

   Client: "I think I am pregnant. I'm so scared to tell my parents, and my boyfriend doesn't even know. My parents will be disappointed. We had planned on me attending college since I was in elementary school. The baby is the most important thing now."

9. **Client:** "My husband has a drinking problem, and I'm afraid he's going to lose his job again. That's why I keep working at my part-time job. I get scared thinking what might happen if we didn't have at least my income coming in."

10. You are working as a social worker at the county health department.

    Client: "Nothing seems to work. I've been up with him for three nights in a row. Just as he calms down and falls asleep, he'll jerk or twitch and wake up. I need some help. We both need some sleep."

Congruence (Genuineness, Authenticity)

Congruence means being consistent. In the helping field, consistency relates to how the helper is feeling, what he or she is thinking, and how he or she is behaving (Cormier & Nurius, 2003). If all three aspects are in line with one another, a person is seen as being congruent. If one or more of these personal aspects differs from the others, the person is incongruent or inconsistent, and therefore sends a message to the receiver that may be confusing. The client may believe, for example, that the social worker's words, such as "I really want to help you," are insincere because at the same time the practitioner is attending to some other task, thus suggesting that the other task is more or at least as important as meeting with the client. The message being sent is therefore incongruent, inconsistent, or confusing.

Genuineness and *authenticity* are additional terms used to describe this helper trait. By demonstrating genuineness, the social worker conveys the message of sincerely wanting to understand, work with, and help the client. The practitioner is not seen as putting up a facade or being someone who is there just to pick up a paycheck, but is seen rather as a person who genuinely wants to help (Raskin & Rogers, 1995). One way to demonstrate this willingness is to engage the client in a collaborative relationship, one in which client and helper work together to understand and resolve the problem for which help is being sought. This is in contrast to the helper who assumes to know all about the person's problem and prescribes a form of treatment without taking the time to learn about the uniqueness of the person, the circumstances, and the particular problem.

Additionally, authenticity implies that the helper responds to questions honestly and without becoming defensive. According to Hammond, Hepworth, and Smith (1977), "an authentic person relates to others personally, so that expressions do not seem to be rehearsed or contrived" (p. 7). Thus, the authentic practitioner will respond to clients in a caring way by using language the client understands rather than behaving in an aloof, rigid, or distant manner and using scripted, stereotypic, or professional jargon when communicating.

Five Aspects of Genuineness

Finally, Cormier and Nurius (2003) summarize five aspects of genuineness, which is the demonstration of "supportive nonverbal behavior, role behavior, congruence, spontaneity, and openness" (p. 69). **Supporting nonverbal behavior** is demonstrated by maintaining eye contact while sitting in a slightly forward position, when culturally appropriate. **Role behavior** is exhibited by practitioners who are comfortable in their position and so feel no need to emphasize their position or status. Further, social workers do not have to "play a role" while serving others because they genuinely want to be there to help. **Congruence,** as previously noted, is being consistent in behavior, feelings, and thoughts. The social worker is able to honestly acknowledge his or her feelings during the interview instead of denying or attempting to cover them up. **Spontaneity** is the ability to react and express oneself naturally. Negative feelings toward the client, however, ought not to be expressed unless they interfere with the helper's ability to be genuine (Rogers, 1957). Finally, **openness** involves the willingness of the practitioner to appropriately self-disclose. The emphasis is on *appropriate* self-disclosure, which is designed to help clients recognize that others have experienced similar situations or feelings, or to encourage a closer working relationship between practitioner and client. Self-disclosure that is motivated simply by the practitioner's need to share has no place in direct practice.

Paraphrasing

Paraphrasing, like empathy, is a verbal response from the worker to the client that in essence conveys the "content" of the messages the worker received from the client. Whereas an empathic response more often expresses an understanding of the "feeling" part of the message, a paraphrase generally focuses on what the client was "thinking" or "doing." Paraphrasing may also be used to convey the facts of what was related. What the practitioner heard and understood ought to be communicated back to the client in a nonparroting fashion. It is best if the social worker uses the key words the client used yet attempts to shorten the response and bring some clarity to the message.

The first two of the following seven scenarios are examples of paraphrases in response to clients' messages. The last five are provided so that you have an opportunity to paraphrase what the client has said.

1. **Client:** "I just don't seem to be able to keep things going. I'm out of money, my car is falling apart, my bills are stacking up, and my job is taking me nowhere. I really want to go back to school, but I can't afford to right now. Yet it seems like I can't afford not to at the same time. I just need a rich uncle to leave me an inheritance."

   Practitioner: "You are hurting for money, your bills are piling up, you'd like to go on with your education, but you don't see any way that you can do that right now."

2. **Client:** "Since we've been meeting, I've been doing a lot better. I've been able to talk with my wife about what has happened to me in the past. I've been able to lead staff meetings at work without thinking that those I supervise are going to resent me, and I find that I don't mind getting up in the morning and going to work."

Practitioner: "You're finding yourself opening up to your wife and giving some direction and support to those you supervise at work."

3. Client: "I caught my daughter with some marijuana and rolling papers. I've been suspicious since this summer when she was staying out late with her friends, and since school started her grades have dropped."

4. Client: "We just moved here from Nebraska. I was told there was a lot of work available in construction. We don't have a place to stay. Me, my wife, and two kids slept in the truck the last two nights. A cop told us we could get some help from you guys. We could sure use it until I get on my feet with work an' all."

5. Client: "My doctor told me I need to see you. I've been injured and unable to work for the past year. I fell off a ladder on an oil rig and landed on my side. It broke my pelvis and fractured my femur. I've able to walk some, but I still need a cane. After about ten to fifteen minutes, the pain gets real bad and I have to sit down. My doctor has me on Tylenol #3. They help a little, but not nearly enough."

6. Meeting with a family, the oldest daughter states:

Client: "Since my mom died, my dad treats me like I'm supposed to take over all the responsibilities. I make supper, I do the dishes, I help the little ones with their homework, and I put up their lunches before I go to bed. I know I've got to help, but so does he. He just says he's too tired and I'm supposed to help."

7. Working as a school social worker, you meet with Ms. Quintero, a Hispanic woman and mother, about her son.

Client: "I don't understand. Pepe goes to school every day. I make sure of that. When he comes home I ask him how things went, what he learned, how was his lunch? You know, all them things that mothers want to know. He always tells me he finished his work at school and his lunch was okay. So, I'm thinking everything is all right. Now you tell me he has not been doing his homework and he's failing."

Summarizing

Summarizing is similar to paraphrasing except that it covers significantly larger amounts of information given by the client. It might be used only two, three, or four times during an interview as a means of reviewing topics, problems, content, or goals that had been previously addressed. Many times summarizing is used to help clients stay on task. As the social worker listens to the client's story, presenting problems, and hoped-for goals, often the client and helper begin to feel overwhelmed. A good summary statement by the helper can bring some organization and structure back to the interview, thus helping the process to move forward rather than become scattered and disjointed.

The following is an example of a summary statement by a helper: "Jim, as I've been listening to you, I've heard you identify three significant problems. They are, first, you're feeling depressed and it seems to be getting worse with time. Second, you and Sue have been fighting about whether or not to vacation at your in-laws or to go to southern California. Third, the two of you have been arguing about religion and which church to attend, if at all, since the children have been asking you about going. All three of these problems are significant. Which one do you see as the most important to work on at this time?"

Clarifying

As clients share their feelings, thoughts, ways of behaving, past experiences, and future hopes, social workers need to make sure they understand the meaning of the words clients have chosen, the context in which the experience happened, the intensity of the client's feelings, and exactly what it is the client hopes to achieve. Oftentimes, clients will assume that the message they conveyed contained adequate information, or that the words they chose to express what was on their mind were completely understood by the practitioner. It is during these moments of the interview process, most often in the first, second, or third meeting with a client, that the social worker is unsure of the exact nature, content, or meaning of the words or messages conveyed. In these situations, the social worker needs to seek clarification from the client to ensure a correct understanding. An easy and efficient way to do this is to ask the client the question, "What do you mean when you say . . . ?" Or ask, "What do you mean when you use the word . . . ?"

Asking for clarification can serve a number of purposes. It signals to the client that you are listening but that the message received was not adequately understood. Therefore, additional information is necessary before you can move forward. Often clients have not had an opportunity to think through their problem. By **clarifying** their thoughts, they must work on sorting through their own interpretation, thus clarifying for themself what it is they thought or experienced before they are able to accurately explain it to another person. Doing so brings greater personal insight. Asking clients to explain the meaning behind the

choice of a word or an experience may also help them understand how the words they choose to use influence their feelings and behavior as well as other people's feelings and behavior.

Last, seeking clarification will help speed up the process of getting to know your client. Asking for clarification will help you discover your client's communication style and how the client thinks and feels about things. The more rapidly you learn this, the better you will be at connecting with the client.

Questioning

One of social work's main tools is asking questions. **Questioning** is often taken for granted and infrequently written about. However, with experience it becomes an art form as the helper asks appropriate, timely, and well-directed questions that help clients explain their story, identify problems, establish goals, and examine their beliefs, feelings, and behavior. Questions help clients arrive at a greater understanding on their own, without being coaxed or lectured. Through the use of questions, clients most often discover their own solutions rather than having their problem solved by their helper. The use of questions may also teach clients a skill they can use in the future, thus creating a sense of strength, accomplishment, and personal resourcefulness.

As novice counselors begin professional relationships, the frequency and type of questions they ask often reveal their anxiety. This is most common during moments of silence or when a difficult subject is broached. At times practitioners ask questions in a rapid-fire fashion, or they jump from one subject to another, usually from a sensitive topic to something less threatening. With experience, the art of asking appropriate, thought-provoking questions will become more natural, and practitioners can use them to assist clients through the process of achieving clarity and identifying options toward solutions to their goals.

Guidelines for Using Questions

Cormier and Nurius (2003) have identified four basic guidelines that make asking questions more effective and efficient. First, ask questions that focus on the concerns expressed by the client. Questions will often come about because they are based on the information the client has already provided. Second, once a question has been asked, give the client time to respond. Pauses between the end of the question and the beginning of the response are most often positive. Those pauses give clients time to ponder their responses. Third, avoid asking questions in rapid succession. Asking one question at a time will keep your client from becoming confused. This is especially important to remember when working with children and elderly persons. Fourth, avoid "why" questions because clients often see them as being confrontative or accusatory.

In addition, be aware of the tone of your voice. A good rule is to frame your question in a tone of voice and with a choice of words that genuinely reflect respect for and an interest in what your client is experiencing and expressing. Remember to be culturally sensitive when asking questions. Finally, avoid using questions that give the impression you are interrogating your client. This will injure the relationship and likely create feelings of distrust, anger, or fear.

Although it may appear on the surface that asking questions is an easy task, we find this is not the case. Skillfully asked questions are used throughout the helping process. In the beginning phase, they assist in developing the relationship. As part of the assessment, questions help to sift through the data to uncover the most relevant information. In planning, questions help to prioritize goals. During the intervention phase, they help clients examine ideas, options, and alternatives. In the evaluation phase, questions help to identify progress and successes that help the client plan for the future. This section takes an in-depth look at the types of questions frequently incorporated in the helping process.

Open- versus Closed-Ended Questions

Two of the most basic types of questions are referred to as open-ended or closed-ended. Open-ended questions allow the client to answer as he or she chooses, giving whatever detail the client deems appropriate based on the client's interpretation of the situation. Practitioners ask open-ended questions in a manner that suggests to clients that they may express themselves as much or as little as they desire.

Open-ended questions are most often recognized by the inclusion of certain words in the sentence, such as *what, how, when, why, could, where,* and *who.* Each of these words encourages the client to give information from his or her own perspective.

According to Cormier and Nurius (2003), "what" questions encourage the client to give information and facts: "What did you think she meant when she said 'I'm tired of living this way?' " "How" questions are associated with emotions and the way feelings are sequenced and processed: "How did you feel when he told you he was seeing another woman?" "Who" questions seek to find out about people, whereas "where" and "when" questions want to find out more about place and time, respectively. "Who was with you when this happened?"; "Do you remember where you were when the phone rang?"

"Why" questions ask the client to give a reason or a rationale for what occurred. Clients may interpret "why" questions as probing by the helper in an effort to find fault, place blame, or accuse them for what occurred. This places the client on the defensive and potentially erodes the therapeutic relationship: "Why did you react that way when he yelled at you?" "Why" questions ought to be used sparingly and when the relationship has developed to the point that a strong sense of trust has been built.

Questions beginning with "could" are asking the client if it is possible to do or say something more: "Could you tell me more about what happened just before you witnessed the accident?"

The following are open-ended questions that follow a client's statement:

1. **Client:** "I'm really nervous about being here today. I've never been to a social worker before."

   Practitioner: "What have you heard about meeting with a social worker that might bring on these anxious feelings?"

2. **Client:** "I was mad at you when you kept asking me if I could stay angry and be okay with it."

   Practitioner: (To other group members) "How were the rest of you feeling about the way I was dealing with Tanya and her anger?"

3. **Client:** "He touched my private parts."

   Practitioner: "Can you tell me any more about where and when this happened?"

4. **Client:** "I could have done some real damage that day. I was so out of control."

   Practitioner: "Could you elaborate on what you mean by 'out of control?' "

5. **Client:** "I want out of this relationship now."

   Practitioner: (Question is asked to show genuine concern) "Tell me why you feel so strongly about leaving the relationship."

Closed-ended questions are best identified as those that typically call for a one-word or short sentence response. They are often used to gather specific information quickly and may require the client to make a polarized or forced (yes or no) choice. Because closed questions are used to gather specific information, they require the social worker to exercise a great amount of control over the direction the interview takes. Practitioners should be cautious about asking closed-ended questions because clients may sense that they are responding to the needs of the helper, or that once they have supplied all the answers, the social worker will provide a solution.

While working in groups of two or three, practice using open-ended questions in response to the following client statements. Remember to ask a question that relates to what the client has just stated.

1. A mother reports to the therapist while her son listens to what she says.

   Client: "He got in trouble again at school yesterday."

2. **Client:** "I make such a fool of myself. I never should have gone there in the first place."

3. **Client:** "I couldn't believe I got the raise. I've never gotten one before, ever."

4. **Client:** "He just stood there laughing at me. You should have seen the look in his eyes. He's never been that way before."

5. **Client:** "She said she wants us to be together."

6. **Client:** "I'm going to do better, I promise. I've just had a rough couple of weeks and couldn't seem to get things going."

7. **Client:** "My mom said they're not supposed to hit me. When they do it, she says it's not my fault."

8. **Client:** "He left Tuesday morning to go to school, just like he always does. When he wasn't home by 6 p.m., I started to worry. I haven't seen or heard from him since."

9. **Client:** "I'm feeling really discouraged about the direction my life is going in. I don't seem to be lifting out of this depression."

10. **Client:** "I'm afraid she's in trouble. I'm not sure why I feel this way. It's just a gut feeling I've had for some time."

Closed questions often begin with the words *is, do,* and *are* (Ivey & Ivey, 2003). Responses are likely to be yes, no, or a specific fact, such as name, age, place of birth, religion, address, and so forth. Examples of closed questions follow:

1. **Practitioner:** "Do you want to be here today?"

   Client: "Yes."

2. **Practitioner:** "Is this your signature?"

   Client: "No."

3. **Practitioner:** "Our records seem to indicate that you've been here before. Are they accurate?"

   Client: "Yes."

4. **Practitioner:** "Do you live with your mom or your dad?"

   Client: "My mom."

5. **Practitioner:** "Is what she said true?"

   Client: "No."

Some clients will take it upon themselves to elaborate on their responses to closed-ended questions. Such might be the case with example number 5 above. When asked if what his mother said was true, the teenage son might respond by saying only "no," but he then might attempt to explain the reasons why he believes what his mother said is not true. An open-ended question is more likely to stimulate interaction between the two if that is what the helper is attempting to achieve.

Socratic Questions

"Nothing is more characteristic of Socrates than talking, and nothing is more characteristic of his talks than asking questions" (Santas, 1979, p. 59). According to Overholser (1988), the Socratic method, with its emphasis on asking questions as one of the three basic components of Socratic dialogue, can be a beneficial technique for helping clients sort out their situations. The Socratic method is specifically incorporated into Ellis's (1994) rational-emotive therapy, in Beck's cognitive therapy (Beck, Rush, Shaw, & Emery, 1979), and in ego psychology approaches (Stein, 1991). But though it is cited in these approaches, little instruction or direction had been offered about the actual components of the "questioning method" until Overholser (1993) described it in detail.

In the days of Socrates, the questioning method was used as a way of demonstrating a person's ignorance and the need to rely on logic (Schmid, 1983). In the therapeutic relationship, questioning is used for very different reasons. Through the use of questions, the client and practitioner engage in a form of exploration (Klein, 1986). The questions are designed to stimulate independent thinking in clients as well as motivate them to discover answers to their problems (Overholser, 1993). This is accomplished through a collaborative relationship between client and practitioner.

Seven Categories of Socratic Questions

According to Overholser (1993), Bloom and Sanders identified and "described seven different types of questions: memory, translation, interpretation, application, analysis, synthesis, and evaluation" (p. 67). **Memory questions** ask a person to recall a past event, to identify specific facts or details. Examples might be: "When did you first experience the symptoms?"; "How long has it been bothering you?"; "When did it last occur?" **Translation questions** ask a person to explain or translate what an idea, event, or piece of information "meant" to him or her. This is done in an effort to increase a client's understanding or to uncover additional information. Examples include: "What does it mean to you?"; "How might you explain that to your wife (probation officer, other significant person)?" **Interpretation questions** help to discover relationships between events, facts, and ideas. Specifically, the practitioner might attempt to present one or more ideas or facts and to allow clients to uncover the relationships between them. An example of this type of question would be: "How is your current relationship with your boss similar to or different from your previous relationships with other supervisors?" Similar to translation questions, interpretation questions seek to find meaning by asking the question, "What does it mean to you?"

Application questions attempt to identify instances in which clients thought about or attempted some action toward the solution of their problems. Seeking for specifics to clients' solution strategies, practitioners might ask: "What have you tried thus far?"; "Did any part of what you tried seem to help?" **Analysis questions** seek to have clients solve their problems by arriving at conclusions based on adequate evidence. These questions also encourage people to use logic and objectivity to support their notions or conclusions. Example analysis questions are: "What evidence do you have to support your conclusion?"; "If you do _____, what do you see happening?"; "What makes the problem better or worse?" **Synthesis questions** encourage clients to use creative thinking, suggesting the search for alternative solutions. Examples include: "What other possible solutions are there?"; "Have you heard of or tried anything else?" Synthesis questions also play a role in helping to define words used with universal definitions. For example: "What does 'being a failure' mean to you?" Finally, **evaluation questions** ask clients to make a judgment based on a standard. First the standard needs to be identified (the use of a "what" question); then the idea or behavior is examined to see how closely it meets the standard (the use of a "how" question). Examples of evaluation questions are: "What would a person have to do to be successful?"; "How well do you fit that description?"; "What does your wife want from you?"; "How well do you see yourself doing that?"

Socratic Questions and the Stages of the Problem-Solving Model

"Systemic questioning refers to the use of a series of questions designed not so much to elicit information about a specific topic as to activate the client's rational self-awareness" (Overholser, 1988, p. 1). According to Overholser (1993), this can be done in an organized fashion by integrating Socratic questions into the stages of the problem-solving model (McMahon, 1996). The goal is to assist clients in the development of problem-solving skills and alternative coping strategies. The basic stages of the problem-solving approach include the following: stage 1—a description of the problem by the client, along with the reasons for seeking help; stage 2—a collaborative assessment of the problem; stage 3—establishing goals (both the client's and others') and determining which interventions might best assist in achieving/accomplishing the goals; stage 4—implementation of interventions; and stage 5—evaluation of the plan.

During stage 1, the types of questions asked by the practitioner are for the purpose of inviting the client to identify and describe the problem. Evaluative and analysis questions at this stage might include "How may I be of help?"; "What helped you to decide to seek assistance at this time?"; "What do you think is causing the problem?"; or "What tells you that _____ is causing the problem?"

From the more general responses about why the person is seeking help and what he or she sees as the possible causes, the practitioner and client can transition into stage 2, asking more concrete and specific questions about the problem and aspects of its source. A continuation of evaluative questions can be used, such as "On a scale from zero to one hundred, how intense is the problem (emotion)?"; "What do you believe your chances are of finding a solution?" In addition, memory questions may be incorporated. For example, "How often does it occur?"; "Are there times when you've been able to make a difference, or when things are better?"; "Are there specific times when it happens?"; or "How intense is it?" Analysis questions also provide client insight by asking them to analyze aspects of the problem. Questions might include the following: "What do you identify as some of the contributing factors to the problem?" or "What makes it better/worse?"

At stage 3, the interview process begins to shift toward goals that the client and/or referring agency or person [parent, partner, judge, school principal] would like to see achieved. Evaluation questions are effective in helping clients decide what it is they want to achieve and what others would like to see happen. Examples include "What specifically would you like to achieve from our meeting together?"; "How will your [other person] know you are doing better?"; "How will you know when it is time to end our sessions?"; or "What does the judge want to see you doing when you return to court?" Memory questions may also help client and practitioner arrive at goals for the future based on what was possible in the past. "Were you able to do that at any time in the past?"; "What specifically happened in the past that leads you to believe you will be able to do it again in the future?" Analysis questions may further assist in breaking down large goals into smaller, more achievable parts. These questions use principles of deductive reasoning (Overholser, 1993): "What is a first step toward accomplishing your goal?"; "No longer feeling depressed is your goal. What is one thing you could do tomorrow that will help you achieve that feeling?"

At stage 4, depending on which model or intervention you use to guide the therapeutic process, application questions assist in examining the potential outcomes of the intervention. You might question the client by asking, "What specifically will you do this week?"; "What else could you try?"; "Exactly how will you go about making the changes?" Synthesis questions help the client to expand on the possible alternatives to problem solving: "What other possible ways are there of doing this?" Analysis questions also examine what has and has not worked in the past: "Were there times when you did _____ that helped?"; "What were the conditions?"; or "What were the conditions when it didn't go so well?"

Finally, in stage 5, when you evaluate the plan that was implemented, analysis and evaluation questions are useful. Analysis questions might ask, "What did you specifically do that helped?"; "Looking back, what do you see that helped the most?" Evaluation questions seek to have clients make a judgment, in this case a judgment about their plan and its implementation. These questions might include the following: "On a scale from zero to one hundred, how well are you communicating now?"; "Do you still see your husband as the only source of the problem?"; "Do you believe your P.O. will recognize the changes you've made?"

Figure 4.3 provides an outline of the problem-solving approach with examples of Socratic questions that may be helpful at each stage. This outline is not meant to be a complete list but may serve as a guide. Over time, the practitioner will become more familiar and comfortable with the use of questions. When used skillfully, they assist clients in problem identification, goal setting, examination of multiple options, and evaluation of progress.

All of these are skills that can be learned and used in the future.

The following section contains examples of client statements followed by model responses for the skills of empathy, positive regard, open- and closed-ended questions, and clarification. These examples are written to allow you to practice each of the skills in preparation for working with clients. We recommend that you review each of the skills as they were described in the chapter, then pair up with a partner and role play receiving and responding to each of the client statements with the appropriate skill. After each response, obtain feedback from your partner regarding your progress and compare your response with the one written in the corresponding section containing model responses. Your responses do not have to be exactly the same as the model responses in order for you to be effective. They are provided as a guide or a reference. Continue the process until you feel comfortable with your skill development. If you are unable to role play these scenarios, practice writing your response and then compare them with the model responses.

Skill Development: Empathy

1. **Thirty-year-old woman who works as a waitress**

   Client: I'm raising my sister's two children right now, and I'm so overtired but they have no other place to go.

   Model Empathetic Response: Taking care of your sister's two children is wearing you down.

2. **Thirty-five-year-old single parent**

   Client: I'm really frustrated with the school my child attends because they think all of his problems are about me.

   Model Empathetic Response: You're angry because the school is blaming all of the problems your child is having on you.

Figure 4.3

Guide to Socratic Questions and the Stages of Problem Solving

Stage 1 Description of the Problem

A. Evaluation Questions

What brought you here today?

How has it been a problem for you?

What changed in your life that made you decide to seek help?

How may I be of help to you?

B. Analysis Questions

What do you think is the cause of the problem?

What tells you that _____ is causing the problem?

What situations make it better/worse?

Stage 2 Collaborative Assessment of the Problem

A. Memory Questions

When did it begin, where does it occur, what are the conditions?

How often does it occur, who is involved?

When is it least likely to occur?

B. Analysis Questions

What exactly do you see as the cause of the problem?

What situations/conditions make it better/worse?

What evidence do you have for this?

C. Interpretation Questions

(with multiple problems) Do your _____ [marital] problems seem similar to your _____ [work] problems? How are your problems alike/different?

D. Translation Questions

What does your _____ [P.O.] expect to have happen from our meetings together?

What do you mean when you say you want to "feel better"?

Stage 3 Establishing Goals and Determining Interventions

A. Memory Questions

Was there a time in the past when you were doing this and it helped?

What was happening then?

B. Evaluation Questions

What would you like to accomplish through our meetings?

How could you tell when you achieved that goal?

You say improved communications is what you want; what will be happening to tell you it is better?

What do your parents [teacher, P.O., judge] want you to be doing?

How will they know you are doing it?

C. Analysis Questions

If you want to achieve a level of 9 out of 10 and you are at a 3 now, what could you do to get to a 4?

D. Translation Questions

What do you believe your parents [teachers] want you to be doing differently?

Stage 4 Implementation of Interventions

A. Applications Questions

What specifically will you do this week?

How will you go about doing _____?

What else could you try?

What do you think will happen if you try _____?

What tells you that doing _____ will help?

B. Synthesis Questions

What other ways could you look at the problem?

Is that the only option you have?

Stage 5 Evaluation of Progress/Plan

A. Analysis Questions

How can you tell it worked/didn't work?

Were there times when it was better/worse?

What do you think was best about your plan?

B. Evaluation Questions

On a scale of zero to one hundred, how well do you believe you accomplished that goal?

How would you rate your level of accomplishment?

What would you do differently, or more of the same, next time?

What have you learned?

Knowing how your wife [boss, coach] feels about this problem, what do you think she would say about how well you are doing?

3. **Twenty-eight-year-old professional woman**

   Client: I'm dating a married man and he won't leave his wife and children. I don't know what to do.

   Model Empathetic Response: Dating a married man is very frustrating, especially when he still stays with his wife and children. You're wondering if you have any future with this man.

4. **Fifty-year-old male truck driver**

   Client: I don't know why I have to come here. All I did was knock my wife around a bit. And she deserved it.

   Model Empathetic Response: You don't like being here and you can't understand why hitting your wife was such a big deal, especially since she had it coming.

5. **Thirty-two-year-old hassled housewife and mother**

   Client: My sister's kids are so perfect and never seem to get into trouble. Mine are always into something. I must be a lousy mom.

   Model Empathetic Response: You're feeling like a failure as a mother because your kids are in and out of scrapes and your sister seems to have angels for children.

6. **Thirty-five-year-old divorced man**

   Client: I want to talk with you about my son, but first I want to know if you have any children yourself?

   Model Empathetic Response: You doubt that I can help you with your son unless I have children of my own and I have experienced some of the same things you have experienced with your son.

7. **Forty-year-old public official**

   Client: Now everything I say to you is in confidence and you won't tell anyone?

   Model Empathetic Response: Sharing personal experiences with another person can be very scary, especially if that person talks to someone else about your problems.

8. **Fifty-year-old housewife who has been married for thirty years**

   Client: I don't want to go back to him. I know he'll hit me again, but I don't feel like I've anywhere else to go.

   Model Empathetic Response: You're scared to go back to your husband because isn't safe, but you don't feel like you have any other options.

9. **Eighteen-year-old African American student at a predominantly white liberal arts college**

   Client: I'm tired of my skin color being the first thing people see about me.

   Model Empathetic Response: You're frustrated because you want people to notice you for more important reasons than your skin color.

10. Mother of three school-age children talking to the school counselor

Client: The therapist we saw last year said that we really were an ideal family. I don't know why the school thinks we're such a bad family.

Model Empathetic Response: You are confused because you were told by a therapist last year that everything was okay with your family, and now people are telling you your family is having problems.

11. Sixteen-year-old boy who is having sexual thoughts about another boy

Client: I've been having thoughts about having sex with another boy. I wonder if I'm a homosexual.

Model Empathetic Response: You're experiencing sexual feelings for another boy and you're wondering if this means you are gay.

12. Thirty-five-year-old dockworker

Client: People say I have an explosive temper, but I think I just express my anger. The other night I got so angry that I threw a fork at my sister and that scared me.

Model Empathetic Response: Sometimes you get so angry that you lose your temper. Throwing a fork at your sister really scared you.

13. Sixty-year-old heart attack patient

Client: I feel like my life is over. It's all I can do to stay here in my bed and wait to die.

Model Empathetic Response: Your recent heart attack has left you feeling discouraged, weak, and out of energy. You're upset with yourself because all you want to do is stay in bed and waste away.

14. Fifteen-year-old boy whose mother and father are constantly arguing

Client: I'm sick and tired of my mom and dad fighting all the time. They don't really care about me or my sister; they're just determined to win a fight.

Model Empathetic Response: You're sad because you don't feel your mother and father care about you. All they seem to be interested in is arguing with each other.

15. Fifty-five-year-old woman who had been married for thirty-five years

Client: My husband left me for another woman, and I feel like I must have done something horribly wrong.

Model Empathetic Response: When your husband left you for another woman after thirty-five years of marriage, you were devastated. You're especially troubled because you believe he left because of something you did.

16. **Twenty-two-year-old student whose girlfriend told him she was breaking up with him**

    Client: I am furious at her. She thinks she's too good for me. When she gets back from vacation, she'll be in for a surprise.

    Model Empathetic Response: You're angry that your girlfriend broke up with you. When she comes back to town, you're going to make her feel bad for dumping you. You're a much better catch than she thinks you are.

17. **Seventy-three-year-old widow**

    Client: How old are you? I'm not sure you have enough experience to help me.

    Model Empathetic Response: You don't believe someone as young as I am can possibly understand what has happened to you and how you feel. You have doubts about my ability to help you.

18. **Nineteen-year-old**

    Client: I don't know whether I should start at the junior college or go the university. What do you think?

    Model Empathetic Response: The decision about where to go has you perplexed, and you would like the decision to be easier.

Skill Development: Positive Regard

1. **Forty-nine-year-old divorcing female**

   Client: I'm not sure I'm going to be able to start a new life.

   Model Positive Regard Response: I know it is difficult now, but the fact that you are here working on your problems suggests you have the strength and ability to give your life direction.

2. **Seventy-six-year-old man**

   Client: I am very lonely since my wife died, but I do enjoy doing volunteer work.

   Model Positive Regard Response: Even though you are hurting because of the loss of your wife, you have the courage to help others and that is great.

3. **Teenager**

   Client: I am not doing very well in school, but I'm honestly trying hard.

   Model Positive Regard Response: You must be proud of yourself for trying hard, and you should feel good that you are doing your best.

4. **Thirty-six-year-old addicted to drugs**

   Client: I just relapsed for the third time, but I came for help sooner this time.

   Model Positive Regard Response: I am glad you had the ability to recognize your relapse and get help sooner.

5. **Forty-six-year-old man with schizophrenia**

   Client: I was able to get all my bills paid off this month.

   Model Positive Regard Response: That is really a nice accomplishment. You should be very proud.

6. **Forty-six-year-old woman with depression**

   Client: I wasn't able to stay at the ladies club dinner, but I did go early and helped with the table decorations.

   Model Positive Regard Response: I'm sorry you weren't able to stay, but it was nice that you could help out with the dinner and feel a part of it.

7. **Sixteen-year-old**

   Client: I am smoking marijuana now and I am beginning to worry about addiction.

   Model Positive Regard Response: I am proud of you for being able to share that problem with me.

8. **Sixty-two-year-old caregiver of her eighty-five-year-old mother**

   Client: I've been taking care of mom for six years now and I'm very tired.

   Model Positive Regard Response: I am glad you can admit that you're feeling tired. It's really important that you are recognizing your feelings and can look objectively at your caregiver situation.

9. **Twenty-eight-year-old woman with a bipolar diagnosis**

   Client: This is the first time I've been able to recognize my depression coming on, and that's why I came in today.

   Model Positive Regard Response: You have made an important step in beginning to be able to control your illness. I'm glad you were able to come in today.

10. **Thirty-six-year-old single mom of three children**

    Client: I'm at the end of my rope—I just can't keep my family going.

    Model Positive Regard Response: I am pleased that you had the strength to begin to look at your family situation.

11. **Young mother**

    Client: I believe my two-year-old may be autistic, and I'm so afraid and don't know what to do.

    Model Positive Regard Response: I can sense your real concern. Autism is a tough problem, and the fact that you are asking questions is the right first step.

12. Thirty-two-year-old father

Client: What would you do if you were in my shoes?

Model Positive Regard Response: I can't know what is going on with you, but perhaps together we can begin to consider some important questions.

13. Frustrated parent

Client: Don't you think a sixteen-year-old girl should be in by 10:00 p.m. on school nights?

Model Positive Regard Response: Every family is different in setting rules, but it is important that we can consider what is best for your family.

14. Forty-two-year-old man

Client: The doctor tells me I have to have the colonoscopy, but I'm scared.

Model Positive Regard Response: It is okay to be scared of that procedure, but you have the ability and opportunity to look at the pros and cons of your own health situation.

15. Eighteen-year-old female

Client: My parents want me to get a divorce now before we have any kids—what do you think?

Model Positive Regard Response: That is a very tough question and probably only you can answer it—but we can talk about your situation so you can consider all your options in a meaningful way.

16. Thirty-nine-year-old mother

Client: My ten-year-old son is mutilating himself by cutting his arms with a pocketknife. He is so depressed—I must be a bad mother.

Model Positive Regard Response: Depression and self-mutilation are very difficult to understand and many parents are afraid to talk about them. You have shown both courage and insight to be here today.

17. Parents of a sixteen-year-old son

Client: Our son is withdrawing from family and friends, and this last week he told us he was hearing voices.

Model Positive Regard Response: It seems like you have a good relationship with your son that he would share with you that he is hearing voices.

18. Fourteen-year-old foster child

Client: It doesn't matter where I live because nobody really cares about me. I only had one foster mom that tried to help me.

Model Positive Regard Response: It must be difficult to be in different foster homes, but it is important that you can recognize that one foster mom was really trying to help you.

Skill Development: Open-Ended Questions

---

1. Male client, second session

Client: I'm not sure I have any strengths at all. My life seems to be a complete mess right now.

Model Open-Ended Response: If your best friend were to describe your strengths, what would that person say about you?

---

2. Depressed female client, first session

Client: What's the point of planning for the future? You can't really control anything and things just turn out the way they're supposed to.

Model Open-Ended Response: Can you describe a time when you did plan for the future and it didn't get messed up?

---

3. Male client, first session, mandated attendance at group session for abusers

Client: I don't see how sitting around in a group like this is really gonna change a thing. Hell, these guys are just as messed up as I am. How can they help me?

Model Open-Ended Response: Let's assume for a minute that the group might be helpful. If the group could be helpful, what kinds of things would you like to change?

---

4. Male group member, third session

Client: Why isn't Raul saying anything in group? Does he think he doesn't have any problems and the group is just for the rest of us?

Model Open-Ended Response: What is it about Raul's silence that raises your concern?

---

5. Female member of a group for child abusers

Client: Frances, you don't know what you're talking about. You come to the group from your nice uptown apartment, but you really aren't like the rest of us.

Model Open-Ended Response: Can you or anyone else in group think of things that you might have in common with Frances?

---

6. Male member of a group for anger management

Client: How do we know that some of the group won't blab about what they hear in our sessions? I don't know them and don't know why I would trust them.

Model Open-Ended Response: What kinds of rules do we need to observe in our group to make people feel more comfortable about the confidentiality of our conversations?

7. **Female experiencing depression, first session**

   Client: I have so many problems I don't even know where to start. How can you help someone with as many issues as me?

   Model Open-Ended Response: Of all of the issues you're struggling with right now, which do you see as the most serious and why?

8. **Female in a domestic violence shelter**

   Client: He is such a good provider. He only gets mad and hits me when I do something bad like burn his dinner. He always apologizes later.

   Model Open-Ended Response: Think back over the past three months. Can you describe how often he gets mad and hits you and under what circumstances?

9. **Seventeen-year-old female**

   Client: My parents want me to have the baby and give it up for adoption, and my boyfriend wants me to have an abortion. I don't really care at this point; I can't make up my mind. Which do you think makes the most sense?

   Model Open-Ended Response: What are the advantages and disadvantages of those two options?

Skill Development: Closed-Ended Responses

1. **Forty-five-year-old female**

   Client: It seems that I'm always scared about something. I worry about my children disappearing, my husband dying, or my mom having to go to a nursing home. I think I'm going crazy.

   Model Closed-Ended Response: Has there ever been a time when you were not feeling this scared?

2. **Twenty-year-old female**

   Client: Why does he act this way? Every time I take him into the store, he asks for this or that and then has a tantrum until I finally give in and buy him something.

   Model Closed-Ended Response: Does he act like this in any other places besides the store?

3. **Thirty-year-old male**

   Client: I really like you. You're funny and so smart and I think we might be a good pair. How about we take in a movie this weekend?

   Model Closed-Ended Response: Are these the two characteristics you look for in a companion?

4. **Male inpatient in a psychiatric clinic**

   Client: I mean, first the Droids were after me, then the Wampuses. I must be pretty important to have them chasing me.

   Model Closed-Ended Response: Have you told Dr. X that these two groups are after you?

5. **Thirty-eight-year-old female**

   Client: I like what you said about I-statements. I used them with my husband yesterday and you would have been proud. He came home from drinking with his buddies and I said: "I hate it that you're a worthless drunk who continues to screw up my life and those of our kids." Pretty good, huh?

   Model Closed-Ended Response: Did your husband respond to your I-statements like you expected he would?

6. **Twenty-five-year-old male**

   Client: This assertiveness stuff is great. I used it on my landlord and it really worked. Tomorrow I'm gonna go in and tell my useless boss that he can't ask me to work late anymore.

   Model Closed-Ended Response: Have you considered the possible consequences of being assertive with your boss?

7. **Thirty-four-year-old female**

   Client: I know we decided that I should ask her out, but I have this nagging concern that it may be a mistake.

   Model Closed-Ended Response: Did you have these concerns when we initially talked about your asking her out?

8. **Twenty-two-year-old male**

   Client: (Just as the session ends) I just thought you should know that I'm thinking about getting back with my old lover. I know she did drugs, but she says she's changed.

   Model Closed-Ended Response: Is this a decision that you can postpone until our next scheduled session?

9. **Fifty-seven-year-old female**

   Client: The other social worker I saw before you got assigned was a real loser. Sometimes I'd smell liquor on his breath and suspected he had a bottle in the drawer. Why doesn't the agency get rid of him?

   Model Closed-Ended Response: Have you shared this information with anyone else in the agency?

Skill Development: Clarification

---

1. **Third appointment for this husband, in counseling because his wife says he "has to or she'll leave"**

   Client: These visits are costing me a bunch. Why don't we swap. I'll do some plumbing for you and you cut me a break on the fees.

   Model Clarification Response: Let me see if I understand you correctly. Are you saying you want to provide me with plumbing services in exchange for our counseling sessions?

---

2. **Forty-five-year-old male mandated to receive anger management counseling following arrest for domestic violence**

   Client: Can I see my records? I want to know what you say about me in there.

   Model Clarification Response: Mark, I don't have a problem letting you see the records I have written, but could you help me to understand how that relates to our current discussion about your anger?

---

3. **Twenty-seven-year-old female diagnosed with major depression and dependent personality disorder**

   Client: I know you said our last session is next week, but don't you think I should continue to see you for another month or so?

   Model Clarification Response: Kathy, could you help me understand your thinking behind your request to continue meeting for another month?

---

4. **Client seeking help to become more assertive**

   Client: I told my husband what you said about him at our last session, and he's really against me coming here anymore.

   Model Clarification Response: Is your husband concerned about us talking about him in the context of your problem?

---

5. **Client referred to a social skills group for single persons**

   Client: If I get into that educational group you mentioned, will I be over my fear of commitment when it's done?

   Model Clarification Response: You're hoping the group will provide you with enough skills to be able to one day enter into a committed relationship with your friend from work?

---

6. **Thirty-seven-year-old male**

   Client: You mentioned that partialization idea last time. Tell me again how it works.

   Model Clarification Response: Would you like to review the concepts on partialization that we discussed in our last meeting, or how they specifically relate to the problem we've been working on?

7. **Male employed by a small business that has no medical insurance coverage, seeking help from the medical social worker**

   Client: Tiny Tim is going to die if he doesn't have the operation, but there's no money and we have no health insurance at Mr. Scrooge's shop.

   Model Clarification Response: Will you please explain Tim's problem and what type of operation the doctors are recommending?

8. **Seventy-three-year-old African American female diagnosed with a progressive, fatal, and nontreatable form of liver cancer**

   Client: It's no use anymore. I'm no use to anyone. I know everyone will be better off when I'm gone.

   Model Clarification Response: What do you mean by "It's no use"; "I'm no use to anyone"; or "I know everyone will be better off when I'm gone"?

9. **Sixteen-year-old Hispanic male whose girlfriend recently left him for another young man**

   Client: What do you think is wrong with me?

   Model Clarification Response: Since I really don't know you, I wouldn't offer an opinion because I would likely be wrong. Please tell me what you think is the source of your problem?

10. **Nineteen-year-old female away from home for the first time, seeing an intake worker at the local community mental health center**

    Client: Sometimes I hear voices that tell me to do bad things. I yell at them but they just come back later.

    Model Clarification Response: What do you mean when you say the voices tell you to do bad things?

11. **Fifty-one-year-old male referred to counseling by his primary care physician**

    Client: I'm taking Prozac for my depression. Why do I have to see a social worker too?

    Model Clarification Response: If you were to come up with an opinion, why do you think your doctor referred you to see me when she has already prescribed Prozac for your depressed mood?

12. **Ex-con just released from jail and talking with his PO**

    Client: I met this sweet thing down at the ice rink yesterday. She told me she's eighteen, but I think she's lying. She wants to see me again. She said she likes older guys like me.

    Model Clarification Response: Help me to understand your point in bringing up this information with me at this time.

13. **Upper-class female business executive who reported being ticketed with a DUI that she said was her first ("It was because I was entertaining some clients. I'm not an alcoholic.")**

    Client: How about you tell the judge that I came to your DUI group and I don't need anymore of this therapy crap?

    Model Clarification Response: Let me see if I understand you. You want me to write a letter to your judge and tell him that you don't need this "therapy crap" any more?

14. **Adult female who begins the first session by stating that she is a "born-again Christian"**

    Client: Are you born again? I think I'd work best with a social worker who was born again.

    Model Clarification Response: Is your point that you would feel more comfortable seeking help from someone who shares similar religious values and beliefs as you do?

15. **Seventeen-year-old male sentenced to drug counseling after being caught in possession of marijuana; marijuana and alcohol were also found in his drug screen**

    Client: Look, don't tell my probation officer about our little secret. The joint wasn't mine anyway, it belongs to a friend. I was just holding it for her.

    Model Clarification Response: What do you mean when you say you were "just holding it for her"?

16. **Thirty-seven-year-old single mother, divorced her second husband two years ago, met a man a couple of months ago, they had an affair that lasted about two weeks, and she has just learned that she is pregnant**

    Client: Do you know of a really good doctor who can do my abortion? I think I'd feel better if I knew it was someone you recommended.

    Model Clarification Response: Do you mean that you would feel more secure seeing a doctor who has experience with this type of medical procedure and in maintaining your confidentiality?

17. **Male immigrant working at a minimum wage job and sending money back to his family in Central America; he is struggling to make ends meet**

    Client: Why doesn't this agency have any evening hours? I have to take off from work to come here, and it costs me money.

    Model Clarification Response: Am I understanding you to mean that it is a struggle for you to get off work in time to make your appointment?

18. **Neighbor of yours who is pressing you to help him solve his problem**

    Client: I got summoned for jury duty again. Can you write me a letter telling the judge that I can't serve because I have to come here each week?

    Model Clarification Response: Help me to understand. Do you want me to write a letter as your friend and neighbor, or as a professional social worker?

APPLICATIONS TO PRACTICE

Case Example

Sharon and George have two children, Cherry age three and George Jr. age five. They have just moved into Hampster, California, and are living in a trailer park. Last week they went out drinking, leaving the children asleep in the trailer. Concerned neighbors made a protective service report, and the investigator has referred the case to you to follow on a voluntary basis. George has a job at a paving company and

Sharon stays at home with the children. The couple have no family or friends in the area. They are willing to have a child care provider in the future when they want to go out and are interested in help regarding the children. There is no history of previous referrals, and the couple seems genuinely concerned and interested in doing whatever they need to do to improve their parenting skills.

Critical Thinking Questions

1. Who will you want to meet with first?
2. What are some things you might say that would show empathy, genuineness, and respect?
3. How will you explain your dual role as a protective service supervision worker and a caring social work treatment provider?

SUMMARY

This chapter identifies a series of skills that are important in direct practice. These include the skills of listening and establishing facilitative conditions through the use of empathy, the expression of positive regard, congruence, and the use of paraphrasing, summarizing, clarifying, and questioning. The chapter emphasizes the importance of recognizing and using nonverbal communications and behavior to understand and communicate your understanding of client situations. Examples of each of the skills are provided, and the chapter ends with an analysis of how Socratic questions can be integrated into the problem-solving process.

Navigating Direct Practice

An access code for Research Navigator™ is packaged within your text. Use this code to register at www.researchnavigator.com and then use the key words listed below to research articles related to the chapter's content. Research Navigator™ helps you quickly and efficiently make the most of your research time.

❏ Nonverbal behavior
❏ Empathy
❏ Positive regard
❏ Congruence
❏ Socratic question

Chapter 5

Knowledge and Skills for Assessment

■ Queenie Martin was covering crisis calls at the Mountain Meadow Mental Health Clinic when she first came in contact with Rashida Motado. Rashida was distraught over the situation with her nineteen-year-old son, Akron, and as a last resort phoned the crisis line. Within in a few minutes, Queenie learned that Rashida believed her son would be dead in a few days because he was depressed and abusing drugs. In the week preceding her call, he had told several friends about his plans to kill himself. The threats were always accompanied by slurred speech and other signs of drug abuse.

Queenie determined that Akron needed to be hospitalized immediately and had the family call the police for help in getting their son to the hospital. The police arrived a short time later and took the young man to a local mental health residential facility where he was committed until he could be further assessed by the staff. After a thorough assessment, the staff decided that Akron should be committed for a period of forty-five days for intensive treatment.

Akron remained in the most restrictive part of the hospital for five days until he was completely detoxed. He was then transferred to a residential treatment facility for follow-up treatment for his addiction. As he continued to "dry out," it was obvious that there remained a depressive element to his mood that also needed to be treated.

A thorough assessment was made of Akron's history of abuse, his mood and psychological state, and the family's style of interaction, along with their strengths and weaknesses. Work at the residential treatment facility then centered on helping both Akron and his family understand the nature of addiction and how important it was to have the family support him on his way back to health. Near the time of Akron's discharge, assessments were also made as to what support was needed when the young man left the treatment facility.

Akron has returned to his home but is still in outpatient treatment. He anxiously awaits the day when he will be able to return to his normal living routine of working and attending college. If the ongoing assessments have been accurate about his needs for reentry into society, and if Akron is sufficiently motivated, he will have a chance to live a productive and fulfilling life.

It is obvious from Akron's case history that assessment has become an important, comprehensive, and often specialized task, especially when an integrated/multidimensional approach is implemented. In this particular case, the crisis social worker was required to assess whether the young man was in need of hospitalization, based on the collateral information provided by his mother. Subsequently, the treatment team had to assess how the patient could best be treated on the locked unit, and also at what point in his treatment he would be ready for a less restrictive treatment facility. When he arrived at the rehabilitation facility, the new treatment team had to assess the young man and his family to decide what the best course of action would be and how much help he

APPLICATIONS TO PRACTICE

Critical Thinking Questions
To complete these critical thinking activities, please refer to the chapter opening vignette on page 105.
1. As the outpatient worker, what information would you want to explore (e.g., chart, telephone contacts with treatment staff, cultural information, drug awareness) prior to seeing the client for the first time?
2. How would you want to begin the interview with this client?
3. What would you want to tell the client about what you knew about him and his family?

would need to receive from his family and the community.

Clearly, assessment plays an important role in the work of a social worker. From the initial stage, when Akron threatened suicide, to the day he left the treatment facility and returned to his family and community, assessment was ongoing. It is important to note that assessment can be defined in two parts. On the one hand, it is an "ongoing process," as demonstrated in this case, in which assessment occurred over the course of the young man's treatment. It is also a "product," as when assessment findings were used to hospitalize Akron; when the hospital treatment team decided he was ready to be moved to a rehabilitation facility; and finally, when the rehabilitation team deemed him ready to reenter the community.

This chapter introduces students to the process of assessment in direct practice. Although this is not a complete review of the topic, it does survey the assessment processes from the different theoretical models previously reviewed. It gives the reader a sense of the importance of assessment from a multidimensional perspective and how this step is incorporated into the overall stages of the problem-solving model, especially as it relates to goal setting and intervention.

Consistent with the planned change or problem-solving model, the first stage of this model has two primary objectives. One is to begin establishing a relationship with the client. The skills found to be effective in accomplishing this task (facilitative conditions and listening skills) are addressed in depth in Chapter 4. The second objective involves gathering information from multiple arenas concerning the client and his or her environment in order to assess the problem. This is most often accomplished in a two-part process. First, clients are invited to share with the social worker the reason for seeking help and addresses what they believe to be the "primary" problem. Typical concerns include such things as how the client is feeling, such as a mood that is experienced as being significantly unpleasant and/or disruptive; a relationship that is not meeting the client's needs; an upsetting event or events in the client's life that have been difficult to cope with; or behavior that has been found to be troublesome either to the client or to those in the environment, or both. Clients are encouraged to tell their story, explaining the reasons why the problem exists and the circumstances that surround the problem.

In the second part of the assessment phase, the practitioner directs questions to uncover information believed to be pertinent and useful in assisting the client to achieve some form of positive change. The social worker's assessment should reflect aspects of those theoretical models that are seen as most appropriate to the client's situation. As one means of assisting in this process, this chapter presents the inner and outer focus model, which can help social workers organize and direct the assessment process. Following this section, specific methods and techniques of assessment drawn from the theoretical models discussed in Chapter 2 are reviewed. Assessment procedures for specific populations and problems are included.

Assessment in Social Work Practice

Assessment is an important task for the social worker. One of social work's pioneers, Mary Richmond, attempted to make the social work profession more scientific by defining assessment. In discussing Richmond's work on assessment, Bisman (1999) states:

> In her *Social Diagnosis* (1917), she provides a lengthy and detailed method for obtaining social evidence, which was used by the social worker for understanding the client's difficulties and deciding "what course of procedure" to follow (p. 39). She states, "social diagnosis is the attempt to arrive at as exact a definition as possible of the social situation and personality of a given client. The gathering of evidence, or investigation, begins the process, the critical examination and comparison of evidence follows, and last comes its interpretation and the definition of the social difficulty (p. 62)." (p. 240)

All of the helping professions struggle with the problem of assessment. In a recent nationally publicized kidnapping case, a local newspaper ran the headline, "Experts Disagree on Illness" (*Deseret News,* Saturday, 10 January 2004). The article continued:

> Wanda Barzee has been declared incompetent to stand trial on charges of kidnapping Elizabeth Smart, but what mental illness does she have? Not even the experts can agree. Both doctors who evaluated Barzee, however, agree there's something wrong with the woman who with her husband, Brian David Mitchell, is accused of kidnapping Smart. One evaluator determined Barzee was a paranoid schizophrenic. The other said she suffered from shared psychotic disorder. (pp. B1–B2)

The problem of determining a definitive assessment for Ms. Barzee may never be solved, but this case illustrates the need for all helping professions to work toward more accurate and useful methods of assessment.

Assessment as a Process and a Product

Throughout the years, social workers have tried to define assessment. Farley, Smith, and Boyle (2003) describe the process as follows:

> Assessment provides a differential approach to treatment based on individual differences and needs. It clearly recognizes the uniqueness of every situation, the importance of treatment planning related to a particular problematic situation, area of family dysfunction, system breakdown, or trouble within a life situation. In addition to the above, an individual's strengths need to be identified and utilized as part of the change process. Defining the problem is clearly a way of individualizing the person.
>
> Assessment is fluid and dynamic. It is ever-changing, beginning at intake and continuing to termination. It is likely to be the emphasis of the worker–client effort to understand the problem in the situation. Assessment often begins with a statement of the

problem by the client. It is guided by what is indicated by the client to be the major problem and may penetrate a range of somatic, psychological, social, cultural, spiritual, and environmental forces. Assessment results in an understanding of the problem. It includes initial impressions that are confirmed, modified, or even rejected in the light of additional information as the case moves from moment to moment. There is a circular quality about assessment. It never ceases during the helping treatment process. It includes judgment about the strength and limitations of the individual in coping with the situation. Assessment addresses itself to strengths, capacities, limitations, motivation and opportunity. Treatment planning and treatment itself are guided by assessment. (p. 70)

Siporin (1975) defined assessment as "both a process and a product of understanding, upon which helping action is based" (p. 219). This idea of assessment is grounded in theory and a sound social work philosophy of building on individual strengths. Pincus and Minahan (1973) wrote that "throughout the planned change process the worker continually assesses situations and makes decisions about what needs to be done and how to do it" (p. 101).

Rauch (1993), on the other hand, discussed assessment as a product when she wrote, "it is presented as a written document entered into the client's record . . . [including] definition of the problem, analysis of the factors supporting the problem situation, identification of strengths and resources, formulation of goals and objectives, and statement of the planned strategies for achieving goals and objectives" (pp. xiv–xv).

When the individual begins to meet with the social worker, a process is set in motion. Usually, the person has a problem needing resolution in order to improve some aspect of the quality of life or social functioning. A skillful social worker will immediately give the client a sense of participation in both the assessment of the problem and in defining the goals the client wishes to achieve. Corey, Corey, and Callanan (2003) favor "a collaborative approach to assessment, one that includes the client as a therapeutic partner" (p. 368). Another team of authors echoes this sentiment: "[A] joint activity among practitioners and clients, assessment relies on the helping relationship" (Bisman & Hardcastle, 1999, p. 57). Therefore, genuine rapport is necessary for any meaningful assessment process.

Theoretical Constructs for Assessment

In addition to the ability to relate to the client, the social worker needs a sound knowledge base of the theories that attempt to explain human behavior as well as of theories that attempt to give meaning to the interaction of social systems and the lives of people. The profession of social work uses many theories. This requires social workers to synthesize and blend theoretical positions that examine the person-in-environment perspective and includes aspects of the biopsychosocial perspective as well as information about a person's, a family's, and/or a group's strengths.

The theory base taught by the social work profession is broad and requires individual social workers to synthesize and understand many different theories. The social work concept of "human behavior and the social environment" requires a good understanding of the psychological and biological forces and the many systems interacting in the environment that in turn affect people's lives.

To assess clients properly, social workers need a theory base from which they can draw and be guided in their efforts to understand the client. The Council on Social Work Education (CSWE), which accredits BSW and MSW programs, requires these bodies to incorporate certain content areas into their curricula. One of these areas is known as human behavior and the social environment (HB&SE). The council has defined the HB&SE sequence in its recent educational policy and accreditation standards (EPAS) as follows:

> Human Behavior and the Social Environment. Social work education programs provide content on the reciprocal relationships between human behavior and social environments. Content includes empirically based theories and knowledge that focus on the interactions between and among individuals, groups, societies, and economic systems. It includes theories and knowledge of biological, sociological, cultural, psychological, and spiritual development across the lifespan; the range of social systems in which people live (individual, family, group, organizational, and community); and the ways social systems promote or deter people in maintaining or achieving health and well being. (CSWE, 2003, p. 46)

The social worker will usually assess the client's problems through one or more theoretical lenses. In the early days of social work, there was a tendency for social workers to join one or the other of two different theoretical camps. One group believed that an individual could be assessed and helped more effectively by changing the person's environment (the settlement house movement). The other camp believed that individuals could be assessed and helped by changing the individual and helping him or her cope more effectively with his or her environment (charity organization societies). As the pioneers in the field of social work tried to become more scientific, they readily adopted the work of Freud and set about using the psychodynamic model as the guide to both assessment and treatment. However, as theorists broke away from Freud, the profession began to incorporate ideas from different theoretical constructs such as ego psychology, behavioral and cognitive psychology, and humanistic and existential psychology. Since the 1970s, the profession has added systems and ecosystems theory as a way of balancing the focus of the profession between the person and the environment. More recently, there has been a call to incorporate the assessment of client strengths as part of the overall picture of the client's world.

Practicing social workers must be able to identify and understand the theory they are using in the assessment process. Chapter 2 contains a review of at least one major theory representing each component of the biopsychosocial perspective. This chapter provides a short review of those theories and theoretical positions as they guide the assessment process. Assessment requires social workers to understand that assessment ideas, techniques, and procedures come from ideas developed over the years. The following material is an attempt to survey and identify some of the major theoretical positions and ideas that have influenced social work assessment.

Another component of the assessment process is the collaboration with clients in the development of goals and the means of achieving them. Goals necessarily derive from the assessment itself and, as noted previously, may change over the course of intervention, thus necessitating that assessment be considered an ongoing process. If during the intervention clients achieve some success, they may feel empowered to establish higher-level goals.

Voices from the Field

Kim Jeanson

Upon graduating from college with my degree in psychology, I entered the workforce as a child case manager for a community mental health center. When I began, I was unsure whether I would be able to work with abused and neglected children because of the high level of emotion they often elicit. However, it quickly became work that I love and feel that I am meant to do. After working for two years as a case manager, I came to the realization that I needed to continue my education in order to assist the clients I see in a deeper manner. I chose the master of social work degree for the versatility as well as the humanness of it. My decision has been one of the best I ever made.

My ability to view clients from a strengths perspective has been very beneficial and has helped me to facilitate change with many people. One client in particular stands out.

During my work at a residential school for boys, I was assigned a very difficult child who was quite aggressive. These aggressive tendencies were often directed at me during our sessions together, with items being thrown at me, things being thrown out the window, as well as his striking me. Through my strengths perspective, and a great deal of supervision, I was able to maintain my positive view of him, and allow him opportunities that most of society has denied him for much of his life. The difference in this boy is amazing. The therapeutic relationship that has come from this once tenuous situation is very strong, and has allowed him the chance to see that he can become connected to those around him and that he truly is not a bad person. This is a life lesson that I hope he is able to take with him in the future.

Three Major Tasks of Assessment

The following material addresses the three major tasks of assessment: (1) developing a rapport with the client that will facilitate his or her genuine engagement in the assessment process; (2) using appropriate theoretical constructs that allow the client and the practitioner to better understand the client's circumstances; and (3) setting goals, along with determining the appropriate interventions to employ.

Assessment Rapport

Although the topic of rapport is covered in depth in Chapter 4, it is addressed here specifically as it relates to assessment. Perhaps the essential ingredient in the process of doing social work at any level is the ability to truly relate to the client in a meaningful and genuine fashion. Rapport is especially essential in the assessment process. Clients have to believe that the social worker is interested in them and is willing to try to understand their feelings, behavior, and perceptions. According to Meyers (1993), "it is well-recognized that people will talk more openly to those whom they trust to hold their confidences, to pay attention to their story, to accept and to understand them" (p. 45).

It is not easy to develop rapport. The case discussed in Case Example 5.1 illustrates the need for the social work professional to be patient and willing to let the client–social worker relationship develop in a way that is meaningful to the client.

Review of Theories and Assessment Models

The following section discusses assessment from the perspective of different theoretical orientations. These orientations reflect the diversity of theories used in social work. In addition, the section introduces the *inner and outer forces model*, a structural assessment model that can be used by social work practitioners engaged in the assessment process.

CASE EXAMPLE 5.1

Developing Rapport with a Client

Gerik, a sixteen-year-old high school junior, was referred to Javon, the school social worker, because he had recently been fighting with his peers, was having trouble in school, and had been arrested for vandalism. Gerik met with Javon because the police had insisted on the visit. Javon was careful to allow Gerik to set the agenda in his first meeting and allow him to verbalize some of his feelings. Javon remained very nonjudgmental and offered the boy the chance to look at some of the difficulties in an open discussion. However, as Gerik began to sense that Javon was really listening to what he had to say and was willing to work with him in an honest, open fashion, it frightened him, and he defended himself by jumping up from his

chair and shouting, "I don't need no help from no one." It looked like Gerik was afraid of forming a close relationship. Javon remained calm and stated that he was willing to work with Gerik and would save an hour block of time each week for the next few months. Gerik again became angry and left the room, slamming the door behind him.

After two weeks, Javon called Gerik and told him he was still saving his time slot and hoped he would come in. Javon was a bit apprehensive the day of the next appointment, but Gerik did show up. After a few minutes of superficial dialogue, Gerik told Javon that no one had ever been interested in him as a person, and he didn't know how to re-

spond to someone who seemed to care.

Javon asked Gerik to help him with the assessment process so that he could understand what Gerik was going through. Gerik verbalized the many struggles he had with an abusive stepmother, a school system that had turned its back on him, and a local police department that was determined to "catch him breaking the law."

In our society, it is not unusual for people to feel alienated, and Gerik was one of those young men who did. Javon was able to develop a good rapport with Gerik and was able to jointly formulate a meaningful assessment and develop some realistic goals.

Inner and Outer Forces Model

Our inner and outer forces model (Farley, Smith, & Boyle, 2003, p. 47) allows for the inclusion of many of the theoretical constructs used by social workers. This model, shown in Figure 5.1, stresses the importance of focusing on the interaction that goes on between people and the context in which they live. It recognizes that inner and outer forces are a complex array of psychological and social events and gives some organizational structure to the assessment process.

This general assessment model has its roots in the work of early social work practitioners who looked at concepts such as "press and stress," with *press* meaning environmental focus coming from social situations and *stress* meaning personality structure. The

Figure 5.1

Inner and Outer Forces Basic Model

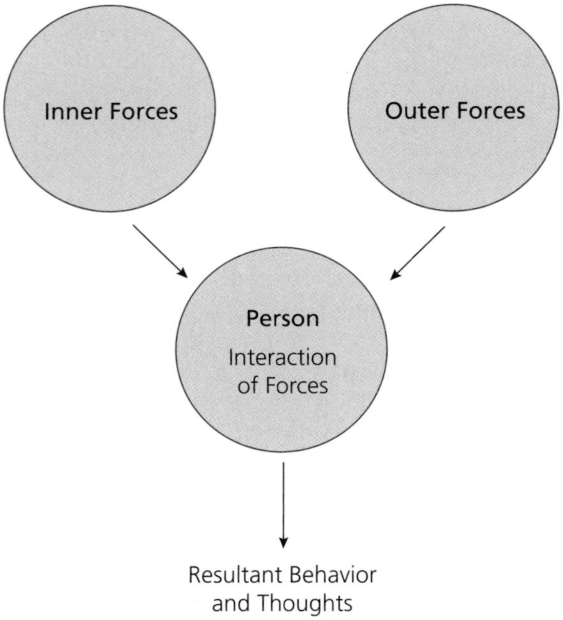

model was inspired by Kurt Lewin's (1951) force field theory, which suggested that all behavior and thoughts are affected by the (driving and restraining) forces prevalent in both the person and the environment. It is also consistent with the person-in-environment focus that is commonly employed in social work and helps social workers to conceptualize an integrative and multidimensional approach by examining potential inner and outer forces that are acting on a client.

One advantage of this model is that these forces can be applied to whatever theoretical construct or constructs social workers employ as their chosen therapeutic domain. For instance, a social worker who places emphasis on Erik Erikson's work and is helping an adolescent can relate both the inner and outer forces to Erikson's material on the task of developing an identity. A social worker committed to a strengths orientation can assess both the inner and outer forces to discover the client's strengths and to identify resources that will assist clients to achieve their goals.

The inner and outer forces model also serves as an aid for assessing complex human behavior. The basic assumption in the inner and outer forces model is that there are forces developed both within individuals and from their environment that influence how they behave, feel, and think. The exact origin of the forces may never be identified, but the important thing is to recognize that forces exist and that they are continually interacting to produce thoughts, feelings, and behaviors.

Because of the wide variation of client groups and the intense interaction among and between these groups, the social work profession has struggled to develop an assessment model that will provide an adequate foundation to assess the many life forces. The inner and outer forces assessment model is simply a way for both the client and the social worker to consider what forces are prevalent in the client's life. It can also be useful in assessing the inner and outer forces that help the person function and have the strength to cope with many problems.

The inner and outer forces model attempts to graphically and simply illustrate key ecosystem concepts. As quoted by Rauch (1993, p. 7), Siporin emphasized the appropriateness of an ecological perspective to social work practice by stressing that the ecological perspective:

1. Helps gain a larger, more unitary and comprehensive unit of attention, a holistic and dynamic understanding of people and the sociocultural physical milieu

2. Permits a strategy of multiple perspectives, a way of thinking about parts and wholes

3. Encourages a theoretically and technically eclectic approach

4. Is directly useful as an assessment instrument and is able to identify consistencies, conflicts, and complementarities in regard to particular systemic attributes

5. Is useful in treatment planning, helping to identify which actions to take to alter intersystemic relationships to optimize the goodness of fit

6. Encourages social workers to develop and use a strong and varied repertoire of assessment instruments and helping interventions because of its multifactorial nature

The inner forces can be defined as having three important sectors, designated as biological, psychological (emotional, behavioral, cognitive), and spiritual. The outer forces comprise two sectors, designated as social (family,

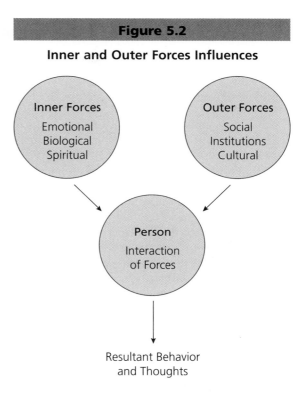

Figure 5.2

Inner and Outer Forces Influences

Inner Forces
Emotional
Biological
Spiritual

Outer Forces
Social
Institutions
Cultural

Person
Interaction
of Forces

Resultant Behavior
and Thoughts

community, institutional) and cultural (see Figure 5.2). Social workers may choose to interject into the model specific theoretical approaches, their knowledge of human behavior, any areas of specialized training, and experience as these apply to the needs of their clients. Social workers can use the inner and outer forces framework in several ways. The framework can assist in both assessing and helping clients cope with problems. The following history in Case Example 5.2 illustrates the assessment and treatment use of the model.

The inner and outer forces assessment model applied in Josh's case is shown in Figure 5.3. The social worker helped to reduce the negative outer forces and increased some positive inner forces, producing more functional

CASE EXAMPLE 5.2

Assessment Using the Inner and Outer Forces Model

Josh, seventeen, and the fifth of seven children, resided in a small rural community. He was referred to the mental health center because he was continually fighting, had received numerous speeding tickets, was doing poorly in school, and had beaten up his stepfather. As Josh described his problems, it was apparent to the worker that the outer forces in Josh's life were overpowering him. The school officials seemed to be set on expelling him, and the local police watched constantly for him cruising Main Street so they could give him a ticket or "harass" him. Josh's stepfather, an aggressive, anxious person, was trying to help Josh by, in his words, "tightening the screws" to make him straighten up.

Although the worker recognized the outer forces precipitating the present referral, consideration was also given to the inner forces influencing Josh's life. Josh admitted that he felt insecure because he had no plans for earning a living. He felt he was a failure in so many areas that he was almost panicked. These feelings of inferiority, insecurity, and anxiety were strong inner forces that required attention from the social worker.

Recognizing that the outer forces needed to be relieved before anything could be done to work on Josh's inner forces, the worker called meetings with school officials, police personnel, and Josh's family. After the worker explained the significant amount of negative pressure brought to bear on Josh by the outer forces, all the people involved agreed to work toward the goals of realistically reducing the pressure they were placing on him. Teachers set up tutorials for

him and gave him positive support. The police agreed to stop singling him out in an attempt to find a problem. This was the same consideration they gave the other young men in town who were not considered "troublemakers." The stepfather also agreed to relax his controls on Josh.

As the outer forces were reduced, Josh's behavior began to change, and he also began to function better in the community. The worker helped him address and change how he responded to some of the negative inner forces, such as feelings of inferiority, that also led to additional changes. Josh completed high school and went on to open an auto body shop in a nearby town. Eventually, he was recognized as a contributing and respected member in the community.

behavior in Josh. The inner and outer forces framework helped the worker assess Josh's problems and suggest a successful treatment course.

The Life Cycle and the Inner and Outer Forces Model

An important addition to the inner and outer forces assessment model is the concept of the life cycle. Theorists in the behavioral sciences recognize that there are stages of human development that seem to be universal. One simple developmental classification consists of childhood, adolescence, adulthood, and old age. Erik Erikson (1963), who adapted his formulation of a life cycle from basic Freudian theory, developed an eight-stage system of classification. At each stage, he identified a life cri-

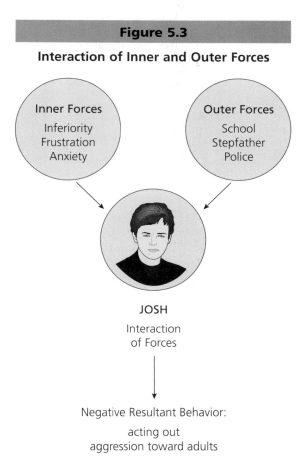

Figure 5.3

Interaction of Inner and Outer Forces

Inner Forces

Inferiority
Frustration
Anxiety

Outer Forces

School
Stepfather
Police

JOSH

Interaction
of Forces

Negative Resultant Behavior:

acting out
aggression toward adults

sis that needed to be overcome for a person to achieve a healthy ego. The ages of each stage, along with the associated crisis, are the following: (1) trust versus mistrust (0–1 years); (2) autonomy versus shame and self-doubt (1–3 years); (3) initiative versus guilt (4–6 years); (4) industry versus diffusion (7–11 years); (5) identity versus identity confusion (12–18 years/[adolescence]); (6) intimacy versus isolation (18–22 years/[young adulthood]); (7) generativity versus stagnation (23–65 years/ [middle adulthood]); and (8) ego integrity versus despair (65+ years/[old age]) (Berk, 2004).

The age range appearing next to the stage has been added to give the reader an approximation of the person's age at a given stage of development. Erikson's formulations are especially useful when combined with the inner and outer forces model, as shown in Figure 5.4. The representation of Erikson's eight stages of life, using the step configuration, provides a sense of climbing and also moving ahead one step at a time. The step diagram is used to illustrate Erikson's epigenetic approach.

With the superimposition of the life stages diagram on the inner and outer forces assessment model, the social worker can consider a person's problem from an organized, integrative approach. For instance, a child in the third grade is reported to be daydreaming too often and not completing his assignments. The child has been referred to the social worker. Using the model, the worker can ask the following questions:

1. What stage of life is the child in? What are the most important developmental tasks for the child at this time?

2. Is it inner, outer, or a combination of forces that seems to be causing the problems?

3. If it seems to be the inner forces, is the main problem in the psychological, emotional, biological, or spiritual realm, or some combination of these? Does the child have feelings of depression that prevent him from working, or does he have something wrong with his eyes that hinders reading? Does the child have a spiritual problem according to the cultural and religious beliefs of his family?

4. If the problem is mainly in the outer forces area, is the child having trouble

Figure 5.4

Inner and Outer Forces and Life Stages

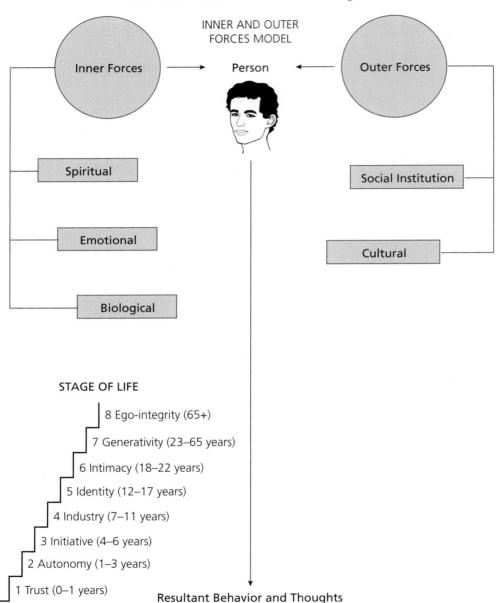

INNER AND OUTER FORCES MODEL

Inner Forces → Person ← Outer Forces

Spiritual

Emotional

Biological

Social Institution

Cultural

STAGE OF LIFE

8 Ego-integrity (65+)

7 Generativity (23–65 years)

6 Intimacy (18–22 years)

5 Identity (12–17 years)

4 Industry (7–11 years)

3 Initiative (4–6 years)

2 Autonomy (1–3 years)

1 Trust (0–1 years)

Resultant Behavior and Thoughts

in the family because of the impending divorce of his parents, a newly blended family, or an unsafe neighborhood with ongoing conflicts? In the cultural area, it might be discovered that the child's Hispanic parents speak only Spanish in the home, making it difficult for him to relate to class material written or spoken in English.

This series of questions that a social worker could ask about a client is shown in Figure 5.5.

Figure 5.5

Inner and Outer Forces and Life Stages: Applied to Child

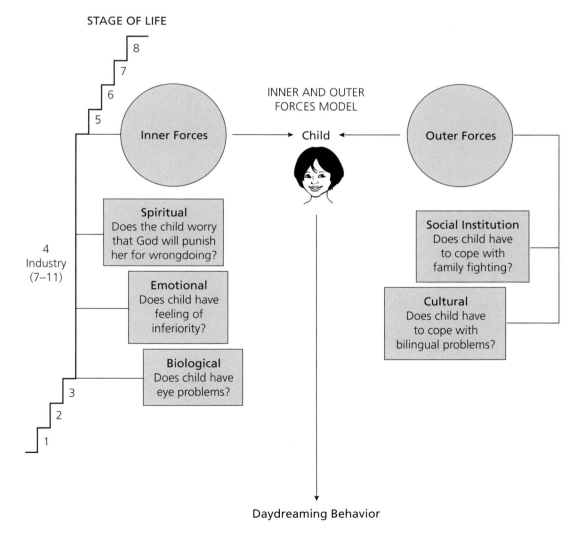

STAGE OF LIFE

INNER AND OUTER FORCES MODEL

Inner Forces → Child ← Outer Forces

4
Industry
(7–11)

Spiritual
Does the child worry that God will punish her for wrongdoing?

Emotional
Does child have feeling of inferiority?

Biological
Does child have eye problems?

Social Institution
Does child have to cope with family fighting?

Cultural
Does child have to cope with bilingual problems?

Daydreaming Behavior

Erikson's stage 4, industry versus diffusion, is highlighted because it most closely relates to the chronological age of the person being assessed. As the diagram is followed horizontally, the main systems of inner and outer forces are considered. This diagram can help social workers assess the problems in a logical fashion. Also, it can assist the social worker in looking across the individual's total experience.

Psychoanalytic and Ego Psychology Assessment

Lemma (2003) suggests that a number of things need to be assessed in psychoanalytic psychotherapy, including the following:

- Client's perspective on the problem or situation
- Client's motivation level
- Client's "internal world and the quality of object relationships"
- Characteristic and nature of the client–worker transference relationship
- Formal and informal networks available to the client
- Client's level of ego strength
- Degree of superego integration experienced by the client
- Nature of defense mechanisms employed by the client
- Level of client's development vis-à-vis character organization
- Client's ways of regulating affect
- Client's physical condition
- Client's culture, heritage, tradition, and related factors

Because psychoanalytic and psychodynamic approaches are more involved, the assessment tends to be more involved as well, ultimately leading to decisions by both the therapist and the client about whether this approach is best. According to assumptions underlying the theory, in order for psychological wounds to truly heal, the root source of the problem must be addressed. As such, psychoanalytic and psychodynamic assessments place primary emphasis on the past.

Many of the ideas of Freud and the ego psychologists who followed him are still used to some extent in social work assessment. Freud's ideas about the biological or instinctual influences of human behavior that had to be held in check by society have given rise to many different forms or protocols for taking social histories. Although there is much-deserved controversy about Freud's theories, evidence suggests that many social workers explore the client's past in order to determine "what went wrong." It is also quite evident that social workers are still interested in the life-stage development of individuals. The developmental stages of Erik Erikson (1963), a student of Freud, are also widely used in social work because they help focus on important areas of development within certain age brackets. Although Erikson used many of Freud's ideas, he minimized the biological instinct drives and neurotic symptomology and focused on the individual's healthy, adaptive qualities. He also believed that personality or human development was based on an "epigenetic process" in which certain personality tasks had to be accomplished at certain ages if the person was to acquire important life skills. If these skills were not acquired, clients must be helped to readdress them in order to solve their dysfunctional behavior.

The value of Freud's work for assessment has been repeatedly challenged. It is, for example, focused on deficits and dysfunctional or problem behaviors and often ignores client strengths. It also is based on a medical model that presupposes the existence of some underlying disease process. Moreover, traditional psychoanalytic models require treatment regimens that involve significant periods of time and therefore conflict with the dictates of managed care. The primary benefit of this work is the attention it pays to the importance of the ego, the value of doing social histories that identify resources and potential sources of help available to the client, and the utility of considering the role physical factors play in the client's well-being.

Behavioral Assessment

Behavioral assessment takes into consideration two significant areas of interest. First is the behavior emitted by the client. Is the client being aggressive, impulsive, or withdrawn; are they on or off task; are they attending to instructions that are being given, or preoccupied with some other stimulus? These behaviors, and many other possibilities, are identified as the target behavior or the behavior that becomes the focal point for change (whether to increase it or decrease it is based on the desired goal).

Once the target behavior is determined, the social worker will conduct a behavioral analysis. This step is to determine the baseline of the behavior. Essentially, this consists of measuring the frequency, intensity, and/or duration of the target behavior. In addition, the assessment also takes into consideration what is happening in the environment, specifically what antecedents and consequences occur around the target behavior. Is a child being prompted by someone or something prior to exhibiting a behavior? Also, what happens immediately following the target behavior? How do people or the environment react?

Recognizing these two areas of importance, the target behavior and its antecedents and consequences, behaviorists have sought to identify structured methods of assessing

these conditions. Merrell (2003) has identified three general categories for observing and recording behaviors. They include naturalistic observation, analogue observation, and self-monitoring.

The *naturalistic observation* method of behavioral assessment is the most direct method available. The assessor observes the client in his or her natural environment and attempts to do so with as little interference or disruption as possible. Typical environments might include a child in his or her home, at school while on the playground or attending class, or at day care. Although the introduction of a new person into the environment will influence how people respond, over time this presence may become less of an influence as the new person becomes integrated into the system.

The *analogue observation* method of assessment attempts to re-create as closely as possible the environment and circumstances in which the behaviors of concern occur. Most often this will take place in the social worker's office, in a laboratory (if research is being conducted), or in some other available setting. Because it is a re-creation of previous events, it inherently carries with it problems of bias, whether purposeful or not. Clients role-play certain situations and infer how they would behave. In this environment, the practitioner has the ability to alter or direct behavior change as a way of positively influencing clients. A key to this method of assessment is to re-create as accurately as possible the conditions of the natural setting. For example, if two brothers are frequently fighting over the attention of their parents, the conditions of the home environment (chairs, toys, and other distractions) ought to be re-created in the office to the extent possible.

With the *self monitoring* method, clients must first be taught to observe and record their target behavior. Then they are instructed to do the observations and recording on their own for a specified time period. One advantage of this type of assessment is that it can incorporate the client's thoughts that precede a valuable assessment device in the application of cognitive–behavioral therapy, especially as it relates to anger, anxiety, and depression. The reliability of the assessment is dependent on the client accurately observing and recording the behaviors as well as any covert changes.

Social Learning Theory and Assessment

Prominent learning theorists developed the construct that as we directly observe desired changes in a person's performance, we must infer that learning, an internal cognitive process, has taken place. In other words, people who have been able to positively change their responses to a particular problem or set of problems have learned to function more effectively.

Behaviorists have offered a much more positive view than psychoanalytic theorists because they insist that the problem area or maladaptive behavior is the problem rather than merely a symptom of an underlying disease. As a consequence, the individual has only to unlearn the maladaptive behavior and/or learn more functional behavior in order to solve the problem.

Social work assessments can use behaviorist theories. Client's overt behaviors are important to note in any assessment process. Also, the notion of imitation or modeling is important to understand as the client describes important people in his or her life. Finally, the social learning principle that inner and outer stimuli constantly interact to create psychological functioning is seminal to the social work assessment process.

Cognitive Therapy Assessment

Cognitive therapy deals specifically with thoughts. Thus, assessment in cognitive therapy looks at thoughts and thought patterns. Cognitive therapy focuses more on the recent past and the present rather than on the distant past (Simos, 2002). Therefore, the assessment is more "now" oriented. Following from that, Simos (2002) has pointed out some areas the therapist ought to examine during the initial assessment. This assessment helps produce "a comprehensive problem list of the major problems across many modalities that a client currently experiences" (pp. 9–10). These include:

- Work relationships
- Relationships with significant others, family, and friends
- Available networks and support systems
- Nutrition and substance usage
- Level of physical activity

Many social workers who implement cognitive theory use the depression, hopelessness, and anxiety inventories developed by Aaron Beck (Beck, 1995). These inventories help establish a baseline and give the social worker an idea of the client's mood, or affect. Willis and Sanders (1997) have written, "assessment involves full understanding of the presenting symptoms and underlying factors, allowing a clear direction for the therapy and establishment of a base-line from which the comparative outcome of the therapy can be measured" (p. 17).

With regard to assessment, Judith Beck (1995) recommends that "preparatory to the first session, the therapist reviews the patient's intake evaluation. A thorough diagnostic examination is essential for planning treatment effectively because the type of Axis I and Axis II disorders (according to DSM) dictates how standard cognitive therapy should be varied for the patient. Attention to the patient's presenting problems, current functioning, symptoms, and history helps the therapist to make an initial conceptualization" and develop an intervention plan (p. 26). Again, the therapist seeks information on the present problems.

Willis and Sanders (1997) do not see a DSM diagnosis as a necessary step in assessment. "The aim of assessment is not to 'label' or 'diagnose' the client but [to] reach some early, and therefore provisional, agreement on the issues to be worked on in therapy" (p. 70).

Assessment in cognitive therapy focuses on the present and recent past and looks specifically at how clients are functioning in the different areas of their lives. It provides an initial agreement about the direction the intervention will take. In using postulates from cognitive therapy, assessment is based on "how the individual perceives, interprets, and assigns meaning to that event" (Beck & Weishaar, 1995, p. 236). The social worker doing the assessment can watch for patterns in how the client thinks about life situations. This theory is useful in understanding why two people who are in the same situation, such as listening to an employer talk about needed improvements in the workplace, will interpret the presentation differently. One individual might believe the presentation was a positive challenge to help the company move forward, whereas the other might interpret the talk as being negative and designed to threaten employees.

Perhaps one of the most practical uses of the cognitive approach is in understanding depression (Beck, Rush, Shaw, & Emery, 1979). The theory presents a practical way of understanding the depression process. The practitioner considers the cognitive triad. The first component of the triad is directed at those irrational thought processes the client has learned or developed that declare himself or herself continually in a negative light. Second, the depressed person thinks that the "world" is treating him or her unfairly. Finally, the depressed person believes that his or her sad plight will continue indefinitely.

A second aspect of cognitive assessment is to examine a client's thoughts to determine if they are based on common "cognitive distortions" (Beck, 1995). Following is a list of twelve typical distortions:

- All-or-nothing thinking (seeing things as extremes, all good/perfect or bad/totally flawed)
- Catastrophizing (predicting the future and seeing it as bad)
- Discounting the positive (telling yourself that the good/positive things/qualities don't mean anything)
- Emotional reasoning (believing something just because you "feel" it is true while discounting contrary evidence)
- Labeling (globally labeling self/others)
- Magnifying/minimizing (evaluating self, others, or situation—unrealistically magnifying the negative or minimizing the positive)
- Mental filtering/selective abstraction (giving too much attention to a single negative detail, while missing the whole picture)
- Mind reading (believing to know what others are thinking without considering other possibilities)
- Overgeneralizing (drawing a negative conclusion beyond the current situation)
- Personalizing (believing others are behaving negatively because of something you said or did without considering other possible explanations)
- Using should/must statements (having a belief of how things absolutely must be

and, when these conditions are not met, overestimating how bad the results are)
- Having tunnel vision (seeing only the negative) (p. 119).

Cognitive assessment is useful in social work because it helps the social worker to be sensitive to faulty and consistent thought patterns that may be present in the client. Identification of problems in cognition will also point to treatment methodologies that can assist clients as they learn to process the world differently.

Person-Centered Assessment

The concepts of the person-centered therapy developed by Carl Rogers have had a major influence on social work practice and assessment. This model posits that human beings have a natural tendency toward self-actualization by moving toward the realization of their full potential. Rogers further declared that if the atmosphere of the therapist–client relationship contained the qualities of congruence or genuineness, unconditional positive regard, and empathy, the client would be able to direct his or her own thoughts, feelings, and behaviors toward self-actualization of more functional behavior.

Despite the ways in which this theory is consistent with social work values, key elements of the person-centered approach conflict with assessment methods traditionally used by social workers. A major conflict is Rogers's premise that clients will be able to assess themselves if the proper therapeutic relationship is established. This notion implies that social workers should not ask questions, have assessment formats, or in any way interfere in the process of relationship building. A second conflict occurs when the social worker attempts to formulate a clear definition of the problem.

Rogers largely rejected the practitioner's role in making professional evaluations, developing a prognosis, and guiding the client in any way. This perspective runs counter to the need for assessment that is evident in most social work areas such as public welfare, community mental health, aging, and corrections.

Despite these limitations, most social workers do accept the importance of establishing a positive relationship with clients prior to any type of assessment. Likewise, the notion that clients have the ability and strength to move toward self-actualization is prevalent throughout social work literature.

Systems Theory Assessment

The systems theory emphasis on understanding the interrelationship between systems and their environment and their subsystems provides a model that fits well with the person-in-environment focus of much of social work practice. The work of Carol B. Germain in blending aspects of systems theory and the ecological perspective has furthered social work's understanding of the behavior of systems of all sizes. Her ecosystems approach focuses on transactions between people and their environment. Germain, as cited by Robbins, Chatterjee, and Canda (1998), wrote,

> The evolutionary, adaptive view of people proposed in this model sees the adaptive achievements of individuals as the outcome of interaction between inherited genetic traits and environmental circumstances. The environment, which is physical and social and further characterized by time and space, can either support or fail to support the adaptive achievements of autonomy, competence, identity formation, and relatedness to others. As a life model, the ecosystems perspective focuses on life transitions such as

developmental stages and changes, external stressors such as unresponsive social and physical environments, and interpersonal stressors such as communication and relationship problems. (Robbins, Chatterjee, & Canda 1998, p. 34)

Systems and ecosystem theories have been useful in social work assessment because they help practitioners look at behavior in clients within the context of systems. Many times clients can improve their functioning by identifying which systems are dysfunctional and then effecting a change in those systems.

Another element of systems theory that is useful for assessment is the notion that people themselves are a system with subsystems that are designated areas such as "biological," "emotional," and "spiritual." These subsystems function as part of the individual's personality and are important to keep in mind while the social worker is doing assessments. Problems for individuals can occur at any level such as individual, group, community, or major societal systems.

Strengths-Based Assessment

The DSM-IV-TR, mentioned in the last section, is based on the medical model worldview that dysfunctional behavior is the result of the disease process and a "deficit-based understanding of human behavior as exemplified by psychopathology" (Graybeal, 2001, p. 233). The strengths perspective helps social workers and clients focus on strengths that can be used to resolve life's difficulties. Graybeal writes:

The strengths perspective (Saleebey, 1992, 1997; Weick, Sullivan, & Kristhardt, 1989) offers a set of guiding principles that shape the lens for viewing human behavior in a very different way. The fundamental premise is that individuals will do better in the long run when they are helped to identify, recognize, and use the strengths and resources available in themselves and their environment. This seems harmless enough, but as the author and his colleagues have witnessed, this simple idea can be seen as very threatening by some (Graybeal, Moore, & Cohen, 1995). Anecdotal information suggests that many have seen the strengths perspective as naive and simplistic, or that it denies advances in the understanding of psychopathology and a biomedical knowledge base and practice models (Saleebey, 1996). This is an unfortunate response, as the identification of strengths is not the antithesis of the identification of problems. Instead, it is a large part of the solution. (p. 234)

A strengths-based assessment helps social workers move away from focusing on problems, symptoms, and diagnoses. Instead, the practitioner emphasizes a client's strengths, resources, and successes. The "ROPES" model of looking for "resources, options, possibilities, exceptions and solutions" was developed by Graybeal (2001, p. 237). Along with the five areas of strengths, Graybeal's model also identifies where the focus is placed as well as providing questions to help both the client and the practitioner identify responses. Figure 5.6 reviews and adapts elements of the Graybeal model.

The strengths-based assessment process can also incorporate the concept of resilience. *Resilience* refers to the proposition that even though some individuals are raised in difficult environments or face formidable circumstances in their adult lives, they have the ability to recover from or adjust to the stress. It is important for social workers doing an assessment to remember the concept of resiliency and to take it into consideration with client systems.

Figure 5.6

Adaptation of the ROPES Model

- **R**esources—focus is on resources: (1) personal, (2) family, (3) social environment, (4) organizational, and (5) community.

  Questions include: What personal, family, friend or religious, organizational, or community, etc., resources/support systems do you have?

- **O**ptions—focus is on the present, with an emphasis on a person's choice.

  Questions include: What resources are available to help you achieve your choice now?

- **P**ossibilities—focus is on the future, with emphasis on imagination, creativity, a vision of the future, and play.

  Questions include: What have you thought of trying but haven't tried yet?

- **E**xceptions—focus is on when the problem was better, or less of a problem.

  Questions include: Are there times in your life when your difficulties are less of a problem?

- **S**olutions—focus is on constructing solutions, not solving problems.

  Questions include: What is working now and what new solutions can you create to solve your problems?

The concept of resiliency was developed by individuals such as Garmezy (1991) and Werner and Smith (1982) who studied children who remained functional and productive even though they had struggled while growing up in homes with extreme poverty or parents dealing with problems of alcoholism or mental illness. Ashford, LeCroy, and Lortie (2001) have summarized the qualities that help protect children against the adversities of life:

- Such children have good social skills; they have a positive mood and are friendly. Other people like them.
- They are able to interact with and engage other people. They approach and interact with adults outside the home. As a result, these children receive encouragement and support from teachers, other relatives, babysitters, and others.
- They possess good problem-solving skills. As a result, they acquire a sense of mastery and learn to think for themselves.
- They have specific interests and are usually very creative (p. 297).

Resiliency is also fostered in families that are fortunate to have an emotionally supportive social network or strong religious beliefs. The social worker needs to consider resiliency in assessment and help the family or individual client to consider the inner strengths they already have or may develop through their work with the social worker.

By the time many clients reach the social worker's office, they have been told many times and by many people that they aren't good enough, that they don't have what it takes, and that they are failures. Identifying and focusing on the client's strengths not only helps the worker in future dealings with the client, but also helps clients recognize those good qualities in themselves and begin to think in terms of assets rather than deficiencies. In the process of identifying strengths, the worker may need to pay special attention to anything he or she sees the client doing well. Workers often find themselves pointing out small or simple positive character traits or behaviors and emphasizing them. This may mean that the worker focuses on the fact that the client is coming in for help—a step in the right direction. Case Example 5.3 illustrates the use of strengths-based assessment.

Cowger and Snively (2002, p. 113) have developed the following guidelines for strengths-based assessment:

1. *Give Preeminence to the Client's Understanding of the Facts.* The client's view of the situation, the meaning the client ascribes to the situation, and the client's feelings or emotions related to that situation are the central focus for assessment.

2. *Believe the Client.* Central to a strengths perspective is a deeply held belief that clients ultimately are trustworthy. . . .

3. *Discover What the Client Wants.* There are two aspects of client wants that provide structure for the worker–client contract. The first is, what does the client want and expect from service? The second is, what does the client want to happen in relation to his/her/their current problem situation? . . .

4. *Move the Assessment toward Client and Environmental Strengths.* Obviously,

there are personal and environmental obstacles to the resolution of difficult situations. . . . Client strengths are the vehicle to creatively negotiate these obstacles. . . .

5. *Make Assessment of Strengths Multidimensional.* Multidimensional assessment is widely supported in social work. Practicing from a strength perspective means believing that the strengths and resources to resolve a difficult situation lie within the client's interpersonal skills, motivation, emotional strengths and ability to think clearly. The client's external strengths come from family networks, significant others, voluntary organizations, community groups. . . .

6. *Use the Assessment to Discover Uniqueness.* The importance of uniqueness and individualization is well articulated by Meyer (1976): "When a family, group or a community is individualized, it is known through its uniqueness, despite all that it holds in common with other like groups" (p. 176). . . .

7. *Use the Client's Words.* Professional and social sciences nomenclature is incongruent with an assessment approach based on mutual participation of the social worker and the client. . . .

8. *Make Assessment a Joint Activity between Worker and Client.* Social workers can minimize the power imbalance inherent between the worker and client by stressing the importance of the client's understanding and wants. . . .

9. *Reach a Mutual Agreement on the Assessment.* Workers should not have secret assessments. All assessments in

CASE EXAMPLE 5.3

Assessment Using the Strengths Perspective

Carlos, a thirty-three-year-old father, was court-ordered to receive in-home parenting services once a week because of a substantiated report of physical abuse against his nine-year-old daughter. At the first appointment with the in-home social worker, Carlos seemed quite depressed about his current situation, including the fact that his daughter would be living with her mother full time until he completed the parenting services.

The social worker observed that Carlos's living conditions were less than desirable. His home was clean, but quite old and sparsely furnished. Carlos confirmed the worker's suspicions that his financial situation was not what he would like it to be. He told the worker about his work at a local food processing plant and said that the company had been forced to lay off some of the workers because of a downturn in the economy. Many of the other workers' hours, including his, had been drastically cut. Until just before his layoff, Carlos had been working more than forty hours per week, but he was now scheduled to work only twenty-four. With the loss of so much of his former salary, he was struggling to pay his bills.

Carlos was remorseful as he told the worker about the night three weeks before when he had slapped his daughter's face several times following a disagreement. The abuse had been severe enough to leave bruises, and Carlos's daughter was immediately removed from his care.

Carlos told the social worker that he was concerned about his daughter's safety because her mother often worked a late night shift, and their daughter was left alone when a babysitter could not be found. He said that the night he hurt his daughter had been his worst day at work for as long as he could remember. Carlos began to cry as he told the worker that he didn't know what he needed to do to "make things right," but that he would do whatever it would take to be able to be with his daughter again.

The worker empathized with Carlos about his situation and told him she would like to brainstorm about some of his strengths for a few minutes. The worker told Carlos that she could see he was a hard

written form should be shared with clients. . . .

10. *Avoid Blame and Blaming.* Assessment and blame often get confused and convoluted. Blame is the first cousin of deficit models of practice. . . .

11. *Avoid Cause-and-Effect Thinking.* Professional judgments or assumptions of causation may well be the most

detrimental exercises perpetrated on clients. . . .

12. *Assess; Do Not Diagnose.* Diagnosis is incongruent with a strengths perspective. Diagnosis is understood in the context of pathology, deviance, and deficits and is based on social constructions of reality that define human problem situations in a like manner. . . .

CASE EXAMPLE 5.3, cont.

worker and that he really cared about his daughter. Carlos slowly nodded his head. He told the worker that he was good with cars and enjoyed working on them and that he had recently applied for a part-time position as a mechanic. She told him that his willingness to seek additional employment in order to alleviate the financial stress in his life was another strength.

The social worker then asked Carlos about his family and friends. Carlos told her that his mother and father lived in the same town and were very supportive of him. He also cited his siblings as being a support. Carlos reported that since his divorce, he had not had many friendships because most of his friends were also friends of his wife. He said that he had be-

come quite good friends though with a man at work who was equally worried about the future of his job. The worker encouraged Carlos to draw on these support systems for the strength he needed during this difficult time.

After more discussion, Carlos and the social worker focused on his motivation to get his daughter back and to have a steadier income. Carlos and the worker decided that Carlos's homework assignment would be to write down at least ten things that he was currently doing well as a person and as a father.

The homework assignment worked well. As Carlos met with the social worker and reviewed his list the following week, several practical approaches emerged. Carlos had

always been able to talk with his parents, and he determined he could build on this strength by sharing some of his struggles with them. The worker and Carlos both felt his ability to share with his parents could have possibly prevented his daughter's abuse that was triggered by his poor employment situation and anger toward his ex-wife. Prior to the abuse, Carlos had always spent quality time with his daughter, and he was determined to build on this strength by consciously planning quality times for the two of them in the future. He also recognized the need to work with and be more supportive of his former wife for the good of their daughter.

Other Assessment Models

Beyond assessment practices that follow specific theoretical perspectives, professionals are also confronted with specialized and commonly recognized protocols. This next section addresses some of those protocols that we believe to be important for social work practitioners to understand, especially as they collaborate with other helping professionals.

Diagnostic and Statistical Manual (DSM)

The first edition of the *Diagnostic and Statistical Manual of Mental Disorders* (DSM) was published in 1952. It was a variant of the *International Classification of Diseases* (ICD), sixth edition text, which contained the classification system used by the World Health Organization (WHO). In this ICD sixth edition, the WHO included for the first time a section on mental disorders (APA, 2000). When DSM-III was published in 1980, it contained significant changes from the two earlier editions. For the first time, the multiaxial diagnostic system was implemented, along with a nontheoretical approach to the classification of disorders. The focus has been placed on describing the features of each disorder, with no attempt being made to describe the possible causative factors, except when physical evidence warrants a definitive statement (such as in the case of dementia due to cerebrovascular disease). Further, DSM does not recommend treatment modalities. DSM is currently in the fourth edition, text revised (American Psychiatric Association, 2000).

The DSM-IV-TR is grouped into sixteen major diagnostic classes such as substance-related disorders, mood disorders, anxiety disorders, schizophrenia and other psychotic disorders, and personality disorders, to name a few. Within each of the sixteen diagnostic classes are found the specific disorders. For example, under the class of "mood disorders" are found the specific disorders of major depression, dysthymia, and bipolar I and II. DSM then lists and describes those predominant features that differentiate one disorder from another.

Since the DSM-III, a multiaxial system of assessment has been implemented; in the mental health field the purpose of this system is to ensure a comprehensive evaluation of the client that includes not only psychological or clinical disorders but also personality disorders, medical conditions, environmental problems, and a method or rating scale for a person's overall level of functioning. Axis I contains the "clinical disorders." These are all of the major disorders, except for mental retardation and personality disorders, that are found in the sixteen diagnostic classes of disorders, along with the section of "other conditions" that may be a focus of clinical attention.

It is assumed that the disorders noted in Axis I are of primary concern unless otherwise noted.

On Axis II are found the personality disorders and mental retardation. Prominent defensive mechanisms may be noted. The purpose for separating out these two disorders was to help ensure that they were evaluated as part of the assessment process.

Axis III was included to report any medical condition that has relevancy to the clinical disorders. It also helps to ensure coordinated treatment efforts for both. Medical conditions may directly affect a mental disorder, as in the case of toxicity from medication that causes delirium, or indirectly, as is often the case with chronic debilitating arthritis and depression.

Significant environmental or psychosocial problems affecting a person's mental disorder, treatment, or outcome are listed on Axis IV. Examples might include separation or divorce, loss of employment, poverty, separation due to military service, abuse, loss of a loved one, or lack of welfare support. This axis was strongly influenced by social workers, who wanted to include the person-in-environment perspective.

Axis V was also included as a way of assessing a person's overall level of functioning. The rating was made according to the Global Assessment of Functioning (GAF) scale (APA, 2000). The rating is often calculated according to two criteria. The first rating is based on the client's "current" level of functioning (or the interest level in the past two weeks). This rating is compared with the second rating, which assesses the client's "highest" level of functioning for a few months during the past year, the supposition being that the goal of treatment is to assist the client in regaining a previous high level of functioning. The rating may also be used to evaluate a client's progress in treat-

CASE EXAMPLE 5.4

Using the DSM

Joyce called the mental health clinic because she was contemplating suicide. She was given an appointment later in the day. At the appointed time, she met with the social worker.

After developing a beginning relationship with the social worker, Joyce noted that she had been feeling terribly sad during the past month and had been unable to study or complete any of her academic work in the community college. In addition, she had barely been able to keep her part-time job at the student union building. She mentioned several times in the interview that she had "no energy."

The social worker asked Joyce about her eating and sleeping habits. Joyce shared that she had not been eating properly and that she couldn't sleep. Actually, she had lost about fifteen pounds in the past few weeks. She had tried using sleeping pills to help her sleep, but they hadn't helped, and she had developed very persistent insomnia.

Finally, Joyce began to cry and told the social worker that she had seriously been thinking about suicide. In her difficult emotional outburst, she said she had been thinking that death would be much better than the struggles she was having.

The social worker believed that Joyce's situation was characteristic of a major depressive disorder found in the DSM-IV-TR. The disorder would be classified as an "Axis I as 296.23 Major Depressive Disorder, single episode, severe without psychotic features." No indications of any personality disorder were found, so no diagnosis was listed in Axis II. However, the social worker thought it best to have Joyce checked by either the clinic's medical team or her own physician to be on the safe side and rule out any Axis III (general medical conditions) diagnosis. Joyce was tested for hypothyroidism and was questioned about any medications she was taking that had side

effects mimicking depression. In her case, none of the other factors were found, and therefore no diagnosis was listed. When she was questioned about any changes in her environment, she reported that her fiancé of one year had decided to leave her for another woman four months ago. She had attempted to find out why but never felt she was given an adequate explanation, which left her feeling empty and confused. On Axis IV was listed estrangement/engagement ended by fiancé. On Axis V, her current GAF score was rated at 25, suggesting the seriousness of her suicide ideation. The highest level rating for the past year was listed at 85, after she reported that she was functioning well in all areas and had a wide variety of interests, with the exception of an occasional disagreement with her ex-fiancé that seemed to end on a positive note.

ment. Case Example 5.4 presents a case history of a person suffering from depression.

Task-Centered Assessment

Task-centered assessment is used in many settings and fits well with the problem-solving model. This kind of assessment is basically a set of guidelines for assessment and practice and is very useful for social work. Task-centered assessment was developed to help social workers conduct brief or time-limited treatment. This approach assists clients and guides social workers in defining those tasks the client consciously wants to complete in order to be able to resolve a problem(s). Both client and practitioner can then develop a "contract" or a plan of action as to how to accomplish the task. The basic construct of task-centered assessment is described in William Reed's work (1978):

> Both our initial and subsequent theoretical work has been based on the premise that the essential function of task-centered treatment is to help clients move forward with solutions to psycho-social problems that they define and hope to solve. The primary agent of change is not the social worker but the client. The worker's role is to help the client bring about the changes the client wishes and is willing to work for.
>
> The assessment process in task-centered practice is critical because it is here that the healing processes begin. People who are struggling and come to the social worker for help have to assess their own situation, with the assistance of the social worker, and define for themselves the tasks they need to accomplish to improve their situation. The emphasis is placed on the person's own problem solving ability. (p. 18)

Case Example 5.5 illustrates task-centered assessment and planning.

In task-centered helping, the worker focuses mainly on those things the client identifies as being a problem. Task-centered work is relatively short term and can be easily assessed by both the social worker and the client.

Substance-Abuse Assessment

Like other assessment models discussed in this chapter, substance-abuse assessment requires some special consideration and skills. Griffin

1993) states that the objectives of psycho-active-drug-involvement assessment include:

- To determine the existence, extent, and intensity of drug use
- To determine what psychoactive drugs are being used
- To establish the duration of the drug use
- To learn whether a coexisting mental disorder complicates the drug use
- To make appropriate treatment dispositions (p. 177)

Griffin notes that when doing drug assessments, social workers need to be aware of their own attitudes toward drugs and drug abuse. Moralism and hostility can impede the proper assessment of an individual struggling with addiction. The social worker's nonjudgmental attitude is especially crucial in building rapport with an addicted person.

Finally, direct questions are the keystone of assessment in this area. The drug abuser is a master at denial and minimizing the existence of abuse. Hepworth, Rooney, and Larsen (2002, p. 227) suggest that when interviewing clients, social workers should be direct and look for concrete answers about substance use. They further elaborate that "asking indirect questions tends to support the client's evasion and yields unproductive responses" (p. 227).

As the social worker assesses individuals suffering from addiction, the client's physical appearance can provide important clues to the severity of the drug use. Such things as neglect of hygiene, use of sunglasses to conceal dilated pupils, or unusual efforts to cover up needle marks give the social worker important information. Collateral reports from referring sources—family members, physicians, employers, or the court system—should also

CASE EXAMPLE 5.5

Using Task-Centered Assessment

Veronica, a thirty-year-old woman, immigrated to the United States from Mexico about two years ago, accompanied by her young daughter. Since then, she and her daughter had been living with her sister, brother-in-law, and their son. Veronica and her sister realized that the living situation was taking a toll on their relationship, and they both felt that Veronica and her daughter should move out.

Veronica contacted the Hispanic Community Agency and made an appointment. During her first appointment, she told the social worker that she needed to find a place to live. The worker asked Veronica about her income, her English language abilities, and how soon she thought she needed to move out of her sister's home. Veronica told the worker that she would like to move out within the next two months, that she had a part-time job that gave her about $400 of income a month, and that she didn't know very much English but really wanted to learn to speak it.

The worker told Veronica that she thought they could accomplish what they needed to do in two months so that she and her daughter could move out of her sister's home. The worker explained task-centered helping and that this intervention would be short term and would end when Veronica accomplished her goal of being more independent. The worker helped her outline the things that needed to be done before she could move out.

The first thing the worker suggested was for the two of them to make an appointment with the housing authority to see if she would be eligible for housing and heat assistance, and the worker told Veronica that she would go with her to translate. Veronica agreed, signed a release-of-information form, and waited as the worker called to make an appointment later that same week. She explained to Veronica that after their appointment at the housing authority, they would know whether she qualified for assistance and then they could look for an apartment.

The worker told Veronica where she could take English classes for free and gave her the assignment to call about the classes and see that there was someone there who could speak Spanish. Veronica agreed to call. The worker then asked Veronica if she wanted to keep the job she had or if she would like to look for a different one. Veronica said she only wanted to work part-time so that she could spend as much time with her daughter as possible and thought she should keep her current job. Veronica told the worker that she traded babysitting with a friend and that allowed both of them to work part-time without their needing to pay for babysitting.

The worker summarized everything they had discussed and told Veronica they would go over her budget at their next appointment. She reminded Veronica of her assignment to call about the English classes and gave her the phone number and name of the person she was to speak with. She confirmed the appointment date they had at the housing authority and made Veronica another appointment to meet with her the following week.

be emphasized. Case Example 5.6 describes the assessment of an individual suffering from drug abuse.

Elder Assessment

With the population of senior citizens on the increase, social workers are going to be called on to assess the elderly and to suggest ways to provide quality of life for them in the aging process. McInnis-Dittrich (2002) states:

> The assessment process gathers a wide variety of information about the quality of an elder's biopsychosocial functioning within the environment in which he or she lives not only from the perspective of the social worker conducting the assessment but from the viewpoint of the elder as well. A productive biopsychosocial assessment of an elder is a dynamic and interactive process. It utilizes the expertise of the social worker as a student of human behavior and the expertise of the elders about their own abilities to survive and thrive in the immediate environment. The information gathered in an assessment is used to pinpoint what, if any, services might improve the elder's quality of life. (p. 79)

It is important to recognize the need to include the elder and his or her family in the assessment process. Because many seniors come to the attention of service providers only in health care settings, there has been a tendency to use the traditional medical model as a conceptual framework in assessment of this population. In other words, the health of a senior is evaluated, medications are prescribed, and then living arrangements are made. Social workers practicing in the field of aging should recognize that even the prescribing of medications requires an approach that includes both the senior and his or her family. For instance,

the senior may not be willing or able to take the medications properly without the help of a family member.

Assessment of seniors requires the social worker to consider a broad spectrum of biopsychosocial forces. Kelley-Gillespie (2003) has developed a model of assessment that includes the following six major life domains: social well-being; physical well-being; psychological well-being; cognitive well-being; spiritual well-being; and environmental well-being (p. 19). Clearly, many of the identified domains overlap and have an impact on one another; however, they may help practitioners to focus on these important domains as they go through the assessment process. Attempts are under way by researchers in the field of aging to apply various measurement tools to further define the domains and to offer practitioners both quantitative and qualitative indicators of what is going on in the life domains of the senior.

Essentially, assessment of elders is a holistic approach. The logic of keeping a ninety-two-year-old woman in her own home may not seem sound, but when her feelings are genuinely considered, her whole quality of life might be well served by having her stay in her own home. For example, Verna was a ninety-two-year-old woman who had lived in her own home for over fifty years, the last thirty of which followed the death of her husband. She had always enjoyed taking care of her home and yard by herself, until the last ten years when she lost her eyesight because of macular degeneration. Her family wanted her to move in with one of them, but she insisted she wanted to stay in her own home. It was obvious to Verna's family that she would need help and support in cleaning her home, keeping a supply of food, and taking care of her yard, and they were willing to accept that responsibility. Verna

CASE EXAMPLE 5.6

Assessment of Substance Abuse

Ron, a twenty-nine-year-old male, was court ordered into substance abuse treatment because of his recent arrest for driving under the influence (DUI) of alcohol. This was his first arrest for DUI, but he did have a previous arrest for possession of an open container of alcohol in his car two years before.

Ron arrived at his first appointment five minutes early and was dressed in business attire. He was very congenial with the receptionist and others in the waiting room. He was met by Nalren, the social worker who would be doing his intake. Nalren showed Ron to a room and engaged Ron in a discussion about his job, his wife, and their young son. When Ron felt comfortable, Nalren began asking him questions about the arrest.

Ron said he normally didn't drink and that this was the first time he had driven while he was intoxicated. He commented that he had come home from a very rough day at work, had a disagreement with his wife, and had then gone to a bar alone. He said he didn't realize he was intoxicated and that he shouldn't have driven; otherwise, he said he would have called a cab. Ron stated emphatically that he didn't have a problem and that perhaps Nalren could just "sign off" the court order and not require him to come to any further counseling.

Nalren had worked in substance abuse for six years and knew that many times those using and abusing substances underestimated their use of substances. He operated from this assumption with Ron. He also realized the need to be direct, such as asking, "When did you last drink?" instead of "Do you think you have a problem with alcohol?" since substance abusers are accustomed to beating around the bush and evading questions about their problem. Nalren told Ron that it would be very important for him to understand his drinking problem and asked pointed questions about his alcohol use, including what typically led to his drinking and how much he normally drank. Ron was initially ambiguous in his answers, but after several minutes, he told the social worker that he normally drank a six pack most days after work. He also reported that he didn't drink as much on the weekends.

As the conversation continued, Ron shared that he had a very demanding job as a lawyer in the same firm where his father was a partner. He also mentioned that if he worked seventy hours a week, he would have the opportunity of being a partner when his father retired, in five years. He did not see what the big deal was about drinking that much because his father had drunk that much for years and had never had a problem. Nalren finished the intake with Ron and made an appointment for him to come in the following week.

In the social worker's written report of his intake with Ron, he concluded that because Ron typically drank after work he felt that would be a good time for Ron to come in for his weekly appointments. He also tried to involve Ron in Alcoholics Anonymous (AA) two additional evenings a week. Ron was also required to take random urine analysis (UA) tests that would occur six to ten times a month. For these random UAs, Ron would be called by the substance abuse agency and told to come in sometime within a four-hour period during that same day. If he failed to come, he would automatically be given a failing report.

accepted their help in a dignified way and always tried to do something positive for those who helped her.

Verna developed all kinds of "helps" around the home that allowed her to function. She had her furniture placed so that she could easily move around without tripping. She put food in certain places in the refrigerator and cupboards so that she could easily find the items she needed to prepare her own meals. She even kept a box of chocolates in a special place to offer guests who might visit.

Verna developed a cancer growth on her eyelid and was taken to the hospital for surgery. The surgery started a downward spiral in Verna's health, and she had to be placed in a care center when she left the hospital. After a short stay in the care center, Verna insisted on returning to her home. Two days after returning home, she told her family that she was "ready to go," and she passed away peacefully in her own home surrounded by her family.

Elder assessment requires social workers to use all their skill to include the senior and his or her family members in the assessment process. Assessment can be pivotal in helping seniors feel empowered and part of the process that will determine their quality of life.

Suicide Assessment

The problem of suicide seems to be on the increase throughout the world, and social workers need to be aware of the behavior patterns of individuals who may be contemplating suicide. Many young people who are at risk for suicide have had difficulty in childhood, adolescence, and young adulthood. Unresolved problems may culminate in suicide attempts.

Perhaps there is no assessment more difficult to make than trying to determine the potential for suicide in a client. Skilled practitioners must be aware of suicide indicators re-gardless of what the client says. The most prevalent themes presented by suicidal individuals are a sense of hopelessness and resignation. Also, two of the most observed behaviors are lack of ability to sleep and weight loss. Beck et al. (1979) describe the suicidal client's responses as follows:

- There is no point to living. I have nothing to look forward to.
- I just can't stand life. I can never be happy.
- I am feeling so miserable this is the only way I can escape.
- I am a burden to my family and they will be better off without me. (p. 214)

Many professionals believe the core of suicidal thinking links in some way to a sense of hopelessness and a deficit in the ability to solve problems. To assess these problems, many different assessment scales have been developed. Some of the more prominent scales have come from cognitive theory. Beck and Weishaar (1995) list some of their own more relevant scales in suicide research and assessment.

Beck has developed key theoretical concepts regarding suicide and its prevention. Chief among his findings about suicide risk is the notion of hopelessness. Longitudinal studies of both inpatients and outpatients who had suicidal ideation have found that a cutoff score of nine or more on the Beck Hopelessness Scale is predictive of eventual suicide. Hopelessness as a predictor of eventual suicide has been confirmed in subsequent studies.

Beck's work has generated a number of assessment scales for depression and suicide, most notably the Beck Depression Inventory, the Scale for Suicide Ideation, the Suicide Intent Scale, and the Hopelessness Scale. The Beck Depression Inventory is the best known of these. It has been used in hundreds of outcome studies and is routinely employed by social workers, psychologists, and physicians to monitor depression in their patients and clients (Beck, 1991, p. 235).

In addition to feelings of despair and hopelessness, other indicators may suggest a possible suicide threat. These indicators are previous suicide attempts; a realistic plan to commit suicide; a family history of suicide; substance abuse; and lack of support systems. The social worker should pay special attention to all of the suicide indicators, especially if they form a constellation of thought patterns.

Suicide rates in adolescents and young adults have been rising dramatically over the past few years. To address the problem of assessing suicide risk, the Adolescent Stress Inventory (ASI) (Griffiths, Farley, & Fraser, 1986) was developed. This inventory differentiates those adolescents who were referred to the hospital because of a suicide attempt from those who were referred to the hospital for medical problems. A discriminate analysis procedure produced the following eight items that differentiate the suicide-attempter's feelings of hopeless about the future: feeling I can't be helped; having thoughts about harming myself; feeling others are to blame for my problems; feeling unsure of my own self-worth; being unable to express my feelings well; having a negative attitude toward life; being fearful; and having thoughts about sex that bother me (Hepworth, Farley, & Griffiths, 1993, p. 61). In addition to these nine items, the suicide-attempters reported problems in the following areas: truancy, drug use, and alcohol use. They also reported problems with the amount of love or harmony in their homes and problems communicating with their fathers (Hepworth, et al., 1993). If the social worker determines that the person being assessed is at risk for suicide, he or she must be ready to mobilize the client's support system and arrange for a psychiatric evaluation and perhaps hospitalization. Suicide

assessment is a difficult situation because a human life is at risk. Suicidal ideation can be thought of as a cry for help and requires fast and thoughtful action on the social worker's part. Also, the practitioner must be aware of the efficacy of using both medication and counseling in the suicide prevention process.

Beginning to Set Goals in Assessment

The third major aspect of assessment is to engage the client in setting realistic goals. As mentioned earlier in this chapter, assessment is both a process and a product. In all elements of these processes, clients need to be encouraged to participate fully and to be able to define the goals they want to set or the direction they want to take in the therapeutic activities.

As noted in the introduction of the various theories and models, the goal-setting process may take on a different quality for each theoretical base. For instance, a person-centered assessment approach would allow and encourage clients to set their own goals completely. The behavioral assessment approach would require a more active participation of both social worker and client to identify the problem and then for the social worker to suggest a specific plan of intervention for the client to consider.

All of the theory summaries and models presented in this chapter have an underlying theme—the client must participate fully in setting the goals and incorporating these goals in his or her own personality structure. Social workers find it frustrating when a client refuses to set goals, but this may be precisely why the person has problems in the first place. The social worker needs to continue to build relationships with these clients and try to free them to deal with the goal-setting process.

The goal-setting process is a major part of planning for termination, which begins in the

Case Example

Mary Jones is eight years old and in second grade at Public School 43 in Megaville, California. Mary comes to school in dirty clothes and often falls asleep at her desk. She is behind in basic math and reading skills and has trouble seeing the board. Your supervisor has asked you to make a home visit to Mary's mother, Johanna, to assess what needs Mary has and whether services need to be provided to the family. When you call Mrs. Jones in the afternoon, it sounds like you have awakened her. You identify yourself as a social work student at PS 43 and ask if you could come out to the house to talk about Mary. Mrs. Jones asks if Mary is causing trouble again and you reply, "No, we've just noticed that she is somewhat behind in her reading and math skills and thought it would be good to visit with you about how to see that she does well in school." Mrs. Jones suggests that you come by the next day about 2:00 PM, and you agree to that appointment. The apartment is in the basement of an old 8plex. Many of the buildings surrounding the 8plex are boarded up and uninhabited. When you knock on the door, there is no answer. You knock again and finally you hear Mrs. Jones say, "I'm coming." Mrs. Jones appears at the door in a bathrobe tied tightly around her waist. It has several stains on it and holes that look like cigarette burns. She asks who you are and you say, "I'm Sara Barnes from the school. We made an appointment for today?" "Oh, yah, come in. I guess I forgot. Sorry about the mess. We just moved in about a month ago and I haven't unpacked much." Mrs. Jones opens the door and invites you in.

Critical Thinking Questions

1. Using the inner and outer forces model, how would you proceed during the interview?
2. Develop a group of questions that you would want to ask.
3. How would you end the interview?

Practice Activity

Working in groups of three, identify who will be the social worker, the mother, and the observer. Using the questions the social worker has developed before class, have the social worker move through the interview gathering information. At the end of the interview, all three group members will then develop an assessment of Mary, using the inner and outer forces model. The interview should take 30–40 minutes, with the development of the inner and outer forces assessment using another 20–30 minutes. Once the task is completed, the observer should be prepared to present the assessment to the class.

Critical Thinking Questions

1. What did you learn from this activity?
2. If you were the social worker, how effective were your questions in getting the information you needed?
3. If you were the observer or client, are some of your questions as effective or less effective than the questions asked by the social worker?
4. As the client, did you feel heard, understood, or valued?

early phase of treatment. To improve social functioning, the individual needs to have the capacity to both set goals and carry them out. Both the client and the practitioner need to assess the inner and outer forces that are acting on the client and then set goals to change the biological, psychological, and environmental systems. Next to the importance of developing a rapport with the client, the goal-setting process, followed by the selection of the appropriate interventions and techniques, is at the heart of direct social work practice. The goal-setting process is addressed in depth in Chapter 6.

SUMMARY

The material in this chapter introduces the new social work practitioner to the concept of assessment. Assessment is a vital part of social work and can be considered both a process and a product. It remains a process the entire time the social worker interacts with the client; but at various decision-making times, assessment becomes a product that directs planning and intervention.

Assessment requires social workers to have the ability to develop a good working relationship or rapport with clients and an understanding of the theoretical lens or model they are using in assessment. Assessment also ushers in the beginning of the goal-setting process so critical for planning. The task of assessment in social work is difficult because the profession deals with people and the social context in which they live. It is no chance occurrence that social work education has a core sequence titled "Human Behavior and the Social Environment" to try to deal with the complexity of human behavior and problems. Material in this chapter highlights the important role of this sequence.

The chapter also includes a simple structural model called *inner and outer forces* to encourage beginning practitioners to organize their

thinking process in assessment. Also, other assessment paradigms such as the DSM, strengths-based, and task-centered assessments are introduced as a way to help social work practitioners and students understand that the lens they use to view the process of assessment is probably a combination of the various theories that have become popular throughout the years.

Finally, a section in the chapter is devoted to the important process of goal setting in assessment. Individuals who have problems and come to the social worker for help need a consistent and supportive atmosphere to help them set their own goals and become more functional.

We have selected only a few basic theories to present in this text. However, social work students can use this introductory material as a way to guide the development of their own theory base, which is essential in the assessment process.

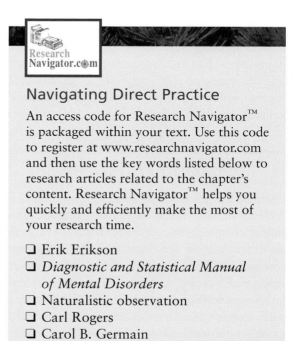

Navigating Direct Practice

An access code for Research Navigator™ is packaged within your text. Use this code to register at www.researchnavigator.com and then use the key words listed below to research articles related to the chapter's content. Research Navigator™ helps you quickly and efficiently make the most of your research time.

❑ Erik Erikson
❑ *Diagnostic and Statistical Manual of Mental Disorders*
❑ Naturalistic observation
❑ Carl Rogers
❑ Carol B. Germain

Chapter 6

Knowledge and Skills for Planning

■ Chris Sharp was a thirty-five-year-old elementary school teacher. Never married, he had taught sixth-grade students for ten years. Chris had always been in control of his life, or so he thought. Then everything seemed to change in a hurry. His retired father had a heart attack, his mother fell and broke her hip, and a long-term relationship he had enjoyed with a woman who taught in the same school district suddenly ended. Chris never thought he would need counseling, but all of a sudden his life seemed to be unraveling before his eyes. He was having trouble sleeping at night and felt a sense of sadness that he had never experienced before. Cautious by nature, Chris was somewhat suspicious of counselors and didn't have much regard for people who couldn't manage their own affairs. He reluctantly called the local mental health center and made an appointment with a social worker.

It is not unusual for clients to feel the same way Chris does in the chapter-opening case example. Many clients seek counseling services only as a last resort and then proceed cautiously, primarily because they have no idea what counseling is all about or what to expect from the experience. Through the processes of engagement, clients become more comfortable with the social worker and begin to share their fears and concerns. Although initially the practitioner is very much a stranger and clients find it difficult to acknowledge that they have lost control over some aspect of their lives, this subsides as they continue into the assessment phase. By the time they begin the planning phase, clients are often ready to move to a different stage. Some clients may still be troubled about the seriousness of their problems and fear they will require months of therapy. Others who were initially concerned that sharing painful secrets will diminish them in the eyes of the social worker will be relieved by the acceptance, nonjudgmentalism, and compassion shown by the worker. Experienced social workers will anticipate these concerns and make every attempt to see that the experience is "user-friendly." One way to make the planning phase of counseling more user-friendly is by developing and following a counseling contract or agreement that is usually negotiated in the first or second session of counseling. The counseling contract is always preceded by a detailed assessment of the services the client requires along with the services that can be provided to the client by the social worker and the agency.

Counseling Contracts

Barker (1999) defines a **contract** as "a written, oral, or implied agreement between the client and the social worker as to the goals, methods, timetables, and mutual obligations to be fulfilled during the intervention process" (p. 103). This definition captures two important characteristics of a contract: it is (1) an agreement between two or more parties and (2) a verbal understanding or written document. A counseling contract will usually have these two characteristics: an agreement between the client and the social worker that is a verbal understanding or a written document.

The word *agreement* has at least four related meanings: (1) the act of agreeing; (2) harmony of opinion, accord; (3) an arrangement regarding a method of action, a covenant; and (4) a properly executed and legally binding compact (*The American Heritage College Dictionary*, 2000, p. 26). A counseling contract is reached when the client and social worker agree to work together on specific goals or problems and concerns. This agreement is the end result of a series of discussions between the client and the social worker regarding what services might be beneficial to the client. This series of discussions is often concluded at the end of the first session of counseling, although it is not unusual for the client and social worker to have two or three sessions before an agreement is reached. The first two or three sessions of counseling are also used to assess the client's strengths and limitations and problem-solving skills. This assessment is crucial in helping the social worker and client design a treatment plan that can be completed successfully while also meeting the client's needs.

A counseling agreement is also a "harmony of opinion or accord" in which the client and social worker agree to work on the same goals or problems and concerns. In the discussions that eventually lead to a counseling agreement, the client will identify a number of goals or problems and concerns. The social worker in turn might add to this list by identifying additional goals or problems and concerns that the client has not considered. For example, the social worker may believe that because of the client's violent past behavior, anger management training should be a goal of counseling. When the social worker identifies

this goal, the client may or may not agree that it should be part of the contract. If the client doesn't share the social worker's point of view, the anger management training goal should not be part of the contract because there isn't harmony of opinion or accord between the client and the social worker. If in subsequent sessions the social worker still believes that anger management training should be reconsidered as a goal, this belief should be discussed again with the client.

An agreement is also "an arrangement regarding a method of action or a covenant." In the contract, the client and social worker agree to work on specific goals or problems and concerns. They should also agree on how these goals or problems and concerns will be resolved. This "arrangement regarding a method of action" implies that the social worker will use his or her knowledge and expertise to help the client while the client agrees to work diligently on his or her goals or problems and concerns. The arrangement should also identify the treatment methods to be used in counseling, such as improving communication skills, developing problem-solving techniques, participating in anger management training, and other methods of action. The client's agreement on methods of action should include working on goals or problems and concerns during each counseling session and between counseling sessions. In other words, the client's methods of action include working diligently during counseling sessions as well as completing specific tasks and activities between counseling sessions that focus on agreed-upon goals or problems and concerns.

An agreement may also be viewed as a "properly executed and legally binding compact." By accepting money from the client, the social worker agrees to provide a service that is equal to and consistent with the fee being charged. By continuing to pay the social worker's fee, the client acknowledges that the services being rendered by the social worker are fair and reasonable and acceptable to the client. The fee-for-service agreement is an exchange of resources. Clients agree to pay for a service they cannot provide for themselves, while the social workers render a service commensurate with their knowledge and expertise. On the other hand, a counseling contract is considered much less binding than a legal contract.

Skills in Developing a Contract

In general terms, the contract between the client and the social worker will include the following:

1. Goals or problems and concerns to be addressed in counseling
2. The treatment methods that will be used to accomplish the goals or address the problems and concerns
3. Number of counseling sessions required for goal accomplishment or problems and concerns resolution
4. Cost of counseling services

The first step in negotiating the contract is identifying the goals or problems and concerns that the client wants to focus on in therapy. One way to begin this discussion is to ask the client to describe his or her current problems and concerns. Many clients can describe their problems and concerns readily or without much hesitation. In their frustration, they often blurt out a series of problems and concerns such as a husband or wife who doesn't understand or appreciate them, an employer who is too demanding and difficult to work with, or a teenage son or daughter who is out of control. For those clients who can't readily identify their problems and concerns, the so-

cial worker can facilitate this discussion by asking them to talk about various aspects of their life such as their family, work, friends, and so forth. Another approach is to ask the client why he or she is here today and what the client hopes to accomplish in counseling. This approach is particularly helpful in identifying, from a client's point of view, the purpose of counseling.

If the client and social worker focus only on problems and concerns, the therapy experience tends to be more negative than positive. One way to instill a more positive note into the therapy experience is to ask the client to list some of the goals that he or she would like to accomplish with the help of the social worker. Goals have a more positive focus than problems and concerns and can include behaviors such as going back to school, learning how to communicate more effectively, pursuing a hobby, or getting more involved in the community through volunteer activities. Another way to establish goals with the client is to ask what positive changes the client would like to make in his or her life. This shift to a positive focus helps mitigate the negative focus that often characterizes the beginning phases of therapy and promotes an important growth and development component in counseling. We strongly believe that the focus of counseling with clients should include goals as well as problems and concerns.

The contract should also identify the treatment methods the social worker will use to help the client accomplish goals and resolve problems and concerns. One treatment method used by many social workers in a variety of treatment settings is cognitive therapy (Robbins et al., 1998). A basic concept of cognitive therapy is the belief that what people think about themselves affects how they feel, and how they feel affects in a significant way their behavior. In *Cognitive Therapy of Depression* (1979), Aaron Beck states that people who are depressed often think about themselves, their world, and their future in negative terms. In cognitive therapy, the social worker helps clients to examine their thought patterns by identifying their negative self-statements, labeling these negative self-statements as specific cognitive distortions, and then helping clients substitute more positive and rational self-statements. In implementing cognitive therapy, the social worker usually has clients keep a daily journal of their self-statements. They then use these journals to examine and correct how these self-statements may affect their feelings and behavior.

Another treatment method many social workers use is the psychodynamic model (Robbins et al., 1998). The psychodynamic method is based on the belief that early life experiences, especially those in infancy and childhood, can have a significant effect on a person's behavior as an adult. A social worker who uses the psychodynamic method will help clients identify and explore how their early life experiences may be affecting their current behavior. For example, a young woman who grew from birth to adulthood in a single-parent family with few male role models might have limited ability to deal with men. Using the psychodynamic method, the social worker would help the client to identify the defense mechanisms such as denial and rationalization that she is using to deal with her world and to explore whether these defense mechanisms are working to her advantage.

The counseling contract should also include the number of sessions that will be required for the client to accomplish goals or resolve problems and concerns. Most public and private counseling centers are using a form of brief treatment in which therapy is limited to six to eight counseling sessions (Farley et al., 2003). During these six to eight counseling sessions, the client and social worker focus on the goals or problems and concerns the client has identified. In many instances, it is reasonable to expect that significant progress can be made in six to eight sessions to help the client accomplish goals or resolve problems and concerns. For example, a couple who wants to communicate more effectively with each other should be able to accomplish this goal in six to eight sessions. This is also true of many other goals such as learning to manage money more effectively, planning a career, and improving parent–child relationships.

Sometimes the client identifies goals or problems and concerns that cannot be accomplished or resolved in six to eight sessions. When this is the case, the client and the social worker can consider at least two options. One option would be to extend the contract for two or more sessions. Many public and private agencies offer this option, although some managed care programs will authorize only six to eight sessions (Farley et al., 2003). When the contract can't be extended beyond six to eight sessions, client and social worker should incorporate a termination plan that enables the client to work on goals or problems and concerns after counseling has ended. This termination plan might include reading self-help books, participating in community education programs, and other activities the client can pursue following the termination of counseling services. This is a desirable outcome because clients should be continually involved in activities that will improve their lives even after counseling has ended.

The cost of counseling services can vary significantly (Farley et al., 2003). Some public agencies do not change clients counseling fees. Every state has a department that provides free services to children and families. In the state of Utah, for example, the Department of Children and Family Services provides free of charge a number of services, including foster care, protective services, and adoptions, that have an important counseling component. Other public agencies such as alcohol and drug treatment centers may use a sliding scale for the services they provide.

In managed care programs, counseling services are generally part of an overall health care package that the client pays for through annual premiums. When the client receives counseling services from a managed care program, the financial arrangements may vary. Some programs charge no additional costs beyond the annual premium that covers these and other health care services, whereas other managed care companies require a co-pay that can vary up to 50 percent of the cost of services. Sometimes managed care programs charge an additional fee for extra counseling sessions beyond the standard contract of six to eight sessions. Still other programs use a sliding scale based on the client's annual income to charge for these additional services (Farley et al., 2003).

Some clients pay for counseling on a fee-for-service basis that is not covered by either a regular insurance policy or a managed care program. When this occurs, the fees charged can vary considerably. Some private therapists use a sliding scale so that each session costs between $20 to $100 depending on the client's annual income. Other therapists charge a standard fee of $100 or more for each session regardless of the client's annual income. If the client plans on having an insurance company pay the social worker, some social workers will charge the fee that is authorized by the insurance provider and wait to be reimbursed when the claim is processed. Other social workers

expect the client to pay for each session and then submit an insurance claim for the client to be reimbursed at a later date.

The counseling contract is finalized with a verbal agreement or written document. Some social workers prefer to finalize the contract on an informal basis, with the client verbally agreeing to work on specific goals or problems and concerns. This verbal agreement between the client and the social worker also includes what treatment methods will be used, how many counseling sessions will be provided, and what the cost will be for each session. After the client has verbally agreed to this contract and the session has ended, the social worker will often write the pertinent information down on a form provided by the agency. This form formalizes the client's agreement with the social worker and the agency and becomes the client's case file.

Some therapists ask the client to not only verbally agree to the agreement but also to affirm that understanding by signing a written document. The written document signed by both the client and the social worker includes what goals or problems and concerns will be addressed, what treatment methods will be used, how many sessions will be provided, and the cost of each session. Some therapists prefer a signed document because it formalizes the counseling contract and reminds both the client and the social worker that they have entered into a formal agreement. The signed agreement can also help both client and social worker maintain a focus for the subsequent six to eight sessions. It is generally advisable to give clients a signed copy of this contract for their personal records and for a review of what will be happening in counseling.

The contract is usually completed by the end of the first counseling session. Sometimes an additional session will be needed to finalize the contract. If a contract has not been finalized by the end of the second session, the lack of readiness on the client's part may be a sufficient reason to discontinue services. In beginning the first session of counseling, the social worker might begin by saying:

> Chris, as we get started, I want to talk to you about what I hope we can accomplish together today. To begin with, I want you to discuss briefly some of the goals or problems and concerns that you would like me to help you with. Then we'll make a list of these goals or problems and concerns and rank them from the most important to the least important. After we have ranked your goals or problems and concerns, then we'll identify the three or four that are the most important and then sign a contract to work on these goals or problems and concerns for the next six sessions. If more time is needed after we have completed six sessions, we'll contract for additional sessions. How does that sound to you?

This short-term goal– or problem and concern–oriented approach to counseling is used today by many social workers and was introduced to the social work profession by William J. Reid and Laura Epstein in their text *Task-Centered Casework* (1972). In this book, Reid and Epstein explained an integrative counseling model that allowed the client and the social worker to focus on specific goals or problems and concerns during therapy. This focus on goals or problems and concerns removed much of the ambiguity of what counseling was all about and led to a written contract that became the basis of what constituted "therapy."

In *The Task-Centered System,* William J. Reid (1978) further refined the task-centered approach to counseling. In the preface, he summarized the main focus of the task-centered approach:

> The task-centered approach is a system of social work practice designed to help people with problems of living. Clients are helped to solve problems through their own actions, or tasks, which they select, plan, and carry out with the assistance of the social worker. The service offered is short-term, structured, and empirically based. (p. ix)

This statement emphasizes three important characteristics of the task-centered approach. To begin with, the model focuses on problems of living that the client identifies. Second, clients are helped to solve their problems of living through their own tasks or actions. And finally, the model is short term and has a strong empirical base. The task-centered approach focuses on the client and what the client wants to change or accomplish in his or her life.

In describing the "problems of living" that are the focus of the task-centered approach, Reid (1978, pp. 35–35) identifies the following: (1) interpersonal conflict, (2) dissatisfaction in social relations, (3) problems with formal relations, (4) difficulty in role performance, (5) decision problems, (6) reactive emotional stress, (7) inadequate resources, and (8) psychological or behavioral problems not elsewhere classified (see Figure 6.1). All of these are problems of living that many people experience in their lifetime. They are also problems of living that can create considerable emotional stress and behavioral problems.

Once the client has identified with the social worker the problems of living that will be addressed in counseling, the task-centered approach focuses on identifying and implementing psychological and behavioral tasks that will help to resolve or ameliorate the specific problems of living. These tasks are actions the

Figure 6.1

Reid's Problems of Living

Reid (1978) has identified several categories of problems experienced by clients that occur in the process of living. Although an individual or family may experience any one of these problems, it is just as likely that more than one will be identified in the process of assessment. For example, a parent having interpersonal conflict with the other parent may also be experiencing difficulty with role performance.

- **Interpersonal conflict:** This includes marital discord, parent–child relationship problems, and other personal concerns.

- **Dissatisfaction in social relations:** This involves a focus on clients' sense of who they are and what they believe is lacking in their life, such as not having enough friends or being uncomfortable around others.

- **Problems with formal relations:** Included here are difficult relationships the client is having with institutions such as the police, the courts, or the school system.

- **Difficulty in role performance:** This focuses on a particular role the client is having problems adequately fulfilling. This might involve having difficulty in the role of being a father to a sixteen-year-old son or being a partner in a gay or lesbian relationship.

- **Decision problems:** These include issues such as whether to marry or whether to go back to school in which the client is having difficulty making decisions or making good decisions.

- **Reactive emotional stress:** This refers to crisis situations, such as the death of a parent, spouse, or child, that impose intolerable stress on the client.

- **Inadequate resources:** This includes the lack of money, housing, clothing, or some other specific resource.

- **Psychological or behavioral problems not elsewhere classified:** This refers to such problems as alcoholism and drug dependence.

client takes with the support and encouragement of the social worker. For example, a client may identify as a problem of living a lack of adequate financial resources. As this problem of living is examined, it may become clear that the problem isn't a lack of money but how money is budgeted and managed. A task that the client agrees to complete with the social worker is reviewing how much money he or she spends each month and for what items and activities. A follow-up task would be to plan a monthly budget that will help the client spend only the money that he or she chooses based on the client's fixed and variable expenses. The

client and the social worker plan and implement similar tasks or activities for other problems of living.

The task-centered approach generally lasts from six to twelve sessions, depending on the client's problems of living. A reasonable approach is to start with six or eight sessions and then contract for additional sessions as needed. This time-limited approach supports the short-term treatment policies that are followed today by many managed care programs (Farley et al., 2003). Another important feature of the task-centered approach is the empirical base that supports the model. A significant part of the early empirical base focused on the effectiveness of the task-centered model in social service agencies in the Chicago area during the 1970s. Farley et al., (2003) and other authors describe in detail more recent empirical studies that support the task-centered approach.

The Importance of Contracts

Contracts are an important part of everyone's life. They are agreements we make with people and with organizations. Some contracts are written down in formal documents, whereas others are verbal agreements that we make with a handshake or a nod of the head. Contracts follow us from the cradle to the grave. Couples sign a contract that gives legitimacy to their marriage and to any children the relationship might produce. Young children contract with their parents to perform certain household tasks in exchange for a weekly allowance. When these same children become adolescents, they contract with the state to follow certain rules and regulations in order to obtain a driver's license. Later as adults they contract with credit unions and banks to purchase automobiles and homes. These same adults will also contract with mortuaries later in life to finance funerals and burials.

Contracts are agreements that include outcomes or consequences. The agreement usually states that if you keep the contract by doing what you say you will do, a specific outcome or consequence will occur. If you agree to pay your home mortgage for twenty years, the home will be yours in twenty years, free and clear of any liens on the property. If you don't pay your home mortgage, the credit union or bank will probably foreclose on the property and you will lose your home. Contracts always spell out outcomes or consequences that are crucial in getting and in maintaining a person's interest in the contract. Most people would not

whimsically enter into a contract that involves a significant time and money commitment, such as purchasing a home over a twenty-year period.

Contracts in counseling are important for many of the same reasons (Hutchins & Vaught, 1997). A counseling contract helps to get and to maintain the client's commitment to improve his or her life. By agreeing to the contract, the client promises to meet the terms of the contract to the best of the client's ability. The client's promise is forged by the contract itself and by the experiences the client has had with other contracts. By agreeing to the contract, the client promises to work with the social worker to improve the quality of his or her life. The operative word here is *work,* because to reach his or her goals the client must take specific steps or actions. At the end of the contract period, the client will have worked to achieve a better life through this joint effort with the social worker.

A counseling contract helps to get and to maintain the client's attention. Like all other contracts, it impresses on the client the seriousness of the agreement the client is making with the social worker and why it is essential that the client abide by the contract if he or she is to realize the desired outcomes or consequences. The bane of all social workers is working with unmotivated clients, clients who for whatever reasons don't want to work to improve their lives. Contracts will not automatically cure this problem, but they will help impress on clients the seriousness of the agreement they are making, especially the part that says clients will work with the social workers. Clients who work to improve their lives, clients who keep their counseling contracts, are the clients who make better lives for themselves. A counseling contract incorporates many of the basic principles of learning theory and provides the client with an educational experience in which tasks and activities are negotiated, designed, implemented, and evaluated by the client and the social worker (Robbins et al., 1998).

In *The Task-Centered System,* Reid (1978) states that contracts with clients have one essential purpose and that is "to set forth explicit agreements between practitioner and client on what is to be done and how" (p. 133). These explicit agreements include the problems of living that will be the focus of counseling; a ranking of the problems of living that identifies the problem to be addressed first in treatment; and the duration of services, including the cost and number of sessions. Reid goes on to say that he prefers oral over written contracts because they save time and are less formal. He does acknowledge, however, that written contracts are preferred when the counseling agreement involves multiple problems of living as well as multiple participants such as an extended family.

The initial contract is usually formulated by the end of the first or second session of counseling. During the course of treatment, the initial contract may have to be modified for a variety of reasons (Reid, 1978). For example, in later sessions a new problem of living might arise that was not identified in the initial contract, such as the death of a loved one. When this occurs, the new problem of living should be added to the initial contract. Often the seriousness of this new problem may require the client and the social worker to change their treatment focus from a problem that was identified in the initial contract to the new problem of living. Sometimes the initial contract has to be modified because the client was too embarrassed in the first session to tell the social worker what the real problem or concern is. The client was afraid his or her disclosure

would shock, disappoint, or even anger the social worker. Now that the client feels more confident that the social worker won't judge him or her too harshly, the client is able to discuss with more freedom what he or she is really concerned about. Or the client may delay telling the social worker about all of his or her concerns until the client has gained more confidence in the social worker's ability to help. This often occurs with clients who have had previous experiences with social workers that were not very successful.

In the task-centered approach, the client identifies problems of living and later ranks them in terms of importance. For example, in the first session a client may identify three problems of living that he wants to address in counseling. One problem of living is classified as interpersonal conflict and focuses on the fractured relationship he has with his wife. Another problem of living is difficulty in role performance and centers on the tumultuous relationship he has with his sixteen-year-old son. A third problem of living is inadequate resources due to a threatened mortgage foreclosure on his home.

After these problems of living have been identified and described, the client is then asked to rank them in order of their importance. In this case, the client ranks as his number one problem the threatened mortgage foreclosure on his home. The second ranked problem is the marital discord between him and his wife, and the third problem is his tumultuous relationship with his son. In the task-centered approach, it is generally best to start with the problem of living that is creating the most distress. Using this as a guide, the social worker would start with the threatened mortgage foreclosure on the client's home. In some situations, it may be best to start on a problem of living that can be resolved more quickly than other problems of living. When a client is faced with multiple problems, he or she and the social worker may choose to focus on the problem of living that can be resolved in the shortest period of time. The sense of success the client gains from resolving this first problem can then be transferred to the other, more difficult problems of living. Clients and families who are identified as multiproblem clients or families need to experience some success in counseling as soon as possible. If this doesn't occur, they may redefine their problems of living as intractable barriers that can't be breached. These problems of living, now redefined as intractable barriers, can quickly lead to a sense of despair and hopelessness. Because of these feelings, the client gives up and stops going to counseling.

Barker (1999) points out that a contract in social work practice is an agreement between a social worker and one or more clients that focuses on treatment goals and the tasks that will be implemented to accomplish those goals. Contracts are time-limited agreements that set deadlines for the completion of specific tasks and activities and the target problems they address. Many social workers believe that formulating a specific contract is the single most important factor in predicting treatment success. This belief is also supported by Hutchins and Vaught (1997) in their book *Helping Relationship and Strategies*. See Figure 6.2 for a simple outline of the components of a contract.

While some practitioners prefer written contracts, others are more comfortable if the worker–client agreement is verbal. One advantage of written agreements is that they make it more difficult to ignore or forget included elements. This can also reduce the likelihood of confusion or misunderstandings that are potentially inherent in verbal contracts. With a written contact, if in doubt, both parties can

Figure 6.2
Components of a Contract

Generally, a counseling contract should include most of the following components:

- Client objectives ranked in priority order from most to least important
- Action steps or tasks to be completed by the client
- Action steps or tasks to be completed by the social worker (All tasks are designed to help achieve the contract's objectives.)
- Schedule or time frame for completion of above tasks
- Techniques and methods to be used in counseling
- Logistical details such as time and place of sessions, costs, and so forth.

"look it up." Verbal contracts, on the other hand, are less formal and tend to be more like friendly agreements. Research conducted on verbal and written contracts suggests that both can be effectively used in counseling (Farley et al., 2003; Hutchins & Vaught, 1997).

In *Helping Relationships and Strategies*, Hutchins and Vaught (1997, p. 224) also emphasize the importance of the counseling contract in treatment. They note the following about counseling contracts:

1. A helping contract specifies behavior to be changed and the positive and negative consequences of accomplishing (or not accomplishing) the change.

2. A helping contract can be between two or more parties, for example, teacher and student; spouses; parents and child; employer and employee; family members; juvenile offender, probation officer; and grandparent–guardian.

3. Clients can contract with themselves to change behavior and receive self-arranged rewards.

4. A helping contract should be specific, concrete, achievable, positive, and future-oriented.

5. A helping contract can be long-range or very short-term.

These characteristics of a counseling contract or agreement are similar to those described earlier by Reid (1978), Maguire (2002), and others.

In reviewing the vital elements of the counseling contract, Farley and colleagues (2003) emphasize the importance of time-limited interventions and refer to the earlier writings of Reid and Epstein (1972) to support that point. In Reid and Epstein's task-centered approach, counseling sessions are generally limited to six to twelve sessions and focus on the problems of living identified by the client. Farley et al., (2003) believe that time-limited interventions are not only favored by many social workers but are also supported by empirical studies. Figure 6.3 indicates some of the reasons for this preference.

We believe that the contract is a vital component of the treatment process and a critical factor in determining treatment success. If the client and the social worker don't agree on specific treatment goals and problems and concerns and the tasks and actions that will be implemented, it is easy for the client and the social worker to become disoriented and lose their way. Counseling contracts help the client and the social worker keep their focus and stay on course. Without this focus, counseling can drift from one topic to another without any progress being made. Even so, there are limits to the counseling contract. Hutchins and Vaught (1997,

Figure 6.3

Advantages of Time-Limited Intervention Strategies

Corcoran and Vandiver (1997, p. 130) cite the following advantages of time-limited intervention strategies:

1. Time-limited service is cost-effective. Results equal to those of open-ended service can be achieved at much less cost.

2. More clients can be served under time-limited patterns. The problem of waiting lists can be reduced appreciably when agencies adopt time-limited services as the primary pattern of service delivery (as many have).

3. Time limits foster clients' optimism when practitioners express confidence that improvement is possible in a short time.

4. Time-limited service facilitates the process of termination by introducing it during the preliminary contracting phase.

5. Time limits sharply demarcate the problem-solving process into the beginning, middle, and ending phases.

6. Funding sources are more willing to approve and pay for time-limited treatment because of the specificity of goals and the limitation of time.

pp. 229–230) cite some of the following limitations:

1. A contract usually focuses on a specific behavior. Consequently, it can overlook other behaviors that also need attention. Several contracts may be needed to help the client deal with multiple behaviors.

2. A contract implies an agreement between two or more individuals. Unfortunately, one individual may be less interested than another in completing the contract.

Individuals who contract with each other should exhibit adequate levels of trust in each other.

3. Outside factors may affect the contract. For example, if a student contracts with a teacher and then that teacher is reassigned to another school, it will be difficult to complete the original contract.

4. Contracts are often written so broadly that it is difficult to know whether the contract has been completed. Specific behaviors such as attendance records are often required to adequately measure the outcome of a contract.

5. Good contracts should not focus on too many behavioral outcomes. Rather, the contract should be measurable and achievable and possible to complete within a specific time frame.

6. It is advisable to contract for positive behaviors rather than the reduction of negative behaviors. Contracts that focus on a positive change should also include a realistic and attractive reward such as buying a particular article of clothing when a mother responds more positively to her children over a one-week period.

7. The individual must be committed to the behavioral change that is described in the contract. The individual must also be committed to forgoing the reward linked to the contract if the contract is not fulfilled.

Identifying and Choosing Goals

This textbook incorporates a strengths approach to counseling, and one of the best ways to negotiate a contract with clients is to ask what they would like to improve about their lives. In the case example that begins the chapter, Chris might begin by saying that he wants to be more helpful to his parents and learn how he can assist them as they struggle with the aging process. He might add that the breakup with his girlfriend has created a lot of emptiness and sadness in his life, and he would like to understand what went wrong and what he needs to do to feel better. Chris might conclude by saying that he isn't sleeping well at night and this is making him more irritable during the day and adversely affecting his teaching. The social worker might add to this list by suggesting that another goal of counseling might be to learn how to deal more positively with the uncertainties of life.

The beginning phase of counseling is what Reid (1978) and Reid and Epstein (1972) call "the problem search." Some clients will quickly list a number of goals they would like to accomplish in counseling. In most instances, these goals first will be presented as problems or concerns. A husband and wife who have recently married may say that they constantly argue about money and that if this bickering doesn't get resolved it will destroy their marriage. The social worker can restate this by saying that one goal of counseling would be for them to understand why they argue about money and how they can communicate more effectively their feelings and concerns. Another client may say that she is so sad and despondent that she can barely make it through the day. This problem can be restated so that the goal of counseling becomes finding ways to bring more joy and happiness into her life. Another client adds that his work is so boring and unfulfilling that he could scream. This problem can be restated so that the goal of counseling is to find ways to make work more rewarding. A related goal might be to consider other employment opportunities that he might find more challenging.

Common Goals of Counseling

The goals of counseling can vary considerably depending on the client and the situation. Systems theory provides a road map that can be used to help the client identify goals (Robbins et al., 1998). Every person interacts each day with a variety of people and organizations that together make up that person's life system. By examining the component parts of this life system, the client can then identify the areas in which help is needed. Common goals of counseling often focus on the following life systems: (1) family relations, (2) other interpersonal relationships, (3) finances, (4) work, (5) education, and (6) crisis management. A common goal of counseling often focuses on the family system. Sometimes the presenting problem is a deteriorating relationship between a husband and wife or the challenges of parenting rebellious teenage children. In the case of Chris, the family system focus may be on aging parents and related health problems such as a heart attack, stroke, Alzheimer's disease, or some other medical condition. The family system is dynamic and fluid and one that requires family members to constantly adjust and adapt. A social worker will often help family members learn new skills to deal with the ever-changing matrix of the family system.

Another common goal of counseling focuses on interpersonal relationships outside of the family system. Sometimes the goal is learning to develop more meaningful interpersonal relationships; more often than not the focus is on improving an interpersonal relationship that has been damaged. In Chris's case, an appropriate goal might be to determine if the estranged relationship with his girlfriend can be repaired. If not, the focus may shift to learning why the relationship failed and then developing more satisfying relationships outside of the family system based on what Chris has learned from the broken relationship.

The client's financial system is becoming an important focus of counseling. With record numbers of individuals and families filing for bankruptcy, financial concerns are a leading cause of divorce and marital and individual unhappiness (Broderick, 1979; Jacobson & Gurman, 1995; Smith, 1992). Sometimes the problem is the lack of money. More often, the more important issue is how money is managed and spent. Social workers are now helping individuals, couples, and families to rethink how they spend their money. Sometimes the solution is a cost-efficient budget that is carefully designed and implemented. Often the meaning that clients attach to money and how money can be used to control and manipulate others must also be addressed and resolved. The client's financial system can no longer be ignored in counseling.

Social workers are also seeing more clients who are identifying work-related goals or problems and concerns. With the downturn in the economy following the September 11, 2001, terrorist attacks, more clients are expressing complaints about their work system (Farley et al., 2003). Some clients find their work tedious or boring; others complain about the extra work they must complete following layoffs and downsizing; and still others worry about the job market and whether they will be employed next month. The uncertainty of the economy, coupled with real and anticipated military conflicts around the globe, keep many people in a constant state of anxiety. Some of these people become clients, and their work system problems and concerns must be addressed.

It is not uncommon for social workers to see clients who have a variety of educational problems and concerns. Restated as educational goals and objectives, these issues often become the focus of counseling. Sometimes the goal is to determine whether to return to school for additional training and, if so, in what field. An accompanying goal is often how to finance this return to school, along with how to handle the associated time-management changes; how will these time constraints affect the client's family system and other interpersonal affairs? The need to rethink educational goals and objectives is often precipitated by real or anticipated work layoffs. Some people will enter and exit the educational system three or more times in their life. Counseling often helps to make these entrances and exits more successful for the client.

Another goal of counseling that many clients identify is precipitated by a significant loss, threat, or challenge that has just occurred in their lives (Kanel, 2003; Smith, 1990). Dealing with a significant loss, threat, or challenge is generally considered to be a part of crisis management. Crisis management will become a part of everyone's life whether or not he or she wants it to. When a crisis does occur, every system the client interacts with will probably be affected. Aging parents become ill and eventually die, accidents occur that will temporarily or permanently disable people, children die unexpectedly, and grieving parents have to put their lives back together. Many clients will see a social worker for the first time because of a crisis they can't manage by themselves. For them, the ultimate act of desperation is seeking counseling services that they never thought they would need. These services are needed because the client's life systems are connected, and a crisis in one part of the system will affect other parts of the life system.

In solution-focused or solution-oriented therapy (DeJong & Miller, 1995), the empha-

sis is on what clients want to change and what is the best way to facilitate the change. Rather than focusing on pathology, solution-focused therapy asks clients what they want to change in their lives and not what the social worker or any other person believes should be changed. In many ways, solution-focused therapy is an extension of Maslow's early work on self-actualization as well as of Rogers's work on self-determination (Robbins et al., 1998). Solution-focused therapy concentrates on developing specific goals that are within the client's reach and the strategies or solutions that will facilitate the completion of these goals (see Figure 6.4). It is a growth-oriented rather than a problem-oriented approach to counseling.

The case example of Chris that began this chapter can be used to illustrate the utility of solution-focused therapy in designing well-formed goals that are important to the client. Chris's parents have health care needs. His retired father suffered a heart attack and his mother fell and broke her hip. In the first session, Chris tells the social worker that his primary goal is to help his parents with their health care needs. A secondary goal is to bring some resolution to the estranged relationship he has with a woman who is also a fellow teacher. These goals are important to Chris and are expressed in his own language. They are goals that describe changes he wants to make in his life. Neither goal would be detrimental to Chris or to any other person.

The second step in creating well-formed goals is to focus on smaller rather than larger goals. Smaller goals are easier to accomplish than larger goals. As smaller goals are completed, the client gains more confidence in his ability to change what he wants to change in his life. In Chris's case, the larger goal of helping his parents with their health care needs

---

Figure 6.4

Suggestions for Goal Setting

Berg and Miller (1992) discuss at length how to make goals of solution-focused therapy clear and precise or, in their terms, well formed. Their suggestions include the following:

1. Select goals that are important to clients. Clients should want to achieve these goals, and the goals should be expressed in the clients' language. The only time the worker should object to the desired goals is when the stated goals will result in danger to the client (such as a goal of terminating his or her life) or to others (such as a goal of physical retaliation for a perceived wrong).

2. Establish small goals; they are easier to achieve than larger goals.

3. Ensure that goals are concrete, specific, and behavioral. This allows both client and worker to observe when progress is being made. For example, "going out to lunch with a friend three times a week" is concrete, specific, and behavioral.

4. Identify goals that describe the presence of something (for example, "taking walks") rather than the absence of something (for example, "no longer feeling discouraged").

5. Develop goals that have beginnings ("arranging a pleasant vacation with my spouse for this summer") rather than endings ("having a happy marriage"). Stating goals as a beginning process helps clients conceptualize the first steps they need to take to achieve the desired outcomes.

6. Select goals that are realistic and that clients can achieve within the context of their lives.

7. Ensure that goals are perceived by clients as involving hard work. Goals call for changes in what clients do, and change is difficult. Clients are generally motivated to work hard to achieve highly desired goals.

---

should be broken down into smaller goals. One small goal would be for Chris to speak to his parents and have them identify specific tasks and activities that he can help them with. His father, for example, might ask Chris to help on Saturday with the yard work that he can no longer do by himself since his heart attack. His mother, on the other hand, may ask him to take her shopping for groceries twice a week to help her in and out of the car and with the groceries. Both of these are smaller goals that address the larger goal of helping his parents with their health care needs.

In solution-focused therapy, goals are concrete, specific, and behavioral. Often they are action oriented and describe what the client

will be doing. In Chris's case, he wants to bring some resolution to the estranged relationship he has with his girlfriend. Again, this larger goal should be broken down into smaller goals. The first smaller goal might be to determine whether the estranged relationship can be repaired. If Chris and the social worker determine that the relationship might be repaired, another smaller goal would be for Chris and the social worker to role-play how Chris might approach his estranged girlfriend. Or, if Chris and the social worker determine that the relationship can't be repaired, the next goal becomes that of helping Chris resolve the sadness and loneliness he is experiencing. A smaller goal to address this larger goal would be for

Chris to call a friend once a week and plan an activity for the weekend that they can both enjoy.

Goals in solution-focused therapy describe the presence of something rather than the absence of something. As Chris role-plays with the social worker a phone call that he plans to make to his estranged girlfriend, he is doing something that will help him accomplish a larger goal. The actual phone call he will make later will determine to a large degree whether the relationship with his girlfriend can be repaired. The phone call is a behavior that will help to determine the presence of something, and that presence is whether the long-term relationship can be repaired.

Well-formed goals also have beginnings rather than endings. In developing tasks and activities to help his parents, Chris is beginning to conceptualize the process that will lead to the larger goal of helping his parents with their health care needs. By role-playing with the social worker the phone call that he will be making to his estranged girlfriend, Chris is also beginning to conceptualize the process that will lead to the larger goal of bringing some resolution to this long-term relationship. As Chris accomplishes one small goal and moves on to another, he continues in this beginning process of achieving his larger goals. This beginning process will take time and will continue to focus on smaller goals.

Well-formed goals are realistic and require hard work on the clients' part. As Chris moves from one small goal to another, it is realistic to believe that he will be able to help his parents with their health care needs. The same is true as he role-plays the phone call he will later make to his estranged girlfriend. This smaller goal will lead him to the larger goal of bringing some resolution to this relationship. The two larger goals that Chris has identified for

himself are realistic and within his capabilities. Both goals will require considerable work and diligence. In accomplishing the two goals, Chris will be asked to complete behaviors that are rigorous and time-consuming. After these goals are completed, he will have more confidence in his ability to change his life, and that is the primary goal of solution-focused therapy.

In their book *Interviewing and Change Strategies for Helpers,* Cormier and Nurius (2003, pp. 262–263) discuss the five following categories of interview leads for identifying goals:

1. Providing a rationale
2. Eliciting outcome statements
3. Stating goals in positive terms
4. Determining what the goal is
5. Weighing advantages/disadvantages of the goal

The first step in identifying goals is to give clients a reason why goals are important to have in their lives. One way to accomplish this task is to ask clients what they have accomplished in life that brings them the most pride and satisfaction. For one client, it might be graduating from college, for another it might be the ability to play the piano, and for another it might be the creation of a beautiful flower garden. Setting goals gives many people a sense of direction and purpose in life. Clients also can gain a sense of direction and purpose by setting goals. And as these goals are accomplished, clients like most other people feel a sense of pride and satisfaction. People who set goals have a better idea of what they want to accomplish in life; people who don't set goals often lack this sense of direction and purpose.

Once clients are more committed to setting goals, the social worker needs to help them identify what goals they want to accomplish. Cormier and Nurius (2003, p. 263) give the following examples as leads to help the client:

"Suppose some distant relative you haven't seen for a while sees you after counseling. What would be different then from the way things are now?"

"Assuming we are successful, what would you be doing or how would these situations change?"

"What do you expect to accomplish as a result of counseling?"

"How would you like to benefit from counseling?"

"What do you want to be doing, thinking, or feeling?"

These questions are designed to help clients identify some desired outcomes or goals they would like to pursue in counseling. If a client has difficulty identifying some desired outcomes or goals, the social worker should spend more time with the client on this task. Some clients may even need to do some additional work between counseling sessions before they can identify some desired outcomes or goals.

Effective goals are stated in positive rather than negative terms. Goals stated in positive terms are easier for the client to commit to than negative goals because they establish a positive mind-set for the client. For example, the negative goal of not arguing with your partner implies that discussing any topic with your partner can lead to an argument, which should be avoided at all costs. A more positive goal would be for you to maintain a calm and steady voice when discussing any topic with your partner. This goal significantly increases the chances that discussions with your partner will be productive for both of you. Or, if a client feels he is wasting too much time watching television, a more appropriate goal than not watching television would be to engage in a productive activity such as reading, listening to classical music, or taking a walk with a friend.

When clients are ready to state their goals, the focus should be on what they want to change about themselves rather than someone else. With most clients, the initial tendency is to externalize the problem to another person and focus on that person's behavior rather than on the behavior of the client. For example, when a client identifies as a goal stopping a sixteen-year-old son from arguing, she externalizes the problem to the son and doesn't assume ownership of the problem. A better goal would be for the parent to talk to the son using a calm voice and to treat the son with respect when they are talking to each other. By setting this goal, the client takes ownership of the problem and focuses on what she wants to change about herself and not the sixteen-year-old son. Another way to look at the situation is to ask who has the greater degree of responsibility for or control over the problem. Obviously in such a situation the parent has more responsibility or control as an adult than does a sixteen-year-old adolescent boy.

The final step in identifying a goal is to weigh the advantages and disadvantages of the specific goal. In the case of the parent, it is clearly advantageous to be able to carry on a discussion with a sixteen-year-old son without having an argument. Part of the parent's role is to help guide the son through the turmoil of adolescence into young adulthood. On the other hand, it may not be to the son's advantage to give up the power and control he experiences by drawing his parent into a heated argument. But because the parent and not the son has assumed ownership of the problem, the advantages to the parent outweigh the advantages to the son. And the advantages that the parent experiences by not arguing with the sixteen-year-old son will be extended to other family members, who will now find family life more peaceful and enjoyable.

In *Direct Social Work Practice,* Hepworth, Rooney, and Larsen (2002) state that "goals specify what clients wish to accomplish and are utilized as a means to facilitate desired outcomes" (p. 328). Their guidelines (pp. 329–335) for selecting and defining goals include the following:

1. Goals must relate to the desired end results sought by voluntary clients.
2. Goals for involuntary clients should include motivational congruence.
3. Goals should be defined in explicit and measurable terms.
4. Goals must be feasible.
5. Goals should be commensurate with the knowledge and skill of the practitioner.
6. Goals should be stated in positive terms that emphasize growth.
7. Avoid agreeing to goals about which you have major reservations.
8. Goals must be consistent with the functions of the agency.

The goals that clients are most likely to accomplish in counseling are those they are emotionally committed to completing. Voluntary clients come into counseling with some measure of commitment. They usually seek counseling because they are unhappy with some aspect of their lives. This discontent is a valuable source of motivation and one that the social worker should help clients use in identifying goals. As these goals are achieved in counseling, the discontent that clients feel is usually replaced with a greater level of well-being and confidence in their ability to change their lives.

Most social workers agree that a key factor in counseling success is working with motivated clients who want to make positive changes in their lives (Farley et al., 2003).

Working with unmotivated clients presents the social worker with a special problem. Because these clients generally lack the motivation of voluntary clients, the social worker needs to help them create a desire to change something in their lives. This can be accomplished to some degree by helping involuntary clients reframe their problems from ones that are imposed on them by the courts, for example, to problems that interest them. For example, a middle-aged man who is referred to a counseling center by a city judge because of repeated DUI arrests may agree to counseling only because if he doesn't the judge won't reissue his driver's license. Getting a driver's license reissued can create some level of motivation for many clients. A better approach would be for the client to consider why he is in counseling beyond the mandatory court order. This can be accomplished in part by having the client discuss some of the other benefits besides getting his driver's license reissued, that he will experience by being sober when he drives. These other benefits might include more success at work, a better relationship with his family, and more financial freedom.

In working with unmotivated clients, it is key to encourage them to identify what they would like to accomplish in counseling. One way to do this is to make clients the "experts" in what they believe needs to be added to their lives. This often allows unmotivated clients to become motivated clients because they are working on what they want to add to their lives and not what the social worker or agency is suggesting or even demanding. All phases of the counseling process—assessment, contract, treatment, termination, and follow-up—are more successful when clients are working on what they want to add to their lives.

Goals in counseling should define the specific changes the client wants to make and how these changes will be measured and evaluated. For example, clients who feel isolated and alone often set as one of their counseling goals to spend more time each week with family members and friends. This goal "to spend more time each week with family members and friends" needs further clarification before it can be measured and evaluated. In accomplishing this goal, the client agrees to call a family member or friend once a week and plan an activity they both can enjoy. If this goal can't be accomplished by the end of the week, the client will complete a backup goal, which might include going to church services on Sunday and interacting there with friends. Completing either of these weekly assignments assures clients that the goal "to spend more time each week with family members and friends" is being accomplished.

Counseling goals should be attainable. It is critical that clients identify goals that can be accomplished with some measure of success. Many clients have sought the services of a social worker because they can't manage by themselves some important aspect of their lives. If these clients identify goals that are unreasonable and unattainable, they add to their preexisting feelings of failure a sense of despair and helplessness. One way to help clients establish attainable goals is to focus on goals that can be accomplished by completing a series of smaller goals. For example, a married couple might tell the social worker that their primary goal is "to have a better marriage." The social worker can bring more specificity to this goal by identifying some of the smaller goals the couple can complete "to have a better marriage." Many marriage and family therapists agree that a couple can build a better marriage by improving their communication, conflict resolution, and problem-solving skills (Broderick, 1979; Stuart, 1980; Brown & Brown, 2002). The larger goal "to have a better marriage" is broken down into three smaller goals that focus on improving their communication, conflict resolution, and problem-solving skills.

Counseling goals should be commensurate with the knowledge and skill of the social worker. This means that the social worker should have the knowledge and skill to help clients with whatever goals they identify. If the goal the client identifies is beyond the knowledge and skill of the social worker, the client should identify another goal. Some clients come into counseling with special requests that are beyond the knowledge and skill of many social workers. For example, a couple might identify as their primary goal their desire to resolve serious sexual dysfunction. That particular goal may be beyond the knowledge and skill of many marriage and family therapists, and it may be best for the social worker to refer the couple to a therapist who specializes in sexual dysfunction issues.

Once again, it is much better to set goals that have a positive focus rather than a negative focus. Instead of teaching a couple how not to argue, it would be better to help them learn how to communicate more effectively. When couples try not to argue, they often avoid issues that need to be discussed because from their point of view every discussion can lead to an argument. Positive goals are important because they put the client in a positive frame of mind. Negative goals usually have the reverse effect. It is much better for clients to concentrate on what they can do to improve the quality of their lives rather than on what they should be avoiding. When clients set positive goals in

Voices from the Field

María Janet Rodriguez

My name is María Janet Rodriguez. I'm from Ponce, Puerto Rico. I left Puerto Rico twenty-five years ago when my husband decided to join the army. During that time, I put my education on hold to move with my husband to Germany.

After living ten years in Germany, the army transferred us to Fort Hood, Texas. The transfer gave me a chance to go back to college and finish my bachelor's degree in social work. Having my degree gave me the opportunity to expand my knowledge and skills, but I felt I needed to earn the master's degree because it provides more knowledge and gives the confidence needed to professionally perform as a social worker.

While working for the South Carolina Department of Social Services in Lexington County as a foster care worker in 1997, I became directly involved with a nine-year-old Mexican girl. As a mother and Hispanic, I understood how this girl was feeling, away from her mother for the first time and in a house—a foster home—full of strangers and part of a very different culture. I complied with my work responsibilities and provided special services to help her cope with her difficulties. Having the opportunity to understand and help someone like this Mexican girl was one of the greatest pleasures in my career. During this period, I learned about and became aware of the needs of Hispanics in this state, South Carolina. It also gave me the motivation to achieve higher work standards.

In the year 2000, I decided to go back to school to earn a master's of social work degree. I am currently making a difference in the lives of my clients and helping the agency I work for to provide culturally competent services to their clients. I am committed to the betterment of the Hispanic population in South Carolina and to improving the community as a whole. Now, with my MSW, I have the opportunity to do something outstanding with my life that I can share with others.

counseling, the smaller goals they will focus on to complete the larger goals will also be positive. This positive framework should be the basis of all counseling experiences.

And finally, goals should be consistent with the functions of the agency. Most agencies exist to provide a specific range of services, and the social worker has an obligation to work within that range. Therefore, an adoption agency is unlikely to support services aimed at improving the marital relationship of a couple seeking to adopt a child. Likewise, an alcohol and drug clinic should not be treating children with severe behavioral problems. This only makes good sense. If the client's request cannot be met by the agency, the appropriate action would be to refer the client to a facility that can meet his or her needs. For this reason, social workers should also be aware of other counseling programs available in the community and what services they provide.

Client Input

Client input is essential to the helping process and to effective counseling. As stated earlier, the counseling experience should be user-friendly and should focus on the goals or problems and concerns the client wants to address. There should never be two sets of goals in counseling: one that the client and social worker work on together and one that the social worker is secretly helping the client accomplish without the client's knowledge. As social workers, we have sometimes heard other therapists in private say something like:

> Although the client believes we are trying to improve his interpersonal skills, what we are really working on is how he relates to authority figures. When we have made sufficient progress in this matter, I will discuss this goal with the client and indicate how important this is to his interactions with others.

If the social worker believes that other goals or problems and concerns in the client's life system should be addressed besides those identified by the client, it is the social worker's responsibility to share this belief with the client and discuss in detail why these other issues should also be included in the counseling experience. For example, as a client discusses in the first session what she wants to accomplish in counseling, it may appear that many of the conflicts she is experiencing have occurred because she has trouble controlling her anger. As the social worker probes for more information, it may become even clearer that the client could benefit from anger management training. If the client doesn't agree with the social worker, the social worker should still proceed with the goals that the client wants to accomplish but keeping in mind that if the anger management issue persists, the social worker should discuss it again with the client and possibly renegotiate the contract. "Beginning where the client is" remains a useful recommendation for practitioners.

One cautionary statement should be made about focusing exclusively on the life system goals or problems and concerns that the client identifies, especially in beginning the counseling experience. The social worker is almost always a perfect stranger to the client and has had little if any contact with the client before counseling begins. Some clients are so embarrassed or traumatized by their problems and concerns that they will not share them with the social worker who to them is still an unknown. These clients may identify other goals or problems and concerns while keeping secret the real conflict they are struggling with. As they gain confidence in the social worker and begin to see the practitioner as someone who really cares and can help, they may feel freer to share their terrible secrets. With this in mind, the social worker should ask the client after each session if he or she is still working on the issues that the client wants to address or if the counseling contract should be renegotiated. Most clients will reply that they are headed in the direction they want to go, but sometimes clients will take this opportunity to introduce new goals or problems and concerns that need to be addressed in their life systems.

In *The Social Work Skills Workbook*, Cournoyer (2000, pp. 274–275) states that setting effective goals is the second critical element of the contracting process, the first element being the clarification of issues. Cournoyer refers to David Campbell's book *If You Don't Know Where You're Going, You'll End Up Somewhere Else* (1994) to illustrate that if clients don't set clear goals, they are likely to end up someplace they didn't want to be. Cournoyer recommends that when practitioners construct goals with clients, they use the SMART format, which stands for goals that are:

1. Specific
2. Measurable
3. Achievable
4. Realistic
5. Timely

Effective counseling goals should also be:

1. Stated as accomplishments
2. Stated in clear and specific terms
3. Stated in measurable or verifiable terms
4. Realistic (have a reasonable chance of success)
5. Adequate, if achieved, to improve the situation
6. Congruent with clients' value and cultural systems
7. Time-specific (include a time frame for achievement)

The vignette in Figure 6.5 is an excellent example of how a social worker can help a client establish goals that are specific, measurable, achievable, realistic, and timely. The vignette also demonstrates how the social worker can effectively use reflective listening, clarification, and other communication skills to help the client establish goals. Effective counseling is both a science and an art. Empirical studies provide the science of counseling, whereas communication skills emphasize the art of counseling. An important part of the art of counseling is to establish a therapeutic relationship with the client. A therapeutic relationship is facilitated by reflective listening, clarification, empathy, and other communication skills that the social worker shares with the client.

What Goals to Work On

In using the integrative model of counseling that focuses on short-term treatment, the client and the social worker generally contract to work on three or four goals or problems and concerns. After six sessions, the client and the social worker may agree that the client's goals or problems and concerns have been resolved, and counseling services are terminated. If work still needs to be done, the contract may be extended for two sessions until sufficient progress has been made to justify terminating services. This focus on six to eight counseling sessions coincides with the preferred provider focus that many health insurance companies now use in which insurance coverage is limited to six to eight counseling sessions (Farley et al., 2003).

In the case example cited at the beginning of the chapter, Chris and the social worker will begin their work together by initiating a goal or problem and concern search that identifies goals they will work on in counseling. These treatment goals, which are generally limited to no more than three or four, are the foundation of the counseling contract that Chris has agreed on with the social worker. In Chris's case, he and the social worker might contract to work on the following goals:

1. Develop specific strategies that will assist him in helping his aging parents to deal more successfully with their health care needs.
2. Determine whether the estranged relationship that Chris has with his long-term girlfriend can be repaired and, if so, determine how the relationship can be improved.
3. Assist him in developing specific strategies that will enhance his other interpersonal relationships, especially those with his students and fellow teachers.

Figure 6.5

Establishing Effective Goals with Clients

Cournoyer (2000, p. 276) presents the following example of an interview between a social worker and client to illustrate how effective goals are established:

Worker: Now that we have a pretty clear list of the issues, let's try to establish specific goals for each one. The first issue we've identified is that your 14-year-old son skips school 2 or 3 days each week. Let's imagine that it is now some point in the future and the issue has been completely resolved. What would indicate to you that your son's truancy issue is truly a thing of the past?

Client: Well, I guess I'll know when Johnny goes to school every day and his grades are better.

Worker: (reflecting goal; seeking feedback) When Johnny goes to school every day and improves his grades, you will feel that it's no longer an issue. Is that right?

Client: Yes.

Worker: (seeking clarification) Okay, now let's try to be even more specific. When you say "Johnny will go to school every day" do you also mean that he will attend all his classes when he's there?

Client: Yes.

Worker: (seeking clarification) What do you think would be a reasonable time frame for accomplishing this goal?

Client: Well, I don't know. I'd like him to start now.

Worker: (sharing opinion; seeking feedback) That would be great progress! But I wonder if that might be expecting too much. Let's see, it's now 1 month into the school year. As I understand it, Johnny skipped school some last year too and this year he is skipping even more. What do you think about a 2-month time frame for accomplishing the goal?

Client: That sounds really good.

Worker: (establishing a goal) Okay, how does this sound as our first goal: "Within 2 months from today's date, Johnny will go to school every day and attend all his classes, except when he's sick enough to go to the doctor"? Let me take a moment to write that down for us. . . . Now about the grades. As I understand, he is currently failing most of his courses. How will you know when that is no longer an issue?

• • •

Once the contract has been negotiated, the client and the social worker begin work on the client's goals or problems and concerns. Because counseling sessions are limited to six to eight sessions, this usually means that the practitioner and client will be working simultaneously on the three or four counseling goals that make up the counseling contract. Each counseling session will focus on tasks and activities the client will complete to accomplish the goals. These tasks and activities also include those the client will complete between counseling sessions. These tasks and activities—learning experiences that the client completes in order to accomplish the counseling goals—are a pivotal part of learning theory and the foundation of behavioral change.

Once the client has identified the goals he or she wants to focus on in counseling, the next step is to decide which goal to work on first. When the client has identified more than one goal, the client and the social worker can proceed in at least one of three directions. One direction would be to identify the goal that will bring the client the most relief or satisfaction and then start working toward that goal. By accomplishing this goal, the client maximizes the relief or satisfaction that can be achieved in the shortest amount of time. Another direction would be to identify the goal that will be the easiest to accomplish and then start working toward that goal. This approach is especially good for clients who have had previous counseling experiences that were less than successful. A final approach would be to work on all the goals simultaneously. With managed care limited to six to eight sessions, this final approach addresses the need to get started on all the goals at the same time.

Identifying Tasks and Priorities

Each goal or problem and concern identified by the client in his or her life system must be broken down into its component parts before the goal or problem and concern can be achieved or resolved. In the integrative model of counseling, tasks or activities are identified and then used to achieve the desired goal or objective. Some of these tasks or activities are psychological in nature, whereas others require a behavioral response from the client. As tasks and activities are completed, the goals of counseling are achieved and the problems and concerns are resolved or at least ameliorated.

Planning for Effective Communication

In many kinds of counseling, including marriage counseling, a common goal for clients is to learn how to communicate more effectively. Effective communication requires the completion of a series of tasks or activities that are based on the fundamental components of learning theory. These tasks or activities begin with basic principles and then lead to more complicated forms of communication such as empathic responses. Each task or activity must be completed in a specific order and with some proficiency before the next task or activity can be addressed.

Many different models (Sevel, Cummins, & Madrigal, 1999; Stuart, 1980; Westra, 1996) teach people how to communicate more effectively. Most of these models stress:

1. Purpose of communication
2. Goals of effective communication
3. Common barriers to communication
4. The client's specific communication barriers
5. Guided practice to remove the client's communication barriers
6. The importance of "I" messages
7. Guided practice in sending "I" messages
8. The importance of empathic communication
9. Guided practice in sending empathic messages
10. Summary and review

Purpose of Communication

In helping clients communicate more effectively, the social worker might begin by having them discuss what they believe to be the purpose of communication. As the discussion

Practice Tip

Many times clients may be skeptical about the social worker's ability to help and understand the problems that need to be addressed. This can lead to the client not presenting the "real issue" until the social worker appears to have listened, shows a willingness to help, and makes statements that show caring. The contract phase of treatment is part of the work phase and takes place after the preliminary assessment. It is important to gain the client's commitment to the fact that there is a problem and that the client wants to change. When preparing the written contract, the expectations should be specific for each person participating in the contract to ensure that progress can be measured. It is also helpful if a contract is for a specific length of time, each member has a copy, and progress is evaluated on a regular basis.

Case Example

James Brown is on probation for breaking and entering several houses and stealing electronic equipment worth several thousands of dollars. James pled guilty. He has just completed a drug treatment program and is ready to return to his job as a chef in an upscale restaurant in Merrivale Ski resort. As a condition of his probation he is to participate in outpatient therapy, remain drug free, and pay restitution. James is a single African American who was raised in a large western city. His mother died a year ago, and his father left home when he was two years old. He has six older brothers and sisters who have a different father and are fifteen to thirty years older than he. Most of them stopped having contact with his mother when she got pregnant with James. James started working with his mother in a restaurant when he was ten. He bussed tables, took orders, worked in the kitchen, and moved into cooking quite naturally. Through contacts the owner had, he was able to attend chef school for two years and then interned under a famous chef for three years. The job of assistant chef at Merrivale was his first real opportunity to begin to create his own dishes. He never used drugs until his mother died, and at age twenty-four he wants to put all this behind him. James shows up to your office dressed in his chef working clothes, black and white checked pants and a white chef shirt. As you usher him into your office, he tells you he has to go to work immediately following the appointment.

Critical Thinking Questions

1. What guesses do you have about what might be the main problem for James?
2. What therapeutic goals might supplement the probation goals he has?
3. In writing a contract, what might you want James to do and what would be your responsibilities?
4. How will you discuss with James your responsibility to report progress to his probation officer and the court?

Research Activity

Using the Research Navigator™ website, www.researchnavigator.com, look up information about the impact of losing a parent. See if there is specific information about African Americans and young adult males regarding the loss of a parent. Make a list of five things that are important to do in counseling this population.

develops, the clients should arrive at the conclusion that one of the basic purposes of communication is to send a message that will be received and understood by others. The message that is sent begins the communication process that may lead to other messages being sent back and forth. The messages that are sent can be conveyed verbally in words and phrases or nonverbally in facial gestures and other body movements.

Johnson and Yanca (2004) state that "effective communication occurs when the persons involved in a situation accurately perceive the messages of the other person and [when] the messages are sent in a way that allows the receiver to take action or respond to the sender in ways that facilitate the purposes of communication" (178–179). They go on to say that the purposes of communication in counseling include:

1. Gathering information needed for the helping endeavor, including client strengths and resources

2. Exploring ideas, feelings, and possible ways to meet needs based on strengths and resources within the client and the ecosystem

3. Expressing feelings or thoughts

4. Structuring the work of the action system

5. Providing support, informing, advising, encouraging, and giving necessary direction

Goals of Effective Communication

Once clients have a better understanding of the purposes of communication, they are ready to move on to the next task in achieving effective communication. As they discuss in their own words what they believe is effective communication, the social worker will guide them to the understanding that each message that is sent has content and feeling associated with it. The goal of effective communication is to understand the content and the feeling that are being communicated by other people in their lives through the messages they send and receive.

Effective communication is a process that includes many different stages. First of all, a message is sent to another person. The message includes words and phrases and is conveyed with an emotional tone such as delight, anger, or confusion. The message can also include nonverbal gestures or cues such as a silly grin or a serious frown. After the message is sent, the person who receives the message must process it for content and feeling. If the receiver chooses to respond to the sender, the return message will also include words and phrases and an emotional tone.

In responding to the sender, the receiver may choose to give the sender feedback to the earlier message, or he or she may send back a message on an entirely different subject. As the communication process continues between the sender and the receiver, the goal of effective communication is to make sure that the message sent is the same message received. In other words, the purpose of effective communication is for the sender and receiver to understand each other by sending back and forth clear and unambiguous messages that have content and feeling.

Common Barriers to Communication

The third step in learning to communicate more effectively is identifying some of the common barriers to effective communication (Hepworth et al., 2002). Some of these barriers include (1) interrupting when the other person is speaking, (2) not looking the other person in the eye, (3) poor body posture, (4) speaking for the other person, and (5) silence. For many clients, a common barrier to effective communication is not letting others finish what they have to say. Many social workers acknowledge that one of their first tasks is to get the client to listen to what others are saying without interrupting. This is especially true in marriage and family counseling. Another common barrier to effective communication is not looking the other person in the eye. For example, during the first session of marriage counseling, it is not uncommon for each partner to look only at the social worker and to avoid altogether any eye contact with each other. As each partner speaks directly to the social worker, it is almost as if the other partner isn't in the room.

Another barrier to effective communication is poor body posture. By slumping his shoulders, turning to the side, and frowning, a husband lets his wife know in an instant that he isn't very interested in what she has to say. Another common barrier to effective communication is speaking for the other partner and telling her what she is thinking and feeling. People find it irritating to have others act as though they already know what people are thinking and feeling without first asking. Among couples, extended periods of silence on the part of one or both partners can also sabotage effective communication. In some instances, these extended periods of silence can even take on a contest quality as each partner tries to out-silence the other.

Identifying the Communication Barriers

After these common barriers to communication have been identified and discussed, the next step is to identify the specific barriers clients are using that keep them from communicating more effectively. With couples, some social workers facilitate this step by audio- or videotaping the first counseling session. By listening to the audiotape or viewing the video, the couple and the social worker can usually quickly identify the communication barriers that are impairing the relationship. Nothing is quite as revealing for a couple as a videotaped interaction they have with each other.

Videotaping the interaction between a couple in the first session of counseling yields considerably more information than would audiotaping. Although an audiotape can pick up the content and feeling of a communication, it misses the nonverbal gestures or cues that are such an important part of communication. Posture, facial features, hand gestures, and other body movements are nonverbal forms of communication that can add to or detract from verbal communication. For example, a husband who has a silly grin on his face as he apologizes to his wife for being late for dinner will probably be viewed as less than sincere by his partner. A wife who continually rolls her eyes in disbelief as her husband explains his fears and concerns will probably infuriate her husband more than console him.

Guided Practice to Remove Communication Barriers

The next step in learning to communicate more effectively is guided practice. In guided practice, the social worker first shows clients what to do and then guides them as they try the new behavior. For example, after observing a couple as they try to communicate during the first counseling session, it may be clear to the social worker that neither partner is listening to the other. When one partner is speaking, the other partner almost always interrupts without letting the other partner finish. After pointing this out to the couple, the social worker suggests a simple technique that will encourage each partner to listen to the other without interrupting. The social worker produces a pen or pencil and suggests to the couple that whoever has the pen or pencil in hand is the one who gets to talk while the other person listens without interrupting. For the rest of the session, the social worker guides the couple in this behavior. After the session is completed, the social worker encourages the couple to practice this behavior between sessions.

During the first session of counseling, it may also be obvious to the social worker that when the partners are talking to each other they look away and don't maintain eye contact. As another example of guided practice, the social worker will encourage each partner for the remainder of the session to maintain eye contact with his or her partner when speaking to him or her. The couple will also be asked to maintain eye contact when talking to each other between counseling sessions. Guided practice should always be part of what couples do between sessions. Couples who make guided practice a part of their everyday lives increase significantly their chances of learning how to communicate more effectively.

The Importance of "I" Messages

People who communicate effectively take ownership of their beliefs and feelings. They don't blame or accuse or belittle others. When they communicate, they focus on how they feel and not on their partner or others in their lives. The following is a list of blaming, accusatory, or belittling messages that can cripple communication:

> You never listen to anything I have to say. I don't know why I even bother talking to you anymore!
> You never give me any credit for what I do. All you do is criticize and make fun of me.
> Why can't you be more like my father? He was such a kind and loving man. I really miss him.

You are really angry today. Why can't you be happy? What's wrong with you?

Clients need to take ownership of their beliefs and feelings. One way to do this is by sending "I" messages to their listeners. An "I" message tells the listener how you feel and not how the listener feels. "I" messages do not blame, accuse, or belittle the listener, because the message is about how the speaker is feeling and not about the listener. Compare the following list of blaming, accusing, and belittling messages with the accompanying "I" messages:

> You never listen to anything I have to say. I don't know why I even bother talking to you anymore!
> I never know if you are listening to me when I talk. Sometimes I get so frustrated that I don't want to try anymore.

> You never give me any credit for what I do. All you do is criticize and make fun of me.
> I wish you would give me even more credit for what I do. I want to feel like I'm more important to you.

> Why can't you be more like my father? He was such a kind and loving man. I really miss him.
> I wish you were even more like my father. He was such a kind and loving man. I really miss him.

> You are really angry today. Why can't you be happy? What's wrong with you?
> I can tell you are really angry today. I feel much better when you are happy. I wish I knew what I could do to help you feel happier.

Guided Practice in Sending "I" Messages

Many people find it difficult to send "I" messages. Over the years, their communication patterns have become more blaming, accusatory, and belittling. For many couples, for example, the lack of appreciation they show for each other is one of the reasons they are having marital problems. It will take a considerable amount of guided practice before many people are able to send "I" messages. Guided practice between sessions will also be required before such couples are able to consistently send "I" messages to each other.

The first step in learning how to send "I" messages is for the listener and the communicator to state back to the other what they hear him or her saying. This is accomplished by saying something like "I hear you saying that . . ." After both are more comfortable paraphrasing what the other has said, the next step is for the communicator to add how he or she feels about the other person's statement. At this point, it is usually best to give each individual a prepared list of blaming, accusatory, and belittling messages like those presented in the previous section. The social worker then helps each individual construct and send a more appropriate "I" message. Couples can often continue to work on changing these blaming, accusatory, and belittling messages to "I" messages between sessions. The final step in sending "I" messages is to focus on the spontaneous communication that takes place in counseling and between sessions.

The Importance of Empathic Communication

Empathic communication is a sophisticated form of communication that requires a great deal of practice (Farley et al., 2003). Although it is discussed in greater detail in other chapters, we provide a brief summary here. When couples communicate with each other, each message they send has at least two parts. One part of the message is the content or facts and the other part is the feeling or emotion being conveyed. For example, a husband may blurt out to his wife when he comes home at night, "I was late again for work today because of that damned traffic! If I can't get to work on time, I might lose my job." The content or fact of the message is that he was late again for work, whereas the feeling or emotion is his anger and frustration. Empathic communication occurs when one partner conveys to the other a message that captures the content and feeling of the partner's earlier message.

Rogers (Robbins et al., 1998) and many other therapists (Cournoyer, 2000; Stuart, 1980; Westra, 1996) consider empathic communication to be a critical factor in establishing rapport and facilitating change in counseling. As the social worker responds empathically to client statements, the client gains greater confidence in the social worker's ability to understand and help. In response to the question "How are you feeling today?," the client replies, "I feel terrible. Nothing ever seems to work out for me. I'm so frustrated I don't know what to do!" This is an opportunity for the social worker to respond with empathy, such as saying, "I'm sorry you feel so bad. When things don't work out the way we plan them, it can be very disappointing." This is an example of reciprocal empathy that captures the content and feeling of the client's statement without parroting the same response.

Couples who learn to respond with empathy to each other's problems and concerns are communicating at a high level. They are able to put themselves in the position of the other partner and experience what the partner experiences and feel what the partner feels. It is not appropriate for anyone to maintain this high level of communication in all of their interactions. Responding with empathy to every message a speaker sends would require a high level of energy and vigilance. Empathy should be used with restraint and discretion. When it is used appropriately, it is a powerful communication tool that conveys understanding and concern. If it is used too often, it creates an atmosphere that is too emotionally charged.

Guided Practice in Sending Empathic Communication

Learning to respond with empathy takes many hours of practice. It also requires that the individuals have some level of commitment to each other. A couple or family whose relationship is in turmoil would probably lack this commitment in the beginning phase of counseling. As their relationship improves, it would then be more appropriate for the social worker to help them develop this skill. As with other communication skills, the social worker will begin with guided practice during the counseling session. This guided practice should be continued between sessions. It should also be an important part of the termination process, in which clients are encouraged to continue the behaviors they have learned in counseling. One of the most important behaviors is responding with empathy to the speaker, whether parent, spouse, or significant other.

This is a cursory look at how the goal of learning to communicate more effectively can be accomplished in counseling. The more important point is that whatever the goal or problem and concern is, the social worker and client must develop together a series of tasks and activities that will accomplish the desired goal. Hundreds of how-to books and articles have been written about communication, budgeting, sexuality, parenting, family life, crisis management, and many other topics. The experienced social worker will become more familiar with these sources and how they can be used to de-

sign tasks and activities to address whatever goal or problem and concern the client wants to address in counseling. These skills are crucial in helping clients learn what they need to know to be happier and more productive.

Characteristics of Effective Goals

Because the goals or problems and concerns in the client's life system are the focus of counseling, they must be negotiated carefully by the client and the social worker. In general, the goals or problems and concerns of counseling should be (1) attainable, (2) growth promoting, (3) short term, and (4) task oriented. The goals of counseling should be attainable and not like the astronomy professor's unanswerable examination question: "Describe the universe and give two examples." Some goals that clients want to focus on in their life systems are either unattainable or unreasonable, such as "I never want to be sad again" or "I want to accomplish everything I set out to do." More reasonable goals would be "I want to understand why I am sad and what I need to do to feel better" or "I want to be more successful at my job." The best counseling goals are those that identify a specific objective, such as "I want to communicate more effectively with my wife" or "I want to get out of debt and learn to manage my finances better."

Goals should also be growth promoting, such as "I want to learn how to be more helpful to my aging parents" or "I want to have more self-confidence when I am around women." Rather than asking the social worker to help with specific goals, many clients want to focus on problems and concerns in their life system, such as "I'm so unhappy with my wife that I hate to go home at night" or "My teenage daughter is driving my crazy." Problems and concerns can be restated so that they are more positive and growth promoting: "I want to have a better relationship with my wife" or "I want to be closer to my teenage daughter." The question about whether the cup is half empty or half full is not rhetorical. It is much better to maintain a positive and growth-promoting focus in counseling than to concentrate only on problems and concerns.

The client and social worker should focus on short-term goals through which some measure of success can be accomplished in six or eight sessions. Whether or not social workers like it, managed care has dramatically changed the way in which counseling services are covered by prepaid insurance plans (Farley et al., 2003). Most managed care plans limit the client to six or fewer sessions with the option of two additional sessions if approved by the insurance company. This means that the client and the social worker must negotiate goals in the client's life system that can be accomplished with some measure of success in six to eight sessions. Because of this short-term focus, the termination phase of counseling has become even more important in the counseling process. Termination is discussed at length in Chapter 14.

The goals of counseling should be specific and clear. They should also include goals that can be subdivided into tasks and activities that relate to the overall goal. These tasks and activities are grounded in learning theory. As each task and activity is completed, the client is that much closer to accomplishing the goal. For example, learning how to manage money more effectively includes a number of related tasks and activities. One of the client's first tasks or activities is to learn more about what he or she spends money on each month. Another task or activity is looking at this list of monthly expenditures and determining which ones are

"needs" and which ones are "wants." As one task leads to another, the client learns how to budget money more effectively and, hopefully, how to get and stay out of debt. Goals that can be subdivided into tasks and activities are the best goals for short-term counseling.

Evaluation and Measurement of Goals

We have many ways to assess whether counseling goals have been accomplished. Four of the more common ways include assessments by (1) the client, (2) the client's family members and friends, (3) the social worker, and (4) standardized instruments. Each assessment plan has its own advantages and disadvantages. Whenever possible, it is advisable to use all four assessment plans in evaluating the degree to which counseling goals have been accomplished.

One way to determine if counseling goals have been accomplished is to ask the client. Evaluations made by the client are subjective and may be biased. Most clients want to believe that counseling has helped them. They have invested considerable time and money in counseling and they want to believe that all this effort has been worthwhile. Because the purpose of counseling is to help clients, it seems reasonable that they be a part of the evaluation process. If a client's goal is to be happier and less depressed after six sessions of counseling, then when services are terminated a logical question is to ask the client whether the goal has been accomplished. The client can answer either yes or no to that goal or give a more detailed response by using the five-point goal attainment scale from the task-centered approach to counseling: (1) no goal achievement, (2) minimal goal achievement, (3) moderate goal achievement, (4) considerable goal achievement, and (5) complete goal achievement (Reid & Epstein, 1972).

The client's evaluation can also include a written narrative of the progress he or she believes has been made in counseling. This narrative might include a daily journal of what happened to the client during counseling and what positive changes the client believes he or she has made in his or her life.

Another evaluation source is the client's family members and friends. The social worker interacts with the client only about one hour a week. Family members and friends generally spend a much greater amount of time with the client, sometimes as much as twenty or more hours a week. They are often in a much better position to address the client's overall well-being than is the social worker. Family members and friends interact with the client in a variety of settings that can include home, work, church, and a host of leisure activities. If the social worker uses the client's family members and friends as part of the evaluation process, it should be with the client's prior approval. In assessing what progress the client has made in accomplishing his or her goals, family members and friends can answer either yes or no to the goal statement or use the five-point goal attainment scale from the task-centered model. Their evaluation could also include a written narrative that describes the positive changes they believe the client has made in his or her life.

The social worker should also be part of the evaluation process. Although they would like to believe they are more objective than clients in assessing how successfully goals have been accomplished, social workers still have a vested interest in the outcome. Social workers want to believe that they are helping to make positive changes in the life systems of their clients. Like the assessments of clients, the assessments of social workers are subjective and may be biased. Even so, social workers still

play an important part in the evaluation process. It can be argued that because social workers have many years of training and experience they are better prepared to give an accurate assessment of what progress clients make in counseling. This is probably true, although their assessments are still subjective or at best somewhat subjective. In answering whether counseling goals have been achieved, social workers can respond either yes or no like clients and the client's family members and friends or use the same five-point goal attainment scale referred to earlier.

Standardized instruments are often used to assess how well counseling goals have been accomplished. Whereas the assessments of clients, clients' family members and friends, and social workers can be subjective, the assessments that are achieved by using standardized instruments are considered more objective and less biased because they are constructed to be more valid and reliable than subjective measures. Validity is a measurement concept that ensures you are in fact measuring the quality or characteristic you believe you are measuring, whereas reliability means that repeated applications of the instrument yield similar results (Rubin & Babbie, 2001). Standardized instruments that are used to assess how well goals have been accomplished in counseling should have acceptable validity and reliability coefficients.

Hundreds of standardized instruments have been constructed that measure many different characteristics such as contentment, self-esteem, marital satisfaction, sexual satisfaction, and family relations. *The Clinical Measurement Package* (Hudson, 1982) has been used for over twenty years by many social workers because it includes nine standardized instruments that can be used to measure the degree to which counseling goals have been accomplished. All nine instruments are scored in a similar fashion and include the same mean and standard deviation score. One of the nine instruments is the Generalized Contentment Scale, which measures varying degrees of happiness or depression. Based on a scale of 1 to 100, the mean or average score on the inventory is 30 with a standard deviation score of 5. If one thousand clients were to complete the inventory, approximately 68 percent would score between 25 and 35, 95 percent between 20 and 40, and 98 percent between 15 and 45. Scores of 30 or less on the inventory suggest that the client is content or happy, whereas scores above 50 suggest varying degrees of depression (Corcoran & Fischer, 1994, pp. 165–167). Scores above 70 suggest severe depression, whereas scores above 90 indicate that the client may be at serious risk for suicide. If the client has set as one of his or her goals a desire to be happier and less depressed, the Generalized Contentment Scale can be administered to the client during the first counseling session and then again when counseling services are terminated. A comparison of before and after scores on the inventory will give the client and the social worker a more objective assessment of whether the counseling goal of being happier and less depressed has been achieved. A beginning score of 50 and an after score of 30 would suggest that the client is much happier than when he or she began counseling.

The Index of Self-Esteem is another standardized instrument included in *The Clinical Measurement Package* (Hudson, 1982). This instrument is used to measure degrees of self-esteem in clients. Based on a scale of 1 to 100, the mean or average score is 30 with a standard deviation score of 5. Scores of 30 or less on the inventory suggest a high degree of self-esteem, whereas scores above 50 suggest vary-

ing degrees of low self-esteem. Scores above 70 suggest very low self-esteem, whereas scores above 90 suggest extremely low self-esteem. The Index of Self-Esteem can be used with the Generalized Contentment Scale to help determine what may be influencing a client's depression. For example, a score of 70 or above on the Generalized Contentment Scale suggests the presence of severe depression. A score of 30 or less on the Index of Self-Esteem suggests high self-esteem. In comparing the two scores, it would appear that the client's severe depression is probably being influenced more by external factors such as the loss of a loved one than by internal factors such as negative thinking. These two scores also suggest that as the client's external situation improves, his or her severe depression should also improve. A score of 70 or above on the Generalized Contentment Scale and a score of 70 or above on the Index of Self-Esteem suggest that the client's severe depression is probably being influenced more by internal factors than by external factors. These two scores also suggest that the client has probably been suffering from severe depression for an extended period of six months or longer. Because the client's severe depression appears to more internalized than externalized, it will probably be more difficult to help the client because his or her severe depression has become a part of the client's everyday life.

The Index of Marital Satisfaction and the Index of Sexual Satisfaction are two standardized instruments discussed in *The Clinical Measurement Package* (Hudson, 1982) that can be used in marriage counseling. The Index of Marital Satisfaction measures the degree, severity, or magnitude of marital satisfaction, whereas the Index of Sexual Satisfaction focuses on the degree, severity, or magnitude of sexual satisfaction. Scores of 30 or below on either instrument suggest a high degree of marital and sexual satisfaction, whereas scores of 50 or above suggest lower degrees of marital and sexual satisfaction. Scores of 70 or above on either instrument suggest seriously low levels of marital and sexual satisfaction, whereas scores of 90 or above suggest extremely low levels of satisfaction. Although these two standardized instruments deal with similar issues, they should be used separately. Although sexual satisfaction is an important part of marital satisfaction, many other factors contribute to marital satisfaction, such as respect, trust, fidelity, and finances. Hudson believes it is best to use each instrument separately because they measure two entirely different issues. Neither scale should be a substitute for the other.

The Clinical Measurement Package (Hudson, 1982) also includes standardized instruments that can be used in family counseling. The Child's Attitude Toward Mother and The Child's Attitude Toward Father are two standardized instruments that measure how children feel toward their parents. Both instruments measure to what degree a child is satisfied with these two relationships. The Index of Parental Attitudes assesses the level of satisfaction parents feel toward their children. The Index of Family Relations, on the other hand, measures the degree of satisfaction that a family member feels toward the entire family. The Index of Peer Relations assesses how you feel about the people you associate with most of the time. As with the other instruments in *The Clinical Measurement Package* (Hudson, 1982), scores of 30 or below suggest high levels of satisfaction, whereas scores of 50 and above suggest lower levels of satisfaction. Scores of 70 and above suggest very low levels of satisfaction, whereas scores of 90 or above suggest extremely low levels of satisfaction.

Standardized instruments such as these (Hudson, 1982) can be used to assess to what degree the client has accomplished goals or resolved problems and concerns. Clients can complete standardized instruments at various points in the counseling process, including beginning, during, after, and in follow-up. The first time a standardized instrument should be administered is when the client begins counseling, preferably at the start of the first session. This beginning or baseline score gives the client and the social worker a measure of how the client is feeling as counseling begins. Standardized instruments can also be administered to the client during counseling. This during score gives the client and social worker a measure of the progress the client is making from one session to another. The same standardized instrument should also be administered at the end of the last counseling session as services are terminated. This after or ending score gives both client and social worker a measure of how the client is feeling at the end of counseling. A comparison of the before and after scores on the same standardized instrument will give some indication of whether counseling has been successful in helping the client feel better. The same standardized instrument can also be administered to the client one or more months after counseling services have been terminated. This follow-up score will give the client and the social worker some measure of the long-term effects of counseling. It is important to assess the long-term effects of counseling, and follow-up scores are an important part of that assessment (Corcoran & Fischer, 1994). If a social worker doesn't assess in some way how the client is feeling one or more months after termination of services, he or she can only guess about the long-term effects of counseling.

It is beyond the scope of this chapter to give a more detailed account of how standardized instruments can be used to assess the degree to which counseling goals have been achieved. However, a comprehensive listing of the standardized instruments often used to evaluate social work practice is found in *Measures for Clinical Practice: A Source Book* by Corcoran and Fischer (1994). The important point is that standardized instruments should be used whenever possible as a part of this evaluation. A positive evaluation by the client, by the client's family members and friends, and by the social worker that is supported by standardized instruments makes a strong case that the client's goals have been achieved and that counseling has been successful. Standardized instruments are an important part of the evaluation process in counseling and are at the core of what has become known as research-directed practice or best practice.

Cultural and Diversity Issues in Planning

Social workers need to be aware of how cultural and diversity issues can affect planning. For example, a white male mental health social worker who is thirty years old may be asked to work with an elderly African American woman who is seventy years old and who suffers from depression. In this situation, the differences are obvious and profound and focus on race, age, and gender. Or a single African American male social worker who is twenty-five years old may be asked to provide marriage counseling to a white couple who are both sixty years of age. In this situation, the differences in race and age are compounded by the fact that the social worker is single and has never been married. It is not uncommon for social workers to work with clients who are different from themselves in either race, age, gender, marital status, education, or cultural background.

When there is an obvious difference between the client and the social worker in terms of race, age, cultural background, or some other important characteristic, it is important that the social worker address this difference with the client in the first session. Waiting until the planning phase to discuss these issues is very likely too late. The following exchange between a marriage social worker who is thirty years old and a couple who are in their seventies illustrates this point:

Practitioner: Mr. and Mrs. Brown, as we begin our first session of counseling I would like to start by asking how you both feel about working with me since I am so much younger than either one of you. How do you feel about that, Mrs. Brown?

Mrs. Brown: Well . . . I'm not really sure. I guess it's okay, although you don't seem to be much older than many of my grandchildren. I don't really know. I'll have to think more about it.

Practitioner: How about you, Mr. Brown?

Mr. Brown: To be honest, your age does concern me. I'm not sure someone as young as you are can really understand what it is like to be old. I think it would be easier to work with someone our own age. I'm sorry, but that's how I'm feeling right now.

Practitioner: Mr. and Mrs. Brown, I appreciate your honesty and your concern. I can understand why both of you would be hesitant to work with someone as young as I am. I have worked successfully with older couples before and I would like to work with you. If at any time either of you feels my age is interfering with our work together, will you please let me know so we can talk more about it? How does that sound to both of you?

Mr. Brown: Sounds okay to me.

Mrs. Brown: That's a good idea. Thanks.

This model of a frank and honest exchange between the couple and the social worker can be used to address many cultural and diversity issues in counseling. In order to do this, the social worker must first of all be sensitive to any real or perceived worker–client differences. It is always best to err on the side of caution in dealing with cultural and diversity issues. If it appears in any way that the client is struggling with these issues, the social worker should address them as soon as possible and reassure the client that the social worker will be sensitive to these cultural and diversity differences.

In *Diversity Perspectives for Social Work Practice,* Anderson and Carter (2003) discuss how the strengths perspective in social work practice can be used in working with diverse populations. According to the authors,

> diversity practice means acknowledging that each individual is (1) like no other in uniqueness; (2) like some others in cultural and other contexts; and (3) like all others in human spirit and potential. Members of social and cultural groups that have survived a history of oppression in the United States have often developed special strengths and adaptive abilities that should be incorporated into the counseling experience. (p. 13)

Anderson and Carter believe these special strengths and adaptive abilities usually come from three sources:

1. Personal transformation qualities as a result of overcoming self-depreciating force

2. Family and community structures that develop self-esteem and provide a network of psychosocial and economic resources

3. Survival determination and skills

Social workers who work with diverse populations should not overlook the personal transformation that many of these clients have already experienced. Rather than focusing on the deficits that may appear on the surface, such as limited education and training, social workers should reinforce the progress these clients have already made in their lives. For many clients, this personal transformation may seem almost beyond belief. Clients from diverse populations have often already made impressive adaptations to life's uncertainties brought on by poverty, illness, or inadequate parenting. Social workers should reinforce these prior successes throughout the assessment, planning, and implementation processes. Even as the client focuses on new goals and problems, the social worker should remind the client of these accomplishments.

Clients from diverse backgrounds often come into counseling with strong family and community support systems. An experienced social worker will make these strong family and community support systems an integral part of the planning process. It is difficult for anyone to make significant changes in life without the support and encouragement of those who love and respect them. Clients need to feel the support and encouragement of those closest to them. For this reason, many social workers will encourage clients to involve family members and friends in the planning experience. The family and community support systems that many clients from diverse populations bring into counseling can be a critical factor in successful counseling.

And finally, many clients from diverse backgrounds already have an impressive array of survival skills and determination that they bring into counseling, such as diligence, honesty, frugality, humor, and fearlessness. These survival skills should be identified early in counseling and employed whenever possible during the planning phase. It can be argued that these survival skills are the core of the client's strengths and abilities. They should be used throughout the counseling experience as the client focuses on his or her goals. Remember the saying, "When the going gets tough, the tough get going." The survival skills and determination that many clients from diverse populations bring into counseling have already made them "tough." These same survival skills and determination will enable the tough to keep going even when new obstacles are placed in their way.

SUMMARY

This chapter focuses on the planning process in direct practice with individuals and families. Many of the knowledge areas and skills identified in the chapter can be used with groups as well. The chapter gives major attention to the use of counseling contracts between social worker and client to help clarify the goals, tasks, and priorities of the planning step.

Another area of significant focus is communication because it represents a common difficulty encountered by many individuals and families. The purpose and goals of and barriers to effective communication are addressed. Specific steps needed to improve communication are described, along with the use of "I" messages.

This chapter concludes with a discussion of how client and social worker can target effective goals and how these goals are measured and evaluated. The use of standardized instruments is discussed, as well as the evaluations made by the client, by the client's family members and friends, and by the social worker. A discussion of cultural and diversity issues in planning ends the chapter.

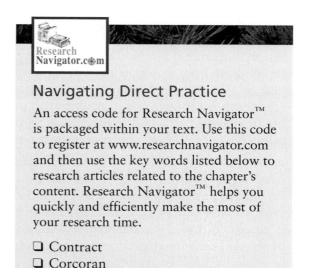

Navigating Direct Practice

An access code for Research Navigator™ is packaged within your text. Use this code to register at www.researchnavigator.com and then use the key words listed below to research articles related to the chapter's content. Research Navigator™ helps you quickly and efficiently make the most of your research time.

❏ Contract
❏ Corcoran
❏ Empathy
❏ Fischer
❏ "I" message

Chapter 7

Knowledge and Skills for Intervention

■ Madison is a social worker for the county drug court. Each person who appears before the judge on a drug- or alcohol-related offense also receives an evaluation by the social worker.

Fahu is a twenty-three-year-old Pacific Islander who has been charged with driving under the influence (DUI). His legal history shows that he has one prior DUI arrest. He has been referred to Madison for a presentencing evaluation to determine if he is an appropriate candidate for the ten-session program focusing on educational aspects of substance abuse. In addition, the judge will want to know if Madison has other recommendations for counseling services that need to be incorporated into the sentencing. One of Madison's primary goals is to assess Fahu's appropriateness as a candidate and his motivation level for receiving help. She also needs to screen him for a severe mental health problem.

Fahu's parents are from Tonga but immigrated to the United States before he was born. He is the fourth of eight children. He indicated that his father had occasionally used alcohol in his twenties, but that excessive drinking had not been a problem for him for years. Fahu has an older brother who has had numerous alcohol-related problems, including three DUI arrests, and the police had removed him from his home following charges of domestic violence.

Fahu completed high school in Smithville, a suburb adjoining a large metropolitan area in the western United States. Following high school, he went to work for various construction companies, mostly building homes. Two years ago he began driving cement trucks. He reports enjoying his job and earning an adequate income, $11.50 an hour with quite a bit of overtime in the summer months. Because of his DUIs, he lost his commercial driver's license (CDL) and is currently unemployed.

Fahu married at age eighteen and divorced four years later. He is the father of two children (a son, age two, and a daughter, age three) who are in the primary custody of his former wife. To date, he has been able to stay current on his child support. However, because of his current unemployment status, he recently moved back into his parents' home.

Fahu reports being very motivated to complete the program so that he can get his CDL restored and return to work. He also projects the attitude of being motivated to take care of his children and wanting to help out with their expenses. In the past, he felt he could handle his alcohol and denied having a problem, but he currently admits to having lost control.

He was first exposed to alcohol at age eleven. Some of the neighborhood boys stole some liquor from one of their parents, and he participated in drinking it with them. He said it made him feel good. He continued to increase his drinking with his friends when he had opportunities to do so. Once he married, he further increased his drinking during the evenings and on weekends. At this time, he reports a preference for beer but will use hard liquor if it is available. He also has used amphetamines to help him stay awake while driving. His alcohol and drug use contributed to the demise of his marriage. On two occasions, he was charged with domestic violence. He indicated that one of the main reasons for the divorce was his alcohol problem. No other significant psychological problems are noted.

The purpose of this chapter is to continue the problem-solving approach with particular emphasis on how interventions are implemented based on the theories selected. Specifically, this chapter addresses those skills and techniques used in the process of planned change. The selection of techniques follows the assessment phase and the establishment of goals agreed to by both the client and the practitioner.

As discussed in Chapter 2, clients' anticipation (expectancy) about the success of their work with a social worker can be an important factor in achieving positive outcomes. Recognizing this and the fact that clients are consumers of our services, it is logical to explain to them the model(s) and techniques of practice we will use and how change can be expected to occur. This allows clients to better understand the purpose for implementing the techniques, which helps increase their level of compliance. Clients' questions and concerns ought to be addressed, and they should voluntarily grant compliance before therapy proceeds. Only on rare occasions should treatment be implemented against the client's consent. Exceptions might include the person who is dangerous to self or others or acutely psychotic and unable to make rational decisions about personal care and safety. These crisis situations generally call for an involuntary admission to a hospital, followed by a civil hearing before a judge to determine the client's mental capacity for making treatment decisions. This is all based on a thorough assessment of the client's mental status and support systems

with a recommendation for the least restrictive environment possible.

The following is an overview of the process of change and the techniques associated with the theories previously discussed. This section is not meant to include all aspects of each theory or perspective, but instead presents the more salient features that will provide a foundation from which to move forward in the development of the individual social worker's direct practice.

Ego Psychology Therapy and Techniques

Although those who use the psychodynamic model differ in their perspectives and emphases (drive, ego, object relations, and self-psychology), they tend to use similar approaches to treatment (Sharf, 2000, p. 4). The uniqueness of ego psychology in its approach to helping is in applying techniques that seek to help strengthen a client's ego (that part of the ego that functions in the conflict-free sphere) or to help make significant changes in the client's personality (that part associated with conflict between the id and the superego in the structural region of the psyche). Two approaches have been identified by Goldstein (1995) as being "ego-supportive" and "ego-modifying." "Ego-supportive intervention aims at restoring, maintaining, or enhancing the individual's adaptive functioning as well as strengthening or building ego where there are deficits or impairments. In contrast, ego-modifying intervention aims at changing basic personality patterns or structures" (p. 166).

Ego-modifying techniques tend to be long term and involve many of the classical psychoanalytic techniques such as insight, transference, dream analysis, and understanding early childhood relationships with important objects.

Table 7.1

Differences between Ego-Supportive and Ego-Modifying Approaches

Criterion	Ego-Supportive	Ego-Modifying
Focus of intervention	Current behavior and conscious thoughts and feelings; some selected focus on past	Past and present; conscious, preconscious, and unconscious
Nature of change	Ego mastery; increased understanding; learning and positive reinforcement; emotionally corrective experiences; neutralization of conflict; better person–environment fit	Insight and conflict resolution
Use of relationship	Experience of the real relationship; positive transference; corrective relationship; worker's relationship with others in client's environment	Understanding of positive and negative transference
Psychological testing	Directive, sustaining, educative, and structured; some reflection	Nondirective, reflective, interpretive
Work with social environment	Environmental modification and restructuring; provision and mobilization of resources; improving conditions	Not emphasized but may be used
Appropriate client populations	Those encountering life transitions, acute or situational crises, or stress; those with ego deficits; those with maladaptive patterns and low anxiety tolerance and impulse control	Those with good ego strength who have maladaptive patterns interfering with optimal functioning; in some cases those with severe maladaptive patterns, defenses, and ego deficits
Duration of intervention	Short term or long term	Generally long term

Source: Reprinted with the permission of The Free Press, a division of Simon & Schuster Adult Publishing Group, from *Ego Psychology and Social Work Practice,* 2nd Edition, by Eda G. Goldstein. Copyright © 1995 by Eda G. Goldstein. Copyright © 1984 by The Free Press. All rights reserved.

By comparison, ego-strengthening techniques may involve counseling for individual change but also incorporate environmental change. Further, less emphasis is placed on the past and the unconscious aspects of the personality and more emphasis is placed on the here and now, current relationships, and the development of a strong therapeutic relationship. It is also geared toward a more short-term helping relationship.

One of the positive aspects of this model is that it is fluid. The social worker may help by first strengthening the ego and later on, based on the assessment and goals, begin modifying the ego, or vice versa. Table 7.1 compares the two approaches of ego psychology as they pertain to the goals for intervention.

Hollis (1972), on the other hand, classified the following major groups of techniques, all of which incorporate the use of communication, when directly working with a client. Techniques used to change the environment are not included in these groupings. Further, she organized the techniques based on "dynamic" considerations rather than on whether they are ego-supportive or ego-modifying. The six categories are:

- Sustainment
- Direct practice
- Exploration, description, and ventilation
- Person-situation reflection
- Pattern-dynamic reflection
- Developmental reflection

The first two techniques are associated with the relationship between the client and the social worker and depend on how much the client will allow the worker to be an influence. The third technique allows clients to express themselves, whereas the last three involve some form of reflection on the client's part. The following paragraphs describe these techniques in more detail.

Sustaining techniques involve the generic communication skills of encouragement (nods of the head, statements such as "yes" and "go on," and an attentive posture) along with empathy, positive regard, and genuineness. **Direct practice** incorporates the use of advice or the offering of suggestions. In one fashion or another, the worker offers an opinion about what action a client might take. Caution ought to be used with this technique; opinions need to be offered in subtle forms. According to Hollis (1972), "their effectiveness depends to a high degree upon the existence of a strong positive relationship between client and worker, which

in turn is promoted by sustaining procedures" (p. 79).

Exploration, description, and **ventilation** are designed to help clients elicit subjective and objective information about significant experiences and to help them express their feelings. Allowing clients to express themselves often provides them relief. The relief achieved through ventilation may also be supported through the use of sustaining techniques. As clients sense the social worker's empathy and encouragement to express themselves, their feelings of anxiety, hopelessness, and guilt tend to lessen.

The **person-situation reflection** technique is designed to help clients reflect on their current situation and on their relationships. Hollis (1972) subdivided this technique into five dimensions: (1) how clients view their health and aspects of the world around them, and how they perceive and understand others, (2) how clients understand their own behavior in terms of how it affects others and themselves, (3) clients' understanding of why they behave as they do in certain situations, (4) their awareness of what causes their behavior as they interact with others, and (5) how they evaluate themselves or some component of their behavior (according to some value system, preference, or self-image). Determining which item to emphasize depends on the assessment and the type of problem clients present. The first two dimensions likely involve problems that are realistic and external to the client, whereas the last three stem from clients' more subjective view of their involvement with the problem.

Pattern-dynamic reflection consists of helping clients to consider, through reflection, those psychological patterns associated with their behavior, along with the defense mechanisms employed with the aid of the social worker. Clients are encouraged to examine the dynamic relationships associated with their behavior. The goal is to have clients look beyond inappropriate reactions and to consider the intrapsychic content associated with the behavior. To do this, the social worker may confront maladaptive and inconsistent behavior.

The sixth technique, **developmental reflection,** is used to encourage clients to reflect on how their psychological tendencies developed. Because it is theorized that people internalize past important experiences to the point that they continue to influence responses today, past childhood experiences are considered and dealt with. Clients explore the relationship between one aspect of their behavior or experiences and another as they occurred in the past. Clients must be given a lot of time to talk about themselves and their situation before the social worker and the clients are able to consider the dynamic developmental and psychological aspects of the problem.

With respect to ego-modifying techniques, the social worker must first assess clients to determine their ability to tolerate in-depth analysis and whether the application of such techniques would prove beneficial. "Individuals whose rigid, maladaptive defenses nevertheless protect them from disorganization may become more disorganized if their defenses are challenged" (Goldstein, 1995, p. 187). These individuals might include clients who are grandiose as a way of protecting themselves from feelings of hopelessness or impulsiveness, or those who have a fragile ego due to psychoses. Techniques in this approach rely on more classical ones such as insight, confrontation, the understanding of transference, and an in-depth look at childhood relationships. The goal is to understand the dynamic relationship of early childhood experiences, feelings, and behavior to current relationships, feelings, and

behavior as they correspond with the stages of development.

Transference/Countertransference

An important technique in psychoanalysis involves the concept of transference. **Transference** is defined as those feelings, fantasies, defenses, and emotional reactions that clients have toward the social worker. The reactions may be positive (feelings of trust, security, confidence, and love) or negative (feelings of anger, betrayal, hurt, and rejection). It is believed that these feelings arise when clients begin to relate to the helper as they did to other significant persons in their lives, especially their parents or primary caregivers. Helpers use this technique to gain an understanding of the past conflictual relationships clients had with others and how the related memories and experiences continue to influence clients' feelings and behaviors in current relationships.

In traditional psychoanalysis, the development of transference is considered to be an essential and normal part of the helping process. Once transference is achieved, the practitioner interprets what is happening so that clients can gain insight and thus work to resolve the conflict, ultimately helping clients to change their personality. Free association and dream analysis that focus on childhood experiences are commonly used techniques to achieve this goal.

In ego psychology, these techniques may be incorporated into the helping process, especially when ego modification is a goal. When ego-supportive techniques are implemented, the practitioner is less likely to encourage the development of transference or to encourage it only selectively. The goal is more likely to be the development of positive transference in order to support and aid clients. In addition, the worker will focus on the here-and-now and discuss rational approaches to solving clients' problems.

Countertransference has been defined as those unrealistic and inappropriate feelings practitioners have toward clients. Like transference, these feelings are also believed to originate at the unconscious level and to be connected to past conflicts in the life of the helper. Congruent with ego psychology, the definition of countertransference has been expanded to include reality-based reactions between social workers and their clients. "The broadening of the meaning of countertransference has an important implication, namely, that the worker's often uncomfortable or potentially hindering reactions may be induced by the client rather than produced by the worker's conflict" (Goldstein, 1995, p. 206). Thus, the social worker may begin to understand how other people in the clients' worlds react toward the clients based on the helper's feelings and experiences. The social worker can in turn use this information to help clients better understand their needs and what they want and to relate more effectively to others. The worker, however, must be careful to accurately assess the difference between countertransference and clients' ineffective use of self in accomplishing their goals.

Insight

Insight, widely used with this model of intervention, is an explanation or understanding provided by the social worker to the client as to the meaning of repressed experiences. Insight focuses on bringing to consciousness and illuminating unconscious conflicts—those that are repressed—and on helping the client understand how those conflicts continue to play out in the client's current life, especially as they pertain to relationships and maladaptive behaviors such as procrastination or excessive stubbornness.

Practitioners are also interested in helping clients understand the defenses they use to deal with situations in their lives. Therefore, another goal is helping clients strengthen and use appropriate defenses, avoid those that are counterproductive, and redirect problematic defenses into more constructive ways of satisfying clients' needs.

Ego Strengthening

Based largely on Erikson's theories, ego psychologists are concerned with strengthening the client's ego and using the person's inherent rationality to identify problems and potential solutions. **Ego strengthening** allows clients to see that out of every crisis or experience comes an opportunity to grow and learn. Clients will also be helped to come to a better understanding of their personal identity though an exploration of their goals, fears, dreams, ideals, and disappointments. Through worker–client interactions, the social worker will help clients let go of roles and ways of behaving that are no longer effective. Clients are taught that they are ultimately responsible for their present situation and the future they face.

Other Techniques

Practitioners using ego psychology theory are likely to use a variety of techniques to help clients improve, including teaching clients new behaviors and skills and reinforcing problem-solving efforts and coping strategies. Social workers will also use the environment to "provide more opportunities and conditions for the use of one's capacities" (Goldstein, 1986). Allowing the client to ventilate feelings is also an acceptable technique. One benefit of ego psychology is the potential to engage in prevention activities that are dedicated to improving the functioning of others—not just the client—in society (Goldstein, 1986).

Behavioral Therapy and Techniques

Behavioral therapy is not based on a comprehensive theory of personality (Liebert & Liebert, 1998). Although attempts have been made to do so (Dollard & Miller, 1950; Mowrer, 1950; Rotter, 1954; Mischel, 1973), few have been adapted to practice. "The important principles that underlie most of these theories are those developed through research on classical and operant conditioning and an observational learning" (Sharf, 2000, p. 292). The goal of behavior therapy is to help clients learn coping skills or eliminate self-defeating habits.

Joseph Wolpe presented several techniques based on Pavlov's principles of classical conditioning, Hull's stimulus-response (S-R) theory of learning, and his own studies on the reduction of anxiety that began with cats (Wilson, 1995). Having established anxiety in the animals using the S-R model, Wolpe (1973) writes that learning has taken place when

> a response has been evoked in temporal contiguity with a given stimulus and it is subsequently found that the stimulus can evoke the response although it could not have done so before. If the stimulus could have evoked the response before but subsequently evokes it more strongly, then, too, learning may be said to have occurred. (p. 8)

Wolpe then sought to reduce or eliminate this learned response through the use of "systematic desensitization" or "counter conditioning."

Systematic desensitization was based on the belief that if the response of anxiety is learned, it could also be unlearned. In order to achieve this unlearning, Wolpe hypothesized, if a response could be identified that when produced was incompatible with anxiety, it could then be paired with the stimulus that evoked anxiety and would essentially block the anxiety or minimize its effects. The principle established from this concept, termed *reciprocal inhibition,* states that "if a response inhibiting anxiety can be made to occur in the presence of anxiety-evoking stimuli, it will weaken the bond between these stimuli and anxiety" (Wolpe, 1973, p. 17). Over time and with enough pairings of the two (anxiety-evoking and anxiety-inhibiting stimuli), the anxiety will diminish and a new, more productive response will be substituted.

What Wolpe found was that the anxiety-inhibiting stimuli initially needed to be paired with a low- or mild-intensity anxiety-evoking stimulus in order to be effective. As anxiety is overcome at the low-intensity level, the person gradually moves up to the next level of anxiety-evoking stimulus. This technique was described as *systematic desensitization* (S-D) because it systematically moved from low- to high-intensity anxiety-provoking stimuli that are paired with anxiety-inhibiting stimuli.

There are three basic procedures in the use of S-D. First, Wolpe found the response of relaxation to be incompatible with anxiety. Borrowing from Jacobsen's (1938) progressive muscle relaxation techniques, Wolpe first taught and then had clients practice this technique until they reached adequate proficiency. For an example of relaxation, see the technique in Chapter 8.

The second step in the process is to create a list of anxiety-evoking stimuli and then rank them, from a low (or mild) level of anxiety evoking to a high (strongest) level of anxiety evoking. An alternative method is to have the client describe evoking stimuli along a time or space continuum, such as the days or hours before an event (e.g., a wedding) or the distance between the client and a feared object (being a block away from a snake as opposed to holding the snake). Clients are asked to rank the intensity of anxiety on a scale from 0 to 100 (0 is no anxiety and 100 is maximum anxiety or panic). Often the distance between anxiety-evoking stimuli average approximately 10 points. Clients also describe, in as much detail as possible, the situations that cause them anxiety.

The third step combines the two previous steps in order to countercondition the anxiety-evoking stimuli. This is done by having clients relax. Once this is achieved, they are asked to imagine, as clearly as possible, the first, lowest level anxiety-evoking stimulus on their list. If they experience any anxiety, they are to signal using the index finger. Clients are then instructed to stop or turn off the anxiety-evoking scene and to relax. When relaxation is once again achieved, they are instructed to return in their mind to the anxiety-evoking scene, again followed by relaxation. This pattern is repeated until clients successfully achieve relaxation. Clients will often report no longer experiencing anxiety when presented with the anxiety-evoking scene.

If after imaging a scene clients report not experiencing anxiety, they are asked to continue to try doing so for another ten seconds and then return to relaxation. They repeat this effort, and if no anxiety is elicited, the next scene on the hierarchy of anxiety-evoking stimuli is presented. If they still are unable to elicit anxiety, the practitioner may describe the scene, in as much detail as possible, to assist the client in achieving this affective state so that they can practice implementing relaxation and controlling the anxiety, once it is experienced. With any given scene, it may take anywhere from two to three presentations to eliminate the anxiety, or it may take the en-

tirety of one, two, or more therapy sessions focused on a single scene before the anxiety is no longer experienced and a sense of control has been achieved.

Once a sense or level of competence has been achieved in the imagined situation, clients are encouraged to practice the newly learned skill in vivo, or in real-life situations. In this process, the skill of being able to relax is important, along with gradient exposure from low to high levels of anxiety-evoking stimuli in order to build confidence and achieve success. The two related behavioral techniques of implosive and flooding therapies (Barker, 1999) are similar to S-D but are not reviewed here.

Assertiveness Training

Systematic-desensitization is the preferred intervention for anxiety and phobias occurring in situations not involving humans. For social anxiety—anxiety in the presence of people—Wolpe developed the technique of assertiveness training. Assertiveness, considered incompatible with anxiety, is for candidates who have difficulty expressing their feelings or their likes and dislikes. As a result, they are often taken advantage of and experience anxiety in social situations. A low sense of self-esteem is also a common characteristic. Assertive behavior is defined by Wolpe (1973) as "the proper expression of any emotion other than anxiety towards another person" (p. 81). Being assertive means being able to express anger and annoyance when appropriate, but also love and friendliness when these emotions are appropriate (Wolpe, 1969).

In the session, the client is asked to rehearse a situation in which assertiveness is needed. The practitioner applies a graduated sequence of behaviors. First, the client is instructed on how to behave (e.g., body posture, facial expression, eye contact, and voice training) (Wilson, 1995). Next, the practitioner takes the part of the "other" person involved in the situation and instructs the client on how to use the newly learned assertive behaviors (bodily expressions as well as verbal expressions). The third step is to have the client practice the new behaviors in the session in order to develop strategies that will carry over into real-life situations.

As with S-D, the clients identify multiple anxiety-provoking social situations and begin with the least anxiety provoking and work toward the most anxiety provoking while developing skills for each (Prochaska & Norcross, 1999). An important rule to follow when using this approach is that it should "never instigate an assertive act that is likely to have serious punishing consequences for the patient" (Wolpe, 1969, p. 67). Goldfried and Davidson (1994) believe that a lack of any assertion by a client encourages the status quo, especially for women who are abused. Rimm & Masters (1974) have recommended a "minimal effective response" that is less likely to be met with a hostile or aggressive response. Clients also ought to be taught to express the minimum amount of negative emotion in order to achieve a desired outcome (Prochaska & Norcross, 1999). Chapter 8 discusses assertiveness training in greater depth.

Applied Behavior Analysis

Applied behavior analysis relies on the principles of operant conditioning, examining the consequences that follow a behavior. These environmental consequences, or contingencies, be they reinforcers or punishers, have an impact on whether a maladaptive behavior will continue or whether a new one will be learned. Environmental contingencies are continually shaping our behavior. Applied behavior analysis attempts to control or alter the contingen-

cies in order to change or correct maladaptive behavior or to teach new adaptive behaviors.

Contingency, Immediacy, and Schedule of Reinforcement

Most behaviorally based programs prefer to have clients increase a desired behavior through the use of reinforcement. In order for reinforcement to be effective, clients need to understand and implement concepts in order to increase the probability that the procedures will succeed. For a reinforcer to be used effectively, a contingency must be established. For this to happen, a relationship must be established between the production of a specific or target behavior and the immediately following introduction of a reinforcer. The reinforcer then becomes contingent upon the production of the desired behavior. The more immediately the reinforcer follows the behavior, the more effective or powerful it is in establishing the behavior. If the reinforcer is not delivered soon after the target behavior is produced, it loses its effectiveness. This is of particular importance when the client is attempting to establish a new behavior.

Once the contingent relationship has been established and the target behavior is being produced, the schedule of reinforcement needs to be determined. Initially, a continuous schedule is recommended, followed by some form of intermittent schedule. This process of moving from a continuous to an intermittent schedule is referred to as "thinning."

According to Sherman (1973), effective contingency management involves six steps:

1. Operationalize the target behavior by stating the problem in "behavioral" terms. It is also necessary to identify the maladaptive responses as well as the conditions under which they occur.

2. Determine whether the target behavior is to be increased or decreased. Further, determine the acceptable level of performance for the target behavior.

3. Assess the target behavior and determine the baseline. The baseline is the rate or frequency level at which a behavior occurs. This will allow you to measure the amount, if any, of change that occurs in the target behavior.

4. Observe the client in his or her natural setting(s) in order to identify the contingencies surrounding the behavior. Note those contingencies that are reinforcers.

5. Identify reinforcers, how they will be administered, and under what conditions they will or will not be given. This results in a change in the conditions (contingencies) that influence the behavior and result in change.

6. Using the baseline data, continue to assess the target behavior for change. If the desired outcomes are not occurring, modifications to the contingencies may be made.

Reinforcers may be administered by a variety of persons, including an outside agency or individual, clients themselves, or a combination of these. When an entire environment is constructed on the principles of operant conditioning, it is referred to as a "token economy" (Atthowe & Krasner, 1968). Those things considered to be positive reinforcers (e.g., TV, free time, a walk, treats, etc.) are made contingent on positive or appropriate behavior. Immediate reinforcement is symbolic; the client is given a token, usually in the form of a chip. Based on a preestablished value system (for example, each red token is worth ten points and the white ones are worth twenty-five points), when the person has earned enough points, she or he may trade in the number of tokens necessary to obtain the desired privilege.

For a **token economy** to be effective, the entire staff must coordinate their efforts to achieve consistency in administering the program. Clearly defined procedures must be outlined and followed to avoid confusion. The staff needs to be reminded to reinforce clients' positive behaviors in order to increase the occurrence of desired behaviors instead of seeking ways to deny rewarding them. Over time the tangible rewards (tokens) need to be replaced with less tangible rewards (compliments) to better simulate the noninstitutional or nontherapeutic environment.

If the goal of treatment is to decrease a behavior while using the token economy procedure, a **response cost** component may be instituted. Each time a target behavior that needs to be reduced is produced, the person is "fined" by having a certain number of tokens or points removed. The fine amount is predetermined. The technique of response cost has been found to successfully treat stuttering, hyperactivity, overeating, smoking, poor academic performance, nail-biting, and antisocial behaviors in young delinquent men (Arnold, Forehand, & Sturges, 1976; Reichle, Brubakken, & Tetreault, 1976; Wolf et al., 1970).

Contingency Contracting

A contingency contract is a formal written agreement between two or more people that defines specific expected behaviors (those to increase and/or decrease), along with the rewards and punishments associated with the behaviors. There are five necessary elements to the contract (Stuart & Lott, 1972). First, it must clearly define what each person is to receive on successful completion of the behavior. Second, the parties involved must be able to monitor the behaviors. Third, if the behavior is not performed to the agreed-upon standard, sanctions that have been previously defined are to be levied. Fourth, bonuses must be given for compliance with the contract, and fifth, compliance or noncompliance must be documented in order to provide consistent feedback about the target behavior and the provision of reinforcers. Compliance with the contract increases when all the parties are involved in its development.

Timeout from Reinforcement

This procedure is classified as punishment because of its effect of decreasing behavior. It essentially removes the person from any opportunity to receive reinforcement for a brief prespecified amount of time. The timeout is called following the occurrence of a target behavior with the goal of decreasing the specific behavior.

Most often, a child is placed on a seat in a corner or a quiet place in a room for a prespecified amount of time. While in timeout, the child is not to receive any form of reinforcement. Adults must be consistent and not interact with the child, even when coaxed to do so, except for an emergency or dangerous situation, for this technique to be effective. Before using this technique, the practitioner needs to carefully examine the target behavior. For example, if the child is seeking to avoid a situation by going to timeout, an alternative technique is recommended.

Shaping

When a new behavior is to be learned, it often needs to be broken down into parts, with each part being taught separately, or successive approximations of the desired end task being taught. The behaviors are taught in a sequence, from beginning to end. As each part is correctly performed, it is reinforced. The next behavior in the sequence is then taught, and when produced it too is reinforced. This continues until the target behavior is learned.

An example of shaping is teaching a child the new behavior of riding a bicycle. First, the instructor shows the child how to adjust the pedals before getting onto the seat. Then the child learns how to correctly place his or her hands on the handlebars. At this point, the child learns to pull himself or herself onto the seat. Once on the bike, the child learns how to balance while peddling. Often this occurs with training wheels attached. When training wheels are removed, an adult will run alongside the new bicyclist while holding onto the back of the seat as the child learns how to coordinate peddling with balance. When the child appears to be steady, the adult lets go of the seat. This letting go begins with short release periods and then increasingly longer periods until the child is able to successfully manage all of the components without assistance. After each step in the process is learned, the child is reinforced with words of praise and recognition.

Premack Principle

If the goal is to increase a behavior that is not often produced, a behavior that is frequently produced can be used as a reinforcer to encourage increased production of the low-probability behavior (Premack, 1965). An example of this might be a child who does not participate in chores around the house. He is frequently found, however, in front of the computer playing games. In order to increase the behavior of helping with the chores, he is informed that his computer time will be allowed only after he has put a certain amount of time into doing chores or after he has completed a prespecified number of tasks. Thus, the computer playing acts as a reinforcer to help increase the amount of chores that are done.

Differential Reinforcement for Incompatible Behaviors (DRI)

The goal of differential reinforcement of incompatible behaviors is to decrease a particular behavior by reinforcing other behaviors that interfere with production of the target behavior. For example, if the behavior of thumb sucking is to be reduced, the child may be rewarded for playing a computer game that involves the use of both hands. While the child is engaged in the game, her hands are not free and she is therefore not sucking her thumb. A child who is found picking at an open wound may be asked to keep his hands in his pockets and reinforced for this behavior.

Modeling Techniques from Social Learning Theory

Based on Bandura's work, modeling has been used as a therapeutic technique to aid in learning new behaviors or assist in the development of coping behaviors. According to Spiegler and Guevremont (1998), there are five basic functions of modeling: teaching, prompting, motivating, reducing anxiety, and discouraging. When teaching a new behavior, the instructor may demonstrate what is expected of the learner. A Little League coach, for example, often models how to properly catch a ground ball.

A prompt is a warning for the subject to be ready to do something. When a person serving as the model or instructor performs a behavior, the subject is cued or prompted to also do something. An elementary school teacher may prompt his students to begin doing math problems when he concludes instruction at the

board and sits at his desk; the Little League coach holds up a bat and a ball, thus signaling that he will be hitting grounders.

Motivation can come from seeing the rewards that another person receives after having completed a task. Young boys and girls who want to become professional athletes or performers may be more motivated to pursue these careers after seeing how the crowd reacts to professionals' performances. Modeling can also be used to help reduce problematic behavior. For example, clients may reduce their anxiety about an object or a situation after they observe someone else successfully dealing with that object or situation. Young boys may not be inclined to jump off a cliff into a lake until they see other boys their age doing it. Likewise, a person may not want to hold a snake, but having witnessed a good friend doing so without harm, may decide it is okay to handle the reptile.

In direct practice, modeling can be applied in a variety of ways. For example, a live model may perform the behavior as the client looks on. Sometimes the model performs the behavior a number of times while the client observes, after which the client performs the behavior. Models may also be symbolic. In this situation, the client might view a video of a model performing the behavior. Pictures in books or magazines, photographs, or movies can also be helpful.

Role playing or behavioral rehearsal (Wilson, 1995) is a form of modeling that allows the client to see how another person might deal effectively with a new or anxiety-provoking situation. It also allows clients to practice newly learned skills or coping strategies while considering different possibilities and alternative plans. Role playing is often used to help clients develop skills of assertion. For example, a timid person might practice job interviewing skills and learn how to respond both verbally and nonverbally to a potential employer's questions.

Techniques from Cognitive Therapy

"Cognitive therapy is an active, directive, time-limited structured approach used to treat a variety of psychiatric disorders. . . . It is based on an underlying theoretical rationale that an individual's affect and behavior are largely determined by the way in which he structures the world" (Beck et al., 1979). The key concept associated with cognitive theory stresses the influence of one's thoughts on their mood and behavior. Specifically, treatment focuses on dysfunctional or maladaptive thoughts and their expression in emotional and behavioral problems. The goal for this theory of intervention is to correct the faulty information processing and incorrect assumptions so that the client will ultimately experience a change in emotions and behavior. To achieve this end, "therapeutic techniques are designed to identify, reality-test, and correct disturbed conceptualizations and dysfunctional beliefs (schemas)" (Beck et al., 1979, p. 4).

Collaborative Relationship

Establishing a positive therapeutic relationship is a key component of this model of therapy. To accomplish this, the core facilitative conditions (empathy, genuineness, and positive regard) are used. It is also important to the relationship that the practitioner and the client work collaboratively on the problem. Unlike some other models of therapy, this concept suggests that both client and practitioner are actively involved in the therapeutic process.

The purpose of this relationship is for the social worker to *join* with the client, as a partner, in understanding and working on the problem. In the beginning, the client's primary responsibility is to identify and report those thoughts and mental images, along with the accompanying emotions and behaviors, that contribute to the problem. The social worker's role at this time is to understand what brought the client in. Social workers are most likely to hear clients describing uncomfortable feelings and/or behaviors or an unsettling or disturbing event in their life. Following the client's description and a thorough assessment of the problem, the practitioner will determine whether to use cognitive techniques, behavior techniques, or a combination of both. The goal of treatment will focus on correcting faulty information processing, those thoughts that are automatic, and modifying maladaptive assumptions.

Homework

Homework assignments are given as part of the intervention process and are to be completed between sessions. Homework serves a couple of purposes. First, it keeps the client involved with and connected to the practitioner between sessions. Second, it helps to speed up the rate of goal attainment by having the client practice newly learned skills.

A-B-C Model

In the process of working toward the goal of cognitive change, both practitioner and client examine the client's automatic thoughts, assumptions, inferences, and conclusions about himself or herself or others based on how the client interprets his or her past, present, or future. A client's thoughts or beliefs are posed in the form of a hypothesis and then examined for evidence that either supports or refutes the validity of the hypothesis.

Through the use of questions and discussion, the social worker elicits specific information about the client's thoughts, feelings, and behavior, especially as they occur during and following upsetting events. To help clients understand how each of these aspects of human behavior occurs, Ellis and Harper (1975) instruct clients on the A-B-C model. "A" represents an activating event or activating experience that the client recognizes. The event might be triggered by a person in the environment, such as your boss's negative remark about your work, or it might result from an object or occurrence such as receiving a grade of D on a paper or looking out the window and seeing that a heavy snowstorm swept through during the night. In each case, the activating event must be recognized or sensed in some way.

As a result of the "A," a person will have some type of thought or belief, "B," about the "A." For clients seeking relief from their mood or to correct a negative behavior, this thought or belief is in some way upsetting. According to Beck and Weishaar (1995), thoughts occur at different levels. At one level, they are identified as being "automatic." Automatic thoughts occur immediately or spontaneously in response to an activating event. Clients can often be instructed to identify automatic thoughts by paying attention to them as an upsetting event occurs or immediately following an event.

The next level of thoughts are referred to as "underlying assumptions" and "attitudes," also referred to as "schema," that were developed through previous experiences. "Assumptions shape perceptions into cognitions, determine goals, and provide interpretations and meanings to events. They may be quite stable and outside the patient's awareness" (Beck & Weishaar, 1995, p. 243). "Automatic thoughts are also generated from underlying assumptions" (p. 243). When possible, the practitioner attempts to identify and correct these faulty assumptions or core beliefs by collaboratively working with clients to identify

them and aiding in the development of skills to alter them.

"C" represents the feeling and behavior consequences that people experience as a result of the belief (B) they hold that was initiated following the activating event (A). Feelings may consist of anxiety, fear, rage, hostility, depression, sadness, euphoria, or comfort, to name a few, or they may constitute any combination or form of these. Behaviors may be evidenced by, but not limited to, avoidance, aggression, withdrawing, or taking excessive risks. These feelings and/or behaviors may result in enough personal and societal distress that the person seeks or is pressured into professional help. See Figure 7.1 for a scenario of the A-B-C model.

Educating the Client

According to Beck and colleagues (1979), the best way to train clients in the cognitive model is through the following five basic steps:

(1) Define "automatic thoughts" (cognition); (2) demonstrate the relationship between cognition and affect (or behavior) using specific examples; (3) demonstrate the presence of cognitions from the patient's recent experience; (4) assign the patient homework to collect cognitions; and (5) review the patient's records [completed homework] and provide concrete feedback. (p. 147)

The practitioner acts as an educator, helping the client to understand the basic tenets of the model and how these tenets apply specifically to the client's problems. One of the first steps with this approach is to provide an explanation of the cognitive model, highlighting the relationship between how clients think about themselves, others, situations, and the future and the way they feel and behave. Examples, as shown in Case Example 7.1, are often used to illustrate this concept.

Figure 7.1

Example of an A-B-C Diagram

Activating event	Belief	feeling and behavior Consequences
Walked into the house. Teenage son called me to come quickly. There was a large bubble in the ceiling from a water leak. Son was poking it with a knife to release pressure.	Why didn't he do something about it before I got home? He's stupid to poke a hole in the bubble; everyone knows you have to get on the roof and clear off the water. Why do I always have to take care of of these things? I'll be up all night fixing this problem, and I'll never get any rest.	—Feelings: Anger Fatigue Frustration —Behavior: Yelled Slammed the door Called him stupid Ordered people around

CASE EXAMPLE 7.1

Educating Clients

Three agency staff members were called into their supervisor's office and told that the agency had just lost a large contract for services that had been paying their salaries. As a consequence, they were told to clean out their offices and leave their keys with the receptionist on their way out. The catalyst or activating event (A) was the same for each staff member. None had seen this coming and all were shocked by the suddenness of the decision. Interestingly, however, the resultant feeling, consequence C, associated with A was unique to each person.

One was scared about the future and worried about what she would do. Another staff member reacted with anger, whereas the third member seemed strangely happy. The differences in emotional reactions to the termination can be accounted for by each person's belief system. The staff member who was scared feared the future and doubted she would ever find a similar position. In addition, she wondered what others would think of her after she lost her job.

By contrast, the angry staff member believed he had contributed greatly to the success of the agency and was being unfairly compensated for his long hours and hard work by being laid off. He was furious at what he perceived to be the treachery and lack of loyalty of his supervisor.

The third staff member, who seemed almost happy about the termination, saw the situation as an opportunity to change her career direction. She decided that she wanted to return to school and become a landscape architect. It is clear that the original A factor was the same for each but that their individual reactions at C were influenced by what occurred in B.

Another way to illustrate the influence of thoughts on feelings and behavior in a concrete way is to ask clients what they were feeling (1) as they drove to their appointment with you and (2) as they sat in the waiting room. Once the feelings are noted, the practitioner then asks what thoughts clients recall having. Making this connection helps demonstrate the relationship between the two: the thought about coming for help and the resulting feelings. The practitioner then helps clients test their hypothesis or the accuracy of their thoughts (Beck et al., 1979). At this point, the social worker can begin to train clients to observe and record their dysfunctional thoughts.

Cognitive Techniques

Once thoughts at "B" are identified, they can be examined through the use of questions to uncover any possible thinking errors (inconsistencies or contradictions). See discussion of Socratic questions in Chapter 4. Cognitive techniques are then used to correct these irrational beliefs (Ellis & Harper, 1975), or cognitive distortions (Beck et al., 1979). Examining and reality-testing automatic thoughts and images is a basic technique in this model. The goal is to help clients more accurately describe and analyze how they see themselves, others, and events in their life. Once thoughts are identified through the collaborative efforts of both practitioner and client, they "should be subjected to the scrutiny of reality testing" (Beck et al., 1979, p. 153). The standard used for testing ought to be that which is deemed to be reasonable for nondepressed, nonpanicky, or nonenraged persons. Facts, not opinions, must be elicited through questions, and clients are asked to identify the evidence they used to validate their conclusions. For example, a client may be asked, "I understand that you thought he was ignoring you, but what

evidence do you have that supports your conclusion?"

Redefining

The technique of redefining (Burns, 1985) encourages clients who are afraid to act to define the problem from a different perspective. Instead of seeing the problem as "I'm no good at taking tests," they would be encouraged to define it as "I need to gain more experience with test taking." The problem ought to be redefined in concrete and specific terms. Redefining is similar to reframing, a technique used by a number of systems-oriented family therapists (Nichols & Schwartz, 2001).

Reattribution

The technique of reattribution invites clients to consider alternative causes for events (Beck & Weishaar, 1995). For people who are inclined to see themselves as solely responsible, this technique encourages them to identify as many factors as possible that may have contributed to their situation. Once alternative factors are identified, the client is asked to accurately place responsibility where it lies. For example, a client might be asked in a follow-up question to her belief that a friend ignored her because he had to have been angry with her to "list other possible reasons as to why he did not acknowledge her besides the possibility that he was purposefully ignoring her."

Decentering

Decentering, another cognitive technique, is used with anxious persons who believe they are the center of everyone's attention and that others know how they are feeling and what they are thinking. Through questioning, clients are encouraged to look for evidence that other people are indeed focusing on them and to consider how others are able to read their mind. Clients are assigned the task of going out into a social setting. Once there, they are to focus their attention on the people around them to determine how much, if at all, others are focusing on them. Further, they are to determine how likely it is that others are aware of their (clients') feelings verses the likelihood that clients are actually focusing on themselves and assuming that others are doing the same. The purpose of this activity is to help clients turn their focus away from themselves and direct it toward others.

Behavioral Techniques

Although the primary goal of cognitive therapy is to modify or change a person's thoughts and assumptions, a key component of achieving this end is the use of behavioral techniques. Behavioral techniques are primarily designed to challenge previously learned assumptions and automatic thoughts as well as assist in the learning of new behaviors. Clients use a form of the scientific method, set up as "experiments" to determine the accuracy or inaccuracy of their thoughts by doing or behaving in a particular way and then examining the results of their activity for evidence that either supports or refutes their hypothesis. Behavioral techniques may also increase a client's repertoire of behaviors and skills that may be used for coping or problem solving.

Activity Scheduling

Homework is a standard technique used with this model. It provides clients with opportunities to test out their assumptions as well as practice newly acquired skills. While clients are performing the assignment, they are often asked to monitor their thoughts (B) and mood and behavior (C). As their skill level progresses, they will learn to examine and then challenge their faulty assumptions and

replace them with more accurate, logical assumptions.

For clients who are immobilized by their thoughts, most often because they are severely depressed or expressively anxious, activity scheduling is an intervention that helps them counteract their inhibiting behavior. Beck and colleagues (1979) recommend that the following four principles be incorporated when activity scheduling is implemented. First, clients need to be informed that no one completes everything they planned for. Therefore, clients need not feel bad when they are not 100 percent successful in accomplishing the task.

Second, clients are encouraged to identify the type or kind of activity that will be addressed at a particular time rather than focus on how much they will accomplish. External factors may influence how much is accomplished and be out of the client's control.

Third, clients need to be reminded that trying to do the activity is the most important aspect, not how successful they are at completing it. Simply trying the activity gives the client and the practitioner needed and helpful information.

Fourth, time needs to be set aside each day to plan for the subsequent day. The evening is a good time, though not right before bedtime as the planning may generate thoughts that keep the client awake. Again, knowing that trying is more important than achieving will help clients overcome any negative thoughts they may have about doing the assignment. The social worker needs to reinforce the idea that in doing the task, clients are not to evaluate how well or poorly they did it, but to observe how they felt and to identify those thoughts (B) associated with the feelings and behavior (C) and activity (A).

The schedule may cover a few days or a week, often with specific activities identified throughout the day. Scheduled activities may simply consist of daily living activities such as rising at 7 a.m., showering, and eating breakfast; 9 a.m.—going for a walk; 10 a.m.—shopping for groceries; and so on, or it may consist of planning a specific event or required tasks such as those involved in business, for example, phoning customers from 9:00 to 9:30, meeting with staff from 9:30 to 10:15, lunching with a colleague at 12:15, and so on.

Mastery and Pleasure

Often clients are asked to rate their mastery of and pleasure in each of the activities in the daily schedule. **Mastery** is the level of performance, or how well the person has done the task. **Pleasure** is the level of enjoyment a person feels at performing the task. The purpose of the mastery/pleasure technique is to help clients who believe they are not doing anything well or are not receiving any enjoyment out of daily tasks to examine the evidence for their assumption. See Case Example 7.2.

Clients will sometimes avoid pleasurable activities. Through recall, the helper and the client look for times and/or events in the past that the client found pleasurable (Beck et al., 1979). The client is then assigned homework to participate in these types of pleasurable activities and to rank the level of mastery and pleasure. The desired outcome is for the client to identify small amounts of pleasure derived from participation in activities as well as a sense of accomplishment or achievement on which to build a change in thought and mood. The information generated by the activity allows the client to more accurately examine and correct negative, distorted thoughts.

Graded Task Assignment

The technique of graded task assignment is used to move a client from doing less difficult to progressively more difficult activities (this is particularly useful for depressed or inhibited clients), as well as to successfully complete assignments. Generally, the successful comple-

---

CASE EXAMPLE 7.2

Mastery and Pleasure

A client once stated that she could not do anything well, especially with regard to keeping up her house. In an effort to examine this assumption, the client scheduled her week and was asked to judge her level of mastery and pleasure. At the following session, she had ranked both mastery and pleasure at 0 for all activities. On review, she was able to identify that she had successfully completed many household chores at a high level of mastery. Yet, like many clients, she did not find much enjoyment from participating in things like dishwashing and cleaning the bathrooms. However, her mood improved when she realized that she had done the tasks well, but she still did not enjoy doing them. When she was able to separate her ability from her enjoyment and, on examination, decided that not liking the tasks had nothing to do with her being a "good" or "bad" mother or homemaker, she was able to find some relief from her depressed mood and thoughts of guilt and of being a failure.

tion of assignments helps to increase clients' level of confidence and improve their mood. Practitioners need to stay close to clients and help them overcome attempts to downplay or ignore their accomplishments.

In graded task assignment, the problem is identified and the solution broken down from complex to more simple steps. Clients are asked to perform the steps and provide feedback as they do so, specifically with regard to their ability to accomplish the task. The client and the practitioner then take a realistic look at client performance and reevaluate goal achievement based on the client's efforts. Clients progressively increase the level of difficulty of the tasks until they reach their goal (Beck et al., 1979). This technique might be applied to a client diagnosed with agoraphobia, or fear of being in public places or doing something embarrassing. The client's ultimate goal would be to go shopping alone at the mall. Although this is a realistic goal, it may be too much to tackle at one time. Therefore, the task would be broken down into smaller, more achievable parts such as driving to the parking lot and staying there until a general feeling of comfort is reached. Later, the client is to walk up to the entrance, then enter the mall, and then venture approximately 100 feet inside. Over time the client will be able to go further and with less assistance. As is evident, this particular technique is similar to systematic desensitization. However, the treatment has an added cognitive component.

Assertiveness Training and Role Play

As in behavior therapy, clients are taught skills that help them deal with others or to identify alternative methods of behaving with people or in situations. In the therapeutic environment, they are allowed to practice the new skills and to receive coaching or view modeling by the practitioner. Social workers using this model also examine clients' specific thoughts associated with the implementation of the new behaviors in an effort to identify and correct any distortions or errors accompanying the behaviors.

Person-Centered Therapy

The process of person-centered therapy begins with the first meeting. Because the focus is on clients, they decide what will be addressed in the session. The helper does not engage in any form of assessment or history taking or pursue any type of agenda that would interfere with the client's goal. The social worker demonstrates respect for the client and listens while exhibiting the qualities of warmth and acceptance. It is completely up to the client to decide which direction the session will go in or whether the session will be filled with conversation, the expression of feelings, or silence. The number of sessions is also up to the client, as well as the frequency of appointments. Therapy continues until clients decide they no longer wish to be in the relationship, which may occur after one session or fifty or more.

"The basic theory of person-centered therapy is that if the social worker is successful in conveying genuineness, unconditional positive regard and empathy, then the client will respond with constructive changes in personality organization" (Raskin & Rogers, 1995, p. 142). The practitioner employs these core qualities to help the client achieve the goal of self-actualization, the ability of people to fully develop their potential (Barker, 1999). Because Rogers believed that humans possess an innate drive toward socially constructive behaviors, the work in the therapeutic relationship is to help the client unleash these forces that contribute to growth (Millon, 1999).

Empathy

"*Empathy* . . . is an active, immediate, continuous process. The social worker makes a maximum effort to get within and to *live* the attitudes expressed instead of observing them, diagnosing them, or thinking of ways to make the process go faster" (Raskin & Rogers, 1995, p. 142). To achieve this, the practitioner must pay attention to what the client is communicating, both verbally and nonverbally, with particular attention to the client's experienced and expressed feelings. By genuinely attempting to understand the client's total experience and communicating that understanding, the practitioner strengthens his or her relationship with the client. Through practice, the social worker will be able to go beyond a parallel understanding of what the client is feeling and thus be able to tap into a deeper level of awareness.

Positive Regard

Positive regard is a nonjudgmental attitude the practitioner holds toward the client. When this quality is sensed and observed as being genuine, clients are more likely to feel at liberty to express whatever feeling they are having at the moment without fear of reprisal or condemnation. Thus, they are able to become congruent, saying what they are truly feeling, resulting in positive therapeutic movement (Rogers, 1986).

Congruence and Genuineness

The characteristics of *congruence* and *genuineness* send the message to clients that the practitioner is being himself or herself. The social worker is not pretending or acting out a part, but honestly wants to help. Because of genuineness, practitioners are also comfortable with their own feelings as they are experienced during the session. According to Rogers (1986), "the therapist is his actual self in his encounter with his client. Without facade, he openly has the feelings and attitudes that are flowing in him at the moment. The therapist encounters his client directly, meeting him person to person. He is being himself, not denying himself" (p. 185). Based on the practitioner's judgment, when it is appropriate the helper's feelings are expressed so that the client–worker relationship is strengthened.

Unlike some traditional models in which the practitioner interprets for clients aspects of their behavior, dreams, or transference, with person-centered therapy clients arrive at insight on their own. Their own personal insight allows them to give "new meaning" to their "own experience" (Rogers, 1942, p. 174) and to understand cause-and-effect relationships or the effects of their behavior from a new perspective.

Rogers does not agree with approaches that allow the helper to diagnose or evaluate in any way. The relationship is to be person-centered, allowing clients to open up communications between the part of them that is the organism and the part that consists of self-evaluation. This permits clients to decide for themselves what is and is not important to them. Knowing that the practitioner accepts them as they are (unconditional positive regard) is enough to allow clients to begin the reevaluation process (Rogers, 1951).

The role asked of clients is to be natural and to assume responsibility for the people they are rather than the people others want them to be. Therefore, the social worker must trust clients and their ability to become what is best for them, based on the genuine feeling clients have as organisms. This corrective process takes place through the relationship established between social worker and client. As the practitioner exemplifies an attitude of positive regard, expresses accurate empathy, and relates to clients as individuals who are congruent with their feelings, clients will begin relating as congruent persons.

Systems Theory, Therapy, and Applied Techniques

"The foremost conceptual influence on family therapy's pioneers was system theory. In fact, family therapy and systems were so closely identified with each other that they became nearly synonymous" (Nichols & Schwartz, 2001, p. 104). According to Nichols and Schwartz (2001), general systems theory (GST), developed by Ludwig von Bertalanffy, was actually developed as a model rather than a theory. It is a "way of thinking or a set of assumptions that can be applied to all kinds of systems" (p. 114). Although many GST concepts have been embraced in family therapy, this model is most often recognized as influencing the early work on family communications, conducted by Gregory Bateson and his colleagues at the Mental Research Institute (MRI), beginning in the late 1950s. "Influenced by the General Systems Theory of von Bertalanffy (1933, 1950), Bateson stressed the importance of circular causality in communication" (Millon, 1999, p. 26). The goal, from this approach, is to correct problems stemming from faulty communications. The practitioner's role is to help reduce and correct repetitive errors that result in miscommunication (Millon, 1999). Contributors to Bateson's early work were Don Jackson, John Weekland, Jay Haley, and Virginia Satir.

Family therapists seem to have best adapted systems theory to practice. Although no single interventive theory or approach is based on GST, its concepts have been incorporated into many modes of family therapy. Consequently, it is important to examine one of the more popular family therapies based on systems theory, namely structural family therapy.

Structural Family Therapy

Salvadore Minuchin's structural family therapy, like the theories for individual therapy, provides an organized and systematic method for intervening with families. Structural family therapy "had the good fortune of developing theoretically at the beginning of psychotherapy's discovery of systems theory and family-oriented techniques" (Carlson & Kjos, 2002, p. 2). According to this theory, families have problems when dysfunctional structures exist and are maintained within the family system. This is most likely to occur when families do not adjust to those changes that necessarily occur as families develop over time. According to Simon (1995), the role of the structural therapist is to assist the family in tapping into those dormant structures already available in order to make the changes that will lead to problem resolution.

To accomplish this task, a primary role of the social worker is to "join" the family to help them make structural change. This change occurs when the worker helps the family to alter their boundaries and the subsystems, or structural relationships, through the use of interventions (Minuchin, 1974; Minuchin & Fishman, 1981). Once the family structure has been positively modified, or altered, the family is able on its own to tap into alternative ways of resolving its problems rather than falling back on the repetitive dysfunctional ways to which they had rigidly clung. Solving their own problem is a task that belongs to the family.

A common supposition of families entering into treatment is that one of its members has a problem. Structural family therapy, as well as other systems-oriented therapies, does not look at the individual as the problem; it looks at the family as a whole and sees a structural problem within the family system. Specifically, this model considers the problem to lie in certain patterns of interaction. The way to improve these repetitive and ineffective interactive patterns is to challenge the symptom: the family structure and the family reality (Minuchin & Fishman, 1981). To improve the structure, various techniques are employed. According to Nichols and Schwartz (2001, p. 251), "the strategy of structural family therapy follows these steps":

1. Joining and accommodating
2. Working with interaction
3. Diagnosing
4. Highlighting and modifying interactions
5. Boundary making
6. Unbalancing
7. Challenging unproductive assumptions

Joining and Accommodating

When practitioners meet with a family, they must integrate themselves into the family system. "Joining a family is more of an attitude than a technique, and it is the umbrella under which all therapeutic transactions occur" (Minuchin & Fishman, 1981, p. 31). To accomplish this, practitioners must demonstrate that they are there to work for the clients as well as with them and sincerely attempt to understand the family's problem, as well as each individual in the family. Practitioners must greet and respect all family members, with special consideration given to the adults. To help maintain family hierarchy and respect, it is best to first ask the parents, not the child, to explain why the family has come for help and to describe the problem.

Just as the practitioner makes accommodations to join the family, family members must tolerate having a practitioner, another person, inside their family system. The family must also accommodate the practitioner's role of helper and leader. The practitioner's failure to adequately join a family will likely result in the family resisting the social worker and blocking any efforts at change.

Working with Interaction

According to this model, the structure of a family is evident in the way members interact with one another. Questioning the family about their style of interaction provides less accurate information than directly observing it during the therapy session. As members interact among themselves, their particular structure begins to emerge (Nichols & Schwartz, 2001). Therapists must be trained to observe the process rather than the content of the interaction. Practitioners encourage family members to interact with one another during the session. For example, if a child is interrupting the conversation, the social worker might ask the parent(s) to please help the child be quiet and wait his turn. Another option might be to ask a mother to respond to her grandmother's or husband's comment regarding the mother's style of parenting. This is referred to as "enactment."

Enactment is a variant of interaction. Its purpose is to see how rules are played out and made manifest through family transactions. Not all family interactions need to be enacted, but

> transacting some of the problems that they [family] consider dysfunctional and negotiating disagreements, as in trying to establish control over a disobedient child, . . . unleashes sequences beyond the family control. The accustomed rules take over, and transactional components manifest themselves with an intensity similar to that manifested in

those transactions outside of the therapy session. (Minuchin & Fishman, 1981, pp. 78–79)

As the leader, the practitioner invites the family to enact or produce those transactions that can be assessed for dysfunction.

According to Minuchin and Fishman (1981), enactment can be viewed in three stages. First, the practitioner observes the ongoing transactions that occur during the meeting. Second, the practitioner asks family members to enact some scenario that it is believed will help to expose dysfunctional transactions and the types of boundaries established, most likely around the problem. Third, the social worker suggests alternative transactions.

The practitioner specifically looks for those processes that manifest enmeshment or disengagement. *Enmeshment* may be demonstrated by "frequently interrupting each other, speaking for other family members, doing things for children that they can do for themselves, or by constantly arguing," among other things (Nichols & Schwartz, 2002, p. 252). Behaviors that manifest *disengagement* might include "a husband sitting impassively while his wife cries; a total absence of conflict; a surprising ignorance of important information about the children; a lack of concern for each other's interests" (Nichols & Schwartz, 2002, p. 252).

Diagnosing

We do not cover this section in depth here because we dealt with it in Chapter 5. However, in short, the practitioner asks that as many significant (those that have substantial access or influence) members of the family as possible attend the initial session, including grandparents, aunts and uncles, and married as well as unmarried siblings living at home or away. The social worker needs to receive input from numerous sources to better help the identified patient with his or her problem. The social worker's goal, in having so many people present is to observe the quality and types of interactions of the whole family as a system, as well as the interactions between and among subsystems. This is the preferred method of doing the assessment (rather than using standardized questions or asking for members' opinions about the types and quality of family interaction) because it allows the social worker to see the system in action and the attempts made to deal with the problem. The practitioner relies on the principles and concepts from systems theory (homeostasis, boundaries, subsystems, feedback, circular causality, etc.) to determine the level of functionality or dysfunctionality within the family interactions.

Highlighting and Modifying Interactions

As families interact, the social worker focuses on the process, usually by observing who says what to whom, identifying who is quiet, and noting how people behave while interacting and how people are positioned. As some type of interaction begins, the helper may request that family members continue with the interaction. For example, a mother may ask a child to sit down and draw a picture or to be quiet while the adults speak. If the child does not respond to the parent, the social worker may then ask the parent to go ahead and quiet the child. The objective is to prevent the mother and child from falling back into the same repetitive pattern of interacting or transacting with each other and to disrupt the existing equilibrium. To accomplish this, the practitioner increases the intensity of the interaction, perhaps by asking a teenager's parents to make their daughter wait her turn while the others speak, or to continue the discussion about her curfew and accompanying restrictions with which she does not agree.

To ensure that the family hears the message—and because they often selectively listen to the practitioner—the intensity of the message may have to increase. The social worker may repeat the message or have the family continue the interaction longer than they normally would. The goal is to help the family find more functional patterns of interacting by disrupting the equilibrium or repetitive, rigid patterns of interacting. This will allow the family to find new ways of dealing with one another.

Boundary Making

"People are always functioning with only part of their repertory. Potential alternatives can be actualized if the individual begins to act in another subsystem, or if the nature of his participation in a subsystem changes" (Minuchin & Fishman, 1981, p. 146). One technique of the structural family therapeutic approach is to alter or influence the subsystems by increasing or eliminating the distance between them, which in turn influences the interaction. By influencing the subsystems to interact differently, the boundaries between them shift, and realignment takes place.

The social worker assesses the family subsystems to determine if the family as a whole or parts of the family subsystems are enmeshed (having diffuse boundaries) or disengaged (having overly rigid boundaries). "In highly enmeshed families the therapist's interventions are designed to strengthen boundaries between subsystems and to increase the independence of individuals" (Nichols & Schwartz, 2001, p. 256). To accomplish this, the therapist may create distance between people. For example, if an enmeshed mother and daughter are identified, the therapist might ask the father and daughter to discuss the daughter's problem while the mother is invited to observe the interaction, thus increasing the distance between the mom and the daughter. Or a couple might be asked to continue talking while their disobedient child is moved away from them. Both parents may also be asked to correct the disobedient child, but to decide together beforehand how they will do it and what is expected. This strengthens the boundary between parents and child. Tasks such as these may also be modified and extended outside of the family sessions.

"Disengaged families tend to avoid or detour conflict, and thus minimize interaction" (Nichols & Schwartz, 2002, p. 257). The social worker's goal with this type of interaction is to block a person from "detouring" and to encourage people to work through their problem by setting up boundaries that allow interaction to happen without outside interference. For example, if a couple has a dysfunctional disengaged relationship, a child may create some form of problem as the parents begin to interact and tension is felt. This move by the child will create a diversion so that the child makes it possible for the enmeshed father to avoid or detour his interaction with his wife. To block this, the social worker may say to the child that she is being "nice by misbehaving when your parents feel stressed by each other, but they are capable of working out their problem, so slide your chair over toward me." The father and daughter may be enmeshed and the father disengaged from the mother because the father believes he does not get the satisfaction he desires from his spouse. Interacting as he does with his daughter allows him to avoid dealing directly with his wife, thus interfering with his ability to find ways to resolve their problems.

Unbalancing

The purpose of this technique is to change the hierarchical relationship of family members within subsystems (Minuchin & Fishman, 1981). To accomplish this goal, the therapist joins with one member of the family or with one subsystem. The person or subgroup that is low in status or hierarchy is empowered by being joined by the social worker. An example might be a mother who is chronically depressed and ignored when it comes to making decisions about the children. In this case, the practitioner may decide to elevate her status and empower her by seeking her advice about what needs to be done regarding a particular child's problem. Another method is to ask her why her family has protected her for so long and to tell her that she needs to begin to make important decisions regarding the everyday activities of the children.

Challenging Unproductive Assumptions

The practitioner may challenge the family about how they perceive others within the system. "Challenging the way family members view reality enables them to change the way they relate to each other" (Nichols & Schwartz, 2001, p. 259). To accomplish this goal, the social worker might instruct or teach the family about structure, or give advice about hierarchies and boundaries. The practitioner might consider using the technique of reframing, helping the clients to see the problem in a different light or from a different perspective. For example, the social worker might describe a child diagnosed with attention deficit hyperactivity disorder as one who has a curious mind and a need to explore. Additionally, the social worker might give a paradoxical directive. With this technique, the often resistant clients are asked to do more of whatever the problem is in order to better understand the significance of it. If they do more, they are demonstrating a greater willingness to

follow instructions and demonstrating an amount of control. If they do less, they achieve an improvement in the problem, which is positive movement toward the goal. For example, the practitioner might ask an obsessive client to obsess more about his problem rather than less, or maybe to a set schedule that is more rigid than his past obsessive behavior. This technique, however, should be used with caution so as not to harm the client. The practitioner should seek supervision from someone who has been trained in using this technique correctly.

Strengths Perspective

Although the strengths perspective has not yet developed into a theory, it does influence how professionals think and what they do (Saleebey, 2002). Practice methods stemming from the principles of the strengths-based perspective are now being described in the literature with such models as family narratives and story, solution-focused therapy, assets-based community development, and resiliency (Nichols & Schwartz, 2001; Saleebey, 2002). The authors have selected solution-focused therapy to illustrate how this perspective is incorporated into practice.

Solution-Focused Therapy

The solution-focused approach to intervention originates with Steve de Shazer and Insoo Kim Berg. It stands in opposition to the medical and problem-solving models that seek to identify a particular cause for a person's or family's problem (such as an inherited gene that predisposes a person to alcoholism or a problem stemming back to early childhood development). This model works instead to find useful ways to build solutions. Proponents of this perspective

Voices from the Field

Jessica Whitney

My name is Jessica Whitney. I was born and raised in Wareham, Massachusetts. I am Deaf. I graduated from Bridgewater State College in Bridgewater, Massachusetts, with a BA in social work. I am the only Deaf person in my family. The support and encouragement from my immediate and extended families is what I rely on during difficult times. I received my MSW from Gallaudet University in May 2004. My educational and internship experiences have given me the enthusiasm and knowledge to work confidently in a school setting. I want to work with Deaf or Hard of Hearing children.

As a Deaf woman, I feel it is imperative for Deaf children to have a Deaf role model. As their social worker, I am empathetic and understand their perspective. For me, working in a mainstream setting would be the ultimate position. Children at Deaf schools are exposed to their language and culture every day. I would like to make this a reality in a mainstream setting as well. I attended both mainstream programs and a Deaf school as a child. My experience has given me a unique advantage when working with the Deaf children.

have built up a repertoire of procedures that have been found to be useful (DeJong & Berg, 2002).

De Shazer learned that discovering the source of the problem and connecting to a workable solution were not necessary to help clients reach their goal. Instead, individuals, couples, and families focus on the desired outcomes and solutions that they want to have happen. According to de Shazer (1985), "the most useful way to decide which door can be opened to get to a solution is by getting a description of what the client will be doing differently and/or what sorts of things will be happening that are different when the problem is solved, thus creating the expectation of beneficial change" (p. 46).

This perspective uses two predominant activities to assist in building solutions. First is

helping clients construct well-formulated goals that are in line with what they want to achieve. Second is finding solutions to their problems. Through listening skills and questioning, the social worker helps clients search for "exceptions," times when the problem did not occur or occurred less frequently (DeJong & Miller, 1995; de Shazer, 1985).

Describing the Problem

DeJong and Berg (2002) have identified basic stages of solution building: describing the problem, developing well-formed goals, incorporating the miracle question, exploring for exceptions, and end of session feedback. When meeting with clients for the first time, the practitioner should greet each person and learn a little about them by asking how they spend their day (DeJong & Berg, 2002). It is also a good idea to explain, using the five basic steps, how the helping sessions will be conducted so that clients have an idea of what to expect. At this point, the social worker turns the focus to the description of the problem by asking, "How may I be of help?" or "What would you like to accomplish from meeting together today?" The practitioner then listens respectfully to what clients have to say about their problem. Asking for details is appropriate, but solution-focused practitioners seek less detail about the problem compared to social workers using a problem-solving or medical model. Clients need to be heard, to be able to tell their story, and the social worker must be willing to listen.

When using this perspective, practitioners ask questions from a "not knowing" stance (DeJong & Berg, 2002) in order to view clients as competent people and to place them in the role of experts regarding their lives and what they want to accomplish as well as how best to achieve their goals. Questions during this beginning stage may seek to find out how the problem affects clients, or just how it is a problem for them. The practitioner may also want to ask clients what they have tried in the past to solve the problem. When clients present multiple problems, it is best to find out which ones they believe to be most important or want to work on first (DeJong & Berg, 2002). To do this, the practitioner might summarize what the client reported and then ask which problem is most important, as illustrated in the following example: "Jason, you have identified a number of problems. They include problems at work, stress in your marriage, and health problems. Which one is most important to you at this time?" As the client narrows down the focus with the social worker's help, the next step is to shift the direction of the interview to what the client wants to be different (i.e., the beginning search for solutions).

Developing Well-Formed Goals

"There are several characteristics of well-formed goals. Among other things, well-formed goals are important to the client, small and concrete, and represent the beginning of something different rather than the end" (DeJong & Berg, 2002, p. 16). To arrive at goals, the practitioner directs questions in a way that invites clients to describe what their life will be like once the problem is solved. DeJong and Berg (2002) recommend the following characteristics of well-formulated goals.

First, to achieve greater compliance, goals need to be important to the client. Although mandated clients have expectations placed on them from the outside world (courts, family social services, parents, partners), and these need to be addressed, it is also important to listen, to respect the client, and to incorporate the client's goals into the therapeutic process. When goals are imposed solely from the outside, clients are less likely to comply.

Second, additional types of questions that assist in the development of well-formed goals are those that invite the client to think about what other people will notice about the client that is different when the problem has been solved. For example, the practitioner might ask, "When you are less depressed, what will other people notice about you that is different?" Another possibility is to ask, "If your probation officer were here, what would she say you will be doing that would tell her you are ready to be released?"

Third, to help clients be more specific and to avoid the notion that their problem occurs "all of the time," ask them what will be different at a specific time or place. For example,

APPLICATIONS TO PRACTICE

Practice Tip

No one model has been proven to be best. As a social worker you will want to know which models have been most effective with the population and presenting problems you are expecting among the clients your agency serves. Social work interventions include assessment, treatment, and evaluation as well as a beginning, middle, and end of each session and the treatment episode. You'll want to experiment with each method of intervention (ego psychology, behavioral therapy, person-centered techniques, etc.) to see how the methods work and how the models are similar and different. Social workers are expected to use competency-based practice skills and best practice models.

Case Example

C.C. and Eric Buchanan have two teenage sons, Marc, age fourteen, and Marvin, age sixteen. Both boys did well in school until the family moved from a large city on the east coast to a small town in Nevada. Recently, the boys were referred to juvenile court for missing school and joy riding. C.C. and Eric bought a small ranch that they were renovating to create a bed and breakfast. C.C. is a registered nurse and Eric works as a contractor. They both love the outdoors and thought the move would be good for the family. The boys want to go back to the east coast, where they did well in school and had a lot of friends. Grandparents are willing to take the boys, but the parents want to keep the family together. The family has been ordered into treatment. Your agency has decided to see the two boys for individual therapy first. Marc has been assigned to you, and you have an appointment with him this afternoon. His parents characterize him as a follower who enjoys building models and carpentry. He participated in football and basketball in school and wants to be an architect. Marc arrives on time for his appointment dressed in loosely fitting cargo shorts, a t-shirt, and Nike shoes that are untied. You invite him into your office and suggest a place for him to sit. Marc slouches down in the chair and stretches his legs out. He is tall and thin with brownish hair. He folds his hands behind his head after pulling the brim of his cap down over his eyes.

Critical Thinking Questions
Based on your knowledge, skills, and values including practice and experience, think about the following issues:

1. What methods of assessment and intervention have you found to be most successful?
2. Which methods do you want to learn more about and why?
3. What models do you consider least effective? What will you need to do to give the various models a "possibility," that is, to engage in using the model without seeing the model as effective or ineffective before you try it?

"When you are home tonight and things are going better between you and your husband, what will you be doing?"

Fourth, goals need to be concrete, measurable, and identified in behavioral terms. Clients often speak of goals in abstract, un-

Practice Activity

With two other students, form a treatment group: a client, a social worker, and an observer. Decide on which model you want to use with this client. Review the assessment and treatment process of the model selected. Spend thirty to forty minutes working out a first interview. After you have completed the first interview using that model, spend five to ten minutes talking about how the model worked from each person's perspective. Take a five- to ten-minute break and then return to the same treatment group. Now engage in a second ses-sion with the client (keeping the same roles). Again, after completing the session of thirty to forty minutes, spend five to ten minutes discussing each role and what worked and didn't work well in the therapeutic process.

Critical Thinking Questions

1. Was the model you selected effective in instilling hope and en-couraging the client to engage in the change process?
2. What other method would you like to try with this client?
3. What model might you use if you were doing family therapy?
4. What would you say to Marc about what infor-mation you would share with his parents? The court?

Be sure to save your notes and the names of your col-leagues from this activity. When you are reading and discussing Chapter 14, you will be returning to this case with the same classmates to participate in the termina-tion session.

---

definable terms such as "not being so stressed" or "being able to communicate better." In re-sponse to these statements, you might ask questions that seek to define the vague goals in more specific ways. For example, the person who wants to be less stressed might be asked to "tell me what you will be *doing* when you're less stressed?" To the couple wishing to com-municate better, you might ask, "When your husband is communicating better with you, what will you notice that he is doing differ-ent?" or "What specific things will you two be doing that indicate your communication has improved?"

Fifth, a key to setting and achieving goals is having clients recognize the part they play in helping to reach these goals. Very often, espe-cially with relationship problems, clients talk about how others need to change. If this oc-curs, listen respectfully to the client's ideas. Then, when possible, ask questions that guide the client to examine his or her role in the change process. For example, when a parent has addressed the need for a change in his teenage daughter's behavior, listen respectfully and agree (if it is appropriate) with his reason-ing. Then you may choose to follow up with a question such as "When she is more respectful with you, how will she see you responding to her that is different from how you respond now?"

Sixth, clients are sometimes anxious and want to reach the pinnacle of their goals im-mediately. Though this may happen, it is more likely to occur over time. Further, what some people want may not be realistic because they are not able to completely control their environment. What has been found to be useful is movement in a positive direction leading toward an ultimate goal. This also helps clients avoid experiencing frustration or failure when change does not happen as quickly as they would like. When a client's goal is to "no longer experience feelings of depression," you may want to help the client by asking "scaling" questions, a common technique that helps clients break up global goals. Using a scale from 1 to 10, you might ask clients how depressed they currently feel. Then, instead of immediately asking about a 10 (which is feeling great, no longer experiencing any depressed feelings), you might ask what your client would be doing differently if the level of depression were to go from a 3 to a 4. An alternative method is to ask what they would be doing at a certain time of the day, such as in the evening or first thing in the morning, because these are the client's worst times of the day.

Miracle Question

A technique that is unique to the solution-focused perspective is to ask clients the "miracle question." While interviewing a woman who reported feeling overwhelmed by her problems, Berg responded: "What do you suppose needs to happen so you could say the time we are spending together has been useful to you?" The client said, "I'm not sure. I have so many problems. Maybe only a miracle will help, but I suppose that's too much to expect." Insoo asked, "Okay, suppose a miracle happened, and the problem that brought you here is solved. What would be different about your life?" (DeJong & Berg, 2002, pp. 84–85). From this experience the miracle question was born; it is now used as a standard technique in practice. It is best asked in a thoughtful and slightly dramatic manner. There are two rea-

sons for asking the miracle question. First, it allows for a deductive view of finding solutions, one that is open to multiple options rather than just one, and second, the question invites people to think about what will happen in the future instead of remaining stuck in the past (DeJong & Berg, 2002). De Shazer (1985) gives an example of how the miracle question is best presented:

> Now, I want to ask you a strange question. Suppose that while you are sleeping tonight and the entire house is quiet, a miracle happens. The miracle is that the problem which brought you here is solved. However, because you are sleeping, you don't know that the miracle has happened. So, when you wake up tomorrow morning, what will be different that will tell you that a miracle has happened and the problem which brought you here is solved? (p. 5)

Once the person begins to identify changes, questioning must continue to encourage the client to be more specific and clear about necessary behavioral change. Novice practitioners are often quick to accept a vague or general response. If clients say they do not believe in miracles, ask them to pretend, because it is an unusual question. Continue to use the questions previously identified that assist in developing well-formulated goals.

Exploring for Exceptions

As clients begin to identify goals, which helps them describe in concrete ways what will be different in their lives when the problem that brought them in is solved, the social worker moves on to the next stage. By the types of questions asked, this stage directs the focus toward the search for times in the client's life when the problem did not exist or when it occurred less frequently or intensely. According to de Shazer (1985), "exceptions" occur during times when the client expected the problem to happen yet it did not. The point to make here is that the problem does not occur 100 percent of the time; clients, however, tend to overgeneralize and focus only on those times when it has happened.

Exceptions may be linked to something clients realize they did, or they may have no clue as to why the exception took place. De Shazer (1985) refers to these as "deliberate" and "random" exceptions, respectively. Through the use of questions, the social worker helps clients to discern, when possible, those variables within their control that aided in the exception. The social worker must listen closely for the difference between the two. The difference will be reflected in the type of feedback the practitioner gives the client at the end of the session.

When exploring for exceptions, the social worker uses a two-phase process. In the first phase, the practitioner questions the client about whether exceptions have occurred. For example, you might ask, "Has there been a time in the last week or month [it is best to keep the time frame in the recent past] when the problem did not occur?" The use of relationship questions may be of help for those clients who are unable to identify an exception. An example might consist of asking the client, "If your spouse, girlfriend, best friend, coworker, neighbor, dog or cat, or parent were here, could they report that you had times when you were doing better this past week or month?"

Once an exception is noted, the second phase is the time to ask for details about the exception. This helps the client see that a random exception was actually deliberate. The practitioner prompts this insight through questions regarding when, what, and where the ex-

ception happened and who was involved. For example, you might ask, "When you felt just a little less depressed on Saturday, where were you and who were you with?"; "What would your husband say that he noticed was different about you when you were doing better?"; "What do you remember doing at the time you were feeling better?" The more detail elicited from the client, especially regarding their recognized and deliberate involvement in the exception, the more precise your feedback and task assignment will be at the end-of-session feedback. Helping clients to identify exceptions will also help the practitioner and clients recognize client strengths on which to build solutions.

Feedback

At the end of each session, therapists using the solution-focused model take an approximate five-minute break from the client to review the content and the process of the session. They organize feedback during this time and give this feedback to the client when they come back together.

Feedback is given in three basic parts: compliments, a bridge statement, and the recommendation of a task (DeJong & Berg, 2002). Compliments are given that focus on the client's strengths and positives. This can encourage the client to work harder. At times, social workers may find this difficult to do, but knowing that it is part of the feedback process encourages practitioners to be more aware of the client's positive features as they conduct the interview. If your compliments are accurate according to the client's belief system, clients will likely affirm what has been reported to them.

At the conclusion of the compliments, the practitioner provides a bridge statement, which connects the compliments with the task that will be suggested. Thus, when developing the bridge statement, the practitioner ought to think in terms of connecting the client's strengths, goals, and exceptions with the task. DeJong and Berg (2002) recommend beginning the statement with "I agree with you that . . . " (p. 118). At this point, include the client's goals, exceptions, and strengths, and then end the statement by saying that you "suggest" a particular task.

The task will usually fall into one of two categories: behavioral or observational (De-Jong & Berg, 2002). With a behavioral task, the practitioner suggests that the client do more of those things that were identified as parts of the positive exceptions that occurred in the past. This is information the practitioner has gleaned during the interview. Observational tasks ask clients to be more observant of those times when the problem is less of a problem or not a problem at all—in other words, exceptions. The main point is to help the client become more aware of those times when the problem is better and to identify what, when, where, and with whom this is happening, with special attention being paid to the client's particular involvement.

The more clearly the client has defined his or her goal, the easier it is to formulate a task. Many social workers find client progress being stymied through the vagueness of the goal. When goals are concrete and specific, the task is clear. Further, when clients recognize that they are part of the problem as well as the solution, progress toward a goal is more likely. When a client believes that another person or situation needs to change before goals can be reached, improvement is less likely because the client does not have perfect control over others.

Multicultural Techniques

Harper and Lantz (1996) identify eight common "cross-cultural curative factors" that can aid in the process of helping people from different backgrounds. These eight factors comprise the following: "worldview respect, hope, helper attractiveness, control, rites of initiation, cleansing experiences, existential realization, and physical intervention" (Harper & Lantz, 1996, p. 9). Attempts to help people through the use of applied techniques to overcome, ameliorate, or cope with problems need to be consistent or congruent with the client's **worldview** of how people get better and what is an approved means of helping. Such congruence may be accomplished by combining Western with non-Western or religious methods or by having the applied technique sanctioned by a respected person from the client's culture.

Hope has been found to be a common denominator among all cultures for people seeking help (Lantz, 1993; Torrey, 1986). Those helpers who understand this cognitive concept will seek to instill hope in their clients through culturally recognized means, such as demonstrating a certain level of training, experience, knowledge, and confidence. **Helper attractiveness,** described by Rogers (1957), consists of those characteristics demonstrated (e.g., genuineness, empathy, and positive regard) by the helper and determined by the client to be important in the helper–client relationship. This practitioner characteristic has been well researched in Western psychology, but cross-cultural researchers have also found it to be of importance among non-Western helpers and healers (Torrey, 1986; Sandner, 1979; Jilek, 1982).

Helping clients reach a level of **control** over their presenting problems is a common goal among many cultures. Control is often achieved by practicing a new behavior. In Western psychology, it might be expressed through the learning of relaxation techniques from biofeedback instruments that are called on during times of stress. Other cultures use different methods. Chinese nationals, for instance, might use skills from tai chi, exercises and stances developed by the Chinese as a form of meditation, as a way of reaching a state of calm and balance (Agnes, 1999). **Rites of initiation** stem from the notion of change brought on by a passage through something. Specifically, Harper and Lantz (1996) report this rite of initiation as a symbolic passage from death (leaving old behaviors) to rebirth (the beginning of new behaviors). An example of this in the Western world is the client who stays in a program until he or she finishes all of the necessary levels and then successfully graduates. This process symbolizes a transition into a new way of living from an old, unhealthy lifestyle.

People from many cultures see **cleansing** experiences as ways of dealing with imperfections, a symbolic cleansing of a person of mistakes made, of failings and shortcomings. Cleansing allows the person to re-turn to a state of balance. For example, among many Native American tribes the sweat lodge is used as a form of cleansing, a way to purify both the spirit and the physical body.

When clients sense a void in their lives or a loss of meaning, **existential realization** helps them reclaim or find that meaning. It is a way "to rediscover 'sacred meanings' camouflaged in the clients' life" (Harper & Lantz, 1996, p. 20). An example of existential realization is when a practitioner is able to help parents find meaning in their lives following the loss of their child. They experience an emptiness or void that needs to be reclaimed or filled, perhaps by helping others prevent the same tragedy they experienced, thus gaining a new purpose for their lives and a sense that some type of good has come about as a result of their loss. **Physical intervention** is the application of some form of physical treatment. Western medicine seeks to correct biochemical imbalances through the use of medications or the surgical correction of some part of the

human body. Some non-Western societies, however, use nonsurgical techniques and strategies as forms of symbolic release or catharsis (Eliade, 1964). The key to using such approaches is to ensure that the methods are culturally valued and relevant to the client's situation.

SUMMARY

Chapter 7 is devoted to identifying the knowledge and skills needed for intervention. These include those drawn from such diverse theoretical perspectives as ego and cognitive psychology theory, behavioral therapy, person-centered therapy, systems theory, the strengths approach, and multicultural theory. Specific techniques are identified under each of the major perspectives, along with explanations of how they are to be employed with clients. Together, they represent a solid repertoire of skills needed by the direct practitioner.

Navigating Direct Practice

An access code for Research Navigator™ is packaged within your text. Use this code to register at www.researchnavigator.com and then use the key words listed below to research articles related to the chapter's content. Research Navigator™ helps you quickly and efficiently make the most of your research time.

❑ Counter transference
❑ Joseph Wolpe
❑ Pavlov
❑ Systematic desensitization
❑ Transference

Chapter 8

Developing Clients' Coping Skills

■ Jerry is a fifty-year-old unmarried high school teacher. For as long as he can remember, he has been anxious and uptight about almost everything in his life. Although he has been teaching for almost twenty-five years, he still has anxiety attacks at least once a month. When these attacks occur, Jerry notices that his heart starts beating faster and he starts perspiring and becomes dizzy. Jerry leaves the classroom when the anxiety attack occurs and tells his students he will be back in a few minutes. After sitting in the teachers' lounge for ten minutes, he is usually able to return to the classroom. Jerry wants the social worker to help him be less anxious and to learn how to relax.

M any different types of coping skills can be used to help clients accomplish their goals or resolve their problems and concerns. Social workers attend in-service training meetings, read professional journals, travel to workshops, and consult with other therapists every week to learn new ways to help clients cope with problems and concerns ranging from alcohol and drug abuse, to child abuse and neglect, to separation and divorce, to Alzheimer's disease. This chapter describes and discusses the following coping skills that are often used to assist clients: (1) cognitive therapy, (2) assertiveness training, (3) anger management, (4) stress management, (5) crisis management, (6) spiritual and humanistic strategies, and (7) other life management strategies.

Cognitive Therapy

People have been writing for centuries about how our thoughts affect our feelings and actions. The Stoic philosophers of the fourth century BC discussed at length the dynamic interaction between thoughts, feelings, and actions. Epictetus wrote in *The Enchiridion,* "Men are disturbed not by things but by the views which they take of them" (Beck, Rush, Shaw, & Emery, 1979, p. 8). This focus on thoughts and how they affect feelings and actions was further refined by Aaron Beck and colleagues (1979) in their text titled *Cognitive Therapy of Depression.* Other authors such as David D. Burns in *Feeling Good: The New Mood Therapy* (1980) and *The Feeling Good Handbook* (1990) continue to develop cognitive therapy and apply it to a variety of common mental health concerns.

One of the basic concepts of cognitive therapy is that the thinking process of many people is distorted. This distorted thinking affects how they see themselves, their experiences, and their future. In turn, this distorted thinking affects their feelings and actions and keeps them from accomplishing their goals or resolving their problems and concerns. The main focus of cognitive therapy is to make people aware of their distorted thinking and then substitute more rational responses for the distorted thoughts. As the distorted thinking is replaced with more rational thoughts, clients' feelings and actions improve. In the case of depression, the client becomes less depressed and begins a journey toward more happiness and self-fulfillment.

Cognitive Distortions

The first step in cognitive therapy is to review with the client the cognitive distortions people commonly use and which ones apply to the client. Burns (1980) identifies ten cognitive distortions:

1. **All-or-nothing thinking:** You see things in black-and-white categories. If your performance falls short of perfect, you see yourself as a total failure.

2. **Overgeneralization:** You see a single negative event as a never-ending pattern of defeat.

3. **Mental filter:** You pick out a single negative detail and dwell on it exclusively so that your vision of all reality becomes darkened, like the drop of ink that discolors the entire beaker of water.

4. **Disqualifying the positive:** You reject positive experiences by insisting they "don't count" for some reason or other. In this way you can maintain a negative belief that is contradicted by your everyday experiences.

5. **Jumping to conclusions:** You make a negative interpretation even though there are no definite facts that convincingly support your conclusion.

6. **Magnification (catastrophizing) or minimization:** You exaggerate the importance of things (such as your goof-up or someone else's achievement), or you inappropriately shrink things until they appear tiny (your own desirable qualities or the other fellow's imperfections). This is also called the "binocular trick."

7. **Emotional reasoning:** You assume that your negative emotions necessarily reflect the way things really are: "I feel it, therefore it must be true."

8. **Should statements:** You try to motivate yourself with shoulds and shouldn'ts, as if you had to be whipped and punished before you could be expected to do anything. "Musts" and "oughts" are also offenders. The emotional consequence is guilt. When you direct should statements toward others, you feel anger, frustration, and resentment.

9. **Labeling and mislabeling:** This is an extreme form of overgeneralization. Instead of describing your error, you attach a negative label to yourself: "I'm a loser." When someone else's behavior rubs you the wrong way, you attach a negative label to him: "He's an ugly louse." Mislabeling involves describing an event with language that is highly colored and emotionally loaded.

10. **Personalization:** You see yourself as the cause of some negative external event, which in fact you were not primarily responsible for.

Negative Self-Statements

The next step in cognitive therapy is for clients to record the negative thoughts and statements they make about themselves each day. In keeping this log of negative self-statements, clients can also record what time of day the thoughts or statements occurred and the circumstances surrounding the event. For example, a client who thinks the negative self-statement "I'm so stupid; I'll never graduate from college!" may also record that the statement was uttered under his breath on Monday morning at 10:00 a.m. when his midterm examination in history was returned with a C– grade. During the next session, the client and the social worker will review the log of negative self-statements the client thought or uttered the previous week and the cognitive distortions used. This focus on the client's negative self-statements and cognitive distortions may continue for one or two additional sessions.

Rational Responses

The final step in cognitive therapy is replacing negative self-statements with more rational responses. The client should work to be able to do this not only every night while reviewing the activities of the day, but also during the day when the negative self-statements are first thought or uttered. For example, the college student who utters the self-defeating statement "I'm so stupid; I'll never graduate from college!" will hopefully correct that negative self-statement with the following rational response, "No, I'm not stupid! That is a cognitive distortion—in fact, an overgeneralization—that I uttered because I got a C– on my history midterm. I'm not stupid; in fact, I usually get As and Bs when I study for an examination. I didn't study for this history midterm and that's why I got a C– grade. When I study, I get good grades. I will graduate from college."

For cognitive therapy to be successful, the client must agree to or "buy into" the two basic premises of the model. The first premise is that the thoughts and ideas we have about ourselves, our experiences, and our future have a significant impact on how we feel and behave. The second premise is that if we want to change how we feel and behave, we must first change our thoughts and ideas. Once clients accept these two premises, they are ready to use cognitive therapy, in which negative self-statements are identified, labeled as cognitive distortions, and replaced with more rational responses.

Cognitive Therapy with Depression

Cognitive therapy has been used for many years to help people who are depressed feel better about themselves. People who are depressed often see themselves, their experiences, and their future in negative terms. Beck and colleagues (1979) refer to this as the "cognitive triad." They also talk about the "schema" or life script that depressed people have written for themselves that is also negative and self-defeating. In working with depressed individuals, the focus is on correcting the negative thinking clients have been using, sometimes for most of their lives. This is done by (1) identifying the negative self-statements that clients think or utter about themselves, their experiences, and their future; (2) labeling these negative self-statements as specific cognitive distortions; and finally (3) replacing these negative self-statements with more rational responses. Clients pursuing this approach should develop a more rational and positive view of themselves, their experiences, and their future.

Beck and colleagues (1979) present a cognitive model for treating depression that lasts fifteen sessions. Before the first session, the practitioner sends the client the booklet *Coping with Depression* and asks the client to read the booklet before the first session begins. On average, clients complete one-hour sessions twice a week for the first four weeks and then once a week for seven weeks. Beck and colleagues believe that the moderately severely depressed to the severely depressed clients require twice-a-week sessions initially. After each session, clients are given homework assignments that support cognitive therapy. These homework assignments are an important part of the intervention and are reviewed and discussed at the next session.

The first session focuses on the following tasks: (1) review the symptoms of depression, (2) assess suicide risk and hopelessness, (3) discuss how thoughts or self-talk affect feelings and behavior, and (4) review the client's level of activity. The homework assignments include (1) keeping a log of daily activities, (2) completing the Minnesota Multiphasic Personality Inventory (used to evaluate psychopathology), and (3) completing life history questionnaire (Lazarus, 1972). The second session focuses on three tasks: (1) review symptoms of depression, (2) review last week's log of daily activities, and (3) discuss the relationship between thinking or self-talk, feelings, and behavior by focusing on the client's specific experiences. The homework assignments include (1) continuing to keep a log of daily activities and (2) identifying problems with family members, friends, and others that may be contributing to the client's depression.

In session three, the client and social worker (1) review the mastery and pleasure activities (client identifies degrees of pleasure associated with a variety of activities) and (2) discuss the client's thoughts or self-talk related to sadness. The homework assignment for the week is to record thoughts or self-talk during periods of sadness, anxiety, anger, and apathy or indifference. The tasks and activities of session four include (1) listing the negative thoughts or self-talk that preceded feelings of sadness, anxiety, fear, and apathy or indifference and (2) reviewing what the client was experiencing when the negative thoughts or self-talk occurred. Homework for the week includes (1) continuing to record negative thoughts or self-talk and (2) completing an activity that the client previously identified as a pleasurable activity and evalu-

ate whether the activity brought the client pleasure.

The main tasks of session five are (1) discussing negative thoughts or self-talk used last week by the client and (2) identifying recurrent or common themes and experiences associated with the negative thoughts or self-talk. Homework assignments include (1) following through on the maxim "Beds are for sleeping" (if the client is not asleep in fifteen minutes after retiring, the client gets out of bed and does something to distract thinking) and (2) continuing to record thoughts or self-talk and how they are related to particular family members, friends, or others. Sessions six, seven, and eight focus on negative thoughts or self-statements from the client's "shoulds" list rather than "wants" list. Homework for the next three sessions focuses on (1) negative thoughts or self-talk and what was happening to the client at the time and (2) alternative explanations for these negative thoughts (e.g., the problem belongs to the spouse and not to the client).

Sessions nine, ten, and eleven concentrate on (1) the client's self-criticism and developing more realistic or rational responses to this self-criticism and (2) pursuing the client's "wants" list and not the "shoulds" list. Homework assignments include (1) replacing negative thoughts or self-talk with more realistic or rational thoughts or self-talk and (2) completing an activity from the client's "wants" list and not "shoulds" list of activities. Sessions twelve, thirteen, and fourteen continue to focus on (1) the client's self-criticisms and the underlying assumptions of the behavior and (2) actions the client can take such as being more assertive in dealing with the criticisms of others. The homework assignments for sessions twelve, thirteen, and fourteen include (1) listing current and future "wants" and (2) reviewing actions the client can take to achieve these current and future "wants."

During the fifteenth and final session, the client and the practitioner review what has been learned or gained in past sessions. One of the most important things the client has learned is that thoughts or self-talk have a significant impact on feelings and behaviors. Another lesson learned is that negative thoughts can lead to feelings of depression and worthlessness. The client has also learned that by replacing negative thoughts with more realistic or rational thoughts, depression lifts and the client is happier and more content. Another lesson learned is that the client's "shoulds" list contributes to depression, whereas the "wants" list helps to relieve depression. The client also learns that completing a pleasurable activity at least once a week often replaces feelings of depression with those of pleasure and contentment.

Suicide Risk

Suicide ideation, gestures, and attempts are often associated with depression. The risk of suicide is especially great with major depressive disorders. Major depressive disorders are common, with a lifetime occurrence of about 15 percent for men and 25 percent for women. Thirty thousand deaths reported each year in the United States are attributed to suicide. In addition, more than 12,000 children and adolescents are hospitalized each year because of suicide threats and behavior. Suicide rates increase with age. Although the elderly attempt suicide less often than younger people, they are more successful, constituting 25 percent of all suicides although they account for only 10 percent of the general population. The suicide rate for men and women seventy-five years of age or older is three time the rate for those thirty years of age or younger (Kaplan & Sadock, 1996).

Because suicide is often a real threat with clients who are depressed, social workers should always evaluate the threat of suicide at the start of the intervention. Scores of 90 or above on the Generalized Contentment Scale (Corcoran & Fischer, 1994; Hudson, 1982), referred to in earlier chapters, suggest that the client is a serious suicide risk and should be evaluated immediately at a hospital or inpatient facility. Burns (1990, pp. 40–41) suggests asking the following questions if a family member or friend appears to be especially despondent or discouraged. The list of questions can be easily adapted to clients.

1. Have you been feeling sad or unhappy?
2. Do you ever feel hopeless? Does it seem as if things can never get better?
3. Do you have thoughts of death? Do you ever think you'd be better off dead?
4. Do you ever have any actual suicidal impulses? Do you have any urge to kill yourself?
5. Do you feel you can resist these impulses, or do they sometimes tempt you?
6. Do you have any actual plan to kill yourself?
7. When do you plan to kill yourself?
8. Is there anything that would hold you back, such as your family or your religious convictions?
9. Have you ever made a suicide attempt in the past?
10. Would you be willing to talk to someone or seek help if you felt desperate? With whom would you talk?

If the answer to several of these questions is "yes," the threat of suicide may be not only real but also imminent. Social workers should always err in the name of caution and seek a thorough suicide evaluation for the client. See Figure 8.1 for another assessment tool that can help practitioners determine a client's risk for suicide.

Another way to assess suicide risk is to memorize three questions and ask clients who seem to feel hopeless:

1. Are you thinking of hurting yourself?
2. How would you hurt yourself?
3. What stops you from hurting yourself?

Intervention Strategies

Many different treatment strategies can be used with suicidal clients. Developing a support system and exploring alternatives constitute a good place to start. With clients who have a low to moderate risk for suicide, it may be appropriate to have them sign a contract agreeing not to attempt suicide for a specific period of time, or to sign a contract in which they agree to contact the social worker before considering suicide. Clients who are moderate or high suicide risks may require hospitalizations and medications. It is also appropriate to notify the client's family members and friends when the risk of suicide is high. Their support and encouragement can be a significant deterrent to suicide. Other safety strategies for working with suicidal clients can include removing all firearms, knives, and other deadly objects from the home; assessing all possibly lethal prescription and over-the-counter medications in the client's possession; and evaluat-

---

Figure 8.1

The SAD PERSONS Scale

A useful assessment tool for suicide risk is the SAD PERSONS scale (Patterson, Bird, & Patterson, 1983, pp. 343–349). The scale identifies ten factors that are often associated with suicide.

1. *Sex.* Males are more likely to complete suicide and choose more lethal means.

2. *Age.* Individuals under age eighteen and over age thirty-five are higher-risk groups.

3. *Depression.* Clients who are depressed are more likely to commit suicide, especially if they begin to feel better and have more energy after being severely depressed.

4. *Previous attempts.* Clients who have attempted suicide before may find it easier to attempt again.

5. *Ethanol.* The presence of alcohol and other drugs is connected with suicide.

6. *Rational thinking loss.* If a person has thought disorders, he or she may not be able to find ways to cope with the crisis.

7. *Social supports lacking.* If a client feels isolated and does not have enough relationships of meaning, there is an increased chance of suicide.

8. *Organized plan.* If a client has an organized plan, this means that the lethality level is high.

9. *No spouse.* Single individuals are more likely to commit suicide.

10. *Sickness.* If a client has a serious physical illness, he or she is more prone to commit suicide.

ing dangerous areas in the homes such as steep stairs and unvented and enclosed areas such as garages.

Cognitive Therapy with Alcohol and Drug Addictions

Cognitive therapy has become an important part of many alcohol and drug treatment programs (Miller, 1999). By identifying and correcting the cognitive distortions that are used to justify excessive drinking, clients gain more control over their use of alcohol. Burns (1990) examines the cognitive distortions used by many clients to support their destructive drinking. For example, one client might say to himself, "Gee, I'll really feel good if I have a beer now. And it will taste so good." Burns labels this cognitive distortion an example of positive "fortune-telling" because the client is predicting something that isn't entirely true. Although some clients experience a brief mood elevation when they start to drink, they almost always end up feeling worse because one beer turns into three or four or more beers. After clients have consumed their fourth or fifth beer, they get angry and depressed and often argue with family members and friends. And to make matters worse, they usually wake up the next morning with a terrible hangover.

Or the client might say, "Life is so boring. I deserve a little fun." This cognitive distortion is an example of emotional reasoning. We all deserve to have more fun in our lives, but drinking won't make life more fun, especially for the chronic drinker. Instead, the client's excessive drinking makes him chronically depressed and bored with life. His drinking problem also creates serious problems at home and at work. There is nothing fun about excessive drinking.

Another client might say, "Gee, that beer tasted good! I think I'll have another one. I'll feel even better!" This is another example of emotional reasoning. Although that first beer might taste good, there is no guarantee that the three or four that follow will improve the client's mood. Excessive drinking doesn't make clients happier; it makes them angrier and more despondent. It also significantly increases the chances that clients will have conflicts with others. Excessive drinking won't resolve interpersonal problems and conflicts but only adds to their frequency and intensity.

Lewis, Dana, and Blevins (2002) employ a model of cognitive therapy they call cognitive restructuring. In this program, clients are encouraged to restate their beliefs and ideas about themselves and their world in a way that more closely represents reality than fantasy. A client who says, "I can't change my behavior," would substitute that statement with, "I won't change my behavior." This corrected self-statement more accurately reflects how the client really feels and helps the client "own" his or her behavior rather than blaming it on someone else or some outside source. The technique is designed to make the client's self-statements more rational by eliminating cognitive distortions such as overgeneralization and all-or-nothing thinking (Burns, 1990). Lewis and colleagues (2002, pp. 60–61) teach clients in their alcohol and drug treatment program to ask the following questions to assess their thoughts and feelings:

1. Is my thinking in this situation based on an obvious fact or [on] fantasy?
2. Is my thinking in this situation likely to help me protect my life or health?
3. Is my thinking likely to help me or hinder me in achieving my short- and long-term goals?
4. Is my thinking going to help me avoid conflict with others?

5. Is my thinking going to help me feel the emotions I want to feel?

In the words of Lewis and colleagues (2002, p. 61):

> Cognitive restructuring of this sort will serve to decrease negative self-statements, negative self-fulfilling prophecies, hopelessness, anxiety, and fear and to increase realistic cognitions, positive self-image, and self-esteem. It requires consistent attention to what the client is saying and a continuous orientation back to reality.

In summary, cognitive therapy with alcohol and drug dependence focuses on three tasks: (1) identifying the self-statements that clients use to justify their alcohol or drug abuse, (2) labeling these self-statements as cognitive distortions, and (3) replacing the self-statements with more rational responses that support clients in their efforts to remain alcohol and drug free. Clients who follow the process of cognitive restructuring every day increase significantly their ability to remain alcohol and drug free.

Cognitive Therapy with Criminal Behavior

One of the more interesting adaptations of cognitive therapy is its use in treating clients in the criminal justice system. In *The Criminal Personality,* Samenow and Yochelson (1976) discuss at length the thinking errors that criminals use to justify and sustain their criminal activities. Mottonen (1987, p. 2) lists fourteen common thinking errors of criminals that have been adapted from Samenow and Yochelson's earlier work:

1. I have to look out for myself.

2. Force or cunning is the best way to get things done.

3. We live in a jungle and the strong person is the one who survives.

4. People will get at me if I don't get them first.

5. It is not important to keep promises or honor debts.

6. Lying and cheating are okay as long as you don't get caught.

7. I have been unfairly treated and am entitled to get my fair share by whatever means I can.

8. Other people are weak and deserve to be taken.

9. If I don't push other people, I will get pushed around.

10. I should do whatever I can get away with.

11. What others think of me doesn't really matter.

12. If I want something, I should do whatever is necessary to get it.

13. I can get away with things so I don't need to worry about bad consequences.

14. If people can't take care of themselves, that's their problem.

Mottonen (1987) adds to this list the following discussion on thinking errors and the criminal personality:

1. I can't stance. When criminals say, "I can't," what they really means is, "I won't." The behavior represents a choice not to live responsibly. Because the responsible world can't provide the excitement criminals want, they distort the "wants" into "needs." When these "needs" aren't met, it is easy to justify not changing. **The goal** is to change the "I can't" attitude to that of "I can."

2. Closed channel. Often, criminals keep their thoughts to themselves and make other people guess what they are thinking. They speak half-truths by saying "yes" or "no" or "I don't know" when they really do have an opinion. It's a way of keeping people in the dark regarding how they really feel. Change can't occur until three things happen. First, individuals start disclosing their thoughts and feelings. Second, they ask for feedback from others. And third, they learn to distrust or question their own thinking. **The goal** is to open channels of meaningful communication with other people and let them help with the lessons of life.

3. **Pretentiousness.** Criminals often view themselves in an unrealistic manner, believing that they can do almost anything and that they are superior to others. Any setbacks are looked on as put-downs or criticisms from jealous people who are not as talented. **The goal** is to reduce this thinking error by reducing the expectations people have for themselves. By putting in place Murphy's Laws—"If anything can go wrong, it will"—the clients let go of the anger they feel when their expectations are not met.

4. **Fear of fear.** Criminals tend to deny fear, considering it a weakness. Fear interferes with the goal of feeling excitement when a crime is committed, and so it is rejected. **The goal** is to understand that being afraid is good. Fear stimulates responsible problem solving. When fear is denied or cut off, criminal behavior takes over.

5. **Power thrust.** Criminals often feel superior because they can dominate others verbally, emotionally, or physically. By being the meanest and most difficult people on the block, criminals believe they can intimidate others into providing them with life's

wants. **The goal** is to make clients aware of how their behavior affects others. Being self-critical helps people develop empathy for others' points of view.

6. **Good person stance.** Criminals minimize the harm they have done to others by acknowledging only the good they *might* have done. Regardless of what they have done to others, these people consider themselves to be good people. As long as criminals see themselves as good persons, they have license to commit whatever acts they choose because the good things in their lives outweigh the bad. **The goal** is to construct a balance sheet of good and evil. The purpose is to show how much harm has been done and how the past life has been wasteful.

7. **Don't get mad—get even.** Getting mad is not enough. Criminals believe that getting even and causing injury is the best way to teach other people to stay out of their way. Usually these people have a short fuse that goes off with very little provocation. **The goal** is to realize how getting even can seriously injure others. It is hoped that these people can learn some self-disgust for this hurtful philosophy.

8. **Lying.** This is the most common error of all. By lying, individuals believe they are doing what everyone else does to get what they want out of life. If everyone else lies, why shouldn't they? **The goal** is to stop lying by being in a group experience with other criminals who lie. In these situations, it is hard to lie because the other group members instantly recognize the lie.

9. **Uniqueness.** Criminals believe that they are unique and deserve special treatment. Because they are special, they are above the law and not subject to the same rules

and constraints as others. Their personal power comes in large part from the belief that they are unique. **The goal** is to watch how "ordinary" people handle life situations with grace and modesty. By watching others, criminals who are self-critical come to recognize that they have the same deficiencies as other people.

10. **Victim stance.** Criminals see themselves as even bigger victims than their victims. Life has not been fair to criminals. If people only knew the terrible things that had happened to them, they would excuse or even applaud the criminal behavior. They take no responsibility for their actions and always blame "the corrupt system" that has made them the people they are today. Some even use psychological and sociological explanations such as growing up in a "culture of poverty" to defend their actions. **The goal** is to counteract the victim stance by examining the choices made, the risks taken, and the contributions the individual made to criminal behavior.

11. **Rigidity.** Life is black or white, yes or no—there are no gray areas. Criminals believe that people are either for them or against them. Women can't be trusted. The police are always out to hurt them. **The goal** is to bring to the client's attention the exceptions that almost always occur in this black-and-white thinking.

12. **Lack of initiative.** Criminals complain of a lack of energy. They are unwilling to do anything they consider boring or disagreeable. Excuses and self-pity, along with psychosomatic aches and pains, are the overriding themes used to avoid living a responsible life. The attitude is, "If I like it, okay. If I don't, to hell with it." **The goal** is to point out that clients have plenty of

energy to do what they really want to do, especially when engaged in criminal activities. These clients are introduced to a new definition of *effort*—doing what you don't want to do and sometimes not doing what you want to do.

13. **Concept of ownership.** When criminals see something they want, it is as good as theirs. The world owes the criminal. They expect everything to be given to them because they are so important. If it isn't given to them, they take it anyway with no questions asked because it is owed. **The goal** is to accept that no one owes the criminal anything, especially not family members and friends. Clients must learn to accept and honor the social boundaries of others.

14. **And finally.** You can never be sure what a criminal is thinking, even when he or she is confined to a jail or prison.

In working with clients in the criminal justice system, the social worker focuses on these and other thinking errors or cognitive distortions and how they are used to justify and sustain criminal activity. Clients keep a log of their inappropriate self-thoughts and self-statements, identify the specific thinking errors they use, and replace their inappropriate self-thoughts and self-statements with more rational responses. Another cognitive approach that is used with clients in the criminal justice system is to encourage them to think more about their victims. By focusing on how people feel and behave after they have been victimized, these clients sometimes gain more empathy for their victims and, hopefully, become more reluctant to engage in criminal activity. Only time will tell if a real change has taken place. In the words of Mottonen (1987), if you are a criminal, "You only have three choices—change, keep doing the crime, or suicide. It's your lifestyle, think about it" (p. 18).

Case Examples

Monica Love is a twenty-year-old college student. She works part time at the college library and takes fifteen hours of course work. As a junior, it is time for her to declare her major. Monica's parents have wanted her to enter the family business when she graduates, but Monica hates retail sales and wants to be a nurse. Recently over the summer break, Monica told her mother about her desire to be a nurse. She thought her mother was supportive but found out the next day that when her mother told her father, he said there would be no more money for tuition unless she went into business management. Monica is an only child and has never voiced her opinions when she disagreed with her parents. Since her father's decree, Monica says she is having trouble sleeping, has lost weight, and spends at least thirty minutes a day crying. She says she know something is wrong for her to feel so bad but doesn't know what to do. A friend suggested she call your agency and make an appointment to speak to someone.

———————

Simon Owl is a twenty-five-year-old factory worker. He has worked in the same job since he graduated from high school and has just been promoted to crew chief. His friends are now teasing him about the promotion and saying he got the job because he was a brown noser. His girlfriend wants him to make a commitment to a wedding date, but he doesn't feel ready. Simon's parents feel it is time for him to move out on his own. Simon feels overwhelmed by all the new expectations and finds that he gets angry at things he used to be able to not worry about. Yesterday at work, Simon got into verbal battles with two of his crew members and then went into the restroom and hit the wall with his hand so hard that he broke it. His boss feels he needs to learn to control his feelings.

———————

Gordon Gray is a seventeen-year-old high school senior at Uptown High School. He is an honor student and earned a letter in basketball. Recently Gordon and his friends have been using alcohol and have been out driving around until 3:00 A.M. Even though it is spring semester before graduation, Gordon's parents are worried that Gordon could fail his morning geometry class because of nonattendance. Gordon is a Cherokee Indian and has a full scholarship to a prestigious college. If he gets picked up for drinking, his parents are afraid he may lose his scholarship. Gordon has agreed to come into your agency and talk to someone but he has told the intake worker he does not have the problem. Gordon believes his parents are just too religious to understand he is just letting off some energy with some friends.

Practice Activity

Get into groups of three and decide who will be the therapist, the client, and the observer. Read the case examples and select one for role playing. Identify what activities will need to be completed in the first interview and make a tentative decision about what types of things you would want to teach the client to manage his or her particular difficulties. Complete a session of thirty to forty minutes and then discuss the outcome of the session from each role perspective for ten minutes.

Critical Thinking Questions

1. How will you introduce the idea of skill training to the client?

2. What ways might you assist the client in seeing the importance of skill training?

3. If the client isn't interested in skill training, how will you continue to provide treatment and continue to move the client into considering skill training?

Assertiveness Training

When clients talk about the goals they want to accomplish or the problems and concerns they want to resolve, many say they want to feel more confident, more self-assured, or more in control of their lives. Some clients describe themselves as meek and indecisive, especially in certain interpersonal situations. For example, a young woman gets very angry at herself when she doesn't stand up to her boyfriend when he makes fun of her political views, or a middle-aged man feels frustrated when he doesn't tell his boss that he can't work late tonight because of family obligations, or an elderly woman feels ignored when her adult children don't listen to what she has to say about child care. These clients want to be heard; they want to be understood; they want to matter to others. What many of them could benefit from is assertiveness training.

According to Kirst-Ashman and Hull (2001), "Assertiveness training leads people to realize and act on the assumption that they have the right to be themselves and express their feelings freely" (p. 67). Assertiveness training is a commonly used method to modify maladaptive interpersonal behavior, especially timid or aggressive behavior (Buttell, 2002; Hull & Kirst-Ashman, 2004). It incorporates both learning theory and behavior modification principles and makes a clear distinction between assertive behavior and aggressive behavior. Aggressive behavior is often punctuated by yelling and screaming and threatening hand gestures and body movements. It is designed to intimidate and coerce people. Assertive behavior, on the other hand, is controlled, purposeful, and focused. It is designed to get the other person to attend to or pay attention to what is being said. Assertiveness training focuses on specific behaviors that

can be learned and applied to a variety of situations.

Alberti and Emmons (2001, pp. 107–111) present the following step-by-step model of assertiveness training:

Step 1. Examine your behavior. Are you satisfied with your interpersonal relationships? Are you asserting yourself enough? Evaluate how you feel about yourself and your behaviors.

Step 2. Keep a log of your assertiveness. Record those situations in which you responded assertively, those in which you didn't, and those that you avoided altogether so you wouldn't have to be assertive.

Step 3. Set realistic goals for yourself. Identify those situations in which you want to be more assertive. Start with a small, low-risk situation in which you have a greater chance of success.

Step 4. Focus on a particular situation. With your eyes closed, imagine how you handled the situation. Imagine vividly the actual details. What were your feelings at the time and afterward?

Step 5. Review your behaviors during the particular situation, such as voice, facial expression, gestures, eye contact, and so forth. Be aware of those behaviors that reflect nonassertive behavior and those that reflect assertive behavior.

Step 6. Observe an assertive model. Watch someone who handles a similar situation with assertive behavior. What components of the person's behavior reflected assertiveness?

Step 7. Consider other assertive responses. Identify other nonverbal and verbal assertive responses that could be used in the particular situation.

Step 8. Close your eyes and imagine yourself using some of these other assertive responses. Through positive imagery, practice using these assertive behaviors with the particular situation.

Step 9. Role-play these assertive behaviors with the social worker or with a friend. Practice role-playing until you become more comfortable with your assertive behaviors.

Step 10. Repeat steps 8 and 9 until you develop an assertive approach that you are comfortable with and that will accomplish what you want to accomplish with others.

Step 11. Be assertive in a real-life situation.

Step 12. Review the real-life situation. Were you assertive? Did you remain calm? What were the consequences of your assertive behavior? What would you do differently the next time?

Step 13. Continue to be assertive in your interpersonal relationships. Don't be discouraged by temporary setbacks. Examine your successes as well as your temporary setbacks. What can you learn from them?

Step 14. Congratulate yourself. Learning to be more assertive isn't an easy task. Pat yourself on the back for a job well done.

Assertiveness training helps clients improve their coping skills and leads to more satisfying interpersonal relationships. It is especially helpful in changing interpersonal relationships in which clients feel they are struggling to be heard and understood or in which there is a significant power differential. Assertiveness training can help timid people be more confident and aggressive people be less hostile (see Figure 8.2). A word of caution should always accompany assertiveness training, and this is alluded to in step 13. Expect some success with assertiveness training but also some setbacks. It may take a number of assertive encounters with certain people before they begin to

---

Figure 8.2

The Benefits of Being Assertive

Lange and Jakubowski (1976, pp. 55–56) discuss the benefits of developing an assertive belief system:

1. By standing up for ourselves and letting ourselves be known to others, we gain self-respect and respect from other people.

2. By trying to live our lives in such a way that we never hurt anyone under any circumstances, we end up hurting ourselves and other people.

3. When we stand up for ourselves and express our honest feelings and thoughts, everyone benefits in the long run.

4. By sacrificing our integrity and denying our personal feelings, relationships are usually damaged or prevented from developing.

5. Personal relationships become more authentic and satisfying when we share our honest reactions with other people.

6. Not letting others know what we think and feel is just as selfish as not attending to other people's thoughts and feelings.

7. When we frequently sacrifice our rights, we teach other people to take advantage of us.

8. By being assertive and telling other people how their behavior affects us, we are giving them an opportunity to change their behavior, and we are showing respect for their right to know where they stand with us.

respond to the client with more care and consideration. Some people may never respond in more appropriate ways to assertive interaction. These are people the client may want to avoid or at least limit interactions with in the future. In general, most people respond with some degree of appropriateness to assertive communication and, as the client becomes more skilled in assertive interchanges, the number of people will continue to increase.

To assist in understanding the concept of assertiveness, Lange and Jakubowski (1976, pp. 14–20) identify and discuss five different types of assertion: (1) basic assertion, (2) empathic assertion, (3) escalating assertion, (4) confrontive assertion, and (5) I-language assertion.

Basic assertion refers to standing up for personal rights, beliefs, or opinions. It does not involve other social skills such as empathy. An example of basic assertion when being interrupted would be to say, "Excuse me, I'd like to finish what I'm saying." When asked an important question that you are unprepared for, a basic assertive response would be to say, "I'd like to have a few moments to think that over." When refusing a request, an appropriate response would be to say, "No, this afternoon is not a good time for me to visit with you." Basic assertion also involves expressing affection and appreciation for others. Examples include "I like you," "I care for you a lot," and "Having a friend like you makes me feel happy."

Empathic assertion occurs when you convey some sensitivity to the other person. It is a type of assertion that recognizes the other person's feelings and experiences. When two people are talking loudly while a meeting is going on, an empathic response for a third party would be to say, "You may not realize it, but your talking is starting to make it hard for me to hear what's going on in the meeting. Would you please keep it down." Or when you are not sure when your new stove will be delivered, an appropriate response would be to say, "I know it's hard to say exactly when the delivery truck will come, but I'd like a ballpark estimate of what time of day." Empathic assertion has considerable power because you are acknowledging the person first before conveying a sensitivity to or understanding of what is happening. This type of assertive behavior also requires the speaker to think carefully about the other person's feelings before responding. This thoughtful consideration minimizes the chance that the speaker will respond too aggressively.

Escalating assertion starts with a minimal response that can be turned up a notch if the person does not respond to the first minimal response. The second or turned-up response is firmer and more focused than the first response. For example, a woman is in a bar with a woman friend, and a man repeatedly offers to buy them drinks. A minimal response to the man would be to say, "That's very nice of you to offer, but we came here to catch up on some news. Thanks anyway." If this minimal response does not stop the man from asking again, a turned-up response would be to say, "No, thank you. We really would rather just talk to each other." If the man persists, an appropriate response would be to say, "This is the third and last time I'm going to tell you that we don't want your company. Please leave us alone!" As the escalating responses become firmer, they also become more assertive and blunt. Most people get the message before "the cannon goes off" and the exchange becomes blunt.

Confrontive assertion is used when other people's words contradict their actions. This type of assertion involves describing what the other person promised to do, what was actually done, and how the speaker feels about it. Examples of confrontive assertion include:

> I was supposed to be consulted before the final proposal was typed. But I see the secretary is typing it right now. Before he finishes it, I want to review the proposal and make whatever corrections I think are needed. In the future, I want to get a chance to review any proposals before they're sent to the secretary.

> I thought we'd agreed that you were going to be more considerate toward students. Yet I noticed today that when two students asked for some information you said that you had better things to do than babysit for kids. As we discussed earlier, I see showing more consideration as an important part of your job. I'd like to figure out what seems to be the problem.

I-language assertion is especially helpful in getting people to express difficult negative feelings. It involves four parts: (1) "When . . . [speaker describes the other person's behavior]," (2) "The effects are . . . [speaker describes how it affects the speaker's life or feelings]," (3) "I feel . . . [speaker describes feelings]," and (4) "I'd prefer . . . [speaker describes what he or she wants]." In responding to a coworker who always interrupts, an appropriate response would be to say, "When I'm constantly interrupted, I lose my train of thought and begin to feel that my ideas aren't important to you. I start feeling hurt and angry. I'd like you to make a point of waiting until I'm finished speaking."

Lange and Jakubowski (1976) believe that the use of videotapes when assertive behaviors are role-played is an effective way for clients to learn assertive behaviors. In constructing these videotapes, the authors make a number of suggestions. To begin with, the role-play actors should be the same sex and as similar in as many ways as possible to the clients who will watch the tapes. Situations role-played in the tapes should focus on everyday experiences that clients can readily identify with. Second, when the tapes are made, assertive role-playing behavior should result in a positive outcome. In other words, the role-play should end in a positive outcome not only for the assertive role-player but also for the other participants in the role-play. Third, the role-play scenes should be short and no more than one to three minutes long. Role-plays of a short duration make it easier for the viewer to maintain a high level of concentration. Fourth, complicated role-plays such as negotiating a new job status with an employer should be broken down to their component parts. These might include approaching the employer, presenting your request, offering suggestions to the employer, and negotiating a new job status. And finally, the important aspects of the role-play should be highlighted on the videotape along with a narrative that describes in detail the component parts of the assertive behavior.

Anger Management

Many clients will seek counseling services because they are not able to control their anger. Some of these clients will even be referred by the courts for anger management because of spousal abuse or other assault and battery charges. Anger is a destructive emotion that consumes many clients and often leads to acts of violence. Uncontrolled anger can even lead to criminal acts that result in incarceration. Social workers should be well versed in anger management techniques because many clients will identify anger as their main problem or concern. Anger management workshops are often used to help clients in a group setting deal more appropriately with their anger. These anger management programs teach clients to control their anger by using a number of learning theory and behavior modification principles.

Most anger management programs will help clients do the following: (1) acknowledge that anger has become a destructive force in their lives; (2) describe the interpersonal situations in which anger is especially difficult to manage; (3) identify the cues that tell clients their anger is nearing the boiling point; (4) implement strategies to control these angry outbursts; (5) evaluate the effectiveness of these strategies; and (6) practice the strategies that work best for each client.

An Anger Management Workshop

Smith and Beckner (1993) and Smith, Smith, and Beckner (1994) designed and implemented a three-session anger management workshop for women inmates at the Utah State Prison. Each session lasted approximately three hours and included homework assignments that inmates completed between sessions.

First Session

The first session began with a general introduction of the workshop objectives, after which the women inmates completed the Novaco Anger Scale (Burns, 1980). The remainder of the session focused on the common symptoms of anger (APA, 2000). This discussion identified the emotional, physical, cognitive, and behavioral symptoms that people experience when they are angry. Also discussed were the ways in which people use anger as an excuse to avoid taking responsibility for their own actions (Dyer, 1976).

The first session ended with a discussion of how the inmates might monitor their anger before next week's session. They were asked to keep a daily record of how they felt according to the following four-point scale: not angry, a little angry, angry, and very angry. The women were also asked to identify symptoms or cues that indicated to them that their anger had reached a dangerous level. The monitoring assignment also instructed inmates to identify the events that might have contributed to their anger.

Second Session

The second session began with a review of the inmates' anger-monitoring assignment. The women were asked to comment on their anger evaluation for each day of the past week, the symptoms that led them to make their assessment, and the events that might have contributed to their anger. The discussion also focused on identifying symptoms or cues that indicated to the inmates that their anger had reached a dangerous level.

The remainder of the session focused on how the women could more effectively manage their anger (Monat & Lazarus, 1991). The anger management strategies included walking away and counting to ten, deep breathing and relaxation exercises, asking for a timeout, leaving the conflict scene and starting a rigorous physical activity, and cognitively reviewing the conflict (Burns, 1980; Tavris, 1982).

The inmates' assignment for the following week was to continue monitoring their anger each day along with the symptoms and events that might be contributing to their anger. The women were also asked to implement an anger management strategy and to write about it.

Third Session

The final session focused on the actions the women had taken during the preceding week to alter their anger and the effects of their actions. The discussion reviewed common strategies for managing anger, focusing on the strategies that seemed most helpful.

The workshop concluded with a general review of what the inmates had learned about anger during the three-session workshop. The session ended with the inmates completing the Novaco Anger Scale for the second time.

Workshop Results

The before and after scores on the Novaco Anger Scale indicated that the women inmates felt significantly less anger at the conclusion of the workshop than they did when it started ($t = 4.39$; df = 10; $p < .05$). In describing the symptoms that made them feel "very angry" or "angry," the women most often identified a flushed or red face, increased heart rate, general agitation, pounding headaches, shakes, clenched jaws, inability to sleep, and obsessive thinking. The situations that caused the women to feel "very angry" or "angry" included confrontations with staff and other inmates, an argument with a friend or family member during a visit, lack of visitors and no mail, and cell shakedowns and inmate cell reassignments. When the inmates were asked what they did to manage their anger, most indicated that they left the conflict scene as soon as possible and tried to cool down in some other area of the prison. Many of these inmates who could not escape the scene of the conflict used breathing exercises and cognitive strategies to control their anger. One inmate said, "I went to my room and told myself off for letting my cousin push my buttons. Then I started laughing."

Myths about Anger

Alberti and Emmons (2001) discuss four common myths about anger. **Anger Myth 1: Anger is a behavior.** Anger is not a behavior; it's a feeling, an emotion. Being angry is not the same as being aggressive. Because angry feelings are often confused with aggressive behaviors, it is difficult for many people to deal appropriately with this natural and very human emotion. If someone says, "I never get angry," that person is mistaken. Everyone gets angry. Some people, however, are very good at not showing their anger. When they get angry, they do not openly express their feelings. Instead, they find nondestructive ways to deal with their anger. As they learn to control their anger, they also learn to control the aggressive behaviors that can follow an outburst of anger. The key to anger management is learning how to deal with anger. Everyone gets angry. And everyone needs to learn how to deal more appropriately with that anger.

Anger Myth 2: You should be afraid of your buried anger! Anger is one of the most difficult emotions to express. Because it is difficult for many people to express their anger, they have been encouraged by others to bury it. Years later when someone encourages them to let it out, they are afraid their angry outburst might seriously harm another person. They continue to suffer in silence out of fear of hurting others. By suffering in silence, however, they also hurt the other person. While the angry person fumes, the other person continues to act in ways that damage the relationship. Until both parties deal more openly with their fractured relationship, both persons will find the relationship tenuous at best. An important part of anger management is unearthing anger and dealing with it openly and honestly. Everyone gets angry and everyone needs to learn how to deal with their anger more appropriately.

Anger Myth 3: The human steam kettle. For many years, the general public has believed the old Freudian myth that human emotions are like a steam kettle. As strong emotions build up inside a person, it is important that these feelings be released before the person explodes into destructive behavior. But the steam kettle analogy is false. What actually happens is that annoying events are stored one at a time in our memory banks. When a particular event is remembered, the anger associated with it is also remembered. The anger experienced, however, is not the sum total of all the experiences stored in the memory bank but only that particular experience. Anger doesn't accumulate. Instead, anger is associated with a particular situation, place, and time.

Anger Myth 4: Venting is good for your health. Anger researchers are at odds when they discuss the value of venting angry feelings. Whereas some believe venting is an essential part of anger management, other researchers contend that venting only intensifies the anger. The latter believe that venting angry feelings through pillow pounding or shouting obscenities only encourages people to handle anger aggressively. According to Alberti and Emmons (2001), "the best and most current evidence clearly supports the view that venting angry feelings is not psychologically healthy" (p. 134). The physical expression of hostility does nothing to solve the problem. A subset of venting myths identified by Carol Tavris (Alberti & Emmons, 2001, p. 134) further illustrates this point:

> Myth: Aggression is instinctive catharsis for anger. Reality: Aggression is an acquired cathartic habit.
>
> Myth: Talking out anger gets rid of it. Reality: Overt expression can focus or even increase anger.
>
> Myth: Tantrums are healthy expressions of anger. Reality: Tantrums, if rewarded, teach the child a method of controlling

others. Emotions are subject to the laws of behavior.

Anger Myth 5: Anger needs to be expressed. Twenty years ago almost every anger management program used physical approaches such as pillow pounding to help people express their anger. Later research—to the dismay of many program directors—showed that when people learned these pillow pounding techniques they used them in and out of therapy, often with devastating results. If a pillow wasn't available to pound, for example, they might pound the nearest person. The focus has now changed to the nondestructive verbal expression of anger in which people are encouraged to speak up when they are angry. Spontaneous verbal expression of anger is now being questioned as well because of the perceived ill effects it may have on the heart and other body organs. Even so, experts agree that the nondestructive verbal expression of anger is much better for people than overt acts of aggression and hostility.

Anger Myth 6: Tell other people, but not the person you're angry with. Many people express their anger toward another person only by indirect, hurtful methods that rarely change the other person's behavior. If the other person's behavior is to change, more direct expressions of anger must be considered. Spouses who are unwilling to openly confront their partners about habits they dislike only reinforce those habits. In dealing with their anger, they often choose a "safe" way to express their frustration—they confide in another family member such as a mother, father, or sister. This "see-how-bad-he-or-she-is" style often has disastrous effects on the relationship. The spouse's anger at the partner builds because the other's behavior doesn't change. At the same time, the partner's resentment also builds because there is no feedback about why the spouse is so hostile. As the angry feelings escalate, both partners are deprived of the opportunity to deal with their angry feelings in a more open and honest manner. If anger is to be managed appropriately, it must be confronted head on in an open and frank interaction between both parties.

A Three-Step Approach to Anger Management

Alberti and Emmons (2001) present a three-step approach to anger management: (1) minimize anger in your life, (2) cope before you get angry, and (3) respond assertively when you get angry. In order to minimize anger in your life, Alberti and Emmons (2001, pp. 142–143) offer the following suggestions:

1. Improve your relationship with others through community service, tolerance, forgiveness, even caring for a pet.

2. Adopt positive attitudes toward life through humor, religion, acting as if today is your last day.

3. Avoid overstimulation from chemicals, work stress, noise, traffic.

4. Listen to others. Practice trusting others.

5. Have a confidant. Make a friend, and talk regularly, even before you feel stress building.

6. Laugh at yourself. You really are pretty funny, you know. (It goes with being human.)

7. Meditate. Calm yourself. Get in touch with your inner being.

8. Increase your empathy. Consider the possibility that the other person may be having a really bad day.

9. Be tolerant. Can you accept the infinite variety of human beings?

10. Forgive. Let go of your need to blame somebody for everything that goes wrong in life.

11. Work toward resolution of problems with others in your life, not "victory."

12. Keep your life clear! Deal with issues when they arise, when you feel the feelings—not after hours/days/weeks of stewing about it. When you can't deal with it immediately, arrange a specific time when you can and will!

Alberti and Emmons (2001, pp. 143–144) conclude with some general observations on anger:

1. Remember that you are responsible for your own feelings. You can choose your emotional responses by the way you look at situations.

2. Remember that anger and aggression are not the same thing! Anger is a feeling. Aggression is a style of behavior. Anger can be expressed assertively—aggression is not the only alternative.

3. Get to know yourself. Recognize the attitudes, environments, events, and behaviors which trigger your anger. As one wise person suggested, "Find your own buttons, so you'll know when they're pushed!"

4. Take some time to examine the role anger is playing in your life. Make notes in your log about what sets you up to get angry, and what you'd like to do about it.

5. Reason with yourself. Recognize that your responses will not change the other person. You can only change yourself.

6. Deflect your cynical thoughts by using thought stopping, distraction, meditation.

7. Don't "set yourself up" to get angry! If your temperature rises when you must wait in a slow line, find alternative ways to accomplish those tasks if at all possible.

8. Learn to relax. Develop the skill of relaxing yourself, and learn to apply it when your anger is triggered.

9. Develop several coping strategies for handling your anger when it comes, including relaxation, physical exertion, "stress inoculation" statements, and other procedures.

10. Save your anger for when it's important. Focus instead on maintaining good relationships with others.

11. Develop and practice assertive ways to express your anger, so these methods will be available to you when you need them.

For the final step of responding assertively when you get angry, Alberti and Emmons (2001, p. 145) offer these concluding suggestions:

1. Take a few moments to consider if this situation is really worth your time and energy, and the possible consequences of expressing yourself.

2. Take a few more moments to decide if this situation is one you wish to work out with the other person, or one you will resolve within yourself.

If You Decide to Take Action

1. Make some verbal expression of concern.

2. "Schedule" time for working things out. If you are able to do so spontaneously, fine, if not, arrange a time to deal with the issue later.

3. State your feelings directly. Avoid sarcasm and innuendo; use honest, expressive language; let your posture, facial expression, gestures, and voice tone convey your feelings; avoid name calling, put-downs, physical attacks, one-upmanship, hostility; work toward resolution.

4. Accept responsibility for your feelings. You got angry at what happened; the other person didn't "make" you angry.

5. Stick to specifics and to the present situation. Avoid generalizing. Don't dig up the entire history of the relationship!

6. Work toward resolution of the problem. Ultimately you'll only resolve your anger when you've done everything possible to eliminate its cause.

Stress Management

Most clients experience a great deal of stress in their lives. This stress can cause anxiety, and this anxiety can lead to serious mental and physical disorders (Kaplan & Sadock, 1996). Anxiety-related problems or concerns are probably the second most common mental disorders next to substance-related disorders (APA, 2000). If clients can learn how to manage their stress, they have developed a coping skill that can help them deal more effectively with a variety of problems or concerns, including stress and anxiety.

Monat and Lazarus (1991) identify a number of different strategies for coping with stress. Three of the most widely used coping strategies use learning theory and behavior modification principles: (1) positive imagery, (2) breathing exercises, and (3) muscle relaxation exercises. In the case example that began this chapter, Jerry states that he has suffered from anxiety most of his adult life. Although he has been a teacher for almost twenty-five years, he has to leave the classroom at least once a month because of panic attacks. He wants to learn how to relax and control his anxiety. Positive imagery, breathing exercises, and muscle relaxation exercises will teach him how to relax. These are normal problem-solving skills that can be used effectively by almost anyone regardless of their age or their infirmity.

Positive Imagery

In positive imagery, the social worker is a guide who takes the client through a detailed narrative designed to relax and calm the client. The scene or activity may be one the social worker suggests or one the client identifies himself or herself. For example, the social worker might suggest that a descriptive narrative of a mountain scene is relaxing and that this might also benefit the client. Or the social worker might ask clients to identify a scene or activity they find calming and relaxing and then develop a detailed narrative of this scene or activity. The positive imagery is shared with the client in a calm, relaxed, and slow-paced voice. Consider the following example of a social worker using positive imagery with Jerry:

> Jerry, the first thing I want you to do is to close your eyes. Now get as comfortable as possible in your chair. Take a deep breath, hold it for a few seconds, exhale, and continue to breathe normally. I want you to imagine in your mind a beautiful and peaceful mountain scene. . . . You are sitting on a log near a crystal clear mountain lake. The lake is in a valley that is surrounded by majestic mountains. The water in the lake is so clear and still that it looks like the surface of a mirror. In fact, as you look into the lake you can see the reflected shapes of the mountains that surround it. Look into the lake and study for a few moments how the mountains are reflected by the smooth and crystal clear water . . . [pause for sixty seconds]. I want you to pay attention to how relaxed and calm you feel. Your entire body is relaxed and calm, and your mind is at ease.
>
> Now I want you to listen to the sounds that surround you. In the pine tree to your left sits a woodpecker. Occasionally the woodpecker taps, taps, taps, taps on the tree searching for bugs. The tapping is rhythmic . . . tap, tap, tap, tap. . . . Notice how the wind moves gently through the pine tree and how the boughs move ever so slightly. You can even hear the quiet stir if you listen closely enough. Concentrate on the gentle stirring of the wind for a few moments . . . [pause for sixty seconds]. Notice how relaxed and calm you feel. Your entire body is relaxed and calm, and your mind is at ease.
>
> You notice the smells that surround you. The first is the smell of pine trees and the fresh and clean scent that fills the air. Breathe deeply through your nose and enjoy the smell of the pine trees. To your right is a small group of mountain flowers. Their scent is faint but sweet as the wind moves across the flowers. Notice how the flowers sway gently in the wind and enjoy their sweet scent. Concentrate on their sweet scent for a few moments . . . [pause for sixty seconds]. Notice how relaxed and calm you feel. You are at peace with yourself and the world. Concentrate on how wonderful you feel . . . [pause for sixty seconds].

This is a brief example of how a social worker might use positive imagery with Jerry. In general, a positive imagery narrative will last at least five minutes. Although the narrative can be extended for a longer period, a shorter narrative gives clients something they can practice and use when feeling stressed out or anxious. Depending on what part of the country a client lives in or comes from, the positive imagery can vary from a mountain scene to a sandy beach to a desert in bloom.

Breathing Exercises

Breathing exercises can also be used to reduce Jerry's stress and anxiety. In many ways, these are some of the most helpful stress management techniques because they can be used in so many different situations, including a crowded bus, train, or airplane, as well as in more secluded or private settings. Breathing exercises are designed to get the client to concentrate on the sensation of breathing. This concentration shifts the client's focus from what he is worried about to his breathing. Deep breathing also provides more oxygen to the brain and can have a calming effect on the body. Consider the following example used by a social worker to help Jerry relax:

> Jerry, I want you to close your eyes. . . . Now get as comfortable as you possibly can in your chair. I want you to clear your mind of whatever you are thinking about and concentrate on my voice. I don't want you to think about anything else except what I am saying to you. Clear your mind and relax for a few moments . . . [pause for sixty seconds].

> Jerry, . . . I want you to take a deep breath and hold that breath for a few seconds. Now exhale and continue breathing normally. Now take another deep breath and hold that breath for a few seconds. Exhale and continue breathing normally. You are feeling relaxed and calm and your mind is at ease.

> Jerry, . . . I want you to breathe deeply and exhale, breathe deeply and exhale, breathe deeply and exhale. As you continue to breathe and exhale, focus on the wonderful sensation of air rushing in and out of your nose. Notice how relaxed and calm you feel. Continue breathing and exhaling for a few moments and focus on the sensation of air rushing in and out of your nose . . . [pause for sixty seconds].

> Jerry, . . . I want you to continue to breathe and exhale, breathe and exhale. As you continue to breathe and exhale, notice the sensation of air rushing in and out of your lungs. Notice how your chest rises and falls as you breathe and exhale. Focus on this sensation of air rushing in and out of your lungs for a few moments. Notice how relaxed and calm you feel . . . [pause for sixty seconds].

As Jerry focuses on his breathing, he stops thinking about what he is worried about and focuses on the sensation of air rushing in and out of his body. This sensation is not only relaxing and calming, but it also increases the flow of blood to the brain and makes him more alert. The breathing exercises can be used for five minutes or longer. These breathing exercises give Jerry a stress- and anxiety-reducing technique he can use in multiple situations.

Muscle Relaxation Exercises

Another stress management technique that can be used in a variety of settings is muscle relaxation exercises. These exercises shift the client's attention from what he is worried about to how it feels when various muscles in the body are tensed and then relaxed. This shift of concentration to how his muscles feel when they are tensed and then relaxed can have a relaxing and calming effect on the client. The exercise increases blood flow to and from the brain and helps the client feel more alert. Consider the following example used with Jerry:

> Jerry, . . . I want you to close your eyes and get as comfortable as possible in your chair. Take a deep breath, hold that breath for a few seconds, and exhale. Continue to breathe and exhale, breathe and exhale. Jerry, . . . I want you to clear your mind of whatever you are thinking about and focus on what I'm going to ask you to do. Jerry, . . . I want you to clench your right hand into a fist and hold it for the count of 10 . . . 1, 2, 3, 4, 5, 6, 7, 8, 9, 10. Unclench your hand and move your fingers back and forth. Now I want you to clench your left hand into a fist and hold it for the count of 10 . . . 1, 2, 3, 4, 5, 6, 7, 8, 9, 10. Unclench your left hand and move your fingers back and forth.

> Now I want you to clench your right hand as hard as you can and hold it for the count of 10 . . . 1, 2, 3, 4, 5, 6, 7, 8, 9, 10. Unclench your right hand and move your fingers back and forth. I want you to continue clenching and unclenching your right hand. As you do, notice the difference you feel in your hand as you tense and then relax it. Continue clenching and unclenching your right hand and notice the difference between being tense and being relaxed.

> Clench your left hand as hard as you can and hold it for the count of 10 . . . 1, 2, 3, 4, 5, 6, 7, 8, 9, 10. Unclench your left hand and move your fingers back and forth. I want you to continue clenching and unclenching your left hand. As you do, notice the difference you feel in your hand as you tense and then relax your hand. Continue clenching and unclenching your hand and notice the difference between being tense and being relaxed.

This muscle relaxation exercise can become progressive as Jerry moves from the hands to the biceps of the right arm to the biceps of the left arm. The progression can then continue to tensing and relaxing the calf muscles in the right leg and then the left leg. A full muscle progression could take ten to fifteen minutes. An adaptation of this exercise is the use of a small rubber ball such as a handball that the client squeezes and then releases. Because the rubber ball is small and portable, it can easily be placed in a coat pocket or purse and used by the client almost anywhere and anytime relief is desired.

Stress Inoculation: A Cognitive–Behavioral Approach

Stress is a part of everyone's life. If clients are to live more productive lives, they must deal more appropriately with stress. According to Meichenbaum (Cormier & Nurius, 2003, p. 479), there are at least four different stressful events:

1. One event that is time limited and not chronic, such as a medical biopsy, surgery, a dental procedure, an oral examination.

2. One event that triggers a series of stressful reactions, such as job loss, divorce, death of loved one, natural or manmade disaster, or sexual assault.

3. Chronic and intermittent events, such as musical performances, athletic competitions, military combat, recurrent headaches.

4. Chronic and continual events, such as chronic medical or mental illness, marital conflict, chronic physical-emotional or psychological abuse, some professions—nursing, teaching, or police work.

Meichenbaum (Sharf, 2000) developed a treatment model to deal with these stressful events that focuses on cognitive and behavioral theory. In stress inoculation training (SIT), clients learn to deal with stress by changing their beliefs about the behaviors and statements they make to themselves regarding stress. In the first phase of stress inoculation training, clients learn that the meanings or cognitions they assign to events—not the event itself—actually create the stress. In other words, how a client defines a particular situation is the critical factor in whether the client views the situation as stressful. For example, a client learns that her fear of walking to work is based on negative self-statements such as, "I am going to be robbed." Or another client learns that her fear of going to college is based on other negative self-statements such as, "I'm stupid. I'll never succeed in college."

The second phase of treatment is skills acquisition in which clients learn to use a variety of coping strategies to resolve the fear and stress they are experiencing. One coping strategy is a series of behavioral techniques that include breathing and muscle relaxation exercises. It is difficult to maintain a high level of stress while trying to relax at the same time. Relaxation exercises mitigate the harmful effects of stress by substituting the pleasant sensation of relaxation. For example, clients who are experiencing stress can say to themselves, "Take this one step at a time and breathe slowly and comfortably." Another coping strategy is a series of cognitive techniques such as positive imagery and behavioral rehearsal. It is difficult to maintain a high level of stress while imagining a peaceful scene or reliving a pleasant experience. The client can replace the negative self-statement of "I'm afraid and I can't do anything" with the statement "I'm going to imagine I'm with my best friend and I will not be afraid."

After clients have learned and practiced these coping strategies, the final phase of treatment is putting them into practice. For the client who is afraid to walk to work, the first step would be to rehearse going to work while breathing slowly and comfortably. In rehearsing this behavior, the client is encouraged to picture in his mind what the sidewalk looks like, how the air smells, and the sounds of cars moving up and down the roadway. After these coping strategies have been rehearsed and mastered, the final step is for the client to actually walk down the street to work. As he walks, the client breathes slowly and comfortably and is attentive to the sights and sounds around the sidewalk and the surrounding area. In some situations, this initial walk might take place with one or two other people. Subsequent walks might include walking with a companion who is ten or fifteen feet behind the client. The final walk for the client would be by himself.

Computer-assisted programs have also been developed and tested that use stress inoculation training. Timmons et al., (2000) evaluated the effectiveness of an SIT computer guidance program that was used to treat individual veterans experiencing maladaptive anger. Timmons and colleagues compared the results of this computer-guided program with a conventional group treatment approach that also incorporated the stress inoculation model. Results indicated that both approaches were equally effective in treating anger with no differences in treatment satisfaction. There were, however, considerable cost savings with the computerized treatment approach.

Crisis Management Strategies

A crisis is a time-limited period of disequilibrium or homeostatic imbalance that is generally precipitated by a significant loss such as the death of a loved one or a separation or divorce. According to Gerald Caplan (1964), a crisis usually follows four stages. The first stage is the initial rise in tension that results from the crisis-provoking event. As this tension begins to mount, the individual will try to resolve the crisis by using familiar patterns of problem-solving behavior. The second stage of crisis is characterized by increased tension because the individual has not yet resolved the crisis. During the second stage, emergency problem-solving skills are often used to reduce the tension. As these emergency activities fail to alleviate the tension, the individual enters the third stage of crisis.

In the third stage of crisis, the tension becomes so great that individuals may experience acute anxiety or depression because they feel so helpless and lost. Entering the final stage of crisis, individuals will either experience a major emotional or mental breakdown or resolve the crisis by using maladaptive patterns of behavior that decrease tension but impair future social functioning. For example, a person who has been laid off from work may ultimately abandon the family if efforts to find employment continue to fail. The individual will usually complete these four stages of crisis within five to eight weeks.

In crisis management, the direct practitioner usually follows either a generic or an individual approach (Smith, 1990). The central thesis of the generic approach is that for each different crisis reaction there are specific psychological tasks and problem-solving activities that every client must complete in order to resolve the crisis successfully. Generic crisis intervention offers an intervention plan designed for all clients experiencing the same crisis regardless of their individual differences. In contrast, the individual approach focuses on the specific psychological tasks and problem-solving activities that each client must accomplish to resolve the crisis. There are no predetermined tasks that every client must accomplish; instead, the social worker's treatment plan concentrates on each client's separate needs.

Clients experiencing the crisis of bereavement may need help with several tasks. These include:

- **Expressing the feelings of sadness and pain associated with the loss.** Social workers should encourage clients to cry if they are so inclined and should help clients recognize that it's okay to express any sort of feelings. These may include anger, guilt, or any other number of emotions that arise in these circumstances.
- **Exploring possible reasons for especially intense or long-lasting bereavement.** Social workers can help clients identify feelings that appear to be an overreaction to the loss and consider the basis for these emotions. The practitioner should also be alert to possible suicidal thoughts associated with these emotions.
- **Reestablishing or reintegrating with social networks.** If necessary, new friends may be needed, or clients may need assistance reconnecting with family and friends. Social workers can identify and suggest opportunities for the bereaved to make new acquaintances
- **Restoring emotional equilibrium.** Here social workers can assist clients as they come to accept the losses they have experienced and begin to return to their normal level of functioning.

Crisis intervention services are also needed by women and men who have survived rape. Depending on how long ago the event happened, the individual may require medical attention, contact with law enforcement, notification of family or friends, and assistance dealing with emotional issues. It is common to experience a variety of emotions, which can include disbelief, anger, stress, fear, depression, and shame, among others. Francis (1993) has identified three phases common to many rape survivors. They include the following:

- **Disorganization.** Client reactions in this phase include anger and fear coupled with doubts about whether they did the right thing or could have done something different that would have avoided the sexual assault.

- **Controlled reaction.** Social workers can anticipate clients becoming calmer and more controlled than immediately after the event. Although some survivors will have other physical and emotional reactions, the period of composure is most common. It is important to recognize that the client is still experiencing intense feelings even if they are not readily apparent.

- **Reorganization.** This a period characterized by some level of adjustment or adaptation to the rape. The length of time before this period occurs can vary from months to years. Survivors who have reached this stage no longer live in fear for their safety and have adjusted to other fears and the loss of self-esteem common to those who have been raped. They will have regained the ability to trust others and incorporated the experience into their sense of self. This process can be aided by the use of support groups and by strong support from the survivor's family.

Principles of crisis intervention theory and practice have been adapted to many other areas of mental health. One especially impor-

Figure 8.3

Characteristics of Potentially Violent Students

1. Express self-destructive or homicidal ideation.
2. Articulate specific plans to harm self or others.
3. Engage in "bullying" other children.
4. Engage in substance abuse.
5. Become involved in gangs.
6. Have harmed small animals.
7. Have engaged in fire setting.
8. Give away possessions.
9. Have been or are victims of child abuse.
10. Have access to a firearm.
11. Have brought a weapon to school.
12. Exhibit poor academic performance.
13. Have been frequently truant from school.
14. Appear withdrawn.
15. Have experienced a significant loss.

Source: Greenstone and Leviton (2002, pp. 52–53).

tant adaptation is using crisis principles to identify students and adults at risk for violent behavior. In *Elements of Crisis Intervention,* Greenstone and Leviton (2002) present a checklist of "early warning signs" that can be used to identify students who might become violent. The more items that are checked, the greater the risk for violent acting-out behavior. A partial list is shown in Figure 8.3.

Greenstone and Leviton's (2002, pp. 54–55) checklist for identifying adults at risk for violent behavior includes the following items:

1. There is a history of causing deliberate encounters with the police or confrontations with other authorities.

2. There is current or historical use of minor children as a tool, pawn, or weapon against the other spouse in a family dispute.

3. The person indicates high levels of personal dissatisfaction with his or her life.

4. The person makes verbalizations concerning homicide or suicide.

5. The verbalizations concern taking and holding of hostages, especially family members.

6. The person has a history of impulsive acts.

7. The person has recently purchased a weapon and ammunition absent a historical interest in such items.

8. The person has a diagnosed psychiatric disorder.

9. The person has a history of violent acts with animals during childhood.

10. Violence in subject's family of orientation is seen as a mode of communication.

Social workers often ask when crisis intervention treatment should be terminated. Treatment should be concluded when the client has completed the psychological tasks associated with resolving the crisis and reached a state of equilibrium in social functioning. This means that the client has returned to at least a precrisis level of functioning. In other words, the client is back to work, spending time with family and friends, and enjoying life once again. Some clients may return to their precrisis level of functioning in six weeks, whereas others require twelve weeks or longer. Because managed care programs rarely authorize more than ten counseling sessions, this means that in some crisis situations the client will not have returned to the precrisis level of functioning before services are terminated. If this is the case, the social worker must design with the client psychological tasks and activities that the client can work on after services have ended that will permit an eventual return to the precrisis level of functioning.

Spiritual and Humanistic Strategies

Historically speaking, social work once had strong spiritual roots derived from both spiritual motivations for helping as well as the sectarian nature of early social service agencies. As social work increasingly focused on professionalization and as more secular agencies developed, this attention to spirituality and religion waned. Unlike earlier social work pioneers, practitioners in much of the twentieth century avoided talking about a client's religion or spirituality. Sometimes this reluctance grew out of a fear that they would be seen as proselytizing. For other social workers, it reflected the concern that inquiring about a client's religion might be perceived as imposing the practitioner's own values on the client. Still others avoided the topic because they doubted it would be a legitimate or productive use of their time with clients. Sometimes practitioners would even redirect the topic if the client raised the issue.

More recently, social work and other helping professions have begun to recognize the immense power these beliefs can have over the ability of clients to withstand trauma and tragedy when things look the darkest. Much of the credit for this new direction goes to writers such as Canda and Furman (1999) and Van Hook, Hugen, and Aguilar (2001), who have understood the power and importance of

Voices from the Field

Edward R. Canda

As a Catholic youth, I learned to examine my conscience and to integrate my spirituality into daily life. That led me to an interest in comparative religious studies and various practices of meditation. I wanted to understand and experience how various religions grappled with the big questions of human life and death, of meaning and purpose. During the late 1960s and early 1970s, protest movements for civil rights and against war raised my conscience about social injustice in the United States and around the world. I began to join my interest in spirituality with social concerns by engaging in occasional social service volunteer activities, social issue debates with friends, and local student activism. A bachelor's degree in anthropology, graduate study of East Asian philosophy in Korea, and a master's degree in religious studies deepened my knowledge of comparative religions somewhat but left me with an-

other big personal question. Studying religions and engaging in spiritual practices provided great benefit to me, but how could I help others through this? So I decided to change to the profession of social work in 1980.

Graduate studies in social work (MSW in 1982 and PhD in 1986) gave me valuable skills and knowledge about how to help, especially regarding my special interests of the time, refugee resettlement and transcultural relations. But despite our profession's ideals of holistic, person/environment practice, I could find little guidance about addressing the spiritual dimension of people's needs and goals. So I conducted my dissertation research to learn from the written and oral wisdom of the leaders on spirituality in social work in order to create a conceptualization of spirituality that would fit social work's mission, practices settings, and ethics.

spiritual values in understanding and helping clients.

Canda and Furman (1999) note that "social work is fundamentally a spiritual profession—one that sets its reason for existence and its highest priorities on service" (p. 4). Many who choose social work for a career have their own religious or spiritual beliefs, which played a role in helping them select this field. The empathy and concern for the worth and dignity of human beings displayed by social workers is

directly related to their spiritual compassion for the suffering of others. Canda and Furman also advocate that "spirituality can be considered an aspect of human experience and functioning, along with the biological, psychological, and sociological aspects" (p. 46). Spirituality helps some people try to make sense out of a sometimes senseless world. For others, it is part of an attempt to better understand themselves and to answer the question "What is my purpose?" (p. 49).

Much has changed since those days in which research, teaching, and practice related to spirituality were rarities and those who engaged in them typically felt isolated. Since the early 1990s, a rapidly swelling momentum of wonderful activity by many scholars and practitioners has led to the development of spiritually sensitive social work. Spiritually sensitive social work respects the diverse religious and nonreligious expressions of spirituality for individuals, families, and communities. It is a joining of heady knowledge, soulful wisdom, heartfelt compassion, and outstretched action. It draws on insights from conventional social work, interdisciplinary studies of religions, perennial wisdom of spiritual teachers across the world, the living testaments of our clients and their communities, and postmodern movements such as transpersonal theory and ecophilosophy. It is a way for social workers to cultivate their inner spiritual lives and to share the fruits for the benefit of others.

Now there are professional organizations for mutual support and networking, such as the Society for Spirituality and Social Work. There are more than 700 related publications in social work and many hundreds of research studies in health and other allied fields. More than 70 MSW programs around the country have courses on spirituality. And similar movements are growing around the world.

At this time when questions of life and death loom ever larger; when competing religious and political ideologues use their religions to rationalize both caring and killing; when clients and students increasingly bring spiritual issues into field and classroom; when practitioners, teachers, and researchers increasingly try to find a fit between their spiritual calls to service and their professional work; when insights from virtually all spiritual traditions in the world are available—this is a time when the movement for spiritually sensitive social work is much needed and very welcome.

For information on many resources and contacts regarding spiritual diversity in social work, see www.socwel.ku.edu/canda.

Spirituality and religious beliefs tend to play even more crucial roles in the lives of clients who are coping with critical events such as a terminal illness, a bereavement, or serious health issues. In these and similar situations, social workers should be comfortable raising the topic of religion or spirituality with clients. Likewise, social workers have come to recognize the importance of these issues for many ethnic and minority groups. For many such groups, the church and religion play a major role in their everyday lives and in efforts to bring about institutional and environmental change. Canda and Furman (1999), in a review of the beliefs and values of several major religions, identify the common threads of compassion for others, commitment to social justice, and commitment to service.

Social workers should be alert to the fact that their clients may have significant religious or spiritual beliefs and values and be familiar with the commonalities across various religious doctrines. At the very least, the practitioner should ask clients about this area and listen carefully when clients identify their religion or other spiritual beliefs as a coping resource. Failure to explore this area prevents social workers from understanding a major area of strength for many clients and a potential area for some others.

Other Life Management Strategies

In addition to the various strategies already described, a number of other strategies have been developed to help clients gain more control over their lives. Many, if not most, can be adapted to social work and used to increase the coping skills of clients. In some cases, asking clients to read the books that describe these approaches can be an adjunct to ongoing therapy or used to help solidify gains following termination. Like other coping skills, these strategies incorporate many of the basic principles of learning theory, especially the belief that people can be taught new behaviors. Consider some of the adaptive strategies identified by Spencer Johnson (1998) in his best-selling management book *Who Moved My Cheese?*:

1. Change happens—they keep moving the cheese.

2. Anticipate change—get ready for the cheese to move.

3. Monitor change—smell the cheese often so you know when it's getting old.

4. Adapt to change quickly—the quicker you let go of old cheese, the sooner you can enjoy the new cheese.

5. Change—move with the cheese.

6. Enjoy change—savor the adventure and the taste of new cheese!

7. Be ready to quickly change again and again—they keep moving the cheese.

Who Moved My Cheese is a story about life and how life can suddenly change. The critical point of the story is that life keeps changing whether or not we want it to. Because life keeps changing, we must see this change in a new light. That new light is not a shroud of gloom but a burst of sunlight because change brings new opportunities and challenges. In many ways, change is the "spice of life" that keeps us interested and focused on what we are doing. Without change, life would be not only predictable but also terribly boring.

Johnson's premise is simple but profound. From his perspective, change is a constant factor in everyone's life and should be accepted and embraced rather than avoided and feared. The only constant in life is that life changes. These changes present people with new challenges as well as new opportunities. In his book, cheese is a metaphor for what people want in life such as a good job, fame, money, or a one handicap in golf. Like the months of the year, what people want constantly changes. The "maze" is where people look for what they want in life. For most of us, the maze includes our spouse, children, family, friends, and work. Johnson describes how two mice named Sniff and Scurry search the maze looking for cheese. The story is delightful and entertaining and an excellent example of how self-help books can be used in social work practice.

Cultural and Diversity Issues

As in all phases of the counseling process, social workers need to be sensitive to cultural and diversity issues and how they may affect how clients develop coping skills. The coping skills discussed in this chapter have been used successfully with clients from a variety of backgrounds, including various ethnic and minority groups. Even so, some of these coping strategies may be better than others with particular groups.

For example, men probably respond better to muscle relaxation exercises than do women, whereas women adapt better to positive imagery. The same is probably true with other cognitive skills. The point is that regardless of which coping skills are used, the social worker must be sensitive to the impact that cultural and diversity issues might have on these strategies. Figure 8.4 provides a useful set of guidelines to

---

Figure 8.4

Guidelines for Multicultural Awareness

1. Attempt to become aware of your own cultural biases.

2. If possible, learn the language of those into whose crisis you might need to intervene. Find a qualified translator if necessary.

3. Ask for clarification if you are not sure what the victim said.

4. Do not assume that you understand any nonverbal communication unless you are familiar with the victim's culture.

5. Do not impose your personal values.

6. If the victim's nonverbal communication is insulting in your culture, do not take it personally.

7. Develop an awareness of anything in your own nonverbal communication that might be insulting in certain cultures.

8. Make every effort to increase your awareness of your own preconceptions and stereotypes of the cultures you may encounter.

9. With your increased awareness, reinterpret the behavior of people from another culture from their cultural perspective.

10. Be willing to test, adapt, and change your perceptions to fit your new experience.

11. Maintain objectivity.

12. Recognize that you cannot change a person's cultural perspective.

13. Do not judge people from another culture by your own cultural values until you have come to know the people and their cultural values.

14. Recognize that your lack of familiarity with a victim's culture might increase the stress in the intervention.

15. Clarify your role, knowledge, and experience with the parties so that you maintain the integrity demanded by your position as intervener.

Source: Greenstone and Leviton (2002, pp. 51–52).

help practitioners increase their awareness of different cultures.

SUMMARY

This chapter focuses on developing clients coping skills using a variety of approaches. These include the use of cognitive therapy, assertiveness training, anger management, stress management, and crisis management. The chapter also highlights working with special at-risk populations such as depressed and suicidal clients as well as those engaging in criminal behavior. Detailed treatment programs for anger management, assertiveness training, and stress management are also presented. The chapter also looks at the role that spiritual, humanistic, and other life management strategies can play in the lives of clients. Suggestions from the work of many different authors are included.

Navigating Direct Practice

An access code for Research Navigator™ is packaged within your text. Use this code to register at www.researchnavigator.com and then use the key words listed below to research articles related to the chapter's content. Research Navigator™ helps you quickly and efficiently make the most of your research time.

❏ Addiction
❏ Anger management
❏ Crisis management
❏ Depression
❏ Spirituality
❏ Suicide

Chapter 9

Empowerment and Strengths-Based Practice

■ Sharon and Bill Parker live with their two children (Amy, age twelve, and Steven, age sixteen) in an inner-city housing unit. Bill works as a day laborer and Sharon picks up shifts as a waitress at a nearby restaurant. Between their income and the low-cost housing, they have been able to pay their bills but little else. They have no insurance for health care. After becoming ill, Amy has been diagnosed with leukemia, and the Parkers will need to be able to negotiate the medical system in order to get Amy the care she needs.

M any of the individuals, families, and communities that social workers work with do not recognize the strength or power they have to create changes in their lives. Very often social workers see clients for the first time when it becomes clear that the client is in need of empowerment. The Parkers, although possessing many strengths, may never have tackled as powerful a system as the institution of health care. This is often the point at which we encounter clients like the Parkers, when they are vulnerable and need the support of someone to help them with their situation.

Empowerment serves as both a process and an outcome in social work practice to help clients recognize and use their own strengths. With empowerment as a process, social workers help clients through activities that use their strengths to create change in their lives. A social worker might, for example, suggest the activity of confrontation to shift a power differential between the Parkers and the health care community. As a product, empowerment serves as the "end outcome whereby a measure of power is achieved" (Boehm & Staples, 2002, p. 450). In this case, the ideal outcome for the Parkers might be the best care possible for their daughter.

Empowerment as a term in treatment "indicates the intent to and the processes of assisting individuals, groups, families, and communities to discover and expend the resources and tools within and around them" (Saleebey, 1997, p. 8). Empowerment also refers to "processes and outcomes whereby less powerful individuals and groups move to reduce discrepancies in power relationships" (Boehm & Staples, 2002, p. 450). For example, the mother who must obtain food for her children might be empowered enough to use reasoning to explain her situation to the food bank. Alternately, she might use advocacy skills to change welfare rules and regulations. To do either, though, she must feel strong enough about herself and her skills to try.

As social workers, it is critical that we be able to empower ourselves. Clients look to us to model those behaviors that we say are so important for them. Without our own use of empowerment, we cannot advocate for our clients or teach our clients to use their own power. Strengths-based practice, as noted in Chapter 2, is often more powerful than a deficit-oriented model of practice. Empowering clients to recognize and use their strengths enables them to move beyond the problem and to help themselves.

Empowerment Guidelines

A social worker often needs to help clients understand how to operationalize their empowerment skills. For any act of empowerment to occur, however, general guidelines important to the process must be followed. Simon (1994, pp. 25–29) identifies the following:

1. *"Shape programs in response to the expressed preferences and demonstrated needs of clients and community members"* (p. 25). Building on the needs and preferences of clients and community members, social workers are often able to make programs work for the clients who use them rather than benefiting the programs themselves. Focusing on intervention from a community perspective could very well be more appropriate for clients than working with one client at a time.

2. *"Make certain that programs and services are maximally convenient for and accessible to one's clients and their communities"* (p. 25). The location of an agency and its access by public transportation is one way the agency shows it respect for clients and its committment to empowerment.

3. *"Ask as much dedication to problem solving from one's client as from oneself"* (p. 25). Asking clients to take responsibility for their own situation through their own problem solving is more helpful than trying to solve the problem for them.

4. *"Call and build upon strengths of clients and communities"* (p. 26). Strengths are the core ingredient in empowerment, and unless we as social workers work with our clients' strengths, change will never be permanent.

5. *"Devise and redefine interventions in response to the unique configuration of requests, issues, and needs that a client or client group presents. Resist becoming wedded to a favored interventive method"* (p. 27). Doing only one form of intervention, such as family therapy, does not allow for the different methods that individual clients may need. In order to help clients, the empowering social worker must employ different interventions to aid that particular client and assist him or her with challenges.

6. *"Make leadership development a constant priority of practice and policy development"* (p. 28). When we make leadership development a constant priority, we are ensuring that our clients and communities are able to develop their own skills and methods to change the environmental situation surrounding them.

7. *"Be patient, since empowerment takes substantial amounts of time and continuity of effort"* (p. 28). Empowerment is a process that takes time. However, in some situations, waiting for things to change is not always possible. It is important to recognize that people achieve more when they are able to make the changes themselves. Social workers who can be patient while helping clients empower themselves will be rewarded when those clients continue to make changes through building on strengths within themselves.

8. *"Take ongoing stock of social workers' own powerlessness and power at work"* (p. 29). There is a saying in our field—that we cannot expect clients to achieve what we have not achieved ourselves. In

order to best understand our clients' struggles with empowerment, we need not only to have struggled with it ourselves but also to have succeeded at it.

9. *"Use local knowledge to contribute to the general good (Geetz, 1983)"* (p. 29). Through the use and understanding of local knowledge of political situations, social workers are better able to create an environment of change for their clients.

These guidelines aid the social worker in ensuring that empowerment activities can occur. However, helping a client carry out the act of empowerment requires more than the social worker following these guidelines. The clients and communities that practitioners work with will generally not have had a lot of experience using their strengths and skills. More often than not, clients will have a lifelong history of feeling powerless. Those individuals within a community will not necessarily understand how to overcome a situation because up to that point they will not have used their strengths and skills as an organized group. Rather, they will have experienced poverty, abuse, and other harmful life experiences (Sheafor & Horejsi, 2003). To begin to enable clients to use their empowerment skills, Saleebey (1997) suggests the following tasks:

1. *Eliminate negative labels for the clients we engage.* When we label clients, we are not really seeing them as the individuals they are. Words and terms are powerful messages we give people, and by using negative labels such as "depressed," we make it difficult for clients and others to see their strengths and abilities.

2. *Promote the individual's awareness of resources in families, institutions, and communities.* Without individuals' knowledge of their resources in all areas, they may view their situation as hopeless. The involvement of others in our struggles creates a sense of hope and support. This hope and support helps individuals move forward knowing they are not alone.

3. *Foster changes in clients' mind-sets to help them see themselves as strong and capable of creating change.* To label a client as weak and incapable of change is to set up the client for failure. As mentioned in the use of negative labels, clients respond to how they view themselves and their capabilities. Clients seek to live up to their own sense of self and what others believe they can do.

4. *Believe in people and their strengths, resources, abilities, and dreams.* Believing in clients is a critical skill all those engaged in practice must learn. Clients learn to see themselves as others see them. Our ability to see all the strengths and resources a client has to offer enables us to help clients move forward to reach their goals.

5. *Reject paternalistic views of individuals that fail to recognize their strengths.* Social workers might be tempted to assume such a caring role toward clients that they do everything for them and do not allow clients to use their own resources and skills. But social workers who make clients' decisions for them encourage clients to feel like children and incapable of fulfilling their own goals. Rappaport (1990) states, "To work within an empowering ideology requires us to identify (for ourselves, for others, and for people with whom we work) the abilities they possess which may not be obvious, even to themselves" (p. 12). Although individuals have often used their strengths before, they have not necessarily recognized them as

strengths. Even those individuals who have struggled through life have strengths that have kept them going (Saleebey, 1997). The individuals we work with may have often used a skill they do not recognize as empowering. It is our responsibility to help clients recognize their skills and put names to them. In other cases, individuals who do not have a particular skill might have the resources to learn it. In these situations, it is our job to help clients recognize the skills needed and to use them in whatever manner is effective for them. Case Example 9.1 gives an idea of how a social worker might aid a client in recognizing his or her own strengths and skills.

The social worker should encourage clients by talking about what they have accomplished and which strengths they used to accomplish it. Empowerment and strengths are closely tied together. We empower our clients, at least in part, through the use of their skills and strengths. To better conceptualize the use of empowerment, we need to look at it from a strengths-based practice perspective. Although the strengths perspective is reviewed in Chapter 7 in a discussion of the solution-focused model, this chapter explores the foundation of

---

CASE EXAMPLE 9.1

Empowering Conversation

Practitioner: I know this must be a very difficult situation with your child so ill.

Ms. Parker: We just do not know what to do. She is so sick and we seem to be getting very little help from the hospital and the doctors. They are treating her because of a policy of giving so much of their services to those without insurance; however, they have not really told us what they are doing and if they are doing everything they can.

Practitioner: I have been very impressed by what you have accomplished so far. You have been able to get Amy into the pediatric ward and have good oncology doctors working with her. What kind of skills did you use to get that done?

Ms. Parker: Well, we were just so upset, we refused to leave until they found her an oncologist. We were stubborn and did not take no for an answer.

Practitioner: What you were was strong and persistent. You were able with your strength of love for your daughter to make something happen. I wonder if you can't just use that same kind of strength to ensure she gets the best care. What would you need to do to accomplish this?

Ms. Parker: Well, for one thing, I would have to not be scared to face these doctors.

They seem so much better than me.

Practitioner: But is that really true? You have worked hard all your life, been able to raise your children well, and know so much more about your child than any of the doctors.

Ms. Parker: I guess I can face them and demand that they tell me what care they are giving her and if it is the most I can do. Would you be willing to go with me when I talk to them?

Practitioner: I would be glad to. Why don't we practice what you are going to say?

a strengths-based perspective without prescribing any particular model.

Strengths-Based Practice

Saleebey (1996) states that the strengths-based practice perspective in social work began, in part, with an approach to case management with people with severe mental illness (Saleebey, 1992; Sullivan & Rapp, 1994; Weick, Rapp, Sullivan, & Kisthardt, 1989). Since then, more and more practitioners and theorists have focused on a strengths-based perspective. Other programs and practices, such as "developmental resilience, healing and wellness, solution-focused therapy, assets-based community development and narrative and story" (Saleebey, 1997, p. 4), have developed along with and as part of the strengths perspective. The strengths practice perspective now plays a major role in social work practice across many interventions. Despite the research that shows the effectiveness of strengths-based practice (Rapp, 1996; Chamberlain & Rapp, 1991), a significant number of theorists still believe that the biomedical model is the best approach. They point to the fact that the biomedical model is the one we as social workers must respond to within the direct practice system. They also point out that clinicians cannot pay attention only to strengths but must also address the problems people are experiencing in order to resolve them. These statements speak to the differences between the biomedical and the strengths models. In one, the major responsibility for client change relies heavily on the social worker (biomedical model), whereas in the other the responsibility is placed more on the client (strengths model). As you review the model, think about how these different approaches might affect the clients with whom you are working.

Strengths-based practice in social work means that "everything you do as a social worker will be predicated, in some way, on helping to discover and embellish, explore and exploit clients' strengths and resources in the service of assisting them to achieve their goals, realize their dreams, and shed the irons of their own inhibitions and misgivings" (Saleebey, 1997, p. 3). The emphasis in this statement is on the social workers' role to help their clients resolve their own problems and achieve their goals. Issues will be resolved through the client's strengths and skills. The practitioner's role is to provide a way to develop or tap into these strengths. In order to go about this, Saleebey (1997, pp. 12–15) cites the following five principles as the foundation of the strengths perspective:

1. *"Every individual, group, family, and community has strengths"* (p. 12). Although it may not always seem as though everyone has strengths, they do. Often we become so overwhelmed that we cannot necessarily identify our strengths or those of others. Sometimes we may need to begin at the beginning and simply note that the client's coming in shows strength, an ability to reach out for help and engage in a situation that might provide aid. As we come to know our clients, we will begin to pick up on other strengths. The following case presents a dilemma for the social worker, who has met the client for the first time and faces the client's lack of hope and belief in herself. As you read Case Example 9.2, put yourself in the social worker's position and find at least three strengths you might call to the client's attention.

2. *"Trauma and abuse, illness, and struggle may be injurious, but they may also be sources of challenge and opportunity"*

CASE EXAMPLE 9.2

The Martinez Family

Mrs. Martinez is forty-three years of age and has three children. She has never married, and none of her children's fathers is involved in their lives. Her oldest son, Rick, age sixteen, is currently in a juvenile detention center for drug use and breaking and entering. Her middle child, Ned, age thirteen, is in and out of trouble at school and has recently been involved in some drug-related activities. Her youngest child, Rose, is developmentally challenged and has been kept behind in school for two years. Recently, Rose developed leukemia and is on massive doses of chemotherapy.

Mrs. Martinez has a job at a clothing factory and makes about $10.00 an hour. She has had difficulty getting to work because of Rose's illness and has run out of sick days and vacation time. Mrs. Martinez is seeking help from a social worker to be able to access services she might need and to work through how she will handle all the current and emerging issues in her life.

(p. 13). It is sometimes hard to understand how a difficult situation can produce strengths and opportunities. Yet, as we think back to times of struggle, it would be unusual not to see something we gained from the struggle. These gains might include a new way of thinking about things, a new insight about ourselves, or a new skill that we learned. These strengths often emerge as we deal with a difficult time in our lives. Using Case Example 9.3, write down two things the client might develop as strengths through the situation.

3. "*Assume that you do not know the upper limits of the capacity to grow and change, and take individual, group, and community aspirations seriously*" (p. 13). Oftentimes we have a set idea about what our clients are capable of doing. Even when they would like more out of their lives, we sometimes hinder their success. Every client needs to be viewed as someone who

---

CASE EXAMPLE 9.3

The Gerry Family

Mr. and Mrs. Gerry have come in for marital counseling. They have struggled with their marriage this past year because Mr. Gerry had an affair with another woman. Although Mrs. Gerry claims that she has forgiven her husband, the issue is always reemerging. Both agree that things have been difficult since that time, and they fight a great deal.

Mrs. Gerry states that she no longer trusts her husband and does not know how to change this feeling.

CASE EXAMPLE 9.4

Kingston Neighborhood

The Kingston neighborhood is a catchment area approximately three miles square. A neighborhood committee council meets every month to deal with issues in the neighborhood. A low-income area with public housing and gang activity, the neighborhood has strong advocates who have been able to shut down two crack houses in the community.

You are the social worker who works with special issues in the community, and you are attending a committee council meeting.

The committee is discussing the gang activity and attempting to come up with solutions to resolve the crime problems. As a council member begins to speak, other members of the council and audience start to

clap and reinforce the speaker. As the conversation continues, issues of political influence begin to emerge. Someone suggests that the council member who was speaking run for mayor. This idea generates much excitement. You are aware that the council member has no experience in politics and did not graduate from high school.

can obtain his or her dreams and aspirations. Our role is not to stop them but to find ways to encourage their progress. Using Case Example 9.4, identify a way in which you feel that this community may be aiming too high, and then name two ways in which you would encourage this community to pursue its dream.

4. *"We best serve clients by collaborating with them"* (p. 14). Many times in the course of social work practice we would like to collaborate with clients but don't, either because it is easier to take care of the issue ourselves or because we don't agree with what the client wants to do. Collaboration is a critical and ethical aspect of practice. Anytime we do not encourage and support collaboration, we are not encouraging or supporting the client. In Case Example 9.5, note when the social worker could have collaborated more with the client.

5. *"Every environment is full of resources"* (p. 15). Although there are times when

certain environments seem less full of resources than others, resources are always present. Whether the situation involves low income, illness, or juvenile delinquency, resources (and strengths) are available in every situation. Name three resources available in the situation shown in Case Example 9.6

Being able to put these principles into action is an important skill that social workers must possess. Working through a strengths perspective means having your own set of strengths that can foster your clients in their empowering processes.

Applying a strengths perspective to a client situation means more, however, than simply recognizing strengths and writing them down on an intake sheet. It requires an orientation to a strengths perspective that forms the primary foundation of the practitioner's approach. Part of this orientation is an understanding of the "post-structural notion that social workers must increasingly respect and

CASE EXAMPLE 9.5

Terri Jones

Terri Jones has suffered from chronic kidney disease for about two years. She has been in dialysis at least three times a week for over a year. Although she has been able to keep her job by working in her home, a new company manager is no longer approving this work arrangement. Terri states that she is afraid to talk with her new manager because she does not know her. Terri is worrying about her resources and how she will manage without a job. As the social worker, you recommend that she bring in her bills to the next session and you will help her with a budget. You also offer to call the company manager to explain the client's situation. When Terri expresses concern that she will not be able to keep her apartment, you tell her not to worry about that now and that you will handle her concerns for her.

engage clients' ways of viewing themselves and their worlds in the helping process. Or, to put it differently, the strengths perspective asserts that the client's meaning must count for more in the helping process and the scientific labels and theories must count for less" (De Jong & Miller, 1995, pp. 729–730). Although we strongly support the use of theory, it is important to recognize that the strengths perspective requires a degree of belief in clients' ability to know for themselves what is best and what is the most appropriate way to achieve this.

Empowering Engagement and Overview

Social workers operating from a strengths perspective are doing so from within a framework of empowerment. This means that the social worker's verbal and nonverbal communications with clients will be designed to emphasize that the seeds of change reside in the

CASE EXAMPLE 9.6

Nora Davis

Nora Davis is fifteen years old and a straight A student at the local high school. She has come to the Planned Parenthood Center because she is pregnant. None of Nora's family or friends knows about the pregnancy. While talking with Nora, you find out that she attends church regularly and does not want to have an abortion. She states that she is too frightened to tell her parents because they will "hate her." She refuses to let you discuss the situation with them. She says she just wants to move away and not let anyone know where she is. When you ask where she would go, she says she would go live with her aunt.

client's untapped strengths and abilities. This sometimes comes as a surprise to clients when they seek help for a specific problem and expect that the problem itself will be the focus of their work with the practitioner. However, accentuating a problem can create both negative expectations and negative outcomes, which clients can seldom overcome once they are set in this negative frame of mind (Saleebey, 1997). Therefore, the initial focus should be on the person and not the problem. Social workers can emphasize this focus through the attitudes they bring to their working environment with the client. Manning (1998, pp. 105–106) recommends a series of empowerment attitudes for the social worker in the mental health field. These observations, however, are just as appropriate in other social work venues.

1. *"Think of and interact with the person, not the label or diagnosis"* (p. 105). The social work field has long questioned the use of labeling or diagnosis as a way of treating a client. Although there can be reasons to use a diagnostic system, from a strengths perspective this would not be appropriate. A strengths focus requires getting to know a client from an interpersonal perspective. By knowing the client as a person, the social worker provides a safe environment for strengths to emerge. Further, a strengths focus presupposes that through getting to know the client the social worker will have a better understanding of the obstacles that hinder the client from recognizing his or her strengths and/or using them. The interpersonal relationship provides the map that guides both social worker and client.

2. *"Respect the person's right to self-determination"* (p. 105). In the process of getting to know clients, the social worker will also come to respect their ideas and their decisions. From a strengths perspective, clients' ability to make their own self-determinations recognizes the main role that clients play in their own treatment. Self-determination is the action that occurs when clients believe in themselves and are capable of making their own decisions.

3. *"Be responsible to the 'whole person,' taking quality of life and environmental factors into account"* (p. 105). When social workers work with a person, they must consider the total context of the client's life. Viewing the client from an internal perspective only negates what is occurring around the client and the effect this environment has on the client's strengths. A person with a strong sense of self can operate from an empowering perspective but must also have the ability to pull supports from the environment to foster this perspective. Whether through family and friends, the success of a job, or the enjoyment of hobbies and talents, individuals find many different ways to draw support from their environment.

4. *"Focus on a strengths perspective rather than on a deficit model for assessment and practice"* (p. 105). A deficit model for assessment and practice examines what is wrong in the person's life and what is not working. This negative focus pulls the client's attention from strengths and successes. By focusing on the strengths perspective, the social worker is supporting the client to achieve his or her goals and supporting the helping relationship that develops.

5. *"Respect the diversity of skills and knowledge that consumers bring to the relationship. Let go of being the 'expert' "* (p. 105). By letting go of being the expert,

social workers set aside their need to be right. By allowing clients to direct the intervention, practitioners support clients' positive development. The intervention becomes part of a collaborative process in which the client and the social worker work together to bring about change.

6. *"Trust consumers' internal motivation to learn and direct their lives"* (p. 106). Social workers need to believe that clients have an innate wish to improve the quality of their lives and to determine what is best for them.

7. *"Respect consumers' ability and right to contribute—to you, to other consumers, to the agency, and to the community"* (p. 106). Too often, practitioners assume that clients are incapable of contributing to other areas because of their troubles in one realm. In effect, their problems are seen as a negative halo that reduces their potential in other areas.

8. *"Recognize the individuality of people, respecting each person's unique qualities, values, and needs"* (p. 106). As a general rule, social workers are very much aware of their clients' individuality. At the same time, there is a tendency to lump people together because they share some characteristics such as a diagnostic label or a particular problem. This lumping undercuts the individuation that the client deserves and needs.

Manning (1998, p. 106) also emphasizes the following role for the social worker from the strengths perspective:

- Develop a client-driven model of care focused on the goals and values held by the consumer.
- Emphasize building connections through roles, involvement, and community to replace lost culture, history, and identity.

- Develop opportunities for meaningful activities that help to build skills, knowledge, and reflexive thinking.
- Enhance consumers' ability to transform their environment rather than adapt to it.
- Engage consumers in taking risks, making decisions, and learning from them.
- Emphasize information, education, and skill-building that increase self-efficacy.
- Involve consumers and family members in decision-making roles in the relationship and within the organization.

Assessment

Numerous principles and tasks need to be carried out in strengths-based practice. One of the primary tasks is the assessment of strengths and skills that the social worker helps the client recognize. In order to carry out this assessment process, we need to recognize what strengths are. Strengths include the following, according to Saleebey (1997, p. 51):

1. What people have learned about themselves, others and their world
2. Personal qualities, traits and virtues that people possess
3. What people know about the world around them
4. The talents that people have
5. Cultural and personal stories and lore
6. Pride
7. The community surrounding the individual.

The social worker asks a series of questions to bring these strengths to the consciousness of the client. These questions might focus on how a client has coped with a situation before, what types of support a client now has, and what the client has established as his or her goals. Social workers ask these questions not in an interviewing sense but as part of the conversational process. In a strengths-based model, the client and the social worker should be able to talk at a conversational level. The social worker should also strongly believe that people are able to make changes in their lives (both social and political), see clients as the only people who can bring insight and understanding to their lives and situations, help clients build self-confidence and experience personal power, help clients identify sources of strength, and work with them to put these strengths into action (Sheafer & Horejsi, 2003).

Assessing from a strengths-based approach requires the social worker to assess not only present abilities but also future strengths and the application of them to achieve goals. The social worker works from the exception perspective, seeing not what the problem is now but what has been successful in the past and how this insight might help clients change the future. Questions that relate to the assessment phase might include those listed in Figure 9.1. These types of questions during the assessment phase move clients away from the problem to contemplate times and moments when the

---

Figure 9.1

Assessment Questions

1. What about the problem is solvable now?

2. How will you know when the problem is solved?

3. How will you feel when the problem is solved?

4. What future goals do you have beyond solving this problem?

5. Tell me about the times when this problem was not present.

---

problem was not or will not be present. By asking these types of questions, we are not only gathering information but also calling attention to times of client strength when they did not have or will not have the problem. Although it is important to allow the client to explain the problem, a strengths-based model of assessment focuses its questions more on times when the problem does not exist.

The manner in which questions are asked is also important from a strengths-based perspective. Your nonverbal behaviors imply to the clients your belief in them and in what they are saying. A comfortable body posture that indicates your openness and willingness to hear what they are saying is critical to the process. Likewise, a facial expression that is open and shows interest encourages clients to think more about their strengths and their ability to resolve the situation. When you are being empowering, your attention—both verbal and nonverbal—needs to be completely on clients and their responses to the questions you are asking. This is essential because you are saying back to them that they have the strength and power to accomplish what they want to accomplish. Case Example 9.7 demonstrates this.

The practitioner is seeking, through the use of both verbal and nonverbal communication, assessment questioning that leads to positive strengths-based responses. The practitioner is examining the uniqueness of the individual. The intervention should focus on the individual and what he or she brings to the treatment. Guidelines for a strengths-based assessment are discussed in Chapter 5 are not repeated here.

Intervention

The intervention process in strengths-based practice begins even before the social worker

---

CASE EXAMPLE 9.7

Empowering Responses to Client Statements

Practitioner: [Sitting at correct distance, three to four feet, with eye-to-eye contact] What was it like when you didn't feel depressed?

Client: [Head down leaning over body] I can't remember as I feel like I have always been depressed.

Practitioner: [Continuing correct body posture and allowing facial expression to change to a smile] Well, what would it be like if tomorrow you woke up and weren't depressed? What would be happening?

Client: [Raises head and smiles a little] I guess everything would be better.

Practitioner: I can see by your facial expression that that circumstance might brighten your day. What picture came into your head when you thought about waking up without being depressed.

Client: [Now not drooping, eyes looking at practitioner] I was just picturing myself as happy and the sun shining.

---

first meets the client. Whether clients have been referred from other sources who provide background data or whether clients have called for an appointment on their own, social workers need to view the information they receive from a strengths-based perspective. How the social worker begins to engage in the situation is part of the intervention. It would be nearly impossible to enter a first session without having formed in your mind a picture of the client from the information gathered. What social workers must do is think about the client in empowering ways, noting already what appear to be the client's strengths and hopes for the outcome. By approaching intervention in this way, the social worker can, through the engagement and assessment process, begin the intervention immediately.

Intervention Techniques

The active intervention phase comes after engagement and assessment. During this period, the social worker moves forward from the as-

sessment questions into those questions, comments, and processes that are more specific and unique to the person's situation. This phase includes the following techniques.

Using Confrontation: As in the chapter-opening case involving the Parkers, many clients will want to learn the use of confrontation techniques. The Parkers have obviously done some of this while initially dealing with the hospital and doctors, but in what additional ways might they use this skill? *Confrontation* as a term has generally had negative connotations. When we think of confrontation, we often think of people arguing or being unable to resolve their differences. In social work practice, however, this is generally the opposite of what confrontation is expected to do. Confrontation in social work practice should enable the social worker and the client to move through issues that may be keeping the client from success.

In order to help a client learn and use confrontation, it is important that social workers be skilled at it and able to use it with their own clients. If practitioners are afraid of confronting others, they will do their clients little good. Confrontation should not be an argument; it is a means to an end, with the ending being a better understanding between the individuals engaged in the process. Confrontation is used in many different situations between a social worker and a client. Among these are identifying discrepancies, pointing out dangerous issues for the client, denying particular circumstances, rationalizing a situation, being unwilling to recognize the consequences of one's behavior, and failing to follow through on stated values or moral responsibilities (Sheafer & Horejsi, 2003).

In client–worker situations, one of the major issues that may come up is the discrepancy between what the client is saying or believing and the behavior the client is carrying out. When behavior and statements conflict with each other, clients may not recognize it themselves. They may be laboring under the impression that their behavior expresses their words. Let's look at an example of this:

> Mr. Parker expresses anger over the time the doctors seem to spend with Amy. He identifies one doctor in particular who comes by only every other day and does not speak to the family while he is there. Mr. Parker says that he is going to give the doctor a "piece of [his] mind" the next time he comes in but instead says nothing to the doctor and remains frustrated. He expresses little during the next meeting with the hospital social worker and will not engage in conversation with his wife about what is going on.

In this case, the father is experiencing feelings (anger and frustration) and not expressing them to the doctor who treats Amy. These types of discrepancies are important to con-

front because they create difficult situations for the client and do little to enable the social worker to help the client.

Other types of situations in which confrontation is important include clients not following through on agreed-upon plans, refusing to help themselves and expecting the social worker to do all the work, behaving in such a way that they create a danger for themselves or others, and letting the opinions of others outweigh what they know is best for them. It may seem inconceivable that we would not want to do what is best for ourselves, but we all have been in circumstances in which we did or said something that was not in our best interest. When we make these decisions, generally it is because of emotional reasons. Often when we are reacting to an emotional need, we cannot see clearly what is happening because emotions have affected our reasoning.

In all confrontations, particular steps need to be followed. Kirst-Ashman and Hull (2002) identify these steps as the following:

1. *Always consider whether your relationship with the client is strong enough to handle a confrontation.* If the situation with the client has reached a point of trust, a social worker should be able to use confrontation in a manner the client finds helpful. Without trust, confrontation can create a defensive situation. Hepworth, Rooney, and Larsen (2002) emphasize the importance of not using confrontation too soon; they also state that in dangerous situations, confrontation should be used no matter how developed the relationship between social worker and client.

2. *A social worker should also consider the client's state of mind before using confrontation.* If a client is upset, he or she probably won't understand what is being

said and why. For example, if Mr. Parker displays a great deal of anger in his discussion with the social worker, the worker may not be able to help Mr. Parker understand how to approach the doctor. He might become angry at the social worker for not "understanding" the situation.

3. *Use confrontation only when necessary* (Compton & Galaway, 1999; Hepworth et al., 1997). When you use confrontation, do it sparingly. An overuse of confrontation can cause the client to not respond to what you have to say or not come back for treatment. Used too often it begins to resemble arguing and can drive the client away.

4. *Use empathy with confrontation* (Hepworth et al., 2002). This suggestion is critical to the effect that confrontation will have on the client. When empathy is used as part of an approach that seeks to help the client accomplish his or her goals, the client will handle confrontation appropriately.

5. *Use "I" statements during the confrontation* (Sheafer et al., 2003). "I" statements used in any context allow for more open discussion because each person is taking responsibility for what he or she feels or does. This allows you to take a nonblaming approach to the situation. If, for example, the social worker says to Mr. Parker, "I am surprised that you are not saying more since it seems as though you are upset" instead of "You need to talk more," the social worker is giving Mr. Parker the opportunity to respond to what the practitioner is sensing rather than simply react to the comments.

6. *If, after a confrontational statement has been made, the client becomes angry, defensive, or upset, it is important to use an empathetic statement at this point.* By giving an empathetic response, the social worker is responding immediately to what the client is feeling and at the same time sending a clear message that what the client thinks is important.

7. *Use nonverbal messages to convey to the client that what he or she is experiencing is important to you.* If, for example, you have an open posture toward the person you are confronting, you are telling that person that you are open to a response and are not afraid to hear what he or she has to say.

Emphasizing Motivation and Commitment: When we emphasize motivation and continuing commitment to the client, we are moving them forward in their own progress toward creating change. Johnson and Yanca (2001) identified three variables that are important for motivation to occur: "the push of discomfort, the pull of hope that something can be done to relieve the problem or accomplish a task, and internal pressures and drives toward reaching a goal" (p. 131). Motivation has often been described as the process that allows the individual to become more willing and able to carry out a plan. In strengths-based practice, client motivation can be enhanced through the use of specific verbal and nonverbal methods that make up a large part of the interaction between the client and the social worker. Through empathy, self-determination, genuineness, and warmth, the social worker can set the stage for positive interchange and, as a consequence, motivate the client for the work to be done. Emphasizing the strengths and successes the client brings sets up an atmosphere of motivation and commitment.

Shebib (2003) suggests the following skills in creating motivation and commitment:

1. Discuss previous actions and any successes achieved.

2. Work with clients to eliminate distorted thoughts and self-defeating talk.

3. Set small steps for achieving goals and celebrate success.

4. Congratulate clients on any change.

5. Convey hope and belief in the client.

Maintaining Focus: Maintaining focus is the process that allows the client to stay centered on the issue and its successful outcome (Poulin, 2005). Often in practice, clients will seek to avoid difficult situations that they believe provide no chance of a successful outcome. By helping clients maintain their focus on the plan they have set for themselves, the social worker encourages clients to continue working toward the successful resolution of the problem. Focusing on positive outcomes and the success they are achieving enables clients to continue making decisions that result in change. The social worker maintains clients' focus by returning them to the situation when they stray off course and reinforcing the decisions and plans they have made. Often this can be done through open-ended and empathetic questioning, which helps the client narrow down the details to figure out the next step. By exploring areas in detail, the social worker and the client stay focused on the important issues emerging in their sessions.

Checking for Ambivalence and Resistance: Ambivalence is a response that many clients experience during the engagement and intervention phase (Poulin, 2005). For any number of reasons, clients may feel ambivalent about the work they need to do or even resist the so-

cial worker's efforts in the session. Oftentimes practitioners deal with this ambivalence by doing nothing. As long as the client comes in to talk and pays lip service to the situation, it is easy to ignore the lack of change or the client's lack of effort to achieve his or her goal. Shulman (1999) refers to this as an "illusion of work." Rather then taking on this difficult situation, we allow it to continue. This is not what social work is about. Social work is about change, and the social worker has a responsibility to persist in bringing the client back to difficult situations.

We deal with this situation by recognizing the ambivalence and talking it through with the client. Ambivalence should be viewed as a normal part of the intervention process. All individuals experience some kind of ambivalence or resistance to change (Poulin, 2005).

Preston (1998) does not believe resistance is an impediment but rather that this resistance, and dealing with it, is therapy itself. Corey (2001) recommends some of the following steps for dealing with resistance in clients:

1. Be positive about what resistance is. It is dealing with changes in the client's life, and this is a normal part of the therapeutic process.

2. Encourage clients to talk about their ambivalence and resistance to elicit feelings about the treatment and changes occurring.

3. Make clients aware that ambivalence and doubt are normal and that they should not be discouraged by their reaction.

4. Design changes in small steps so clients can accomplish more and feel more successful in the work they are doing.

Rehearsing: Rehearsal is a process of trying out, through role-play, the action steps clients hope to take in the future (Poulin, 2005). Clients and the social worker can recognize and deal ahead of time with any obstacles, such as ambivalence and resistance. In this technique, the worker generally plays the other person the client is dealing with; the worker then provides feedback after the role-play is done. This supports clients and helps them move forward in their action plan. More about rehearsal and role-play can be found in preceding chapters.

Story and Narrative Building: Story and narrative building are techniques most commonly associated with narrative therapy. This model is discussed in Chapter 10. From a strengths-based perspective, story and narrative building enable the client to look at the situation from a positive perspective rather than as a problem that is unsolvable. By listening to their individual stories, clients can imagine a new story told from a reframed perspective. Clients who might have interpreted their lives in negative ways can, through reframing and story building, take a completely different approach to their lives and their possibilities.

In story and narrative building, the client is helped to "develop a new story from the seeds of (preferred) unique outcomes" (Nichols & Schwartz, 2004, p. 344). For the social worker, this would mean questions such as:

- How is what you are picturing now different from the picture you had before?
- What are you doing differently in your new story?
- Who will be happy for you with this positive outcome?

These questions ask clients to think about a new story they have written for themselves through the positive changes they have made. Clients create a new story by thinking through several questions the social worker asks. These questions encourage clients to tell about their victories over problems in the past and the accomplishments they are achieving now. Through narrative and story building, clients are strengthened as they acknowledge their new lives and the positive meaning in them. Stories and narratives are often reinforced through the confirmation of client change by other people. A social worker might suggest to clients that they ask others who have seen a change to comment to them on what is different. This then reinforces the story.

Building and Using Natural Helping Networks: An important component of the intervention phase in strengths-based practice is the building and using of natural helping networks. Friends and family, along with social support groups, can play a major role in building up the client's confidence and lending support to the changes the client has undertaken. These interpersonal relationships give clients a strong sense of self and support for their situation. Social workers help clients build and use these natural helping networks by encouraging clients to think about who in their lives is supportive of them or who is close and would be willing to support them, and then encouraging clients to take action by reaching out to these people as supports.

Complimenting Success: Compliments are not something practitioners give just to make the client feel good; instead, compliments must be based in reality (DeJong & Berg, 2002). This technique helps clients acknowledge their successes and become more confident about themselves. Compliments also allow the social worker to gather more information about a situation. The client's response to a compliment can provide more and new data that can lend insight into the client's situation. DeJong and

Berg (2002, pp. 35–36) identify different types of compliments:

1. "Direct compliments," which consist of those reactions a social worker has to a client in direct response to something the client has accomplished.

2. "Indirect compliments," which are generally stated in the form of a question and may express admiration, or they may simply ask a question to which the social worker knows the answer will be positive.

3. "Self compliments," in which the client acknowledges something he or she has successfully achieved. A social worker's response would generally reinforce self-compliments with an indirect compliment.

All these types of compliments work well in helping the client achieve success and build on it.

Ending

During the ending phase of a strengths-based approach, the social worker needs to be aware of the client's feelings about ending the relationship. This can be a difficult period for both the social worker and the client, but the focus on the client's strengths, resources, successes, and natural helping networks does a lot to alleviate endings. In a strengths-based approach, it is critical for clients to decide to end the intervention. This may occur because a set amount of time has passed or because clients feel they are at a good ending point. Either way, clients must be involved in the decision-making process. Strengths-based practice does not support dependency, and clients should, through the intervention process, have been a part of all decision making and feel good about their own sense of independence.

Poulin (2005) identifies two main practice skills unique to the ending process. These are (1) generalizing, in which clients are helped to transfer what they have learned to other situations and experiences, and (2) identifying the next steps, in which clients plan for what will happen after the intervention is over. In generalizing, the social worker might review the progress with the client and talk specifically about those things that can be seen in the context of other situations. In identifying the next steps, the social worker might have the client visualize the plan after the ending or might help the client specify how the changes will be maintained. Additionally, some strengths-based practice approaches recommend continued follow-up for a certain period of time to ensure that clients are maintaining their changes.

In the next section, we discuss the empowerment perspective as it relates to specific oppressed populations. Although the underlying principles of this perspective are pertinent to each population, significant differences in each population require specific applications of the basic model. These are discussed in each population section.

Empowerment of Women

To understand the role of empowerment in women's lives, we must first understand the powerlessness that women often face. Within societies around the world, the role of women is seen as less important than that of their male counterparts. Social work has long considered women to be more vulnerable due to their limited access to resources and the exclusion of women from positions of power (Busch & Valentine, 2000). However, women's powerlessness incorporates more than this. Rappaport (1985) defines empowerment as:

> a sense of control over one's life in personality, cognition, and motivation. It expresses

Voices from the Field

Dennis Saleebey, DSW

When I graduated from the MSW program at UCLA, I was smitten with the psychodynamic appreciation of human behavior and social work practice. The idea that you could discern what was wrong with people when they did not have a clue, gave an immature young man a little gloss of confidence and sophistication. But in my first job as a social work officer in a large Air Force hospital's psychiatric service (inpatient and outpatient), I began to realize that people—their snares and troubles, their hopes and dreams—were not captured well by this orientation. But it was not until a fortuitous meeting with a young street minister in Fort Worth and later a move to the University of Kansas, that I began to realize that my approach to helping had been narrow and problem drenched. In the years since then, I have been lucky to be working with and learning from colleagues, practitioners, and scholars who are involved in developing approaches to practice funded by a firm belief in what people know, what they want and hope for, and what resources they have within and around them. A practice based on possibility and promise rather than exclusively on pathology and problems is exciting and challenging. Working with residents in three public housing communities over the years also was, on a daily basis, a remarkable demonstration of how resilient and resourceful people are, even under very challenging conditions.

I urge you as you work with individuals, families, groups, and communities to be aware of, account for, affirm, and act on their strengths, assets, resources, and wisdom. As soon as clients begin to share their narrative you can begin the search for and discovery of strengths. In the end, that is all you really have to work with as you collaborate with clients in helping them articulate and move toward their hopes and dreams.

---

itself at the level of feelings, at the level of ideas about self-worth, at the level of being able to make a difference in the world around us. . . . We all have it as a potential. (p. 17)

This definition broadens the perspective and takes into account the notion of internal feelings of powerlessness brought on by both internal and external factors. Women, according to Glenmaye's (1998) theory, share three conditions that add to their sense of powerlessness:

- *Alienation from the self.* Alienation from the self refers to the "estrangement of a woman from her inner self" and an "estrangement from personhood itself" (Glenmaye, 1998, p. 32). Women often internalize inferior feelings and negativity, which affects their self-esteem and sense of self-worth. This in turn alienates women from their real selves and allows oppressive factors such as stereotyping, cultural domination, and sexual objectification to rule their lives (Glenmaye, 1998).

- *The double-bind.* The double-bind refers to the position women are often placed in when they must decide between their own needs and society's stereotype of them. Glenmaye (1998) shares the example of a woman who chooses to stay home with her children. Some people will see her as lazy and incapable of making a living, but if she chooses to work, some people will see her as not caring about her children. In almost every decision a woman makes, Glenmaye states, a woman "will feel guilty, inadequate and at some deep level of being, a failure as a woman" (p. 33). This is the double-bind situation; society's views of women place them in a no-win situation.

- *Institutional and structural sexism.* Institutional and structural sexism is active within U.S. society. Male domination of social, economic, and other systems often preclude women from power positions. Glenmaye (1998) states that the "unequal distribution of power is manifest in laws, economic resources, personal status, and the many ways in which women are physically and sexually victimized by male violence" (p. 34).

These factors alienate women from more powerful positions and add to their sense of self-alienation.

The question then remains as to how social workers can help empower women in our society. Although many articles, books, and chapters have been written on this subject, certain factors stand out as important to the process of empowerment in an intervention. Gutiérrez's

(1990) model for empowering women of color is significant for all empowerment strategies in an intervention process. Her model incorporates the idea of group work as the preferred venue for an empowerment process. She notes that small groups are a "perfect environment for raising consciousness, engaging in mutual aid, developing skills and solving problems and an ideal way for clients to experience individual effectiveness in influencing others" (p. 151). This same point has been reinforced by Coppola and Rivas (1985), Garvin (1985), Hirayama and Hirayama (1985), Pernell (1985), and Sarri and duRivage (1985).

Gutiérrez (1990) also emphasizes the importance of the "collaborative helping relationship" (p. 151). Through this relationship, the "interaction should be characterized by genuineness, mutual respect, open communication and informality" (p. 151). The client can also gain self-empowerment through the relationship by the way in which the social worker helps the client transfer her success in the sessions out into the real world.

The techniques in Gutiérrez's (1990, pp. 151–152) model are as follows:

1. *"Accepting the client's definition of the problem"* (p. 151). When you accept the client's definition of the problem, you are opening up control of the situation to the client. She is empowered to guide the intervention's process. This gives women an opportunity to control their lives in a stressful situation.

2. *"Identifying and building on existing strengths"* (p. 151). In identifying and building on a client's existing strengths, social workers are reinforcing the client's already existing strengths and recognizing her abilities beyond the present situation. For women, recognizing their struggles

and their success within society reinforces them outside of the helping situation in the real world.

3. "*Engaging in a power analysis of the client's situation*" (p. 152). This power analysis involves an in-depth reading of the client's situation. It begins with "analyzing how conditions of powerlessness are affecting the client's situation" (Gutiérrez, 1990, p. 152). This analysis considers not only the conditions within the personal situation but also those outside in society that are producing powerlessness. The second step in the power analysis is to "identify sources of potential power in the client's situation" (p. 152). These sources of power can be found both within the person's present situation and within the larger society. Oppression and power in the external world are important factors that impinge on women's lives, and to ignore these is to not work from an empowerment perspective.

4. "*Teaching specific skill*" (p. 152). When social workers teach specific skills to clients, they are giving them powerful methods with which to overcome their own powerlessness and to gain control of their present situation. Skills such as problem solving, parenting, and organizing can all be used by women to empower their situations.

5. "*Mobilizing resources and advocating for clients*" (p. 152). When we mobilize resources and advocate for clients, we are teaching them the same skills if we do it in an empowering way. Having clients be a part of mobilizing resources and advocating for themselves leads to empowerment and the ability to transfer these skills to other situations. Mobilizing and advocating are important skills women need to function in our society.

Empowerment of Older Individuals

Intervention with older individuals in our society has for a long time hinged mainly on medical issues. As the older adult population increases, so do their needs for medical services. Around the mideighties, the population of persons sixty-five and older was 12 percent. By 2030 this population will have increased to 22 percent (U.S. Bureau of the Census, 1985). The needs of those eighty-five and older are creating the most concern because they live longer and are still in need of daily care. In addition to daily care and medical services, Smith and Eggleston (1989) state, older adults wish to feel useful and contribute to society, to not be socially isolated, and to have as normal a daily life as possible. Considering the physical situation and needs of older adults, it is not surprising that they often feel powerless. Older individuals tend to be devalued in society largely due to their loss of employment in our work ethic–oriented culture. They are often seen as using up the resources the current generation of workers is providing. Although attitudes differ from culture to culture, older adults in our society are not generally revered. They are sometimes considered "throw-away people," individuals for whom society has no use. Our society makes few efforts to provide for them in an empowering manner.

Empowerment intervention with older adults needs to place self-determination at the center of the conceptual framework (Fast & Chapin, 1997). Self-determination allows the older person to take back control of his or her life. Although there may be many situations in which self-determination does not seem possible, it is important for the social worker to recognize those situations in which the older adult can make decisions. Because many decisions are medical, the medical model prescribes that the expert professional make the decision for the older person. From an empowerment and strengths-based perspective, however, decision making involves the individual in mutual collaboration whenever possible. Social workers also need to be able to identify those situations in which clients can make decisions or to create situations that increase the likelihood of their involvement in decision making. Fast and Chapin (1997, pp. 122–128) suggest that the following strengths-based and empowerment perspective practice methods be used with older adults:

1. *"Personalized assessment and planning"* (p. 122). In personalized assessment and planning, the older adult is viewed as a unique individual with unique qualities and strengths. The relationship between the older adult and the social worker should be based on mutual trust. When social workers are assessing or planning with an individual from a strengths-based perspective, they are looking for and acknowledging individual qualities and finding ways to give the client some control over his or her life. This is furthered by using the client's strengths to make daily and long-term decisions.

2. *"Assertive outreach to natural community resources and services"* (p. 124). As part of being social workers, we need to reach out assertively to natural community resources and services. Seeking out natural helping resources is a concern for older adults, which is why including them in the process is so important. They may not have many personal resources or they may have them but not be able to acknowledge it. The social worker needs to work with

clients to identify those resources and to help them become more comfortable with their use. Additionally, the social worker's personal help in navigating community resources can make a big difference to the older adult. Although it is important for clients to decide whether to have you accompany them, it is also important to always offer. Thus, the client decides whether or not to use you in this capacity.

3. *"Emergency crisis planning"* (p. 127). In working with older adults, it is important to help them set up emergency crisis planning. This allows the client to make some decisions before an emergency occurs. With preplanning, the client's wishes can be carried out if he or she is in an acute medical state, and natural helping networks are considered before a crisis has occurred.

4. *"Ongoing collaboration and caregiving adjustments"* (p. 128). The social worker working with an older adult needs to have an ongoing plan for continued contact and collaboration. This does not mean the social worker never ends the relationship, but it does suggest that helping to find resources and services is not enough. It is important to reinforce the client's strengths and power through continuous contact. This contact also aids in dealing with those caregiving situations in which adjustments must be made, as often happens at some point in the process.

Empowerment of Gays and Lesbians

Oppression and the powerlessness of lesbian and gay individuals are prevalent throughout many societies. DeLois (1997) calls our attention to the fact that lesbians and gays "are already actively involved in their own empowerment" (p. 65). She suggests that each time a person comes out into the open about his or her sexuality, this individual has already been involved in the empowerment process. However, everyone is not out, and those who are have much to fear, including "loss of family, loss of job, loss of child custody, retreat into depression and alcoholism; and the constant threat of verbal and physical assault" (DeLois, 1997, pp. 64–66). This places lesbians and gays in the center of social oppression and powerlessness.

In working with lesbians and gays, social workers need to be as clear as possible about their own feelings and beliefs. To be able to work from an empowerment and strengths-based perspective, social workers need to support and empower their gay and lesbian clients to accept themselves for who they are. They also need to work with their clients to identify those areas in which clients feel the most powerless and find ways to validate their sense of identity and value as people. Barret and Logan (2002, p. 61) suggest that practitioners:

- Explore and challenge their own homoprejudice
- Connect lesbian clients with the feminist community
- Understand and appreciate how difficult it is to accept a homosexual orientation

DeLois (1997) recommends the following empowerment practice concepts for working with gays and lesbians:

1. *Establishing a trusting alliance between the worker and the client within a safe environment.* The relationship between the worker and the client must have a foundation of trust and support. Social workers need to provide their gay and lesbian clients with not only an accepting environment but also one that supports their sex-uality. Social workers have a responsibility to provide their clients with an intervention that uses empowering approaches as well as ones that take proactive stances on the legal and political rights of clients.

2. *Helping clients become aware of the effects of societal factors in their lives and moving them forward in a coping manner.* Clients are sometimes not aware of how societal factors affect their internalized lives. Helping clients to figure out this influence and how to cope is an important process in empowering practice.

3. *Working with clients to help establish their advocacy and mobilization skills to fight for their political and legal rights.* Social workers need to work within the political and legal systems to advocate for fair treatment of gays and lesbians. They also need to help their clients understand the role of advocacy in their lives and help them mobilize resources for active participation in societal change.

4. *Making sure that social workers themselves understand the history of oppression of gays and lesbians in the United States.* It is an important responsibility for social workers to engage in knowledge building around gay and lesbian issues. The greater the social worker's understanding of a situation, the more likely he or she is to serve clients in their best interests.

5. *Seeking change within organizations to challenge the obstacles for gay and lesbian clients and to provide a nonheterosexist practice.* Social service agencies must provide the right environment for not only the client but also gay or lesbian social workers. An agency has a responsibility to support clients and workers who are gay or lesbian and also to advocate for

their rights both within and outside the organization.

Empowerment of People of Color

People of color have long had to deal with issues of racism and oppression. In her study of poor communities of color, Okazawa-Rey (1998) notes that members of her study "face the issue of powerlessness rooted in racial and economic inequality" (p. 52). This overarching sense of powerlessness has consequences that keep people in oppressive situations. Lum (1986) states that:

> the *color factor* has been a barrier that has separated Black, Latino, Asian and Native Americans from others. Anglo-Saxon and European minority groups have successfully integrated with each other and become assimilated into the mainstream of American society and power. But by and large minority people of color have been without equal access. The history of racism, discrimination, and segregation binds minority people of color together and contrasts with the experience of White Americans. (p. 1)

This lengthy history of racism and oppression has been challenged over the years but has yet to yield the types of change that open up societal systems to equality for all.

Social work practice has been part of the societal movements to create change, and yet during the last two decades it has done little to promote this type of change within practice texts. Leigh (1984) notes that helping interventions that include empowerment processes need to educate people about oppressive societal systems and create support groups to help them understand their legal rights and to work with their self-worth issues. Lum (1986) notes

the importance of social workers having "minority" knowledge, which consists of a "range of information, awareness, and understanding of the minority situational experience. It includes history, cognitive-affective-behavioral characteristics and societal dilemmas of people of color" (p. 25). This perspective, which calls for educating clients as well as ourselves about relevant issues related to powerlessness and oppression, is the type of empowerment practice needed with people of color.

Okazawa-Rey (1998) has developed the following practice principles for working with people of color:

1. *Expand definitions of problems to incorporate the micro, meso, and macro factors affecting communities of people of color.* Although Okazawa-Rey was speaking about the issue of health, the same is true in other situations. Issues affecting clients of color need to be looked at from a holistic view of factors (social, economic, cultural) that may be affecting the situation. These other factors play into the presenting situation, and they must be examined in order for a social worker to work from an empowerment basis with a client.

2. *Use both the client's cultural and personal backgrounds to empower the client.* It is critical to not only examine issues within the context of a client's cultural and personal backgrounds, but also to find answers that incorporate the perspectives found within these contacts. Support groups, persons with similar situations, and cultural helping networks all provide a strong base that people of color can call on for help.

3. *"Analyze and understand the structural inequalities that affect the lives of people of color"* (p. 62). Clients need to understand

that inequalities and oppression in their lives may be contributing to their situation. Rather then allowing clients to blame only themselves for the situation, the social worker needs to help them understand what other factors are affecting the situation. Clients need to be involved in this analysis of the effects of inequality and oppression.

4. *Work together collectively with clients to take action within their communities.*

Individuals need to share their concerns and situations. Through working together as a collective, people can become a greater force for change. Through these groups, individuals generate more power for themselves as well as for the group. This collective power can lead groups to take action to confront and change societal oppression.

Skill Development: Empowerment

Using the following case examples, practice your empowerment skills responses.

1. **Fifty-eight-year-old woman**

   Client: I just don't think I can take it anymore. Ever since the death of my husband, I feel like dying myself.

   Model Empowering Response: It's very difficult to lose someone and I know that you feel like dying yourself. I have felt fairly comfortable about your safety since I recognize all the strength you have. It's important now to talk about your feelings and to try to understand if you are still safe.

2. **Twenty-three-year-old woman**

   Client: My sister broke up with her boyfriend two weeks ago, and she has been really drinking heavily. I've been going out with her, and my drinking has gotten heavy too.

   Model Empowering Response: It sounds like you have been trying to support your sister and yet you now feel caught up in her situation. Drinking has not been a problem for you before, so let's figure out how you can continue to be a support without the drinking.

3. **Thirty-five-year-old-woman, crying**

   Client: It's awful when you can't stand your own child. I have no control over him, and sometimes I wish he wasn't mine.

   Model Empowering Response: You have been very successful at managing him with his ADD. It sounds to me like you are feeling worn out and frustrated. Let's talk about all the good you have been able to accomplish with him.

4. Phone call from client

Client: I need to tell you that I'm having an affair but I don't want my wife to know. So let's just keep this a secret between us.

Model Empowering Response: I'm pleased you feel you can share things with me, but as you know I stated in the first session that there could be no secrets between myself and one of you. I think it is important that you consider how committing to your marriage will affect your life. We need to talk about your commitment during the next session.

5. Forty-eight-year-old man

Client: I just can't get along with my boss at work. He hates me, and nothing I do at work is right.

Model Empowering Response: There are so many things you do that are right in your life that it's hard for me to believe you do nothing right at work. Tell me more about your relationship with your boss.

6. Twenty-four-year-old man

Client: I'm ashamed to tell you this, but I hit my son so hard the other night that it caused bruises.

Model Empowering Response: There are times when we may feel like hitting our children, but at no time is it appropriate. When you first came in, I mentioned to you that I would not be able to maintain confidentiality if child abuse is involved. This is one of those times. However, I would like you to call the child protection agency yourself while I am sitting here with you. This will give them a chance to hear from you what happened and give you a chance to express how bad you feel about it.

7. Client noticing social worker is staring out window

Client: I think you're not listening to me. You seem to be thinking about something else.

Model Empowering Response: I must honestly tell you that you are right. I had a difficult phone call from a family member right before you came in, and I am having a difficult time concentrating. Your situation is very important to me, and I admire the fact that you were able to be so honest with me when you realized things were not working.

8. Thirty-four-year-old man

Client: We never can agree on the amount of money to spend. He yells at me if I spend too much, and I yell at him when he spends too much.

Model Empowering Response: It sounds to me like finances may be a problem between you, and I think it is important that you are able to recognize this. What might be the best way you can handle it?

9. **Sixty-seven-year-old man**

   Client: I've been sick with cancer for the last six months, and now they tell me that I may only have three months to live.

   Model Empowering Response: I recognize that you have been fighting to survive so hard these last six months and now they are telling you that you have only three months to live. This is a very scary situation, and I wonder if you can think about what you would want these next three months to look like.

10. **Father during a family session**

    Client: We want you to make Sandy behave. I don't think we need to talk about us when it is her problem. That's why we come to you.

    Model Empowering Response: I know it's important to you that I concentrate on Sandy. I wonder if you can think about all the times you have been able to problem-solve together and come up with a way to make this situation better for all of you. Think first about how you would want the situation to be.

11. **Woman talking to child welfare worker**

    Client: Get out of my house. I'm not going to talk to you anymore about my children.

    Model Empowering Response: You sound very protective about your children and family situation. I can understand that, however, I am required to talk with you about this and I hope we can find a way to sit down and resolve the situation together.

12. **Woman during first session**

    Client: Do you have any children of your own?

    Model Empowering Response: It sounds like it's important to you that I also have children and I think it was good that you were able to ask me. I don't have children yet.

13. **Fourteen-year-old male**

    Client: I plan to go out partying with my friends tonight. You said this was confidential, so I guess I can tell you I'm gonna smoke some weed.

    Model Empowering Response: I am glad that you feel safe enough to tell me about what you are going to do tonight. However, I remember that there were a lot of good things that happened for you when you did not smoke. Can you remember those?

14. **Thirty-three-year-old woman**

    Client: I can't seem to get along with my boyfriend. He's always cheating on me but I really love him and want to work it out.

    Model Empowering Response: You sound like you want to make things work but that he isn't as committed to it as you are. What would you want your situation to be like with your boyfriend?

15. Fifty-eight-year-old man

Client: I feel so bad about myself. I'm not worth anything.

Model Empowering Response: You sound down on yourself today. I wonder if we can talk about those things that made you feel so good about yourself during the last visit. You seemed to believe in yourself more when we last talked.

16. Woman following her second session

Client: I'm really sorry but I can't pay you for tonight's session.

Model Empowering Response: I am glad that you came to the session and are willing to talk about your payment situation. I think it is important for you to not get more in debt now than you are. We need to find a way that you can continue counseling and yet be able to pay for your treatment.

17. Woman following a group session

Client: I don't think you've helped me at all. I've just been wasting my time talking to you.

Model Empowering Response: You sound very angry over what has been happening in the sessions. It is important that we can talk about your feelings around this subject. What have you wanted to happen that hasn't?

18. Sixty-four-year-old woman

Client: You're a wonderful therapist. You've helped me a great deal.

Model Empowering Response: I am happy you think we have done good work together. But most of that is because of the hard work you have done.

SUMMARY

This chapter examines the definitions of empowerment and strengths-based perspectives and their importance to direct social work practice. Empowerment in social work practice has been written about from various viewpoints. However, some commonalities generalize to all empowerment practice. These include (1) the importance of the agency and/or program maintaining an empowerment perspective in working with clients, (2) soliciting client involvement in collaborative efforts, (3) the building of strengths, (4) the focus on client uniqueness, (5) the building on clients' strengths and their communities, and (6) awareness of the social worker's own personal issues of powerlessness and empowerment.

Although strengths-based practice is carried out through different models, certain principles underlie this practice no matter which model is used: (1) every individual, group, family, and community has strengths, (2) everyone has the ability to grow in strength, (3) the practice relationship and the social worker's collaboration with clients are important to success, and (4) the social worker must be aware of all the different kinds of resources a client might have. Strengths-based practice can be offered through a social work continuum including

APPLICATIONS TO PRACTICE

Case Examples

You have just been hired as the director of social work services at a small nursing home. The owners want the residents to experience a better quality of life and participate in decisions about their treatment and activities. The previous owners were taken to court for not having adequate client participation in the programming. You're excited about the opportunity to develop a sense of community among the residents. When you interviewed several of the residents, they seemed uninterested in participating in any changes. In fact, some said they wanted the old owners to come back.

The community board at your agency, The Helping Way, has asked the director to come up with counseling methods that will empower the clients to be more self-sufficient. For more than ten years your agency has

been a domestic violence shelter. The board wants the agency to participate in some community funding between local churches and service agencies that would target housing and employment for the abused parent. Each supervisor is to come up with ideas about areas of community need and prepare a short report for the director within two weeks. The person submitting the best plan will be given funding to an upcoming out of town workshop that will focus on domestic violence services.

The Dipsie County Juvenile Court Probation Department has just been awarded a grant to develop programs to empower youth to make better choices, complete high school, and engage in employment opportunities. The program will be limited to first-time offenders during

the start up. The director has asked you and the other supervisors to develop a budget proposal built on community needs and national programs who have already been operating to provide these services.

Critical Thinking Questions

Answer the following questions related to each of the previous cases:

1. What activities would be necessary to complete each of these assignments?
2. How would you present the new program to your constituents?
3. How would you present the new program to the other stakeholders in services to this group?
4. At what point would you want to include ideas and suggestions from the community about this program and why?

Research Activity

Using the Research Navigator™ website, www.researchnavigator.com, find articles and program information about one of the case examples. Prepare a short draft that identifies some of the current programs related to the case example.

engagement, assessment, intervention, and ending. During the intervention phase, specific techniques can help you build clients' strengths and power. These include confrontation, motivation and commitment, maintaining focus, checking for ambivalence, rehearsal, story and narrative building, building and using natural helping resources, and complimenting success.

When working with oppressed groups, the social worker needs to understand the importance of several different practice components. These include building a solid, trusting relationship; accepting clients for who they are and what they bring; focusing on strengths of not only the client but also of the client's community; working collaboratively and collectively; assessing clients and their situation from a holistic perspective, including self, family, community, and society; teaching clients specific skills that will work within their environment; and helping clients mobilize resources and advocate for themselves. The final section of the chapter is devoted to potential client

statements and empowering responses the social worker might make.

Navigating Direct Practice

An access code for Research Navigator™ is packaged within your text. Use this code to register at www.researchnavigator.com and then use the key words listed below to research articles related to the chapter's content. Research Navigator™ helps you quickly and efficiently make the most of your research time.

❑ Glenmaye
❑ Gutiérrez
❑ Intervention
❑ Saleebey
❑ Strengths-Based Practice

Chapter 10

Strengthening Family Functioning

■ Steven, age thirteen, was brought to the family counseling center by his mother. Previously a good student, Steven was now receiving failing grades and refusing to attend school. His mother, Mrs. Levett, who had been separated from Steven's father for six months, was at her "wit's end." Difficulties with Steven began approximately a year ago and according to the mother was a "sudden thing," with Steven bringing home bad grades from school and then being suspended for fighting. In the ensuing months, things escalated and Steven was suspended two more times. Mrs. Levett states that she believes his behavior is what led, in part, to the separation between her and her husband.

Family practice has always been a part of social work intervention. Beginning with settlement houses and charity organization societies, early social workers in both these areas worked with individuals through their families. Settlement houses began in the late 1800s and wed the family as a foundation to create change within the community and society. Settlement houses sought to bring together neighborhoods (generally of immigrant families) to fight for changes in their social conditions (Popple & Leighninger, 2002). Additionally, they served as centers where individuals and families could share their cultural backgrounds and learn new skills that acculturated them into U.S. society. Settlement house workers viewed difficulties within the family as the result of societal issues beyond the individual's control. Charity organization societies, on the other hand, were founded by philanthropic organizations to provide funding and services to families in need. Reverend Gurteen, an Episcopalian minister, set up the first Charity Organization Society in 1877 in the United States. Funding from philanthropic individuals and organizations was given to needy families along with moral advice on how the individual and family should be leading their lives. This advice giving was based on the belief that individuals were responsible for their own situations (Popple & Leighninger, 2002).

Work with families also occurred through the Family Service Association (FSA). The FSA began in 1911 and focused on casework with families and children. Mary Richmond, an early pioneer of casework and a member of the charity organization movement, sought to bring social work intervention to families during these early years of family casework. As society became more involved in individual well-being, social welfare agencies supported by the government began to spring up across the country. Social workers were the main professionals concerned with child welfare, and their work was directly related to families' and children's well-being. These initial programs in family social work have spread to include many other areas. Whether the work is with hospitalized children, the elderly in nursing home care, or child protective agencies, social workers spend much of their time focused on the family.

The purpose of this chapter is to provide an overview of family practice and the concepts that influence how family work is carried out. The roles of engagement and assessment are addressed as well as intervention techniques. The chapter includes a look at the different cultural and ethnic factors that affect family practice.

Family Therapy

During the 1940s and 1950s, **family therapy** became a major type of treatment intervention. Significant theorists (from different backgrounds, including psychiatrists, psychologists, and social workers) across the country began to talk of using families as the means of resolving psychological issues for individuals. While Bowen and Minuchin, on the East Coast, were developing their own approach to treatment of families, several others (Bateson, Haley, Satir) were on the West Coast doing the same. In family therapy, systems theory took a lead role in suggesting that because individuals operate predominantly within a family system, the family itself could serve as the client for the intervention. This theory postulated that individual issues did not form within a vacuum but in relation to others. For family therapists, individual issues are part of the larger system (the family) and its function.

General Systems Concepts

From seeing the family as part of a larger system, several other concepts began to emerge in family therapy based on general systems theory. Some of the common general systems concepts that appear across many different models of family therapy include homeostasis, feedback loops, boundaries, closed/open systems, subsystems, roles, and rules (covert and overt).

Homeostasis

Homeostasis refers to "the tendency of any system to try to maintain itself in a state of equilibrium or balance" (Hull & Mather, 2005). In a family system, there is a balance of the structure and functions within the family. For example, a family pattern may be for the husband to drink, the wife to nag, and the children to act out this conflict. Upsetting this pattern would unbalance the family system and thereby nudge the family to seek new ways of keeping these relationships and behaviors in balance. For example, a father and husband stops drinking but the wife unconsciously wants to keep the same power structure in the family. To ensure this, she finds other things to nag her husband about, and the children continue to act out in response to the parents' ongoing conflict. The balance of behaviors and patterns in the family can be either healthy or, as in this example, unhealthy.

Feedback Loops

Feedback loops refer to interactions that occur among family members. For example, a family may have a particular pattern of communication when a crisis occurs. For example, a mother initiates the chain of messages to alert family members to the fact that her son and daughter-in-law are having major financial problems. The mother may first tell her daughter. The daughter in turn becomes upset (feedback loop) and goes to her father for comfort (feedback loop). The father may then call his mother (the son's grandmother), who in turn calls her grandson's wife and scolds (feedback loop) her about upsetting the family. This type of pattern may recur every time a crisis occurs. The feedback loops are continuing loops of communication, with one setting off another. Family practice therapists must make every effort to understand a family's specific patterns and responses of communication.

Boundaries

Boundaries are those invisible lines of separation that individuals or families give themselves in terms of communication and physical space. Some families have well-defined boundaries and leave no room for anyone else to enter the family in a personal or physical way. Activities are contained within the family and very little communication is received or sent outside the family system. In a family or with an individual with loose boundaries, other people may know intimate details or be allowed to enter the individual or family space without limits. These invisible boundaries serve as "gatekeepers" for information going in or out of a system (Becvar & Becvar, 2003).

Closed/Open Systems

Family systems can be either open or closed. When a family system is closed, outsiders are not allowed in and those from the inside do not participate in outside activities. A family might, for example, not allow the children to participate in extracurricular activities or to have other children over to the house. When a system is open, there is an exchange of activities. Children and adults take opportunities to involve themselves with others. People may be in and out of the family home on a regular basis. A system may be too open or closed, as when the child is never at home or is never allowed to leave the family to do things independently. Healthy families strike a balance between an open and a closed system.

Subsystems

Subsystems within a family occur when a few members group together sometimes in opposition or competition with other members. A subsystem may also be composed of one person within the family who operates on his or her own. Subsystems are often formed according to generation, gender, and similar interests. The parents in a family generally form a subsystem that excludes others from certain information and activities. Similarly, the children in a family may form a subsystem and collaborate in keeping certain information away from their parents. Individual family members can be a part of several different subsystems. Subsystems are a normal part of family life, and only when alliances are destructive do they need to be rethought. For example, an unhealthy subsystem occurs when a parent and a child exclude the other parent from participating in their activities. The parent and child form a closed subsystem to the other parent.

Roles

Roles are those patterns of behavior carried out by a family member according to a set of defined expectations. A family member can play many roles, including, but not limited to, parent, son, breadwinner, and chauffeur, for example. The roles a member assumes may hinder or help that individual within a family according to how behavioral roles are assigned. For example, a father's expected role may be that of breadwinner in a family, yet if the father loses his job and becomes dependent on his wife, he may feel worthless because he is not carrying out the expected role.

Rules

"The rules according to which a system operates are made up of the characteristic patterns within the system" (Becvar & Becvar, 2003, p. 69). Rules reflect the values of the system as well as explain the behaviors expected of each person in the family. Within a family system, there are both overt and covert rules. Overt rules are those that are obvious and publicly ac-knowledged and discussed. For example, a family may have overt rules about curfews, asking permission regarding an outing, agreeing on the purchase of all items over $300, and the time of meals. Covert rules are unspoken but known by all members of a family. For example, when children are expected to make straight As or go to their grandparents' for dinner every Sunday but are not directly told of these expectations, these are covert rules. Covert family rules may be much more difficult to identify if one is outside the family looking in.

Unique Models

Unique models began to develop in family therapy as theorists began to test out their own ideas and implement their understanding of general systems concepts. Some of the more common models include structural family therapy, experiential therapy, strategic family therapy, cognitive–behavioral therapy, psychoanalytic family therapy, and postmodern therapies such as feminist therapy and narrative therapy. The following section gives a brief overview of these different models and how their theories affect family practice.

Bowenian Family Therapy

Bowenian family therapy was developed by Murray Bowen in the 1950s. As a psychiatrist at the National Institute of Mental Health, Bowen headed a project that evaluated the treatment of families placed in a hospital with their schizophrenic family member. To Bowen, the importance of the family did not end when someone grew up and left the family; family ties continued to be significant no matter what the family situation. Theoretically, Bowen believed that the "family as a multigenerational network of relationships, shapes the interplay of individ-uality and togetherness using six interlocking concepts (Bowen, 1966): differentiation of self, triangles, nuclear family emotional process, family projection process, multigenerational transmission process, and sibling position" (Nichols & Schwartz, 2004, p. 121).

Key to Bowen's theory was the differentia-tion of self. This concept refers to the individ-ual's ability to be free of family-of-origin issues and to be autonomous and well functioning in current family relationships. Through relation-ships and current individual functioning, the family is able to move beyond its generational issues and work toward autonomy for individ-uals. The genogram (covered later in this chap-ter) is a tool often used for assessment related to this and other theories.

Structural Family Therapy

In structural family therapy, the focus is on the structure of the family (the subsystems, bound-aries, hierarchy, and roles) and how structure affects the family dynamics. Salvador Minuchin is commonly connected with this therapy. Be-sides adapting concepts from general systems theory, Minuchin also incorporated aspects from ecological systems theory, network ther-apy, and several other approaches (Franklin & Jordan, 1999). Minuchin (1974) believed that family structure was "the invisible set of func-tional demands that organizes the way in which family members interact" (p. 51).

According to Minuchin, a family structure might be defined by subsystems, how the boundaries are set, or which roles are played. By influencing these structures during family therapy meetings so that past repetitive pat-terns of interactions are disallowed, Minuchin believed that change could occur within a fam-ily along with movement toward more healthy interactions. For instance, if in a family one parent and a child are enmeshed and the other parent has no involvement, the therapist might set out to change the seating in the room. This might entail the practitioner moving the child from a seat next to the enmeshed parent to a seat next to the uninvolved parent. Through such activities, Minuchin seeks to point out the dysfunctional structure and encourage change by altering the types of interaction.

Experiential Therapy

Experiential family therapy, based on aspects of humanistic psychology, emphasizes the expression of feelings and the importance of interpersonal interactions. Most often associated with this model of family therapy are Virginia Satir and Carl Whitaker. Whitaker strongly believed that individual growth is as much a part of the therapy as family integration (Nichols & Schwartz, 2001). With this approach, family members are encouraged to be creative and open to change through their mutual experiences with one another. Therefore, the focus of the practice is on the here and now, with little time spent on past history. The goal of practice becomes individual growth toward self-actualization. Creative changes in individuals and the family are believed to emerge as part of this growth. Within the intervention itself, the therapist models and uses "use of self" to help the family explore other ways of being. The "use of self" refers to the way in which social workers use themselves and the impact of the situation to respond to clients in an empathetic manner. Through creative techniques, therapists are able to help their clients give meaning to their families and push forward for solutions. Therapists are also seen as being able to create change through their own wisdom and creativity.

Strategic Family Therapy

This family intervention model is often credited to the work of Jay Haley, who believed that clients' ideas create and maintain problems in families. In strategic family therapy, the focus of the intervention is on understanding the identified patient's symptoms and giving them meaning. Symptoms were seen as the result of hierarchical difficulty in a family. In the case of a parent–child coalition, Haley thought that symptoms or problems in a family emerged to maintain a particular structure (Hull & Mather, 2005). The symptom then becomes the focus of the treatment, with the family finding ways to change that symptom and hence the situation in the family. The family is also viewed as being the best able to understand their situation.

The stategic family therapist generally works on sequences of behavior and communication patterns to change the symptoms. Often, directives (direct instructions) are given to clients in order to change behavior and create different constructs within the family. These directives often come in the form of homework assignments or exercises done outside the session. One specific strategy used by strategic therapists to create change is the "paradoxical directive" (Nichols & Schwartz, 2001). Paradoxical directives "prescribe more of the symptom" in order for the family to create a change. For example, the therapist might assign parents whose child is experiencing enuresis to increase the problem by giving the child more liquid. Haley theorized that prescribing more liquid to increase the symptom (bed-wetting) would cause the parents to take steps to decrease the problem.

Cognitive–Behavioral Therapy

Cognitive–behavioral family therapy involves the modification of thoughts and actions by influencing an individual's conscious patterns of thoughts (Meichenbaum, 1977). Based in large part on behavioral therapy, it was later linked to the role of cognitive behavior. Among the techniques used are positive and negative reinforcement, punishment, and extinction, as well as the cognitive therapy concepts of cognitive distortion, thought stopping, and schemas. "Behavioral family therapy aims to change specific targeted family problems though the identification of behavioral goals, social learning theory techniques for achieving these goals and the use of social reinforcers to facilitate this process" (Nichols & Schwartz, 2001, p. 276). By way of comparison, cognitive–behavioral therapy focuses on the following goals: (1) defining family problems in behavioral terms, (2) educating family members about the role of antecedents, consequences, and cognitions affecting behavior, (3) teaching intervention methods, and (4) acting out and evaluating cognitive and behavioral changes (Franklin & Jordan, 1999, p. 82).

Psychoanalytic Family Therapy

"The goal of psychoanalytic family therapy is to free family members of unconscious restrictions so that they'll be able to interact with one another as whole, healthy persons" (Nichols & Schwartz, 2001). Psychoanalytic family therapy is based on the premise that early childhood relationships affect who we are now and how we act with other individuals. The focus of this approach in family therapy is to work through the conflicts experienced during childhood and gain insight into how these past relationships influence present relationships. Psychoanalytic family therapists do not give up the idea of individual work but rather embrace it as the foundation of the present family relationships.

Feminist Therapy

Feminist therapy is a postmodern approach to treatment. In postmodern approaches, there is no real "reality," only "subjective reality," in which individuals account for their lives according to the transitory meaning they give to their being. In postmodern practice, the session is often "characterized by collaboration, not-knowing, curiosity, and reflecting" (Franklin & Jordan, 1999, p. 149). It proceeds based on the belief that the meanings one has toward others or experiences in life change as people react to what is being said. Feminist family therapy sees the inclusion of gender issues as well as power relationships as essential to effective treatment. From a feminist viewpoint, the larger society imposes its traditional beliefs about male and female roles on the therapeutic session, and as long as the family therapist accepts these traditional norms, very little can be done to remedy the power differential between family members. Franklin and Jordan (1999) identify five elements that must be considered in order to practice feminist therapy:

1. In this society, gender inequality is highlighted, and many times women are oppressed by society's patriarchal nature.

2. The individual's experiences of men and women are considered the cornerstone of all social science understanding through research; here the use of interviews and ethnographies to validate feelings is highlighted.

3. This method has a social action component with the primary emphasis on improving the conditions that women experience.

4. Feminism questions the roots of traditional research and the ways gender bias exists in this research, noting that as products of the society, researchers cannot be objective observers.

5. Feminists feel that researchers and subjects should not be separated, generally

favoring more interactive models for establishing information (Concian, 1991). (pp. 329–330)

Narrative Therapy

Narrative therapy has become a highly recognized approach to working with families in recent years. Narrative therapy is also founded in postmodern constructivism. Narrative family therapists believe that "experience generates expectation and expectation then reshapes experience through the creation of organizing stories" (Nichols & Schwartz, 2001, p. 387). Through the stories people tell, they give meaning to their lives and relationships. As these narratives unfold, we decode the messages that individuals give to their experiences, and these messages generally demonstrate the views people have of themselves. Consider, for example, the reaction of two different people who are informed that they have lost a job promotion. One individual is an adult who was reared in a loving and supportive environment. The other adult was reared in a neglectful and critical environment. The first individual may consider that factors having nothing to do with him or her, such as the needs of the company, went into the decision. The latter person is much more likely to look at the situation and conclude, "I screwed up. What did I do wrong?" How these two individuals explain their lives has a lot to do with past experiences. As professional social workers, it is critical to be aware of how clients' past experiences influence them. If a man sees his own life as a failure, it will be that much harder for him to move forward by creating more positive meanings and explanations of his life. A narrative family therapist seeks to have both the family as a whole and the individual members of the family give new meaning to their experiences. By telling a new story about the family, the family can let go of their preconceived ideas of themselves and try on a more positive and functional meaning.

Practice with Families

As you begin to work with a family, you will likely integrate different concepts and techniques from several of the different models previously described. Working with a family is very different from working with an individual. When you work with an individual, you are dealing with one person, one assessment, one set of goals, and one treatment plan. When you are dealing with a family, you are dealing with a variety of individuals with different perceptions of the issue and their own goals. There are several things to keep in mind in family work.

1. Family work requires the social worker to form a relationship with several people at one time. You need to form a relationship with each family member during the first couple of sessions. This process of relationship building takes time and requires concentrated effort. Imagine being in a room with five different people who have different opinions and trying to form a relationship with all of them at once. The ability to connect with an entire family is a difficult skill to learn, yet it brings enormous benefits. You need to view everyone's perception as valuable, which you accomplish by ensuring that you hear and understand each member. Building a relationship with a family incorporates the skill of empathizing with all members of the family as well as being in touch with their feelings and thoughts. Make sure you take time to speak with everyone and let each person have his or her say as part of this process.

2. Social workers need a broad range of assessment skills to gather all the data they need from families. Assessment is a major part of all practice. It allows us to pursue an understanding of the individual from a biopsychosocial perspective. In family practice, you must not only assess the individuals within the family, but you must also assess the family itself in terms of its characteristics. The family has a life cycle and must contend with different issues at different stages in that cycle. Additionally, the assessment of the family needs to be made in terms of subsystems, interactions, communication, and roles. Families bring with them their own identity. For instance, family members may constantly argue with one another and interrupt one another continuously. This may be their way of interacting, and understanding this process is important to the assessment. How particular subsystems interact also becomes important in understanding the communication between family members. Whether it is the parents who work together as a team or a parent and a child in a coalition, it is important to know how these subsystems work as well as how to create change.

3. Social workers who work with families must be able to handle communication issues among family members. Family members need to be able to communicate among themselves so that they can resolve issues as they emerge now and in the future. Social workers cannot be responsible for all the communication within a session. However, they need to assess the family's styles of communication because this knowledge becomes vitally important when family members start to work through problems with one another. Social

workers also need to be skilled at teaching effective communication. They will be helping individual family members talk with one another and work out issues through listening and communication skills. Helping family members to create healthy interactions requires social workers to be able to stand outside of the interaction and give direction. For example, if a mother and father are constantly fighting, the social worker will need to be able to slow down the interaction, help each listen to the other, and help them respond to each other in a nondefensive manner. These are the types of skills social workers need in family practice situations when working with several individuals.

4. Family work requires the ability to engage different family members around a common goal. Often when a family enters into treatment with you, many different goals will emerge. Your job will be to help them bring together these goals into one broader goal. Take, for instance, a traditional family consisting of a working mother, a working father, a twenty-two-year-old daughter living on her own, a fourteen-year-old daughter, and a seventeen-year-old son. The father is a high school football coach and the son is the quarterback for the team. Mom and oldest daughter are very passive, whereas the fourteen-year-old daughter is very verbal in blaming the father for all the family's problems. They have come for family help because the fourteen-year-old has been acting out at school, slipping out of the house and drinking, and being picked up by the police. The father clearly wants the daughter to straighten up and behave, whereas the mother says she just wants the fighting to stop. The son wants his fourteen-year-old

sister to stop embarrassing him, the eldest daughter says nothing, and the fourteen-year-old keeps repeating that her father is too strict and tries to control everything.

The first step to finding a common goal is to allow each family member to voice his or her goal in coming for help. The second step is to move the family in the direction of looking for a broader goal that ties them all together. Ask the question, "As a family, what would be the best thing to happen from coming here for help?" Attempt to broaden their thinking by seeing the family as a whole with one possible clear goal. This family might agree on the goal of "bringing the family together without having all of the fighting that occurs in the house."

5. Social workers need to maintain a neutrality. As we form relationships with our clients, we get to know them as unique individuals with thoughts and feelings with which we can empathize. When there are several people in the room, we spend time building relationships with them all. We must be careful not to get caught up in seeing one person's side of the story more clearly than another's. If we do, our relationships will become unbalanced. This unhealthy response may start in a session, with you supporting one person more then another. Although sometimes it is appropriate to be supportive of one client more than others, your support cannot be one-sided. It is important to stay in touch with all family members and be able to support each of them equally at different times. Becoming one-sided in your perception of the family will push members out of their relationships with you and cause them to feel misunderstood in the process. They can become defensive and uncooperative in

the sessions, leaving you with very little support for moving toward a common goal.

Initial Contact

Your initial contact with a family sets up a critical relationship that can either help or hinder the practice process. Whether this is a referral, a request, or a court order, you need to handle the initial contact in a warm and empathetic manner. This does not imply that you do not deal with a mandated referral in clear and concise ways, but all clients (and families) deserve our respect. If the meeting is predicated on a telephone call, take that call in as professional a manner as you would if you were meeting the clients in person. Even in phone calls, social workers can show themselves as warm and caring. Through tone of voice and the questions asked, the practitioner can convey to the family member concern for his or her welfare. Even when the family member is angry, it is important to be empathetic. An example of this appears in Case Example 10.1. Social workers must not become defensive in such conversations. This is a skill more easily learned if you first understand that the clients' anger is not personally directed toward you, even though you may take the brunt of that anger. If you are being empathetic to all members of a family, you will be open to hearing all their feelings expressed and can be nondefensive in your process of interaction. This then allows the clients to show expression.

In preparation for the initial visit, review any information you may have on the family. Although information cannot be shared without the family's permission, files or reports the family has authorized for release are appropriate for review. This information can give you insight into the family's way of interacting. Do not prejudice yourself by the information you

CASE EXAMPLE 10.1

Initial Family Telephone Call with Nonvoluntary Client

Practitioner: Hello, this is Ms. Marks with the Family Counseling Center.

Mr. Graf: My name is Mr. Graf and I am calling because my son is having some problems. The court told me we had to go through some family counseling or something.

Practitioner: Thank you for calling, Mr. Graf. The court has sent your referral over and I will be happy to make an appointment.

Mr. Graf: You need to know that I don't appreciate the court or anybody else telling me what to do with my kid. And I don't appreciate having to go somewhere to talk about my family.

Practitioner: It sounds like this is a very difficult situation for you. You would like to handle your family business yourself.

Mr. Graf: It isn't anyone else's business.

Practitioner: I can understand your anger at this situation. I would really like to work with you to see if there are some things we can work through together. Maybe if we meet, there will be some things I can help you with.

Mr. Graf: You can help me by signing off on my court order.

Practitioner: I would like to do that. Let's make an appointment and see if we can't get started on the process.

review. Your experience with the family can be very different from what you read about them.

Initial Interview with a Family

During the initial contact, two things begin to occur: the engagement process and the assessment process. The initial interview adds to these engagement and assessment processes. This section begins with a discussion of the engagement process and its importance to the ongoing treatment process.

Possibly the most important outcome of an engagement process is the "therapeutic alliance," through which a working relationship occurs (Worden, 2003). Working relationships become the foundation through which the family and the family practitioner begin to resolve problems and find solutions that are built on the strengths found within the family. "The key to building an alliance is to accept people where they are, to listen respectfully to their

points of view and appreciate their attitudes" (Nichols & Schwartz, 2001, p. 87). Through the building of this alliance, the process of treatment can continue.

During the initial session, you will want to begin to accomplish a variety of goals. Some of these include:

1. Establishing guidelines for the sessions. During the initial session, it is important to set guidelines for the work you are about to do. Some of these guidelines are simple agreements about when you will meet, who will attend, and how to handle any changes that emerge. You will also want to discuss how the sessions will be run, the role of each person, the purpose of the meeting, the importance of everyone sharing their ideas, and the emphasis on the problem being a family problem rather than any one person's problem. This focus on the family ensures that the members

start to see this as a systemic rather than an individual problem. To help them move in this direction, you might say, "It sounds to me as if the whole family has an investment in this problem because of its effect on each of you. Let's talk about how this involves the family."

Other critical guidelines include those that have to do with respecting one another during the session, such as not calling one another names, giving each person time to be heard, not interrupting during the session, and accepting one another's point of view whether they agree with it or not. Using the following client comments, practice how you might remind the family member of the guidelines without demeaning the person:

- "I really think you are an idiot. You are the one who is causing all the problems."
- "I don't think you should be allowed to talk like that." (interrupting conversation between child and practitioner)
- "Why don't you ever try to make good grades? You should be more like your brother."

2. Building therapeutic alliances with all family members. The social worker needs to build a therapeutic alliance with all members of a family. Whether you begin by simply acknowledging the person or by engaging him or her in conversation, always be working toward building this relationship. In family work, some members may believe you are not listening to them if you are engaging another family member. This is often the case for the family member who has been singled out as the problem. Making sure the family understands the importance of engaging everyone may be

as simple as saying, "I want to get to know everyone and how each of you sees the situation in the family. To accomplish this, I will be talking with each of you during the session." Worden (2003) suggests the following guidelines for the family therapist:

- The therapist is responsible for promoting an atmosphere conducive to change.
- In so doing, the therapist actively forms a therapeutic alliance in collaboration with the family. Therapy is a conjoint effort between the therapist and family with the therapist as a participant, observer and facilitator.
- The therapist may lead or show the way to change through supporting, questioning, challenging or provoking the family, but he or she gives utmost respect to the family's capacity or willingness to change.
- Consequently, change is ultimately the responsibility and choice of the family. (p. 55)

This role provides the practitioner with the ability to form therapeutic alliances and move through the process of change the family decides to undertake. The role of facilitator helps the practitioner elicit information and at the same time engage the family in a discussion about their issues and goals.

3. Eliciting information from each member about what they see as the problem and what their goals might be. During the first session, the practitioner needs to build a rapport with and seek information from each family member. When you are trying to establish rapport with all family members, it is best to refrain from being overly confrontational. However, in some situations it is necessary to ensure that the

family is aware of the guidelines. One of these times may be when a family member tries to dominate the session. As discussed earlier, it is often helpful to establish early on that everyone will get a chance to speak. Thus, the social worker may at times need to remind everyone of the rules and that each person will need to wait his or her turn. One possible response when a family member tries to dominate is to explain, "I think what you are sharing is very important, but it is also important that I get others' views. So I would like to take turns in this process." If this does not stop the domination of the conversation, you might try nonverbal methods. One nonverbal technique is to turn your chair slightly to cut off your direct line of vision to the talker's face. Another is to put out your hand in the person's direction to let him or her know you are talking with someone else.

Each family member's opinion is important in the session. Gathering different information allows you all to assemble a larger picture of what may be going on in the family. From a postmodern constructivist stance, all realities are subjective, and there is truth in what all individuals believe because it is that individual's own truth. Guided by this premise, you will be able to allow for this subjective experience and understanding because it is essential to gathering information. By being open to what all members have to say, you are accepting them as they are and trusting in their beliefs.

4. Assessing patterns of family functioning through listening and observation. The assessment of family functioning is a critical piece of the initial session process. Important factors to be considered include who speaks to whom, how family members sit in relation to one another, the overt and the covert rules, the roles played in the family, and where the family is in relation to the family life cycle and whether it is an appropriate place for them to be. This kind of information gives a broader perspective on family patterns and the issues that need to be addressed. As they become more comfortable, family members will begin to discuss the dynamics of their relationships and you will be able to gauge their problematic interactions. Understanding these dynamics helps the social worker decide what types of questions will be the most helpful to the family. Noting subsystems within the family will tell you who currently communicates with whom and what about. Understanding interactions provides a window into the lives of individual family members and their strengths as well as their concerns. Rules and roles tell much about the family itself and how individual members fit or do not fit into the family situation.

5. Building on the strengths of the family and its members. As discussed in the previous chapter, the practitioner and the family need to build on the strengths of family members and on the strengths of the family itself. These strengths can be used not only to aid individual members but also to give the family as a whole an understanding of what they might accomplish together. Strengths can be found in many different aspects of the family's life, including individual strengths, environmental strengths, support system strengths, and family strengths. Individual strengths include a person's ability to listen, communicate, be dependable, problem-solve, have a positive attitude, and get along with oth-

ers. To test environmental strengths, we need to be asking how the family interacts with outside institutions and environmental factors. We also may ask ourselves the following types of questions: Does the family need help negotiating environmental walls? Are they able to make outside systems work effectively for them? Who are their support systems and how are they used? How might these systems be used to help the family achieve their goals? What are the family members able to do for themselves and how has the family worked to resolve issues before?

6. Focusing the session on the family as a system, not just blaming a specific member. During the initial session, the practitioner should direct family members away from a blaming perspective. Often, one person in the family takes the blame for all the family problems. We know through research and experience that blaming is very unproductive in family therapy (Nichols & Schwartz, 2001; Green, 2003). Although certainly one family member sometimes emerges as the identified patient, this does not necessarily mean the problem stems from this person. From a family practice perspective, difficulties arise when a family can no longer maintain a healthy homeostasis. Due to a situational change or a family life cycle process, the family sometimes works to maintain its balance through dysfunctional methods. Thus, an identified family member may emerge as the problem and draw the focus away from other important family issues. During the first session, point out that when things occur within a family, everyone is affected. The conversation needs to move away from that one member. For example, in dealing with the Levetts introduced in the case study at the beginning of this chapter, the social worker might want to meet with both the mother and the father (even though they are separated) and ask them about ways they have resolved other family situations. This approach pulls the focus away from Steven and may allow both mother and father to talk about other things that might be affecting Steven's behavior. The mother and the father may in turn talk about concerns they have not only about Steven but also about problems between the two of them. This focus emphasizes that more than one thing is going on in a family and that seemingly separate issues can actually be interrelated.

7. Encouraging continuation of family sessions. The practitioner needs to make clear, toward the end of the first session, the importance of continuing the sessions and working together as a family to resolve the perceived problems and to achieve their goals. It is not always easy to get a family to agree to return. The time you have spent with the family will need to have conveyed to them how important their work as a family is and how, through working together, they can achieve their goals. The relationships you have established with each member will, more than anything else, determine their willingness to return.

The way you greet the family during the initial interview can be very important. Introduce yourself and see who takes the lead in introductions. Generally, this is a parent, but observe which one seems to be in charge of the situation. If it is the mother who takes charge, how does she introduce herself? Then notice who speaks next. Also, be aware of the types of interactions going on in the family during this introduction.

Following the greeting, the family should be allowed to sit where they choose, whether in the therapist's office or in the family home. This may give you an idea of the patterns of interaction within the family. Who sits next to whom? How are family members rearranging the seats as they sit? How are they interacting as they take their places? Is someone directing them as to where to sit? Following the seating process, you may want to begin with some light conversation commenting on something that might be of interest to at least one of the family members. It could be about a football game if someone has an interest in football or it could simply be a comment on the weather. Although this type of discussion should not continue long, it is not idle conversation. This pause before the issues are discussed gives the family time to get comfortable and begin to relax. At some point, you will want to point out guidelines for the sessions. It is often easier to do this early on in the initial session because guidelines provide a structure that is safe for the family and give everyone an idea about how sessions will be handled.

Generally, you would now begin to elicit information from the family members about the problem. Opening up this question to everyone allows the person who is going to take the lead to come forward. Starting the discussion by asking, "What brings you in today?" or "Why do you think you are here?" is an appropriate way to begin. You also need to ensure that you ask everyone in the family the question. This sends the message that everyone's opinion is important and that all are involved. It also allows each family member some time to adjust to what is happening and to start to form some opinions

about the therapist. Working with everyone helps build empathy and trust. If you focus on one family member, others will feel left out and might be reluctant to build a relationship with you. As this process evolves, it begins to pull blame away from one person, if this is going on. By asking each person the question, you remove the family's focus from the identified problem family member.

Following this questioning process, begin to identify the situation as a family issue. You can do this in several different ways. One method is to explain to the family that generally a problem is not caused by just one person and that all family members are involved with what is happening. A second approach is to pull the attention away from the identified family member by focusing on other individuals in the family and how this situation is affecting them. A third technique is to bring attention to a relationship in the family and focus everyone on this. Case Example 10.2 provides an example. The social worker has moved the focus from Steven as the problem to a discussion of how the mother and father deal with difficult situations. This allows for a refocusing of the problem and a chance for the social worker to see how the mother and father interact between themselves.

After identifying the situation as a family issue, it is appropriate to begin to point out some of your observations, including family strengths. One way of doing this is to begin your statement with a comment on a strength.

- "I can see how important Steven is to both of you and how you want to help him."

CASE EXAMPLE 10.2

Refocusing Responsibility to the Family

Practitioner: I know we have been talking about Steven's problem, but I would like to shift this focus and ask both you [Mrs. Levett] and Mr. Levett about how the two of you have attempted to resolve difficult situations in the past.

Mrs. Levett: Well, we do talk about the situation. Ever since the problems started we have been trying to work them out.

Mr. Levett: *You* tried to work them out. I was never allowed to be involved. We never talked about anything.

Mrs. Levett: That's not true.

Practitioner: It sounds to me like there are two different opinions here. Perhaps we can begin now to talk with one another about resolving difficult situations. Let's take some time for the two of you to discuss this.

- "It sounds to me like you have the ability to discuss things between yourselves."
- "Although you say you never talk, Mr. Levett, I am very impressed by the efforts you have been making."

Families and individuals have strengths in many different areas, such as special skills, personal characteristics, interactional patterns, emotional strengths, and efforts the family is making.

During this first session, you need to give the family hope about the outcome. Commenting on the fact that they have taken the first step of seeking help reinforces the family as well as instills hope. You can also provide hope by commenting on strengths and by pointing out ways in which the family has resolved past problems themselves. The following examples illustrate this technique:

- "I recognize you are here because of different issues, but it sounds like the way you resolved the last conflict you had was very effective and those same skills can aid you now."
- "The way in which you and your son talked through that problem illustrates to me that you can resolve other conflicts."

Toward the end of the first session, try to establish an overall goal on which family members can agree. As discussed earlier, having a broader perspective often helps in defining a family goal. The following are questions you might ask yourself as you listen to what the family would like to accomplish: What do the family members want for the family? What would the family like to accomplish from being in the sessions and how might they do this? What was the one general conclusion family members could say they came to after this initial session? These types of questions bring the family around to not only seeking a common goal but also determining their commitment to the continuation of the family practice process.

Assessing Family Situations

We talk about assessment at several different points in this book. Collins, Jordan, and Coleman (1999) suggest that the "goal of assessment and problem definition is to explore, identify, and define dynamics within and beyond the family that contribute to problem development" (p. 22). This type of assessment means more than understanding the dynamics within the family; it means looking at the environmental impact on the family as well as the other factors affecting the family's life. As in other social work practice, an assessment would not be complete without looking at the individual family member. This kind of assessment is important if you want to understand what is happening not only in the family but also between family members. Methods for gathering individual assessment are discussed in Chapter 5. In a family assessment, several basic areas need to be addressed, including the identifying problem, stage of family life cycle, family functioning, and environmental factors.

Identifying Problem

Although we examined the role of the identifying problem in the discussion of the initial session, it is important to review its relevance to the family assessment. The family would not be seeing a practitioner if they had not identified a problem; however, different family members will have different ways of describing this problem. Understanding how each family member views the problem is an important step in the assessment process. "Exploring the presenting problem begins with simply hearing the family's account in their own words" (Nichols & Schwartz, 2001, p. 93). Giving all family members an opportunity to express themselves also lets you gather more in-

formation. Who expresses their feelings the strongest? What is the reaction of the family member who is being blamed, if there is one? How do the members interact with one another over the discussion of the issue?

Listening to every family member discuss the problem gives you a broad view of the problem, but it is also important to try to get more information about how the family has tried to resolve it. What have they done so far? Who has worked together on it? What were the outcomes of these efforts? Although it may seem as though you are overemphasizing this question, in reality you are following the family's initial lead. As you gather data from family members, you can begin to paint a bigger picture of how this issue operates in the family.

Stage of Family Life Cycle

Perhaps one of the first things to be assessed in a family situation is the family life cycle. A family life cycle parallels an individual's developmental life cycle, and the practitioner assesses a family's life cycle by examining the family's development over time and comparing it to the norm of traditional development. The family life cycle, as developed by several different theorists, ought to be viewed with flexibility. Figure 10.1 illustrates an adaptation of the traditional family life cycle.

Clearly, the life cycle has for some time been defined according to a traditional middle-class American family pattern. Today, relationships do not necessarily follow this norm. With almost half of all marriages ending in divorce, many individuals either remain single or go through a series of different relationships while raising a family. Many gay and lesbian partners do not follow this cycle at all. Likewise, individuals from different cultures may experience these steps in a different manner. Consequently, when you are assessing families in

Figure 10.1

Family Life Cycle

1. Marriage	• Committing to the relationship
	• Formulating roles and rules
	• Differentiating as a couple while separating from families of origin
	• Making compromises and negotiating around concrete and personal needs
2. Families with young children	• Restabilizing the marital unit with a triangle
	• Accepting the child and integrating that child into the family
	• Reconsidering relationship with each other and with work
3. Families with school-age children	• Allowing greater independence
	• Opening family boundaries to accommodate new social institutions
	• Understanding and accepting role changes
4. Families with teenagers	• Dealing with teen independence through boundary adjustments
	• Adjusting to a new definition of personal autonomy
	• Rule changes, limit setting, role negotiation
5. Families with young people leaving home	• Preparing teen for independent living through schooling and job skills
	• Accepting youth's independence
6. Middle-aged parents	• Adjusting to the "empty nest"
7. Aging family members	• Involvement with grandchildren and partners of the children
	• Dealing with problems of aging

Source: Adapted from Collins, Jordan, and Coleman (1999, p. 63).

light of the family life cycle, it is critical that you are open to variations. Many of these variations have cycles of their own, such as the divorce cycle, illustrated in Figure 10.2.

Figure 10.2	
Stages of Divorce	
Phase of Divorce	**Developmental Issue**
1. The decision to divorce	• Acceptance of one's own part in the failure of the marriage
2. Planning the breakup of the system	• Working cooperatively on problems of custody, visitation, and finances
	• Dealing with extended family about divorce
3. Separation	• Mourning loss of intact family
	• Restructuring marital and parent–child relationships and finances; adaptation to living apart
	• Realignment of relationships with extended family; staying connected with spouse's extended family
4. The divorce	• Mourning loss of intact family; giving up fantasies of reunion
	• Retrieval of hopes, dreams, expectations from the marriage
	• Staying connected with extended family

Source: Adapted from Goldenberg and Goldenberg (1991, p. 24); Carter and McGoldrick (1988, p. 22).

Because a divorce proceeds in stages, just like the family life cycle, a family going through divorce will be facing two sets of developmental stages at the same time. This dual process can come at any time during the family life cycle. It is critical for professionals to be aware of all the stages and issues a family may be experiencing in order to better understand what they are going through and to compare them to the expected stages of development. Understanding these stages then gives the social worker the opportunity to deal with the issues from a developmental perspective.

Family Functioning

Assessing family functioning is a critical part of the assessment process. Family functioning entails many different factors including "communication, problem solving, beliefs, alliances/coalitions, and supports" (Thomlison, 2002, p. 85). We emphasize the importance of assessing communication in other parts of this book. However, this section explores the information received in a family session. This communication needs to be assessed in terms of both verbal and nonverbal expressions. The practitioner needs to understand the "metacommunication" in all the information shared within a family. *Metacommunication* is a term that means "a message about a message, typically nonverbal (a smile, a shrug, a nod, a wink), offered simultaneously with a verbal message, structuring, qualifying or adding meaning to that message" (Goldenberg &

Goldenberg, 1991, p. 326). This is an important method of assessment to determine whether family members are hearing what is said or what is meant. Good communication calls for a congruency between the verbal and nonverbal messages. Are family members saying the same thing with their words as they are with their posture and expression? Or do words and expression appear to mean the opposite, confusing other family members? Items to observe about the family's communication include:

1. Who is talking to whom?

2. What are the nonverbal messages saying about family members?

3. Is there interruption during the communication? Who is interrupting and why?

4. What is not being discussed during the session?

5. How are family members communicating with the practitioner?

During the assessment, it is also helpful to gather information on the family's problem-solving skills. Not only will you want to learn about the ways in which the family has tried to resolve the present issue, but you will also want to gather information about how they have solved other issues.

1. Do they seem to understand the problem-solving process?

2. How has it worked before in this family?

3. What factors appear to be hindering problem solving at this time?

4. How do they attempt to carry it out?

Understanding a family's belief pattern is critical to the practitioner's work. The belief pattern develops an "internal working model" (Vosler, 1996, p. 53) that guides both the family as a whole and the individuals within the family. It sets out a framework within which a

family functions. For example, a family might operate from the belief that it is better for children to be seen than heard. Thus, in the family session, the children may not speak up, or if they do, they are frowned on. In another family, the activities of individual family members should center on the family instead of the external world. This might indicate that the family is enmeshed and unable to allow for outside interference, which may greatly hinder the initial impact a social worker can make on the family. These beliefs are tied to the rules and rituals families have for their members. For example, if every Sunday the family goes to grandma's house for lunch, the whole family understands the importance of extended family and the unacceptability of not attending.

Many internal models are the direct result of family-of-origin models. Husbands and wives bring these internal models into the marriage, and they are either adopted by the partner and incorporated into the present belief system or they are discarded for new ones that the couple develops themselves. There is no one correct internal working model (Vosler, 1996). Therefore, the models brought into the family sessions need to be understood within the context of the family and its cultural background.

We have discussed alliances and coalitions, in part, by talking about subsystems within a family. Alliances tell social workers who is involved with whom and around what issues. Coalitions can be either functional or dysfunctional. In a family in which the mother and father form a coalition that decides the rules and carries out the parental responsibilities jointly, the children have a clear understanding of what is expected and cannot manipulate one parent over another. In a family in which one parent has a coalition with a child, the parent who is not included in the coalition will feel left out and sometimes disengaged from the family. Healthy coalitions and alliances generally occur

Voices from the Field

**Dorothy S.
Becvar**

I entered the field of social work knowing that I wanted to work with families. This decision evolved out of several significant experiences. I had been employed for two years in a school for children with learning disabilities and often had experienced the frustration of having efforts to help students be undermined as a function of a failure to recognize the importance of also helping the families with whom the students lived. In addition, I had been through a divorce and had learned firsthand the benefits of receiving help from someone trained in family therapy, in this case a clergyman. And with the encouragement of the latter, I had been trained as a leader of Family Clusters, a church-based enrichment model for groups of whole families (Becvar, 1984). Finally, as a copresenter of a preconference institute on Family Clustering at the 1976 annual conference of the American Association of Marriage and Family Therapy (AAMFT), I had met the man who was to become my second husband, Ray Becvar. Ray, whom I married just prior to my first semester in graduate school, was one of the first to bring family therapy to St. Louis, and as he explained systems thinking to me, I immediately knew that I had found concepts that captured the way I already viewed the world.

When I began my studies in social work, family therapy was just beginning to emerge as a separate profession (Becvar & Becvar, 2003) and counted among its adherents representatives from all of the mental health disciplines. It was an exciting time, with opportunities to attend workshops presented by the creators of the major models of family therapy. Thus, I had a double opportunity for learning as I earned my MSW with a concentration in family practice in 1980, and my PhD in family studies in 1983, while at the same time acquiring knowledge about family therapy from the seminal theorists and therapists in the field both in person and through their publications. In the years since then I have taught in schools of social work as well as departments of marriage and family therapy. I have published articles and books in the literature of both fields. I am licensed as a clinical social worker and as a marriage and family therapist. Since entering the field, I have always maintained a private practice, either full-time or part-time. For me, there never has been a conflict between my dual identity as a

when a line is drawn between people of different generations, with children in one group and parents in another.

It is also important to be aware of any support systems available to the family. Extended family, work, friends, church, or other supports can be helpful at particular times in the intervention. Although you would not normally contact any of these support systems yourself without permission, family members

social worker and a family therapist, although I am well aware that tensions between the two disciplines often are experienced by others (Becvar, 1995).

Nevertheless, students today often have the opportunity to learn about family therapy as part of their social work curriculum. Indeed, a focus on the family is basic to the social work profession, and a family therapy orientation that is characterized by a systemic perspective provides a means for understanding relationships, including people in the context of their families and families in the context of the larger society, as well as the relationships between institutions and societies. As we are able to embrace the notions of recursion and complementarity, to operate from a both/and perspective, and to recognize the degree to which reality is subjective, perceptual, and cocreated, I believe our ability to help those who come to us for assistance is enormously enhanced. I certainly am grateful for the opportunities to learn and to work that have been provided to me as both a social worker and a family therapist.

If asked to give advice to students who are studying social work and also may be interested in marriage and family therapy, I would recommend that they become familiar with the educational requirements for licensure in both professions and then tailor their course of study accordingly. I also would recommend that they become student members of both NASW (National Association of Social Workers) and AAMFT (American Association for Marriage and Family Therapy) in order to learn more about each profession. Finally, consulting with an experienced professional, preferably one who is approved to do supervision, might be an important means of finding answers to their specific questions. Indeed, I believe that for those just starting out in the field as well as for those who have been practicing for some time, access to supervision always is essential.

References

Becvar, D. S. (1984). Family clustering for growth and development. In M. H. Hoopes, B. L. Fisher, & S. Barlow (Eds.), *Structured family facilitation programs.* Rockville, MD: Aspen Systems.

Becvar, D. S. (1995). Family therapy and the social work curriculum: Fit or misfit? *Journal of Family Social Work, 1*(2), 43–55.

Becvar, D. S., & Becvar, R. J. (2003). *Family therapy: A systemic integration* (5th Ed.). Boston: Allyn & Bacon.

can call on them at different times for assistance. For example, a mother or father might call on his or her own parents for support in dealing with a problem situation. Work might become involved if the family needs time off for therapy sessions, and friends often play a critical role in supporting the process of the intervention. Knowing which institutional supports can help, such as the church or school, can relieve some of the pressure the family may be feeling. Formal and informal supports can be critical to working with families successfully. Building these supports may be one of the tasks the family will need to complete in order to achieve their goals.

Environmental Factors

Many external environmental factors must be addressed during an assessment. Included in this assessment is Maslow's (1967) hierarchy of needs. The most basic focus in this hierarchy is on essential needs such as food, clothing, shelter, and medical care, as well as emotional support (Holman, 1983). Then the focus may shift toward the assessment of external needs such as social networks and institutions such as work, church, family, and friends. Another environmental factor that plays an important role is the family's economic situation. Families who are focused on survival have very little time for resolving emotional issues within the family. A family that seeks help because of financial difficulties may have few available resources. Therefore, the family's employment situation and the income being generated may be the most appropriate place to focus your initial efforts. The following basic questions will assist in determining the level of intervention needed to help the family:

1. Are they living in a safe environment?

2. Do they have enough food and clothing?

3. What is the family's employment situation?

4. Are there ways the social worker can be helpful in ensuring more economic support for the family?

5. In what ways does the family interact with the outside environment?

6. How dependent is the family on external resources?

Another important environmental factor to consider is the culture, background, and ethnic identity of the family and how this affects their view of their environment. Cultural diversity and ethnicity issues vary from family to family, and being aware of their impact is crucial to the whole process of family intervention. Practitioners must understand the meaning of the concepts of culture and ethnicity before working with families. "Culture refers to the culmination of values, beliefs, customs and norms that people have learned, usually in the context of their family and community. Ethnicity relates to a client's identity, commitment and loyalty to an ethnic group" (Jordan & Franklin, 1995, p. 169). In reviewing how to work with families of different cultures and ethnicity, practitioners need to recognize some basic issues that often affect these families. For instance, because certain minority groups experience higher levels of poverty and discrimination, they are less likely to use mental health and other community services (Ho, 1987, pp. 14–18). Although families should not be stereotyped, some basic realities should not be overlooked. One of these realities is that certain families may have greater basic survival needs than a need to work through dysfunctional interactions.

Cultural competence, according to Lum (1999), is "the set of knowledge and skills that social workers must develop in order to be effective with multicultural clients" (p. 3). Lum (1999) and Fong and Furuto (2001, p. 6) have identified four components of culturally competent practice, which include cultural awareness, knowledge acquisition, skill development, and inductive learning. Cultural awareness requires that social workers understand and be able to identify clients' significant cultural values. Knowledge acquisition involves the practitioner's recognition that the client's cultural values are strengths to be acknowledged in the helping process. Skill development is the practitioner's ability to adapt services to the unique values held by the client. Finally, inductive learning refers to the need for social workers to continue to seek appropriate resources, interventions, and services that are consonant with the client's values.

Dillard (1983) recommends that social workers understand the following points about cross-cultural counseling:

1. Nonverbal communication constitutes a larger proportion of the communication with diverse clients than verbal messaging.

2. Eye contact is beneficial in most but not all cultures.

3. Both open-ended and closed-ended questions are permissible in almost all cultures.

4. Reflection of feeling is often effective, but people in some cultures will be uncomfortable with this technique.

5. Most cultures have no problem with the use of paraphrasing.

6. Self-disclosure must be used carefully when you work with people from different cultures.

7. Clients from cultures expecting a social worker who is directive will want the helper to give interpretations and advice.

8. Periodic summarization is appropriate in most, if not all, cultures.

9. Confrontation can be an appropriate tool in many situations, but some racial groups may misconstrue this technique as evidence of bias.

10. All cultures respect the core skills of genuineness and openness.

Although these ten points are important, most important is your ability to do "culturally competent practice."

The following sections focus on specific minority and ethnic families, specifically African American, Latino, Native American, and Asian, as well as culturally different families and those with same-sex orientation.

African American Families: Although stereotyping is never appropriate, some facts about African American families are important to remember. In 1999, 47 percent of African American families were in "married couple families," compared to 82 percent in white families. In the same year, 45 percent of African American families were maintained by women with no spouse present, compared to 13 percent of the same situation in white families (U.S. Bureau of the Census, 1999). Reasons for figures like this may in part be related to the high mortality rate of young African American males, among other factors.

Ho (1987) describes the African American family as stressing the following values and qualities: "collectivist, sharing, affiliation, deference to authority, spirituality and respect for the elderly" (p. 188). The collectivist, sharing, and affiliation values are related to the characteristic of "extendedness" in the African American family (Staples, 1971), meaning that African Americans are much more likely to live within an extended family situation in which several different households link together (Farley & Allen, 1987). African American families may also be characterized by flexible family roles (Billingsley, 1992; Hill, 1971).

In terms of gender roles, African American women tend to be seen as the economic supporter as much as the husband (Jones, 1985). This role identification may affect what the family social worker does within the session. Again, although there are always exceptions, this kind of information is important to have before meeting with African American families.

Collins and colleagues (1999, p. 221) recommend the following in working with African American families:

1. Offer services to the extended family network or to groups of families who support each other.

2. Take into account the needs of single, female heads of households, including transportation problems, accommodation to work schedules, and babysitting needs.

3. Consider flexible hours for meetings so that extended family members may also attend. Also, consider transportation and lodging needs for extended family.

4. Services should be brief and time limited to encourage attendance of families who may distrust the mental health system.

5. Treatment focusing on psychoeducational and social skills methodology may be used, as well as direct communication with the family about treatment issues.

6. The family social worker must be willing and able to acknowledge racism and issues that may impede self-disclosure by African American family members.

7. African American family members value mutuality and egalitarianism; thus, the family social worker should provide services that respect the client family and include the family in the decision-making process.

Latino Families: The Latino population is the fastest rising minority group in the United States. The difficulty in determining the actual population growth is associated in part with the issue of what it means to be Latino. *Latino* is a term that refers to Mexicans, Puerto Ricans, Cubans, and other descendants of these groups. Enormous diversity exists among the Latino groups. It is beyond the scope of this book to cover all the different ethnic and cultural groups identified under this heading. Therefore, we have selected Mexican Americans as the focal group because they represent the largest Latino group in the United States.

Mexican Americans are most often divided into two groups: new immigrants (both documented and undocumented) and those born in the United States. Mexican Americans are overrepresented in low-wage positions, have the lowest educational attainment, and have the largest number of people living in a single household when compared with other groups in the United States (Demo, Allen, & Fine, 2000). Families tend to live in concentrated areas and serve as social supports and networks for other families (Staples & Mirande, 1980). Within the Mexican American culture, the family is often emphasized over the individual. Kinship networks are important support systems for the individual.

Mexican American cultural beliefs emphasize "male machismo" and "female virtue," gender characteristics that tend to reinforce a patriarchal family system that in turn supports a power differential between male and female roles in the family. Due in part to this power differential, domestic violence has been found to be high in Mexican American families (Torres, 1986).

Other problems not uncommon in Latino families include drug addiction, juvenile delinquency, and teen pregnancy. An important aspect in intervention with Latino families, particularly with elderly Latinos, is the role of *curanderismo* or folk healing. The practice of *curanderismo* is common in many Latino communities and often takes the place of more traditional forms of health and mental health care (Applewhite, 1995). Some guidelines for working with Latino families include the following:

1. Be respectful of the traditional roles in the family and do not challenge them. Helping families to see how these traditional roles affect them provides more insight for the family.

2. Be open to extended family input and help from natural support networks.

3. Be aware of the special issues that arise within Latino families.

4. Be able to speak the family's language of origin or be able to include an interpreter in your services.

5. Be open to the use of folk healing involvement.

Native American Families: Native Americans have long suffered at the hands of their white counterparts. Poverty and unemployment run high in Native American families as well as alcoholism and suicide rates. Research shows that Native American families are interdependent with their extended family and tribal community. High priority is placed on children and their upbringing. Roles within the family differ among tribes, but the role of women has always been a major and positive feature of Native American families.

Green (1999, p. 242) has outlined the following general cultural tendencies in Native American families:

- Family structure varies from tribe to tribe and from rural to urban areas, but extended units in various forms are common.
- Children often have multiple caregivers and may live with various relatives based on convenience.

- Cooperation and sharing are highly valued; individualism, assertiveness, and impulsiveness are discouraged.
- Noninterference and respect for the rights and choices of others are highly valued. Confrontation is rarely perceived as appropriate.
- Pacing activities according to the needs and expectations of others is more important than observing clock time and abstract schedules.
- Elders have important ceremonial and sometimes political roles; their views count.
- Religious values and ritual practices infuse Native American life and are regarded as critical components in preserving Native American identity and in promoting healing.

These cultural aspects of Native American life make it critical that we observe the following guidelines when working with these families:

1. Demonstrate respect for the family, extended family, and tribal traditions.

2. Be prepared to deal with problems that arise in the Native American family most often, including poverty, unemployment, alcoholism, and suicide.

3. Develop knowledge and skills in working with spirituality.

4. Show appreciation for the role and importance of family elders.

5. Avoid the use of confrontation and increase the use of collaboration in resolving issues.

Asian Families: Asian American families, like other cultural groups, comprise a great variety of different backgrounds. However, some general cultural characteristics exist within these families. In most Asian American families, the family is the center of life and family members share a close bond. Individualism is discouraged. Family members are to act in congruence with the family and beliefs of family elders. Family cohesion is achieved through togetherness and the integration of different family members' activities (Brammer, 2004).

In many ways, female and male roles are unequal; the woman is expected to defer to her father first and then to her husband. At the same time, women are highly valued and favored for their subservient roles in many family situations.

Green (1999, p. 299) notes some of the following cultural aspects of Asian American families:

- Strong, mutual support, including cooperation, interdependence, and harmony, are expected within the family and the community.
- A strong hierarchical, stable pattern of family and community relations is the setting for mutual support, expressed through a strong sense of obligation and duty to others. This duty overrides individual preferences.
- Relations with those outside the family are an extension of family interests expressed most pointedly in family influence over the choice of friends or a mate.
- Problems are solved within the family, and a code of family pride and honor limits the degree to which internal problems should be known outside the family or shared with professional helpers such as social workers.
- There is great family pressure to succeed, especially through education. Failure is a failure of obligation to one's family.

- Ambiguity in social relations is a source of anxiety.

The following guidelines are appropriate when working with Asian American families:

1. Recognize and maintain the importance of the family because personal issues are generally a private matter and not shared with external resources.

2. Be sensitive to the client's cultural values regarding the importance of the family. To the extent possible, employ collaborative strategies with the family and community rather than striving for goals that elevate the importance of the individual above the family.

3. Be aware that an individual's sense of self is strongly tied to the family and that the community places pressures on the individual to conform to norms.

Gay and Lesbian Families: Although many family therapists treat gay and lesbian families exactly the same as heterosexual families, some differences must be addressed. First is the fact that being gay or lesbian is a difficult lifestyle. Looked down on by a homophobic society, many gay and lesbian families find themselves without resources often available to heterosexual couples. Until recently, most states did not grant marriage licenses to gay and lesbian couples, notwithstanding a recent spate of exceptions to this rule. Therefore, same-sex couples experience a "loss of heterosexual privileges" due to their differences (Barret & Logan, 2002).

Demo and colleagues (2000, p. 208) summarize recent research that compares gay and lesbian couples with heterosexual couples. They conclude that same-sex couples had:

- An equal desire to be in committed, enduring romantic relationships.
- Comparable levels of feeling attracted to their partners, satisfaction with the relationships, and less difficulty breaking up when serious problems develop.
- An equal valuing of egalitarian relationships, although whether such relationships were enacted varied from study to study, and a rejection of the traditional husband–wife, masculine–feminine division of labor in favor of flexibility and sharing of housework, household expenses, and roles. Lesbian couples more than gay couples equally shared household labor.
- Similar levels and kinds of conflicts (e.g., over finances, driving styles, and affection and sex) but with unique ones related to gender (merger for lesbians, competition for gay men), sexual orientation (disclosure to family members), and race–ethnicity (strong conflict when extended family ties were strong).
- Similar predictors of satisfaction with and stability of relationships, such as interdependence and problem-solving abilities. Most studies reported relatively high levels of satisfaction among their respondents.

Important guidelines for working with gay and lesbian couples include:

1. Be sensitive to the external factors that place pressure on the couple and the family.
2. Recognize those similarities to heterosexual families that exist for gay and lesbian families.
3. Be aware of your own feelings regarding the family and work on any prejudices you may have.

4. Make sure the family has support systems in place, as these may be weakened with the extended family due to the relationship.
5. Recognize their loss of privilege.

Tools for Assessing Families

Numerous tools can be used in the assessment of families. Among these are the basic information forms you will use during the first session that provide a good basis for the beginning phase of assessment. Different agencies handle these forms in many different ways. Figure 10.3 shows an example of an intake form.

Ecomap: The ecomap depicts the family in its environmental situation, identifying and characterizing the significant community context in which the family exists. It demonstrates the flow of resources and energy into a family system as well as the outflow of family energy to external systems (Hartman & Laird, 1983, p. 159). An ecomap helps the practitioner obtain information about family relationships both inside and outside the family. It is used during the assessment stage to help the social worker understand how the family system interacts with the outside world. It can also be used with the family to help them understand how their family system inputs and outputs energies.

To begin using an ecomap, it is important to introduce it to the family in a manner that depicts how useful it can be. For example, you might say, "I'd like to draw a picture now that can tell us all a lot about your family and your relationships with groups of people or organizations outside your family." Emphasize how a picture can sometimes make things clearer because it is a visual representation of the family.

Figure 10.3

Family Assessment Form

Name: _____   Phone Number: _____

Family Members and Ages: _____

Address: _____

1. Identifying Information: _____
   _____
   _____

2. Identified Problem or Concern: _____
   _____
   _____

3. Descriptive data such as ages, marriages, employment, education: _____
   _____
   _____

4. Culture, Religion: _____

5. Family Functioning:

   Roles: _____
   Communication: _____
   Problem Solving: _____
   Beliefs: _____
   Alliances/Coalitions: _____
   Supports: _____

6. Family Strengths and Problems: _____
   _____

7. Individual Strengths and Problems: _____
   _____
   _____

8. Summary/Hypothesis: _____
   _____

9. Goals: _____
   _____
   _____

10. Intervention Plan: _____
    _____
    _____

11. Date of Assessment and Plan for Update and Review: _____
    _____

Source: Adapted from Thomlison (2002, p. 85).

Figure 10.4

An Ecomap

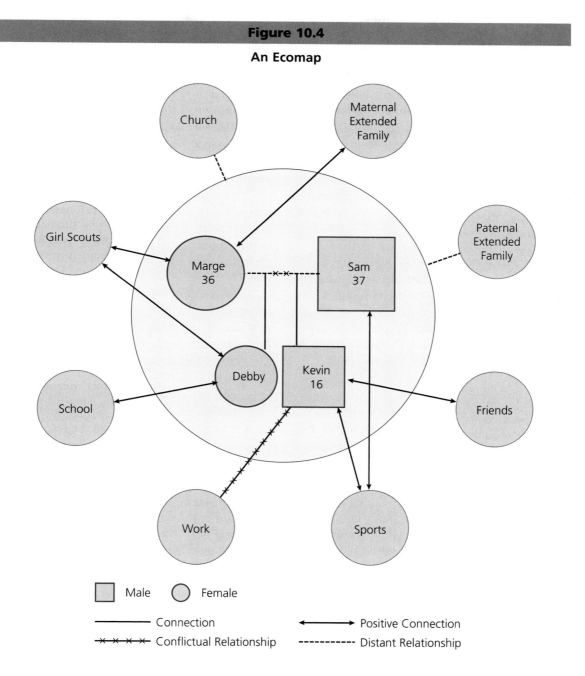

Creating an ecomap involves drawing a large circle in the middle of a page and then drawing family members within that circle. Boxes generally represent males and circles generally represent females. Outside of the larger circle, smaller circles are drawn to depict the external systems with which the family interacts. The ecomap in Figure 10.4 depicts a family with two parents and two children, a boy and a girl. Lines indicate relationships within the family and between the family and outside systems. As you can see from the lines and outside systems, the family is directly or indirectly involved with numerous other systems. Common connections can be identified between Marge and the daughter Debby in Girl Scouts and between Sam and the son Kevin in sports. The conflictual line between mother and father indicates a lack of shared involvement, suggesting that the parents need to address certain issues.

Genogram: A genogram is "a schematic diagram of a family's relationship system, in the form of a genetic tree, usually including at least three generations, used in particular by Bowen and his followers to trace recurring behavior patterns within the family" (Goldenberg & Goldenberg, 1991, p. 325). This tool, which incorporates commonly used symbols, provides the social worker and the family with a visualization of the family relationships and patterns that may be influencing the family at this point in time. It also enables them to examine the "ebb and flow of the family's emotional processes in their intergenerational context" (Goldenberg & Goldenberg, 1991, p. 160). The genogram is also a place to depict for discussion religious affiliation, occupations, ethnic or cultural issues, illnesses, or important life events, if relevant (Goldenberg & Goldenberg, 1991). It also can contain a pictorial of generation-to-generation types of issues in each partner's family of origin. The genogram in Figure 10.5 illustrates a hypothetical family's relationship patterns. Joan, the identified client, is shown with three generations on her side of the family. Both Joan and Jerry were married previously and have children by those marriages. The practitioner would want to know what

those relationships were like in the blended family. Although the children no longer live in the home, they may play an important role in it. Additionally, the genogram shows a pattern of divorce in the family, and this may have some effect on the present marriage because this is the second marriage for Joan and Jerry. What effect does a previous marriage to an alcoholic have on Joan and how she perceives her present marriage?

This tool can be effective in helping families identify recurring or transgenerational problems in the family. It may also help the family understand what issues are affecting them and how they might deal with things differently in the future.

Both ecomaps and genograms can be useful tools for helping assess family situations and identify possible avenues for intervention. Like any other tool, they should be used when the family situation warrants and not employed in all family assessments. Once an assessment is completed and planning has identified goals that the family wishes to work on, the next step is to employ the intervention processes and techniques that show the greatest promise for achieving the family's goals.

Processes and Techniques

Family practice involves numerous intervention processes and techniques. Although many of these are tied to particular models of family therapy, others can be used in all family practice.

Family Sculpture

Family sculpturing is a technique that can be used in both assessment and intervention. Originated by David Kantor and Fred Duhl, the family sculpture is a way for the family to express their perceptions of how family members operate and behave toward one another

Figure 10.5

Genogram

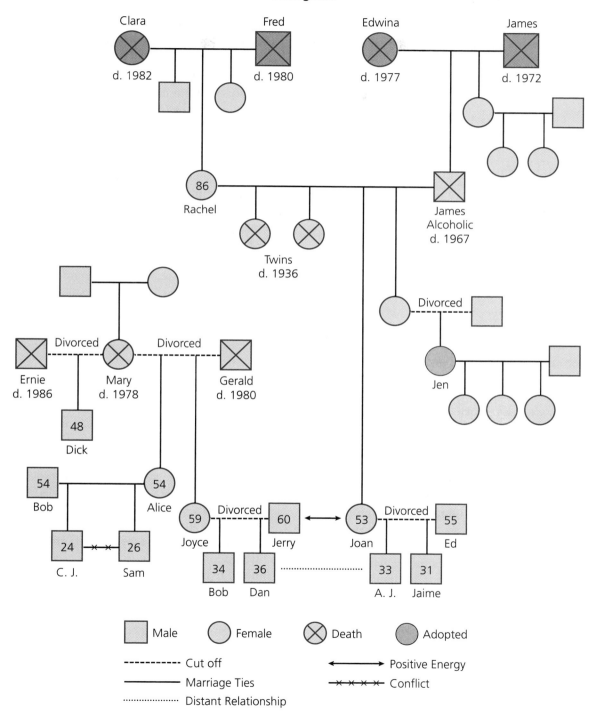

(Nichols & Schwartz, 2001). The family sculpture is a presentation, in human form, of the behaviors and relationships between family members through the use of space, posture, and attitude. A family might be introduced to the act of sculpturing in the following way:

> Have family members stand in a room posed in ways that depict the nature of their relationships. Members take turns arranging family members in relationship to one another; body gestures, distance, and physical actions convey the meaning of the sculpture. Each family member takes charge of their particular sculpture, instructing family members what positions to assume. Essentially, the sculptor treats family members as if they were made of clay. (Collins et al., 1999, p. 32)

Following the sculpturing family members are asked how they feel about the way they were placed, and anyone who wishes may try creating another sculpture. Sometimes a family sculpture can bring out information another person was not aware of, or it may show how different members of the same family view the same situation from a different perspective. By placing an individual in a physical stance, the person can begin to experience what the other person is feeling and become more in touch with his or her own issues. Once each person has had an opportunity to express how he or she felt when placed in the sculpture of the other person, all family members have learned a great deal about what is happening in the family, which often provides an impetus for members to share their feelings with one another.

Homework Assignments

Homework assignments are given to family members to complete outside of the therapeutic environment and between sessions. Homework assignments are used in many different types of treatment and can be employed in family work to help members give up the solutions they have been trying and to try different things to change the family's communication and interaction. Generally, the intent of homework assignments is to help family members relate to one another and understand their role in a particular situation (Nichols & Schwartz, 2001). Common homework assignments might include the parents spending time alone with each other, family members taking turns listening to one another without interrupting, or having an enmeshed family member do something on his or her own.

Questioning

Questioning can be a useful intervention tool with certain families. Three types of questioning are frequently employed: circular, strategic, and reflexive.

1. *Circular questioning:* Circular questioning occurs when the social worker attempts to gather "differences in perception about events or relationships from different family members" (Goldenberg & Goldenberg, 1991, p. 320). For example, a father might be asked how he believes his wife perceives their son's behavior. This type of questioning allows family members to hear how others perceive the same occurrence. This circularity demonstrates to the family that interaction in the family is circular and not linear. It helps family members recognize their differences and get new information on a topic, which could then lead to new behavior.

2. *Strategic questioning:* Through strategic questioning, the social worker challenges family members about something that needs to be changed. In this type of ques-

tioning, the social worker has assessed and determined what needs to be changed in the family and is now asking direct questions that confront family members about the assessment. For example, a social worker may have assessed that a husband uses alcohol as a way of manipulating his wife's behavior (Worden, 1994). As a follow-up question to the discovery of this information, the social worker might ask, "How long will you continue to use alcohol to manipulate your wife's behavior?" If the husband denies the statement in the question, the social worker may then point out the ways in which he or she arrived at this conclusion and may ask more questions of the husband that reassert this assessment.

3. *Reflexive questioning:* Social workers ask reflexive questions to encourage family members to reflect on their behavior and to consider new options (Worden, 1994). Unlike strategic questions, reflexive questions "assume that family members are autonomous individuals" who make their own decisions about changing (Worden, 1994, p. 81). These questions play a guiding role in aiding family members to construct their own view of the family problem. For example, the social worker might ask a wife, "What do you think is the reason for your husband's drinking?"

Multiple Family Therapy

Multiple family therapy groups were begun by Laqueur in 1950. These groups involve four to six families who are seen on a weekly basis together. These early multiple family sessions were conducted like therapy groups, using members of other families to confront one another. Today, multiple family therapy groups can be used in this manner but more often are imple-

mented in a psychoeducational manner. For example, in an adolescent residential drug treatment setting, several families might be brought into a group and given educational information about drugs. Information and skill building, along with communication within families, may also be addressed. Families would serve as support for one another and would also challenge any myths or dysfunctional behavior.

Changing Family Communication

The process of changing family communication occurs as part of the ongoing process of intervention. Families can get into many different types of communication patterns that do not work, including interrupting, constant arguing, lecturing, blaming, and other dysfunctional patterns. The following methods have been found to be effective in helping clients work through issues:

1. *Memesis:* This is the process by which the social worker "imitates family members' moods, tones of voice, postures, communication and behavior" (Franklin & Jordan, 1999, p. 29). The goal of this type of imitation is to have the social worker join with the family. For example, a social worker might sit in a way similar to the way family members sit, thus providing a similarity between them and creating an alliance between the social worker and the family.

2. *Enactment:* Enactment is the process by which family members are asked to act out a problem situation, or the enactment may occur naturally in the session. After the occurrence, the social worker attempts to model or give suggestions for change in the process. For example, a family may show a sequence pattern in how the parents become embroiled in an argument about a

child. The social worker would then give them ideas about how to handle the situation differently.

3. *Tracking:* Tracking is the processes by which the social worker "uses the words, symbols, history, and values of the family in communicating with them" (Franklin & Jordan, 1999, p. 29). Tracking allows the social worker and the family to better understand one another. By using similar concepts and language, the family has a better sense of being heard.

APPLICATIONS TO PRACTICE

Case Example

The Rodriguez family are third generation Latinos who live in a suburb of a large eastern city. The neighborhood is mixed both culturally and racially. Mr. and Mrs. Rodriguez have been married for twenty years and have two children, a girl, Maria, age seventeen, and a boy, Miguel, age fourteen. Maria is active in modern dance and chess club, and Miguel plays Little League baseball and soccer. Juan Rodriguez owns his own Mexican restaurant where his wife, Consuela, oversees the books and serves as the hostess.

Maria wants to attend college out of state. The parents are concerned that Maria is hanging out with a group of gringos who are popular at school but aren't doing as well scholastically as Maria. The friends want Maria to travel with them to the Southwest to visit colleges during spring break. When both parents oppose this plan, Maria ran away to her friend's house and refused to come home. After three weeks of pleading with her, the parents sent their parish priest to talk with her and the other family. Maria

agreed to go home if her parents wouldn't bring up the problem again. The parents agreed to drop the issue but have noticed that Maria stays out late and has stopped doing homework. When the parents ask her about her homework, Maria says it doesn't matter since she isn't going to college. The parents have planned for Maria to attend college all her life. Juan called you to make an appointment at the urging of his priest and said everyone would attend the family therapy sessions.

Practice Activity

Based on the information given, complete the family assessment form found in Figure 10.3, an ecomap, and a genogram. Be prepared to discuss your materials in class.

Critical Thinking Questions

1. Which model do you think would work best with this family and why?

2. What special issues would be important to address in the first session based on the family ethnicity and referral process?

3. How would you want to have each family member sit? Discuss his or her views? Feel heard?

4. At the end of the session, how might you improve the chances that all members will feel heard and want to return for subsequent sessions?

4. *Paradoxical directives:* Paradoxical directives occur when the social worker "gives a client or family a directive he or she wants resisted" (Goldenberg & Goldenberg, 1991, p. 328). This is a special technique that should be applied only in those cases in which the social worker and the client have established a good working relationship and the social worker is using the strategic model of family practice.

5. *Reframing:* Reframing is the relabeling of old behavior into a new, more positive light. For example, a son who is always getting into trouble could be seen as "needing attention" rather than as "a problem maker." This reframing then leads to family members responding differently to the behavior than they did before.

6. *Role playing:* Role playing is a technique through which different family members take on particular roles in the family and demonstrate how communication and behavior are carried out. Role playing can also involve role reversal, in which family members take on roles of other family members and see what it is like to be the other person in a particular situation. For example, a father and son may change roles and have a conversation regarding the son's curfew time. This gives both of them the experience of seeing the situation from another perspective.

SUMMARY

In this chapter, we discuss the role of family practice in relation to direct practice. A review of systems theory shows that the different types of family practice models use many similar concepts. The chapter also addresses some of the primary theories used in family therapy, including Bowenian, structural, experiential, strategic, cognitive–behavioral, psychoanalytic, feminist, and narrative family therapy.

In addition, the chapter looks at the initial contact between the social worker and the family and identifies a variety of issues important for assessing family systems. These include problem identification, stages of the family life cycle, family functioning, and environmental factors. The chapter also provides information on ecomaps and genograms, tools for assessing families.

Cultural considerations are a key element in all practice. Learning to be culturally competent is essential to providing ethical professional services. Finally, a variety of processes and techniques used by family practitioners is reviewed. These include family sculpture, homework assignments, questioning, multiple family therapy, and changing family communication.

Navigating Direct Practice

An access code for Research Navigator™ is packaged within your text. Use this code to register at www.researchnavigator.com and then use the key words listed below to research articles related to the chapter's content. Research Navigator™ helps you quickly and efficiently make the most of your research time.

❑ Carl Whitaker
❑ Family therapy
❑ Feedback loop
❑ Feminist therapy
❑ Homeostasis
❑ Virginia Satir

Chapter 11

Improving Group Functioning

■ Maria Hernandez worked as a clinical social worker in outpatient services at the community mental health center. Her services involved helping families and their children with drug and alcohol abuse problems. Over time, Maria began to notice that the families with whom she worked shared many commonalities, and she wondered about the possibility of using a group format rather than only seeing clients individually. She decided to bring together a multiple family group for psychoeducational services. The group would be provided information about drug use and abuse while giving families an opportunity to share their experiences.

Although Maria was unsure about how to go about this process, she knew that the uppermost limit she wanted was four families. This group would include all family members from each family. She estimated that she would have approximately twenty individuals in the family group at each session. Maria then selected the four families from her caseload that seemed to share similar situations and issues. She planned an eight-week session during which these families would come together to share information and support one another regarding the effects of drugs and alcohol in the family.

Group practice in social work developed with the creation of the settlement house movement. Whereas charity organization societies worked with individuals and families through diagnosis, treatment, and resource development, settlement house workers worked with groups of individuals, aiding them in socialization, education, recreation, and community organizing. This early type of group work focused on activities to "spur members to action" (Toseland & Rivas, 2001, p. 49). Social workers were skilled in bringing individuals together around common goals and in helping them through recreation, education, socialization, and community building to achieve their goals. Anderson (1997) contends that three major trends influenced the development of group work around the start of the twentieth century: social reform and self-help, recreation, and progressive education.

Social reform and self-help emerged on the scene as a result of the tumultuous events in the period 1890 to 1910. With the increasing industrialization of society, the enormous numbers of immigrants coming into the country, and the development of imperialism, the United States was at a turning point in its ability to foster the democratic, egalitarian society on which it was supposed to be founded. Individuals began to emerge during this period, such as Jane Addams, who sought, for the good of society, to bring back to democratic society mutual aid and the intermingling of races and classes. She focused her efforts on social ills as well as elevating society to a higher level of humanity (Anderson, 1997). It was individuals such as Jane Addams who brought group work to the forefront of the helping profession to create changes in society through socialization and community building.

Recreation emerged during this period as a result of the development of organizations such as the YMCA, YWCA, settlement houses, Girl Scouts, Boy Scouts, and Jewish Community Centers (Anderson, 1997). These early recreation organizations gained momentum with the establishment of more defined work days, which went along with the industrialization of the country. As individuals had more time for themselves outside of work, activities began to evolve to fill this time. This movement focused its efforts on all individuals and did not define any one group as needing the services more than others. The efforts were aimed at bringing individuals together to socialize and create activity (Anderson, 1997). Social workers such as Grace Coyle sought ways to incorporate the recreation process into the ongoing development of individuals through socialization with others. Others focused on the process of group work as a therapeutic method (Toseland & Rivas, 2001).

Progressive education at the turn of the century sought to bring about better public education through different means. Anderson (1997) notes that two of its guiding principles—"learning by doing" and "learning through small group democratic problem-solving processes" (p. 20)—fostered group work not only in public education but also in the social reform movement. This focus also supported the movement toward a democratic society and the involvement of individuals who could work together.

The 1930s had a profound effect on social work and its relationship to group work. Group work became formally associated with social work at the 1935 Conference of Social Work. Several different types of experiments were conducted around this time that tied group work to the mental hygiene movement. Group work was clearly moving away from recreation only purposes and was being used in hospitals and mental institutions for therapeutic reasons. During World War II in particular, groups became an essential method for dealing with veterans because of the lack of trained mental health workers. The process of group work continued in many different modes in the following years, being used in therapy, recreation, education, and socialization. Its confusing relationship with social work became more clearly defined in 1955 when the American Association of Social Workers (AASW) became one of the major organizations to form the National Association of Social Workers (NASW). Group work also became a way of uniting neighborhoods and communities around particular issues during the 1960s. Today, group work still struggles to find a specific identity in social work but continues to be widely used in the profession and taught in the education of social work.

Group Work

Today, group work in social work practice includes two separate foci, one devoted to using groups for therapeutic purposes and another concerned with the use of groups for other purposes such as community development, planning, and administrative efficiency. Toseland and Rivas (2001) define group work as "goal-directed activity with small treatment and task groups aimed at meeting socioemotional needs and accomplishing tasks. This activity is directed to individual members of a group and to the group as a whole within a system of service delivery" (p. 12). This definition considers the importance of both treatment and task groups and the importance of working with both the individual in the group as well as the group itself.

Types of Group Work

The different types of group work can be traced back to the early and differentiated beginnings of the method. These early methods were both task oriented and therapeutic. They laid the groundwork for the many different kinds of group work that emerged. One of the major writings associated with the development of social group work is "Social Group Work Models: Possession and Heritage" published in 1962 by Papell and Rothman. This article identifies three specific models of group work: the social goals model, the reciprocal model, and the remedial model. The social goals model "focuses on socializing members to democratic societal values" (Toseland & Rivas, 2001, p. 52) and emphasizes the importance of the group decision and the value of group activities in understanding democracy. Organizations such as the YWCA, Girl Scouts, and settlement houses continue to use this method to bring about change through groups (Toseland & Rivas, 2001).

The reciprocal model seeks to form a self-help, mutual aid system that helps its members find a balance between their needs and those of society. The group often serves as a mutual aid for members to achieve their goals. The emphasis is on working with the group as a therapeutic environment for change.

The remedial model emphasizes the improvement of the individual from a problem-solving perspective and focuses on restoring or rehabilitating the members' behavior. The social worker plays a major role in these kinds of groups and intervenes in the group directly. An example might be a therapeutic group in a mental health setting, a clinical setting, or a neighborhood center (Toseland & Rivas, 2001).

Although these early definitions of group work set the stage for different types of groups, those of particular importance to social workers today are treatment groups and task groups. Toseland and Rivas (2001) see treatment groups as having five different purposes: support, education, growth, therapy, and socialization. Task groups they see as being differentiated by selected characteristics. Those whose purpose is serving clients include teams, treatment conferences, and staff development. Those whose purpose is serving organizational needs include committees, cabinets, and boards of directors. Social action groups, coalitions, and delegate councils are task groups that serve the community. In this chapter, we discuss the two basic types of groups, treatment and task.

Task Groups

Task groups can be defined as those groups "whose overriding purpose is to accomplish a goal that is neither intrinsically nor immediately linked to the needs of the members of the group" (Toseland & Rivas, 2001, p. 15). By this definition, the goal of the group is to benefit a broader group of people than the members themselves. Task groups generally focus on changing some aspect of the environment through producing documents, reports, policy ideas, and platforms for special issues. Anderson (1997) concludes that the acronym TACIT is helpful for understanding the steps in the group problem-solving process and how task groups operate. TACIT stands for task orientation, accommodation, communication, integrative problem solving, and task completion. These are the stages in the group development process beginning with the coming together of the group (task orientation), the adjustment of group members to one another and the issue (accommodation), the (communication) pattern that then flows between members, the process of confronting and resolving the issue

---

Figure 11.1

Typology of Task Groups

Client Needs	Organizational Needs	Community Needs
(1) Teams	(1) Committees	(1) Social action groups
(2) Treatment conferences	(2) Cabinets	(2) Coalitions
(3) Staff development	(3) Boards of directors	(3) Delegate councils

Source: Toseland & Rivas (2001).

(integrative problem solving), and the ending of the group (task completion).

There are many different types of task group work. Toseland and Rivas (2001) divide these groups into three major categories, (1) those that meet client needs, (2) those that meet meet organizational needs, and (3) those that meet community needs. See Figure 11.1 for the groups that have been identified under each of these classifications.

Leadership in Task Groups

It is not unusual for task groups to be led by social workers. As part of the definition of the profession itself, social workers are trained to bring together groups for the purpose of achieving goals. The role of the social worker in task groups is to provide a structure for the meeting and the accomplishment of a goal. A social worker does this through a series of different behaviors. Anderson (1997) defines these behaviors as including directing, providing, processing, and catalyzing.

1. **Directing.** Refers to the behaviors of the social worker in the task group. These might include "setting goals, assigning roles and tasks, prescribing norms, managing time, stopping, interceding and suggesting procedures" (p. 257).

2. **Providing.** Refers to behaviors that foster growth and the accomplishment of the task. This might include "expressing affection, praising, communicating genuineness and empathy, and showing concern for each member and the group as a whole" (p. 257).

3. **Processing.** Refers to behaviors that help the group to understand and see the process that is going on, such as "explaining, clarifying, interpreting, giving feedback, and labeling processes" (p. 257).

4. **Catalyzing.** Refers to being able to motivate members, increase interaction, and express emotion. Some of these include "reach[ing] for feelings, challenging, and confronting" and "encouraging work, challenging obstacles to work, and sharing feelings" (p. 257).

Task Group Composition

The composition of the group depends on whether it is a group that anyone can join, such as a coalition (a group organized around social issues), or a group to which one has to be elected or selected to be part of the organization, such as a board of directors. In groups in which the members have joined on their own, the social worker may have to spend a lot of time dealing with personalities and interactions among members. This work is critical to the ongoing process of the group, but when they are not able to select the members, social workers often have to rely on themselves to move along the process of the group. Ideally, groups whose membership is open to anyone will have the diversity of talents and skills needed to accomplish the task.

In groups in which members are selected, the focus needs to be on those prospective members who can add something to the group. For a board of directors of a nonprofit agency, for example, members need to possess characteristics that will benefit the agency. A board of directors made up of all social workers does not necessarily have the variety of skills so necessary to the running of a nonprofit organization. Likewise, a board of directors for a nonprofit agency made up of all businesspeople will need a more balanced view of how social services operate in the community.

Procedures and Exercises

The social worker can use many different techniques and exercises in task groups to help resolve issues, focus on goals, facilitate member involvement, move members along in their tasks, and pull together the pieces for the end goal. We have talked about some of the functions a leader carries out in the task group, but we also need to consider the techniques of task group work. The techniques presented here include:

1. Decision making
2. Nominal group techniques
3. Brainstorming
4. Brainwriting
5. Parliamentary procedure

Decision Making: Decision making in task groups occurs, at least in part, as a component of the problem-solving process. The process of decision making allows the group to discuss various aspects of an issue and to come to

some conclusions about what is to be done. The decision-making process is an initial aspect of group discussion. In many cases, discussion is structured around a specific focus that has been decided on by the group. Although freewheeling discussion is sometimes a part of task group meetings and is at times desirable, for the most part the discussion relates to the issue at hand. Members of the group will generally have open discussion and follow through with additional means of decision making (Fatout & Rose, 1995).

As the discussion evolves, the decision will often emerge as part of the process. Fatout and Rose (1995) generally refer to the decision emergence as "a gradual, even natural, development of a decision consensus" (p. 117). Consensus is reached when there is general agreement among all members about a particular decision. Although consensus is preferable in many situations, some of the disadvantages include the length of time it takes to come to a unanimous decision and the necessity of having members who are comfortable sharing power with others.

In more hierarchical situations, the decision-making process will depend on a vote. Voting is a process by which task groups can make decisions through egalitarian methods. When the voting process is not a simple majority vote but requires a high percentage of members voting yes, such as two-thirds or three-quarters, it will be harder to obtain a yes vote. Fatout and Rose (1995) state that the higher the percentage of yes votes needed to pass a motion, the less likely there will be a positive vote. When higher percentages are used, the task group is more often concerned with the decision consequences and less likely to give an affirmative vote. This does not mean that higher percentages should not be used, but it is important to understand the implications.

Nominal Group Techniques: Nominal group techniques (NGTs) are used to reduce possible conflict in a group and to continue the generation of ideas. Generally in this process, group members are given an initial statement of the problem and asked to list ideas they have about the issue on a separate piece of paper. They are generally given a specific amount of time (e.g., five minutes) to carry out this task. After the initial period of working alone, the leader asks each member to list his or her ideas, and these are recorded on a flip chart. Ideas that are similar are combined and expanded to include all the thoughts being generated. Each idea is discussed for two to three minutes. These ideas are then rank-ordered (highest to lowest priority) by each group member. The rank orderings are then calculated, highest priority being given to items considered highest priority by the most members in the group. This then gives the rankings for the ideas proposed. NGT is an effective means of winnowing large numbers of options down to those that members believe are most important. On the flip side, it takes time to run through the successive steps needed to identify the final choices.

Brainstorming: One of the major techniques a task social worker will use is brainstorming. According to Toseland and Rivas (2001), "brainstorming is used to increase the number of ideas generated by members" (p. 360). It increases the number of alternative solutions through a "synergistic group effect" (Stewart & Shamdasani, 1990). Brainstorming can be either unstructured or structured. Unstructured brainstorming allows for individuals to speak as thoughts come to them and and to not be hampered in the process. In structured brainstorming, the social worker sets particular guidelines. These would generally include

the following, according to Fatout and Rose (1995):

1. The generation of numerous ideas is encouraged so that there will always be enough to make sure at least one or two are appropriate.

2. Criticisms or judgments about ideas are withheld so that members will feel comfortable and free about presenting them.

3. Joining the different ideas presented is encouraged because this promotes the use of two or three ideas at a time.

4. Wild and unusual ideas are encouraged in order to encourage all group members to participate.

The use of brainstorming tends to increase the number of ideas generated and in turn increases the quality of those chosen. Additional benefits, according to Toseland and Rivas (2001, p. 364), include the following:

- Dependence on a single authority figure is reduced.
- Open sharing of ideas is encouraged.
- Members of highly competitive groups can feel safe.
- A maximum output of ideas occurs in a short period of time.
- Members' ideas are posted immediately for everyone to see.
- Ideas are generated internally rather than imposed from outside the group, which increases the feeling of accountability.
- Brainstorming is enjoyable and self-stimulating.

It is important that members be allowed to suggest ideas without others evaluating or commenting on the wisdom of a particular item. Members who freely criticize the suggestions of other members tend to inhibit the generation of new ideas. Brainstorming works best when all members are able to contribute their ideas, piggyback on the suggestions of other members, and feel safe to offer creative options.

Brainwriting: Another decision-making method that can be employed in task group work is brainwriting. This method can be used easily with large groups. The first step is to divide the larger group into smaller ones and then prepare these smaller groups to work both together and independently. The second step is to give each group a problem or situation on which they will focus their discussion. For example, a group of substance abuse agency practitioners may be asked to identify what they perceive as the greatest needs for in-service training based on the challenges they face in their work. All the small groups may be limited to one main topic, or each group may be asked to consider a different topic. In the example of the practitioners, all groups responded to the same issue (challenge), and each group member listed his or her challenges on a piece of paper. Following this process, the papers are set in the middle of each table and members of the group select a page that is not his or her own. Their responsibility is to add to the responses of the first writer. This piggy-backing and responding process continues until everyone in the group has written on each person's page. Members then share in their small groups the items they listed and the comments of others, and then the group responds to the topic. One person from each group is asked to take notes on the discussion and later to summarize this material for the larger group. Often this summary will be written on large sheets of paper, which will later be discussed within the large group. Following this process, the larger group holds a discussion to process the information and then comes to a decision. In the case of the substance abuse practitioners, the larger group used the smaller group reports to generate a list of in-service training needs that supervisors and administrators would use in planning educational opportunities for the coming year.

Parliamentary Procedure: Parliamentary procedure is an efficient method of allowing large groups to function in a structured way and to make decisions. Begun in the 1300s in the English Parliament, these procedures have evolved to the present day. In the United States, *Robert's Rules of Order* (Roberts, Evans, Honemann, & Balch, 2000) are generally used by task groups to carry out their work. Toseland and Rivas (2001) note that most parliamentary procedure is determined by motions brought by group members. These motions include the following:

1. Privileged motions are motions carried out as part of the agenda of the meeting, such as adjournment and recess.

2. Incidental motions are those calling for a clarification in procedures. These might include "point of order" and "point of information."

3. Subsidiary motions deal with the motions on the floor. These might include amending or tabling a motion.

4. Main motions deal with major issues of the group. Main motions take precedence over pending motions, not including privileged, incidental, and subsidiary. An example of this would be the consideration of a tabled motion.

These procedures provide a structured means of going about a group's business. Generally used in larger groups, parliamentary procedure is designed to ensure that all members of the group have an opportunity to debate and discuss proposed decisions. These activities allow members to feel assured that their ideas will be heard and that the group will follow an agreed-on procedure for considering their suggestions. On the other hand, members may feel that they have not been as big a part of the process as they wanted. Addressing issues in such a structured way can create hesitancy in members who feel they do not have much to offer to the debate or who are uncomfortable speaking in front of large groups. Because decisions are made by the majority, parliamentary procedure can lead to hard feelings when one side overrides the objections of the minority. Further, parliamentary procedure is not an efficient or effective way of dealing with complex issues. For real problem solving dealing with very involved or complicated issues, it is often better to ask a small subgroup to come up with a proposal that can be brought to the larger group for a final decision.

Treatment Groups

Treatment groups can be defined as "groups whose major purpose is to meet members' socioemotional needs. The purposes for forming treatment groups might include meeting members' needs for support, education, therapy, growth, and socialization" (Toseland & Rivas, 2001, p. 15). These groups are generally seen in a therapeutic setting such as a hospital, a private practice, an agency, or an outpatient setting. The following is an explanation of the types of groups in this category:

1. Support groups are groups that bring together individuals for mutual assistance, interest, or activities. They can occur in many different settings including church, school, social club, family, community organization, and service organization, to name a few. The purpose of the support group is to help individuals deal with life stresses by providing them with effective coping skills. These groups help sustain and provide encouragement for their members. Effective coping skills are developed through the interaction of group members with one another.

2. Education groups provide group members with information. Generally, a portion of the group time is set aside for the social worker to present material on a particular subject. An example of this is a family group that meets to gather information about the use of drugs by adolescents. In addition to presenting didactic material, the practitioner gives the group the opportunity to discuss the information among themselves and to learn from one another's experiences. Toseland and Rivas (2001) suggest that when group members are selected, the social worker should consider the knowledge level of group members on the subject so that all members can participate.

3. Growth groups are designed to assist members achieve their highest potential. They are not designed to work on remedial issues, as is the case with therapy groups. At the same time, members do work together to improve and enhance one another's and their own lives. The concept for these groups is based in part on Maslow's (1971) model of self-actualization. In this model, individuals seek further growth after basic physiological, safety, love, and self-esteem needs are met. In a growth group, each member's striving for self-actualization is encouraged through the interaction between members. It is through these interactions that members can expand their behaviors

4. Therapy groups seek to help members resolve personal problems, cope with life transitions and traumas, and work through psychological issues. In therapy groups, problems may be similar (such as a group for depressed individuals) or very different (such as a general inpatient psychiatric group) depending on the individuals in the group. Generally, members will work both individually on their own goals and together on group goals. The social worker is seen more as an expert who can aid clients in resolving their issues. Oftentimes, the social worker will work with one individual at a time and engage others as they move along. There has been a lot of discussion about how to select members for a therapy group. Yalom (1995) recommends that for a group to be effective, members should have equal ego strength in order to work together in the same emotional environment. By ego strength, we mean the capacity to reason, understand others, and maintain a degree of self-awareness and self-control. Because of this and other reasons, it is not unusual for a social worker to interview and assess members for a group before it begins.

5. Socialization groups help members to "learn social skills and socially accepted behavior patterns so they can function effectively in the community" (Toseland & Rivas, 2001, p. 27). Much of the activity in socialization groups is in the form of exercises or games. Role playing, for instance, allows members of a socialization group to practice their new skills with other members before trying them out in the "real" world. One example of a socialization group is the recreational group in a Boys and Girls Club. Through activities, young people are taught how to interact with one another, communicate more accurately, and learn how to operate within groups.

Leadership in Treatment Groups

Leadership in treatment groups can range from the directive role (therapy groups) to the non-directive role (support groups). Often the social worker's role is determined by both the type and purpose of the group. Some groups, such as the socialization group, can have both directive and nondirective leaders. Much of the leader's role is determined by the competence of the members and the complexity of the program activities (Toseland & Rivas, 2001). Social workers in treatment groups must understand very clearly the purpose of the group and the manner in which individuals want to accomplish this purpose. Social workers in direct practice are often involved with treatment groups, and many of these groups will require them to take an active leadership role. In this role, social workers need to be clear about what their responsibilities and activities will be within the group. Many group members will not understand the way in which treatment groups work, and part of the practitioner's role will be to ensure their understanding.

Corey (2004, p. 97) defines the social worker's functions early in a therapy group as follows:

- Teaching participants some general guidelines and ways to participate actively that will increase their chances of having a productive group
- Developing ground rules and setting norms
- Teaching the basics of group process
- Assisting members in expressing their fears and expectations and working toward the development of trust
- Modeling the facilitative dimensions of therapeutic behavior

- Being open with members and being psychologically present for them
- Clarifying the division of responsibility
- Helping members establish concrete personal goals
- Dealing openly with members' concerns and questions
- Providing a degree of structuring that will neither increase member dependence nor promote excessive floundering
- Assisting members in sharing what they are thinking and feeling about what is occurring within the here-and-now context
- Teaching members basic interpersonal skills such as active listening and responding
- Assessing the needs of the group and facilitating in such a way that these needs are met

As the group continues to move through the therapeutic process, it will be important for the social worker to facilitate group members' efforts toward their therapeutic goal. Some members will not progress in the same way as others, and as the group goes through the different stages of group work, members will need group leadership. How a social worker works through the stages of group work is addressed later in this chapter.

Treatment Group Composition

The composition of treatment groups has undergone much discussion over the past several decades. Depending on the type of treatment group, the composition may be open to selection by the social worker, or it may be preset. In support groups, for example, members often select themselves based on the issues they have in common. A support group for individuals who are going through divorce is an example of this. In socialization groups, individuals often self-select because they want to learn a new skill. For example, a basketball league for children ages six to eight would include all children in that age range.

In therapy groups, the selection of members can become complicated. Groups in inpatient settings, for example, might be open-ended so that new members join a therapy group as soon as they enter the inpatient setting. The group might be closed-ended with a particular issue such as depression. Depending on the agency or setting, these groups may be automatically self-selected or may be selected by the social worker based on specific criteria. It is an advantage, in most cases, for a social worker to be able to select those individuals who are right for a group.

Toseland and Rivas (2001) suggest that there are good reasons to have both common characteristics and diversity in a group. Whether a group is made up of heterogeneous individuals or homogeneous individuals can make a difference in how effectively a group operates. Homogeneous groups are often composed of individuals similar in age or interest or issues. Homogeneous group members tend to identify more with one another and become cohesive more quickly in the development of the group. Heterogeneous groups are often made up of individuals with different "coping skills, life experiences, and levels of expertise" (Toseland & Rivas, 2001, p. 167). This allows group members to operate as though the group were a "macrocosm" of the real world, with different individuals who need to be interacted with on a regular basis. This allows group members to practice their skills and to learn from one another. The combination of both heterogeneity and homogeneity in a group can create a structure that is very effective. Individuals with similar characteristics and issues can become more cohesive, and yet with heterogeneous characteristics of skill and expertise they can teach one another how to interact differently in the real world.

Techniques and Exercises

Treatment groups use many techniques and exercises, and many of these can be traced to the social worker's theoretical underpinnings. For example, if the social worker takes a behavioral approach with a group, he or she is likely to focus on brief interventions, learning new skills, modeling, coaching, and behavioral rehearsal. In this section, we focus on those techniques and exercises most commonly used in group work. These include:

1. Techniques for building cohesion
2. Techniques for dealing with reticent group members
3. Techniques for dealing with difficult behavior
4. Techniques for dealing with disagreement
5. Techniques for fostering self-awareness

Techniques for Building Cohesion: Cohesion is an important factor in successful group work. Without it, group members do not build trust and are therefore unwilling to share and obtain feedback about their personal situations. There are many different ways to build cohesion among group members. One of the first things a social worker needs to do is to use what are often referred to as "icebreakers," whereby group members get to know one another on a more personal basis. One method of doing this is to divide the group into dyads. Each dyad partner spends some time getting to know the other person and then introduces that person to the group during introduction time. Another icebreaker is to have group members write down something about themselves that they are willing to share with the group. The social worker then reads these out

loud, and the group spends time trying to figure out who wrote down what information.

Besides these initial exercises, the group builds cohesion based on a sense of belonging and a willingness to be part of the group. To foster feelings of belonging, individual members need to be willing to spend some of their emotional time in the process of sharing their own personal lives and their feelings and reactions. Social workers can help members move in this direction by inviting direct exchange between group members rather than having them address comments to the practitioner. Encouraging open and honest discussion also leads to better cohesion as group members are able to share their thoughts and feelings.

Another method for building cohesion is to focus the group members in the here-and-now so they can deal with what is happening in the group at that moment. Using a there-and-then focus (outside-the-group occurrences) will limit the cohesiveness among members, and individuals will work only on their own issues through the social worker.

Techniques for Dealing with Reticent Group Members: Reticence is often evident in the beginning of a group. It may stem from the reluctance on the part of certain individuals to become involved, or perhaps some members are being forced to attend the group (as in a court-ordered case). Whatever the reason, the most important thing for the social worker to do is to address the issue of reluctance right away. This may be done through statements such as, "I feel there is more that needs to be talked about than is being done now," or "I sense a reluctance on the part of some members to take part in the group. Let's talk about what that reluctance is about." You might also talk about how you are experiencing the reluctance. For example, you might say, "I am feeling very uncomfortable and I think some of you are feeling that way also." Another way to deal with reluctance is to invite questions about what will happen in the group, what the role of the leader will be, and what responsibilities members will have. As members of the group come to understand how the group functions, they become less reluctant to be part of the group and more willing to address their own issues.

Techniques for Dealing with Difficult Behavior: In dealing with difficult behavior, the social worker should be alert to what may be triggering the behavior. Seldom do group members become difficult without a reason. Knowing this reason and being able to address it through the group process can do a lot to extinguish the behavior. Problematic behavior should be considered as emerging from the individual member. Such behavior may be a reflection of that person's idiosyncratic nature or perhaps a symptom of a concern shared by multiple members. Rarely is the social worker the cause of the difficult behavior, and leaders are advised not to personalize it.

When addressing difficult behaviors, it is important to remember that this is a learning opportunity not only for the person but also for the group. Bringing about change in individuals can be facilitated when the difficult behavior is examined in the group process. This calls for a gradual approach to enlisting the individual's participation in dealing with the difficult behavior.

One issue that often comes up in group is how to deal with someone who monopolizes the conversation. In these cases, the social worker or other members of the group must address this concern as appropriately as possible. A mechanism for handling these situations involves the social worker pointing out posi-

tive aspects of what the individual is saying and yet stating that it is important for those who are not talking to engage more in the conversation. Additionally, individuals who monopolize conversations can be asked to receive feedback from others about what they said but without commenting. This gives other members of the group the opportunity to talk and yet addresses the issue of having the monopolizing person sit and listen.

Another method for dealing with difficult behavior is to call the person's attention to the agreements you will have made at the beginning of the group. These agreements include various statements related to how members are to be part of the group. Reminding members of these guidelines can help the group observe the ground rules.

Techniques for Dealing with Disagreement: As the group moves through the stages of the group process, disagreements can arise. As in other situations, it is best for the social worker to recognize these disagreements and make use of the here-and-now by addressing these conflicts directly. Disagreements most often emerge as a person notes a problem with something going on in the group. It is important for those who are experiencing the disagreement to deal with it directly in the group. One way of doing this is to ask those who are in disagreement to work through the issue as part of the group process. Toseland and Rivas (2001) suggest that the skills of moderating, negotiating, mediating, and arbitrating, implemented before a disagreement arises, can help dissipate strong emotions. Additional ways of dealing with disagreements and conflicts are discussed in a later section of this chapter.

Techniques for Fostering Self-Awareness: Self-awareness is a critical component of successful group work. As individuals come to recognize themselves, their thoughts, feelings, and behaviors, they can better adapt themselves to what is going on both inside and outside of themselves. For members to become self-aware, they must address their issues in a personal way. Members who are uncomfortable with what they see as their personality should be encouraged to discuss this in group and possibly go as far as playing out this personality with another group member while being observed. Reid (1997) states that this personal learning can take several forms, including (1) insight into understanding who someone is personally through an examination of previously unacknowledged feelings and traits and (2) through interpersonal learning within the group process as the person acts out behaviors that other group members reflect on.

Group Development

A group might be closed-ended (beginning and ending within a particular time frame, with members starting and finishing together) or it might be open-ended (members join and leave the group at different times, and the end of the group is not identified by any particular date). Groups, especially closed-ended groups, go through defined developmental stages. These stages have been addressed by many different theorists. Corey (2004) lists the following developmental stages: (1) pregroup issues or formation of the group, (2) initial stage or orientation and exploration, (3) transition stage or dealing with resistance, (4) working stage or cohesion and productivity, and (5) final stage or consolidation and termination.

Anderson (1997) lists the following stages and the issues that arise at that stage: (1) preaffiliation/trust; (2) power and control/ autonomy; (3) intimacy/closeness; (4) differen-

tiation/interdependence; and 5) separation/ termination. Reid (1997) likens the developmental stages to those of a human being with the following layout: (1) childhood, (2) adolescence, (3) adulthood, and (4) death.

Garland, Jones, and Kolodny (1976) define the stages as (1) preaffiliation and power and control, (2) intimacy and differentiation, and (3) separation. These different stages can be identified as beginning, middle, and end stages. Table 11.1 provides an overview of how these different theorists present the developmental stages of groups.

Beginning Stage

The beginning stage is the time of planning and group formation. In the planning stages of group work, the practitioner takes time to solidify who will be in the group and works with the information available to help shape the group's objectives. Generally, the number of members in a treatment group is between six and eight. Decisions about who will be in the group must be based not only on the individual group member but also on how different members will get along with one another. Social workers who take their time with this part of the group process are likely to have more success in their groups.

Planning the Group

Among the things to be accomplished in the planning of a group are:

1. Establishing group objectives
2. Recruiting and screening group members
3. Developing physical space and materials

Establishing Group Objectives: Group objectives are based on the group's purposes. In order to best understand how these objectives influence the planning of the group, it is

			Table 11.1		

Developmental Stages of Groups

Developmental Stages	Reid (1997)	Garland, Jones, & Kolodny (1976)	Anderson (1997)	Corey (2004)
Beginning	Childhood	Preaffiliation and power and control	Preaffiliation/trust	Pregroup issues or formation of group
			Power and control/autonomy	Initial stage or orientation and exploration
Middle	Adolescence	Intimacy and differentiation	Intimacy/closeness	Transition stage or dealing with resistance
	Adulthood		Differentiation/ interdependence	Working stage or cohesion and productivity
End	Death	Separation	Separation/ termination	Final stage or consolidation and termination

important to ask the question, "What are the reasons for the establishment of this group?" Whether this is a task group or a treatment group, the practitioner must give meaning to the group's creation. Is the goal to educate members about mental illness or an attempt to organize a neighborhood around a property issue? Is this going to be treatment group for sexually abused adolescents or a planning meeting of the agency's finance committee? These questions solidify the reason for which the group is being developed. A common meaning allows the group members to understand the direction the group takes. Although all members of the group make a decision about their own role within the group, an overall meaning provides them with boundaries for their roles and their personal goals.

Establishing group objectives is also related to the group sponsor. An organization, a social worker, or potential members themselves may come forward with the idea for the group. This idea, along with the purpose of the group, lays the foundation from which people operate. An organization concerned about drug use among adolescents likely will have different group objectives than if the group were established by the adolescents themselves. Ultimately, a group's purpose is influenced by both the ideas of the sponsoring individual or organization and the wishes of the members.

Recruiting and Screening Group Members:
Group membership may emerge as part of the social worker's efforts, the organization's efforts, or the individual's efforts. Many times, a worker in an agency or organization will see a need for a particular group and then set about establishing that group while seeking potential members. In some cases, it may be best to further develop the objectives before recruiting members. Without a clear understanding of what these objectives are, there is a likelihood that certain members will not fit well with the group. Selecting members whose objectives match the group's purpose and preliminary objectives makes it easier to facilitate involvement and increase communication. On the other hand, if group members are chosen early, the group objectives can become more specific to its members' needs and wants through their input.

The process of recruiting members is different for each group. In treatment groups, members are sought as the social worker establishes the need for the group. The practitioner's caseload and those of other social workers and agencies may suggest potential members. With a clear purpose and objectives, it is easier for the social worker and other practitioners to assess who may be best suited for the group. As potential members of the group are being identified, the social worker can begin gathering data about the members and about their objectives and goals for the group. This also allows all potential members to talk with the social worker to see whether they fit with the group.

In task groups, potential members are often recruited for their expertise, their power, and their interest in carrying out the objectives of the group. Sometimes the social worker must work with others to select appropriate members. In other situations, leaders can make their own decisions about who will best help the group complete its tasks. In some groups, such as neighborhood communities, selecting members may not be possible as all neighborhood members have a right to be a part of the task solution. In contrast, on a board of directors the social worker or members of the organization might select particular people to be involved in the group because of their individual and professional characteristics. As individuals are deciding whether to become involved in a group, it is often helpful to share with them the information you have about the organization or agency. This allows potential members to screen themselves out if they do not fit with the objectives or do not have an interest in the group.

Developing Physical Space and Materials:
The environment in which the group meets is critical to the group process. Cramped quarters or a depressing atmosphere can affect a group's attitude and mood. Social workers must also be sensitive to the issue of privacy, and the space selected must ensure that privacy. Additionally, the space needs to be appropriate for face-to-face interactions. A room with desks attached to the floor is an inappropriate space for group activities.

The materials used in the group process will depend on the type of group. In some treatment groups, preparing materials is not important because the group itself will direct the process and only the verbal and nonverbal actions of the group will be employed. In psychoeducational treatment groups, it will be necessary to develop materials that can be presented as part of the group's learning process. Task groups in particular will use materials prepared by the leader and by members themselves to do their work. In some groups, it may be appropriate for members to sit at a table so materials can be spread out and used by everyone. However, in some cases a table may be inappropriate because it hampers nonverbal communication (Toseland & Rivas, 2001). The environment of the meeting room must be matched with the goals of the group.

Forming the Group

The formation of the group also occurs during the beginning stage. This initial coming together of group members can be a tenuous situation. Individuals join a group with a preconceived notion of what it will be like. Their expectations and their previous experience with similar groups will structure their behavior. Garland, Jones, and Kolodny (1965) associate this period with the terms *approach* and *avoidance*. This is the point at which members of the group are frightened to join, not knowing how they will be received or if they will fit in. Their behavior is distant and cautious because they want to be a part of the group and yet do not want to risk rejection. Wanting to be a part of the group reflects a desire to belong and be accepted by others. Many people want to share their experiences and to be brought together as part of a group. During this stage, the social worker needs to facilitate a safe environment, one that can build on the trust of all members. This can be achieved by supporting all group members and establishing norms within the group. As members become more comfortable in the situation, they can then begin to express more about themselves and their beliefs.

With this comfort, issues of power and control begin to emerge. Members vie with one another over such things as group goals and decision making, and it is common for some challenges to be aimed at the practitioner. Subgrouping may occur as members affiliate with others in the groups. This is often a conflictual period in which members and alliances challenge one another and their roles within the group. This conflict is important because it begins to stabilize the norms and patterns of interaction that the group will employ throughout its existence. It is the social worker's role as leader to bring members through this period and into an environment in which they can be more invested. As norms are established, individual's roles in the group are established. People have a sense of where they are in the group and how their behavior plays into the ongoing group process.

Helping members through this stage involves several activities. These include:

1. Clarifying the guidelines and purpose
2. Facilitating member involvement and communication
3. Establishing individual and group contracts
4. Asserting the self in a conflict situation
5. Processing the group following a conflict situation

Clarifying the Guidelines and Purpose: One of the first things to be done in a group is to help clarify the guidelines. These guidelines may contain rules about how the group will be run, the expectations of group members, issues of confidentiality, and discussion of trust. These guidelines and initial conversations answer questions for members and also help the social worker establish a safe environment. The more that group members feel from the beginning that they are protected from harm by set guidelines and a clear purpose, the easier it is for them to express themselves. On the other hand, protecting group members too much can take away from the individual expression of needs and issues in the group.

Group purpose is defined not only by the social worker but also by each of the members. Purpose is an ongoing process by which individuals in the group through interaction with one another can shift the purpose. Evidence indicates that when group purpose and individual personal purpose work together, the group can be more successful (Berelson & Steiner, 1964).

Of paramount importance in the clarification of guidelines and purpose is the establishment of trust. As group members become comfortable with the guidelines and are clear about the purpose, they begin to trust more in the workings of the group even during the conflict stage.

Practitioners need to be aware when a group is beginning to show a lack of trust. According to Corey, Corey, Callanan, and Russell (2004, p. 78), some of the signs of this include:

- Participants are slow to initiate work.
- Members say very little when called on for their reactions.
- Members keep negative reactions to themselves, share them only with a few, or express them in indirect ways.
- Members deflect by telling detailed stories.
- Participants intellectualize.
- Members are vague and focus on others instead of on themselves.
- There are long silences.
- Participants put more energy into "helping" others or giving others advice than in sharing their personal concerns.
- Some maintain that they do not have any problems that the group can help them with.
- Others are unwilling to deal openly with conflict or even to acknowledge the existence of conflict.

Lack of trust does not lend itself to moving a group past their conflict and into the next stage. A lack of trust can also produce judgmental attitudes from some members, with name calling and put-downs as part of this process. At this point, practitioners need to assert themselves and set guidelines for these behaviors if they have not been previously set. Additionally, building trust is helped along through the use of attending skills such as listening, empathy, genuineness, and self-disclosure (Corey & Corey, 2002).

There are no easy ways of establishing trust in a group. However, as mentioned earlier, some groups have used exercises in the beginning stage to break the ice and build trust. These exercises help members become acquainted with one another and open up the lines of communication. One such exercise is called "top secret." Toseland and Rivas (2001) describe this as follows: "Members are asked to write down one thing about themselves that they have not or would not ordinarily reveal to new acquaintances. The leader collects the top secrets and reads them to the group. Members attempt to identify the person who made each revelation, giving a reason for their choice" (p. 193). This exercise allows members to share personal information in a nonthreatening way. As members come to know one another, this exercise can be used again to build trust.

Facilitating Member Involvement and Communication: Social workers can begin to facilitate members' involvement through the use of exercises such as "top secret." Additionally, leaders can draw out members through their own discussion of the group and its purposes. Letting group members know from the beginning that this is their group allows individuals to voice opinions about the direction they would like to see the group take. Always including all members in the discussions is critical. To be inclusive, the social worker needs to solicit thoughts and feelings on an ongoing basis from all group members. Showing genuine interest in what everyone has to say and supporting their points is a great way to facilitate their involvement and communication. Although some in the group will wish to dominate the conversation, others will hesitate to say anything. Being able to balance these interactions becomes critical to group success. Being able to personally ask for someone's thoughts while at the same time closing out the comments of another group member is a tactful skill that practitioners must learn in order to heighten communication. When dealing with people who monopolize the conversation, it is important to let them express their points and then move the conversation to other people in the room. For example, as one person continues to talk, you might say, "I think that is an interesting point. Let's see what other members think about what you are saying." And then if necessary call on another member of the group by name so the person who is monopolizing realizes he or she no longer has the floor.

Think about the factors that are likely to make new members feel more comfortable in a group. These include comments from the leader supporting the purpose of the group, demonstrations of empathy toward the anxiety that often accompanies new experiences, and possibly the leader's enthusiasm for what is about to happen. Being enthusiastic and clear about the group elicits conversation from group members. By engaging in these behaviors, the leader is modeling communication and expected interaction patterns. As the group members become aware of the leader's expectations, goals, and purpose, they will seek to be a part of this if it also meets their objectives. Assuring them that the group will

function for them is part of the recruitment process discussed earlier. Furthering their commitment by helping members identify their own goals for the group encourages more of their involvement and communication. As individuals fit their own goals within the structure of the group, their commitment and involvement become clearer. For example, in a psychoeducational group for families with troubled teens, a mother may see that her goal of having a better relationship with her son can be achieved through her involvement in the group and its purpose. This encourages her participation in the group and her communication with other group members about their similar situations.

Establishing Individual and Group Contracts: Contracts in group work can be both verbal and written. Generally, contracts are verbal agreements made between the social worker and the group members. In essence, contracting in groups involves three skills, according to Schwartz (1976): clarifying purpose, clarifying roles and responsibilities, and reaching for members' feedback. Although we have discussed clarification of purpose as it relates to the group, we have yet to stress the importance of members' interchange with social workers regarding this purpose. It is especially important in involuntary groups that members are given the opportunity to respond to the purpose (Anderson, 1997). Their response in negotiating this purpose becomes critical to their involvement in the group and what they may gain from it. If their own objectives do not fit with this purpose (this should be a part of the recruitment and screening process in the early stage), then it is best that everyone concerned understand this now. It also gives members the opportunity to make a commitment to the group and to recognize the leader's interest in members' involvement and collaboration in the group process.

When social workers clarify roles and responsibilities in negotiating the contract, they are sharing their expectations of what will happen within the group. Practitioners can clarify their role by being honest with the group about how they will interact as a social worker. In some groups, the social worker may serve as the expert providing information to group members. In other groups, the role may be one of facilitating the conversation. Members' roles emerge early in the group process, and their ability to fit their role with the contractual agreement is critical. Typically, members' roles can be divided into those that enhance task achievement (task roles) in the group and those that facilitate the ongoing functioning of the group (maintenance roles). Behaviors associated with task roles include such things as seeking the opinions of others, teaching others, and elaborating on the ideas of others. Behaviors that further the maintenance role include compromising, listening to others, and relieving tension. One member may play more than one role, and this list of roles is by no means exhaustive. Further, some roles may not be carried out in every group. However, the early involvement of members in fulfilling particular roles is critical to the contractual process in the group.

The third skill needed in setting up contracts involves reaching for members' feedback. Reaching for feedback means that the social worker shows receptivity to differences of opinion and encourages members to voice their thoughts on the group's purpose and goals. In some groups, especially involuntary ones, members often have initial mistrust and doubts about the group. This mistrust can be reduced if members feel free to give feedback and to voice their opinions about what will happen in the group (Anderson, 1997). Al-

though on some level this may be threatening to social workers, without it the group's likelihood of success is doubtful.

Asserting the Self in a Conflict Situation: During the initial formation of the group, as mentioned, there can be conflicting agendas and opinions among members. Conflict also occurs as a result of the power and control struggle early on in a group. We often think of conflict as something bad, but in reality it can have a positive function in any group. Conflict or disagreement over issues fosters investment in the process. If the conflict is handled appropriately, it can increase members' sense of connection to others, strengthen their commitment to the group process, and encourage them to continue with the group. A major task for the social worker leading the group is to employ conflict resolution skills that help further the aims of the group. Examples of those skills include: personalizing; role reversal; empathy; questioning; moderating, negotiating, and mediating; and invoking the contract (Anderson, 1997; Toseland & Rivas, 2001).

1. **Personalizing.** *Personalizing* a problem allows the social worker to redirect responsibility to the person with the problem. It involves feeding back to the members their role in the conflict in the group through sentences such as, "You feel angry that what you are saying is not being heard"; "You feel you have risked personal information and no one is responding to you"; and "You feel hurt because your ideas are not being taken seriously." These types of comments encourage members to voice their feelings in the group situation and take responsibility (Anderson, 1997).

2. **Role Reversal.** *Role reversal's* basic skill involves asking a member to assume the role

of another individual in his or her life. This individual can be a member of the group or someone outside of the group, such as family member or significant other. Members who are able to place themselves in the shoes of another may find that it helps engender a degree of empathy and insight into the other person. In conflict situations, a heated discussion often flares when neither side is listening to the other and simply says what it wants to say. In cases like these, role reversal slows down the process and establishes a situation in which each person stops to listen to what is being said in order to repeat it. A social worker might ask the two conflicting parties to take turns talking and to repeat what each hears the other person say before beginning.

3. **Empathy.** *Empathy* can have a strong impact on conflict when those in the conflicting roles begin to hear that they are being listened to and understood. The social worker does this through the use of "I" statements and repeating in an empathetic way what is being said. For example, a social worker might say, "I sense that you are feeling hurt by what was said to you"; "I feel your sense of grief over the loss you are experiencing"; or "I hear you saying that the group isn't trying to understand you." This allows the member to let go of the anger and concentrate more on the feelings creating the anger.

4. **Questioning.** *Questioning* involves reaching for the feelings and thoughts that underlie the conflict. An example might be, "Marta, you seem quite upset about what Nadia said. How did what she said make you feel?"

5. **Moderating, Negotiating, and Mediating.** These three skills are necessary for resolving conflicts and disagreements in some cases. *Moderating* allows social workers to keep boundaries in meetings so that conflict does not get out of hand. *Negotiating* is used to help two or more members come to a general consensus about their conflict. *Mediating* is used when members cannot reach an agreement together and the social worker needs to negotiate a more formal agreement that helps each side find a middle ground with which they can live (Toseland & Rivas, 2001).

6. **Invoking the Contract.** One of the easiest ways to handle unproductive conflict is to *invoke the contract* by asking group members if this behavior is what was agreed to by the group in the beginning. This allows the members in conflict to receive outside information from other group members. It reminds members of the purpose of the group and how they may be veering off course through these conflicts (Anderson, 1997).

Processing the Group Following a Conflict Situation: Once a conflict is ended, it is important for the social worker not to ignore this occurrence but to bring it directly into the group by talking about the process, how the group handled it, and what it means for the group. These experiences are learning ones for the group and its members. Discussing the process of the conflict and how it was handled can help members create positive change in future situations. Group members can use the skills they have learned from this experience to handle other situations both inside and outside the group.

Group Work Assessment

Assessment in group work, as in individual work with clients, is an ongoing process and needs to begin early in the intervention. Social workers need to assess (1) the individuals in the group, (2) the group as a whole, and (3) the environment in which the group operates.

Assessment of Individuals: Members of a group will come from a variety of backgrounds. One person's environment will not be the same as that of others. Each individual brings with him or her a unique set of characteristics and environments. Depending on the type of group, what individual members wish to discuss or work on can vary greatly. According to Toseland and Rivas (2001), it is important to understand the intrapersonal life of the member, the interpersonal interactions of the member, and the environment in which the member functions. Knowing these three areas allows the social worker to anticipate how the member will function in the group and how their characteristics will affect others. Generally, by the beginning of the group the social worker will have an idea of members' characteristics and backgrounds. This knowledge can come from pregroup discussions, observations of their actions within the group, charts of behavior maintained by the social worker or member, self-reports, and testing and scales including rapid assessment instruments. Sometimes understanding the environments in which clients live will require more personal inquiry, and a portion of this might be done individually rather than in the group. Whenever possible, it is best to perform these kinds of assessments before the group begins.

Assessment of the Group as a Whole: Observation of the group includes an assessment of communication and interpersonal actions, patterns within the group, the alignments and divisions between members, and the roles members are undertaking as part of the group. It is important in this process not to lose track of how individuals behave and react to one another. Relationships and loyalties may shift throughout the life of the group, and these must constantly be assessed in order to enable the group to move forward. Undertaking this kind of assessment requires a lot of understanding about group work in general. How individuals interact with one another and the effect these interactions have on the group deserve special consideration.

Assessment of the Group Environment: Assessment of the group environment is contingent at least in large part on the assessment of the individuals and of the group as a whole. The group environment, or one in which successful group work is occurring, requires ongoing work by both the social worker and group members. A group environment needs to allow for open and direct discussion while providing its members safety. An environment characterized by interpersonal criticism and hostility is unlikely to encourage members to open up and share their feelings and thoughts.

Middle Stage

With the completion of the initial phase of group work, the middle or working stage begins. Note that not all groups move into the middle stage. For a variety of reasons, some groups can become stuck in the initial stage and never move beyond the superficial or away from power and control issues. This is not necessarily a reflection on the worker's skill; it may be attributed to who the group members are or to their reluctance to invest themselves in the group. The middle stage of group work is when members are most often confronted with the difficulties of working through their issues or their tasks. This is the stage of intimacy and differentiation, a time when most of the group work is done. During the working stage, the social worker needs to help move the group through the process so that they are "straightforwardly addressing and resolving conflict, openly disclosing personal problems, taking responsibility for their problems and making pro-group choices" (Hepworth et al., 2002, p. 537).

Brandler and Roman (1999) suggest that the middle stage consists of three parts: "(1) an early phase closely related to beginnings during which residual issues are evident, (2) a middle phase during which the group struggles to separate from the beginning issues and proceed with the work of the group, and (3) a final phase during which separation from beginnings is effected and group cohesiveness is achieved, which allows for working through all developmental tasks specific to middles" (p. 42).

Early Middle Stage: During the early part of the middle stage, members are often concerned with some of the issues from the initial stage such as "trust, testing, approach and avoidance, and clarification of contract" (Brandler & Roman, 1999, p. 42). These activities slowly begin to change from cautious and hesitant into ones that are more confrontational and connected. Individuals begin to become comfortable with one another and feel freer to "have direct and meaningful interactions with one another including confrontations" (Corey et al., 2004). Group members become more comfortable sharing personal information and dealing with conflicts. It is a period when the worker needs to be gently pushing the members along. Encouraging their open conversation and discussion of feelings leads the members into more intimacy with one another.

Middle Middle Stage: During this period, the group becomes more spontaneous and open to working with one another about intimate issues (Brandler & Roman, 1999). Focus is on the here-and-now and the there-and-then. By this we mean that what is happening in the group (here-and-now) is associated with what is happening in the real world (there-and-then). Group members move toward the achievement of the task or the resolution of the problem. This is the time when cohesion is critical to the group's success. Cohesion is the sense of connection or bond that group members have with one another. When cohesion is present, the members identify with the group and with one another (Shulman, 1999). Cohesive groups maintain their memberships, complete tasks, solve problems, conform more to norms, and resolve issues between members in safe and secure ways. Cohesiveness is a positive aspect of the group in that it indicates the positive affiliation between members and the ability of members to listen to one another. This group stage encourages "a level of cohesion that allows for two or more individuals to work simultaneously on common issues, as opposed to members' taking turns by doing their individual work in a group setting" (Corey et al., 2004, p. 131).

During this stage, group members have honest and open conversations with one another, including confrontation. "Conflict in the group is now accepted as part of the process, and members do not fear it" (Corey et al., 2004, p. 131). Through this process of confrontation and dealing with the here-and-now, members begin to resolve issues and complete tasks. Members distinguish more clearly between group goals and individual goals. Members begin to differentiate themselves from the group and focus on their personal growth or accomplishments. Although they continue to support the group, they also individualize their work in the group.

End Middle Stage: In the end of the middle stage, group members are working more and more through their own issues and achieving the goals they have set for themselves and the group. The major goal of this work is accomplishing the goals and feeling satisfied with the group's work. There is a "heightened awareness and intensity in the work" (Brandler & Roman, 1999, p. 45) as individuals move toward separation and termination.

In treatment groups,

> the primary task of the worker during the middle stage is to help members accomplish the goals they have contracted to achieve, which is accomplished by (1) helping members overcome obstacles to goal achievement in their own lives, (2) facilitating group dynamics that support members' efforts, and (3) helping the organization and the larger community to respond to members' efforts. (Toseland & Rivas, 2001, p. 255)

In task groups, there is more concern with "creating new ideas, developing plans and programs, solving problems that are external to the group, and making decisions about the organizational environment" (Toseland & Rivas, 2001, p. 323). Brandler and Roman (1999, p. 46) suggest that the social worker's responsibilities during this middle stage require them to be able to do several things, including clarify communication; mediate differences; confront group members; identify commonalities to build deeper levels of cohesiveness, mutuality, and bonding; and identify and respect difference to build independence and individuality.

1. **Clarify Communication.** The social worker's role in clarifying communication requires an understanding of the use of role reversal and "I" statements. It is up to the social worker during this stage to help group members reflect on what has been said and how they heard it. The social worker may also help members respond. Although during the middle stage members are becoming more and more independent, the worker still has a significant role in helping members think through what they heard and to structure responses that reflect the members' thinking and feelings. Helping members to further clarify their roles or the changing of their roles in the group is another responsibility of the social worker. As members begin to identify new roles, the worker will help them implement those roles in the group.

2. **Mediate Differences.** During this middle stage, more and more differences between group members will emerge as the cohesion in the group makes talking about differences less risky. The worker helps resolve disputes and bring group members to a consensus. Compton and Galaway (1999) suggest that the social worker must help members see one another's points of view and the value of them. The social worker brings the members together to a mutually agreeable decision and highlights the importance of the relationship among the members.

3. **Confront Group Members.** Confrontation is used during the middle stage to move individual members and the group as a whole further along in their goals. It helps members deal with resistance and motivation (Toseland & Rivas, 2001). Confrontation can be very difficult. Workers as well as members are often hesitant to confront one another on issues because of the negative responses and reactions it can bring. However, confrontation, when done

in an empathic way, can be productive (see Chapter 12). Starting the confrontation with a positive statement about the person helps prepare the individual for the confrontation. For example, a social worker may want to tell a member that he or she is being extremely negative about what is happening in the group. The social worker might say, "I can sense how angry you are with the group's situation. Let's talk about that anger because it's coming out in the group as negativity right now and bringing other people down."

4. **Identify Commonalities to Build Deeper Levels of Cohesiveness, Mutuality, and Bonding.** It is important during this stage to bring out commonalities among the members. One member might be struggling with confusion over the task to be accomplished while another member is feeling left out of the activities. The worker might bring these two individuals closer together by saying, "It seems as though both you and John are struggling with the project. Perhaps the two of you could talk to the group about how you would like to work toward its completion." In other cases, using words of praise and validating the members' experiences in the group can build cohesiveness. Taking an interest in each individual and encouraging them to support one another also creates bonding. You might say, "Jim, you are doing such a good job of sharing your experiences. I think Bonnie has a similar situation in her relationship with her husband. Perhaps you could ask Bonnie some questions that would help her share her experiences in a similar way."

5. **Identify and Respect Differences to Build Independence and Individuality.** This skill

requires social workers to use their "use of self." Responding authentically to members of the group and sharing empathetically encourages members' independence and open communication with other group members. Additionally, the social worker will want to identify members' differences, not just their similarities. At this point in the group, differentiation needs to begin. Differentiation calls for members to begin to identify themselves as separate from the group. This movement from close intimacy to the identification of self is much like the process that occurs during childhood. For differentiation to occur, there must be a strong supportive foundation that encourages this to happen. The social worker, in helping bring about this differentiation, needs to be sensitive to each member and to encourage his or her personal growth. For example, the social worker might say, "Carol, you have really worked hard today on your fear. I am sure this way of dealing with your fears will carry over into your work and home situations."

In Case Example 11.1 we can see that strong emotions are beginning to emerge. The worker is using the emotions to help family members begin to deal with one another. There are similarities in all the families and Mr. Sampson has correctly pinpointed what is going on by noting that there is something no one wants to talk about. The worker uses this opening to lead the Sampson family into a discussion of what this is about and then to use this discussion to help other families and their members think about their own elephants.

End Stage

The ending stage is a significant one for group members. As the group moves into this stage,

CASE EXAMPLE 11.1

Middle Group Stage

The following is an example of a middle stage interaction in a group. This is the group Maria Hernandez in the opening vignette formed composed of four families dealing with drug and alcohol abuse.

Practitioner: Last week we talked about how the use of alcohol is often stimulated by peer pressure among friends at school. We know that some individuals may be able to handle the use of alcohol, whereas others are not. What are some of the things you have been thinking about in regard to this fact?

Mr. Sampson: I know my son just can't seem to quit. He's addicted and other kids aren't. Is it because he drinks more? What causes that?

Practitioner: We do not always know why a specific individual becomes addicted. However, there is strong evidence that some people are capable of developing an addiction to any number of substances. This susceptibility to addiction can be influenced by several factors including genetics, life experiences, personality, and peer influences.

Mr. Covey: I heard that sometimes drug and alcohol abuse can be hereditary. Is that true?

And if so, I don't know where my daughter could be getting it from.

Sandy Covey (age 16): Yeah, right! Like you and Mom don't drink!

Practitioner: It sounds like you are angry with your parents, Sandy. I wonder if others are feeling the same way. Is anyone angry with someone in their family?

Mike Todd (age 15): I'm angry at my Dad. He's always drinking, and then he calls me a drunk. I wish he would just look at himself.

Mr. Todd: I'm not the problem; you are. At least it's legal for me to drink!

Practitioner: It sounds like there is a lot of anger going on in most of the families. How do you deal with anger?

Mrs. Todd: I don't like to fight, so I try to make sure it doesn't get out of hand. Like yesterday, Mike was upstairs reading a book and his Dad wanted him to rake the leaves. They got into a shouting match and neither of them got what he wanted.

Practitioner: It's difficult when there are drug and alcohol problems in families, and sometimes that makes us angry

at a lot of things. What do you think, Mr. Todd?

Mr. Todd: I know I haven't been able to be in a good mood since Mike started drinking too much like he does.

Mr. Sampson: I know what you mean. It's like this big elephant in the room that no one wants to talk about, so we fight about other things. Stupid things.

Mr. Covey: I don't want to fight with her, but that seems to be all we do.

Practitioner: It sounds like there is a lot of anger and a lot of fighting going on at home. Let's try to deal with just one situation and see what we all can learn. Mr. Sampson, you said it was like a big elephant in the room. I think you mean the drinking Sheri is doing. Is that right?

Mr. Sampson: Yeah, but really any of the drinking that goes on in the house. It's like everyone is afraid to talk about it.

Practitioner: Let's have the family talk to one another about it now. Would you like to start, Mr. Sampson?

they will be completing their work on both a practical and an emotional level depending on the type of group. In task groups, the products (e.g., reports, recommendations) of the group are completed, and discussion of the results and their implementation become key (Toseland & Rivas, 2001). In treatment groups, individual growth is reviewed and decisions on how to maintain these changes are made (Toseland & Rivas, 2001).

Social workers need to be very aware during this stage of the reactions to termination. A group that has been working steadily and accomplished success on both individual and group levels may return to argument and denial of the group's success. These are all reactions to the process of termination. In task groups, the risk of these kinds of reactions is not as great. In treatment groups, however, individuals have shared deep personal issues, which has led to intimacy among group members. The loss of this type of deep relationship can cause strong emotional reactions. Recognizing that some members will react negatively is important to being able to handle the termination process.

Corey and colleagues (2004, p. 164) suggest that the following tasks need to be completed during the ending stage:

- Members are encouraged to face the inevitable ending of the group and to discuss fully their feelings of separation.
- Members are encouraged to complete any unfinished business they have with other members or the leaders.
- Members are taught how to leave the group and how to carry with them what they have learned and especially how to talk to significant people in their lives.
- Members are assisted in making specific plans for change and in taking concrete steps to put the lessons they have learned into effect in their daily lives.

- Leaders help members discover ways of creating their own support systems after they leave the group.
- Specific plans for follow-up work and evaluation are made.
- Consideration is given to how members might discount a group experience and to teach members relapse prevention strategies.

Although several of these tasks are reflective only of treatment groups, the majority can be relevant for task groups as well. These tasks highlight the importance of the ending stage and its relevance to continuing the success achieved in previous stages. Communication in the ending stage tends to concentrate on the evaluation of the group, review of the group's and members' accomplishments, and plans for what will happen after the group. Attention to things outside of the group become more important, and the relationships built during the other stages of the group process begin to wane.

Case Example 11.2 shows a therapeutic group in the ending stage of group development. This is an outpatient group for individuals going through divorce. From this example we can see how some group members discount their changes while others feel positive about themselves. The worker asked for other group members' opinions when talking with Henry. Henry related to Bob, and Bob's opinion seemed to have the most effect on Henry. This was an example of the importance of reviewing and evaluating the work that was done by highlighting changes that have occurred.

Multicultural Issues in Group Work

Multicultural issues are important factors to consider when doing group work. Social

CASE EXAMPLE 11.2

Ending Group Stage

Practitioner: Well, we have two more weeks to work together. I think it would be good to discuss how we've done with our goals for the group and for each of us personally.

Karla: I feel like I have accomplished several things, including getting control of my anger at my ex-husband.

Terri: I don't think I have gotten over my anger, but it is better to be angry than depressed like I was when I started group.

Practitioner: It sounds as if both of you have moved on to different places with the divorce.

Henry: I wish I could say the same thing. I don't feel any different than I did when I came in. I think I've made some friends, but I don't think it has helped.

Practitioner: That must feel very disappointing to you. What do others think about this?

Bob: I don't know if you have changed much or not. I suppose only you might know. But I think you talk a lot more in group than when you first came, and you have helped me with some of my issues.

Karla: I think you have changed. You seem much more interested in things than you did before.

Practitioner: It sounds like some are seeing changes in you. What do you think about that, Henry?

Henry: I suppose it could be true. I know Bob and I have worked on similar issues, and he seems to be moving forward. I just don't know about myself.

---

workers must themselves be willing to look at their own ways of viewing and interacting with members from different cultural backgrounds. It is critical for social workers to be in touch with their own identity and the ways in which diversity affects them and other members of a group. Corey (2004) states that "multicultural counseling focuses on understanding not only racial and ethnic minority groups (African American, Asian Americans, Latinos, Native Americans, and white ethnics) but also women, gay men and lesbians, people with physical disabilities, elderly people, and a variety of special needs populations" (p. 15). This broad-based definition of multiculturalism places the social worker in the position of needing to acknowledge these differences and share the value of diversity with the group.

In this diverse pluralistic society, social workers will be dealing with many different forms of diversity when working with groups. Research suggests that this is a positive factor. For example, McLeod, Lobel, and Cox (1996) found that groups with racially diverse members outperformed those that included only whites. These findings suggest, in large part, that it is in the best interest of the group if there is diversity and if the social worker knows how to use it in a productive manner. A logical first step is to acknowledge the diversity among the group members. Talking about this diversity as an asset because of the variety of perspectives it brings to the issues in the

Voices from the Field

I am a thirty-six-year-old African American male currently completing my MSW from Grand Valley State University in Grand Rapids, Michigan. I am also employed as an eligibility specialist for the Family Independence Agency (formerly Department of Social Services), where I work with a diverse population of clients seeking assistance from federal and state low-income programs and services. As an African American male working in the field of social work, I am a rarity. Many of my coworkers and colleagues speak in theory about cultural awareness and diversity, yet they cannot make the connection from textbooks to clients. Our profession at times has not re-

Kenneth McCoy

flected the diversity that we promote in our mission statements and organizational philosophy. Thus, creating a homogenous profession in thought, theory, and demographics often does not reflect those whom the profession seeks to help. I work to help fill this void in our profession. I look to offer an African American male's perspective, not to challenge what currently exists, but to enhance the way we help. My education, experience, and training have given me the tools and confidence to effectively help those whose voices often go unheard. As social workers, we have an obligation to be leaders in helping bring about change for all.

group is one way of introducing the subject. Another way to begin the discussion is to ask members to identify some personal characteristics about their cultural background and how these might influence them in the group. Some group members will not identify with their cultural background, and meeting others who do have a strong connection may put them in touch with their own. For example, in a group made up of different cultures and racial backgrounds, the social worker asked members to speak about their own cultures. After two or three Hispanic members from the neighborhood had spoken, another Hispanic member noted that he had not thought about the reasons why he reacted as he did, but in listening to his neighbors he could also iden-

tify with the cultural norms and roles that affected him.

Social workers need to have knowledge not only about their own culture but also about the cultures of others with whom they will work. To know only your own culture does a disservice to those individuals from different backgrounds. There are many ways to gain knowledge about other cultures. Reading literature and information on the culture is a good place to start. Probably the most effective way is to place yourself in one-on-one relationships with those with whom you will work. Asking for help in understanding a different cultural background is another effective way to get started building one's knowledge.

Social workers need to be sensitive to how the diverse cultures in a group may work together. For example, cultural tensions among or between specific groups may inhibit their ability to work together in a group format. Differences in interpersonal interactions and behavior may pose special problems. Members for whom eye contact is important may fail to understand why people of another culture consider regular eye contact to be rude or intrusive. Those who do not believe in talking about feelings may find the pressure of other members to share emotions to be inappropriate. Men and women have different ways of communicating that may pose a problem when males dominate a meeting or use confrontation in ways that female members find abusive.

Group members from cultures that believe in and use natural helpers such as folk healers may find other members suspicious or disparaging of these approaches. Those who attribute emotional illness to spirits or other atypical sources may be seen as odd by those with no knowledge of such belief systems. These and

APPLICATIONS TO PRACTICE

Case Example

Your hospital psychiatric center has just opened and you will be in charge of the patient meetings, both reporting the goals for the inpatient treatment and running the groups on the unit. The hospital has a contract to provide inpatient services to veterans of the recent Iraqi combat who are having trouble readjusting to the community, their family, and/or employment. The psychiatrist wants the team to discuss the patient first and then have the patient come in; you would then deliver the decision. You would like to have the patient in on the discussion to hear what staff members are reporting. You know that some of the patients might not be able to actively participate but think as many as possible should be given the opportunity. You have gotten the psychiatrist to agree to a trial plan of including all patients in the team discussion, with the proviso that if he doesn't want a particular patient to attend you will not oppose his decision. The two of you have a good relationship, and he has agreed that the decision to exclude the patient will be the exception. He will discuss his decision with you after the reviews.

Critical Thinking Questions

1. How will you prepare the staff for the patient assessment meetings?
2. What explanation will you give regarding which patients will attend and which will not?
3. What data do you want to collect and report?
4. At what point will you want to discuss the development of a standard protocol regarding the patients?

Research Activity

Using the Research Navigator™ website, www.research navigator.com, find psycho-educational group programs for families who might benefit from drug and alcohol education. Develop a rough outline of an eight-session format and be prepared to discuss the information in class.

other differences offer a wonderful opportunity for group members to become more culturally aware and to break down some of the we–they feelings that differences sometimes engender.

One way of helping to bridge cultural gaps in groups is to recognize the vast commonalities among people regardless of their background. For example, most groups value the family as an important institution and most benefit from the informal resources that families can provide. All individuals develop coping skills and mechanisms that are designed to allow them to deal with sometimes unbearable personal losses and challenges. Group members can be helped to understand that some behaviors that appear unusual are simply attempts to manage difficult events and experiences. Ultimately, social work clients of whatever race, ethnicity, gender, or sexual orientation are likely to have to grapple with a common set of problems and possess a variety of strengths that can be brought into play.

Social workers also need to be aware that some of their commonly employed approaches may prove ineffective or counterproductive with certain groups. Harper and Lantz (1996), for example, point out that offering gay and lesbian clients traditional resources may be a mistake. Agencies and practitioners who commonly help straight clients may contribute to the discrimination and maltreatment that gay men and lesbian women frequently encounter. Mixing gay and straight members in a group may or may not be wise, depending on the other members' ability to tolerate differences. The strong prejudices and negative attitudes toward gay men and lesbian women of some group members may render such an otherwise appropriate intervention ineffective.

SUMMARY

This chapter focuses on how social workers use groups for task and treatment purposes.

Issues of leadership are discussed with respect to both task and treatment groups. Topics include leadership in task groups, task group composition, and procedures and exercises useful for decision making in task groups.

The chapter also discusses leadership and group composition in treatment groups, along with a variety of techniques and exercises for dealing with situations that occur in these groups. Group development is described starting with the beginning stages and running through to the end stage. Assessment of individuals, the group as a whole, and the group environment are covered in this context. Finally, the chapter identifies salient points about cultural diversity in groups and the benefits and risks associated with group differences.

Navigating Direct Practice

An access code for Research Navigator™ is packaged within your text. Use this code to register at www.researchnavigator.com and then use the key words listed below to research articles related to the chapter's content. Research Navigator™ helps you quickly and efficiently make the most of your research time.

❏ American Association of Social Workers
❏ Jane Addams
❏ Parliamentary procedure
❏ National Association of Social Workers
❏ Rivas
❏ Toseland

Chapter 12

Intervention with Larger Systems

■ Reuben Johnson had talked himself blue in the face. Despite two full years of quiet discussions and negotiations with city officials, no progress had been made in getting an elevator installed in Elm Grove City Hall. The mayor and other officials stated they simply did not have the money to add an elevator to the seventy-five-year-old building, a former post office. As director for Disability Advocates, a not-for-profit organization dedicated to improving services for people with physical disabilities, Reuben had found these two years frustrating.

Meeting with his board of directors, Reuben laid out the situation and sought their feedback. "Should I bag it and accept the city's arguments or try something new? I'm not sure what else I can do," he told board members. "What do you recommend?" Fred Valesquez, chairperson of the board, spoke first. "Reuben, the name of our organization is Disability Advocates, and I think we need to crank up our advocacy efforts to the next level." Other members echoed a similar refrain, and by the end of the meeting Reuben had a new strategy approved by his board—namely, social action.

Over the next few weeks, Reuben coordinated a series of activities designed to achieve his goal. First, people with disabilities in the community began a letter-writing campaign targeting both the newspapers and city officials. Members of the city council received dozens of letters urging them to make City Hall accessible to people with disabilities. A group of individuals with physical disabilities met the editor and editorial board of the local newspaper and asked them to support their effort. This led to a newspaper editorial urging the city to find the funds for an elevator.

In addition, every meeting of the city council was attended by citizens committed to the goal of making City Hall accessible. In fact, so many chose to attend that the city had to move the meetings to a local gymnasium. Local television stations that normally only summarized city council meetings began to cover the meetings in more detail. Reuben and others spoke passionately about the need for the city to help its citizens with disabilities participate fully in city activities. After two months of nearly relentless attention to the topic, the mayor and city council agreed to use funds from the city's contingency account to pay for installation of an elevator. Six months later, Reuben joined city officials at a public ribbon-cutting ceremony announcing the opening of the new elevator. Once again, advocacy had paid off for Reuben and his organization.

Direct practice, while focusing primarily on working directly with individuals, families, and groups, sometimes requires the social worker to intervene with larger systems such as organizations and communities. The need to intervene with organizations and communities is often related to barriers that impede the ability of client systems to effectively and efficiently meet their needs. When this occurs, direct practitioners may become involved in eliminating the environmental barriers that prevent people from getting access to needed resources and services. The barriers may be physical, as in the preceding case, or in the form of policies and procedures, uncoordinated delivery of services, or other obstacles. Typically, direct practitioners are expected to devote their time primarily to meeting the psychosocial needs of their clients. As we have seen in earlier chapters, the focus tends to be on helping clients who are experiencing intrapersonal and interpersonal problems. Efforts are devoted to assisting people by developing and strengthening their coping skills, empowering them to help themselves, and improving family and group functioning. This is the reason for the existence of a large proportion of the social agencies in which social workers are employed.

However, sometimes the only way to accomplish one or more of these goals is to help clients deal with environmental barriers blocking their progress. In this chapter, we cover several aspects of modifying environmental barriers. As the first step, we identify the kinds of barriers that clients and social workers may encounter. Then we look at the most basic role social workers play in larger systems, namely working for improved coordination of services. In particular, this chapter examines the role of case manager in great detail.

The next large system intervention role discussed is that of advocate. Being an advocate for a client is identified as a direct practice role in Chapter 1. The level and degree of advocacy carried out by direct practitioners will depend on a variety of factors and requires them to have specific knowledge and skills to be effective.

This chapter also looks at other environmental change strategies including social action, social planning, and organizational change. The chapter concludes with a discussion of how cultural and diversity issues affect these activities.

Although the emphasis in the remainder of this chapter is on activities with larger systems such as communities and organizations, it is crucial to remember that the universal skills used in working with individuals remain applicable to other areas of social work practice. Good listening skills, genuineness, empathy, and the ability to summarize, for example, are just as useful whether approaching individual clients or community decision makers. These skills discussed in Chapter 4 and those covered in Chapter 7 (i.e., partialization and strengths-based practice) can be effective when dealing with legislators, agency administrators, or others connected with environmental barriers. In the end, these skills apply regardless of the size of system with which the social worker is working.

Identifying Barriers

Environmental barriers can take many forms ranging from clearly visible obstacles such as the missing elevator to very subtle, almost invisible items that achieve the same outcome. The NASW Code of Ethics, introduced in Chapter 3, says, "the primary mission of the social work profession is to enhance human well-being and help meet the basic human needs of all people, with particular attention to the needs and empowerment of people who are vulnerable and oppressed, and living in poverty" (1999, p. 1). In addition, "fundamental to social work is attention to the environmental forces that create, contribute to, and address problems in living" (1999, p. 1). Clearly, social workers are obligated to help clients overcome barriers that interfere with their "well-being" or attainment of "basic human needs." To accomplish this goal requires several things of social workers, the first of which is to recognize when these barriers are operating. Unfortunately, multiple barriers can exist. The following pages highlight a few of the more troublesome ones: (1) physical, (2) policy and procedural, (3) emotional/social, (4) cultural, and (5) informational.

Physical Barriers

Spotting physical barriers is sometimes easy. In the case that opened this chapter, the absence of an elevator created multiple problems for people with disabilities. City services located on upper floors were simply inaccessible, meaning that those with disabilities had less opportunity to avail themselves of these resources. Even going to court was a problem for those with physical disabilities. They either had to be carried to court or those with more mobility had to crawl up the stairs to the courtroom. The easiest environmental barriers to recognize are those that physically prevent clients from exercising the same rights as other members of society. Although the advent of the Americans with Disabilities Act has produced substantial access for many people, there remain thousands of public facilities with no or limited access for those with disabilities. This includes buildings owned by various levels of government as well as restaurants, other recreational facilities, and housing.

In addition, there are likely many more thousands of facilities to which access is severely limited. For example, those using accessible entrances must often travel hundreds of feet farther than other users because only a portion of a building's entrances have doors that open automatically or at the touch of a button. Existing elevators may be too small to handle a motorized wheelchair or the building has no signage printed in braille. Bathrooms are not accessible or the only bathroom available is on a different floor. The fact that social workers can recognize these shortcomings illustrates the fact that a practitioner does not have to wait for the client to point out a barrier before taking action to deal with it.

Unfortunately, many people are oblivious to physical barriers because, lacking a particular disability, they do not see something as an obstacle. For example, those with normal hearing may not consider that their office's audible fire alarm system is a potential problem for those with a hearing disability. People who are deaf will not hear the alarm when it sounds. Adding a visual alarm to the system would be an important way to help hearing-impaired clients and workers. When clients bring such shortcomings to the attention of the social worker, the practitioner is obligated to try to help them overcome these barriers.

Sometimes no one thinks about a potential problem until it actually develops. In the middle of a fire alarm, for example, everyone left the building except for a client in a wheelchair. He was on his way back to his social worker's office when the alarm sounded and, unfamiliar with the building layout, became confused. The elevator that had brought him to the second floor automatically shut off when the fire alarm sounded. He was effectively stranded in a back hallway with no way to exit the building. No one had thought about this problem beforehand, and the absence of an agency plan for helping these individuals in the event of a fire could have been catastrophic. Fortunately, the incident convinced the staff to develop a proactive plan to ensure that everyone would be able to get out of the building when necessary. As this case illustrates, lack of foresight can be a major problem that creates or perpetuates physical barriers for clients.

Another major stumbling block in many communities is the lack of adequate transportation permitting clients to access available services. Social workers can help address this problem by encouraging agencies to locate services on public transportation routes or close to other services that their clientele is likely to use. Another option is to offer transportation vouchers or other financial assistance in getting to the agency. At the very least, social workers must be capable of anticipating transportation barriers and their potential impact on clients.

Policy and Procedural Barriers

Some barriers are incorporated in policies and procedures of agencies and other service providers. Laws that prohibit social workers from explaining all of a client's options because legislators imposed their own religious beliefs on everybody else are another example. So are laws and policies that prevent undocumented workers from receiving public services or those that restrict abortion to cases only in which the mother's life is at risk.

Another policy barrier to accessing services affects women clients of childbearing age. The lack of available child care is a major issue for these women because most programs make no provisions for this dilemma (Kline, 1996). To give an example of how important this factor can be, a study by the National Center on Addiction and Substance Abuse (1996) found that when child care was provided for women in treatment for substance abuse, the mothers were five times more likely to continue treatment for a full year. In addition, they stayed three times as long as women not provided this service.

Other policy and procedural barriers are much harder to detect. Again, clients may alert practitioners to their existence, as when they point out that a particular agency turns away Spanish-speaking clients because they have no translators available. Although the agency director may not consciously set out to cause a problem for these clients, the failure to anticipate their needs is no less a barrier.

At other times, barriers are discovered when a client fails to recognize a resource. This can happen when an agency actively tries to keep a low profile and discourages certain clients from using its services. For example, Burnette (1999) identified lack of knowledge about the existence of health and social service providers as "the most frequently named barrier to service use" (p. 28) by custodial grandparents from Latino families.

The antidote to this shortcoming is, of course, expanding awareness of the services and resources provided by specific agencies. Another method involves encouraging agencies to engage in outreach activities designed to inform and assist clients in the use of the available resources (Burnette, 1999).

Sometimes barriers reflect the individual or collective biases of those who work in the community. An example that tends to affect minority populations occurs periodically in the law enforcement arena. Although not official police policy, some law enforcement agencies actively engage in the practice of stopping African American drivers for what is called DWB (driving while black). In such situations, the police automatically stop people of color driving in certain neighborhoods on the assumption that they do not belong there. When concerned members of the community recognize these discriminatory practices, it can lead to advocacy for changes in law enforcement. Advocacy, an important tool for direct practitioners, is discussed later in this chapter.

Emotional/Social Barriers

Sometimes the barriers to client use of existing services are located within the individual and family. For example, people in need often do not use services that could help them. This may arise from embarrassment about needing help or it may reflect fear of bringing shame on one's family. Some people equate accepting help with taking charity, and many are too proud to do this even if their needs are desperate. Some members of society exacerbate this reluctance by holding and expressing negative attitudes toward those seeking welfare or other forms of public assistance. Even the reactions of grocery store checkers to clients paying for their food with food stamps can discourage using this form of help. The messages that social workers convey to clients when we greet them can have a positive or negative effect on their willingness to return.

Emotional barriers for clients may be increased or lessened just by the actions of social workers. If practitioners express interest in clients' ideas and seek to involve them fully in the change process, they help to reduce clients' emotional barriers. For example, Kruzich, Friesen, Williams-Murphy, and Longley (2002), in a study of African American families with children in residential treatment centers, found a great deal of variance in how the centers treated parents. Some encouraged family involvement in treatment planning, whereas others showed little interest in communicating with families about their children. Many parents felt a lack of respect from the staff, whom they perceived as not valuing them. As noted in a later section on cultural barriers, the poor quality of service and questionable practices experienced by many cultural groups help create a reluctance to use services that are otherwise appropriate. Such artificial barriers are just as real and problematic for these clients as if the agency had placed a concrete barrier in their way.

Cultural Barriers

Another invisible barrier occurs when certain client groups are at greater risk for specific problems and society has not attempted to address those risks. For example, the death rate from alcohol-related causes for Native American women is higher than for other women, and "Hispanics/Latinas come in second highest in use of alcohol, binge drinking, and heavy alcohol use" (Coridan & O'Connell, 2002, p. 4). At the same time, African Americans tend to have a higher prevalence of mental disorders than whites but are underrepresented as outpatients and overrepresented in inpatient facilities (U.S. Department of Health and Human Services, 2000). The stigma associated with getting help for substance abuse and other mental health disorders suggests the importance of using outreach and other marketing efforts, particularly involving practitioners from these groups.

Practitioners should also be aware of the ways in which social programs create problems for certain groups of clients. For example, when agencies provide coeducational treatment programs for women substance abusers, they often use the same methods they use with men. This practice often sets up women to fail. The high occurrence of past child sexual and physical abuse among this population places these women at risk, particularly in recovery groups that practice a high degree of confrontation. Women clients often find this approach a reminder of past abuse, which in turn causes them to lose trust in social workers and agency services (Wright & Donoghue, 1997).

Further, Kruzich and her colleagues (2002), in the study mentioned earlier, found that African American families facing out-of-home placement of their children experienced concerns different from those of non–African American families. These included doubts about whether the children's placement would be beneficial, worries about staff overmedicating their children, and fears about the lack of cultural competence of those working with their children. A related concern was stereotyping by staff, along with concerns that their children would be misdiagnosed and labeled based largely on the child's ethnicity. It is easy to understand how experiences such as these would discourage clients from exploring or using resources they see as unresponsive. It is also easy to recognize how social workers demonstrating an interest in clients and empowering them through involvement in case planning and treatment can help alleviate such trepidation. Chapter 9 discusses empowerment strategies in greater detail.

African American clients and their families also face related barriers that can prevent them from receiving critical services. Evidence suggests that these families receive unequal treatment from mental health providers. For instance, African American clients often get more cursory assessments coupled with more severe diagnoses. In addition, they are "more likely to receive psychiatric medications, more doses, and more injections of antipsychotic medication than were Caucasian" clients (Segal, Bola, & Watson, 1996, p. 284). This is particularly significant when viewed in light of a surgeon general's report that many ethnic minority patients need *lower* doses of such medications (U.S. Department of Health and Human Services, 2001).

Anxiety among potential African American clients about over- or inappropriate medication prescription can work as a powerful disincentive to seek out mental health resources. Social work practitioners should be sensitive to how such fears can serve as a barrier to clients seeking help. In addition, social workers can play a role in helping clients better understand why a given medication is being used, along with how it works and any side effects.

Along with these issues in the mental health area are similar problematic treatments in other areas of practice. For example, African American children are more than twice as likely to be placed in special education programs in schools than their numbers in the population would suggest. In addition, they are much more likely to receive corporal punishment (Harry & Anderson, 1994). Similar findings exist for African American adolescents, who are more likely to be placed in the juvenile justice system or in other out-of-home settings (McCabe et al., 1999). The different treatment received by African American clients clearly creates unnecessary barriers to their use of various social services. Few clients would willingly seek out services that actively discriminate against them on the basis of their skin color or other cultural factors.

Other barriers to service exist for specific groups of clients. For example, Ying (2001) found that despite increased risk of mental health problems for refugees from Southeast Asia, many obstacles impede their ability to get needed help. These include lack of accessible services; agencies that rely primarily on concrete rather than psychosocial services; and clients who have little, if any, awareness of mental health, mental illness, and its treatment. The result of these barriers is that clients needing help seek out physicians or natural healers. Moreover, the delay in getting services in such situations can exacerbate the original symptoms.

Informational Barriers

Perhaps the most common barrier to using resources available in the environment is simple lack of knowledge of their existence. Individuals new to a community are less likely to be familiar with the types of resources that might be available. This is especially a problem for refugees and others arriving from areas where social service resources are generally nonexistent. Of course, social services are not the only resources about which clients may need information. Others might include inexpensive sources of clothing, food, and household items (Ying, 2001). Clients may also need help with knowing how to use public transportation, where to enroll a child in school, and the existence and location of support groups for clients experiencing similar challenges.

It is entirely possible that a new social worker will not know of pertinent resources in a community, which makes seeking consultation and supervision important activities for the novice. Generally, agency staff with longer service will be able to help new workers identify potential resources or, at the very least, point them in the right direction. New workers can also make use of local and national resource directories, including those available on the Internet. The latter resources can be particularly helpful when documenting the needs of particular client groups such as minorities or families in poverty.

When working with certain refugee populations, in particular those who may encounter multiple health care providers, the social worker can serve as an educator helping clients understand the differences among health practitioners. This helps produce clients who are more aware of their options while orienting them to a process that may be completely foreign to them. It is also appropriate to tell clients that others in their situation have sought help from various community resources. This can help lessen the social stigma some cultures associate with mental health problems.

Whether social workers discover them or clients bring barriers to the practitioner's attention, the important thing is to acknowledge their existence and determine what strategies would be most effective in eliminating the obstacles. As already noted, barriers can take many forms, ranging from those that are visible to those that cannot be known without working directly with clients. Social workers can help overcome many of these barriers through direct practice with clients. Others will need to assume an advocacy role, an approach addressed later in this chapter. Sometimes the barriers can be resolved through coordination and case management activities.

Case Management and Coordination

Some of the barriers clients face evolve from the multiple organizations or agencies providing needed services. For example, it is not unusual for certain clients to need services or resources provided by various agencies in a community. These might include counseling, medication, housing, financial aid, and emotional support. Without careful coordination, clients may fall through the cracks between different agencies, never receiving the help they need. One of the approaches used in such situations is known as **case management**. Case management is designed to coordinate the provision of services from multiple sources for the benefit of the individual client. Rothman (2002) defines *case management* as "a service for highly vulnerable client populations to ensure that they receive the help they need within the fragmented American service delivery system" (p. 467). Too often, clients find their access to resources impeded and require the assistance of social workers who provide case management services. Clients who fall into these situations include those with chronic mental health diagnoses such as schizophrenia, people with severe physical or developmental disabilities such as brain trauma and mental retardation, or the frail elderly. Clients with some of these conditions will require services throughout their lives if they are to remain in the least restrictive environment. In addition, case management services have been used in the child welfare field, particularly with respect to permanency planning (Mather & Hull, 2002). Here the goal is to ensure that every effort is made to help keep families together and make sure that each child has the opportunity to live in a stable home. Achieving this requires a type of service that integrates and coordinates all aspects of work on behalf of the client system.

Rothman (2002) and other authors (Walsh, 2000; Rose, 1992; Frankel & Gelman, 2004) identify a series of activities that case managers perform in order to achieve the goal of ensuring that clients receive needed services: (1) case finding, (2) assessing the client's needs, (3) establishing appropriate goals, (4) planning the intervention, (5) linking clients with resources, (6) monitoring and reassessment, and finally (7) evaluation. As should be evident, these steps also characterize the problem-solving process used routinely in social work.

Case Finding

Case finding is concerned with ensuring that those who need case management services have access to them. Sometimes this process is straightforward, as when other agencies or individuals refer the client to you or your agency. At other times, outreach is needed in the form of notifying other agencies and organizations about the availability of an agency's services. This could involve sending fliers or letters announcing case management services or speaking to groups that might know of clients needing this type of help. The bottom line is that without knowing about the availability of

case management, clients cannot use the resource.

Assessing Client Needs

Assessing client needs includes identifying the client's situation and challenges as well as considering the extent to which your own agency's services match a client's needs. If it is clear that the client will benefit most from the services of another agency, a referral is provided. If, on the other hand, the client requires case management services, then you have a potential match. During the assessment process, social workers gather pertinent biopsychosocial/cultural information covering such diverse areas as financial resources, medical conditions, client level of functioning, and availability of social/emotional resources (e.g., family, friends). This may involve interviews with the client, family members, other providers, or anyone whose knowledge will assist in understanding the client's situation. Group meetings with some of these sources may be needed. The goal is to identify all unmet needs so that the assessment is as comprehensive and inclusive as possible. It is critical to involve the client to the greatest extent possible in this process and the other steps that follow. It is also important to explore client strengths. Figure 12.1 shows a case management assessment designed to emphasize the client's strengths.

Establishing Appropriate Goals

In case management, we refer to goals as service goals, which include both long- and short-term items. Service goals might include maintaining the client in the community, locating suitable employment, completing a rehabilitation plan, and establishing a long-term plan for health care. Goals should be attainable with clear time lines established for their accomplishment.

Figure 12.1

A Strengths-Based Case Management Assessment

Case Manager's Name:_____   Date:_____

Client's Name:_____

Category	Current Status: Where am I?	Desires/Aspirations: What do I want?	Resources— Personal/Social
Housing/living situation			
Financial situation			
Employment/ education			
Social supports			
Health			
Leisure/recreational supports			

What are my priorities?

1.   3.

2.   4.

Case Manager's Comments:_____

_____

Case Manager's Signature:_____
Date:_____

Client's Comments:_____

_____

Client's Signature:_____
Date:_____

Source: Adapted from S. M. Rose (1992).

Planning the Intervention

Planning the intervention encompasses several steps. First, it is essential to identify what services, if any, the case manager will provide. Some case managers provide therapy or counseling, whereas others have such services provided by different practitioners. Second, a case plan will also identify which informal and formal resources are most likely to be helpful in meeting client needs. This step presupposes that the case manager has a solid awareness and understanding of other services appropriate for the client. Having an up-to-date list and description of such resources is important.

A third step is to identify the obstacles that clients may encounter in accessing certain resources. For example, are there income limitations, eligibility issues, or other factors that need to be addressed before the client can use this agency's services?

One purpose of the goal-setting and planning process steps is to create a service plan that will specify who will do what by when. We underscore the importance of such a plan because tasks for which no one is responsible generally do not get done. Figure 12.2 shows a service plan developed for a client. This case plan sheet would be completed and signed by both the social worker and the client. The short-term goals represent steps that must be taken in order to achieve the client's long-term goal. If the long-term goal is to locate employment, for example, short-term goals might consist of activities such as reading the want ads in the newspaper, accessing any on-line job sources, preparing a résumé or other document listing strengths and experiences, and contacting the local WorkForce Services Office. If the client needs to obtain some preparation for employment such as education or training, these steps would also be built into the short-term goals.

As should be clear by now, it is often necessary to break up long-term goals into specific, achievable, short-term steps. There are a couple of advantages to doing this. First, each step is manageable and will not overwhelm a client who is already struggling with life events. Second, keeping track of progress on short-term goals is helpful in monitoring. A client who is having trouble completing a short-term goal may need assistance. Lack of achievement may indicate resistance, lack of motivation, or confusion. Perhaps the goal should be further subdivided or potential obstacles and solutions identified and rehearsed to ensure a greater sense of competence on the client's part.

The column labeled "Responsibility" indicates who is responsible for completing a particular short-term goal. Responsible individuals could include the client, case manager, family member, or some other collateral support person. If others besides the client and case manager are responsible for completing a short-term goal, their signatures should be added to the bottom of the plan sheet.

Case management is often used with clients facing multiple challenges. Because of this, it may be necessary to revise the case plan to deal with changes in such things as clients' situation, their ability to complete a step, availability of needed resources, and other unforeseen circumstances. In other words, remember that the case plan is written on paper, not in concrete.

Linking Clients with Resources

Once the planning process has been completed, the next step is to link clients with the resources they need to attain their goals. As you may recall, this is where the role of case manager overlaps with that of broker (see Chapter 1). Typically, resource systems fall into two

Figure 12.2

Example of a Case Management Service Plan

Client:_____ Case Manager:_____ Date:_____

Planned Frequency of Contact:_____

Life Domain Area of Focus:　　　____Housing/Living Situation　　____Employment/Education
(Mark all that apply)

　　　　　　　　　　　　　　　____Social Supports　　　　　　　____Leisure/Recreation Supports

　　　　　　　　　　　　　　　____Financial Situation　　　　　　____Health

Client's Long-Term Goal:

Measurable Short-Term Goals toward Achievement	Responsibility	Target Date	Actual Date	Comments

Client Signature:_____ Date:_____ Case Manager Signature:_____ Date:_____

Source: Adapted from S. M. Rose (1992).

categories, either formal or informal. Formal resource systems include other agencies or organizations that have established programs related to a client's needs. Informal resource systems include the client's family and other social contacts. This might include friends, coworkers, church connections, or any other individual or group that may be of assistance.

Linking clients to resource systems includes several activities, such as "matching of clients to agencies, initial telephone contact, orienting the client, preparing papers, and visiting agencies" (Rothman, 2002, p. 468). The process of matching clients to agencies or other service providers again requires that the case manager know whether the client can qualify to receive services from any specific agency.

In many cases, the case manager will accompany the client to an appropriate agency, both to support the client's efforts and to help iron out any unforeseen difficulties that might be encountered. If, for example, the agency is going to require the client to produce certain documents or records, the case manager can help the client assemble these items. In addition, the worker can help the client understand what to expect from the first contact with the new agency.

Helping clients access informal systems must take into account two things, namely the appropriateness of these systems and their capability of providing needed services. If family members are estranged or relationships are characterized by long-standing animosity, attempting to reconnect client and family may prove counterproductive. Likewise, if family members contribute to the existence of the client's difficulty, they will not prove useful.

However, even if family members or others can help, the social worker needs to consider how well they can sustain that effort. For example, caring for a family member with a severe psychiatric disorder may quickly tax the emotional resources of the family. In such cases, consideration must be given to providing respite services that would allow the family caretakers time off so that burnout does not occur. Thus, the case manager is also concerned with expanding and supporting the capabilities of informal resource systems to help meet client needs.

The case manager provides a liaison function with all of the resource systems with which the client is connected. Liaison is concerned with helping the client and resource system communicate with each other and share critical information. A related purpose is maintaining effective working relationships between and among agencies because they will need to work together in the future.

If the case manager is going to be providing direct services to the client, such as therapy or counseling, attention must be paid to how this will be accomplished. Harris and Bergman (1988) identify the tasks that are important for the case manager: (1) building a therapeutic relationship with the client, (2) modeling behaviors that help the client achieve important life goals, and (3) changing the client's environment, such as removing barriers and helping the client use available resources. To the extent possible, this role is also concerned with helping clients use their own personal resources to overcome barriers encountered in the environment.

Monitoring and Reassessment

A key step in case management is monitoring the client's situation to ensure that the services needed were provided in a timely and effective manner. It is not uncommon for a client whose needs are not met to drop out or just stop coming without telling the social worker about the problem. In case management, the social worker is responsible for following up to see that this does not happen.

In addition to following up with the client, the case manager will contact the service-giving agency to get their perspectives on the client's progress. It may be prudent to talk with family members or others who are involved in the client's life to ascertain their views on how the client is doing. When such discussions are appropriate, the social worker must make sure to get the client's permission to contact other people.

In the process of monitoring services, it is also important to reassess the client's situation. For example, the case manager should be concerned about whether the client is achieving the service goals originally established. It is neither unusual nor unexpected to have to modify goals, locate additional or different resources, or provide other services not originally envisioned. Keep in mind that case management services are often used with clients who are facing lifelong challenges and that changes are often needed to continue meeting client needs.

Of course, if the case manager is providing services to the client directly, this is another source of information for monitoring. Is the client making progress or experiencing setbacks? Does the client need to learn new skills that the case manager is capable of providing? This underscores the importance of maintaining good case records that can be reviewed during the monitoring phase.

The case manager may also have to work with other agencies to further the achievement of client service goals. This can involve advocacy to deal with unexpected barriers to service created by another agency's decision, or creating interagency agreements about service provision, including possibly contracts for services. This might be the situation when one agency chooses not to provide a given service but instead purchases it from another organization. Often this is more cost-efficient than trying to set up a service that will be used by only a small number of clients.

Evaluation

Whereas monitoring is an ongoing function of the case manager, evaluation tends to occur at the conclusion of case management services. Evaluation can happen with clients whose difficulties are of a temporary nature and who are now able to function independently. As in the other steps in the case management process, clients should be fully involved in such evaluations. In many case management scenarios, however, evaluation does not occur as an ending step because clients continue to receive services for their entire lives.

Evaluation, when it does occur, has another benefit that goes beyond the individual client. Evaluation is at the heart of efforts to substantiate that interventions are effective and responsive to client needs. Efforts to evaluate case management services have shown that they are a successful means of rendering help to certain groups of clients. Results show that those receiving case management services experienced increased functional capacity, lower rates of hospitalization, reductions in symptomatology, higher quality of care, and an improved quality of life compared to those not receiving such care (Gorey et al., 1998; Mueser, Bond, Drake, & Resnick, 1998; Scott & Dixon, 1995).

Case managers may work as individuals or as members of a team dedicated to helping the client. The team can comprise professionals from other disciplines or people with different kinds of expertise. Frankel and Gelman (2004) note that "most social workers who specialize in direct practice do case management" (p. 7).

They also point out that case management activities are often performed by those from other professions such as nursing. Settings in which case management is performed can range from child welfare agencies, criminal justice systems, and mental health organizations, to name a few.

Ethical Issues in Case Management

As in other aspects of direct practice, case management involves some ethical considerations that must be addressed. Frankel and Gelman (2004) identify confidentiality as a key concern. Because case management involves multiple agencies and individuals, it opens up the possibility of breaching confidentiality guidelines of the social work profession. Confidentiality issues should be discussed with the client at the beginning of the helping process. This is not only consistent with the NASW Code of Ethics, but it is also required by the Health Insurance Portability and Accounting Act (HIPAA). Clients have the right to approve sharing of their records and should know specifically with whom these data will be shared. Data to be protected begin with the client's name and go on from there.

Other ethical challenges exist. For example, the client's right to self-determination can collide with the case manager's concern that the client lacks the competence to make appropriate decisions regarding what services are necessary. This is always a gray area in which the case manager's judgment has the potential to violate a client's rights. Likewise, a client must be informed about any potential harm or risks entailed by accepting case management services. Because one benefit of case management for agencies is that it helps control costs by ensuring that clients receive only the resources they need, clients will likely lose the ability to draw the same help from different resources.

Another ethical situation involves the use of a type of case management that Moxley (1997) calls system-driven case management. The increased emphasis on managed care and the influence of managed care organizations on social work practice cannot be denied. Moxley believes that case management has been adopted by such organizations to achieve benefits for the managed care system and not necessarily for the client. He states that this model of case management focuses on reduction of duplication, increased efficiency, rationing of expensive services, substitution of less expensive care for more costly approaches, and deviance management. This last refers to using case management instead of incarceration or hospitalization, approaches that can benefit clients but also contain costs to the criminal justice and health care systems (Moxley, 1997, pp. 16–19).

In contrast, Moxley (1997) cites the consumer-driven case management model as more readily consistent with social work ethics. In this model, the goal is to personalize services to meet individual client goals instead of the one-size-fits-all approach of the system-driven model. The consumer-driven approach emphasizes a responsiveness to clients' needs that ensures clients are making the decisions about the care they receive. It also focuses on the case manager playing a supportive role in helping the client deal with environmental barriers and creating new support mechanisms where none existed before. The emphasis is on empowering clients to take control of their lives and reduce dependence on the case manager.

This chapter emphasizes a model of case management more in keeping with the consumer-driven approach. However, the two models do continue to exist, and direct practitioners can expect to encounter both in their practice. For a more detailed look at the topic of case management, see Frankel and Gelman (2004) and Rothman (2002).

Advocacy Roles

Social work has a long if inconsistent history of using advocacy to assist clients. Although early social workers maintained a significant focus on changing the larger environment to benefit immigrants and other groups, later practitioners were less involved in such efforts. Direct practice, as we indicated earlier, tends to focus most specifically on work with individuals, families, and groups. This focus might suggest that social workers no longer engage in advocacy roles. Fortunately, this is not the case. Even with a primary concern of helping individuals, families, and groups, there is ample opportunity and need for social workers to become advocates.

Brill (1998) defines advocacy as being composed of two components. First, social workers plead the cause of their clients to others, who may include other social workers, public officials, landlords, or anyone else whose decisions are creating barriers for the client. Advocacy on behalf of specific individuals, families, or groups is usually called **case advocacy.** Second, social workers engage in supporting, defending, or otherwise lobbying for a cause. As might be expected, this approach is called **cause advocacy** or sometimes **class advocacy.** The cause could be changes in agency policy, new laws, or other broad efforts to create new resources for client systems. The goal of cause or class advocacy is not to aid a specific client but rather to represent everyone who shares certain characteristics. These characteristics might include ethnicity, disability status, gender, or any other distinctive element that applies to a class or group of people. The civil rights movement of the 1960s was an ex-

ample of cause advocacy. In that case, the goal was to ensure that people of color received the same constitutionally guaranteed rights that were accorded to other classes of people. Current efforts to ensure that constitutional and other legal rights available to other citizens apply equally to gay men and lesbian women are also examples of cause or class advocacy.

From a more practical standpoint, advocacy is action taken by the social worker to ensure both people's rights and their access to needed resources. By definition, it encompasses both case and cause advocacy. Because direct practice typically focuses on working with individuals, families, and groups, this chapter talks more about advocacy on behalf of specific clients. Examples of advocacy include helping a family receive a favorable decision from one's own agency regarding specific services they badly need. This could be temporary shelter, health care, or pro bono counseling. It could also include working to set up a health care service for refugees. The direct practitioner can also perform an advocacy role by supporting and accompanying a client asking agency decision makers, such as agency supervisors or administrators, to make an exception to policy. Though the social worker does not take an active role in pressing for a particular decision, this approach has a major benefit of helping to increase the client's power to achieve goals. As indicated earlier, empowerment of this type is an important goal of social work and is discussed at greater length in Chapter 9.

At times, case advocacy becomes cause advocacy, as happens when rights won for one's own clients are available to others in a similar situation. When advocacy leads to a change in policy, everyone benefits equally. For example, consider a social worker who advocated with her own agency to provide transportation assistance for a family with whom she was working. Unable to get to their court-mandated counseling sessions, the parents were in danger of being found in contempt of court and having their children removed from the home. Once a precedent of providing transportation assistance had been set, the agency subsequently created a small line item in the budget that could be used in similar situations. This way other families could receive the help they needed without the social worker having to advocate for the specific client system.

Ethical Implications of Advocacy

Advocating for clients does have some ethical implications. First, social workers are not sanctioned to engage in advocacy without the client's permission, regardless of how important the goal. Advocacy involves potential risks to the client, and no one should be subject to those risks without a clear awareness of them and having given consent. The consequences for the client can be serious. An example is a social worker whose client lives in an apartment in which hot water is only infrequently available because of old plumbing and fixtures. The client has mentioned the problem to the landlord on several occasions, but the situation never improved. The social worker offered to meet with the landlord to advocate for the client. Together they considered the pros and cons of such a role for the practitioner. On the one hand, the social worker might be able to get the situation improved. On the other hand, the landlord might decide to evict the client and rent the apartment to someone else. The client pointed out that this was a relatively inexpensive place to live and that if she had to move, her housing costs might increase by 50 percent or more. Weighing the relative risks, the client decided to put up with the inconvenience and asked the worker not to intervene. On a positive note,

the landlord finally got around to fixing the problem after another year had passed.

Client self-determination requires that they be involved in all such decisions, even if the risks appear small. This can become more complicated when the client has diminished capacity to understand what is going on. At the same time, the social worker must use all means possible to ensure that clients have maximum opportunity to make choices based on what is best for them.

Another ethical limitation to advocacy concerns the rights of others. Social workers cannot advocate for clients if by doing so they ignore or harm the rights of others. This is true even if the client actively solicits our service toward this goal. Neither can we engage in advocacy activities that threaten general societal rights. For example, we cannot set fire to the police station because a client, or even a group of clients, experiences discrimination in law enforcement. Our methods must be within the ethical guidelines of our profession.

Another general guideline in the use of advocacy is to employ it in such a manner that it does not increase client dependency on the social worker. This requires encouraging and helping clients do as much for themselves as possible. If advocacy requires a particular knowledge or skill possessed by the social worker, our role may be one of leading the client. If advocacy can be achieved by the client with the social worker behind the scenes, this is preferable.

Deciding When to Advocate

There are many situations in which advocacy is an appropriate activity for direct practitioners. Several of these are listed in Figure 12.3.

Knowledge for Advocacy

Advocacy requires both knowledge and skill in the application of specific activities. For example, social workers must know to which legal

Figure 12.3

Appropriate Advocacy Situations

1. When clients are denied services or other resources to which they have a legal right

2. When clients are denied services or resources ordinarily available to other groups

3. When services are not currently available to meet the needs of multiple clients

4. When decisions affecting clients are made in an arbitrary or capricious fashion

5. When clients face discrimination in obtaining needed resources

6. When societal conditions "are destructive to people" (Brill, 1998, p. 214)

7. When clients seeking services or resources are treated inhumanely

rights clients are entitled. It would be foolhardy to demand that an agency provide a legal right that has no standing under the law. Many rights, however, are guaranteed under the U.S. Constitution, such as due process and freedom of speech. Other rights may be covered by individual laws such as the Americans with Disabilities Act. In any case, it might be appropriate to talk with an attorney if in doubt.

In addition, the practitioner must be aware of an organization's policies before arguing that the agency has not acted appropriately. Because most agency policies tend to be written down, this is one avenue to explore before taking an active advocate role.

A third consideration is the process or procedure for complaining or appealing the decision at issue. The appeal process may be discussed in an agency policy manual, incorporated in laws or regulations, or simply be chal-

lenged by following an organization's chain of command. In the last case, a decision by a line worker may be appealed to that person's immediate supervisor. If the supervisor's decision is not believed to be fair or accurate according to policy, the supervisory decision might then be appealed to the agency director. Most decisions in many organizations can be appealed through either formal or informal channels. Rarely is the first word in such situations the last word. In any event, the social worker must be knowledgeable about the process in order to use it appropriately.

A fourth category of things to consider involves the adversary (Connaway & Gentry, 1988). Adversaries are people or organizations that block or hinder the client from reaching a goal. For example, before meeting with an adversary, advocates should consider whether the adversary is likely to have similar values, goals, or objectives. Will the adversary be open to persuasion? Who is the best person to provide this persuasion? How will this individual act if the advocate uses confrontation? How much influence and power does the adversary have either to agree to the request or to block it? What is the adversary's degree of vulnerability with respect to the problem? For example, has the adversary ignored agency policy or laws or engaged in behavior that is considered unprofessional? If any of these is the case, the adversary is more vulnerable to change efforts.

As Connaway and Gentry (1988) note, social workers must also consider the client's situation as part of the planning process when considering use of advocacy. Most important is the client's vulnerability. Two aspects of vulnerability are significant. First, the more emergent the client's situation, the more emphasis there is on quick action. Homeless clients, or those without the basic necessities of life, are at greater risk than, say, a family that needs marital counseling to strengthen their relationship.

Further, practitioners must take into account how vulnerable the client is if the adversary reacts negatively to the advocacy efforts. Can the client be harmed by denial of other benefits or resources? Will it create additional problems that will make matters worse?

A second aspect of the client's situation deals with the resources at the client's disposal. These resources include clients' ability to advocate for themselves, their tolerance level for dealing with conflict or confrontation, their past experience dealing with similar situations, and their strength of commitment to achieving their objectives (Connaway & Gentry, 1988).

When each of these considerations has been factored into the equation, it is time for the social worker and the client to make a decision. Is advocacy the appropriate approach to take? When the decision is made to go ahead, the social worker must then employ a variety of skills to achieve the goals of advocacy.

Skills for Advocacy

Advocacy requires particular skills that are responsive to the task of removing environmental barriers. These include (1) persuasion, (2) education, (3) bargaining, and (4) legal action.

Persuasion

Persuasion skills are used to convince someone else to make a decision, change a decision, or in some other way move in a direction that benefits the client. Persuasion is a collaborative approach that requires preparation, fact gathering, and listening. For example, practitioners must be acutely aware of the problem and be able to articulate this clearly to the adversary. Then they must be able to discuss the situation marshaling all of the available facts. The goal is to ensure that the adversary fully understands the situation and knows that the worker and client have a similar understanding. A third step is to anticipate and/or listen attentively to the position of the adversary. This achieves several things, including demonstrating sensitivity to the adversary's needs and situation and a willingness to listen and understand. Of course, it also allows the social worker to identify arguments or ideas he or she might use in responding to the adversary's position.

Next, advocates must clearly spell out what they want to happen. This is a topic that the social worker and the client have already discussed and is something that will accomplish the client's goal. In some situations, it may be wise to identify what will occur if the adversary does not agree to the desired course of action. These options may include further appeals or possibly even a lawsuit.

Several factors can influence the likelihood of an adversary agreeing to a client's request. Obviously, the less one is asking from the adversary the easier it is for the adversary to comply with the request. Asking a landlord to replace a water heater is much more likely to be met with a positive response than requesting that all windows in an apartment be replaced. Also, if adversaries believe that they share common interests with the social worker and the client, it will be easier for them to agree with a given proposal. The approach the social worker takes can also have a bearing on the adversary's position. For example, it is better to use collaborative tactics of persuasion when this is possible. No one likes being beaten over the head, and such tactics often can backfire, with the adversary becoming even more determined not to give in.

If collaboration and cooperation do not work, other methods may be used. Clear statements of opposition to the adversary's position are one alternative. "I do not find your proposal at all responsive to my client's needs" is an example of such a statement. In unusual situations, it may be necessary to go further by stating an intention to challenge the adversary's position in every way possible. These ways might include filing appeals, grievances, or lawsuits or engaging in social actions such as picketing. Keep in mind that the least confrontive approaches should be used before resorting to more aggressive tactics. Also remember, it is essential that the client agrees with aggressive tactics before the social worker attempts to use them.

Finally, summarize any discussions between the advocate and the adversary so that the problem, proposed solution, and areas of agreement are restated (Halley, Kopp, & Austin, 1998). If the adversary has agreed to a request or a suitable compromise has been reached, it is time for the social worker and the client to thank the adversary and make an exit. If the meeting was not successful, it is time to consider some of the other options described earlier.

Education

Persuading others is an important skill for social workers, but it is not the only one available to advocates. For example, practitioners can **educate** adversaries when it appears clear that they are operating from a position based on misinformation. This involves presenting data in a clear and convincing manner while being able to challenge and correct the adversary's information. In other situations, the social worker, client, and adversary may be able to use problem-solving skills to reach an agreement. This involves applying the problem-solving model of engagement, assessment, planning, implementation, evalua-

tion, and termination to tackle a complex problem.

Bargaining

Another skill useful in advocacy is bargaining. **Bargaining** is a process that involves two or more parties, often with different power levels, who are focused on producing a win–win compromise. As Netting and colleagues (1993) note, "in order to negotiate, both the action and the target system must perceive that each has something the other wants, otherwise there is no reason to come together" (p. 256). Likewise, before entering into the negotiations needed to reach a bargain, each party must be willing to give up something to get something else. Obviously, this works only if you have something to bargain with. Because compromise is the heart of bargaining, if nothing can be sacrificed for the greater goal, bargaining is likely to be unsuccessful.

An essential step before entering into the bargaining process is to have a plan that identifies exactly what the client system really wants (Kahn, 1991). With this as the bottom line, bargaining tactics then involve asking for more in order to have something to give up in exchange for getting what the client wants. Negotiations never start at the bottom line because failing to achieve this will often leave one or more parties bitter.

Bargaining can be used in a number of situations. It can be effective, for example, when used to help a teenager and her parents reach an agreement about a reasonable curfew on school nights. It may also help parents and their child who has been expelled from school reach an agreement with the school administrators imposing the sanction. Rather than expulsion, perhaps the family would agree to a suspension or other less serious consequence in exchange for something the school system values. The value sought could be specific behavior that the adolescent will exhibit in school, or the parents' dropping the threat of a lawsuit against the school.

Legal Action

More stringent skills involve taking **legal action:** using internal or external appeal procedures, threatening to embarrass the adversary or his or her agency by calling public attention to their shortcomings, or using other pressure tactics (Connaway & Gentry, 1988). However, none of these skills should be employed unless the client is fully aware of the potential consequences that such tactics might elicit.

Advocacy is an important role for direct practitioners, especially when clients are prevented from exercising the same rights accorded others or when they are denied resources they need to survive. Some of the practice skills employed by advocates are the same ones useful for working with individuals, families, and groups (e.g., educating, persuading, bargaining). Others begin to move into what has historically been called social action or community organization (e.g., appeals, legal action, picketing, public embarrassment). These latter approaches tend to be more effective when advocating for classes of people rather than for individual client systems.

Other Environmental Challenges

Although direct practitioners spend the greatest portion of their time dealing with individuals, families, and groups, occasionally it will become necessary to consider pursuing organizational and community change. This chapter identifies advocacy, particularly case advocacy, as an important activity for the direct practitioner. Although case advocacy can be effective

in achieving results for an individual client, there is no guarantee that the gains achieved for client A or family B will be available for future clients. It is not uncommon for an agency or organization to make an exception for a specific case but not to change the policy or procedure so that others can benefit from the decision. This may be because systems tend to maintain the status quo despite temporary imbalances or setbacks.

Failure to maintain changes is a common problem when working with client systems, regardless of size. With individual clients and families, we can incorporate activities that help prepare them to retain the benefits they have enjoyed as a result of working with us. This task is more difficult with larger systems targeted as part of case advocacy. As a consequence, direct practitioners may find themselves trying to create more permanent change in such systems. After all, it makes little sense to keep advocating for each new individual when the solution is a permanent change that benefits all clients.

A second situation that may require practitioner involvement is when a larger system refuses to make critical changes in its policies or practices that are harmful to human beings. These practices may affect an entire community or a specific group within the community. An example is a water treatment facility that had received a contract to clean up groundwater contaminated with pollutants. Their original plan called for cleaning the groundwater by removing the pollutants and then pumping the pollutants into a nearby river. The river, an already contaminated tributary, ran through portions of the community that were economically depressed. When the plan became public knowledge, a wide variety of groups protested the idea of removing the contaminants from one area and relocating them to another. Suc-

Voices from the Field

Paula Allen-Meares

When I entered the MSW program at the University of Illinois at Urbana–Champaign, I enjoyed learning about the diverse methods and populations unique to the social work profession. While my field placement at the Illinois Department of Children and Family Services (IDCFS) focused my interests on families in need of assistance, I remained fascinated by and open to learning about additional fields of service delivery.

My position at IDCFS required my participation in meetings at local schools, and it was there I first became aware of the unlimited possibilities of social work in an educational setting. My interest was fueled, and I found myself searching for a school social work position. In that role my multidisciplinary perspective grew.

It is this perspective that remains critical to today's school social workers. In order to be effective in an educational setting, school social workers must embrace a multidisciplinary perspective, function as a member of a team, have knowledge about the spectrum of students' learning needs and developmental challenges, and possess cultural competencies to address the growing and changing student demographics. To be successful, school social workers must use empirically validated interventions, be accountable and outcome focused, and constantly document the vital contribution they make to the educational process.

cumbing to the pressure, the water treatment facility abandoned the plan.

Although the plan for dealing with contaminated groundwater might not seem like a social work issue, it does in fact fall under the social work ethical standard of responsibility to advocate for the "general welfare of society, from local to global levels, and the development of people, their communities, and their environments" (NASW, 1999, p. 26). The quality of life of people in a community is the concern of social workers by virtue of our ethical standards. When this quality of life is threatened, social workers may appropriately meet this threat through joint action with other groups.

Another situation that may occur is the opportunity to work for changes in macro systems that will result in benefits to whole groups of people. For example, when new programs are proposed at the legislative level, social workers have the chance to join with others to support the proposal. A proposal to fund more substance abuse programs is a much more positive step than simply locking up more users. Increased funding for domestic violence services might be another goal that as a social worker you might want to support. In these kinds of situations, it is common for organizations such as the National Association of Social Workers to actively lobby for the proposals. This is a wonderful opportunity to show support by writing letters or otherwise contacting legislative representatives, whether local, state, or federal.

Other Environmental Change Strategies

In order to deal with the kinds of environmental challenges discussed in the previous section, several change strategies must be addressed. The following section looks at change models involving social action, social planning, and organizational change.

Social Action

Social action is a term used by Rothman (2001) to describe advocacy-type efforts designed to create "fundamental changes in the community, including the redistribution of power and resources and gaining access to decision making for marginal groups" (p. 33). Marginal groups can include those characterized by poverty, oppression, and other forms of discrimination. Activities associated with social action range from more confrontational approaches such as demonstrations, boycotts, strikes, and picketing to legislative advocacy. Efforts to achieve fair treatment for farmworkers and to protect the environment have often involved the more confrontational kinds of activities. More recently, these activities have been supplemented by others that tend to be less controversial. These methods include coalition building, involvement in political campaigns, letter writing, negotiating, grant writing, and other steps designed to empower those with little influence in society.

One reason for the change in tactics of social action is the backlash from the more confrontational and adversarial approaches such as civil disobedience and marches. These tactics have their place, but they tend to polarize some who would otherwise be potential allies. A second reason is that most social workers are providing direct practice services, and social action is not an expected part of their positions. Lacking both time and organizational sanction to engage in more confrontational aspects of social action, they can still play an important role in other ways.

The ability to organize with like-minded colleagues is a key element of social action. Though individuals can certainly have a major impact on events, groups tend to bring more credibility and strength to change efforts. Therefore, social action works best when individuals or organizations band together to tackle the need for change. As Rothman (2001) notes, power can come in the form of "a lot of money or a lot of people" (p. 39). Lacking the first source of power, social workers often use the latter. As you might expect, the ability to work together with others becomes an important skill in building such coalitions. Working as part of a larger group requires the ability to listen well, communicate clearly, and play appropriate roles needed to help the group function effectively. Group roles are addressed at greater length in Chapter 11.

Social action also requires a degree of courage because those with power in the community are often the target of the change effort. Challenging those individuals can be both personally and professionally risky. Social workers are asking those with power to share it with others, which may be contrary to their own perceived best interests. Few of those holding power will view this effort as laudatory. On the other hand, successfully achieving these kinds of major changes is extraordinarily empowering for the beneficiaries and participants.

Tactics for bringing about change through social action can be quite inventive. For example, Haggstrom (2001) mentions the possibility of drawing public attention to an organization or other decision-making group. Decision makers who are skirting the law or other regulations may be very reluctant to have anyone look too closely at their actions. Similarly, coalitions can produce favorable outcomes for decision makers in exchange for making the desired changes. A decision by coalition members to patronize a business in exchange for the business hiring more residents from the local neighborhood can benefit both sides. Of course, the inherent threat of the coalition's boycotting the business may underlie the latter's apparent beneficence.

It is clear that simply winning the battle is insufficient if no ongoing change occurs. If, for example, the goal is to increase the decision-making role of the recipients of social or other services, permanent changes must be made that allow this to continue. Placing recipients on decision-making bodies such as boards and committees gives them a much more permanent role. Ensuring that policy changes are publicized and included in official documents is another way to help ensure that changes last. A third method is eternal vigilance. Keeping an eye on what decisions makers do is a continuous, but necessary, task. For example, many people, when the police officer is out of sight, tend to return to their old driving habits. Decision makers are not a great deal different.

Social Planning

Social planning is concerned with eliminating social problems in the community, particularly things such as crime, violence, poor-quality housing, and inadequate health care (Sheafor & Horejsi, 2003). Lauffer (1981) called social planning "the development, expansion and co-ordination of social services and social policies" (p. 581). The activities of the direct practitioner in this arena are "fact gathering,

data analysis, policy analysis, sharing technical information, and program planning" (Sheafor & Horejsi, 2003, p. 117). An agency director who decides to begin offering substance abuse services because this appears to be a growing problem in her community is doing social planning. An agency board of directors that decides to open a branch office in a low-income neighborhood to better reach clients who lack access to its existing services is also doing social planning. A social worker sitting on a community board responsible for overseeing building proposals is in a position to influence social planning. So is the direct practitioner who marshals facts and figures showing that the problem of domestic violence is worsening among the clients his agency typically serves and who asks that the agency consider developing a plan to deal with the change.

The emphasis here has been on the direct practitioner playing a peripheral role in social action and social planning, but this is not always the case. Many social workers are employed in agencies dedicated to bringing about better communities and a better society. Still others serve as advisors to political leaders or as elected officials in their own right. These are crucial social work roles that constitute indirect practice in contrast to this text's emphasis on direct practice. Both are important roles for social workers.

Organizational Change

Almost all social workers at one point or another in their careers will be part of a social service organization. This can be a social service agency, a protective service agency, a criminal or juvenile justice organization, or any number of other structures. They may also be part of a private nonprofit organization or a private for-profit agency. The agency may be publicly funded in whole or part. Finally, it may be operated by a church or other religious organization. Regardless of how it is structured and operated, each organization at some point will cause practitioners to question the organization's policies or practices. Getting the social worker's own organization to change might seem reasonably easy. After all, the social worker is a valued member of the staff, perhaps even a supervisor. However, it is in the nature of systems to maintain their stability and fend off attempts at change.

Because practitioners are part of the organization, they have a vested interest in it surviving. It is not the social worker's goal to destroy it or damage it but rather to help it do a better job of meeting the needs of clients. The efforts made to achieve this end will therefore be different from those employed in traditional social action. The next section describes some of the ways that social workers can pursue organizational change from within their agency.

A Force-Field Analysis

Whether the direct practitioner is considering starting a new program, changing existing policies and procedures, or undertaking some other change effort at the organizational or community level, one of the most effective tools is a force-field analysis. The force-field analysis model, originally developed by Lewin (1951), is also the basis for the inner and outer forces model described in Chapter 5.

The concept is relatively simple but provides an excellent way of identifying those forces that impede and those that facilitate a proposed change in an activity or action. The first step is to specify or articulate the activity or goal you are pursuing. Is this a new program serving a particular population or a change in a specific agency policy? The second step is to visualize the environment in which your pro-

posed change will take place. Is this an agency or a community, a neighborhood, or some combination? The third step is to identify all the forces in that environment that you think will oppose your proposal. Once listed, these become the forces that impede your ability to accomplish your goal. Potential opposing forces might include an agency administrator reluctant to spend additional money to begin a new program and staff members who wish to preserve the status quo at all costs. Other impeding factors might be the cost of developing new services and the lack of staff with adequate education and training to offer needed services.

The fourth step is to identify and list those forces in the environment that will facilitate or otherwise assist in the change effort. These forces include your own capability to create change based on such factors as a personal relationship with the decision maker, a willingness to lobby an agency board of directors, or other skills that can help you achieve your goal. Forces outside yourself may include articulate clients who are willing to speak out on behalf of your idea because they will use the services created. They may also include powerful people in the community or organization who are known to favor the kinds of proposal you are considering.

Keep in mind that the reason such a proposal is not already in place is that there is always a relative balance between restraining and driving forces (Homan, 2004). That means that the change effort must identify sufficient additional driving forces to offset the normal restraining forces. New forces that can be harnessed might include money, a group of like-minded people, public opinion, media attention, personal support by opinion leaders, and anything else that your creative mind can devise.

The fifth step in the process is to evaluate the relative power of each of the forces on both sides of the field. The combined power of the restraining and driving forces will be the major factor in whether you achieve your goal. This analysis should give you a fairly accurate sense of whether you can bring enough power to bear to change the situation. If you decide that the goal is both realistic and achievable, the last step is to select a plan that will accomplish your goal. This strategy must be carefully thought out so that each restraining force can be either neutralized or overcome (Meenaghan & Gibbons, 2000). Used correctly, this model can be useful whether the goal is organizational or community change. In the following section, we look at the topic of creating new programs.

Creating New Programs

Believing that an agency should offer a new program or undertake a major revision of an existing service is not uncommon among practitioners. Most social workers find areas of shortcomings that they think could be reduced or overcome by specific changes. However, creating a new program in any organization should be attempted only after careful consideration. Hasenfeld (2001) states this point clearly when he observes that "no new agency or program should be initiated unless it is propelled by the existence of a concrete and viable need" (p. 460). This position is buttressed when one thinks of the resources required to launch or maintain any program. These include the obvious things such as money and staff, but to these Hasenfeld adds the knowledge and competence to implement the service, the availability of complementary services offered by other agencies (such as referring agencies), and an adequate supply of clients.

Proving there is a need for a new program requires gathering data from various sources (Hasenfeld, 2001). These activities, data, and sources include:

- Completing a needs assessment (a formal analysis of the existence of specific needs)
- Analyzing existing reports such as census data, victimization surveys, and other information compiled by public and private sources
- Collecting information from potential beneficiaries of the proposed service
- Identifying existing agencies that might be able to provide the proposed program
- Collecting information from other agencies that offer similar services or serve a similar population to determine gaps or other service shortcomings

The rationale for gathering these data should be clear. Any program requires substantial resources, and no agency wants to begin something only to find out later that another organization is already providing the service at a lower cost. Neither would an agency director or board be happy to learn that the number of clients needing a specific service was too small to justify the expenses involved.

It is sometimes easier to begin a program when there is a natural constituency interested in the issue. For example, if the practitioner documents the lack of suitable transportation for persons with physical disabilities, working toward change would be facilitated by having a committed group in the community behind the idea. Although data alone can be persuasive, having support from others, particularly potential users of a service, can greatly strengthen the likelihood of support. As a result, another step in the process is determining whether such a group exists or can be formed.

New programs also require great clarity about the target population to be served, the specific problems or issues needing attention, and the services that match to the problems. They also need careful consideration about the actual cost of providing the services, the expertise and availability of potential staff, and the physical facilities and equipment required. Money needed to start a program can come from redistribution of existing resources, grants or contracts from public or private sources, fees from clients, and/or donations. Service providers might be reassigned from other programs, hired from the outside, or recruited from among volunteers (Hasenfeld, 2001). Physical facilities and equipment can be donated, reused from a previous program, or borrowed on a temporary basis.

Another matter that needs attention is the question of how and where services will be offered. Will this be an outreach program offered away from the agency's home building, or simply another service offered within the existing facility? Will the hours served by staff be the same or different? For example, is the new program to be offered in the evenings or on weekends? Will the staff require any special expertise such as fluency in Spanish or competence in the area of substance abuse or domestic violence? What structure will the new program take and how will services be organized differently after the new initiative is launched? What level of supervision will the staff in the program need? This last is particularly important because the person providing supervision is accountable for the work of supervisees (Hasenfeld, 2001).

Locating an adequate supply of clients to use the service must be considered. For example, relationships will need to be strengthened with potential referring agencies. Advertising of services may be needed, such as fliers,

posters, or the news media. Talking to groups or organizations that might be aware of clients needing the service can also be useful. For example, if the service is to individuals with severe mental health challenges, it may be helpful to speak with leaders of the local chapter of the National Alliance for the Mentally Ill (NAMI).

Another consideration is establishing an evaluation plan that will help determine whether the services provided are accomplishing their purposes. Decisions need to be made about what records will be kept, how success will be defined, and who will complete the evaluation. An evaluation component is often required by funding agencies or others whose approval of the program is sought.

If programs are to be continued over time (as opposed to short-term projects), they must receive legitimation and sanction from the community (Hasenfeld, 2001). This means that members of the community accept the need for the program and support its existence. A successful program may have a cadre of people who are pleased with having participated, and such client groups are helpful in creating support. Similar support can come from agencies satisfied with the services provided. Other public relations activities helpful for creating support include open houses, periodic press releases, public presentations to various community groups, and creation of an advisory board composed of influential citizens.

Although this may seem like a lot of work, it is absolutely essential to be prepared. Agency boards and administrators, granting agencies, and public officials asked to support a new program will need convincing that the proposal is sound. Organizational resources are so constrained that few new programs can be implemented without careful attention to all of these concerns. Failing to do the necessary homework either dooms a proposal to failure or sets up the agency for later problems should the new program be started. Ignoring concerns such as how to keep the program going in the future will undermine the likelihood that the program will have a future.

Changing Policies and Practices

Every organization has some policies or practices that practitioners find objectionable. These may involve services offered to clients, expectations of workers, or ways of carrying out various agency tasks. Sometimes these policies or practices are simply annoying and do not really affect the practitioner's ability to help clients meet their goals. An example might be a policy that the social worker must have all case notes entered into clients' files before being eligible to take compensatory time. This kind of rule is unpleasant but generally does not prevent us from helping our clients. Other policies can be much more problematic. An agency director, for example, might have strong personal views about what a social worker can say to a client. In one agency, the director did not want staff mentioning abortion as an option to pregnant women seeking agency help, even when the issue was what to do about the pregnancy. This position was effectively an unwritten agency policy. Agency practitioners objected to this position because it limited options for some of the clients, which in their view violated the NASW Code of Ethics requirement that clients be given the right to make choices fully informed about all the possibilities. In practice, they simply ignored the director's wishes and provided the information that their profession believed was appropriate for clients to have in order to make an informed decision.

Changing organizational policies and practices can be easy or difficult depending on several factors. Policies that agency administrators are heavily invested in are more difficult to change. Changes that involve threats to funding, those that might bring bad publicity, and other proposals that undermine the agency's purpose will usually be resisted firmly. A request to change a practice that evolved over time without anyone recalling why it developed will probably be much easier to change. Having said that, we must acknowledge that some administrators will be reluctant even in these situations, reasoning that if the practice has been around for a while, there must have been a good reason for adopting it.

An example of an organizational policy that was relatively easy to change involved an agency that had a practice of locking the door to the supply closet so that staff had to make requests to get a tablet of paper or a new pen. Even paper clips and staples were stored under lock and key. The staff found the practice annoying because it meant they had to make a formal request for every supply item. When they inquired about the reason for this practice, the staff were told it was a fiscal decision because staff would use up all the supplies and cost the organization a lot of money.

A new agency director came in and began to hear complaints from the staff about several things they disliked. Among them was the locked supply closet. Not only did it cost them additional time and inconvenience to get needed supplies, but also the practice sent a message that the staff could not be trusted. Although the fiscal officer of the agency strongly supported the locked closet, the new director listened to staff arguments and ordered the door unlocked. Although supply costs did rise somewhat after this decision was made, the gain in goodwill among the staff more than compensated for the increased costs.

In a similar vein, an organization had been working to ensure that all staff were computer literate and that computers were used for all agency communication. The agency policy called for every staff person to have a computer that would be networked to a printer located on each floor of the three-story building. Because of this policy, staff members would type a letter, run down the hall to the printer, insert letterhead paper in the printer, run back to their office, and press the print button on the computer. Then they would run back down the hall to pick up the letter. While there they would insert an envelope, return to their office, hit the print command to print out the envelope, and return again to the printer room. If the printer malfunctioned for any reason, they would repeat the above steps. If someone else printed out a document in the time staff members were between office and printer, the steps would have to be repeated. This policy had been in place for several years despite the inconvenience it entailed.

Finally, several unit directors pointed out the increased productivity that could be achieved by eliminating the running around required by the policy. The director liked the idea of staff accomplishing more and agreed to acquire individual printers for each staff member who wanted one. As expected, most staff members requested a printer. Soon they were using the networked printer only for longer documents, a practice that prolonged the life of this very expensive piece of equipment. Savings on replacing this larger printer less frequently helped offset the costs of providing each staff member with an inexpensive but durable printer he or she could use without leaving the office.

As we have said, changes that carry a high price tag are less likely to be acted on unless there is a real advantage to doing things differ-

ently. Smaller cost changes in policies and practices can be achieved more readily. Even if the cost is modest, however, some administrators will be reluctant to undertake a policy change. One way of encouraging them to consider a new approach is to seek permission to do it on an experimental basis. An experimental effort could be run for six months and its success carefully evaluated. Success with reasonable costs can then be used to buttress arguments for permanent change.

Another measure of how much resistance will arise when proposing changes is the extent of impact. A change in one aspect of a single agency program is less threatening than changes that will affect the entire unit or agency. In addition, changes that involve modifying the basic mission or goals of an organization will meet with greater resistance than those that amount to tinkering with procedure.

The practitioner's organizational distance from the decision maker also has a bearing on how readily a change will be adopted. The greater the levels of bureaucracy between the two, the more likely that change will be resisted (Patti, 1980). A couple of factors explain this phenomenon. First, the degree of investment and excitement about an idea typically diminishes the further it gets from the initiator. Second, the amount of information that goes up the chain of command in an agency becomes progressively smaller. Each level of administration provides a shorter, more concise summary of the proposal until the very heart of the proposal may be lost. Figure 12.4 diagrams this process of diminishment.

When a new policy proposal might have multiple consequences for an organization, it is sometimes best to suggest establishing a committee to look at all aspects of the idea and report back to agency administrators. Administrators may be more willing to ask a commit-

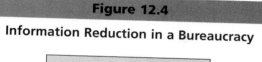

Figure 12.4

Information Reduction in a Bureaucracy

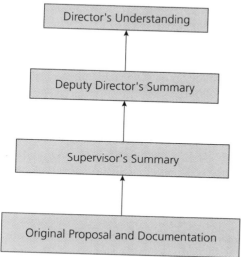

from many different fields is more likely to accept and encourage change than a simpler bureaucracy. The more complex an agency, the more changes it will undergo over time. Third, highly formalized organizations tend to have greater resistance to change. This may be due to the tendency to rely on rules and policies to guide individual and group actions. As workers lose the flexibility to innovate because of the multiplicity of rules, they introduce less change into the organization.

Surviving and prospering within an organizational context is a challenge for many social workers. The larger the agency, the more like a bureaucracy it can become. Effective practice in such organizations requires several things (Sheafor & Horejsi, 2003; Resnick & Patti, 1980), which are identified in Figure 12.5.

Although some social workers may see themselves as relatively powerless to bring about organizational change, they are often in the best position to know when change is needed. It is true that administrators in larger systems often have some power to create change, but that fact does not diminish the direct practitioner's ability to get things done. A social worker's ability to influence an organization is affected by the factors mentioned previously. At the same time, characteristics such as level of access within an organization can increase the practitioner's ability to cause change. For example, access to other people in the organization, to critical information, and to resources such as equipment and money increases change-causing ability. The social worker's level of access tends to be a function of length of time in an agency because seasoned staff gain greater access to these items with each passing year. This observation was at the heart of Pruger's (1973) classic article on the successful bureaucrat, namely that staying

tee to consider something if they know the report will come back to them. Not only does it buy time, but it also helps ensure that the idea will be thoroughly reviewed before any attempt at implementation.

Finally, several other variables can affect an organization's receptivity to change. Hage and Aiken (1980), who studied organizations for many years, identified the influence of each of several factors: degree of centralization, level of agency complexity, and degree of formalization of the agency. Based on their studies of various bureaucratic organizations, they concluded the following. First, decentralized agencies generally find it easier to change, if only because the change is more likely to occur in a smaller arena. Agencies with greater centralization may also have more layers of bureaucracy or administration to go through to bring about change. Second, a complex organization staffed by specialists and professionals

Figure 12.5

Tips for Surviving in a Bureaucracy

- Observe the agency chain of command. This generally means keeping supervisors informed about your activities and any potential problems you are addressing. Do not go over your supervisor's head except in the most drastic of circumstances. If your supervisor believes you have done an end run to the boss, the consequences can be serious.

- Maintain your competence and ensure that your skills and knowledge are always needed by the agency.

- Find ways to go above and beyond what is asked of you. Demonstrate that you bring a lot to the agency beyond your competence as a practitioner.

- Keep a sense of humor. Much that occurs in bureaucracies is actually quite funny if you do not take things too seriously.

- Recognize how slowly organizations change and respect the time it takes to get things done.

- Do not be afraid to question why certain rules exist. There may be good reasons or none at all. Either way, you are in a better position if you know.

- Recognize that one characteristic of every organization is that it has a goal to survive. Things that threaten this survival tend to be opposed.

- Understand that efforts to change an agency will always find some staff who are opposed, some who are in favor, and more who are neutral.

- Seek support from colleagues when trying to change a bureaucracy—it will be essential to success.

- Consider initial opposition to a proposal as an opportunity to improve the proposal and gain further support by incorporating the ideas of others.

- Undertake change efforts only if there is a very good chance that you will be successful. Nothing is more disappointing and discouraging than fighting a battle you cannot hope to win.

- Consider incremental changes a victory. Few organizations change overnight.

---

power in an organization leads to greater influence.

Other factors inherent in an agency have a bearing on the amount of power a direct practitioner can exert on the organization. These include the items listed in Figure 12.6 (Kanter, 1987). This list illustrates just a few of the factors that can enhance a social worker's power to bring about change from within an agency. Changing an agency from within is just one more way of eliminating environ-mental barriers that hamper effective service giving.

Cultural and Diversity Issues

Some of the examples provided in this chapter have indicated that people of color and other groups face more and greater environmental barriers than do whites. For example, there are major differences in the type of mental health care afforded ethnic and racial minorities

APPLICATIONS TO PRACTICE

Case Example

The state legislature has just met to develop the state budget. The proposed budget calls for severe cuts in day care subsidies that will impact the mothers you have been helping to find employment. You have lobbied the legislature, had mothers speak in front of the service committee, and got others to write letters to legislative members, but nothing has been successful as yet. Your organization has worked with several other agencies that are concerned about these cuts,

and the pressure to maintain the current budget on day care subsidies has been heavy. One of the more radical groups of the coalition, Save Our Rights to Employment (SORE), has decided to go to the state capitol to have a sit-in demonstration in the governor's office. Your boss has received a call from the governor's office stating that any employees encouraging this action will be fired. You have notified your employees to continue to engage in the activities they are al-

ready trying, but you feel as though time to ensure the funding is running out.

Critical Thinking Questions
1. What other actions could you engage in to further the cause?
2. How will you manage your messages to the employees and their anger about the governor's edict?
3. What actions will you take related to the coalition?

Research Activity

Identify an issue or barrier that you feel strongly about. Using the Research Navigator™ website, www. researchnavigator.com, find out what is being done nationally and locally about this

issue. If there is a local organization working on this issue, call and ask them if you could talk with the director, observe a board meeting, or talk to people who are experiencing the problem. Prepare a short

report for class that outlines what is being done, what more needs to be done, and what you are going to do in the next month to advocate about this issue.

(Jackson, 2002). A study by NASW of clients served by social workers reflected this difference, finding, for example, that people of color were twice as likely to receive service from larger agencies than from private practitioners (NASW, 2001). Awareness of these barriers and disparities demands that social workers engage in culturally competent practices that help clients achieve their goals.

One approach to cultural competence is to learn about traditional methods of healing

used by the groups with whom you work. This can be a Koranic healer used by some Arab groups or a *curandero* employed by many Spanish-speaking people (Al-Krenawi, 1998). Ethnic groups often have professional healers, and social workers can work with such individuals rather than trying to replace them (Green, 1999). Traditions of each group may include a deep spirituality that forms the basis both for definitions of illness and acceptable treatments. Ensuring that you have a strong

---

Figure 12.6

Factors Increasing the Direct Practitioner's Organizational Power

- The agency has relatively few rules to guide practice.

- The practitioner's position involves few established routines.

- A great variety of tasks is inherent in the practitioner's position.

- The agency provides frequent rewards for innovation.

- The practitioner has frequent contact with agency administrators and decision makers.

- The practitioner is involved in agency-level committees and task forces.

- The practitioner has frequent contact with other practitioners.

- Few or none of the practitioner's predecessors are present in the agency.

---

knowledge base about the different cultures with which you most commonly work is one way to avoid becoming a barrier yourself.

Another approach is to use professional theories and techniques differently depending on the culture. For example, Al-Krenawi (1998) reports the ways in which he adapted his Western style of practice to work with Arab Bedouin clients who expected him to be more directive, provide advice, and offer instructions on how to proceed. He advises that "practitioners would do well (1) to learn about, value, and show respect for their clients' culture, and especially for their traditional and religious approaches to psychological healing; and (2) in their own practice to draw upon and support the conjoint use of the

traditional healing methods (e.g., rituals) in the patient's religion and culture" (p. 17). Figure 12.7 summarizes some of the ways in which social workers can adjust their practice to clients from different cultural groups (Al-Krenawi, 1998, p. 18).

This list is not intended to be an exhaustive or comprehensive guide to effective practice with diverse groups. Social workers will learn as they work with various groups experiencing environmental barriers that it is essential to improvise, acquire further knowledge about

---

Figure 12.7

Guidelines Regarding Diversity

1. Make conscious efforts to understand the culture, beliefs, values, and religion of the clients with whom we work.

2. Identify with the client the role of their nuclear and extended family, particularly in terms of family rituals and significant members.

3. Identify community resources such as spiritual leaders or other community-level rituals.

4. Clarify the client's own understanding of the symptoms or problem. For example, how has the client attempted to resolve or improve the situation?

5. Take into account both the client's definition of the problem as well as those of others in the client's world such as family or natural healers.

6. If traditional healers have been consulted, ask about their suggested treatment.

7. Consider what role being ill or disturbed has in the client's family. Does it carry stigma or benefits?

8. Adapt an active and directive role when this is consistent with the expectations and values of the client.

---

each group, and carefully monitor practice results. In this way, the practitioner is less likely to become another obstacle to people receiving the help they need.

SUMMARY

This chapter begins with a recognition that many problems experienced by clients are the result of, or involve, barriers in the environment. Barriers can be of several types, including physical, policy and procedural, emotional/social, cultural, or informational. Overcoming these barriers requires a variety of skills and roles. In particular, the chapter looks at case management and coordination roles and advocacy roles in depth. Other environmental challenges and change strategies are identified, including social action, social planning, and organizational change. The force-field analysis is identified as a tool that can be used by direct practitioners seeking change in larger systems.

The chapter also discusses ideas for creating new programs and for changing organizational policies and practices. Both ethical

issues and cultural and diversity considerations are also addressed.

Navigating Direct Practice

An access code for Research Navigator™ is packaged within your text. Use this code to register at www.researchnavigator.com and then use the key words listed below to research articles related to the chapter's content. Research Navigator™ helps you quickly and efficiently make the most of your research time.

- ❏ Advocacy
- ❏ Hasenfeld
- ❏ Health Insurance and Portability Accounting Act
- ❏ Kruzich
- ❏ National Association of Social Workers
- ❏ National Center on Addiction and Substance Abuse

Chapter 13

Knowledge and Skills for Evaluation

Jorge is new to his position as a therapist at the Mountain View Mental Health Center. Having completed his MSW degree six months earlier, he is just starting to understand the agency and its expectations. His supervisor has talked with him recently about beginning to evaluate his practice with clients, saying that it is both agency policy and a factor in his own annual personnel review. Jorge knows the agency largely provides brief therapy in which social workers and clients set specific goals to deal with clearly defined problems. Typically, clients come for about six sessions before termination. Jorge decides to go back and look at some of his textbooks to see what methods might make the most sense for evaluating brief therapy with clients. Following this review, he prepares some notes that he will discuss with his supervisor at their next session. He proposes to do two things that could prove helpful in determining whether clients are benefiting from his work with them. The first is to use a system similar to that discussed by De Jong and Hopwood (1996). This method involves asking clients after each session to rate on a scale of 1 to 10 where they are now compared to where they were when they first came to therapy. A rating of 1 means that the client's problems are the very worst they have been, whereas 10 indicates that the initial problems have been completely resolved. By collecting these data after each session, Jorge will be able to see through the eyes of the clients what progress they feel they have made.

The second method Jorge thinks he might use is either a single-subject design or a goal-attainment scaling approach. He learned about both of these as a student and knows from his review that a client's situation might be a factor in which of these approaches he can use. Now Jorge feels more or less ready to discuss evaluation with his supervisor.

This chapter is devoted to the proposition that evaluating one's practice is an obligation inherent in the role of social worker. It is considered just as important as doing assessments or selecting and carrying out an intervention. In the following pages, we address several perspectives on evaluation, including definitions of evaluation, the rationale for evaluating direct practice, and the ethics of evaluation. We then identify several practice evaluation approaches considered most appropriate. These include single-system designs, goal-attainment scaling, target-problem scaling, task-achievement scaling, satisfaction studies, and quality assurance.

In addition, we consider the role of group designs in practice evaluation, focusing on both experimental and quasi-experimental designs. Finally, we address cultural and diversity issues impinging on evaluation and conclude with some general recommendations about evaluation.

Defining Evaluation

Evaluation is the process of determining the effectiveness of our work with clients and is concerned with whether the outcomes the worker and client hoped for have been achieved. To a lesser degree, it is also concerned with the activities carried out by clients and social workers as they work to bring about change. On the one hand, activities are important because they should be consistent with the goals and objectives set in the helping process. In other words, the behaviors of the client and the worker should help achieve the outcomes desired. They should also reflect professionally accepted actions that have been generally recognized as tools to bring about change. When practitioners use methods that have not been validated and researched, they run the risk of harming clients and placing themselves in danger.

On the other hand, the methods used to help clients tend to have less importance than the outcomes because it is possible for both worker and client to do everything expected and still generate no change in the outcome. The client remains depressed and angry, or the family continues its disintegration. In this chapter, we are concerned primarily with outcomes, or the changes that occur in the lives of the clients we serve.

Rationale for Evaluation

The inclusion of evaluation as a step in the problem-solving process underscores the idea that it is widely recognized as a legitimate component of our helping activities. Evaluation becomes as essential a skill as asking questions, identifying problems, selecting interventions, and using empathy. From this standpoint, evaluation is a logical or rational activity for any helping professional. It is one of the ways we determine what works for us as helpers and what clients found most helpful. As such it is a means to improve our social work skills and knowledge.

In addition, the NASW Code of Ethics (1999) (discussed in Chapter 3) identifies practice evaluation as an ethical obligation of all social workers. As you may recall, the code specifically requires that social workers "monitor and evaluate policies, the implementation of programs, and **practice interventions**" (p. 25; emphasis added). Moreover, the code requires that social workers use the results of evaluations in their professional practice. The reasons for including these obligations in the code are commonsensical. First, clients deserve to be helped using approaches that have proven effective with other clients facing similar problems or challenges. Clients should not be guinea pigs for practitioners who want to test out their own unique theories and techniques. Second, careful evaluation of our practice allows us to share this information with others. This is the way that knowledge is built in any profession—through evaluating interventions and sharing the results with others. As such, evaluation supports the ethical principle of competence, a key concept undergirding the Code of Ethics (Nugent, Sieppert, & Hudson, 2001).

Another reason for conducting evaluations is the demand for accountability placed on social workers by managed care companies, which encourage interventions that produce the desired outcomes. These organizations often approve social work interventions only for problems for which past research has shown effective treatments are available. Ineffective treatments and interventions are unlikely to be approved by managed care corporations.

Besides managed care, other funding agencies require accountability and evaluation of social work interventions. Some of this focus was driven by the 1993 Government Performance and Results Act, which requires federal agencies to establish measurable goals and assess outcomes (Ginsberg, 2001). These requirements extend to organizations and agencies that receive federal funds through such things as grants and contracts. The same is true of other funding bodies such as foundations, which expect ongoing monitoring and evaluation of whatever type of intervention is being proposed.

Accountability extends well beyond managed care to the social worker's own agency and those with which it has contracts for services. Social service and mental health agencies face budget constraints that make wasting resources unacceptable. Resources include the activities of social work staff. In other words, if social workers engage in methods or approaches that are ineffective, they are creating further problems for their own employer. Social workers who fail repeatedly to help clients achieve their goals and objectives are likely to be replaced.

In addition, agencies are concerned about whether services are delivered as efficiently as possible. If the same outcome can be achieved through fewer sessions or different interventions, the service organization is likely to increase the use of those approaches. Inefficient treatments end up using resources that could be spent on other needs.

Another reason for evaluation is the benefits it brings to our clients. When clients see change occurring in the direction of their goals, this can serve as further motivation (Poulin, 2000). At the same time, lack of progress can indicate to the client that additional effort is needed. Several studies have demonstrated that clients enjoy participating in the evaluation process and may be more interested in evaluating effectiveness than are their social workers (Young & Poulin, 1998).

Fortunately, social work research and practice texts are paying much greater attention to the knowledge and skills needed to evaluate one's own practice. Most texts now provide content dealing with practice evaluation, particularly single-subject designs, which can serve as a resource for practitioners.

Ethical Issues in Evaluation

In Chapter 3, we discussed the importance of social workers engaging in ethical practice. Ethical issues also influence the evaluation process in several ways. Thus, the social worker must be alert to ways in which decisions in this arena may have ethical implications and adhere to this obligation when evaluating practice. One example of this is ensuring that client information is safeguarded and that clients remain anonymous (Yegidis & Weinbach, 2002). This is especially true when we use computers to help us with data analysis. Access to client records maintained on a computer must be restricted to prevent this information from being available to other staff.

Likewise, clients should not be coerced in any way to participate in an evaluation. Although the social worker may not intend to coerce clients into participating, the very fact that clients have a prior relationship with the practitioner may result in their feeling some degree of pressure to become involved in the evaluation.

In addition, evaluators are supposed to be neutral and objective when completing this task. This is made more difficult in practice evaluation because the social worker is the one who engaged in the behavior now being evaluated. This places a special burden on the social worker to report findings honestly even if the findings suggest that the helping process did not achieve success.

Another ethical requirement when reporting findings is to acknowledge their limitations. For example, the types of evaluations used in practice usually do not allow us to generalize our findings to any other group or individual. Nor do they allow us to attribute causality to our own interventions regardless of how positive the outcome. Thus, we should be extremely cautious not only in reporting our findings but also in generalizing them to other clients with whom we work.

Social workers have an obligation not to harm their clients. Should our evaluation indicate that things are getting worse for the client instead of better, ending the relationship must be considered an option (Yegidis & Weinbach, 2002). Although this outcome is not likely, it cannot be ignored.

As in other aspects of direct practice, social workers should not engage in deception unless there is absolutely no alternative. Clients must give their informed consent to participate in research and evaluation, and deception effectively prevents this from happening (Wilkinson & McNeil, 1996).

Larger agencies or social service organizations may have an internal **institutional review board (IRB)** that is tasked with the responsibility of ensuring that evaluations and other research protect the rights of participants. In such cases, the agency may have a blanket system of evaluation that meets the standard of protecting human subjects. At other times, a social worker may need to request approval from the IRB prior to engaging in an evaluation.

Although observing these ethical standards and procedures may seem burdensome, they are designed to prevent injury or harm to the subjects of evaluations. They were instituted in response to some horrendous examples of research conducted without any regard for the well-being of participants. Both federal and state laws require that these protections be accorded to each and every person who is the subject of research.

Evaluation Approaches for Direct Practice

One real benefit of evaluating direct practice in the twenty-first century is the wealth of tools available to practitioners. Thirty years ago, evaluation approaches were limited, and many social workers had no idea how to go about evaluating their practice. Today this topic is addressed at both the BSW and MSW levels of education, in part because of accreditation requirements of the Council on Social Work Education (CSWE). CSWE is the national body responsible for evaluating the quality of baccalaureate and master's programs in social work, and it has required that these educational programs prepare students "to evaluate their own practice" (2003, p. 36).

Among the evaluation tools discussed in this chapter are single-system designs, goal-attainment scaling, target-problem scaling, task-achievement scaling, satisfaction studies, quality assurance methods, and group designs. We also briefly discuss the advantages and disadvantages of each approach.

Quantitative versus Qualitative Evaluation

Evaluation designs can be considered as falling along a continuum, with one end representing quantitative approaches and the other qualitative methods. Quantitative designs are those that "translate observations into numbers and statistics that are presented in the forms of graphs, frequency distributions, and other statistics. In some cases, numerical data and statistics are used to infer facts about the phenomena being studied through the use of inferential statistical tests" (Ginsburg, 2001, p. 32). Qualitative designs are those whose "focus is on variables and characteristics that are essentially non-numerical" (p. 33). Although these two approaches would seem substantially different, there is significant overlap on some dimensions. For example, it is not unusual for social workers using qualitative measures to convert their findings into numbers.

Two of the commonly employed approaches discussed in this chapter (target-problem scaling and goal-attainment scaling) fall more on the qualitative side of the continuum. Other methods such as quasi-experimental and designs that use multiple baselines fall on the quantitative end (Alter & Evens, 1990). More important, however, is the fact that both approaches provide helpful methods that can be used by social workers who want to evaluate their own practice.

Limitations Inherent in Practice Evaluation

It is important to understand that most of the evaluation methods described in the following pages are designed only to tell us whether clients achieved their goals and whether critical tasks necessary for goal attainment were performed. Although the benefits of practice evaluation are clear, the limitations inherent in most practice evaluation approaches are also significant. For example, we cannot generalize the results of our findings to other cases or other situations because methods such as single-system designs do not meet the criteria needed for such assumptions. Even if our intervention proved enormously successful with a client experiencing anxiety, we cannot assume that this intervention will work as well with other anxious clients. The ability to generalize from one situation to another requires

that we have comparative data and use methods designed specifically for this purpose. We discuss these methods more directly later in this chapter.

A second major limitation is the inability to attribute causation to our interventions. Although it would be nice to say that our work with the client produced the changes she or he experienced, this is simply not possible with most practice evaluation methods. Establishing causality between two events such as treatment and outcome requires that we meet a variety of criteria, most of which cannot be accomplished with simple practice evaluation approaches. For example, one important criterion is that "the observed empirical correlation between two variables cannot be explained away as the result of the influence of some third variable" (Rubin & Babbie, 2001, p. 294). When we are working with clients, we are aware that other things are going on in their lives simultaneously. They are getting older, experiencing different things, interacting with others, thinking, and feeling. In reality, many more things are going on in their lives than our intervention. Consequently, we cannot claim that it was our assistance that produced the change we see in the client. Although it is entirely possible that our help was the only factor resulting in achievement of the client's goals, it also possible that other experiences, alone or in combination with intervention, caused the change. We explore this area later in the chapter when we address group designs. In the meantime, as you consider each of the following practice evaluation strategies, please keep these admonitions in mind.

Single-System Designs

As Yegidis and her colleagues note, single-system designs are intended to help us answer the question "Does what I am doing with this client or with this client system seem to be making a difference?" and "If it does seem to be making a difference, is the change consistent with my intervention goals?" (1999, p. 269). Single-system designs, as their name implies, are most often used with individual cases. They can be employed with small groups and families in situations in which the problems being addressed fit the single-subject model. Different authors may refer to this model using various terms, including *single subject, n = 1,* "single case time-series, single system research, and ideographic research" (Yegidis et al., 1999, p. 269). One reason for using the term **single-system** design is that it clarifies that it can be used with other systems besides the individual client.

The process for using these designs is straightforward. Social workers collect data from clients (and sometimes others), analyze it, and then interpret the results to help them make appropriate decisions about practice effectiveness. The sources of data can be quite varied. For example, clients may complete logs that provide a day-by-day history of what behaviors occurred and when. Family members such as spouses or siblings can keep similar records of target behaviors. Sometimes organizational records can provide this information. A school will have records of class absence and grades, both of which might be important dependent variables. Employee absence or other agency records may also be available and helpful, depending on the particular objective. Still other data sources may come about through behavioral observation, in which specific behaviors are identified as targets for change, the client is observed, and a record made of incidence of the target behavior. The observation can be completed by the client, family members, teachers, or others in a position to correctly identify and record occurrence of the behavior. For example, a teacher might count the number of times each period that Johnny gets out of his seat without asking. A parent might record the times a child with a curfew comes in on time. The practitioner might record the number of times each member of a couple says something derogatory about the other person or the frequency with which a shy group member opens up to other members.

Another source of data may come from rating scales or other instruments designed to measure change in a particular area. Examples include scales designed to measure self-esteem, depression, anxiety, and many other individual characteristics. Two common instruments are the Beck Depression Inventory (Beck, 1991) and the Global Assessment of Functioning (GAF) scale in the *Diagnostic and Statistical Manual of Mental Disorders* (4th ed., Text Revision) (APA, 2000). Typically, many of these instruments are used by the practitioner and completed by the client. In some instances, other agencies or organizations may be responsible for giving and analyzing these instruments. Rating scales typically fall into two categories, those that the practitioner creates for the individual client and those that are standardized. There are advantages in using standardized instruments with established reliability and validity.

Decisions about which data sources to use are made during the assessment phase of the problem-solving process. Clients should be involved whenever possible in the process of considering what will be used to measure progress. Practitioners need to be thinking about an evaluation plan at this early stage in the helping process and should be familiar with the options available.

As an evaluation tool, single-system designs can be used to evaluate changes in behavior as well as less obvious things such as client beliefs or attitudes. They are based on the assumption that changes in the system can be seen and measured to some degree (Yegidis & Weinbach, 2002). We discuss specifically five kinds of models that fit under the term *single-subject design*: AB, B, ABA, ABAB, and ABCD. Other options are available and can be used as needed.

AB Designs

To understand single-subject designs, we must first define two research concepts, A and B. When clients first come to us, they often report situations they are finding intolerable in their lives. These could be marital discord, parent–child conflicts, or other situations that have been going on for some time. To be most helpful from an evaluation standpoint, clients would ideally provide us with specific information about how often these situations occur or their level of seriousness, or both. Data on the frequency, intensity, and duration of the problem give us a starting point from which to determine when change is occurring. For example, consider a child who has skipped school an average of two days each week during the preceding semester. This information allows us to construct a **baseline** from which we can determine future change. The baseline or preintervention phase is the "A" in the AB design and represents the starting point. In this case, the twice-a-week truancy rate can be compared with the days absent after we begin the intervention. The intervention phase is the "B" part of the AB design.

Figure 13.1 shows how this design might look if employed in the case of the truant youngster. As is evident, the A phase or baseline period shows that the child was absent from one to three days a week in the five-week period prior to intervention. After intervention

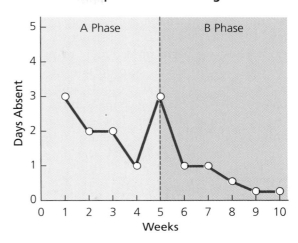

Figure 13.1

Example of an AB Design

began, the frequency of absences dropped to one and then to none. Because the reason the family sought help was the child's absences from school, this is definitely an improvement and *suggests* that the intervention worked. It would be useful to know whether this improvement in attendance continued for the rest of the school year. However, the agency might not engage in follow-up, so there is no way of ascertaining whether the improvement carried over past intervention. AB designs work well only when there is either a record of problem behavior prior to intervention or when a record can be constructed. Attempts to reconstruct such things as the number of arguments or the frequency of drinking binges after the fact are of limited effectiveness because people's recall may not be accurate. In the case of truancy or absences from work, records often do exist and a retrospective A phase can be created.

When an A phase or baseline cannot be determined, we must consider other models. A common alternative is the B design.

B Designs

Often clients come to us without the luxury of a baseline period. They seek help now and would not be amenable to going away for a few weeks so that we can construct the A period. Thus, we begin immediately to provide whatever help seems appropriate to their needs. This means that we have only the B phase to use for charting changes in the problem behavior or situation. It is equally important in B designs that we carefully define the problem and measure changes over time.

For example, a family has been struggling with frequent arguments between the father and the oldest daughter. The goal of intervention is to help these two begin to communicate in ways that do not automatically result in argumentation. Figure 13.2 shows a B-only design for this family. The chart shows that arguments between father and daughter did decrease in the weeks following intervention, although they were not completely eliminated by the end of the ten-week period. In such situations, the family may wish to contract for additional sessions or they may be satisfied with the progress and forego more treatment. Again, this design is common when no prior baseline can be established, a situation not unusual in much of social work practice.

ABA Designs

ABA designs are used in situations when a regular AB design is followed by a period in which no intervention occurs. Perhaps the client goes on vacation for a month during the summer and thus will not be receiving any help for a while. Such a period could also be caused by the practitioner leaving for similar reasons. Assume the social worker is working with a couple who are having difficulty making a decision about whether to put the woman's mother in a nursing home or similar facility.

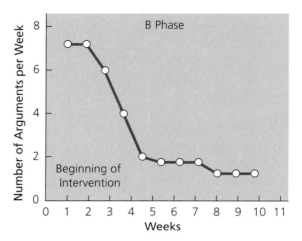

Figure 13.2

Example of a B Design

They have been caring for the woman for two years and recently have been at odds over what to do. The husband wants her placed in a facility, whereas the daughter wants to try keeping her at home a little longer. The tension between the couple is growing and has led to some nasty fights. The couple agree to see a family therapist for six weeks to see if they can reach some agreement that will satisfy both of them. They see the practitioner for four weeks and seem to have found a way to discuss the matter without resorting to arguments and fighting. At the end of the four weeks, the couple leaves for a brief vacation. On returning they report having spent the last week arguing about the same issue.

Figure 13.3 shows how the practitioner might chart this situation. This chart shows a high level of conflict in the three weeks before intervention, a steady decline during intervention, and a sharp rise during the couple's vacation period. This suggests that the couple have not really learned to resolve their issues. They are fine when in therapy but return to old behaviors

Figure 13.3

Example of an ABA Design

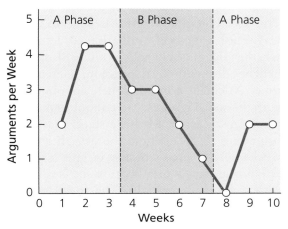

effort will be needed to stabilize the change effort and help ensure longer-lasting results.

ABAB Designs

ABAB designs involve two baseline and two treatment or intervention phases. For example, if the ABA design shown in Figure 13.3 was used and treatment continued for another four-week period, we would end up with an ABAB design. There are two real advantages to this design. First, the additional intervention period serves to solidify gains made in the first treatment phase. Clients have the opportunity to practice new behaviors and expand the situations in which these behaviors are used. Second, from a research standpoint it is easier to see that the change in client behavior is related directly to the intervention. It also helps practitioners identify whether clients have developed dependency on them or have been able to continue improvement on their own. Figure 13.4 shows what happens when we add a second intervention period to the preceding case.

afterward. The goal of intervention is to help people resolve their problems and learn how to deal with future challenges outside of the therapeutic relationship. In this situation, additional

Figure 13.4

Example of an ABAB Design

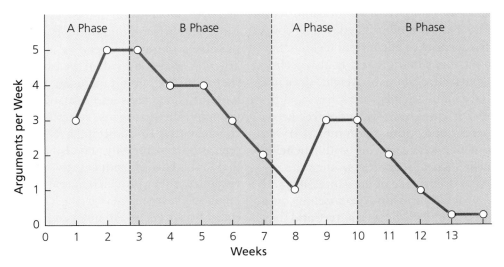

ABCD Designs

It should be clear by now that these designs can be varied in several ways to help evaluate the effectiveness of any given intervention. Each of these designs is based on the assumption of using a single type of intervention across each of the B phases. In other words, only one treatment is administered during the B phase. The treatment may be relaxation, assertiveness training, counseling using a specific approach, systematic desensitization, or some other method considered appropriate for helping the client system. However, it is not uncommon to encounter situations in which different treatments are integrated with one another to help clients achieve their goals. This may occur because several possible interventions have proven effective for a particular problem. For example, it is common to treat people suffering from depression with both counseling and medication.

Consider the case of Michelle, a thirty-four-year-old administrative assistant, who makes an appointment to see a social worker because she is feeling depressed. After an initial interview, the social worker learns that Michelle ended a long-term relationship with her boyfriend about a month ago, which coincided with the onset of her current feelings. She is sad about this situation and is also feeling bad about herself. She is overweight, does not seem to have many friends, and is having difficulty with her employer. The employer keeps moving her around within the company trying to find someone who can work with Michelle.

Michelle's social worker considers the relatively recent occurrence of the depression and offers to provide individual counseling over the next two months. Michelle agrees and they make weekly appointments. The initial goal is to work on reducing Michelle's feelings of un-

happiness over her current situation. However, after four appointments Michelle reports not feeling much better. In fact, she says she has lost her appetite and is having trouble sleeping. The social worker refers Michelle to a colleague for a medical evaluation to determine whether she might benefit from medication to help her deal with the depression. In the meantime, Michelle continues her appointments with the social worker. After about four weeks on the medication, Michelle states that she is beginning to feel better. She asks her social worker if she knows of any weight loss programs that truly work, because she is still concerned about her weight. The social worker suggests a couple of programs, and Michelle elects to join one of them.

In this scenario, the social worker has introduced three specific interventions over the course of the case. The first was counseling, to which was added antidepression medication, and finally a weight reduction program. In an ideal world, we might like to have each of the treatments given independently of one another. This would help determine which seemed to have the biggest impact on the client's situation. In Michelle's case, the counseling continued over the duration of the treatment. From a cause-and-effect standpoint, it is almost impossible to know the relative effectiveness of any one of the individual treatments because they occurred simultaneously. On the other hand, it is not unusual for a social worker to use multiple treatments, either sequentially or concurrently. In addition, a client might be seen as part of a family and also alone as an individual. This introduces two **independent variables,** either of which, alone or in tandem, might be responsible for the change experienced by the client. An independent variable is the factor that we believe produces a particular outcome. Thus, in direct practice, counseling or therapy with a client experiencing low self-esteem would be considered the independent variable. By contrast, the client's score on a self-esteem scale would be the **dependent variable** because this is thought to be affected by the therapeutic activities of the practitioners. Figure 13.5 shows how Michelle's situation might be graphed. Numbers on the left-hand side of the graph indicate the number of times a day Michelle feels depressed. She notes that the depression began when the relationship with her boyfriend ended, and this is represented by the diagonal line beginning at the zero point on the horizontal scale.

Multiple Goals and Baselines

Although the previous examples have considered only a single goal, it is certainly possible to measure achievement of more than one goal using single-system designs. Let's use as an example a child who is wetting the bed

each night and getting in fights with his sister. For simplicity's sake, Figure 13.6 uses a simple AB design to demonstrate how two goals—eliminating bed-wetting and sibling arguments—can be accommodated on a single graph. Keep in mind that this method can accommodate as many goals as will logically fit on the graph.

Advantages and Disadvantages of Single-System Designs

Generally speaking, single-system designs are easy to use when specific goals have been identified and change can be measured in some fashion. They are also inexpensive, an important factor in view of limited resources, and can be easily understood by both staff and workers (Yegidis & Weinbach, 2002). Moreover, they are more timely than many evaluation tools, largely because they can provide almost immediate information, whereas

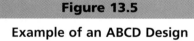

Figure 13.5

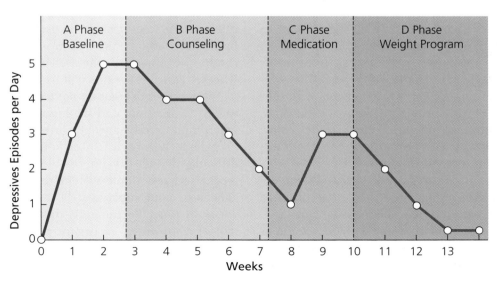

Example of an ABCD Design

Figure 13.6

Example of Multiple Goals and Baselines

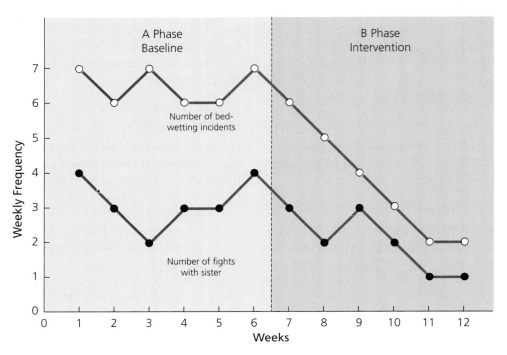

follow-up studies may provide data only months or years later. In the long run, information gleaned from single-system designs can begin to show patterns that can inform our practice. For example, if repeated single-system evaluations show that clients with substance abuse problems improve after a combination of individual and group therapy, this information appears to support the effectiveness of these interventions.

A major drawback of single-system designs is that results cannot be generalized to other situations. Just because a particular client is successful in coping with depression or anxiety does not mean that our approaches will work equally well with other clients, even

those experiencing similar problems. Neither can single-system designs be used to assess a particular method of intervention. Nor can the results be used by themselves to predict whether entire programs will be effective.

Some types of cases do not lend themselves to easy evaluation, and the models work best when supported by agency norms and policies (Yegidis & Weinbach, 2002). For example, it is difficult, though not impossible, for a social worker to use single-system research if the agency or your supervisor believes it to be a waste of time. Fortunately, this is becoming less of a problem as organizations become more sophisticated about evaluating social work practice.

Goal-Attainment Scaling

As we established in our discussion of the advantages and disadvantages of single-system designs, this method of evaluation is not appropriate for every situation. As a result, practitioners and researchers have developed other tools that can be employed to assist in evaluating our practice. One of these is called **goal-attainment scaling (GAS)**. GAS is an evaluation tool that has been used to assess changes in systems ranging from individuals to organizations and that is employed by a variety of human service providers (Bloom, Fischer, & Orme, 1995). The process of using GAS involves carefully identifying the client's

problems, assessing and assigning relative weights to each problem, listing the anticipated goals for each of the problems, collecting data on the actual outcomes achieved, and developing an average rating for the client or clients. Figure 13.7 discusses each of these steps in detail.

GAS gives us another mechanism to help assess what kinds of progress the client system is making on each of them. Figure 13.8 shows a completed goal-attainment scaling sheet for an adolescent who is in conflict with his parents on several dimensions. As might be expected, this sheet is created at the conclusion of goal setting. At the end of the intervention, the social worker places some indicator in the appropriate column and row for each goal. This

---

Figure 13.7

Goal-Attainment Scaling

Step 1: *Identify client problems.* This takes place through interviews with the client and/or others who are familiar with the situation, as well as through any other available sources of information. This might include test results, data from various assessment instruments, and the social worker's own observations.

Step 2: *Select client problems to work on.* This is a joint process with the client in which multiple problems are culled to produce a list of the most serious concerns needing attention. These problems run the gamut from such issues as "interpersonal conflict, reactive emotional distress, problem solving, problems of role transition, human sexuality, child rearing/child care, and so on" (Bloom et al., 1995, p. 81). Each of these problems is redefined as a goal and given a weight that suggests its relative importance to the client.

Step 3: *Identify scale of behaviors to be used.* In this step, we are listing behaviors that represent levels of progress toward full achievement of each goal. Identify the expected level of success that reflects a reasonable estimate and then move to the most unfavorable outcomes and most favorable outcomes.

Step 4: *Complete the goal attainment scaling sheet.* Enter the goals, weights, and levels on a blank goal attainment sheet (see Figure 13.8) along with the points associated with each level of attainment.

Step 5: *Evaluate outcomes.* Gather data on the client system's success on each of the problem areas and enter this on the scaling sheet.

Step 6: *Calculate the overall GAS scores and each scale score.* This step involves multiplying the weight of each goal by the number for the level of goal achievement (see Figure 13.8).

could be a check mark or, depending on the age of the client, a sticker of the sort used by teachers to signify good work. In this case, the adolescent's progress is shown by the achievement levels that are highlighted on the sheet. Using the relative weight of each goal, multiplied by the points shown in the level column, allows calculation of an overall GAS score. For example, the first goal was weighted at 10 points and the expected level of achievement (0 points) was reached. The second and third goals, each weighted at 8 points, show improvement that was better than expected (+1 point). A simple calculation would look as follows: $10 \times 0 = 0$, $8 \times 1 = 8$, $8 \times 1 = 8$. Thus, the overall GAS score for this case is $0 + 8 + 8$ or 16, a favorable outcome by most standards.

Advantages and Disadvantages of Goal-Attainment Scaling

A major advantage of goal-attainment scaling is its flexibility, reliability, and inherent face validity (Alter & Evens, 1990). GAS can be used to track goal achievement at all levels including work with larger systems. One of the benefits of GAS is the ability to graphically list multiple goals and their relative importance to the client. This gives both client and worker an opportunity to think about what problems really are more serious and which ones are less consequential. This method also provides a mechanism to scale goals from the worst possible outcome to the best possible outcome while simultaneously identifying a reasonable level of goal achievement. Unlike single-subject designs, which focus on changes in behavior or

---

Figure 13.8

Completed Goal-Attainment Scaling Sheet

Goal-Attainment Scaling Sheet

Levels of Success	Problems and Weights		
	Mike will discontinue his angry outbursts (Weight = 10)	Mike will complete his chores (Weight = 8)	Mike will participate in family activities (Weight = 8)
Most unfavorable outcome (−2)	Continued high frequency of outbursts (2+ per day)	Never completes chores	Never participates in family activities
Less than expected success (−1)	Outbursts occur less often (1 per day)	Completes chores only when asked repeatedly	Participates in family activities rarely
Expected success level (0)	Outbursts occur infrequently (1 per week)	Completes chores with one reminder	Participates in one family activity extra at least weekly
Better than expected level (+1)	Outbursts occur rarely (1 per month)	Completes chores without being asked	Participates in family activities whenever asked
Most favorable outcome (+2)	Outbursts no longer occur	Asks if he can help with other chores	Participates in family activities without being asked

attitude, GAS is concerned with the client's goals. By doing so, it helps empower clients, who are the ones responsible for identifying and achieving their own goals (Poulin, 2000). Regular use of the chart can help clients see the progress they are making toward achieving their goals.

Disadvantages to this model include the possibility that either the problems themselves or the relative weights will not precisely capture the client's real situation. For example, it is possible that the relative weights of a goal may change during the intervention phase, requiring updating of the goal-attainment scaling sheet. Another limitation arises because some goals cannot be scaled as easily as others. GAS can cease to be useful if the goals and the various levels of achievement are not precisely defined. Vague goal statements can seriously undermine the value of this evaluation tool. For example, setting goals such as "feel happier" or "will have better self-esteem" are often too vague to be useful (Nurius & Hudson, 1993).

Target-Problem Scaling

Target-problem scaling is used in situations in which the social worker and the client have identified a problem that is targeted for elimination or reduction (Alter & Evens, 1990). This evaluation method is most useful when it is difficult or impossible to quantify outcomes. The first step is to state the problems in behaviorally specific terms. Each problem is to be assessed using the following scale:

Extremely serious (ES)
Very serious (VS)
Serious (S)
Not very serious (NVS)
No problem (NP)

This step is completed by clients, who are in the best position to know the relative severity of the initial problems for which they are seeking help.

The next step is to employ the interventions considered appropriate to each problem. This is followed by "repeated ratings of the extent to which the problem has been ameliorated, reduced, or eliminated" (Alter & Evens, 1990, p. 63). Whoever is doing the ratings uses the following rating scale:

1 = Worse   2 = No change   3 = A little better
    4 = Somewhat better   5 = A lot better

Finally, a global rating is assigned based on an average (mean) of all the problems.

Most often both the client and the social worker complete the rating process, although others in the client's environment can assist when this is appropriate. For example, a parent might help evaluate the extent to which a child's problem has been controlled or eradicated. Figure 13.9 shows an example of a target-problem rating sheet. In this case, the client is dealing with low self-esteem coupled with high levels of anxiety in social situations, which together are gradually limiting her functioning at home and at work.

As might be evident, this system can be expanded to include multiple problems using the same framework. It is also possible to list problems for different clients on a single sheet. This might be the case for members of the same family or for group members.

Advantages and Disadvantages of Target-Problem Scaling

A big advantage of target-problem scaling is that it does not intrude on the helping process and fits well into the usual problem-solving process. Its relative simplicity means that it

Figure 13.9

Target-Problem Rating Scale

Target-Problem Rater: Self	Target-Problem Rating Severity Level			Target-Problem Rating Change Scale		Global Rating
	Start	Time 1	Time 2	Termination	Follow-up	
High anxiety in social situations	ES	S	NP	5	5	4.5
Low self-esteem	S	S	NVS	3	4	

can be used even with clients who have limited educational development, verbal skills, or both. Reliability is good and the instrument can be used with multiple problems.

Like all evaluation methods, target-problem scaling has some drawbacks, one of which is its narrow focus on problems. Overt attention to clients' problems tends to run counter to a strengths-based philosophy of intervention. In addition, there is little information available regarding validity except for face validity (Alter & Evens, 1990).

Task-Achievement Scaling

The methods previously discussed are useful for evaluating progress in achieving goals and reducing problems, but these are not the only tools available. Moreover, they are not always the most appropriate tools for certain kinds of social work practice. Some kinds of practice are focused on the social worker's completion of specific tasks. These tasks in turn are directly related to achievement of client goals. Consider the case of a social worker helping an adolescent client currently living in an inpa-

tient psychiatric facility. The client has completed a three-week course of intensive therapy that included group sessions, individual psychotherapy, and medication. She is going home in a couple of days but will need some assistance in several areas. Before she can be released, however, the social worker has several tasks to complete. For example, the client's parents must be notified about her scheduled discharge so that they can provide transportation. The social worker will take responsibility for ensuring that this contact is made. Next, the client must be given information on an outpatient group that she is supposed to join to help her maintain her stability once she is discharged. Information to be provided by the social worker includes meeting location, times, cost, and contact information. Finally, the social worker is responsible for regular liaison with the client to ensure that progress made in the treatment center carries on afterward. Thus, the worker will need to establish a schedule of appointments and/or follow-up visits in the community.

These tasks are all related to the ultimate goal of helping the client maintain herself following discharge from the treatment center. One way the social worker can evaluate the extent to which these tasks are completed is using the task-achievement scale. An example of task-achievement scaling is shown in Figure 13.10.

Reid and Epstein (1972) developed task-achievement scaling as an adjunct to their work with clients using task-centered casework. Although the example here involves tasks the social worker is to complete, it is just as appropriate to use this model to evaluate the extent to which clients complete tasks needed to reach their goals. Thus, this method could be used to help a client keep track of and follow up on important activities that must be completed. An example of client tasks might include:

1. Complete application for medical assistance.
2. Schedule medical examination for six-month-old daughter.
3. Make appointment to learn about obtaining GED.

There is no time frame provided for task-achievement scaling, and it is assumed that the tasks will be completed within whatever time frame was established during earlier stages of the problem-solving process.

Advantages and Disadvantages of Task-Achievement Scaling

Task-achievement scaling is an excellent system for keeping track of important tasks required to help clients achieve their goals. Whether the tasks are to be completed by the social worker or the client is irrelevant because the system works equally well for both.

You may already have considered a potential disadvantage to this method. For example, it was noted earlier that a task or activity can be completed with the goal still not reached. The assumption underlying task-achievement scaling is that completing the task will lead to the goal. Sometimes this just does not happen. At other times, clients may not complete the tasks fully. This might suggest the client is insufficiently motivated or that some barrier prevented full completion. The practitioner must work with the client to identify what is responsible for incomplete tasks, plan to overcome barriers, or change the tasks.

Figure 13.10

Task-Achievement Scaling

Social Worker Task	Extent of Achievement	Rating
Notify parents regarding discharge date and time	Parents notified and will come to social worker's office on arrival	5
Provide client with information on outpatient support group	Client given preprinted handout with times and dates of meeting	5
Schedule appointments and home visits with client	Two appointments scheduled	3

Rating Scale: 5 = Completed, 4 = Substantially completed, 3 = Partially completed, 2 = Not completed, 1 = No opportunity

Satisfaction Studies

Satisfaction studies are simply ways for the social worker to obtain feedback from clients or others receiving service. Generally speaking, such studies consist of a survey instrument that contains questions directly related to specific social worker behaviors. For example, a social worker might want to know how good a job she did in providing training for new foster parents. How the foster parents experienced the training could be important information that might help improve future activities of this sort. It is important that satisfaction studies be used appropriately. If the social worker wanted to know how much the foster parents learned during the training, a satisfaction survey would not necessarily provide this information. Testing knowledge acquisition generally requires some other mechanism such as comparison of pretest and posttest scores on a valid test of information related to the subject matter (in this case, foster care). In some cases, the practitioner would use both the knowledge test and a satisfaction survey because they will likely garner different information.

Satisfaction surveys typically use a set of closed-ended questions, inquiring about the behavior of the social worker (or other agency staff), but it is wise to provide open-ended questions that clients can use to describe their experiences in their own words. Although open-ended questions are not as easily tabulated and aggregated, they can reveal information not captured by closed-ended questions. Any single client response to an open-ended question may be idiosyncratic, but a content analysis of such responses for all respondents can identify themes or consistent issues. These identified patterns can be used to improve services and may suggest other questions for future surveys.

Whenever possible, it is better to try to locate an existing satisfaction survey with known validity and reliability than to construct one on your own. One option is the Client Satisfaction Inventory (CSI), which has both construct and content validity, along with a high degree of reliability (Nugent et al., 2001). Keep in mind that satisfaction surveys are not restricted to gathering information from clients. They can also be used to solicit opinions from other agencies, referral sources, and any other individual or organization from which feedback can improve services. Figure 13.11 depicts a client satisfaction instrument that uses typical questions.

Advantages and Disadvantages of Satisfaction Surveys

A major advantage of satisfaction surveys is their ease of use and simplicity. Costs for creating surveys are minimal, and depending on what is being surveyed, they can be used on a continuing basis. Clients feel empowered when given the opportunity to provide feedback to the social worker and/or the agency. Clients, after all, are the consumers of our helping efforts and have a unique perspective. Gathering feedback from them is inherently logical. In addition, patterns or trends can be detected as the information from surveys is aggregated from year to year. Equally important, interpretation of the results is generally easy (Royse, 2004).

The primary disadvantage of satisfaction surveys is the fact that "in practically every study clients say that they are satisfied with services. The vast majority of published consumer satisfaction studies show that clients

Figure 13.11

Example of a Client Satisfaction Survey

Prairie Valley Hospital
Client Satisfaction Survey

Recently, you received services from the social services department of Prairie Valley Hospital. At Prairie Valley Hospital we are interested in your opinions about the quality of care you received. Please take a moment to complete this survey and help us to improve our services. Thank you.

In responding to each question, please use the following scale:

5 = Strongly agree
4 = Agree somewhat
3 = Undecided
2 = Disagree somewhat
1 = Strongly disagree
0 = Not applicable

1.____The services I sought from the social service department were provided.

2.____Social services staff responded promptly to my requests for assistance.

3.____Social services staff fully explained procedures to me.

4.____Social services staff listened to me.

5.____Social services staff completed tasks on time.

6.____Social services staff answered my questions completely.

7.____Social services staff understood my concerns.

8.____Social services staff treated me with courtesy.

9.____I would recommend the social services staff to friends and family.

10.____Overall, I am satisfied with the services provided to me.

Please feel free to add any comments you feel would help us improve the services you received.

_____
_____
_____
_____
_____

almost invariably report high levels of satisfaction" (Royse, 2004, pp. 263–264). Such findings have been noted in various countries across the globe and with clients experiencing many different problems. The therapeutic model used by the practitioner does not seem to have any influence on how satisfied clients are with the services provided. These results can likely be explained by a combination of factors. First, clients may have had few if any choices with respect to the practitioner, agency, or service provided, leaving them with no basis for comparison. Second, those who complete such surveys are generally those who completed the helping process. This would not include those who drop out early, nor does it include people who choose not to return their surveys. Even those who do return the survey may rate the worker or agency positively out of apprehension about possible repercussions.

Royse (2004) suggests that one way to compensate for positive bias is to set the threshold of acceptability higher. To do this, the social worker could decide in advance that any survey results showing that fewer than 70 percent of clients were pleased with the service or agency would be considered an indication of dissatisfaction. Without such a threshold, one might erroneously conclude that the majority of clients are happy with the agency or worker.

Surveys in general suffer from limitations such as low return rate and incorrect addresses, and they may be affected by the educational achievement of the client (Royse, 2004). Finally, the surveys employed often lack known reliability or validity because they are typically unique to, and created by, the specific agency or worker.

Another limitation of satisfaction surveys employed at the conclusion of a case is that the information cannot be used to improve service to that specific client. Although the results may help us design better programs and services in the future, they offer this respondent no help. Compare this fact with the way in which single-subject designs are used to monitor progress during the intervention. Monitoring allows for midcourse adjustments, which is usually not possible with satisfaction surveys. Some attempts to overcome this disadvantage have been tried by practitioners who ask clients to complete a questionnaire at the end of each session. When this method is employed, the practitioner is able to use this information in forthcoming sessions with the same client system.

Quality Assurance

The intent of quality assurance (sometimes called quality control or quality improvement) is to ensure that services are provided in accordance with an organization's standards. Thus, they are used less to evaluate outcomes than to determine to what extent practitioners are following the procedures and policies set by the agency. Quality assurance may mean examining whether social workers followed the steps necessary in handling particular cases. It may also focus on whether specific time limits were adhered to, such as responding to all child protective service referrals within twenty-four hours. In other situations, the focus may be on the extent to which each case file contains necessary information such as assessment results or DSM code. Social workers may be evaluated on whether their case notes are current or whether they are completing their assessments on time. Almost any aspect of practice can be subject to quality improvement evaluations.

The general procedure with quality assurance is first to have a set of standards to which staff are to adhere, followed by periodic check-ing to see if those standards are being met. Thus, a sample of each social worker's case files may be reviewed every month or on a random basis. When such reviews determine there is a problem, the goal is to help the social worker meet the standard. This may involve additional training or supervision. Continued failure to meet quality assurance standards can be used to discipline the individual, including termination.

Group Designs

Before introducing the common practice evaluation approaches described in this chapter, we identified several limitations inherent in these methods. Although these limitations do not lessen their value for helping to evaluate practice effectiveness, they do interfere with our ability to determine cause and effect. To overcome this limitation, group designs may be employed. Group designs are used to help us make what is called a **causal inference**. In other words, group designs help us determine what caused the outcome witnessed in the client. As the term implies, group designs are used to compare groups of clients.

Group designs also attend carefully to those factors that enhance the generalizability of our findings. One such factor is the focus on internal validity or, more appropriately, threats to internal validity. These issues are discussed later as part of the advantages and disadvantages of group designs.

Experimental Designs

Experimental designs get their name from the fact that they are the premier method of conducting experiments in most areas of science. Two characteristics set experimental designs apart from other methodologies: the use of **control groups** and **randomization**. A true experiment would ensure that clients are randomly assigned to either a group receiving help (experimental group) or a group receiving no assistance (control group). Random assignment means that every client has an equal chance of being placed in one group or the other. Randomization would be compromised, for example, if all the women were placed in one group and the men in another, or if high-functioning clients were assigned to one group and the low-functioning placed in the second group. Random assignment can be done by several methods ranging from a simple coin toss to using a table of random numbers.

The purpose of using randomization and a control group is to ensure that the two groups are sufficiently comparable to fairly test our intervention. Because no factor other than chance is responsible for whether a given client is in one group or another, we have achieved the basis for a two-group comparison.

Pretest–Posttest Control Group Design

This design involves a comparison of two comparable groups, one of which receives an intervention while the control group does not. Both groups take the pretest and the posttest, and the difference between the two groups is attributable to the intervention. This is a strong design because it eliminates many factors that could threaten the validity of our findings. If both groups are comparable, the only factor responsible for change should be our intervention.

Posttest-Only Control Group Design

If a social worker is concerned about the influence that prior completion of the pretest may have had on the outcome, one way of eliminating this is to use a posttest-only control group

Voices from the Field

Barry R. Cournoyer

I earned a master's degree in social work in 1974. I loved the experience and learned a great deal. My professors were engaging, committed, and dedicated to both teaching and service. My field practicum instructors generously shared their practice wisdom and, of course, I learned most of all from the clients I served. In the early 1970s, few professors and even fewer social workers engaged in research or incorporated findings from practice-relevant research studies in their teaching or service. Most assumed that adherence to core social work values and principles and good intentions would lead to positive outcomes. At that time, relatively few social workers thought we needed to include evidence of practice effectiveness or systematically evaluate the outcomes of our own services to clients.

Some thirty years later, it's a dramatically different world. The challenging nature of contemporary social problems and the practice context require social workers who can seek, discover, analyze, and apply emerging knowledge in service to others and then sys-

tematically evaluate the effects. In the twenty-first century, a compassionate heart is insufficient. We have too many examples of profound harm done in the name of "good intentions."

Today, our clients need critical thinking, responsible, scholarly professionals who conscientiously adhere to the ethical principles that social workers "critically examine and keep current with emerging knowledge relevant to social work, . . . routinely review the professional literature and, . . . base practice on recognized knowledge, including empirically based knowledge, relevant to social work" (NASW, 1999, Sections 4.0l.b & c) . . . and . . . "monitor and evaluate policies, the implementation of programs, and practice interventions" (NASW, 1999, Section 5.02.a). Contemporary practitioners must be knowledge workers as well as service providers. Our efforts to help others must be informed by evidence of practice effectiveness and guided by evaluation of the services we provide. In sum, we must be *evidence-based social workers*.

design. In this model, the pretest is skipped entirely and comparisons are made of the experimental and control groups only on the posttest. This eliminates the ability to determine how the two groups would have done on the pretest, but it is assumed that random as-

signment eliminated any differences between the groups.

Quasi-Experimental Designs

Many times it is not possible to assign clients randomly to a control or an experi-

Evidence based social work is the mindful and systematic identification, analysis, and synthesis of evidence of practice effectiveness as a primary part of an integrative and collaborative process concerning the selection and application of service to members of target client groups. The evidence based decision-making process includes consideration of professional ethics and experience as well as the cultural values and personal judgments of consumers. (Cournoyer, 2004, p. 4)

Through practice-effectiveness review groups and practice research networks, organizations such as the Cochrane and the Campbell Collaborations, and reference to research-based practice guidelines, evidence-based social workers (1) formulate practice-effectiveness questions that relate to the clients they serve, (2) search for and discover relevant nomothetic information, (3) analyze and synthesize the evidence, and (4) disseminate the findings to colleagues and consumers. Evidence-based practitioners then use evidence of what works in a collaborative process of problem identification and goal specification—much as social workers did thirty years ago. However, once the goals are

clear, evidence-based social workers introduce nomothetic evidence of practice effectiveness as part of the exploration with clients about how best to pursue those goals. We inform clients about the potential risks and benefits associated with different intervention approaches and encourage them to consider that information as we jointly decide how to proceed. When an intervention strategy is determined, we then attempt to implement it in accord with practice guidelines and systematically evaluate its ideographic effects and outcomes. Both nomothetic and ideographic knowledge are fundamental to evidence-based social work. Ultimately, knowledge about what works must apply to the particular individual, family, group, organization, or community we serve.

References

National Association of Social Workers. (1999). *Code of ethics of the National Association of Social Workers.* Retrieved May 19, 2004, from www.socialworkers.org/pubs/code/code.asp

Cournoyer, B. R. (2004). *The evidence based social work (EBSW) skills book.* Boston: Allyn and Bacon.

mental group. It may seem unethical or problematic from a public relations standpoint to deny someone treatment. In such cases, an alternative is to use quasi-experimental designs. Three of these designs are discussed in the following sections: nonequiv-

alent control groups, time series, and multiple time series.

Nonequivalent Control Groups

Nonequivalent control groups are used when it is not possible to randomly assign clients to experimental and control groups. Despite this limitation, it is still useful to seek a comparison group as similar as possible to the experimental group. Direct practitioners working with youth in a residential treatment center, for example, might want to test out an adventure-based counseling program that had been used successfully at other such facilities to build self-esteem and mutual support. Consisting of group activities that involve rock climbing, camping, physical agility, and canoeing, this program could be tested on one cabin at the residential treatment center while another cabin would be used for comparison purposes.

Ideally, it would be desirable for the two cabins to have residents with similar difficulties and abilities to begin with; otherwise, the comparisons would likely be less useful. To test the effectiveness of the adventure-based counseling program on self-esteem, for example, the social workers would give both cabins pretests that measured this variable. Following the intervention with the first cabin, both groups would complete posttests. Figure 13.12

shows this comparison. The mean self-esteem score for residents in cabin A increased following the intervention, whereas there was almost no change in the score for cabin B, which did not participate in the adventure-based counseling program. Although the graph shows only the mean self-esteem scores here, it would have been easy to chart the individual members' pre- and posttest scores.

Time Series Designs

In time series designs, social workers make several observations both before and after the intervention takes place. Suppose practitioners are interested in knowing if their work with nursing home residents is having the desired effect. The behavior of concern is the apparent "forgetfulness" of residents with respect to current events. Practitioners might assess residents' awareness of current events with a test given every Monday for four weeks followed by a four-week current affairs educational group. After the educational group is over, practitioners again give the residents a test on the following four Mondays.

Figure 13.12

Example of a Nonequivalent Control Group

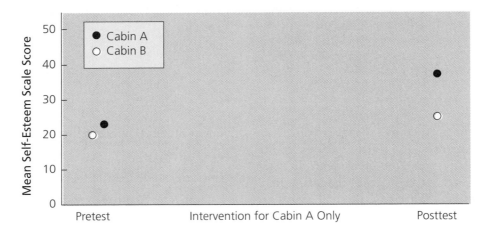

One advantage of using repeated measures to test before and after the intervention is the fact that they can help identify patterns that might confound our results. For example, it is possible that residents' awareness of current events fluctuates periodically, and using only a pre- and a posttest would have missed this instability. Figure 13.13 shows how a time series design might look.

From this graph one can see that although there were variations in knowledge scores from week to week, before implementation of the current events group, the overall level of knowledge remained relatively low. Following the intervention, variations continued, but at a much higher level. This suggests that the current events group had the desired effect of increasing residents' knowledge of what is going on in the world around them.

Multiple Time Series Designs

A multiple time series design involves using the time series approach but with the addition of a nonequivalent control group. This model com-
pares the group receiving the intervention with another group that did not receive it. However, there is no assumption of random assignment of residents to the two groups that would be needed to consider the groups equivalent as in an experimental design. In the preceding case, the practitioner might decide to begin the current events group on one specific wing of the nursing home and use another wing as the nonequivalent control group. This design works as long as there are no real differences between wing A and wing B. However, if wing B has a larger proportion of residents suffering from Alzheimer's disease, a fair comparison between the two wings would be impossible. Figure 13.14 shows a multiple time series design. Wing B (black line) shows a variation in scores in the weeks prior to intervention with accuracy rates between 22 percent and 30 percent and a similar pattern after the current events group was over. Wing A (blue line) scores showed a similar variation prior to intervention and then show solid gains afterward. The fact that wing A scores were higher and remained

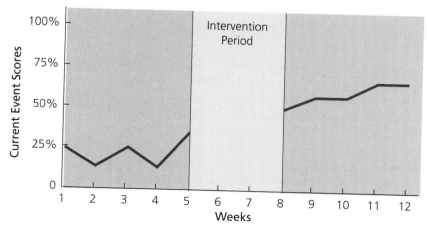

Figure 13.13

Example of a Time Series Design

Figure 13.14

Example of a Multiple Time Series Design

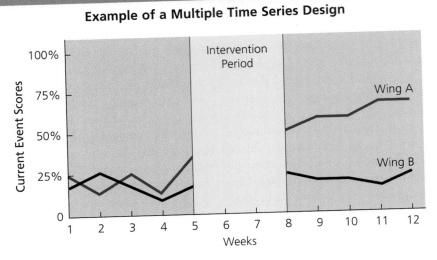

higher following intervention suggests that the current events group was effective.

Advantages and Disadvantages of Group Designs

Some of the capabilities inherent in group designs, namely the possibility of drawing causal inference and generalization, have been previously discussed. Causal inference is the ability to determine that one event is likely the cause of another. Or, put differently, group designs help the practitioner say with some degree of certainty that the intervention is the most likely cause of the change in the client system. Generalizability is the ability to suggest that the methods and results obtained with a particular group may be applicable to other similar groups. Both are important advantages of group designs.

Perhaps the primary disadvantage of group designs is the need to observe a higher standard of care when designing and carrying them out. We pointed out earlier the importance of randomization and control–comparison groups for group designs as well as some inherent problems in meeting these requirements. A second category of limitations is actually of two types: threats to the internal validity of a design and threats to the external validity. If present and not attended to, these threats may impair our ability to attribute causation or to generalize our findings, or both. Each category of threats is discussed below.

Threats to Internal Validity

Internal validity is a concept concerned with eliminating alternate explanations of why change occurred. An internally valid evaluation would have few if any factors (other than the treatment) that could be responsible for the outcome. By their very nature, group designs must control for these alternative explanations because without this ability one can never assert that an intervention helped produce the change in the client's situation. Several threats to internal validity require attention, including instrumentation, maturation, mortality, selection bias, statistical regression, diffusion of treatment, testing, and history (Rubin & Babbie, 2001).

Instrumentation: We have talked previously about the importance of using valid and reliable measures when assessing and evaluating clients. This is an extremely critical step in group designs because it helps eliminate one of several threats to internal validity, namely **instrumentation**. Instrumentation can be a problem if the instruments used for assessment have limited reliability or validity because it is not possible to be sure that they are consistently measuring exactly what they are supposed to measure. An example would be using a client satisfaction questionnaire to determine the effectiveness of a substance abuse treatment program. The instrument being used is not valid for measuring changes in drug use.

Maturation: **Maturation** is a term used to refer to the passage of time. For example, it is commonly observed that rates of juvenile delinquency tend to go down as individuals mature. The actual process of growing older (sometimes wiser) can produce changes in a client's thinking as well as perceptions, behaviors, and feelings. With the passage of time, many people get better whether or not they receive help.

Mortality: **Mortality** occurs when clients drop out of treatment prior to the planned termination point. Let's say the social worker begins with twelve adolescents in a program designed to discourage drug use. Both pre- and posttests of the clients' intentions to use drugs in the future, coupled with school and police records, might be employed to help determine whether the group program is effective. Along the way, four members of the group drop out and the social worker finishes the group with eight members. Perhaps the dropouts felt frustrated at their lack of progress or maybe they felt they had achieved their desired goals. The point is that the social worker does not know why they left, and

the dropouts will not be part of the group completing the posttest. If six of the remaining participants improved their score on the posttest and two did not, the practitioner might be tempted to say that 75 percent (six of eight) of those who participated showed gains. However, if the four who dropped out did so because they were not making progress, the actual success rate is probably more like 50 percent (six of twelve). Because the ultimate goal is to test the effectiveness of an intervention, we recommend trying to contact dropouts to get their participation in the posttest. Ignoring them threatens the validity of the claim of a 75 percent success rate.

Selection Bias: **Selection bias** impinges on the ability to draw inferences because the outcomes witnessed may have more to do with characteristics of the clients who were helped than with anything the direct practitioner did to help. For example, a program that accepts for treatment only those clients with a high potential for recovery is engaging in what is called **creaming.** If the social worker wants to say that the substance abuse group treatment was effective, it will be necessary to compare that group to other groups either receiving no treatment or receiving different kinds of interventions. When bias in selecting clients for inclusion in a group occurs, it makes it harder to draw comparisons with other groups. Those with higher potential for recovery may have greater motivation, more support from family and friends, or other resources that could make a real difference in the outcome.

Statistical Regression: We know that the very mention of the word *statistics* causes many social work students to immediately break out in hives, migraines, and leprosy. However, statistics play a major role in practice evaluation and particularly in group designs. **Statistical**

regression refers to the tendency of extreme scores (very high or very low) on any instrument to change over time, absent any intervention whatsoever. The direction of change is toward the mean or average score obtained by those who complete the instrument. To convey the direction of movement, this phenomenon is called **regression toward the mean.**

Assume for a minute that an agency is offering a series of groups that focus on improving marital functioning. In work with clients who participate in the group, the agency is using an instrument such as the Index of Marital Satisfaction (Nurius & Hudson, 1993) to help assess how happy the couples are about their marriage. The instrument is being employed in the assessment phase and again as a means of evaluating change. Hopefully, those who said they were very dissatisfied with their marriage will have more positive feelings after the group ends. The agency would also hope that those who had higher levels of marital satisfaction will retain or improve their scores. Unfortunately, statistical regression can become a real annoyance in such situations. For example, those who had low satisfaction scores at the start are likely to have higher scores later even if they did not participate in a group. Equally bad, those who scored high levels of satisfaction in the beginning could score lower at the conclusion of the group. Either way, extreme scores can be predicted to change over time and therefore threaten the social worker's ability to identify causality.

Diffusion of Treatment: If a social worker wished to compare two intervention approaches to working with clients who are noncompliant in taking their medication, it would be preferable that each approach be sufficiently different from the other. Perhaps this would involve using an educational group approach with eight clients and a cognitive behavioral approach with another eight. In an ideal world, these group approaches would be considered sufficiently different to allow for comparison purposes. Often, however, different intervention approaches have remarkably similar characteristics, resulting in overlaps that prevent a real comparison of different treatments. For example, both of these approaches emphasize learning and thinking processes. In addition, diffusion of treatment might occur because social workers leading the group are likely to exhibit empathy, genuineness, and other similar positive attributes used in the cognitive behavioral approach. It is also possible that the two leaders have read the literature on the other approach and have adopted some of the techniques or ideas associated with it. In the end, the similarities in intervention activities between the two groups may well prevent comparison of one group with another. In fact, the common elements of the two approaches may be responsible for the outcomes rather than the unique features of the specific treatment used.

Testing: **Testing** is an internal threat to validity because the very act of being tested can have unexpected influences on clients (or on anyone, for that matter). If you know you are going to be tested on something, the natural tendency is to try to prepare for the event. Consider a situation in which the social worker is using a pretest–posttest model to determine whether adolescents taught about HIV and other sexually transmitted diseases (STDs) improve their understanding of the risk factors involved. Between the pretest and the posttest, some or all of the members may look up answers to the questions they missed or did not understand on the pretest. This gives at least part of the group an additional intervention (educational group plus looking up answers). This undercuts the social worker's original intent to use an educational group alone to test that method's efficacy.

History: **History** is an interesting situation in which events occurring outside of the intervention have an unexpected impact on the dependent variable. For example, suppose practitioners were trying to compare success rates of two methods of weight control (educational group versus support group). History could affect one of these groups in at least two different ways. First, consider what would happen if the educational group's session is interrupted by a fire across the street from the meeting location. Members witness the event and, at least for a time, are focused on the fire rather than on what is going on in the group. Unless the social workers plan to create a fire for the support group (not recommended), this event will likely have an impact on the educational group beyond that planned for at the beginning. In other words, the different experiences of our groups mean they are no longer comparable.

A second problem occurs when external events may actually produce the observed outcome. If social workers are working with a group of adults in an inpatient treatment center for depression, they hope their use of a group combined with individual therapy will have a positive impact on the clients' moods. In an ideal arrangement, they would like to ensure that the therapy is the only intervention in use. In real life, this is often impossible to ensure. Suppose the treatment center has a new chef who prepares excellent food or a new recreational therapist is hired with lots of popular ideas about activities for the group members. It may turn out that the clients' improved moods are due more to these unforeseen events than to our group treatment. To summarize, any event either internal or external to the group can influence the outcome and raise questions about the internal validity of our evaluation.

Another difference between single-system and group designs is the ability to generalize our findings to other groups. For example, it would be helpful to know that the anger management intervention used effectively with one group of spousal abusers is likely to be effective with others. To help ensure this generalizability, social workers must recognize and deal with threats to external validity.

Threats to External Validity

Threats to external validity can reduce or eliminate the ability to generalize research findings to other groups and situations (Grinnell & Unrau, 1997). This section identifies six such threats: (1) differences in clients, (2) practitioner effects, (3) measurement differences, (4) different dependent variables, (5) interaction of history and intervention, and (6) different interventions.

Differences in Clients: It is logical that **client differences** might affect the ability to generalize from one group to another. A section at the end of this chapter notes how cultural differences can have an impact on the evaluation process. Gender differences, cognitive skills, and values may all confound efforts to successfully use the same intervention on different groups. Ultimately, practitioners must always be cautious and alert to how differences among clients might affect generalizability.

Practitioner Effects: **Practitioner effects** refer to the fact that all practitioners are different from one another in some respects. These differences may be in skill level, style of intervention, and beliefs, to name just a few. Awareness of this factor is especially important as social workers attempt to use theories or approaches discussed in the literature. The fact that an approach worked well when used by one practitioner does not mean it will work as well for others.

Measurement Differences: **Measurement differences** is a term that covers a variety of situations threatening our ability to generalize. Suppose a social worker has worked successfully in the past with several groups of clients with substance abuse problems. However, in one of the current groups the old methods do not seem to be working well. Methods that work well in some situations may not work as well when there are differences in such things as client problem (cocaine addiction versus alcoholism), intervention (group size or number of sessions), or outcome (measurement instruments used) (Nugent et al., 2001).

Different Dependent Variables: Two practitioners working with clients sharing the same characteristics may use different definitions of success. One practitioner working with alcoholic clients may believe success has been achieved when a client has no recurrence of a problem for six months following therapy. Another may define success as sobriety for one year after the conclusion of treatment. Obviously, if practitioners use different measures of the dependent variable, the results of the two interventions can differ.

Interaction of History and Intervention: We noted earlier the role that history can play in threats to internal validity. History poses a similar threat to external validity. Even if it were possible to create two groups identical in all respects and the practitioner's interventions did not differ, events happening in the external environment can play a role in a group's dynamics and achievements. For example, events such as September 11, 2001, a war in Iraq or some other location, or dramatic changes in the economy can influence group members. Instead of focusing on the intervention and dealing with their problems, clients may be worrying about loved ones, fearing for their jobs, or wondering how world events will affect them. Historical influences can have subtle effects on how well

the intervention works and the possible outcomes, both of which are hard to detect.

Different Interventions: A common observation is that attempts to replicate interventions can result in different outcomes. This occurs because, as Nugent and colleagues (2001) suggest, "any intervention applied to different clients or client systems in different settings by different practitioners will be different from the original intervention in varying ways and degrees. This reduces the likelihood of identical outcomes or results in comparison to the original case" (p. 97). Perhaps the most effective way of eliminating threats to external validity is replication. This is a good argument for continuing to evaluate our efforts. Every time an intervention is replicated and evaluated with similar results, it helps rule out various threats to external validity. Repetition is a building block of good science and good practice.

Cultural and Diversity Issues in Evaluation:

Cultural and diversity issues play a role in all aspects of our practice, including research and evaluation. Our own biases may lead us to include or exclude certain people from our evaluations. Decisions practitioners make to note, for example, the demographic characteristics of clients such as race, gender, or marital status are inherently subject to some degree of bias. Asking clients to identify with one racial group may be inappropriate for those who consider themselves biracial. Clients who are aware that race is not a biological concept and in fact does not exist may be particularly offended by a requirement that they identify themselves using an inappropriate designation. It is also important to use cultural labels that the groups find acceptable. In addition, it is entirely possible that the variable of race is of little or no importance to those on whom we gather data (Ginsburg, 2001). Rather than conclude that a specific finding is related to the client's culture, it is appropriate to consider whether socioeconomic factors may have played a larger role (Williams, Unrau, & Grinnell, 1998).

Lumping diverse groups (such as Hispanics or Asians) into one racial category may result in misleading findings because the needs, interests, norms, and values of different groups can be vastly different. Likewise, hundreds of Native American or First Nations tribal groups exist, many with different values, traditions, and beliefs. Failure to take these within-group differences into account can raise questions about the external validity of our research (Yegidis & Weinbach, 2002). Transgendered individuals may object to being categorized as

APPLICATIONS TO PRACTICE

Case Example

You are a social worker at Teen Support, an agency that provides counseling services for status offending youth (individuals who are truant or engaging in behavior that the law requires people to be a certain age to legally engage in: smoking, drinking, driving, or leaving home). All services are provided at no cost to the family but must be completed within sixty days. Completion may consist of referral to another agency or case closure. All the families assigned to you include as an identified client, a truant youth between the ages of twelve and fifteen. Your supervisor wants you to track these families and develop a way to look at outcomes for treatment. You have a caseload of fifteen juveniles and their families and have been using a behavioral–cognitive intervention model. The boss wants you to write up a short treatment evaluation protocol and submit the evaluation model to her for approval within the next week. Once the model is approved, you are to begin to use it on all cases referred to you within the next three months. The agency wants data from this project to include in the annual report, which is compiled six months from now and distributed to community funding sources in nine months.

Critical Thinking Questions
1. What model of evaluation would be the most effective for this assignment?
2. Once you have selected your evaluation model, what limitations will you want to address in the protocol to increase reliability of outcome data?
3. How will you decide on your sample?
4. What variables will you want to control for?

Research Activity

Using the Research Navigator™ website, www.research navigator.com, look up research studies about working with teenage truancy. Select a minimum of five articles and review the treatment methods considered to be the most effective with this population. Also evaluate whether an existing evaluation study could be replicated with your clients.

either male or female, whereas gay and lesbian clients may see the reference to marital state as inherently reflecting heterosexual bias.

Evaluation instruments used must also be neutral in terms of gender, culture, or other characteristics. This means that social workers should look carefully at any instruments used to assess and evaluate change in clients following intervention. Those that have been validated only on white people or on men should not be used routinely with other types of clients.

To the extent possible, the evaluation activity should be a joint project of the social worker and client system because too often diversity groups are simply left out of the planning for specific evaluations. This is especially important if you hope to use your findings to evaluate the success of specific programs. For a more exhaustive look at ways to ensure that your research and evaluations are culturally and gender sensitive, see Williams, Unrau, and Grinnell (1998).

General Recommendations

Evaluation of practice is now a given in most areas of social work practice. At the same time, much has been learned about how to improve the quality of evaluation efforts. As noted earlier in this chapter, most evaluation tools require that goals and objectives be clearly defined to eliminate as much ambiguity as possible. This step is important both for purposes of intervention and for evaluation.

Although the evaluation methods described earlier in this chapter are all important tools, it is usually best to rely on multiple measurements whenever possible. Combining, for example, single-system designs and client satisfaction surveys will provide more information than either method alone. In particular, the combination of methods helps overcome some of the disadvantages and shortcomings of individual approaches.

Similarly, using experimental and quasi-experimental designs helps us to eliminate many of the shortcomings of single-system designs. Whenever possible, social workers ought to use the most sophisticated evaluation tools at their disposal and report findings at conferences and other venues where this knowledge can be shared with peers.

Social work practitioners should be committed to using evaluation tools that are valid and reliable. When the tools in use do not have all the desired psychometric properties (e.g., high validity and reliability), practitioners must take this into account when interpreting the results. Poulin (2000) recommends that measures also should be relevant to the expected outcomes and capable of detecting change when it occurs. A relevant measure is one that helps determine whether the outcome desired has been achieved. Using a satisfaction survey to determine whether a group for abusers felt that the group was worthwhile is an example of an irrelevant measure. Members of the group may have enjoyed the experience and still not changed their abusive behavior toward their spouses and significant others. By itself, the satisfaction survey does not produce information that helps us know whether the abuser has changed his or her ways.

Capability to detect change is an important feature of any instrument because if a measure is lacking in this regard, it may never be possible to know whether things changed in the desired direction. Sometimes a measure lacks the degree of sensitivity we desire, and only repeated use will help make this determination. This is another reason why practitioners should try to use instruments that have a history of sensitivity to change instead of inventing their own.

Finally, practitioners should remind themselves that the process of evaluation will sometimes provide unforeseen results. Evidence of lack of progress or nonachievement of objectives can be disappointing. Discovering that an intervention had an unintended negative result is disheartening. However, such potential outcomes are the cost of doing business for any practitioner. They help us sharpen our thinking, reexamine our approaches and techniques, and become more effective social workers. Moreover, evaluation of one's own practice is an important characteristic of an ethical practitioner. We have discussed in several chapters the importance of using theories, models, and techniques that have proven to be effective rather than relying on idiosyncratic methods. This is the heart of the effort to employ evidence-based practice whenever possible. Moving toward a future in which evidence is a major criterion on which we make choices will take concerted effort from social work practitioners. Recommended steps in this direction include evaluating our own practice using the best tools available. Although evaluating one's own practice will not produce the quality of research that allows us to consider it evidence based, it does allow us to learn what works for us and in what situations. Another step is to stay current with the literature in social work and related fields, especially literature that focuses on evaluation of practice. A third recommendation is to participate in conferences and workshops dealing with social work practice. As consumers of such learning opportunities and as readers of the literature in our field, we must critically evaluate what we read and are told. As one of our old friends continues to say, becoming an evidence-based practitioner requires that we repeatedly ask the questions "Does it work?" and "How do we know?" when presented with research purporting to demonstrate the efficacy of particular practice approaches or programs.

SUMMARY

This chapter defines *evaluation* and explores some of the reasons it is such an important part of the helping process. Ethical issues in evaluation activities are also discussed. The chapter also introduces single-subject designs in a number of different configurations that are useful for evaluating direct practice. Other methods identified include goal-attainment scaling, target-problem scaling, task-achievement scaling, satisfaction studies, and quality assurance. These methods are categorized into those that meet the standard for quantitative designs and those that are more qualitatively oriented. The advantages and disadvantages of different evaluation methods are also discussed.

More sophisticated group designs are also reviewed, including experimental and quasi-experimental approaches. Advantages and disadvantages of group designs are identified, along with threats to both internal and external validity. Finally, cultural and diversity issues in evaluation are described.

Navigating Direct Practice

An access code for Research Navigator™ is packaged within your text. Use this code to register at www.researchnavigator.com and then use the key words listed below to research articles related to the chapter's content. Research Navigator™ helps you quickly and efficiently make the most of your research time.

❏ Dependent variables
❏ Government Performance and Results Act
❏ Statistical regression
❏ Validity

Chapter 14

Knowledge and Skills of Termination

■ Johnnie is a thirty-five-year-old single woman who has requested help for depression. Rosario, a social worker in a mental health center, contracted to work with her for six sessions. At the start of the second session, Johnnie told Rosario she would not be able to continue because of a family emergency. During the weekend, her eighty-year-old mother suffered a heart attack and was hospitalized. Her mother was going to be released on Friday, and Johnnie was flying home the same day to take care of her. Johnnie didn't know how long she would be gone. The doctor had told Johnnie that her mother would need someone to help her for at least a month. Johnnie told the social worker she was sorry they couldn't continue working together because she was starting to feel better.

Termination is recognized as a critical stage in the problem-solving framework used in social work and other helping professions. Handled appropriately, it can further achievement of a client's goals and help ensure continuation of changes that occurred during the intervention phase. All treatment models pay attention to the termination process. This chapter looks at how different theories and therapies view termination. In addition, it reviews some general termination guidelines, identifies common types of termination, and discusses tasks at termination. The chapter also considers termination situations in which clients achieved their goals and those in which this did not fully occur. Finally, the chapter de-

scribes how issues of cultural diversity can influence the termination process.

Different Views of Termination

In beginning this discussion of termination, it is important to provide an overview of how termination is conceptualized in a variety of treatment models. Those discussed in this chapter include (1) ego psychology, (2) task-centered, (3) cognitive, (4) solution-focused, (5) behavioral, (6) systems, (7) crisis intervention, (8) person-centered, and (9) family therapy models.

The Ego Psychology Model

The ego psychology model of treatment is based on a number of important beliefs or assumptions that are discussed in Chapter 2. Unlike more recent models, ego psychology is not designed to be a short-term intervention. Thus, termination is likely to come only after a significant number of sessions between social worker and client. In the ego psychology model, services generally end when the initial symptoms disappear, when the client has developed insight into past problems and situations, and when relationships in various areas of the client's life improve. Perhaps key to this model is the great importance placed on the therapeutic relationship between client and social worker (Welch & Gonzales, 1999). This therapeutic relationship is the linchpin, so to speak, of change in therapy. The longer the relationship between social worker and client, the greater the significance of termination when it does occur.

In the final session or sessions, reviewing progress the client has made can be an ego-enhancing experience. It can serve as a means to support and reinforce client achievement and provide hope that the changes can be maintained. Clients also may find it valuable to consider areas in which progress has not been as great. These may be targets for future work as clients use newfound insight to delve into previously unexamined areas of their lives.

The ego psychology model pays perhaps greater attention than most models to the emotional responses that both client and social worker have to the termination. This attention derives from the critical role that the relationship between worker and client has played in bringing about change and from the level of intimacy that has been engendered. Traditionally, practitioners expected the client to have strong emotional reactions to termination, especially if the client's problems were related to issues of dependency or prior losses of significant others (Patterson & Welfel, 2000). Anticipating this, the social worker would focus on how the client felt about the termination. Likewise, the practitioner might anticipate that the client would regress by "reverting back to problematic patterns or initiating new counseling goals" (p. 111) and take the opportunity to help the client develop insight into what would be viewed as a typical reaction to endings. Fortunately, most recent research has downplayed the negative aspects of terminations and suggests that clients are just as likely to have positive reactions to the ending (Marx & Gelso, 1987; Quintana, 1993).

Also consistent with the ego psychology model is the expectation that the social worker may have emotional reactions to termination. This reaction could take the form of resisting the termination or simply feeling a keen sense of loss. Goodyear (1981, p. 348) notes that the practitioner's reaction is likely to be more difficult under certain circumstances, such as:

- When termination signals the end of the significant relationship
- When termination arouses the counselor's anxieties about the client's ability to function independently
- When termination arouses guilt in the counselor about not having been more effective with the client
- When the counselor's professional self-concept is threatened by a client who leaves abruptly and angrily
- When termination signals the end of a learning experience for the counselor
- When termination signals the end of a particularly exciting experience of living vicariously through the adventures of a client
- When termination becomes a symbolic recapitulation of other farewells in the counselor's life
- When termination arouses in the counselor conflicts about his or her own individualism

This is not to say that every social worker operating from the ego psychology model will experience a strong emotional reaction to termination. Many can and will take pride in their contribution to the client's progress and deal handily with any sadness engendered. They can also share the client's happiness at the changes that have taken place. Social workers who do find themselves struggling with strong emotional reactions should seek consultation with peers or a supervisor.

Task-Centered Model

The task-centered model is a short-term approach to treatment that focuses on problems of living (Reid & Epstein, 1972; Reid, 1978). Treatment generally lasts six to eight sessions, although more sessions can be added at the discretion of the client and the social worker. The task-centered model includes a contract that is negotiated between the client and the social worker during the first session. The contract generally includes the goals of treatment, the psychological and behavioral tasks that will be used, the number of sessions, and the cost of therapy. The contract is either verbally agreed to or signed and is the focus of all subsequent sessions.

The termination process in the task-centered model begins in the first session with a discussion of how many sessions will be required to accomplish the goals of treatment. After the contract has been negotiated and agreed to by the client and the social worker, all subsequent sessions focus on a target problem and the psychological and behavioral tasks that must be completed for the problem to be resolved. When these tasks are completed, the social worker can ask the client if the target problem has been resolved. The client can answer either yes or no or use the following goal-attainment scale: (1) no goal achievement, (2) minimal goal achievement, (3) moderate goal achievement, (4) considerable goal achievement, and (5) complete goal achievement (Reid & Epstein, 1972).

Ending treatment is the last stage of the task-centered model. According to Reid (1978), the next-to-last session should focus on the final tasks that need to be completed in the last session. These tasks include the following: (1) review and assess what was accomplished during treatment in relation to the client's problems; (2) plan directions for the client's continuing work on these problems, if further work is needed; and (3) help the client see that the problem-solving methods he or she

has learned in the period of service can be applied generally to problems of living.

The review gives the social worker the opportunity to praise the client for the progress made in their work together, recognizing that it was often difficult to achieve. This review also gives the client and the social worker the chance to discuss whether additional work is needed. A significant strength of the task-centered model is the planning that takes place in the last treatment session regarding the problems and concerns the client may experience after services are terminated. During the last session, social workers should stress how important it is for clients to continue to work on their problems and concerns and especially their goals. Clients who work on their problems and concerns between sessions are those who make the most progress in therapy. And clients who continue to work on their problems and concerns after services are terminated are those most likely to benefit from the long-term rather than short-term effects of counseling.

Cognitive Therapy

Cognitive therapy is based in part on the belief that what clients think about themselves, or their self-talk, has a significant impact on how they feel and behave (Corsini & Wedding, 1995). The first step in cognitive therapy is to have clients agree, or at least consider, that what they think about themselves has a significant effect on how they feel and how they behave. Once clients have agreed to consider this point of view, the next step is to have them record on a daily basis their self-talk. This is usually done by having them write down in a notebook the self-statements they either utter or think about themselves throughout the day. After recording their self-talk for a week or longer, the client has a baseline of negative and positive thoughts that he or she can review and assess with the social worker. The goal of cognitive therapy is to replace these negative self-statements with more rational responses by acknowledging the negative self-statement, labeling the statement as a specific cognitive distortion, and then offering a more rational response.

In *Cognitive Therapy of Depression*, Beck and colleagues (1979) make the following statement about termination:

> The issue of termination should be touched on periodically throughout therapy. From the beginning the therapist stresses to the patient that he will not stay in treatment indefinitely, and that he will be shown how to handle his psychological problems on his own. "Positive transference reactions" are not encouraged; rather, the therapist attempts to present himself realistically in the process of therapy. This "demystification" of therapy has the effect of countering the patient's dependency on the therapist and any belief in the "magic" of therapy. Throughout therapy, the patient is encouraged to become more independent and self-reliant. As therapy progresses, the patient plays an increasingly active role in identifying target problems and choosing strategies. This sets the stage for the patient's becoming his own therapist. (p. 317)

Beck and colleagues (1979) point out that a common concern of patients is that they will become depressed again after services are terminated. In addressing this concern, they cite the following case example:

Patient: Can you guarantee that I won't become depressed again?

Therapist: You are likely to become depressed again.

P: How then am I any better off than I was when I started therapy?

T: What have you learned here?

P: Well, I've learned to control what causes me to be depressed—my negative thoughts and attitudes.

T: What you have now are the tools to control how often you get depressed, how severe the depression will be, and how long you will stay depressed.

P: I never want to be depressed again.

T: That is certainly understandable, but the nature of depression is such that it's often hard to prevent its occurrence. But the intensity, frequency, and duration are under one's control. In fact, the recurrence of a mild depression could be of benefit. What are some of the advantages of becoming depressed after you leave treatment?

P: I could practice the techniques I've learned. . . . I could prove to myself that I can overcome depression and so I won't be afraid that I couldn't handle it.

T: The way you are describing it, then, is that a mild bout with depression could strengthen you. (p. 320)

This exchange between client and social worker emphasizes that cognitive therapy has an important educational component that teaches clients new ways to deal with depression. In terminating services, Beck and colleagues stress the educational component of cognitive therapy and review with clients the new skills they have acquired and how these skills will help them deal more appropriately with depression. They also spend time discussing the situations in the future that could cause clients to relapse into depression. As these situations are identified and discussed, clients develop relapse strategies for dealing more appropriately with these future problems.

Solution-Focused Therapy

Solution-focused therapy asks clients what is happening now and how the situation should be changed or modified. In may ways, solution-focused therapy builds on the important social work premise of "beginning where the client is." Unlike treatment models that focus on pathology or what is wrong with clients, solution-focused therapy asks clients what they want to change or, to borrow a phrase from Carl Rogers, "who they want to become."

The initial step in solution-focused therapy is developing well-formed goals that are reasonable and within the client's grasp. Termination in solution-focused therapy begins in this first session when the social worker asks the client, "What do you want to change in your life as the result of coming here?" (DeJong & Berg, 2002). After each session, a couple, for instance, would be asked what progress they are making on their goal of having a more satisfying marriage.

As the couple continue to make their relationship more satisfying, the social worker re-introduces termination in a later session by asking, "What further changes need to be made in your relationship in order for both of you not to come and talk to me anymore?" (DeJong & Berg, 2002). The focus now shifts to the final changes the couple want to make before services are terminated. In this final stage of termination, the couple give each other and the social worker feedback on the changes that have occurred in their relationship and how many more sessions they need to complete other changes. The last session of solution-focused therapy is spent discussing the changes that have occurred and what clients will be doing to sustain these changes after services have ended.

Behavior Therapy

The main premise of behavior therapy is that maladaptive behaviors are learned and can therefore be changed or modified through additional learning. In behavior therapy, termination begins in the first session as clients tell the social worker what they hope to accomplish in their work together. As their work together continues, the client learns new skills, and at an appropriate point services can be terminated. When services are terminated in behavior therapy, social workers encourage clients to continue to use the new skills they have learned, such as being more assertive.

Systems Therapy

Social workers who use a systems approach to therapy are grounded in the basic principles of systems theory (Robbins et al., 1998). When a social worker uses a systems approach to therapy, termination begins in the first session as the inner and outer forces of the client's life are assessed and evaluated. As the deficiencies in the inner and outer forces of the client's life are identified, treatment strategies are designed to resolve or at least ameliorate these deficiencies. As the inner and outer forces in the client's life are strengthened, the client moves that much closer to the termination of services. When services are terminated, the final session focuses on what the client needs to do to keep improving these inner and outer forces.

In the final session, many social workers impress on clients the importance of maintaining a balance in their lives that will support these inner and outer forces (Farley, Smith, & Boyle, 2003). In other words, clients are encouraged to maintain a balance between self, family, work, and other aspects of their inner and outer lives. Spending too much time on any one area of their lives will probably be harmful.

Crisis Intervention Therapy

Crisis intervention therapy is a model that is used to improve the psychosocial functioning of individuals during a period of disequilibrium (Kanel, 2003). A crisis can be precipitated by a loss, a threat, or a challenge. Many crisis reactions are caused by significant losses such as the death of a loved one, a divorce or separation, or the loss of a job. This loss is compounded because the individual has not developed the coping or problem-solving skills that are necessary to resolve this particular crisis.

The goal of crisis intervention is to return the client to a precrisis level of functioning (Smith, 1990). This is accomplished by completing specific tasks and activities that are linked to the crisis. The termination process in crisis intervention therapy begins in the first session as the social worker tells the client that the crisis will be resolved by completing certain tasks and activities. As their work together continues and clients complete more of these specific tasks and activities, clients are that much closer to resolving the crisis. The crisis will be resolved when the client returns to a precrisis level of functioning.

The final session of crisis intervention therapy usually focuses on the four following questions: (1) What precipitated or caused the crisis?; (2) Why couldn't the client resolve the crisis by himself or herself?; (3) What new problem-solving and coping skills has the client acquired in resolving the crisis?; (4) How will these new problem-solving and coping skills help the client in the future? (Smith, 1990). The client and the social worker answer these questions together. If the client and the social worker agree that sufficient progress has been made in resolving the crisis, services can be terminated. One guiding factor in termination is determining whether the client has returned to a precrisis level of functioning.

Person-Centered Therapy

Person-centered therapy is an approach to helping people that was formulated by Carl R.

Rogers in 1940 (Corsini & Wedding, 1995). The fundamental concept of the model is helping clients to become self-actualized or to reach their full potential. The guiding principle of the model is a therapeutic relationship based on trust between the client and the social worker. This relationship of trust is facilitated by genuineness, nonjudgmental caring, and empathy. By continually providing these facilitative conditions, the social worker helps clients reach their full potential.

The nondirective character of client-centered therapy means that the client plays a major role in deciding when termination is appropriate. As a consequence, the termination process is "more open-ended" (Patterson & Welfel, 2000, p. 111). In general terms, clients approach termination as they become more aware of the incongruencies between who they want to become and their actual behavior. Following this same line of thinking, clients—not social workers—are the ones who introduce the idea of terminating services. Once clients introduce the topic of termination, the social worker uses the facilitative conditions of genuineness, nonjudgmental caring, and empathy to help clients make a decision regarding the termination of services that is in their best interests.

Family Therapy

Family therapy is both a theory and a treatment model (Corsini & Wedding, 1995). Unlike most other models, the identified patient in family therapy is not the focus of therapy but a reflection of what is happening to the entire family. The identified patient carries the symptoms for the family; consequently, the family—not the identified patient—should be the focus of treatment. The primary goal of family therapy is to help the family and its individual members function more effectively.

The termination phase of family therapy begins as the family learns more effective ways of asking for what they want from one another. In general, family therapy is terminated when most of the agreed-on goals of the family have been reached. Termination of services may be initiated by the family or by the social worker. The final decision to terminate services rests exclusively with the family. An important part of termination in family therapy is anticipating the reoccurrence of previous family problems and how those family problems can be effectively resolved. According to Corsini and Wedding (1995), "termination is easier in family therapy than in individual therapy because the family has developed an internal support system and has not become overdependent on an outsider, the social worker. The presenting complaint or symptom has usually disappeared and it is time for disengagement" (p. 380).

General Termination Guidelines

Services are usually terminated when clients have accomplished most, if not all, of the goals they have contracted with the social worker. Many social workers believe it is best to terminate services when all of the goals have been accomplished, whereas others believe it is acceptable to terminate services when some goals still remain (Farley et al., 2003; Shulman, 1999). Other social workers believe the client should continue in some type of supportive relationship even though the primary goals have been accomplished (Smith, 1990).

In the beginning phase of their work, the client and the social worker discuss what measures they will use to determine how successfully the client's goals have been accomplished. As mentioned in Chapter 6, these evaluation measures often include a before-and-after assessment by the client, by the client's family members and friends, and by the social worker. These assessments can be completed using either standardized rapid assessment instruments or tools devised by the family and the social worker. When these assessments suggest that the previously identified goals have been accomplished, it is then appropriate to begin the termination of services that was first discussed in the initial session.

Social workers who choose to terminate services while a goal still remains to be accomplished believe this approach is important because it requires the client to continue to work on a personal goal even though services have ended. When this approach is used, one of the main purposes of termination becomes that of identifying the tasks and activities the client can continue to work on afterward. This type of termination incorporates a basic tenet of learning theory: that learning is a lifelong pursuit (Robbins et al., 1998). When this approach is used, before services are finally terminated the social worker may see the client one month later in a follow-up session to discuss what the client has accomplished.

When terminating services, some social workers will discuss with their clients other assistance or learning opportunities they might consider. For example, when a couple has reached the last session, the social worker might discuss with them the advantages of joining a marital enrichment group that will give them additional help with their relationship. Or a divorced client would be encouraged to join a divorced men's group at the YMCA for additional support and encouragement. Other social workers might encourage clients to read self-help books such as *The Road Less Traveled* (Peck, 1978), *Feeling Good* (Burns, 1980), *Men Are from Mars,*

Women Are from Venus (Gray, 1992), or *Who Moved My Cheese?* (Johnson, 1998) as part of an ongoing enrichment program. Clients might also be asked to review a list of classes that are taught through various community education programs to determine if any of these classes might help them with their personal goals.

When services are ended before the client's goals have been accomplished, the social worker should leave the client with a strategy that can be used to assess the progress that is made following the termination of services. Learning this strategy involves some guided practice with the social worker so that the client can make reasonable assessments of his or her progress on a month-to-month basis following termination.

Standardized instruments can be used to help clients assess the progress made following the termination of services. For example, the Generalized Contentment Scale (Corcoran & Fischer, 1994; Hudson, 1982) is a twenty-five-item inventory that measures varying degrees of happiness and depression. The inventory is easy to score and interpret. With some guided practice by the social worker, clients can learn how to calculate their scores each month following the termination of services and then compare these scores with the scores they had when services ended. For example, a score of 50 calculated at the end of therapy and then compared with a one-month follow-up score of 35 suggests that the client's mood has significantly improved following the termination of services. A two-month follow-up score of 30 compared with the after-therapy score of 50 suggests that the client's mood continues to significantly improve. By comparing the after and follow-up responses, clients can assess the progress being made after services are terminated. Clients can continue to make these personal assessments for many months after sessions have ended.

Types of Termination

Services can be terminated for a variety of reasons, including the following: (1) the client moves; (2) the client chooses not to continue with the social worker; (3) the negotiated contract is successfully completed; (4) the negotiated contract expires with additional work still remaining; (5) the social worker moves, becomes ill, or retires; and (6) the social worker chooses not to continue with the client. The situation described in the case example that begins this chapter is not uncommon. We live in a society that is more mobile than ever before. Due to fluctuations in the economy, clients may lose jobs, accept new employment, go back to school, or pursue other educational or training opportunities. Many of these employment changes require clients to relocate to other cities, states, or even countries. Some clients, like Johnnie, move because they have to take care of elderly parents, or maybe a separation or divorce forces them to return home to live with parents, relatives, or friends. Sometimes they become physically ill themselves and return home for medical treatment. For whatever reason, services are often terminated because the client moves out of the area and is not able to continue (Welch & Gonzales, 1999).

When services are terminated because clients move, social workers can ask if their clients want to be referred to other social workers who practice in the community to which they are moving. Whereas some social workers will ask clients if they want to be referred, other social workers will discuss with their clients why they believe it is important for them to continue in a professional relationship in their new location. This is probably a good practice to follow. Many clients are reluctant to make that initial request for help because they are embarrassed to admit that they have lost control over their lives. Once that initial request has been made and the ice has been broken, so to speak, clients are not as reluctant to ask for services. This is especially true when clients are satisfied with the services they have already received. For social workers to make proper referrals, they should be familiar with the services that are available in the area to which the client is moving. Some social workers may even have colleagues who practice in the area. Those who do not can call the local mental health center to find out more about the services available.

Services can also be terminated because the client doesn't want to continue anymore. There are several reasons why a client may not want to continue. In some cases, the client and the social worker simply don't hit it off. Maybe the client feels the social worker isn't understanding enough or is too judgmental or is "too much" or "too little" of something else. Sometimes the client doesn't want to continue because the process creates too much anxiety or is too painful. Other clients may want to terminate services because they do not consider them beneficial, the financial costs are too high, or they don't have the time to continue because of hectic schedules. When clients are reluctant to continue for one of these reasons, it is important to discuss their concerns and determine if the therapeutic relationship can be improved. Sometimes the situation improves and sometimes it doesn't. When it doesn't improve, services often have to be terminated (Greenson, 1967; Wolberg, 1967).

In the best-case scenario, services are terminated when the negotiated contract is successfully completed. This is the end for which clients and social workers strive. Managed care has dramatically changed how services are being offered (Farley et al., 2003). In most instances, the number of sessions are predetermined and usually limited to six to eight sessions. Any additional sessions must be approved by the managed care program supervisor. Managed care mental health services rarely include more than ten to twelve sessions. Most managed care social workers believe that the goals their clients want help with can be accomplished in six to eight sessions.

When the negotiated contract is successfully completed, the social worker and the client can take pride in the work they have accomplished. It is difficult for most clients to make positive changes in their lives, so as these changes occur, clients should be congratulated for their hard work and diligence. They should also be reminded that if services are needed again, they shouldn't hesitate to ask for help. When clients successfully complete their sessions, the chances increase dramatically that they will return if additional services are required. When the negotiated contract has been successfully completed, it is advisable to complete the three following tasks as part of the termination process. The first task is to review with clients the goal, problem, or concern that led them to seek assistance. The second task is to discuss what new skills clients have learned that helped them accomplish their goals. The final task is to discuss with clients how these new skills will help them as they leave and continue on with their lives.

More often than not, services are terminated in managed care programs even though the client still needs to do additional work. Services ended because the allotted number of sessions had been completed and no additional sessions were approved. For this reason, the termination of services in managed care programs has taken on an added importance. Social workers need to make sure that clients are equipped to do additional work after services have been terminated (Farley et al., 2003).

If clients need to continue working on their goals or problems and concerns following the termination of services, and most clients do, the final session should focus on what clients can do to help themselves after services have ended. In general, the client and the social worker should focus on three related activities. The first activity is to design with clients the tasks and activities they can complete by themselves. A task or activity that is easily within the grasp of most clients is reading self-help or other appropriate books that will support what has already been accomplished. Another task is to encourage clients to take advantage of community programs that can help them. City and county libraries offer a variety of programs that can help clients with their goals or problems and concerns. Free monthly lectures that address personal concerns as well as local and national issues can provide clients with stimulating experiences that also include the opportunity to meet new people. A final task is to refer clients to other resources in the community. The YWCA and YMCA, for example, offer a variety of group experiences that can help clients with such issues as how to budget money or how to communicate more effectively. Similar programs are also sponsored by area hospitals as well as community mental health centers.

The restrictions imposed by managed care programs become moot when clients are willing and able to pay for services out of their own pocket. Mental health services offered in the 1940s and 1950s were characterized by a fee-for-service that the client paid because very few insurance companies covered these kinds of services. With the advent of community mental health services in the 1960s, more insurance companies started adding mental health coverage to their insurance benefits. Over the years, this coverage has evolved into present-day managed care programs. Even so, clients who are willing to pay for services out of their own pocket can continue sessions beyond the restrictions normally imposed by managed care. Although the termination of services is still an issue for these private paying clients, it is not as immediate an issue as it is with managed care.

When clients elect to self-pay for services, another question that should be addressed is how long the intervention should last. Some clients who pay for their own sessions continue in therapy for many months and sometimes for many years. It is not uncommon to hear about a celebrity or some other prominent person who has been in analysis for five or more years. Other self-paying clients will only be in therapy for six or fewer sessions. In these cases, there is no one-size-fits-all approach to mental health services. Some social workers will have their clients continue seeing them for many months because they are serious suicide risks (Wolberg, 1967). Other social workers will offer long-term therapy because clients need continuous support and encouragement. Without this continuous support and encouragement, some clients may become suicide risks. Whether therapy is short or long term, the welfare and safety needs of clients should always be the main reason why one approach is chosen over another.

Services can also be terminated when the social worker moves, retires, or becomes ill. This doesn't happen very often but when it does it can be traumatic for the client. Most social workers know well in advance whether they will be moving or retiring. On the other hand, illness is a matter that cannot be planned for in advance. When a social worker has to terminate services for one of these reasons, it is important to discuss the matter with the client well in advance and have a number of options the client can choose from, including referral to another social worker. When clients lose their social worker, they may feel sad or even rejected. Ego psychology theory places great importance on helping the client deal with these feelings as a critical part of the termination process (Wolberg, 1965; 1967).

If a social worker knows well in advance that a move or retirement will occur in three or four months, he or she has at least three options to consider in working with clients. One option would be to continue with current clients and not accept any new clients during the last one or two months of employment. A second option would be to continue working with new clients as long as the new clients know about the impending move or retirement. If this strategy is used, the social worker should tell clients about the social worker who eventually will be taking over the client's care. It would also be advisable for the social worker to introduce clients to the new social worker at least one month before the social worker departs. A third option would be to change assignments two or three months before leaving. For example, the social worker could ask to be assigned to complete interviews that generally last one or two sessions. After these intake interviews are completed, clients are transferred to other social workers for treatment. Focusing exclusively on intake interviews would be an appropriate assignment for a social worker whose departure is imminent.

Another infrequent but potential reason why services are terminated is that the social worker just cannot connect with the client and, recognizing this situation, refers the client to another social worker. Before social workers terminate services with a client they just can't connect with, at least two options should be considered. One option would be a frank discussion with the client about what is happening and how the social worker is feeling. Sharing this information with a client can open up a dialogue that can be beneficial for both parties. Rather than saying, "For whatever reason, I just don't seem to like you," it would be better for the social worker to begin the discussion by saying, "Have you noticed that you and I have a difficult time communicating with each other?" Whereas the first response is accusatory and judgmental, the second response is more measured and will probably facilitate a better exchange of ideas and feelings between the social worker and the client. Another option for the social worker to pursue before terminating services would be to stop working with the client for two or three weeks. This temporary suspension of services can give the social worker time to reflect on his or her unacceptable feelings toward the client, talk with a colleague or supervisor, and decide what would be best for both social worker and client. The temporary suspension would also give the client a reprieve from the rigorous and often demanding task of making positive life changes. If both of these options fail to improve the social worker's ability to help the client, then it is probably best to refer the client to another practitioner.

The General Tasks of Termination

The general tasks of termination include the following: (1) review with the client the purposes for seeking assistance, (2) discuss why the client was not able to accomplish the goals or resolve the problems or concerns without the social worker's help, (3) identify the new problem-solving skills the client has acquired, (4) discuss how these new problem-solving skills will help the client accomplish future goals or resolve new problems or concerns, (5) explore how these new problem-solving skills can be further enhanced and developed after services have ended, and (6) discuss how the client is feeling about terminating contact with the social worker (Smith, 1990; Farley et al., 2003; Patterson & Welfel, 2000).

Why Clients Ask for Assistance

Clients ask for assistance for many different reasons. One of the most common reasons is that they need help with a goal or problem and concern they can no longer accomplish or resolve by themselves. Most people want to believe that they are "the captains of their own ship" or that "the world is their oyster." When people find out that a goal seems beyond their reach or that a problem or concern is beyond their grasp, they often feel helpless or at least more vulnerable than they want to feel. After a series of failed attempts to accomplish the goal or resolve the problem or concern, they become more discouraged and may finally ask for help. These clients are generally quite motivated because of the distress they are experiencing.

Some clients seek assistance because they were either forced to or felt they were coerced in some way. Working with involuntary clients is a common experience for most social workers. Clients who have physically abused a spouse or some other family member may be referred by the court for anger management. Or clients with repeated DUI arrests are given one last chance to control their alcohol and drug abuse or go to jail or prison. Sometimes a reluctant husband is told it's either marriage counseling or his wife will file for divorce. Although some of these clients are motivated to change, more often than not they are just angry because their spouse or the judicial system has forced them to seek assistance.

Other clients seek assistance because they have always been in a helping relationship and don't know what else to do. Some of them have been involved with the mental health system, public welfare services, or correctional institutions for many years. They may have been in and out of counseling and suffer from chronic depression or anxiety, have disabled children who require special services, or are convicted sex abusers who must be continually monitored. The goals or problems and concerns they bring with them have bothered them for years and are still not resolved.

Whatever the reason, the first step of the termination process is to review with the client the reasons for seeking help. In keeping with the strengths-based focus of this book, the social worker may need to restate or reframe with clients what led them to this point. Rather than seeking assistance to stay out of jail or prison because of repeated DUI arrests, the client asks for help to gain more control over her use of alcohol and drugs. Or the husband who began marriage counseling because he was afraid his wife would divorce him asks for assistance to improve his relationship with his wife. By putting a positive focus on why the client asks for assistance, services can be perceived as an experience that may improve the client's life and may likely improve it again in the future if needed.

Why Problems Weren't Resolved without Social Work Intervention

The second step of the termination process is to review with clients why they couldn't accomplish their goals or resolve their problems or concerns without services. This generally occurs because clients lacked the special knowledge, skills, or training required to ac-

Voices from the Field

John Nickisson

My name is John Nickisson. Originally from the United Kingdom, I came to the United States in 1981, and since that time I have continued to travel around the world and throughout the United States. I lived in China in 1987 and the Marshall Islands in 1990, and I have also lived in New York State, Colorado, Massachusetts, and Michigan. I am married with two children, have an undergraduate degree in community health education, and a graduate degree in psychology. I began my MSW at Grand Valley State University, Michigan, in the fall of 2002 and will graduate in 2006. Thanks to one influential professor in my present program, I consider myself a budding critical theorist. Ongoing research and teaching at the college level are also very much a part of my life.

My field of expertise is called co-occurring disorders (or dual diagnosis). The treatment philosophy is client-centered and calls for the integration of mental health and substance use treatment. In addition, the impact of other co-occurring issues is also continually assessed and addressed.

As a clinician since 1987, I have worked with a wide variety of adults, children, and families with diverse issues, backgrounds, histories, stories, and worldviews; however, my preference is working with those with co-occurring disorders. I believe that my MSW and subsequent clinical certification, in conjunction with my clinical, academic, and personal life experiences, will provide me with the tools I need to have an impact on present treatment methodology toward a more integrated and client-centered philosophy.

complish the goal or resolve the problem or concern. This lack of knowledge, skills, or training is discussed with the client in this stage of the termination process and reinforced as the main reason the client couldn't deal with the situation without help.

Many clients seek help for the first time because they are in a crisis. A crisis is usually a loss, a threat, or a challenge that the client has not experienced before. Clients who are struggling with a new crisis often do not have the coping or problem-solving skills to resolve the problem by themselves, prompting them to seek services. Crisis situations can include the death of a loved one, a serious illness or accident, loss of employment, or any other unexpected or unplanned for situation. The goal of crisis management is to help the client regain, as much as possible, what has been lost, threatened, or challenged (James & Gilliland, 2001). The ultimate goal of crisis management is to return the client to his or her precrisis level of functioning (Smith, 1990).

Other clients are simply overwhelmed with a litany of problems that haven't been resolved for months and maybe even years. These clients seek services with the hope that the social worker can help them find some of the resources they desperately need (Reid & Epstein, 1972). Some clients seek help because they don't have the problem-solving skills to resolve a marital conflict or a problem at work or a disagreement with a teenage son or daughter. They are interested in learning how to be a better spouse, employee, employer, or parent. From their point of view, the social worker has special skills and abilities that they hope will be shared with them. They are seeking help to acquire the coping and problem-solving skills they lack (Hutchins & Vaught, 1997). They want to learn how to improve their lives.

Knowledge, Skills, and Training Acquired

The third step in the termination process is reviewing with the client what new knowledge, skills, or training was acquired in sessions and how this has helped accomplish goals or resolve problems or concerns. Clients in crisis learn many things about themselves and about their world as a result of working with a social worker. To begin with, they learn that, to quote Robert Burns, "the best laid schemes o' mice and men often go astray" (Johnson, 1998, p. 9). Many things about our lives we can't control, such as the death of a loved one. We can anticipate how we might feel, but until the loss occurs our work is still basically an intellectual exercise. A truth many clients learn is that the world is not as predictable as they once thought and that bad things do happen to good people (Kushner, 1981). This is a basic tenet of humanistic and existential theory and a concept that Frankl discussed at length in his book *Man's Search for Meaning* (1959). In crisis sessions, clients also learn the skill of examining what has been lost and how that loss can be replaced to some degree. This new knowledge and skill from crisis intervention should be reviewed with the client.

Another skill that many clients acquire is learning to trust the social worker and to accept help. Some people are closed off and guarded with others and don't freely share their goals or problems and concerns. They bottle up their emotions, and when the top blows off they don't know what to do. For many clients, one of the most valuable experiences of therapy is learning to trust and confide in another person and letting themselves be vulnerable and dependent to some degree. This new skill should also be identified and discussed in this step of the termination process.

Future Use of Knowledge, Skills, and Training

Social workers commit a serious error if they don't encourage clients to continue to use their newfound knowledge, skills, and training after the professional relationship ends. The importance of clients continuing to apply what they have learned following the termination of services can't be overemphasized. For example, a couple who have learned the importance of discussing the component parts of their relationship, such as how they communicate, show affection, resolve conflict, and so on, should continue this review even though services have ended. For example, a couple might agree in the termination phase to discuss the component parts of their relationship at least every two or three months.

Clients who have experienced a crisis and resolved to some degree the loss, threat, or challenge they have experienced should be encouraged to apply the same skills they have learned if another crisis should occur. One of those newly acquired skills is asking for help and then trusting and confiding in another person. The gains that clients acquire will become short term as opposed to long term if they don't continue to work on their goals or problems and concerns afterward. This is a basic concept of learning theory (Robbins et al., 1998). One reason why clients lose the long-term benefits of their work with the social worker is that they stop practicing what they have learned when services are terminated. In other words, they stop learning.

Research studies continue to show that the gains of therapy are often short term because clients don't continue to practice their new skills (Farley et al., 2003). Some years ago a marital enrichment study conducted at the University of Utah's College of Social Work demonstrated this fact only too well (Taylor, 1980). After ten weeks of marital enrichment sessions in which couples spent eight hours each Saturday and Sunday working on their relationships, before-and-after measures showed that all couples scored significantly higher in communication skills, conflict resolution, and marital satisfaction at termination. One- and two-month follow-up evaluations showed that the significant gains in communication skills, conflict resolution, and marital satisfaction continued. When follow-up evaluations were completed three months later, however, the significant changes had evaporated and the couples were back to the scores they started with before the marital enrichment workshop began. This is just another example of why social workers need to encourage their clients as strongly as possible to continue to use their new knowledge, skills, and training even though services have been terminated.

Expanding New Knowledge, Skills, and Training

During the time they are receiving services, clients learn a lot about themselves and about their world. One goal of the termination process is to help them expand on the new knowledge, skills, and training they have acquired. One of the best ways clients can accomplish this goal is through self-study. Sometimes referred to as bibliotherapy, self-study focuses on the self-help literature and how this literature can help clients after counseling has been terminated. Hundreds of self-help books have been written over the years. Most social workers have developed their own list of self-help books that they encourage clients to read. Some of these books have become self-help classics and are described in this and earlier chapters. Self-help books borrow extensively from learning, ego psychology, humanistic, cognitive, and existential theories and can provide excellent examples of how these theories can be integrated.

Community education programs can also be used to expand the knowledge, skills, and training clients have acquired. Almost every public school district offers evening education programs for adults. The classes taught in these programs focus on many topics that can benefit clients after services are terminated. For example, a review of evening classes offered by a local school district found classes on parenting, communication skills, personal finance, family relations, and other related topics. Many of these classes are taught by mental health professionals in the community. For clients interested in improving their physical as well as mental health, there were classes on yoga, meditation, exercise, weight training, and the martial arts. For those clients interested in pursuing the arts, there were classes on oil painting, watercolor, drawing, pottery, and calligraphy.

In some cases, clients might be encouraged to pursue additional education or specialized training. If they are unsure of their interests, clients can also be referred to a vocational education specialist who can help with other employment and training opportunities.

How the Client Feels about the Termination of Services

The last step in the termination process is discussing with clients how they feel about the termination of services. As we have seen, clients can experience many different feelings as the professional relationship draws to an end. Most clients will feel a sense of accomplishment now that they have completed important goals or resolved serious problems or concerns. They often express gratitude to the social worker for his or her help and assistance. This gratitude should be graciously accepted even as the social worker comments that clients deserve most of the credit because they worked hard to improve their lives.

Clients may be pleased with the additional time and money they have at their disposal now that work with the social worker has concluded. For some it will seem like a burden lifted because of the intensive work that goes into making changes in one's personal life and relationships.

At the same time, some clients approach the end with apprehension and even fear. They are not sure they can continue without the social worker's assistance. These feelings are sometimes the result of services that have to be terminated too soon because of the limits of managed care. This is one reason why helping clients to develop a plan they can follow afterward is critical for helping to ensure long-term benefits. When clients have a plan they can follow after services are terminated, they often feel they have a better grip on the apprehension and fear that can accompany the termination of services.

Other clients might experience a sense of abandonment by the social worker (Patterson & Welfel, 2000). They have told the social worker things about themselves that they have never shared with another human being. They might wonder how the social worker will use this information and whether it will remain confidential. Or they may see the termination of services as a personal rejection by the social worker. Whatever the case, it is essential that the social worker explore with clients their feelings or concerns about termination. If clients are experiencing strong reactions to this phase, these feelings must be addressed honestly and the clients reassured that the social worker still has the highest regard for them. Sometimes one or two monthly follow-up sessions can ameliorate the sense of abandonment or rejection that some clients experience. Overall, however, most clients do not perceive termination as a crisis situation. Indeed, most successfully negotiate this phase and do not let their emotional reactions interfere with the progress they have made (Patterson & Welfel, 2000).

How the Social Worker Feels about the Termination of Services

Most social workers view the termination of services in a positive light. This is especially true when the client has overcome serious personal problems with the help and guidance of the social worker. Helping clients correct serious personal problems while also assisting them on the road to personal growth and development is the main reason most social workers got involved in counseling in the first place. The social worker's sense of accomplishment can be magnified many times over when the client is a couple or a family.

Social workers may feel some sadness when they terminate the relationship with their clients. This is to be expected because social workers have come to know their clients as complete persons and not just people with personal problems. After weeks of working together with clients, most social workers find their clients to be engaging and interesting people, and they look forward to seeing them. It is natural that these positive feelings develop and grow. Without these positive feelings, an essential ingredient to successful counseling—the rapport that must develop between social workers and their clients—would never occur.

Social workers should view termination as the next step their clients must take on their road to personal growth and development. It is essential that clients try out their new problem-solving skills without further help and guidance from their social workers. When termination is viewed as a necessary step in the growth and development of clients, it is easier for social workers to separate themselves from their clients. This separation completes the counseling process and starts the client on a new personal journey.

Planning for the Ending

As discussed earlier, planning for the termination of services begins in this first session. In this first session, clients identify the goals or problems and concerns they want to work on. From that point on, the social worker and the client work together on the tasks and activities that will accomplish goals or resolve problems and concerns. As each goal or problem or concern is achieved or resolved, the client moves that much closer to the termination of services. This progress should be monitored each session by the social worker and the client. In managed care programs, the movement toward the termination of services is reinforced by the fact that help is limited to six to eight sessions. As each session is completed, the client is that much closer to termination.

The detailed planning for termination of services must begin no later than the next to

last session. It will take at least one session to complete the six tasks of termination discussed earlier. With managed care programs limiting the number of sessions, the social worker and client must spend sufficient time to plan what the client can continue to work on when services are terminated. If the social worker is successful in getting clients to continue working to improve their lives following the termination of services, chances are much better that the accomplishments they have made will be long term rather than short term. There is even the chance that with proper termination planning, the accomplishments made by the client can continue to grow and develop after the sessions end. A thoughtful and detailed termination plan will help clients move toward this goal.

The importance of termination planning can't be overstated. Because the social worker's time with the client is so limited, it is essential that the client's progress continue after services have ended. Reference has already been made to how self-study literature, community education programs, high school and college evening education, and other services can be used to help the client. When these activities are incorporated into termination planning, the client continues the quest for personal growth and development that will hopefully become a lifelong journey. The social worker must help the client develop a detailed plan that can be followed after counseling services are terminated. Without this detailed plan, what the client has gained from the counseling experience will most likely diminish over time.

Maintenance/Stabilization of Change

We have discussed at length how proper termination planning can help clients maintain the changes they have made to their lives through

APPLICATIONS TO PRACTICE

Practice Activity

Go back to the case in Chapter 7 (p. 242) about C. C. and Eric Buchanan and their two sons, Marc, fourteen, and Marvin, sixteen. Look over your notes from the two sessions you and your treatment group prepared. Get together in the same practice group and, maintaining the same roles, engage in a brief discussion of where the treatment left off and how you want to proceed in the termination process. Remember to refer to the general guidelines and tasks for termination. Engage in a session of thirty to forty minutes. After completing the session, discuss what seemed to work well and what might have been done differently. Have the observer report to the class the outcome of the session.

Critical Thinking Questions

1. Think about a time you said good-bye to someone who had helped you and who you enjoyed working with. What was hard about saying good-bye? What did you do to feel better about losing this friend?

2. What has happened when you weren't able to say good-bye to someone with whom you were close? How did you manage your feelings?

3. What do you think might help this client in the saying good-bye process?

Research Activity

Using the Research Navigator™ website, www.research navigator.com, look up client termination specific to the model you and your treatment team used for this case activity. For discussion in class, identify two to three things about the model and population that are important in the termination process.

Practice Tip

Some client groups have a high incidence of failing to return after the first session. It is important to discuss termination at the end of each session so the client is aware of the benefits of treatment and feels hopeful that you can assist him or her in making the changes desired.

   Toward the end of the first session, you may want to ask:

1. Is this what you thought counseling would be like?

2. Are you feeling as though we can work together to resolve this issue?

3. Would you like to return next week at this same time to continue to work on this issue?

4. Do you have suggestions about how I can be more helpful?

You will also want to compliment the client about what has happened during the interview:

1. You've really worked hard this last hour. I appreciate your willingness to discuss this problem and consider alternatives.

2. You've really been thinking about what you want to be different.

3. I look forward to working with you.

their relationship with the social worker. The goal is a simple one: help the client develop a plan that will build on what has been gained once services are terminated. One plan that has become an important part of the maintenance of change is relapse prevention. Although relapse prevention is being used in many areas, its roots began in the treatment of alcohol and drug addictions (Farley et al., 2003).

Relapse prevention focuses on helping clients identify those situations that might encourage them to abuse alcohol and drugs after services are terminated and ways in which this relapse can be prevented. For example, some alcohol and drug addiction occurs because clients self-medicate themselves with these substances. They suffer from depression or anxiety and use alcohol and drugs in an attempt to feel better. Some clients experience so much stress in their lives that they use alcohol and drugs to relax. In relapse prevention, one goal is to help clients identify the early signs of depression, anxiety, and stress and then take corrective action that doesn't include using alcohol and drugs. One corrective action might be to increase their level of physical activity, which often has a beneficial effect on depression, anxiety, and stress. Another corrective action might be to use relaxation exercises such as positive imagery or deep breathing to mitigate the effects of depression, anxiety, and stress.

Another aspect of change maintenance is environmental manipulation. With severe alcohol and drug addiction, the client sometimes has to consider changing employment or even relocating to another city, especially if employment has become part of why alcohol and drugs are being abused. Many sales, marketing, and advertising positions require employees to spend inordinate amounts of time socializing with clients after regular working hours. When they socialize, alcohol and drugs are often available. If the client can't avoid these situations because of work, the first step in relapse prevention would be to help develop strategies to not drink and use drugs in these situations. In a worse-case scenario, the strategy may include finding other employment.

Maintenance or stabilization of change is used in a variety of other areas besides alcohol and drug treatment. The goal remains that of helping the client anticipate situations that may threaten the progress already made. Generally this is done by helping clients understand what problems and situations brought them in to seek help. Very likely, clients will encounter these same situations or others like them again when services are terminated. When that happens, clients need to respond in a way that will help them continue on the path of growth and development and not be diverted to a side trail that can lead to problem reoccurrence (see Figure 14.1).

The principles identified in Figure 14.1 can be used in a number of different case situations. Consider the case of a woman whose two major stresses in life are (1) being criticized at work by her boss and (2) returning home at night to a messy home. When either one of these situations occurs, the woman is flooded with conflicting feelings and emotions. On the one hand, she is angry at her boss for criticizing her at work and at her children who do not help by keeping the home clean and tidy. On the other hand, she is frustrated by her inability to control these two situations and draws the conclusion that the fault must be hers and not the fault of her boss or family. Overwhelmed by her feelings of inadequacy, she retreats to her bed, where she feels better and tries to forget what has happened at work and at home.

Figure 14.1

Relapse Prevention and Addiction Counseling

The relapse prevention model (Marlatt & Gordon, 1985) is a self-management program specifically for clients who are recovering from addictions. The goal of the program is to teach clients to anticipate and cope with situations that may lead to relapse. The program can be used on any addictive behaviors and can be incorporated into the treatment planning that takes place when services are terminated. The model (Miller, 1999) is based on four assumptions:

1. Addiction is an overlearned, maladaptive habit pattern.

2. Behavioral determinants and consequences have an impact on behavior.

3. People are not responsible for developing a habit or for not simply being able to stop it.

4. Escape from the addiction cycle hinges on changing habits through participation and responsibility.

   Relapse is a two-step process. The first step is lapse, when clients violate the goal they have set for themselves, such as staying drug free. Step 2 is relapse, or returning to the pretreatment level of drug abuse. Lapse occurs when clients have one joint of marijuana after two months of sobriety and then view themselves as utter failures at staying sober. Relapse follows when clients return to their pretreatment abuse of marijuana. When relapse occurs, it should be viewed as a mistake that clients can learn from rather than a personal failure.

   Marlatt and Gordon (Miller, 1999) outline a number of treatment strategies that can be used to pre-

vent relapse. These strategies can be used to help many clients during the termination phase. In using the model, social workers are encouraged to help their clients identify the following:

1. Situations that are high risk for them.

2. Skills to cope in high-risk situations.

3. Relaxation and stress management skills.

4. Positive outcome expectancies: realistic outcomes of addictive behavior (sometimes described in self-help groups as "follow the drink through [to its inevitable outcome]").

5. Immediate and delayed effects of the addictive activity.

6. Action to take if a relapse occurs.

   Marlatt and Gordon (1985) list a number of relaxation and stress management skills that can be used by clients in relapse prevention. These skills include breathing exercises, positive imagery, and physical exercise. The client first learns to recognize the various signals that suggest stress is reaching a dangerous level, such as rapid heart rate, perspiration, shaking, high-pitched voice, and dizziness. Before the stress reaches a dangerous level, the client uses one or more of these relaxation and stress management skills to lower stress and reduce the risk of relapse. Another relaxation and stress management skill is using cognitive theory to help the client recognize the distortions in thinking that may lead to relapse.

The social worker helps the woman develop a strategy to cope with these two high-risk situations. Her strategy at work includes breathing deeply when her boss is criticizing her and trying to remain as calm as possible. The follow-up strategy is to excuse herself by telling her boss she needs to use the restroom. In the restroom, she enters a stall and continues to breathe deeply for two or three minutes. As she breathes deeply, she imagines in her mind a peaceful scene at a beach she likes to visit. When she is calmer and more relaxed, she leaves the restroom and returns to her desk. Her strategy with her family is to remind them when she comes home that they have already agreed to help with the housework and then ask them to take a few minutes to tidy up while she is in the bathroom. While in the bathroom, she breathes deeply and imagines in her mind again the peaceful scene at the beach. When she feels calmer and more relaxed, she leaves the bathroom and rejoins her family. Approaches like this are used when it is not possible for the client to avoid situations that provoke anxiety reactions.

Another maintenance of change strategy is used with clients who are experiencing such addictive behaviors as smoking. The strategy involves helping the client examine the positive and negative outcomes that will occur by stopping the addictive behavior. This is accomplished, in part, by completing a "decision matrix chart" (Miller, 1999) that compares the immediate consequences of quitting the addictive behavior with those of continuing the abuse. For example, some of the positive reasons to stop smoking include increased self-efficacy, social approval, improved physical state, and financial gain. Some of the positive reasons to continue smoking include immediate gratification, removal of withdrawal discomfort, and weight loss. By completing and analyzing the decision matrix chart, clients can better evaluate the immediate consequences of stopping or continuing an addictive behavior such as smoking.

A follow-up step is to add to the decision matrix chart another category that examines the delayed consequences of stopping or continuing an addictive behavior. Some of the delayed reasons to stop smoking include enhanced self-control, improved health (absence of disease), financial gain, and absence of social disapproval. The delayed consequences of not stopping include continued gratification. The negative consequence of stopping smoking is denial of gratification, whereas the negative consequences of continuing to smoke are decreased self-control, health risks, financial loss, and continued social disapproval. By identifying and discussing the delayed consequences of stopping or continuing an addictive behavior, clients have additional reasons to stop the abusive behavior.

Another strategy is to prepare the client for the possibility that problems will recur in the future. By anticipating this possibility, the client can learn to view the recurrence as an opportunity to learn and grow rather than a personal failure. A logical place to start is for the client and the social worker to examine the high-risk situations most likely to lead to recurrence. By role-playing with clients how they might handle these future situations, the social worker can help prepare them for this eventuality. For example, clients might be helped to use some of the relaxation and stress management skills that were identified in earlier sessions.

In summary, social workers who want to help clients maintain the changes they have made might want to consider the following tasks, which are adapted from Miller (1999, pp. 117–118).

- Help clients see recurrence as both an event and a process.
- Identify high-risk factors and coping strategies; be aware of cues that can set off cravings.
- Find different ways to cope with negative emotions.
- Learn to cope with cognitive distortions.
- Be aware of social pressure to act in specific ways.
- Develop a social network supportive of their behavior change.

- Develop a balanced lifestyle.
- Develop a plan to deal with future recurrence of problem situations.

A Short-Term Treatment Approach to Termination

Murphy (1965) discusses a number of interesting issues regarding termination, one of which is the idea of temporarily terminating services when a stalemate occurs and the client stops making progress. Stalemates occur when clients repeat the same themes again and again without making any real change in their lives. In such cases, a brief suspension of sessions can achieve several goals. First, it may help the client realize the importance of working on identified needs and making progress toward the original goals. Second, it may help clients who have trouble identifying those goals or problems and concerns they want to address. If this impasse continues for more than two sessions, the social worker might suggest that services be temporarily terminated until clients can identify the goals or problems and concerns they want to focus on. Social workers can then indicate to clients that they should resume contact in a month or two when they have a better idea of what they want to work on in therapy.

Sometimes in short-term intervention, the problem is not clients' inability to identify goals or problems and concerns but the inability to get clients to work on them. When clients repeatedly fail to do their homework assignments and come to sessions unprepared, or when their participation in sessions is less than enthusiastic, it is important for the social worker to address these problems as soon as possible. More often than not, a frank discussion with clients is all that is needed to get

them to be more involved. If this doesn't work, the social worker might suggest a temporary termination or separation of one or two months until the client is better prepared to continue working with the social worker.

Even though the social worker and the client are terminating their relationship, this does not necessarily mean they will not work together in the future. Clients may continue to have some concerns that at some point they will seek help to resolve. Sometimes a new crisis overwhelms their capacity to cope, and they return.

In short-term practice, it is assumed that clients will have goals or problems and concerns that they will continue to work on even after services are terminated. One of the most important steps in termination is designing tasks and activities that the client can work on after services end. This reinforces the concept of self-improvement as a lifelong pursuit and not just a part of therapy that is abandoned when services are concluded. Reference has already been made to how self-help books and community education can support this lifelong pursuit of self-development even after services are terminated.

Even though short-term services are limited to six to eight sessions, the social worker should never minimize the emotional loss or even rejection that many clients experience when sessions end. A critical concept of ego psychology theory has always been the "positive regard" that the client can develop for the social worker (Corsini & Wedding, 1995). It is not difficult to understand how this positive regard can develop as a result of traditional interventions in which the relationships can last for six months or longer. A shorter period of service can also generate positive regard for the social worker, especially if the client was in crisis and the social worker guided him or her through the morass of feelings that surround a significant loss. In the short-term model of intervention, the social worker needs to give clients permission to return later if services are needed. The social worker also needs to give clients permission to try their new problem-solving skills on their own. By redefining the experience, clients can say that they have gained a new support person to call on again even though services have been terminated. In other words, rather than losing the social worker, an important person has been added to the client's support system.

Cultural and Diversity Issues

The social worker has to be sensitive to cultural and diversity issues and how they can affect the termination of services. Social workers should be alert to the possibility that their own lack of cultural sensitivity may contribute to clients' decisions to terminate prematurely. Likewise, using theoretical models that clients, especially women, see as gender inappropriate may cause them to seek another practitioner.

For clients who terminate as scheduled, Devore and Schlesinger (1999) advocate openly addressing cultural and diversity issues during termination, especially if these issues played a role in the actual intervention. This is also an opportunity for social workers to learn more about how clients perceived the practitioner's sensitivity to diversity. Such a discussion is consistent with our own need to increase our self-awareness and to seek feedback when appropriate.

In *Diversity Perspectives for Social Work Practice,* Anderson and Carter (2003) state that termination is a closure of the relationship between client and worker. If client goals have been reached, success will most likely be noted by ending treatment. Termination can also mean a readjustment of previous goals and intervention approaches that result in a new series of sessions. Anderson and Carter (2003) then go on to say that arriving at a final destination as part of termination may have a special meaning for ethnic clients:

> *Arrival* at a destination defines successful termination. Involvement or rejoining the client to his or her ethnic community is an example of an arrival point. That is, when an ethnic person is reunited and reconnected to his or her ethnic community, there is an arrival after a long journey away from one's roots. Measurable growth, insight, and change between contact and termination process stages is an accurate indicator of the progress made. *Recital* involves reviewing positive changes that have occurred in the helping process by taking a retrospective view and reflecting on what has happened at certain points in the client's life. *Completion* is the achievement of goals and resolution of issues, attended by a sense of accomplishment. (p. 71)

Many authors (e.g., Anderson & Carter, 2003; Farley et al., 2003) believe that one of the most important treatment strategies that can be used with clients of color is to help them connect or reconnect with their ethnic group. Reestablishing ties with their ethnic group provides clients of color with a support system that is invaluable during and subsequent to the intervention. The emotional, physical, and other resources that can be provided by their ethnic group can help clients maintain and build on the positive changes that occurred in their work with the practitioner.

SUMMARY

This chapter focuses on the knowledge and skills needed by the social worker during the termination phase of the problem-solving process. It also identifies the ways in which different theories and treatment models approach termination. General termination guidelines are introduced and various types of termination discussed. Tasks of termination are reviewed, along with methods to maintain change and prevent relapse. The importance of developing a detailed plan for the client to follow after the termination of counseling services is also discussed and emphasized. Cultural and diversity issues in termination are also briefly considered.

Navigating Direct Practice

An access code for Research Navigator™ is packaged within your text. Use this code to register at www.researchnavigator.com and then use the key words listed below to research articles related to the chapter's content. Research Navigator™ helps you quickly and efficiently make the most of your research time.

❑ Behavior therapy
❑ Family therapy
❑ Person-centered therapy
❑ Systems therapy

Writing Skills for Social Workers

Bonnie Lantz, University of Utah

Social work professional writing began with writing case narratives for most records and using process recording for instructional purposes. Although some agencies may continue to rely on records that serve as a narration of a client's story, most organizations that depend on external funding and accreditation must meet specific guidelines in recording. Records and reports are expected to summarize and synthesize the many hours of treatment into a focused chronology of assessment, diagnosis, treatment progress, and recommendations. It is no longer acceptable to have only relationship and treatment skills. Social workers must document work products to ensure that work meets federal, state, and professional regulations and funding guidelines.

Most students enter social work with basic writing skills. This appendix is presented to provide the social work student with familiarity with and examples of professional writing that meets the requirements for professional social work assignments. The appendix is divided into four sections: Section I, General Overview of Social Work Writing; Section II, Writing for Course Work; Section III, Record Keeping, Court Reports, and Evaluations; and Section IV, Professional Social Work Best Practice Guidelines. Each of these sections will present basic information, suggestions, examples, and exercises. Students are encouraged to access campus writing centers, books and articles about professional writing, and web resources to supplement the materials presented. It is also important to ask for critique and suggestions from other students, agency colleagues, and social work educators to improve your writing skills as you develop professional focus. Finally, becoming a proficient professional writer requires the same practice, experience, and feedback that are required in learning most skills.

Section I: General Overview of Social Work Writing

Professional writing relies on critical thinking and the writer's background in culture, course work, and life experiences. Throughout primary and secondary education, students are expected to produce written assignments and are given feedback from an instructor about how well the student has mastered what was learned and how the student expressed the learning in writing. Although the student may have had assistance from other adults who reviewed the assignment and the written work product and may have offered suggestions or provided technical editing regarding spelling, sentence structure, and punctuation, most learning prior to professional training has had only one rater and reviewer—the instructor. Some students master getting good grades by figuring out what the instructor wants. Essentially the student is writing for the instructor. By entering a profession, a student must learn to write for a variety of purposes and must follow certain presentation patterns, which may include making judgments about what information means.

In professional writing, whereas the basic rules of writing are upheld, other elements are added to the writing assignments in the classroom as well as the agency. Professional writing includes consideration of the purpose, audience, ethics, subjective and objective information, scientific application, positive statements, and active voice. Although the masters student may write research papers in much the same way as he or she did as an undergraduate; writing for records (assessments, treatment plans, and progress notes), court reports, and evaluations require different standards. All professional writing is expected to be clear, specific, and organized in a way that allows the reader to follow the same logic the writer followed in making conclusions. Certain standards must be understood and followed so that clients are fairly represented in all written formats.

Purpose and Audience

Think about the purpose of the written document. Does the instructor want a chronology of events from a client interview? Are you writing a treatment plan and monitoring progress for you and the client, or will the court or a review board be reading the record too? Are you recording your feelings and thoughts to see your progress toward professional acculturation?

Before writing, consider the purpose and who will use the writing. Next, make notes and give consideration to who, what, when, where, and how. The *why* of things is something that will not be addressed until the other questions are answered. *Why* questions imply making a judgment, and professional writing has a separate section for discussing what the information you have collected means. Usually *why* information is labeled as professional outcomes, discussion, or outcome expectations.

Taking notes can assist you in the development of an outline, which includes who is doing or has done what, as well as how and where the actions took place. Look at the following example and determine who, what, when, where, and how.

Mary Smith is a twenty-three-year-old school dropout. She was the driver of the getaway vehicle for three robberies committed by her boyfriend, Shawn Knight, during the past six months. All three robberies took place in fast food restaurants where Mary had previously worked. Mary is currently on probation and Shawn is in jail pending his trial. Because Shawn has a history of committing over 50 armed robberies, he is likely to be incarcerated if found guilty. The purpose of this report is to inform the court of the progress Mary has made in weekly counseling and to review her current treatment plan.

Who _____
What _____
Where _____
When _____
How _____

From this writing the reader knows that this is a report about Mary Smith (who) currently on probation for driving the getaway vehicle (what) for fast food restaurant robberies (where) during the past six months (when). The reader doesn't know how the events happened but may guess that Mary became involved in the robberies at the request of her boyfriend, who has committed forty-seven more robberies than Mary.

Notice that the written report is free of adjectives and conjecture about why. The purpose of the report is to provide facts or information to the court. The treatment plan, counseling session dates and attendance, and progress report will follow this opening statement and will be discussed in Section III.

Ethics

Professional social workers are expected to write original documents and to cite ideas as well as materials written by another person. Any information that is incorporated into a written assignment or report must be properly cited to avoid plagiarism. With the advent of technology there has been a proliferation of websites that offer for free or for a fee, papers and documents for a variety of assignments. Computer programs are also available to instructors that can scan a paper and evaluate whether material has been taken from another source. It is important to know that paraphrasing someone's work or changing some of the words also requires a citation. When a student hands in an assignment whether it is for school, publication, or client records, the expectation is that the material is original work completed for this particular assignment and that any part of the document that is not original is credited to the actual author. In some cases an instructor may allow students to work together on an assignment, with students contributing components of the writing or students each participating in different ways (e.g., research, presentation, report writing). If a student has previously developed a paper about a particular topic, he or she may wish to incorporate parts of the paper into the new assignment. This should not be done unless the student has discussed the utilization of the previous materials with the instructor and received approval for supplementing the new assignment with previous work. The National Association of Social Workers Code of Ethics is very clear about the expectation that professional social workers maintain honesty and personal integrity in all aspects of their lives.

Written or oral ethical violations can lead to serious consequences, including being dismissed from a college program or employment, losing one's license, and court actions being overturned when those actions were based on inaccurate reporting of the facts. If the student or employee knew or should have known the standard, he or she is generally held accountable for his or her actions or inactions.

Objective versus Subjective Information

Professional social workers are expected to separate clients' needs and treatment from their own values and experiences. The client has a right to be treated with dignity and respect and to expect that any materials written about him or her will reflect accurately what has happened. Objective information can be expressed in words or numbers and represents what the social worker observed or is reported as what the client and others have said. Objective reporting should be free of pejorative words (e.g., jerk, pig, slob), evaluations (e.g., great, wonderful, awful) and should relate to the reader only what you actually saw or heard, although it may also include what you smelled or tasted. After the writer provides the information or facts, the research paper, record, or report may include what the observer thinks these facts mean. This second process represents what the information means based on the observer's experience, training, and research. These types of characterizations are considered the professional's opinions and are allowed and considered to be more subjective; that is, they are based on professional interpretations rather than specific factual evidence. If you are certified as an expert witness in court, you will be allowed to give your opinions about the information you provide. It is important to consider the meaning of whatever words you put into professional writing so that the connotative and denotative value accurately represent the facts.

Review the following example and rewrite it so it is based on facts rather than subjective opinions.

> Susan Regelman is the queen of cocaine. She is high all the time and doesn't care who sees her acting crazy. Susan was so loaded one night she screamed and yelled all night, which she says was really just talking to the callers on the radio talk show. When I arrived at Susan's house she was wearing filthy clothes, and her kids were running around in filthy clothes that looked like they hadn't been changed for weeks. Dirty dishes and rotten food was all over the house. Because this was a horrible place for these poor little kids to be and Susan fell asleep while I was talking to her, I called the police and had them pick up the kids and take them to a wonderful shelter home where they were bathed and fed and loved before they were tucked into warm and comfortable beds for the night. I think this mother should be locked up and never be allowed to see her kids again because she obviously doesn't care for them.

How did you do? Changing these types of comments into an objective report can be quite difficult. Here's an example of how it might be written more objectively.

Susan Regelman has lived in Oakville for 10 years. She has a record of being picked up for being high on drugs and has been found in possession of cocaine on seven occasions during the last year. Police reports include laboratory tests that found Susan using cocaine each of the seven times she was stopped by the police. Neighbors report that last night they were awakened at 3:00 a.m. by loud noises coming from Susan's house. The noise sounded like Susan yelling, and they could also hear a commentator on the radio. The children, Jeremy, age 3, and Mariah, age 4, were out in the yard playing in the grass. When I arrived, Mrs. Regelman turned down the radio, invited me in, and said I could sit in the living room with her. As I sat down, I noticed that Mrs. Regelman was blinking her eyes and squinting. When I asked her if she was having a problem, Mrs. Regelman said, "I can't see the chair." I offered to help her find a place to sit, but she waved her arms and said, "No, I was just in that chair. I'm sure I can find it again." As she walked she weaved from side to side. She appeared to fall into the chair and then closed her eyes and started snoring. When I tried to talk to her she did not move or acknowledge that she heard me. In the living room floor were 10–15 plates that contained small amounts of food. There were ants, bees, and flies throughout the house with about fifty ants and flies on the plates. The children were playing quietly on the front lawn in a small child's plastic swimming pool. I called the police to take the children into protective custody and the paramedics to have Mrs. Regelman checked to make sure she would be all right. Based on my findings, I would recommend the children remain in custody until a thorough investigation can determine whether the children will be safe in Mrs. Regelman's custody. I would also like to see if there are relatives who might take the children on a temporary basis and arrange for a visit between Mrs. Regelman and her children during the next week.

So, how did you do? Although you may not have thought to fill in the missing information, which happens through reading records and reports and talking to collateral sources (neighbors and family members), there are several things that you probably were able to do. First, characterizations such as "the queen of cocaine," "high all the time," "filthy clothes," and "horrible place" are all loaded with negative meaning and not supported by facts. Next, the modifiers related to the shelter home such as "wonderful," "loved," and "warm and comfortable" are all loaded with positive meaning and not supported by facts. By using those kind of adjectives in what are supposed to be objective descriptions, the reporter's evaluation may be completely discounted as not representative of actual facts. The closing statement regarding the desired outcome, "I think the mother should be locked up and never be allowed to see her kids again," may reflect how you feel, but it is not indicative of a recommendation that can be followed. The idea that further investigation is needed to provide documentation about what action should be taken is more in keeping with the development of objective information. Finally, the statement "she obviously doesn't care for them," reflects the worker's feelings and judgments rather than facts.

Scientific Application

Social work is a profession based on research that uses both qualitative (information in the form of words, pictures, sounds, visual images, or objects) and quantitative (calculable, computable information in the form of numbers) methods. There is an expectation that data collected follow certain protocols, and the social worker is aware of the strengths and limitations of the methods utilized. Social workers rely on observation, clients' self-reporting, and data triangulation to collect facts and then collate these facts with professional knowledge to formulate an opinion that is then articulated in oral or written form. Observations that are audio or video recorded are more accurate than notes taken by the observer. In many cases, observation will rely on the notes of the observer, so it is important not only to focus on what you actually see and hear but also to transfer the notes into a report or record as soon as possible after the interview. Photographs may be used to supplement a report. Less reliable are clients' self-reports or reports of other untrained observers or people who know the person you are gathering information about and have either a positive or negative position based on their relationship with the person who is the subject of the report. Any information that is not gained through direct observation can be strengthened in terms of credibility through triangulation. *Triangulation* represents using multiple sources for information and balancing both positive and negative statements to try to more accurately represent what is happening. An example of triangulation would include the following steps. A new client, Peggy Sue Perkie, reports that she is in a lot of pain and that she cannot get a doctor to prescribe pain pills. She is getting desperate, and a friend told her that maybe you knew a doctor who would prescribe medication based on your recommendation. You would want to have the client clarify the kind of pain, the frequency of pain, and her history of medication and treatment to increase the information you have available from her to make a professional judgment. Who else might be able to corroborate Peggy Sue's story? Family, friends, or close associates? What about the doctors she has talked to? If you think you will want to seek information from other individuals, it is important to discuss this with Peggy Sue and have her sign releases of information so that you can review records, talk to people, and gather a cross section of information. Without clarifying the client's story with her and talking to other people, you are left with only the information the client has reported to you to make a decision. Self-reporting is often based on what the individual wants and wants you to know and hear and may not be accurate or complete. Probing for additional information from the client, talking to doctors and associates, reviewing records, and having the client complete clinical surveys or inventories are all processes that triangulate or supplement the data to improve the accuracy of the self-report.

Positive Statements and Active Voice

Writing needs to include strengths and action-oriented words. Social workers today are encouraged to empower their clients by using a strengths-based approach that focuses on the desired positive behavior or outcome. Rather than use the deficit as the behavior the client will change, for example, "John will stop yelling at the teacher," it is better to use a positive statement such as "John will monitor his voice and speak in conversational tones when talking with the teacher." Behavior is learned, which means people can learn new behavior. Review the following examples and change them from negative statements to positive statements:

1. Molly will quit biting her nails. _____

_____

2. John will stop wetting the bed. _____

_____

3. Carrie will not be late to school. _____

_____

Another important skill in writing is to state things in the active voice. This means to specify what someone does rather than using the passive voice, which has the verb acting on the person. Following are examples of active voice:

1. Joan hit the ball.

2. Marty rated the candidates.

3. Phil hit George with a bat.

Following are examples of passive voice:

1. Options were considered by the researcher.

2. Traffic was stopped by the little boy.

3. The table was broken by the father.

Reports that are clear and specific are easier to understand. Papers or comments that focus on what happened allow the reader to create a more accurate picture of the events. Using active sentence structure makes your statements more authoritative and expresses your confidence in your report.

Section II: Writing for Coursework

Writing for coursework includes two major types of writing: (1) free-writing used in journals and recording impressions; and (2) writing papers, which may include case examples with assessments, treatment plans, evaluation applications, and research findings or application papers. Social work is a practice profession. Everyone who practices social work is expected to be able to separate personal feelings from client situations and to apply knowledge, skills, and values to micro, mezzo, and macro circumstances. One of the ways students learn to separate themselves from the people they are helping is to be clear about who they are and to begin with understanding what the client says from the client's perspective. Social workers are also expected to actively encourage the client to speak up on his or her own behalf and to encourage the client to participate to the fullest extent possible in all decision-making situations. Because many times people are attracted to social work because they want to help others and have had some success in life listening and giving advice to others, they see social work as an avenue to learn how to be better at what they feel they are naturally able to do. However, the actual profession of social work is built on a foundation of the social worker using knowledge, skills, and values to encourage empowerment and to advocate change through social policy, research, supervision, community organization, planning, and advocacy. Because the individual professional social worker uses him- or herself as a part of this change process, it is important for the social worker to be aware of strengths, challenges, beliefs, and abilities. Keeping a diary related to practice situations and writing a response to something one has read, heard, or seen are two ways to assist you in becoming aware of thoughts or ideas that might impact providing objective client-centered services. Some of the kinds of questions a professor might ask a student to respond to in writing include:

1. What led to your selection of social work as a career?

2. Think about your position in your family of origin. Where did you fit in terms of the power and your adherence to the rules? Who did you feel closest to?

3. What clients do you think you'll have the greatest difficulty in helping and what might you do to improve your skills and understanding of working with this type of individual?

Free-writing assignments are often given at the beginning or ending of the class time, and students are encouraged to write a response based on what immediately comes to mind.

In keeping journals, professors may ask a student to write about feelings, practice experiences, how the learning is fitting together, or growth experiences (to name a few types of journal assignments). This type of writing allows the student to monitor growth and change and to be able to see how the course work is coming together or becoming integrated in thinking and practice.

Case Examples and Applications

Often a professor wants a student to show not only that he or she understands the material presented but that he or she can also apply the material to a practice situation. In these cases the professor may give the student a case example or suggest the student select a current case he or she is working on. Then, after a brief summary of the case, the professor wants the student to show the application often in one of the following ways:

1. Using the identified case, provide an assessment, treatment plan, and discussion of how you would evaluate success.

2. Select a social policy that you would like to analyze and then apply one of the models we studied in class.

3. Select two theories of human behavior and apply the theories to an individual, couple, or family.

In each application, it is important to read the written instructions carefully to be sure you understand what is expected. Ask other students and the professor if you don't clearly understand the expectations because this type of writing is quite different than the type of writing you have been doing throughout your other educational programs. Here, the instructor wants to see that you understand the material and can apply it to a real or hypothetical situation.

Research and Findings

This type of paper may include an application. Here the professor wants to know that you understand a topic and know how to find and apply the research to a particular subject. There is usually an expectation that you will use citations from refereed professional journals rather than books, newspapers, or magazines. A refereed professional journal is considered the most credible source of research articles and current areas of study. These journals have policies whereby a group of professionals with the same specialty as the article represents review the article, without knowing who wrote it, and then decide whether it merits acceptance for publication. Thus, not only are the articles written by individuals actively doing research, but they are also reviewed by peers of that writer. This type of assignment is usually expected to be written based on some style manual. Currently most programs rely on APA style guidelines, which are described in the *Publication Manual of the American Psychological Association, 5th Edition.* Students should purchase or have regular access to this manual if they are writing research papers or publishable articles. The paper should follow the style and format presented in the manual. Your paper should include a title page, the body of the paper, and a reference list. Most professors will suggest a type font and type size and may even specify margins, indentation

rules, spacing, and page numbering. If these things are not specified, the writer should select a 12-point easily readable font (e.g., Times Roman or Arial), double-space the paper, and submit the document as a single-sided copy. Always save a copy of the document until you are finished with the program so that you have proof of your work. If the professor specifies the length of the paper, it is important that you understand whether the length given is an estimate or an expectation. The writing suggestions given in earlier sections of this appendix all apply especially regarding using proper spelling, grammar, punctuation, and sentence structure; using active voice; and clarifying and following all instructions. Professional programs model experiences that you will have in the practice world. Grants and other funding sources often specify what materials they want you to submit, how many pages may be submitted as the maximum, and due dates and forms that need to be followed.

Integration

Social work is a profession that views the person in the environment and includes course work in human behavior and the social environment, social policy, research, practice, and practicum. Programs are expected to have both foundation and advanced course work. Content is expected to include information about social and economic justice, diversity, and populations at risk. The program should also provide opportunities for each student to integrate all course work into a unified whole and to apply knowledge, skills, and values representative of the social work profession. At times, these expectations will be expressed in an oral or written exam, practice exercise, or written assignment. When a student is asked to write about a subject or client from each of the social work content areas, the student will need to be able to look at a micro, mezzo, or macro case situation and then express that situation in relationship to each of the study areas. This type of assignment would probably include a brief summary of a client (individual, community, or organization) with sections about each social work area of study.

Papers that adhere to the assignment, use correct style and grammar, and are organized in a logical manner receive the highest grades. Another component of a well-written paper is to include an introduction that tells the reader what the paper is about, the body of the paper, and a summary of it at the end that focuses on what the writer has presented. Even with spell checkers, grammar checkers, and thesauri available on computers, students still need to proofread materials and rely on a dictionary to better understand the nuances of words. Spell checkers will not pick up words that are properly spelled but wrong or omitted. Although a thesaurus will provide a lot of word choices, it will not give you awareness of the exact meaning of the word. Many of your professors have vocabularies larger than the students' and have a better understanding of words' etymologies. You will improve your grades by keeping these suggestions in mind.

Section III: Records, Court Reports, and Evaluations

In the next two sections, case examples are presented in a narrative format to allow students to relate to written case examples in the development of writing samples that relate to the specific type of writing. It should be noted that case narratives, although useful for teaching purposes, are not useful in college papers, agency records, or court reports. The role of the professional is to gather information, decide what is important, and then develop a treatment plan or recommendations based on the core issues.

Records

Most agencies have forms that are used to guide the recording process. Some records are paper charts and others are computerized. Most recording includes an assessment of the problem, a problem statement, goals and objectives, treatment plans, and progress notes. Charting may also include developing a formal diagnosis, usually based on the current DSM (Diagnostic and Statistical Manual) or the ICD-CM (International Classification of Disease—Clinical Modification) and CPT (Physicians' Current Procedural Terminology). A fee schedule, payment history, clinical surveys, and other forms such as current information about the client's insurance, address, and so forth may also be included in the standard agency or private practitioner chart. Supervisors may keep records of supervisee training, assignments, and conferences. Administrators may use minutes and agendas, planning documents, and task lists to develop and direct the agency mission, budget, and services. Records are kept so that clients, social workers, administrators, and internal and external auditors and reviewers can understand the services provided and can determine whether the services meet the regulatory guidelines. If a client is reassigned or a supervisor or administrator leaves the agency, the next person providing the service can use the record to be informed about what has happened so far and what might be the next step in the service delivery.

It is important for recording to be kept current, and it is best if the recording is completed during or immediately following the service delivery. Attending to recording expediently means that the facts and transactions are fresh in the social worker's mind and therefore are less likely to be missing important elements. Because of the pressure of external funding audits, many agencies have taken the position that "If it's not written down, it didn't happen."

Read the following case scenario and then prepare a problem statement, treatment plan with at least two goals and objectives, and a session progress note.

Maggie Bell comes into counseling at the Midtown Counseling Center and after filling out the forms, relates the following information. Curtis and Maggie Bell grew up in the same neighborhood and were high school sweethearts. They attended the same college out of state and lived in dorms during their undergraduate experience. They married three years ago and have one child, Bonnie, who is 6 months old. Curtis continues to work as an engineer, and Maggie has quit her job as a graphics designer to be a full-time mother. Before they married, they agreed to attend the Lutheran church and raise their children Lutheran even though Curtis was raised Roman Catholic. Bonnie has not yet been baptized because Curtis's parents are pressuring the couple to baptize Bonnie at St. Mary's, where Curtis's family were among the founding members. Maggie states that she and Curtis used to talk everything through before making final decisions but just found out that Curtis and his parents have set Bonnie's baptism for a month from Sunday at St. Mary's. Curtis has told her that, "It's no big thing. We'll just have Bonnie baptized twice if you're going to make such a big deal about it." Maggie reports that she had an easier time standing up to Curtis before she had the baby, and she currently finds herself crying most of the day, wondering if she can stand being married anymore. Curtis has also mentioned that his parents

want to pay for Bonnie to attend St. Mary's private school. Maggie knows the program is superior to the public school but doesn't want Curtis's parents running their lives and making decisions about their child's future.

Problem statement: _____

_____

Objective: _____

_____

Goal #1: _____

_____

Goal #2: _____

Progress note: _____

_____

How did you do? What is the main idea of the problem? Mary wants to communicate her ideas and needs to her husband and develop problem-solving skills. The objective could be that Maggie wants to reshape communication and problem-solving skills with her husband that consider some of the changes that have happened regarding income, home activities, and care of and decision making about their child, Bonnie. Goals might include:

1. Maggie will talk with Curtis about her desire to have couples counseling to work on communication and problem-solving skills.

2. Maggie will invite Curtis to attend the next session, and the counselor will administer a couples communication and problem-solving skills survey to evaluate the couple's current level of skills.

In most social work methods, the social worker develops the problem statement, objective(s), and goal(s) in cooperation with the client. Often these statements are written down, and the client usually receives a copy of the agreement and signs the contract. Progress notes might include the information gathered, agreements, and progress made. In the previous case, the story narrative told by the client might be included in the notes along with the contract. Then the progress note might say:

> Maggie openly discussed her concerns and actively participated in the development of the treatment plan. She is sure that Curtis will come in with her next week and states that she wants to improve communication and problem-solving skills.

Remember that it is not necessary to record everything that is said. The record should reflect the main discussion and points that are considered important to the ongoing treatment plan.

Court Reports

Social workers are often called on to write a letter to the court that includes information about how the client is functioning, summarizes the client's treatment progress, and makes recommendations for future court actions. Social workers may testify in divorce custody hearings, child welfare hearings, and juvenile and adult criminal proceedings. Because court reports are often the foundation for critical life decisions (e.g., whether someone will remain in prison, whether a parent or relative will be granted custody of a child, or what treatment a person should receive), it is imperative that the social worker maintain objectivity in the gathering of information and the reporting of the facts and opinions regarding the case (see Section I, Professional Writing). Court reports are usually divided into four sections:

1. Purpose of report
2. Observations
3. Opinions
4. Recommendations

Using the following example, write a court report divided into these four sections.

Jerome Fogg is a 37-year-old male who is before the court for sentencing on a felony drunk driving charge (DUI). Jerome was referred to Ferndale Counseling for an assessment of the level of his alcohol use and treatment services and recommendations. Jerome's blood alcohol level at the time of the automobile accident was .24, or three times the legal qualification for being considered drunk (.08). Jerome states he has been drinking socially since he was 10 and first got drunk when he was 12. His parents knew he was drinking and often provided access to beer and vodka for Jerome and his friends because they wanted him to learn to "drink like a man." Jerome has been referred to court seven times in the last five years for drunk driving and has spent time in jail and prison for automobile homicide, illegal transfer of liquor across state lines, bigamy, and domestic violence. He is currently on parole and lives with his parents and works on the family farm. Jerome reports that his wife and family left town about five years ago. They are not divorced because he doesn't know how to contact her to serve the papers. He has married two other women since his wife left and defrauded both of them out of approximately $30,000. His last incarceration was related to these marriages and the fight that ensued when the two women found out about each other. Jerome participated in alcohol counseling while in prison and has previously completed outpatient alcohol treatment programs. Before going to prison Jerome indicated he was working as a carpenter and drank only on the weekends with family and friends. Jerome doesn't think he has an alcohol problem and believes he can quit anytime he wants. The accident was just a mistake in judgment. The car in front of him was stopped at a stop sign and the driver had taken her foot off the brake. He didn't see her car and plowed into the back of it. The investigating officer said he was going 50 miles an hour in a 25 mile-an-hour residential area. The driver suffered whiplash and has had to have three surgeries to correct displaced cervical vertebrae. At the time of the accident, Jerome was driving without a license in an unregistered automobile that was not insured. Jerome indicated he had purchased the vehicle at the auto auction and had been repairing it. He was finally able to get it running the day of the accident so when he ran out of beer, he drove to the convenience store that was about three blocks from his house when the accident happened. Jerome stated he knew he shouldn't drive but was too drunk to walk to the store.

The counselor had Jerome complete the SASSI drug use evaluation form and asked Jerome a number of questions to assess the level of Jerome's alcohol and substance abuse involvement. Jerome reported no ongoing health problems and stated that he knew he shouldn't drink and drive but he didn't think he had a drinking problem. Previous counseling reports indicate that Jerome was uncooperative with treatment planning and goals. He did not see abstinence as necessary and was not willing to consider not drinking as he feels that non-drinkers are sissies and "I'm no sissy." He is willing to come into counseling as long as the program doesn't expect him to quit drinking and is sure he can continue to work with his family on the farm. "My mom and dad are happy to have the help, and I enjoy being home again where I can drink, work, and do what I want."

As you develop the report, think about what is important for the court to know. How will you write the report so that the information is clear, concise, objective, and logical? What recommendations do you want to make?

After you have finished writing your report, you may want to compare it to the sample that follows.

Purpose of report: Jerome Fogg is before the court for sentencing on a felony drunk driving charge. Blood alcohol level at the time of the accident was .24.

Observations: Mr. Fogg was referred to Ferndale Counseling for assessment and recommendations. An interview assessment and the SASSI evaluation were used to evaluate Mr. Fogg's alcohol use and ability to benefit from outpatient treatment.

Mr. Fogg states he does not have an alcohol problem. He has attended other alcohol counseling programs, both in prison and outpatient. This is Mr. Fogg's seventh arrest for drunk driving and the first incident in which the drunk driving included both extensive damage to the other vehicle and personal injury to the other driver. The SASSI evaluation indicates that Mr. Fogg meets the diagnostic criteria for alcohol abuse (305.33). Mr. Fogg states he is willing to attend treatment but will not stop drinking and can live and work on his family's farm if he is released.

Opinions: Mr. Fogg has a long history of drinking alcohol and has had several drunk driving events for which he was referred to the court. He is unwilling to stop drinking and therefore will continue to pose a risk to the safety of others in the community. Mr. Fogg plans to live with his family members who support his drinking. Even though

Mr. Fogg does not have a driver's license, he does have access to vehicles, and when his judgment is impaired by drinking, he has been unable to resist driving. Although Mr. Fogg has been in prison and jail previously and has received substance abuse counseling, he has not stopped drinking.

Recommendations: Mr. Fogg needs either to be monitored at home on house arrest or to be returned to prison. Counseling, whether provided at prison or on an outpatient basis, must focus on separating drinking from driving. Mr. Fogg indicates he will not stop drinking. If he is placed on house arrest, he will be able to pay off fines and restitution.

How did you do? Were you able to condense the interview into the most important points? What about the recommendations? Were you able to consider what might be the best plan given the circumstances? It is important to remember that your role in providing a court report is to advise the judge, not to make the court's decision.

Evaluations

Professional social workers are often asked to perform a biopsychosocial evaluation, which serves as the foundation for treatment, case planning, and case decision making. An example of this kind of evaluation is a discharge plan that recommends acute care discharge and identifies a plan for posthospital care. Consider the following case example.

Doris Diamond is an 86-year-old female who has lived alone in the same home in which she was born since her parents and husband died and her children have grown and established their own families in other communities. Doris was hospitalized four days ago when she was found unconscious in her

home. A neighbor stopped by to visit Doris when she didn't come to church. The neighbor, Marian Daniels, broke a window to get into the house and called the paramedics when she couldn't get Doris to respond.

When Doris entered the hospital she was dehydrated and awakened within 3 to 4 hours of receiving IV fluids. She reported that she fell about a week ago and couldn't get up. She felt dizzy and remembers having a hard time staying awake. Occasionally she awakened with pain in her arm and leg on the left side. A physical examination showed cuts and bruises but no broken bones. An EET and CT scan indicated the patient had experienced a mild stroke.

Mrs. Diamond has lived alone for the past 20 years. She has many friends and is active in church and the senior citizen center. Mrs. Diamond was trained as a nurse and took care of her parents until their deaths 35 years ago. She and her husband Hugh had two children, Nancy, who is currently 50 and lives in California, and George, who is married and lives in Ohio with his wife. Mrs. Diamond's husband, Hugh Diamond, died 20 years ago in an industrial accident. After the accident Mrs. Diamond traveled extensively. She visits her children once or twice a year, and both children and their families come home to celebrate Christmas and Mrs. Diamond's birthday.

There is no history of genetic or biological disorders. None of Mrs. Diamond's family has received counseling or psychiatric treatment. Mrs. Diamond is of above average intelligence and oriented to place and time. She is active in the community and continues to travel alone and with groups.

At this time, Mrs. Diamond is going to need some rehabilitation care. She prefers to live in the Townline Rehabilitation Center until she can return home. During her placement in the Rehab Center, Mrs. Diamond will engage in an active physical and recreational rehabilitation regimen with a focus on building strength.

Notice that this type of report or evaluation is more of a narrative format. Usually there are components that must be included such as the reason for the report, biopsychosocial information, and recommendations.

Section IV: Recommendations for Best Practice

Social work professional writing is as important to social work practice as oral communication and treatment skills. Because no one form has been developed to use for every client or situation, social workers must read directions, follow protocols, and learn and practice professional writing skills. Records, letters, court reports, and evaluations must be clear, concise, and relevant to the purpose expected. Social workers should expect to develop professional writing skills through study, practice, and experience. All written communication should take into consideration the client and the audience. Social workers are expected to be able to set aside their own personal beliefs and values and create written documents that are fair and objective. This means limiting the descriptive adjectives and reporting direct observations on the basis of what they actually saw. Reports should follow whatever formats or recording sheets and

checklists an agency uses. Remember that most recording is now subject to audit by funding and accreditation organizations. Charts that do not include written verification of the specific services provided may cause the agency to lose revenue or licensure to continue business. Within all written documentation is the ethical requirement that the report is accurate and that in course work the student gives credit to the source of the idea and words. Any work a student gives to a professor is expected to be original work prepared for the current assignment unless the student has received permission to build on previous work or provides citations to represent the use of materials that someone else wrote. With the proliferation of electronic resources, students are expected to cite whether the referenced materials were located on web sources or from peer-reviewed articles in professional journals. In the social work profession plagiary or dishonesty can lead to dismissal from education, employment, or licensure.

Most students and professionals are able to focus on the mastery of social work practice skills and through practice and experience are able to shape their basic knowledge, skills, and values to meet the social work professional mandates for effective oral and written communication. Professional writing skills will continue to need refinement throughout your career. This appendix has been developed as a basic orientation to the demands of developing accurate, clear, concise, and logical written communication as a priority to effective social work professional practice.

Educational Policy and Accreditation Standards

Council on Social Work Education

Contents

PREAMBLE

Social work practice promotes human well-being by strengthening opportunities, resources, and capacities of people in their environments and by creating policies and services to correct conditions that limit human rights and the quality of life. The social work profession works to eliminate poverty, discrimination, and oppression. Guided by a person-in-environment perspective and respect for human diversity, the profession works to effect social and economic justice worldwide.

Social work education combines scientific inquiry with the teaching of professional skills to provide effective and ethical social work services. Social work educators reflect their identification with the profession through their teaching, scholarship, and service. Social work education, from baccalaureate to doctoral levels, employs educational, practice, scholarly, interprofessional, and service delivery models to orient and shape the profession's future in the context of expanding knowledge, changing technologies, and complex human and social concerns.

The Council on Social Work Education (CSWE) Educational Policy and Accreditation Standards (EPAS) promotes academic excellence in baccalaureate and master's social work education. The EPAS specifies the curricular content and educational context to prepare students for professional social work practice. The EPAS sets forth basic requirements for these purposes. Beyond these basic requirements of EPAS, individual programs focus on areas relevant to their institutional and program mission, goals, and objectives.

The EPAS permits programs to use time-tested and new models of program design, implementation, and evaluation. It does so by balancing requirements that promote comparability across programs with a level of flexibility that encourages programs to respond to changing human, professional, and institutional needs.

The EPAS focuses on assessing the results of a program's development and its continuous improvement. While accreditation is ultimately evaluative, in social work education it is based on a consultative and collaborative process that determines whether a program meets the requirements of the EPAS.

FUNCTIONS OF EDUCATIONAL POLICY AND ACCREDITATION

1. Educational Policy
The Educational Policy promotes excellence, creativity, and innovation in social work education and practice. It sets forth required content areas that relate to each other and to the

purposes, knowledge, and values of the profession. Programs of social work education are offered at the baccalaureate, master's, and doctoral levels. Baccalaureate and master's programs are accredited by CSWE. This document supersedes all prior statements of curriculum policy for baccalaureate and master's program levels.

2. Accreditation
Accreditation ensures that the quality of professional programs merits public confidence. The Accreditation Standards establish basic requirements for baccalaureate and master's levels. Accreditation Standards pertain to the following program elements:

- Mission, goals, and objectives
- Curriculum
- Governance, structure, and resources
- Faculty
- Student professional development
- Nondiscrimination and human diversity
- Program renewal
- Program assessment and continuous improvement

3. Relationship of Educational Policy to Accreditation
CSWE uses the EPAS for the accreditation of social work programs. The Educational Policy and the Accreditation Standards are conceptually integrated. Programs use Educational Policy, Section 1 as one important basis for developing program mission, goals, and objectives. Programs use Educational Policy, Section 3 to develop program objectives and Educational Policy, Sections 4 and 5 to develop content for demonstrating attainment of the objectives. The accreditation process reviews the program's self-study document, site team report, and program response to determine

compliance with the Educational Policy and Accreditation Standards. Accredited programs meet all standards.

EDUCATIONAL POLICY

1. Purposes

1.0 Purposes of the Social Work Profession

The social work profession receives its sanction from public and private auspices and is the primary profession in the development, provision, and evaluation of social services. Professional social workers are leaders in a variety of organizational settings and service delivery systems within a global context.

The profession of social work is based on the values of service, social and economic justice, dignity and worth of the person, importance of human relationships, and integrity and competence in practice. With these values as defining principles, the purposes of social work are:

- To enhance human well-being and alleviate poverty, oppression, and other forms of social injustice.
- To enhance the social functioning and interactions of individuals, families, groups, organizations, and communities by involving them in accomplishing goals, developing resources, and preventing and alleviating distress.
- To formulate and implement social policies, services, and programs that meet basic human needs and support the development of human capacities.
- To pursue policies, services, and resources through advocacy and social or political actions that promote social and economic justice.
- To develop and use research, knowledge, and skills that advance social work practice.
- To develop and apply practice in the context of diverse cultures.

1.1 Purposes of Social Work Education

The purposes of social work education are to prepare competent and effective professionals, to develop social work knowledge, and to provide leadership in the development of service delivery systems. Social work education is grounded in the profession's history, purposes, and philosophy and is based on a body of knowledge, values, and skills. Social work education enables students to integrate the knowledge, values, and skills of the social work profession for competent practice.

1.2 Achievement of Purposes

Among its programs, which vary in design, structure, and objectives, social work education achieves these purposes through such means as:

- Providing curricula and teaching practices at the forefront of the new and changing knowledge base of social work and related disciplines.
- Providing curricula that build on a liberal arts perspective to promote breadth of knowledge, critical thinking, and communication skills.
- Developing knowledge.
- Developing and applying instructional and practice-relevant technology.
- Maintaining reciprocal relationships with social work practitioners, groups, organizations, and communities.
- Promoting continual professional development of students, faculty, and practitioners.
- Promoting interprofessional and interdisciplinary collaboration.
- Preparing social workers to engage in prevention activities that promote well-being.

- Preparing social workers to practice with individuals, families, groups, organizations, and communities.
- Preparing social workers to evaluate the processes and effectiveness of practice.
- Preparing social workers to practice without discrimination, with respect, and with knowledge and skills related to clients' age, class, color, culture, disability, ethnicity, family structure, gender, marital status, national origin, race, religion, sex, and sexual orientation.
- Preparing social workers to alleviate poverty, oppression, and other forms of social injustice.
- Preparing social workers to recognize the global context of social work practice.
- Preparing social workers to formulate and influence social policies and social work services in diverse political contexts.

2. STRUCTURE OF SOCIAL WORK EDUCATION

2.0 Structure

Baccalaureate and graduate social work education programs operate under the auspices of accredited colleges and universities. These educational institutions vary by auspices, emphasis, and size. With diverse strengths, missions, and resources, social work education programs share a common commitment to educate competent, ethical social workers.

The baccalaureate and master's levels of social work education are anchored in the purposes of the social work profession and promote the knowledge, values, and skills of the profession. Baccalaureate social work education programs prepare graduates for generalist professional practice. Master's social work education programs prepare graduates for advanced professional practice in an area of concentration. The baccalaureate and master's levels of educational preparation are differentiated according to (a) conceptualization and design; (b) content; (c) program objectives; and (d) depth, breadth, and specificity of knowledge and skills. Frameworks and perspectives for concentration include fields of practice, problem areas, intervention methods, and practice contexts and perspectives.

Programs develop their mission and goals within the purposes of the profession, the purposes of social work education, and their institutional context. Programs also recognize academic content and professional experiences that students bring to the educational program. A conceptual framework, built upon relevant theories and knowledge, shapes the breadth and depth of knowledge and practice skills to be acquired.

2.1 Program Renewal

Social work education remains vital, relevant, and progressive by pursuing exchanges with the practice community and program stakeholders and by developing and assessing new knowledge and technology.

3. PROGRAM OBJECTIVES

Social work education is grounded in the liberal arts and contains a coherent, integrated professional foundation in social work. The graduate advanced curriculum is built from the professional foundation. Graduates of baccalaureate and master's social work programs demonstrate the capacity to meet the foundation objectives and objectives unique to the program. Graduates of master's social work programs also demonstrate the capacity to meet advanced program objectives.

3.0 Foundation Program Objectives

The professional foundation, which is essential to the practice of any social worker, includes, but is not limited to, the following program objectives. Graduates demonstrate the ability to:

1. Apply critical thinking skills within the context of professional social work practice.

2. Understand the value base of the profession and its ethical standards and principles, and practice accordingly.

3. Practice without discrimination and with respect, knowledge, and skills related to clients' age, class, color, culture, disability, ethnicity, family structure, gender, marital status, national origin, race, religion, sex, and sexual orientation.

4. Understand the forms and mechanisms of oppression and discrimination and apply strategies of advocacy and social change that advance social and economic justice.

5. Understand and interpret the history of the social work profession and its contemporary structures and issues.

B6. Apply the knowledge and skills of generalist social work practice with systems of all sizes.[1]

M6. Apply the knowledge and skills of a generalist social work perspective to practice with systems of all sizes.

7. Use theoretical frameworks supported by empirical evidence to understand individual development and behavior across the life span and the interactions among individuals and between individuals and families, groups, organizations, and communities.

8. Analyze, formulate, and influence social policies.

9. Evaluate research studies, apply research findings to practice, and evaluate their own practice interventions.

10. Use communication skills differentially across client populations, colleagues, and communities.

11. Use supervision and consultation appropriate to social work practice.

12. Function within the structure of organizations and service delivery systems and seek necessary organizational change.

3.1 Concentration Objectives

Graduates of a master's social work program are advanced practitioners who apply the knowledge and skills of advanced social work practice in an area of concentration. They analyze, intervene, and evaluate in ways that are highly differentiated, discriminating, and self-critical. Graduates synthesize and apply a broad range of knowledge and skills with a high degree of autonomy and proficiency. They refine and advance the quality of their practice and that of the larger social work profession.

3.2 Additional Program Objectives

A program may develop additional objectives to cover the required content in relation to its particular mission, goals, and educational level.

4. Foundation Curriculum Content

All social work programs provide foundation content in the areas specified below. Content areas may be combined and delivered with a variety of instructional technologies. Content is relevant to the mission, goals, and objectives of the program and to the purposes, values, and ethics of the social work profession.

4.0 Values and Ethics

Social work education programs integrate content about values and principles of ethical

---

[1]*Items preceded by a B or M apply only to baccalaureate or master's programs, respectively.*

decision making as presented in the National Association of Social Workers Code of Ethics. The educational experience provides students with the opportunity to be aware of personal values; develop, demonstrate, and promote the values of the profession; and analyze ethical dilemmas and the ways in which these affect practice, services, and clients.

4.1 Diversity

Social work programs integrate content that promotes understanding, affirmation, and respect for people from diverse backgrounds. The content emphasizes the interlocking and complex nature of culture and personal identity. It ensures that social services meet the needs of groups served and are culturally relevant. Programs educate students to recognize diversity within and between groups that may influence assessment, planning, intervention, and research. Students learn how to define, design, and implement strategies for effective practice with persons from diverse backgrounds.

4.2 Populations-at-Risk and Social and Economic Justice

Social work education programs integrate content on populations-at-risk, examining the factors that contribute to and constitute being at risk. Programs educate students to identify how group membership influences access to resources, and present content on the dynamics of such risk factors and responsive and productive strategies to redress them.

Programs integrate social and economic justice content grounded in an understanding of distributive justice, human and civil rights, and the global interconnections of oppression. Programs provide content related to implementing strategies to combat discrimination, oppression, and economic deprivation and to promote social and economic justice. Programs prepare students to advocate for nondiscriminatory social and economic systems.

4.3 Human Behavior and the Social Environment

Social work education programs provide content on the reciprocal relationships between human behavior and social environments. Content includes empirically based theories and knowledge that focus on the interactions between and among individuals, groups, societies, and economic systems. It includes theories and knowledge of biological, sociological, cultural, psychological, and spiritual development across the life span; the range of social systems in which people live (individual, family, group, organizational, and community); and the ways social systems promote or deter people in maintaining or achieving health and well-being.

4.4 Social Welfare Policy and Services

Programs provide content about the history of social work, the history and current structures of social welfare services, and the role of policy in service delivery, social work practice, and attainment of individual and social well-being. Course content provides students with knowledge and skills to understand major policies that form the foundation of social welfare; analyze organizational, local, state, national, and international issues in social welfare policy and social service delivery; analyze and apply the results of policy research relevant to social service delivery; understand and demonstrate policy practice skills in regard to economic, political, and organizational systems, and use them to influence, formulate, and advocate for policy consistent with social work values; and identify financial, organizational, administrative, and planning processes required to deliver social services.

4.5 Social Work Practice

Social work practice content is anchored in the purposes of the social work profession and focuses on strengths, capacities, and resources of client systems in relation to their broader environments. Students learn practice content that encompasses knowledge and skills to work with individuals, families, groups, organizations, and communities. This content includes engaging clients in an appropriate working relationship, identifying issues, problems, needs, resources, and assets; collecting and assessing information; and planning for service delivery. It includes using communication skills, supervision, and consultation. Practice content also includes identifying, analyzing, and implementing empirically based interventions designed to achieve client goals; applying empirical knowledge and technological advances; evaluating program outcomes and practice effectiveness; developing, analyzing, advocating, and providing leadership for policies and services; and promoting social and economic justice.

4.6 Research

Qualitative and quantitative research content provides understanding of a scientific, analytic, and ethical approach to building knowledge for practice. The content prepares students to develop, use, and effectively communicate empirically based knowledge, including evidence-based interventions. Research knowledge is used by students to provide high-quality services; to initiate change; to improve practice, policy, and social service delivery; and to evaluate their own practice.

4.7 Field Education

Field education is an integral component of social work education anchored in the mission, goals, and educational level of the program. It occurs in settings that reinforce students' identification with the purposes, values, and ethics of the profession; fosters the integration of empirical and practice-based knowledge; and promotes the development of professional competence. Field education is systematically designed, supervised, coordinated, and evaluated on the basis of criteria by which students demonstrate the achievement of program objectives.

5. ADVANCED CURRICULUM CONTENT

The master's curriculum prepares graduates for advanced social work practice in an area of concentration. Using a conceptual framework to identify advanced knowledge and skills, programs build an advanced curriculum from the foundation content. In the advanced curriculum, the foundation content areas (Section 4, 4.0–4.7) are addressed in greater depth, breadth, and specificity and support the program's conception of advanced practice.

ACCREDITATION STANDARDS

1. Program Mission, Goals, and Objectives

1.0 The social work program has a mission appropriate to professional social work education as defined in Educational Policy, Section 1.1. The program's mission is appropriate to the level or levels for which it is preparing students for practice and is consistent with the institution's mission.

1.1 The program has goals derived from its mission. These goals reflect the purposes of the Educational Policy, Section 1.1. Program goals are not limited to these purposes.

1.2 The program has objectives that are derived from the program goals. These objectives are consistent with Educational Policy, Section 3. Program objectives are reflected in program implementation and continuous assessment (see Accreditation Standard 8).

1.3 The program makes its constituencies aware of its mission, goals, and objectives.

2. Curriculum

2.0 The curriculum is developed and organized as a coherent and integrated whole consistent with program goals and objectives. Social work education is grounded in the liberal arts and contains a coherent, integrated professional foundation in social work practice from which an advanced practice curriculum is built at the graduate level.

> **B2.0.1** The program defines its conception of generalist social work practice, describes its coverage of the professional foundation curriculum identified in Educational Policy, Section 4, and demonstrates how its conception of generalist practice is implemented in all components of the professional curriculum.

> **M2.0.1** The program describes its coverage of the foundation and advanced curriculum content, identified in Educational Policy, Sections 4 and 5. The program defines its conception of advanced practice and explains how the advanced curriculum is built from the professional foundation. The master's program has a concentration curriculum that includes (a) concentration objectives, (b) a conceptual framework built on relevant theories, (c) curriculum design and content, and (d) field education that supports the advanced curriculum. The program demonstrates how the depth, breadth, and specificity of the advanced curriculum are addressed in relation to the professional foundation.

2.1 The social work program administers field education (Educational Policy, Section 4.7 and Section 5) consistent with program goals and objectives that:

2.1.1 Provides for a minimum of 400 hours of field education for baccalaureate programs and 900 hours for master's programs.

2.1.2 Admits only those students who have met the program's specified criteria for field education.

2.1.3 Specifies policies, criteria, and procedures for selecting agencies and field instructors; placing and monitoring students; maintaining field liaison contacts with agencies; and evaluating student learning and agency effectiveness in providing field instruction.

2.1.4 Specifies that field instructors for baccalaureate students hold a CSWE-accredited baccalaureate or master's social work degree.[2] Field instructors for master's students hold a CSWE-accredited master's social work degree. In

---

[2]*This and all future references to "CSWE-accredited baccalaureate or master's social work degree" include degrees from CSWE-accredited programs or programs approved by its Foreign Equivalency Determination Service.*

programs where a field instructor does not hold a CSWE-accredited baccalaureate or master's social work degree, the program assumes responsibility for reinforcing a social work perspective.

2.1.5 Provides orientation, field instruction training, and continuing dialog with agencies and field instructors.

2.1.6 Develops policies regarding field placements in an agency in which the student is also employed. Student assignments and field education supervision differ from those associated with the student's employment.

3. Program Governance, Administrative Structure, and Resources

3.0 The social work program has the necessary autonomy and administrative structure to achieve its goals and objectives (Educational Policy, Section 2.0).

3.0.1 The social work faculty defines program curriculum consistent with the Educational Policy and Accreditation Standards and the institution's policies.

3.0.2 The administration and faculty of the social work program participate in formulating and implementing policies related to the recruitment, hiring, retention, promotion, and tenure of program personnel.

3.0.3 The chief administrator of the social work program has either a CSWE-accredited master's social work degree, with a doctoral degree preferred, or a professional degree in social work from a CSWE-accredited program and a doctoral degree. The chief administrator also has demonstrated leadership ability through teaching, scholarship, curriculum development, administrative experience, and other academic and professional activities in the field of social work.

3.0.4 The chief administrator of the social work program has a full-time appointment to the program and sufficient assigned time (at least 25% for baccalaureate programs and 50% for master's programs) to provide educational and administrative leadership. Combined programs designate a social work faculty member and assign this person sufficient time to administer the baccalaureate social work program.

3.0.5 The field education director has a master's degree in social work from a CSWE-accredited program and at least two years post-baccalaureate or post-master's social work degree practice experience.

3.0.6 The field education director has a full-time appointment to the program and sufficient assigned time (at least 25% for baccalaureate programs and 50% for master's programs) to provide educational and administrative leadership for field education.

3.1 The social work program has sufficient resources to achieve program goals and objectives.

3.1.1 The program has sufficient support staff, other personnel, and technological resources to support program functioning.

3.1.2 The program has sufficient and stable financial supports that permit program planning and achievement of program goals and objectives. These include a budgetary allocation and procedures for budget development and administration.

3.1.3 The program has comprehensive library holdings and electronic access, as well as other informational and educational resources necessary for achieving the program's goals and objectives.

3.1.4 The program has sufficient office and classroom space, computer-mediated access, or both, to achieve the program's goals and objectives.

3.1.5 The program has access to assistive technology, including materials in alternative formats (such as Braille, large print, books on tape, assistive learning systems).

4. Faculty

4.0 The program has full-time faculty, which may be augmented by part-time faculty, with the qualifications, competence, and range of expertise in social work education and practice to achieve its goals and objectives. The program has a sufficient full-time equivalent faculty-to-student ratio (usually 1:25 for baccalaureate programs and 1:12 for master's programs) to carry out ongoing functions of the program.

4.1 The program demonstrates how the use of part-time faculty assists in the achievement of the program's goals and objectives.

4.2 Faculty size is commensurate with the number and type of curricular offerings in class and field; class size; number of students; and the faculty's teaching, scholarly, and service responsibilities.

B4.2.1 The baccalaureate social work program has a minimum of two full-time faculty, with master's social work degrees from a CSWE-accredited program with full-time appointment in social work, and whose principal assignment is to the baccalaureate program. It is preferred that faculty have a doctoral degree.

M4.2.1 The master's social work program has a minimum of six full-time faculty with master's social work degrees from a CSWE-accredited program and whose principal assignment is to the master's program. The majority of the full-time master's social work program faculty have a master's degree in social work and a doctoral degree.

4.3 Faculty who teach required practice-courses have a master's social work degree from a CSWE-accredited program and at least two years post-baccalaureate or post-master's social work degree practice experience.

4.4 The program has a faculty workload policy that supports the achievement of institutional priorities and the program's goals and objectives.

5. Student Professional Development

5.0 The program has admissions criteria and procedures that reflect the program's goals and objectives.

> **M5.1** Only candidates who have earned a bachelor's degree are admitted to the master's social-work degree program.

5.2 The program has a written policy indicating that it does not grant social work course credit for life experience or previous work experience.

5.3 In those foundation curriculum areas where students demonstrate required knowledge and skills, the program describes how it ensures that students do not repeat that content.

> **5.3.1** The program has written policies and procedures concerning the transfer of credits.
>
> **M5.3.2** Advanced standing status is only awarded to graduates of baccalaureate social work programs accredited by CSWE.

5.4 The program has academic and professional advising policies and procedures that are consistent with the program's goals and objectives. Professional advising is provided by social work program faculty, staff, or both.

5.5 The program has policies and procedures specifying students' rights and responsibilities to participate in formulating and modifying policies affecting academic and student affairs. It provides opportunities and encourages students to organize in their interests.

5.6 The program informs students of its criteria for evaluating their academic and professional performance.

5.7 The program has policies and procedures for terminating a student's enrollment in the social work program for reasons of academic and professional performance.

6. Nondiscrimination and Human Diversity

6.0 The program makes specific and continuous efforts to provide a learning context in which respect for all persons and understanding of diversity (including age, class, color, disability, ethnicity, family structure, gender, marital status, national origin, race, religion, sex, and sexual orientation) are practiced. Social work education builds upon professional purposes and values; therefore, the program provides a learning context that is nondiscriminatory and reflects the profession's fundamental tenets. The program describes how its learning context and educational program (including faculty, staff, and student composition; selection of agencies and their clientele as field education settings; composition of program advisory or field committees; resource allocation; program leadership; speakers series, seminars, and special programs; research and other initiatives) and its curriculum model understanding of and respect for diversity.

7. Program Renewal

7.0 The program has ongoing exchanges with external constituencies that may include social work practitioners, social service recipients, advocacy groups, social service agencies, professional associations, regulatory agencies, the academic community, and the community at large.

7.1 The program's faculty engage in the development and dissemination of research, scholarship, or other creative activities relevant to the profession.

7.2 The program seeks opportunities for innovation and provides leadership within the profession and the academic community.

8. Program Assessment and Continuous Improvement

8.0 The program has an assessment plan and procedures for evaluating the outcome of each program objective. The plan specifies the measurement procedures and methods used to evaluate the outcome of each program objective.

8.1 The program implements its plan to evaluate the outcome of each program objective and shows evidence that the analysis is used continuously to affirm and improve the educational program.

PROGRAM CHANGES

The EPAS supports change necessary to improve the educational quality of a program in relation to its goals and objectives. The EPAS recognizes that such change is ongoing. When a program is granted initial accreditation or its accreditation is reaffirmed, the program is, by that action, accredited only at the level or levels and for the components that existed and were reviewed at the time of that action. Prior to the next scheduled accreditation review, changes may take place within the program. Although it is not necessary to report minor changes, programs notify the Commission on Accreditation (COA) of such changes as new leadership, governance, structure, off-campus programs, etc. Depending on the nature of the change, the COA may request additional information. Prior to the implementation of a substantive change the program submits a proposal and receives approval. Substantive changes are defined as those that require a waiver of one or more aspects of EPAS.

Abbott, E. (1919). The social caseworker and the enforcement of industrial legislation. In *Proceedings of the National Conference on Social Work, 1918* (pp. 312–318). Chicago: Rogers & Hall.

Agnes, M. (Ed.). (1999). *Webster's new world dictionary* (4th ed.). New York: Macmillan.

Alberti, R. E., & Emmons, M. L. (2001). *Your perfect right* (8th ed.). Atascadero, CA: Impact.

Alexander, J., & Parsons, B. (1982). *Functional family therapy.* Pacific Grove, CA: Brooks/Cole.

Al-Krenawi, A. (1998). Reconciling western treatment and traditional healing: A social worker walks with the wind. *Reflections* (Summer), 6–21.

Allen-Meares, P., & Lane, B. A. (1993). Grounding social work practice in theory: Ecosystem. In J. B. Rauch (Ed.), *Assessment: A source book for social work practice* (pp. 3–13). Milwaukee, WI: Families International, Inc.

Alter, C., & Evens, W. (1990). *Evaluating your practice.* New York: Springer.

The American Heritage College Dictionary. (2000). Boston: Houghton Mifflin.

American Psychiatric Association (APA). (2000). *Diagnostic and statistical manual of mental disorders* (4th ed., text revision). Washington, DC: Author.

Anderson, J. (1981). *Social work methods and processes.* Belmont, CA: Wadsworth.

Anderson, J. (1997). *Social work with groups.* New York: Longman.

Anderson, J., & Carter, R. W. (2003). *Diversity perspectives for social work practice.* Boston: Allyn and Bacon.

Andrews, A., Guadalupe, J., & Bolden, E. (2003). Faith, hope and mutual support: Paths to empowerment as perceived by women in poverty. *Journal of Social Work Research and Evaluation, 4*(1), 5–18.

Applewhite, S. (1995). Curanderismo: Demystifying the health beliefs and practices of elderly Mexican Americans. *Health and Social Work, 20,* 405–418.

Arlow, J. A. (1995). Psychoanalysis. In R. J. Corsini & D. Wedding (Eds.), *Current psychotherapies* (5th ed., pp. 15–50). Itasca, IL: F. E. Peacock.

Arnold, S. C., Forehand, R., & Sturgis, E. T. (1976). Effects of a response cost procedure on the academic performance of retarded students. *Journal of Behavior Therapy and Experimental Psychiatry, 7,* 191–192.

Asay, T. P., & Lambert, M. J. (1999). The empirical case for the common factors in therapy: Quantitative findings. In M. A. Hubble, B. L. Duncan, & S. D. Miller (Eds.) *The heart and soul of change* (pp. 23–55). Washington, DC: American Psychological Association.

Ashford, J. B., LeCroy, C. W., & Lortie, K. L. (2001). *Human behavior in the social environment.* Belmont, CA: Brooks/Cole.

Atthowe, A. J., & Krasner, L. (1968). Preliminary report on the application of contingent reinforcement procedures (token economy) on a "chronic" psychiatric ward. *Journal of Abnormal Psychology, 73,* 37–43.

Austin, D. (1983). The Flexner myth and the history of social work. *Social Service Review, 57*(3), 357–377.

Axelson, J. (1999). *Counseling and development in a multicultural society* (3rd ed.). Pacific Grove, CA: Brooks/Cole.

Bandura, A. (1965). Influence of models' reinforcement contingencies in the acquisition of initiative responses. *Journal of Personality and Social Psychology, 1,* 589–595.

Bandura, A. (1969). *Principles of behavior modification.* New York: Holt.

Bandura, A. (1977). *Social learning theory.* Englewood Cliffs, NJ: Prentice-Hall.

Bandura, A. (1986) *Social foundations of thought and action: A social cognitive theory.* Englewood Cliffs, NJ: Prentice-Hall.

Bandura, A., Adams, N. E., & Menlove, F. L. (1968). Factors determining vicarious extinction of avoidance behavior through symbolic modeling. *Journal of Personality and Social Psychology, 8,* 99–108.

Bandura, A., Blanchard, E. B., & Ritter, R. (1969). The relative efficacy of desensitization and modeling approaches for inducing behavioral, affective, and attitudinal changes. *Journal of Personality and Social Psychology, 13,* 173–199.

Barker, R. L. (1999). *The social work dictionary* (4th ed.). Washington, DC: NASW Press.

Barlow, D. H., Craske, M., Cerny, J. A., & Klosko, J. (1989). Behavioral treatment of panic disorder. *Behavior Therapy, 20,* 261–282.

Barret, B., & Logan, C. (2002). *Counseling gay men and lesbians.* Pacific Grove, CA: Brooks/Cole.

Beck, A. (1991). *The Beck depression inventory manual.* San Antonio, TX: Psychological Corporation.

Beck, A. T., Rush, A. J., Shaw, B. F., & Emery, G. (1979). *Cognitive therapy of depression.* New York: Guilford.

Beck, A. T., & Weishaar, M. E. (1995). Cognitive therapy. In R. J. Corsini & D. Wedding (Eds.), *Psychotherapies* (5th ed.; pp. 229–261). Itasca, IL: F. E. Peacock.

Beck, J. (1995). *Cognitive therapy: Basics and beyond.* New York: Guilford Press.

Becvar, D., & Becvar, R. (2003). *Family therapy* (5th ed.). Boston: Allyn and Bacon.

Bellak, L., Hurvich, M. M., & Gediman, H. (Eds.). (1973). *Ego functions in schizophrenics, neurotics, and normals.* New York: Wiley.

Berelson, B., & Steiner, G. A. (1964). *Human behavior.* New York: Harcourt Brace Jovanovich.

Berengarten, S. (1986). *The nature and objectives of accreditation and social work education.* Austin: University of Texas School of Social Work.

Berg, I. K., & Miller, S. D. (1992). *Working with the problem drinker: A solution-focused approach.* New York: Norton.

Bergin, A. E., & Garfield, S. L. (Eds.). (1994). *Handbook of psychotherapy and behavior change.* New York: Wiley.

Berk, L. E. (2004). *Development through the life span* (2nd ed.). Boston: Allyn and Bacon.

Billingsley, A. (1992). *Climbing Jacob's ladder: The enduring legacy of African American families.* New York: Simon & Schuster.

Bisman, C. D. (1999). Social work assessment: Case theory construction. *Families in Society: The Journal of Contemporary Human Services, 80,* 240–246.

Bisman, C. D., & Hardcastle, D. A. (1999). A model for using research methodologies in practice. *Journal of Teaching in Social Work, 19,* 47–63.

Blanck, G., & Blanck, R. (1994). *Ego psychology: Theory and practice* (2nd ed.). New York: Columbia University Press.

Bloom, M., Fischer, J., & Orme, J. G. (1995). *Evaluating practice: Guidelines for the accountable professional* (2nd ed.). Boston: Allyn and Bacon.

Boehm, E., & Staples, L. H. (2002). The functions of the social worker in empowering: The voices of consumers and professionals. *Social Work, 47*(4), 449–460.

Bouchard, T. J. Jr., Lykken, D. T., McGue, M., Segal, N. L., & Tellegen, A. (1990). Sources of human psychological differences: The Minnesota study of twins reared apart. *Science, 250,* 223–228.

Brammer, R. (2004). *Diversity in counseling.* Pacific Grove, CA: Brooks/Cole.

Brandler, S., & Roman, C. (1999). *Group work.* New York: Haworth Press.

Brill, N. I. (1998). *Working with people.* New York: Longman.

Broderick, C. (1979). *Couples.* New York: Simon & Schuster.

Brown, J. H., & Brown, C. (2002). *Marital therapy: Concepts and skills for effective practice.* Pacific Grove, CA: Brooks/Cole.

Burnette, D. (1999). Custodial grandparents in Latino families: Patterns of service use and unmet needs. *Social Work, 44*(1), 22–34.

Burns, D. D. (1980). *Feeling good: The new mood therapy.* New York: Signet.

Burns, D. D. (1985). *Intimate connections.* New York: Morrow.

Burns, D. D. (1990). *The feeling good handbook.* New York: Plume.

Busch, N., & Valentine, D. (2000). Empowerment practice: A focus on battered women. *Affilia 15*(1), 82–95.

Buss, A., & Plomin, R. (1984). *Temperament: Early developing traits.* Hillsdale, NJ: Erlbaum.

Buttell, F. (2002). Group intervention models with domestic violence offenders. In A. R. Roberts & G. J. Greene, *Social workers' desk reference* (pp. 714–716). New York: Oxford.

Campbell, D. (1974). *If you don't know where you're going, you'll end up somewhere else.* Niles, IL: Argus Communications.

Canda, E. R., & Furman, L. D. (1999). *Spiritual diversity in social work practice: The heart of helping.* New York: Macmillan.

Caplan, G. (1964). *Principles of preventive psychiatry.* New York: Basic Books.

Carkuff, R. R. (1969). *Helping and human relations. Vol. 1: Practice and research.* New York: Holt, Rinehart, and Winston.

Carlson, J., & Kjos, D. (2002). *Theories and strategies of family therapy.* Boston: Allyn and Bacon.

Carver, C. S., & Scheier, M. F. (1996). *Perspectives on personality* (3rd ed.). Boston: Allyn and Bacon.

Chamberlain, R., & Rapp, C. A. (1991). A decade of case management: A methodological review of outcome research. *Community Mental Health Journal 27,* 171–188.

Chess, W. A., & Norlin, J. W. (1991). *Human behavior in the social environment: A social systems model.* Boston: Allyn and Bacon.

Coffey, D. S. (1999). *The exploration of affiliation and control in the client-case manager relationship in intensive case management.* Unpublished doctoral dissertation, Bryn Mawr College.

Collins, D., Jordan, C., & Coleman, H. (1999). *An introduction to family social work.* Itasca, IL: Peacock.

Compton, B., & Galaway, B. (1999). *Social work processes* (6th ed.). Pacific Grove, CA: Brooks/Cole.

Concian, F. (1991). Feminist science: Methodologies that challenge inequality. *Gender and Society,* 6(4), 623–642.

Connaway, R. S., & Gentry, M. E. (1988). *Social work practice.* Englewood Cliffs, NJ: Prentice Hall.

Cooper, M. G., & Lesser, J. G. (2002). *Clinical social work practice. An integrated approach.* Boston: Allyn and Bacon.

Coppola, M., & Rivas, R. (1985). The task action group technique: A case study of empowering the elderly. In M. Parenes (Ed.), *Innovation in social group work: Feedback from practice to theory* (pp. 133–147). New York: Haworth.

Corcoran, K., & Fischer, J. (1994). *Measures for clinical practice: A source book* (2nd ed.). New York: Free Press.

Corcoran, K., & Vandiver, V. (1997). *Maneuvering the maze of managed care: Skills for mental health practitioners.* New York: Free Press.

Corey, G. (2001). *The art of integrative counseling.* Pacific Grove, CA: Brooks/Cole.

Corey, G. (2004). *Theory and practice of group counseling.* Pacific Grove, CA: Brooks/Cole.

Corey, G., Corey, M., & Callanan, P. (2003). *Issues and ethics in the helping professions* (6th ed.). Pacific Grove, CA: Brooks/Cole.

Corey, G., Corey, M., Callanan, P., & Russell, J. M. (2004). *Group techniques.* Pacific Grove, CA: Brooks/Cole.

Corey, M., & Corey, G. (2002). *Groups: Process and practice.* Pacific Grove, CA: Brooks/Cole.

Coridan, C. & O'Connell, C. (2002). *Meeting the Challenge: Ending Treatment Disparities for Women of Color.* Alexandria, VA: National Mental Health Association.

Cormier, S., & Nurius, P. S. (2003). *Interviewing and change strategies for helpers* (5th ed.). Pacific Grove, CA: Brooks/Cole.

Corsini, R. J. (Ed.). (1981). *Handbook of innovative psychotherapies.* New York: Wiley.

Corsini, R. J., & Wedding, D. (1995). *Current psychotherapies* (5th ed.). Itasca, IL: F. E. Peacock.

Council on Social Work Education (CSWE). (2001). *Educational policy and accreditation standards.* Alexandria, VA: Author.

Council on Social Work Education (CSWE). (2003). *Handbook of accreditation standards and procedures* (5th ed.). Alexandria, VA: Author.

Cournoyer, B. (2000). *The social work skills workbook* (3rd ed.). Belmont, CA: Brooks/Cole.

Covey, S. R. (1989). *The 7 habits of highly effective people.* New York: Simon & Schuster.

Cowger, C. D., & Snively, C. A. (2002). In D. Saleeby (Ed.). *The strength perspective in social work practice* (3rd ed., pp. 106–123). Boston: Allyn and Bacon.

Danzinger, P. R. (2001). Defining and recognizing elder abuse. In E. R. Welfel & R. E. Ingersoll, *The mental health desk reference* (pp. 478–483). Hoboken, NJ: Wiley.

Davey, G. (1987). *Cognitive processes and Pavlovian conditioning in humans.* New York: Wiley.

Davison, G. C., & Neale, J. M. (1990). *Abnormal psychology* (5th ed.). New York: Wiley.

De Jong, P., & Berg, I. K. (2002). *Interviewing for solutions* (2nd ed.). Pacific Grove, CA: Brooks/Cole.

De Jong, P., & Hopwood, L. E. (1996). Outcome research on treatment conducted at the Brief Family Therapy Center, 1992–1993. In S. D. Miller,

M. A. Hubble, & B. L. Duncan, *Handbook of solution-focused brief therapy*. San Francisco: Jossey-Bass.

De Jong, P., & Miller, S. D. (1995). How to interview for client strengths. *Social Work, 40*(6), 729–736.

DeLois, K. (1997). Empowerment practice with lesbians and gays. In L. Gutierrez, R. Parsons, & E. Cox (Eds.), *Empowerment in social work practice* (pp. 65–71). Pacific Grove, CA: Brooks/Cole.

Demo, D. H., Allen, K. R., & Fine, M. A. (2000). *Handbook of family diversity*. New York: Oxford.

de Shazer, S. (1985). *Keys to solution in brief therapy*. New York: Norton.

Deutsch, M., & Krauss, R. M. (1965). *Social psychology*. New York: Basic Books.

Devore, W., & Schlesinger, E. (1999). *Ethnic-sensitive social work practice* (5th ed.). Boston: Allyn and Bacon.

Dillard, J. (1983). *Multicultural counseling*. Chicago: Nelson/Hall.

Dodes, L. (2002). *The heart of addiction*. New York: HarperCollins.

Dollard, J., & Miller, N. E. (1950). *Personality and psychotherapy*. New York: McGraw-Hill.

Dowrick, P. W. (1991). *Practical guide to using video in the behavioral sciences*. New York: Wiley.

Dyer, W. E. (1976). *Your erroneous zones*. New York: Avon.

East, J. F. (1999). Hidden barriers to success for women in welfare reform. *Families in Society, 80*(3), 295–304.

Egan, G. (1998). *The skilled helper: A problem-management approach to helping* (6th ed.). Pacific Grove, CA: Brooks/Cole

Egan, G. (2002). *The skilled helper: A problem-management and opportunity-development approach to helping* (7th ed.). Pacific Grove, CA: Brooks/Cole.

Eliade, M. (1964). *Shamanism*. London: Routledge and Kegan Paul.

Ellis, A. (1973) *Humanistic psychotherapy: The rational-emotive approach*. New York: Julian Press.

Ellis, A. (1994). *Reason and emotion in psychotherapy*. New York: Birch Lane Press.

Ellis, A., & Harper, R. A. (1975). *A new guide to rational living*. North Hollywood, CA: Wilshire Books.

Emmelkamp, P. M. G. (1994). Behavior therapy with adults. In A. E. Bergin & S. L. Garfield (Eds.), *Handbook of psychotherapy and behavior change* (4th ed., pp. 379–427). New York: Wiley.

Erikson, E. H. (1950). *Childhood and society*. New York: Norton.

Erikson, E. H. (1963). *Childhood and society* (2nd ed.). New York: Norton.

Erikson, E. H. (1968). *Identity, youth and crisis*. New York: Norton.

Ewen, R. B. (2003). *An introduction to theories of personality* (6th ed.). Mahwah, NJ: Lawrence Erlbaum.

Experts disagree on illness. (2004, January 10). *Deseret News*, sec. B, pp. 1–2.

Eysenck, H. J. (1964). *Crime and personality*. Boston: Houghton Mifflin.

Farley, O. W., Smith, L. L., & Boyle, S. W. (2003). *Introduction to social work* (9th ed.). Boston: Allyn and Bacon

Farley, R., & Allen, W. (1987). *The color line and the quality of life in America*. New York: Oxford University Press.

Fast, B., & Chapin, R. (1997). The strengths model with older adults: Critical practice components. In D. Saleebey (Ed.), *The strengths perspective in social work practice* (pp. 115–131) New York: Longman

Fatout, M., & Rose, S. (1995). *Task groups in the social services*. Thousand Oaks, CA: Sage.

Fong, R., & Furuto, S. B. C. I. (Eds.). (2001). *Culturally competent social work practice: Skills, interventions, and evaluations*. Boston: Allyn and Bacon.

Fox, S. S., & Scherl, D. J. (1972). Crisis intervention with victims of rape. *Social Work, 17*(1), 37–42.

Francis, S. (1993). Rape and sexual assault. In B. S. Johnson, *Adaptation and growth: Psychiatric nursing*. Philadelphia: Lippincott.

Frankel, A. J., & Gelman, S. R. (2004). *Case management* (2nd ed.). Chicago: Lyceum.

Frankl, V. E. (1959). *Man's search for meaning*. New York: Pocket Books.

Franklin, C., & Jordan, C. (1999). *Family practice*. Pacific Grove, CA: Brooks/Cole.

Freud, S. (1911). Formulations on the two principles of mental functioning. In J. Strachey (Ed. & Trans.), *The standard edition of the complete psychological works of Sigmund Freud* (Vol 12, pp. 218–226). New York: Basic Books.

Freud, S. (1953). The interpretation of dreams (Part II). *The standard edition of the complete psychological works of Sigmund Freud* (Vol. V). London: Hogarth Press.

Freud, S. (1957). Volume on the history of the psychoanalytic movement, papers on metapsychology and other works. In J. Strachey (Ed. & Trans.), *The standard edition of the complete psychological works of Sigmund Freud* (Vol. XIV). New York: Basic Books.

Freud, S. (1963). *Introductory lectures on psychoanalysis* (Parts I and II). J. Strachey (Ed.). Reprinted by permission, George Allen & Unwin Pub. And W. W. Norton & Co.

Freud, S. (1963). *Introductory lectures on psychoanalysis* (Vol. XVI, Part III). London: Hogarth Press.

Freud, S. (1965). *The interpretation of dreams.* New York: Avon Books. (Original work published 1900)

Freud, S., & Krug, S. (2002). Beyond the Code of Ethics, Part I: Complexities of ethical decision making in social work practice. *Families in Society, 83*(5/6), 474–482.

Furman, R. (2002). Jessie Taft and the functional school: The impact of our history. *Canadian Social Work Journal, 4*(1), 7–13.

Garfield, S. L. (1994). Research on client variables in psychotherapy. In S. L. Garfield & A. E. Bergin (Eds.), *Handbook of psychotherapy and behavior change* (4th ed., pp. 190–228). New York: Wiley.

Garfield, S. L., & Bergin, A. E. (1994). *Handbook of psychotherapy and behavior change* (4th ed.). New York: Wiley.

Garland, J., Jones, H., & Kolodny, R. (1965). A model for stages in the development of social work groups. In S. Bernstein (Ed.), *Explorations in group work* (pp. 12–53). Boston: Milford House.

Garland, J., Jones, H., & Kolodny, R. (1976). A model of stages of group development in social work groups. In S. Bernstein (Ed.), *Explorations in group work* (pp. 17–71). Boston: Charles River Books.

Garmezy, N. (1991). Resilience in children's adaptation to negative life events and stressed environments. *Pediatric Annals, 20,* 459–466.

Garver, C. S., & Scheier, M. F. (1996). *Perspectives on personality* (3rd ed.). Boston: Allyn and Bacon.

Garvin, C. (1985). Work with disadvantaged and oppressed groups. In M. Sundel, P. Glasser, R. Sarri, & R. Vinter (Eds.), *Individual change through small groups* (2nd ed., pp. 461–472). New York: Free Press.

Geertz, C. (1983). *Local knowledge.* New York: Basic Books.

Gilbert, N., Miller, H., & Specht, H. (1980). *An introduction to social work practice.* New York: Prentice-Hall.

Gilliland, B. E., & James, R. K. (1993). *Crisis intervention strategies.* Pacific Grove, CA: Brooks/Cole.

Ginsberg, L. H. (2001). *Social work evaluation.* Boston: Allyn and Bacon.

Glenmaye, L. (1998). Empowerment of women. In L. Gutierrez, R. Parsons, & E. Cox (Eds.), *Empowerment in social work practice* (pp. 29–50). Pacific Grove, CA: Brooks/Cole.

Goldenberg, H. (1983). *Contemporary clinical psychology.* Monterey, CA: Brooks/Cole.

Goldenberg, I., & Goldenberg, H. (1991). *Family therapy* (3rd ed.). Pacific Grove, CA: Brooks/Cole.

Goldfried, M. R., & Davidson, G. (1994). *Clinical behavior therapy* (Rev. ed.). New York: Wiley.

Goldstein, E. (1986). Ego psychology. In F. J. Turner (Ed.), *Social work treatment* (3rd ed., pp. 375–406). New York: Free Press.

Goldstein, E. (1995). *Ego psychology and social work practice* (2nd ed.). New York: Free Press.

Goodyear, R. J. (1981). Termination as a loss experience for the counselor. *Personnel and Guidance Journal, 59,* 347–350.

Gorey, K. M., Leslie, D. R., Morris, T., Carruthers, W. V., John, L., & Chacko, J. (1998). Effectiveness of case management with severely and persistently mentally ill people. *Community Mental Health Journal, 34*(3), 241–250.

Gottesman, I. I., & Shield, J. (1972). *Schizophrenia and genetics.* New York: Academic Press.

Gray, J. (1992). *Men Are from Mars, Women Are from Venus.* New York: HarperCollins.

Graybeal, C. (2001). Strength-based social work assessment: Transforming the dominant paradigm. *Families in Society: The Journal of Contemporary Human Services, 8,* 233–242.

Graybeal, C., Moore, V., & Cohen, M. (1995). The transformation of a social work program: A narrative of liberation. *Reflections: Narratives of professional helping, 1*(2).

Green, J. (1999). *Cultural awareness in the human services.* (3rd ed.). Boston: Allyn and Bacon.

Green, J. B. (2003). *Introduction to family theory and therapy.* Pacific Grove, CA: Brooks/Cole.

Greenson, R. R. (1967). *The techniques and practice of psychoanalysis.* Vol. 1. New York: International Universities Press.

Greenstone, J. L., & Leviton, S. C. (2002). *Elements of crisis intervention* (2nd ed.). Belmont, CA: Brooks/Cole.

Griffin, R. E. (1993). Assessing the drug-involved client. In J. B. Rauch (Ed.), *Assessment: A source book for social work practice* (pp. 173–183). Milwaukee, WI: Families International.

Griffiths, J. K., Farley, O. W., & Fraser, M. (1986). Indices of adolescent suicide. *Journal of Independent Social Work Practice, 1,* 49–63.

Grinnell, R. M., & Unrau, Y. (1997). Group designs. In R. M. Grinnell Jr. (Ed.), *Social work research and evaluation.* (5th ed., pp. 259–297). Itasca, IL: Peacock.

Gutiérrez, L. (1990). Working with women of color: An empowerment perspective. *Social Work 35*(2), 149–153.

Hage, J., & Aiken, M. (1980). Program change and organizational properties. In H. Resnick & R. J. Patti (Eds.), *Change from within: Humanizing social welfare organizations* (pp. 159–182). Philadelphia: Temple University Press.

Haggstrom, W. C. (2001). The tactics of organization building. In J. Rothman, J. L. Erlich, & J. E. Tropman, *Strategies of community intervention* (pp. 27–64). Itasca, IL: Peacock.

Hall, J. A., Carswell, C., Walsh, E., Huber, D. L., & Jampoler, J. S. (2002). Iowa case management: Innovative social casework. *Social Work, 47*(2), 132–141.

Halley, A. A., Kopp, J., & Austin, M. J. (1998). *Delivering human services: A learning approach to practice* (4th ed.). New York: Longman.

Hammond, D., Hepworth, D., & Smith, V. (1997). *Improving therapeutic communication.* San Francisco: Jossey-Bass.

Harper, K. V., & Lantz, J. (1996). *Cross-cultural practice: Social work with diverse populations.* Chicago: Lyceum.

Harris, M., & Bergman, H. C. (1988). Clinical case management for the chronically mentally ill: A conceptual analysis. *New Directions for Mental Health Services, 40,* 5–13.

Harry, B., & Anderson, M. G. (1994). The disproportionate placement of African American males in special education programs: A critique of the process. *Journal of Negro Education, 63,* 602–619.

Hartman, A., & Laird, J. (1983). *Family-centered social work practice.* New York: Free Press.

Hartmann, H. (1958). *Ego psychology and the problem of adaptation.* New York: International University Press.

Hartmann, H., Kris, E., & Loewenstein, R. M. (1947). Comments on the formation of psychic structure. In A. Freud et al. (Eds.), *The psychoanalytic study of the child.* New York: International University Press.

Hasenfeld, Y. (2001). Program development. In J. Rothman, J. L. Erlich, & J. E. Tropman (Eds.), *Strategies of community intervention* (pp. 456–477). Itasca, IL: Peacock.

Hendricks, I. (1943). The discussion of the "instinct to master." *Psychoanalytic Quarterly, 12,* 561–565.

Hepworth, D. H., Farley, O. W., & Griffiths, J. K. (1993). Assessing and treating suicidal adolescents and their families. In J. B. Rauch (Ed.), *Assessment: A source book for social work practice* (pp. 91–103). Milwaukee, WI: Families International.

Hepworth, D. H., Rooney, R., & Larsen, J. (2002). *Direct social work practice: Theory and skills* (6th ed.). Pacific Grove, CA: Brooks/Cole.

Herlihy, B. (2001). Managing boundaries. In E. R. Welfel & R. E. Ingersoll, *The mental health desk reference* (pp. 465–471). Hoboken, NJ: Wiley.

Hill, R. (1971). *The strengths of black families.* New York: Emerson Hall.

Hinckley, G. B. (2000). *Standing for something.* New York: Three Rivers Press.

Hirayama, H., & Hirayama, K. (1985). Empowerment through group participation: Process and goal. In M. Parenes (Ed.), *Innovations in social group work: Feedback from practice to theory* (pp. 119–131). New York: Haworth.

Ho, M. K. (1987). *Family therapy with ethnic minorities.* Newbury Park, CA: Sage.

Hoffman, K. S., & Sallee, A. L. (1994). *Social work practice.* Boston: Allyn and Bacon.

Hollis, F. (1972). *Casework: A psychosocial therapy* (2nd ed.). New York: Random House.

Holman, A. (1983). *Family assessment: Tools for understanding and intervention.* Newbury Park, CA: Sage.

Homan, M. S. (2004). *Promoting community change.* Belmont, CA: Brooks/Cole.

Howard, K. I., Kopta, S. M., Krause, M. S., & Orlinsky, D. E. (1986). The dose-effect relationship in psychotherapy. *American Psychologist, 41,* 159–164.

Hubble, M. A., Duncan, B. L., & Miller, S. D. (1999). *The heart and soul of change: What works in therapy.* Washington, DC: American Psychological Association.

Hudson, W. B. (1982). *The clinical measurement package.* Homewood, IL: Dorsey.

Hull, G., & Mather, J. (2005). *Understanding generalist practice with families.* Pacific Grove, CA: Brooks/Cole.

Hull, G. H., Jr., & Kirst-Ashman, K. K. (2004). *The generalist model of human services practice.* Pacific Grove, CA: Brooks/Cole.

Hutchins, D. E., & Vaught, C. C. (1997). *Helping relationships and strategies* (3rd ed.). Pacific Grove, CA: Brooks/Cole.

Ivey, A., Normington, N., Miller, D., Morrill, W., & Haase, R. (1968). Microcounseling and attending behavior: An approach to pre-practicum counselor training. *Journal of Counseling Psychology, 15,* 1–12.

Ivey, A. E., & Ivey, M. B. (1999). *Intentional interviewing and counseling* (4th ed.). Pacific Grove, CA: Brooks/Cole.

Ivey, A. E., & Ivey, M. B. (2003). *Intentional interviewing and counseling* (5th ed.). Pacific Grove, CA: Brooks/Cole.

Jackson, R. L. (2001). *The clubhouse model.* Pacific Grove, CA: Brooks/Cole.

Jackson, V. H. (2002). Cultural competency. *Behavioral Health Management, 22*(2), 20–26.

Jacobson, E. (1938). *Progressive relaxation.* Chicago: University of Chicago Press.

Jacobson, N. S., & Gurman, A. S. (Eds.). (1995). *Clinical handbook of couple therapy.* New York: Guilford Press.

James, R. K., & Gilliland, B. E. (2001). *Crisis intervention strategies* (4th ed.). Belmont, CA: Brooks/Cole.

Jilek, W. (1982). *Indian healing: Shamanic ceremonialism in the Pacific Northwest today.* Laine, WA: Hancock House.

Johnson, L., & Yanca, S. (2001). *Social work practice.* Boston: Allyn and Bacon.

Johnson, L. C., & Yanca, S. J. (2004). *Social work practice: A generalist approach.* Boston: Allyn and Bacon.

Johnson, S. (1998). *Who moved my cheese?* New York: G. P. Putnam's Son, 1998.

Jones, J. (1985). *Labor of love, labor of sorrow: Black women, work, and the family from slavery to the present.* New York: Basic Books.

Jordan, C., & Franklin, C. (1995). *Clinical assessment for social workers: Quantitative and qualitative methods.* Chicago: Lyceum.

Jordan, C., Lewellen, A., & Vandiver, V. (1994). A social work perspective of psychosocial rehabilitation: Psychoeducational models for minority families. *International Journal of Mental Health, 23*(4), 27–43.

Kadera, S. W., Lambert, M. J., & Andrews, A. A. (1996). How much therapy is really enough: A session-by-session analysis of the psychotherapy dose-effect relationship. *Journal of Psychotherapy: Practice and Research, 5,* 1–22.

Kahn, S. (1991). *Organizing.* Washington, DC: NASW.

Kanani, K., & Regehr, C. (2003). Clinical, ethical and legal issues in e-therapy. *Families in Society, 84*(2), 155–162.

Kanel, K. (2003). *A guide to crisis intervention.* Belmont, CA: Brooks/Cole.

Kanter, R. M. (1987). Power failure in management circuits. In J. M. Shafritz & J. Steven Ott, *Classics of organization theory* (2nd ed.). Chicago: Dorsey Press.

Kaplan, H. I., & Sadock, B. J. (1996). *Concise textbook of clinical psychiatry.* Baltimore: Williams & Wilkins.

Kaplan, H. I., & Sadock, B. J. (1998). *Synopsis of psychiatry* (8th ed.). Baltimore: Williams & Wilkins.

Kazdin, A. E. (1978). *History of behavior modification: Experimental foundations of contemporary research.* Baltimore: University Park Press.

Kelley-Gillespie, N. (2003). *Perceptions of quality of life of the elderly.* Unpublished doctoral dissertation, University of Utah, Salt Lake City.

Kirst-Ashman, K. K., & Hull, G. H., Jr. (2001). *Generalist practice with organizations and communities* (2nd ed.). Belmont, CA: Brooks/Cole.

Kirst-Ashman, K. K., & Hull, G. H., Jr. (2002). *Understanding generalist practice.* Pacific Grove, CA: Brooks/Cole.

Klein, S. (1986). Socratic dialogue in the meno. *Southern Journal of Philosophy, 24,* 351–363.

Kline, A. (1996). Pathways into drug user treatment: The influence of gender and racial/ethnic identify. *Substance Use and Misuse, 31*(3), 323–342.

Knox, K., & Roberts, A. R. (2002). Police social work. In A. R. Roberts & G. J. Greene, *Social workers' desk reference* (pp. 668–672). New York: Oxford.

Krill, D. F. (1983). Existential psychotherapy and the problem of anomie. In F. J. Turner (Ed.), *Differential diagnosis and treatment in social work* (3rd ed.). New York: Free Press.

Kruzich, J. M., Friesen, B. J., Williams-Murphy, T., & Longley, M. J. (2002). Voices of African American families: Perspectives on residential treatment. *Social Work, 47*(4), 461–470.

Kübler-Ross, E. (1969). *On death and dying.* New York: Macmillan.

Kushner, H. S. (1981). *When bad things happen to good people.* New York: Avon.

Lambert, M. J., & Anderson, E. M. (1996). Assessment for the time limited psychotherapies. *Annual Review of Psychiatry, 15,* 23–47.

Lange, A. J., & Jakubowski, P. (1976). *Responsible assertive behavior.* Champaign, IL: Research Press.

Lantz, J. (1993). *Existential family therapy.* Northvale, NJ: Jason Aronson.

Lauffer, A. (1981). The practice of social planning. In N. Gilbert & H. Specht (Eds.), *Handbook of the social services* (pp. 583–597). Englewood Cliffs, NJ: Prentice Hall.

Lazarus, A. (1972). *Behavior therapy and beyond.* New York: McGraw-Hill.

Leigh, J. (1984). *Empowerment strategies for work with multi-ethnic populations.* Paper presented at the Council on Social Work Education Annual Program Meeting, Detroit, MI.

Lemma, A. (2003). *Introduction to the practice of psychoanalytic psychotherapy.* New York: Wiley.

Lenson, B. (Ed.). (Undated). *The black book of executive politics by Z.* New York: National Institute of Business Management.

Lewin, K. (1951). *Field theory in social sciences.* Westport, CT: Greenwood Press.

Lewis, J. A., Dana, R. Q., & Blevins, G. A. (1994). *Substance abuse counseling: Individualized approach* (2nd ed.). Pacific Grove, CA: Brooks/Cole.

Liebert, R. M., & Liebert, L. L. (1998). *Liebert and Spiegler's personality: Strategies and issues* (7th ed.). Pacific Grove, CA: Brooks/Cole.

Lindemann, E. (1944). Symptomatology and management of acute grief. *American Journal of Psychiatry, 101,* 141–148.

Lloyd, J. (1980). *Placement prevention and family reunification: A handbook for the family-centered service practitioner* (Rev. ed.). Iowa City: National Resource Center on Family-Based Services.

Loewenberg, F. M., Dolgoff, R., & Harrington, D. (2000). *Ethical decisions for social work practice.* Itasca, IL: Peacock.

Long, V. O. (1996). *Communication skill in the helping relations: A framework for facilitating personal growth.* Pacific Grove, CA: Brooks/Cole.

Longres, J. F. (1995). *Human behavior in the social environment.* Itasca, IL: F. E. Peacock.

Lum, D. (1986). *Social work practice and people of color.* Monterey, CA: Brooks/Cole.

Lum, D. (1999). *Culturally competent practice.* Pacific Grove: Brooks/Cole.

MacCluskie, K. C. (2001). Responsible documentation. In E. R. Welfel & R. E. Ingersoll, *The mental health desk reference* (pp. 459–465). Hoboken, NJ: Wiley.

Maguire, L. (2002). *Clinical social work.* Pacific Grove, CA: Brooks/Cole.

Maheu, M., & Gordon, B. (2000). Counseling and therapy on the Internet. *Professional Psychology: Research and Practice, 31*(5), 484–489.

Mahler, M. S. (1968). *On human symbiosis of the vicissitudes of individuation.* New York: International Universities Press.

Mancuso, J. C. (Ed.). (1970). *Readings for a cognitive theory of personality.* New York: Holt, Rinehart and Winston.

Manning, S. (1998). Empowerment in mental health programs: Listening to the voices. In R. Gutierez,

R. Parsons, & E. Cox (Eds.), *Empowerment in social work practice.* Pacific Grove, CA: Brooks/Cole.

Marlatt, G. A., & Gordon, J. R. (1985). *Relapse prevention: A self-control strategy for the maintenance of behavior change.* New York: Guilford.

Marx, J. A., & Gelso, C. J. (1987). Termination of individual counseling in university counseling centers. *Journal of Counseling Psychology, 34,* 3–9.

Maslow, A. (1967). *Toward a psychology of being.* New York: Van Nostrand Reinhold.

Maslow, A. H. (1968). *Toward a psychology of being.* (2nd ed.). New York: Van Nostrand-Reinhold.

Maslow, A. (1971). *The farther reaches of human nature.* New York: Viking Press.

Mather, J. H., & Hull, G. H. (2002). Case management and child welfare. In A. R. Roberts & G. J. Greene, *Social workers' desk reference* (pp. 476–480). New York: Oxford.

McCabe, K., Yeh, M., Hough, R. L., Landsverk, J., Hurlburt, M. S., Culver, S. W., & Reynolds, B. (1999). Racial/ethnic representation across five public sectors of care for youth. *Journal of Emotional and Behavioral Disorders, 7,* 72–82.

McCartney, K., Harris, M. J., & Bernieri, F. (1990). Growing up and growing apart: A developmental meta-analysis of twin studies. *Psychological Bulletin, 107,* 226–237.

McGill, D. (1992). The cultural story in multicultural family therapy. *Families in Society: The Journal of Contemporary Human Services, 73,* 339–349.

McInnis-Dittrich, K. (2002). *Social work with elders: A biopsychosocial approach to assessment and intervention.* Boston: Allyn and Bacon.

McLeod, P., Lobel, S., & Cox, T. (1996). Ethnic diversity and creativity in small groups. *Small Group Research, 27*(2), 248–264.

McMahon, M. O. (1996). *The general method of social work practice: A problem-solving approach* (3rd ed.). Boston: Allyn and Bacon.

McMurtry, S. L., & Hudson, W. W. (2000). The client satisfaction inventory: Results of an initial validation study. *Research on Social Work Practice, 10*(5), 644–663.

Meenaghan, T. M., & Gibbons, W. E. (2000). *Generalist practice in larger settings.* Chicago: Lyceum.

Meichenbaum, D. (1977). *Cognitive behavior modification.* New York: Plenum.

Merell, K. W. (2003). *Behavioral, social, and emotional assessment of children and adolescents* (2nd ed.). Mahwah, NJ: Erlbaum.

Merikangas, K. (1990). The genetic epidemiology of alcoholism. *Psychological Medicine, 20,* 11–22.

Meyer, C. H. (1993). *Assessment in social work practice.* New York: Columbia University Press.

Miley, K. K., O'Melia, M., & DuBois, B. (2004). *Generalist social work practice* (4th ed.). Boston: Allyn and Bacon.

Miller, G. A. (1999). *Learning the language of addiction counseling.* Boston: Allyn and Bacon.

Millon, T. (1999). *Personality-guided therapy.* New York: Wiley.

Minuchin, S. (1974). *Families and family therapy.* Cambridge, MA: Harvard University Press.

Minuchin, S., & Fishman, H. C. (1981). *Family therapy techniques.* Cambridge, MA: Harvard University Press.

Mischel, W. (1973). Toward a cognitive social learning reconceptualization of personality. *Psychological Review, 80,* 730–755.

Monat, A., & Lazarus, R. (Eds.). (1991). *Stress and coping: An anthology.* New York: Columbia Press.

Mottonen, D. (Ed.). (1987). *What does your future hold?* Salt Lake City, UT: Valley Mental Health, 1987.

Mowrer, O. H. (1950). *Learning theory and personality dynamics.* New York: Ronald Press.

Moxley, D. P. (1997). *Case management by design.* Chicago: Nelson-Hall.

Moxley, D. P. (2002). Case management and psychosocial rehabilitation with SMD clients. In A. R. Roberts & G. J. Greene, *Social workers' desk reference* (pp. 481–485). New York: Oxford.

Mueser, K. T., Bond, G. R., Drake, R. E., & Resnick, S. G. (1998). Models of community care for severe mental illness: A review of research on case management. *Schizophrenia Bulletin, 24*(1), 37–70.

Murphy, W. F. (1965). *The tactics of psychotherapy.* New York: International Universities Press.

National Association of Social Workers (NASW). (1973). *Standards for social service manpower.* Washington, DC: Author.

National Association of Social Workers (NASW). (1999). *Code of ethics of the National Association of Social Workers.* Washington, DC: Author.

National Association of Social Workers (NASW). (2001). Client profiles differ by setting. *NASW News, 47*(1), 12.

National Association of Social Workers (NASW). (2004). *Guidelines for recommendations in professional review for ethics violations.* Washington, DC: Author.

National Center on Addiction and Substance Abuse. (1996). *Substance abuse and the American woman.* New York: Author.

Netting, F. E., Kettner, P. M., & McMurtry, S. L. (1993). *Social work macro practice.* New York: Longman.

Newman, B. M., & Newman, P. R. (1995). *Development through life: A psychosocial approach* (6th ed.). Pacific Grove, CA: Brooks/Cole.

Nichols, M., & Schwartz, R. (2001). *Family therapy: Concepts and methods* (5th ed.). Boston: Allyn and Bacon.

Nichols, M. P., & Schwartz, R. C. (2004). *Family therapy* (6th ed.). Boston: Allyn and Bacon.

Nichols, M. P. (1987). *The self in the system.* New York: Brunner/Mazel.

Norcross, J. C., & Newman, C. F. (1992). Psychotherapy integration: Setting the context. In J. C. Norcross & M. R. Goldfried (Eds.), *Handbook of psychotherapy integration* (pp. 3–45). New York: Basic Books.

Nugent, W. R., Sieppert, J. D., & Hudson, W. W. (2001). *Practice evaluation for the 21st century.* Belmont, CA: Brooks/Cole.

Nurcombe, B., & Gallagher, R. M. (1986). *The clinical process in psychiatry: Diagnosis and management planning.* London: Cambridge University Press.

Nurius, P. S., & Hudson, W. W. (1993). *Human services: Practice evaluation and computers.* Pacific Grove, CA: Brooks/Cole.

Okazawa-Rey, M. (1998). Empowering poor communities of color: A self-help model. In L. Gutierrez, R. Parsons, & E. Cox (Eds.), *Empowerment in social work practice* (pp. 52–64). Pacific Grove, CA: Brooks/Cole.

Overholser, J. C. (1988). Clinical utility of the Socratic method. In C. Stout (Ed.), *Annals of clinical research* (pp. 1–7). Des Plaines, IL: Forest Institute.

Overholser, J. C. (1993). Elements of the Socratic method: I. Systematic questioning. *Psychotherapy, 30,* 67–74.

Papell, C., & Rothman, B. (1962). Social group work models: Possession and heritage. *Journal of Education for Social Work, 2,* 66–77.

Parad, H. J. (1971). Crisis intervention. In R. Morris (Ed.), *Encyclopedia of social work,* (16th ed., Vol. 1). New York: National Association of Social Workers.

Patterson, L. E., & Welfel, E. R. (2000). *The counseling process* (5th ed.). Pacific Grove, CA: Brooks/Cole.

Patterson, W. M., Bird, J., & Patterson, G. A. (1983). Evaluation of suicidal patients: The SAD PERSONS scale. *Psychosomatics, 24*(1), 343–349.

Patti, R. J. (1980). Organizational resistance and change: The view from below. In H. Resnick & R. J. Patti (Eds.), *Change from within: Humanizing social welfare organizations.* Philadelphia: Temple University Press.

Paulson, B., Truscott, D., & Stuart, J. (1999). Clients' perceptions of helpful experiences in counseling. *Journal of Counseling Psychology 46,* 317–324.

Peck, M. S. (1978). *The road less traveled.* New York: Touchstone.

Pernell, R. (1985). Empowerment for our clients and for ourselves. In M. Parenes (Ed.), *Innovations in social group work: Feedback from practice to theory* (pp. 107–117). New York: Haworth.

Pickens, R., et al. (1991). Heterogeneity in the inheritance of alcoholism. *Archives of General Psychiatry, 48,* 23.

Piercy, F. P., & Frankel, B. R. (1989). The evolution of an integrative family therapy for substance abusing adolescents. *Journal of Family Psychology, 3,* 5–25.

Pincus, A., & Minahan, A. (1973). *Social work practice: Model and method.* Itasca, IL: F. E. Peacock.

Pinderhughes, E. (1995). Direct practice overview. In *Encyclopedia of Social Work* (19th ed., Vol. 1, pp. 740–751). Washington, DC: NASW Press.

Popple, P., & Leighninger, L. (2002). *Social work, social welfare, and American society.* Boston: Allyn and Bacon.

Poulin, J. (2000). *Collaborative social work.* Itasca, IL: Peacock.

Poulin, J. (2005). *Strengths-based generalist practice.* Pacific Grove, CA: Brooks/Cole.

Premack, D. (1965). Reinforcement theory. In D. Levine (Ed.), *Nebraska symposium on motivation* (pp. 123–180). Lincoln: University of Nebraska Press.

Preston, J. (1998). *Integrative brief therapy: Cognitive, psychodynamic, humanistic and neurobehavioral approaches.* San Luis Obispo, CA: Impact.

Prochaska, J. O., & Norcross, J. C. (1999). *Systems of psychotherapy* (4th ed.). Pacific Grove, CA: Brooks/Cole.

Prochaska, J. O., & Norcross, J. C. (2003). *Systems of psychotherapy* (5th ed.). Pacific Grove, CA: Brooks/Cole.

Pruger, R. (1973). The good bureaucrat. *Social Work, 18*(4), 26–27.

Quintana, S. M. (1993). Toward an expanded and updated conceptualization of termination: Implications for short-term individual psychotherapy. *Professional Psychology: Research and Practice, 24,* 426–432.

Rapoport, L. (1962). Working with families in crisis: An exploration in preventive intervention. *Social Work, 7*(3), pp. 48–56.

Rapp, C. A. (1997). The strengths model: Case management with people suffering from severe and persistent mental illness. In D. Saleebey (Ed.), *The strengths-based perspective in social work practice.* New York: Longman.

Rapp, C. A. (2002). A strengths approach to case management with clients with severe mental disabilities. In A. R. Roberts & G. J. Greene, *Social workers' desk reference* (pp. 486–491). New York: Oxford.

Rappaport, J. (1981). In praise of paradox: A social policy of empowerment over prevention. *American Journal of Community Psychology, 9,* 1–25.

Rappaport, J. (1985). The power of empowerment language. *Social Policy 17*(2), 15–21.

Rappaport, J. (1990). Research methods and the empowerment agenda. In P. Tolan, F. Chertak, & L. Jason (Eds.), *Research-ing community psychology* (pp. 51–63). Washington, DC: American Psychological Association.

Raskin, N. J., & Rogers, C. R. (1995). Person-centered therapy. In R. J. Corsini & D. Wedding (Eds.), *Current psychotherapies* (5th ed., pp. 128–161). Itasca, IL: Peacock.

Rauch, J. B. (Ed.). (1993). *Assessment: A source book for social work practice.* Milwaukee, WI: Families International, Inc.

Reed, W. J. (1978). *The task-centered system.* New York: Columbia University Press.

Reichle, J., Brubakken, D., & Tetreault, G. (1976). Eliminating pervasive speech by positive reinforcement and time-out in a psychotic child. *Journal of Behavior Therapy and Experimental Psychiatry, 1,* 179–183.

Reid, K. (1997). *Social work practice with groups.* Pacific Grove, CA: Brooks/Cole.

Reid, W. (1978). *The task-centered system.* New York: Columbia University Press.

Reid, W. J., & Epstein, L. (1972). *Task-centered casework.* New York: Columbia University Press.

Rescorla, R. A. (1972). Informational variables in Pavlovian conditioning. In G. H. Bower (Ed.). *The psychology of learning and motivation* (vol. 6, pp. 64–99). New York: Academic Press.

Resnick, H., & Patti, R. J. (Eds.). (1980). *Change from within: Humanizing social welfare organizations.* Philadelphia: Temple University Press.

Rimm, R. J., & Masters, J. (1974). *Behavior therapy.* New York: Academic.

Robbins, S. P., Chatterjee, P., & Canda, E. R. (1998). *Contemporary human behavior theory: A critical perspective for social work.* Boston: Allyn and Bacon.

Roberts, H. M., Evans, W. J., Honemann, D. H., & Balch, T. J. (2000). *Robert's rules of order.* (10th ed.). New York: Perseus.

Rogers, C. R. (1942). *Counseling and psychotherapy.* Boston: Houghton Mifflin.

Rogers, C. R. (1951). *Client-centered therapy.* Boston: Houghton Mifflin.

Rogers, C. R. (1957). The necessary and sufficient conditions of therapeutic personality changes. *Journal of Consulting Psychology, 21,* 95–103.

Rogers, C. R. (1959). A theory of therapy, personality, and interpersonal relationships, as developed in the client-centered framework. In S. Koch (Ed.), *Psychology: A study of a science. Study I. Conceptual and systemic, vol. 3: Formulations of the person and social context* (pp. 184–256). New York: McGraw-Hill.

Rogers, C. R. (1961). *On becoming a person.* Boston: Houghton Mifflin.

Rogers, C. R. (1968). *General systems theory* (Rev. ed.). New York: George Braziller.

Rogers, C. R. (1986). Client-centered therapy. In I. L. Kutash & A. Wolf (Eds.), *Psychotherapists' cookbook: Therapy and technique in practice* (pp. 197–208). San Francisco: Jossey-Bass.

Rogers, C. R., Gendlin, E., Kiesler, D., & Truax, C. (1967). *The therapeutic relationship and its impact: A study of psychotherapy with schizophrenics.* Madison: University of Wisconsin Press.

Rose, S. M. (1992). *Case management & social work practice.* New York: Longman.

Rothman, J. (2001). Approaches to community intervention. In J. Rothman, J. L. Erlich, & J. E. Tropman, *Strategies of community intervention* (pp. 27–64). Itasca, IL: Peacock.

Rothman, J. (2002). An overview of case management. In A. R. Roberts & G. J. Greene, *Social workers' desk reference* (pp. 467–472). New York: Oxford.

Rotter, J. B. (1954). *Social learning and clinical psychology.* Englewood Cliffs, NJ: Prentice-Hall.

Royse, D. (2004). *Research methods in social work* (4th ed.). Pacific Grove, CA: Brooks/Cole.

Rubin, A. (1992). Case management. In S. M. Rose, *Case management and social work practice* (pp. 1–20). New York: Longman.

Rubin, A., & Babbie, E. (2001). *Research methods for social work* (4th ed.). Belmont, CA: Wadsworth.

Rychlak, J. R. (1981). *Introduction to personality and psychotherapy* (2nd ed.) Boston: Houghton Mifflin.

Saleebey, D. (1992). *The strengths perspective in social work practice.* White Plains, NY: Longman.

Saleebey, D. (1996). The strengths perspective in social work practice: Extensions and cautions. *Journal of Social Work, 41*(3), 296–306.

Saleebey, D. (1997). *The strengths perspective in social work practice* (2nd ed.). New York: Longman.

Saleebey, D. (2002). Introduction: Power in people. In D. Saleebey (Ed.), *The strengths perspective in social work practice* (3rd ed., pp. 1–22). Boston: Allyn and Bacon.

Samenow, S. E., & Yochelson, S. (1976). *The criminal personality.* New York: Jason Aronson.

Sander, F. M. (1979). *Individual and family therapy.* New York: Anderson.

Sandner, D. (1979). *Navajo symbols of healing.* New York: Harcourt, Brace, and Jovanovich.

Santas, G. X. (1979). *Philosophy in Plato's early dialogues.* Boston: Routledge & K. Paul.

Sarri, R., & duRivage, V. (1985). *Strategies for self help and empowerment of working low income women who are heads of families.* Unpublished manuscript, University of Michigan, School of Social Work, Ann Arbor.

Scharff, J. (Ed.). (1989). *The foundations of object relations family therapy.* New York: Jason Aronson.

Scharff, J. S., & Scharff, D. E. (1998). *Object relations: Individual therapy.* Northvale, NJ: Jason Aronson.

Schmid, W. T. (1983). Socratic moderation and self-knowledge. *Journal of the History of Philosophy, 21,* 339–348.

Schwartz, W. (1976). Between client and system: The mediating function. In R. R. Roberts & H. Northen (Eds.), *Theories of social work with groups* (pp. 171–197). New York: Columbia University Press.

Scott, J. E., & Dixon, L. B. (1995). Assertive community treatment and case management for schizophrenia. *Schizophrenia Bulletin, 21*(4), 657–668.

Segal, S. P., Bola, J. R., & Watson, M. A. (1996). Race, quality of care, and antipsychotic prescribing practices in psychiatric emergency services. *Psychiatric Services, 47,* 282–286.

Sevel, J., Cummins, L., & Madrigal, C. (1999). *Student guide and workbook for social work skills demonstrated: Beginning direct practice CD-ROM.* Boston: Allyn and Bacon.

Sharf, R. S. (2000). *Theories of psychotherapy and counseling: Concepts and Cases* (2nd ed.). Belmont, CA: Brooks/Cole.

Sheafer, B. W., & Horejsi, C. R. (2003). *Techniques and guidelines for social work practice* (6th ed.). Boston: Allyn and Bacon.

Sherman, A. (1973). *Behavior modification: Theory and practice.* Pacific Grove, CA: Brooks/Cole.

Shoshani, B. S. (1984). *Gordon Hamilton: An investigation of core ideas.* Unpublished doctoral dissertation, Columbia University, New York.

Shulman, L. (1991). *Interactional social work practice.* Itasca, IL: Peacock.

Shulman, L. (1999). *The skills of helping individuals, families, groups, and communities* (4th ed.). Itasca, IL: Peacock.

Simon, B. (1994). *The empowerment tradition in American social work.* New York: Columbia University Press.

Simon, G. M. (1995). A revisionist rendering of structural family therapy. *Journal of Marital and Family Therapy, 27,* 17–26.

Simos, G. (2002). *Cognitive behavior therapy: A guide for the practicing clinician.* New York: Taylor & Frances.

Siporin, M. (1975). *Introduction to social work practice.* New York: Macmillan.

Smith, L. L. (1978). A review of crisis intervention theory. *Social Casework, 59*(7), 396–405.

Smith, L. L. (1990). Crisis intervention: Theory and practice. In J. E. Mezzich & B. Zimmer (Eds.), *Emergency psychiatry* (pp. 305–328). Madison, CT: International Universities Press.

Smith, L. L. (1992). How couples misuse money. *Family Therapy, 19*(2), 131–135.

Smith, L. L., & Beckner, B. M. (1993). An anger management workshop for inmates in a medium security facility. *Journal of Offender Rehabilitation, 19*(3/4), 103–111.

Smith, L. L., Smith, J. N., & Beckner, B. M. (1994). An anger management workshop for women inmates. *Families in Society, 144*(3), 172–175.

Smith, M. L., Glass, G. V., & Miller, T. I. (1980). *The benefits of psychotherapy.* Baltimore: Johns Hopkins University Press.

Smith, V., & Eggleston, R. (1989). Long-term care: The medical model versus the social model. *Public Welfare, 47,* 27–29.

Specht, H., & Courtney, M. (1994). *Unfaithful angels: How social work has abandoned its mission.* New York: Free Press.

Spiegler, M. D., & Guevremont, D. C. (1998). *Contemporary behavior therapy* (3rd ed.). Pacific Grove, CA: Brooks/Cole.

Staples, R. (1971). Toward a sociology of the black family: A decade of theory and research. *Journal of Marriage and the Family, 33,* 19–38.

Staples, R., & Mirande, A. (1980). Racial and cultural variations among American families: A decennial review of the literature on minority families. *Journal of Marriage and the Family, 42*(4), 403–414.

Stein, H. (1991). Adler and Socrates: Similarities and differences. *Individual Psychology, 47,* 241–246.

Stewart, D., & Shamdasani, P. (1990). *Focus groups: Theory and practice.* Newbury Park, CA: Sage.

Stuart, R. B. (1980). *Helping couples change: A social learning approach to marital therapy.* New York: Guilford.

Stuart, R. B., & Lott, L. A. (1972). Behavioral contracting with delinquents: A cautionary note. *Journal of Behavior Therapy and Experimental Psychiatry, 3,* 161–169.

Substance Abuse and Mental Health Services Administration. (1997). *Cultural competence guidelines in managed care mental health services for Asian and Pacific Islander population.* The Asian American and Pacific Islander Task Force. The Western Interstate Commission for Higher Education Mental Health Program.

Sue, D. W., Ivey, A. E., & Pedersen, P. B. (1996). *A theory of multicultural counseling and therapy.* Pacific Grove, CA: Brooks/Cole.

Sue, D. W., & Sue, D. (1990). *Counseling the culturally different: Theory and practice* (2nd ed.). New York: Wiley.

Sullivan, W. P. (2002). Case management with substance-abusing clients. In A. R. Roberts & G. J. Greene, *Social workers' desk reference* (pp. 492–496). New York: Oxford.

Sullivan, W. P., & Rapp, C. A. (1994). Breaking away: The potential and promise of a strengths-based approach in social work practice. In R. G. Meinert, J. T. Pardeck, & W. P. Sullivan (Eds.), *Issues in social work: A critical analysis* (pp. 83–104). Westport, CT: Auburn House.

Tavris, C. (1982). Anger defused. *Psychology Today, 16*(11), 25–35.

Taylor, G. M. (1980). *Marriage enrichment: A strategy for strengthening relationships.* Unpublished doctoral dissertation, University of Utah.

Thomlison, B. (2002). *Family assessment handbook.* Pacific Grove, CA: Brooks/Cole.

Thorndike, E. L. (1898). Animal intelligence. An experimental study of the associative processes in animals (*Psychological Review,* monograph supplements No. 8), New York: Macmillan.

Timmons, P. L., et al. (2000). Stress inoculation training for maladaptive anger: Comparison of group counseling versus computer guidance. *Computers in Human Behavior, 13,* 51–64.

Tolman, E., & Honzik, C. H. (1930). Introduction and removal of reward and maze performance in rats. *University of California Publications in Psychology, 4,* 257–275.

Torres, S. (1986). *A comparative analysis of wife abuse among Anglo-American and Mexican-American battered women: Attitudes, nature, severity, frequency, and response to the abuse.* Unpublished Doctoral dissertation, University of Texas at Austin.

Torrey, E. (1986). *Witch doctors and psychiatrists.* New York: Harper & Row.

Toseland, R., & Rivas, R. (2001). *An introduction to group work practice.* Boston: Allyn and Bacon.

Tsuang, M. T., & Faraone, S. V. (1990). *The genetics of mood disorders.* Baltimore: Johns Hopkins Press.

Ursano, R. J., Sonnenberg, S. M., & Lazar, S. G. (1991). Concise guide to psychodynamic psychotherapy. In R. E. Hales (Ed.), *Concise guides* (12–17). Arlington, VA: American Psychiatric Association.

U.S. Bureau of the Census. (1985). *Demographic and socioeconomic aspects of aging in the United States* (Current Population Reports, Series P-23, #38, pp. 1–16). Washington, DC: U.S. Government Printing Office.

U.S. Bureau of the Census. (1999). Household and family characteristics. *Current Population Reports.* Washington, DC: U.S. Government Printing Office.

U.S. Department of Health and Human Services. (USDHHS). (2000). *Special report to the U.S. Congress on alcohol and health.* Rockville, MD: Author.

U.S. Department of Health and Human Services. (USDHHS). (2001). *Mental health: Culture, race and ethnicity—A supplement to mental health: A report of the Surgeon General.* Rockville, MD: Substance Abuse and Mental Health Services Administration, Center for Mental Health Services.

Van Hook, M., Hugen, B., & Aguilar, M. (2001). *Spirituality within religious traditions in social work practice.* Pacific Grove, CA: Brooks/Cole.

Von Bertalanffy, L. (1968). *General systems theory* (Rev. ed.). New York: George Braziller.

Vosler, N. (1996). *New approaches to family practice.* Thousand Oaks, CA: Sage.

Walsh, J. (2000). *Clinical case management with persons having mental illness.* Belmont, CA: Brooks/Cole.

Walsh, J. (2002). Clinical case management. In A. R. Roberts & G. J. Greene, *Social workers' desk reference* (pp. 472–476). New York: Oxford.

Watson, J. B. (1924). *Behaviorism.* New York: Norton.

Weick, A., Rapp, C., Sullivan, W. P., & Kisthardt, W. (1989). A strengths perspective for social work practice. *Social Work, 34*(4), 350–354.

Welch, B. (1999). Boundary violations: In the eye of the beholder. *Insight 1,* 1–4.

Welch, B. (2003a). After five years, fresh insight. *Insight, 3,* 1–6.

Welch, B. (2003b). HIPAA privacy regulations present new risks. *Insight, 2,* 1–6.

Welch, I. D., & Gonzales, D. M. (1999). *The process of counseling and psychotherapy.* Pacific Grove, CA: Brooks/Cole.

Welfel, E. R. (2001a). Protecting clients' rights to privacy. In E. R. Welfel & R. E. Ingersoll, *The mental health desk reference* (pp. 447–452). Hoboken, NJ: Wiley.

Welfel, E. R. (2001b). Responsible interactions with managed care organizations. In E. R. Welfel & R. E. Ingersoll, *The mental health desk reference* (pp. 496–502). Hoboken, NJ: Wiley.

Welfel, E. R., & Heinlen, K. T. (2001). The responsible use of technology in mental health practice. In E. R. Welfel & R. E. Ingersoll, *The mental health desk reference* (pp. 484–490). Hoboken, NJ: Wiley.

Werner, E. E., & Smith, R. S. (1982). *Vulnerable but invincible: A longitudinal study of resilience and youth.* New York: McGraw-Hill.

Westra, M. (1996). *Active communication.* Pacific Grove, CA: Brooks/Cole.

Wiger, D. E. (1999). *The clinical documentation sourcebook: A comprehensive collection of mental health practice forms, handouts, and records* (2nd ed.). New York: Wiley.

Wilkinson, W. K., & McNeil, K. (1996). *Research for the helping professions.* Belmont, CA: Brooks/Cole.

Williams, M., Unrau, Y. A., & Grinnell, R. J. (1998). *Introduction to social work research.* Itasca, IL: Peacock.

Willis, F., & Sanders, D. (1997). *Cognitive therapy: Transforming the image.* Thousand Oaks, CA: Sage.

Wilson, G. T. (1995). Behavior therapy. In R. J. Corsini & D. Wedding (Eds.), *Current psychotherapies* (5th ed., pp. 197–228). Itasca, IL: Peacock.

Wolberg, L. R. (1965). *Short-term psychotherapy.* New York: Grune & Stratton.

Wolberg, L. R. (1967). *The technique of psychotherapy* (2nd ed.). New York: Grune & Stratton.

Wolf, M. M., et al. (1970). The time-game: A variable interval contingency for the management of out-of-seat behavior. *Exceptional Children, 37*(2), 113–117.

Wolpe, J. (1969). *The practice of behavior therapy.* New York: Pergamon Press.

Wolpe, J. (1973). *The practice of behavior therapy* (2nd ed.). New York: Pergamon.

Worden, M. (1994). *Family therapy basics* (1st ed.). Pacific Grove, CA: Brooks/Cole.

Worden, M. (2003). *Family therapy basics.* Pacific Grove, CA: Brooks/Cole.

World Health Organization. (2004). Quoted in *Deseret News* (March 13), Church sec., p. 10.

Wright, T., & Donoghue, K. (1997). Obstacles to culturally sensitive services for drug-addicted women and their children. In T. Wright & K. Donoghue, *AIA monograph on cultural competency.* Berkeley, CA: Author.

Yalom, I. (1995). *The theory of practice of group psychotherapy.* New York: Basic Books.

Yegidis, B., & Weinbach, R. (2002). *Research methods for social workers.* (4th ed.). Boston: Allyn and Bacon.

Ying, Y. (2001). Psychotherapy with traumatized Southeast Asian refugees. *Clinical Social Work Journal, 29*(1), 65–78.

Young, J. E., Beck, A. T., & Weinberger, A. (1993). Depression. In D. H. Barlow (Ed.), *Clinical handbook of psychological disorders* (2nd ed., pp. 240–277). New York: Guilford.

Young, T., & Poulin, J. (1998). The helping relationship inventory: A clinical appraisal. *Families in Society, 79,* 123–133.

Zinn, M., & Wells, B. (2000). Diversity within Latino families: New lessons for family social science. In D. Demo, K. Allen, & M. Fine (Eds.), *Handbook of family diversity* (pp. 252–273). New York: Oxford University Press.